# GRENDEL™

## war child

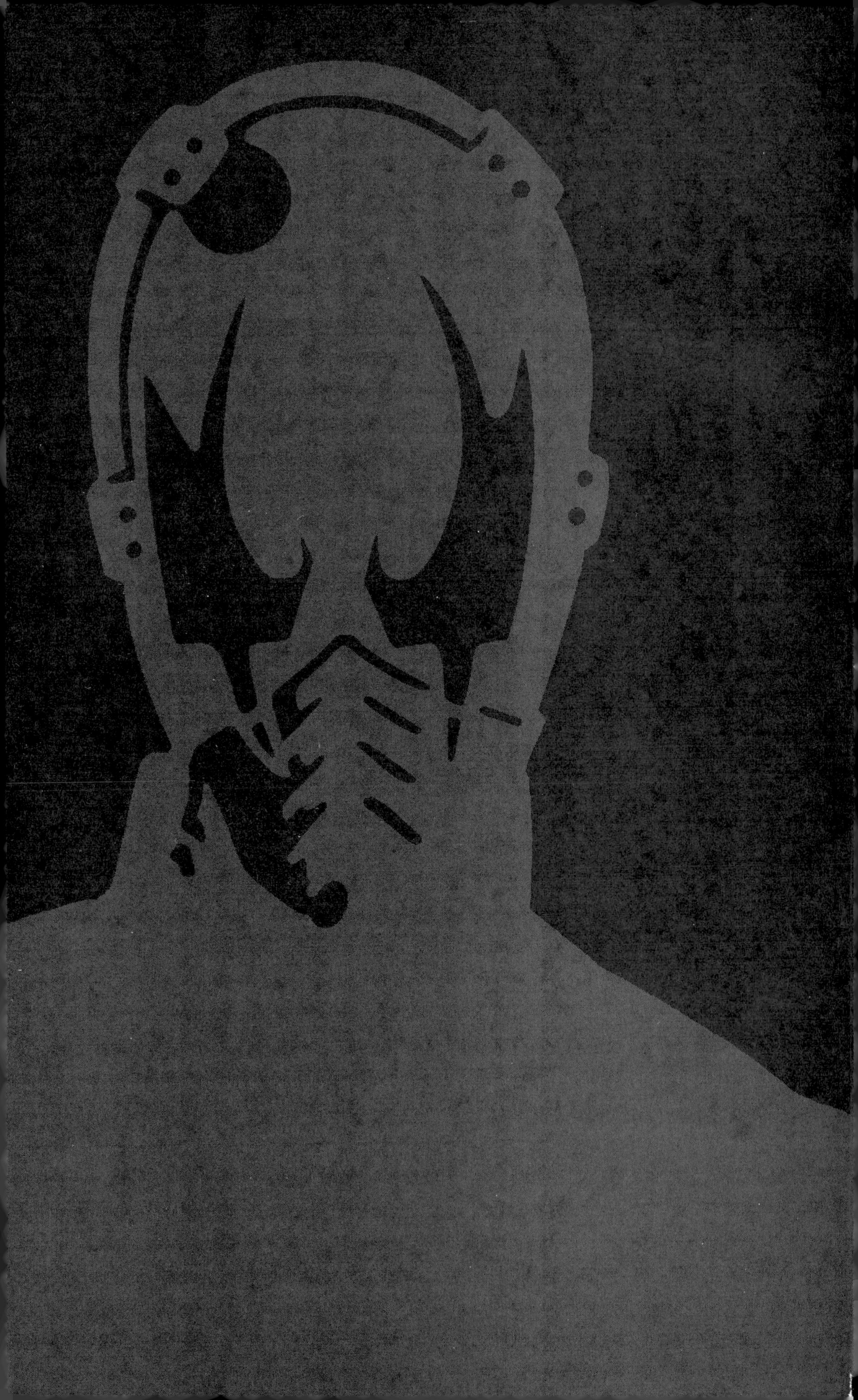

# GRENDEL™
## war child

Created, written, and inked by
**MATT WAGNER**

Pencilled by
**PATRICK McEOWN**

Inking assist by
**MONTY SHELDON**

Color art by
**BERNIE MIREAULT**
**KATHRYN DELANEY**

Lettering by
**KURT HATHAWAY**

Chapter art by
**SIMON BISLEY** (Chapters 1-4)
**MATT WAGNER** (Chapters 5-10)

Collection cover art by
**MATT WAGNER**

Edited by
**DIANA SCHUTZ**

Collection edited by
**KIJ JOHNSON**

Collection designed by
**CARY GRAZZINI**

**DARK HORSE COMICS**

**Mike Richardson**
Publisher

**Neil Hankerson**
Executive V.P.

**David Scroggy**
V.P. of publishing

**Lou Bank**
V.P. of sales & marketing

**Andy Karabatsos**
V.P. of finance

**Mark Anderson**
General counsel

**Diana Schutz**
Editor in chief

**Randy Stradley**
Creative director

**Cindy Marks**
Director of production & design

**Mark Cox**
Art director

**Sean Tierney**
Computer graphics director

**Chris Creviston**
Director of accounting

**Michael Martens**
Marketing director

**Tod Borleske**
Sales & licensing director

**Mark Ellington**
Director of operations

**Dale LaFountain**
Director of m.i.s.

Published by Dark Horse Comics
10956 SE Main Street
Milwaukie, OR 97222

First trade paperback edition: November 1993
ISBN: 1-878574-89-2

One thousand copies of this book will be produced
as a special signed, limited-edition hardcover.
Limited edition: July 1994
ISBN: 1-878574-94-9

10 9 8 7 6 5 4 3 2

# INTRODUCTION

Beginnings and endings.

This storyline marks the end of an era even as it signals the re-birth of a concept.

Originally slated to appear as issues #41-50 of the original *Grendel* saga, this roller coaster through hell was meant to act as a segue into an entirely different world than the one wherein we began. Confused? Then let's go back to the beginning.

After the initial success of the original Grendel tale, *Devil by the Deed*, my publishers at the time asked me if I was interested in continuing the character in a monthly book. Seeing as how *DbtD* ended with the death of the title antagonist, this left me with the opportunity of continuing the concepts of Grendel, as opposed to the character of Hunter Rose. In fact, once I began what eventually turned into this ten-year project, I realized this was indeed the only way for me to maintain interest in a monthly book. By constantly moving the concepts forward, by continually dashing people's expectations of how things ought to be, and by eternally reinventing the character in familiar yet newly challenging guises, I found I had accidentally stumbled on a unique formula for success in what was rapidly becoming one of the most volatile entertainment markets around.

Still, even with such a wide-open field of story possibilities, I knew that someday my muse would yearn for other narrative pastures. (You see, I *do* have this other property that people find rather likable. Maybe you've heard of it?) I had been looking for some new direction to take my blossoming epic when a stray comment from a friend led me down the path we tread today. I knew I couldn't just keep continuing the linear next-person-picks-up-the-mask course that the first several segments had entailed. So, when Bernie Mireault asked me one day if "Grendel" could ever inhabit a crowd, my response was, "Sure. Hell...why not the whole world, then?"

Thus I proceeded to spend well over half the original series' duration building things up to have Grendel conquer the globe. Additionally (here's those dashed expectations again), I thought it might be fun to completely turn things on their collective ear and have Grendel actually become a *respected* name in this futuristic setting. Still and all, the moral ambiguity that has always been one of the hallmarks of this book would remain. Is Grendel now the most honored of terms or still one of the most heinous? Depends on who you speak to, I guess.

After so many years of striving to become more experimental with each progressing narrative, I also thought it would be fun to take the series out with a real blast. We hadn't had anything quite like this adventure for quite some time and so I decided to pull out all the stops. Biker gangs, pirates, zombies, mutants, vampires, and ultimate weapons — I deliberately tried to include as many adventure serial clichés as I could in what would eventually become *War Child*. The result was just as bombastic as I had hoped and makes for an exciting, break-neck read. You actually consume the almost 300-page tale in a single sitting! (Go on, give it a try.)

As I said earlier, the story structure was meant to provide me with an escape valve for the pressures of my other creative interests. The resultant endless-tableau-within-an-endless-tableau has given me the opportunity to open up the Grendel concepts to other creative teams. *Grendel Tales* promises to continue what has become a tradition of daring entertainment and thought-provoking fiction.

I hope you enjoy this "last" chapter of *Grendel*. Although it may have all the markings of an ending, I can assure you this is only the beginning.

M.WAGNER

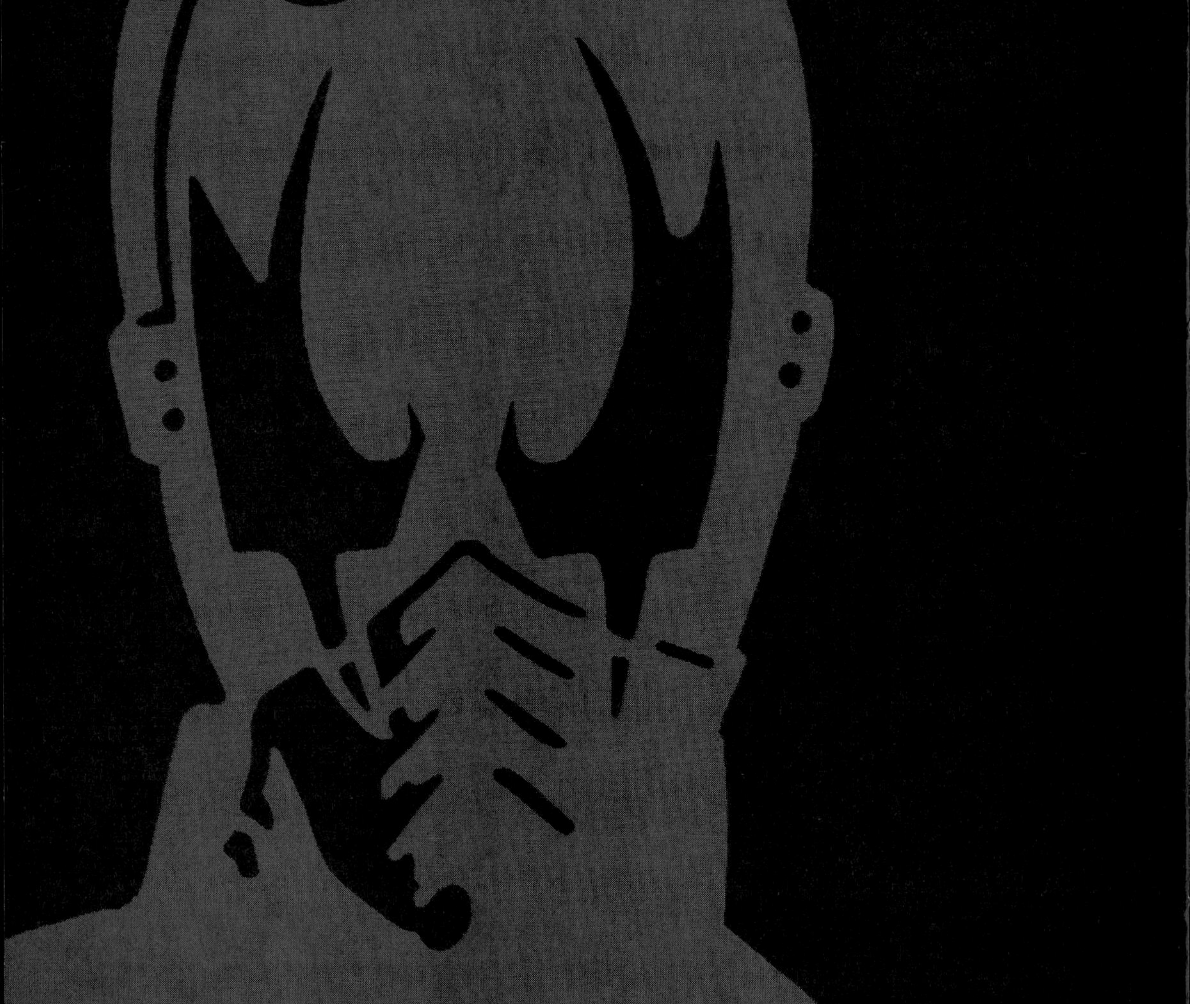

# OUR STORY SO FAR . . .

In the latter days of the twenty-seventh century, the battle-scarred earth is finally united under the rule of a single man, Orion Assante. His fifty-year reign as world monarch gives rise to a new class of military elite — the Grendels.

Grendels enjoy a privileged status in society and adhere to strict codes of military ethics. They are fanatically dedicated to honoring the will of their Khan — which they proclaim with the rallying cry "Vivat Grendel!" Since the death of Orion I, however, the warrior caste has become fragmented and clannish due to the lack of an immediate successor to the throne.

The rightful heir, Orion's only son Jupiter, has been cloistered away in an underground military complex deep in the Dakota Black Hills. His political captivity is at the hands of his stepmother, presiding regent Laurel Kennedy Assante, whose power-driven scheming has made a prisoner of her daughter Crystal, as well.

# CHAPTER 1
# DEVIL
## *in the desert*

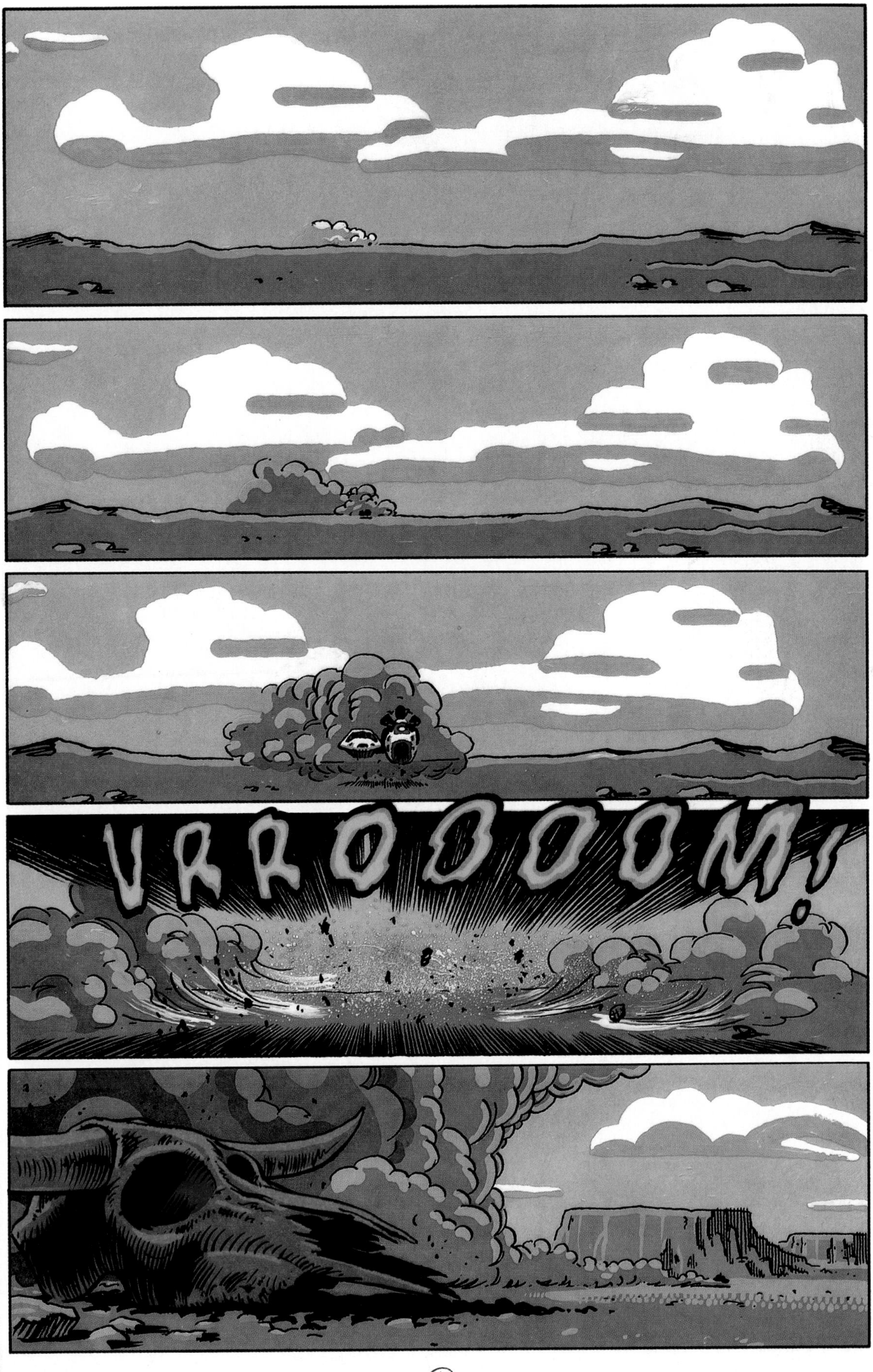
VRROOOOOM!

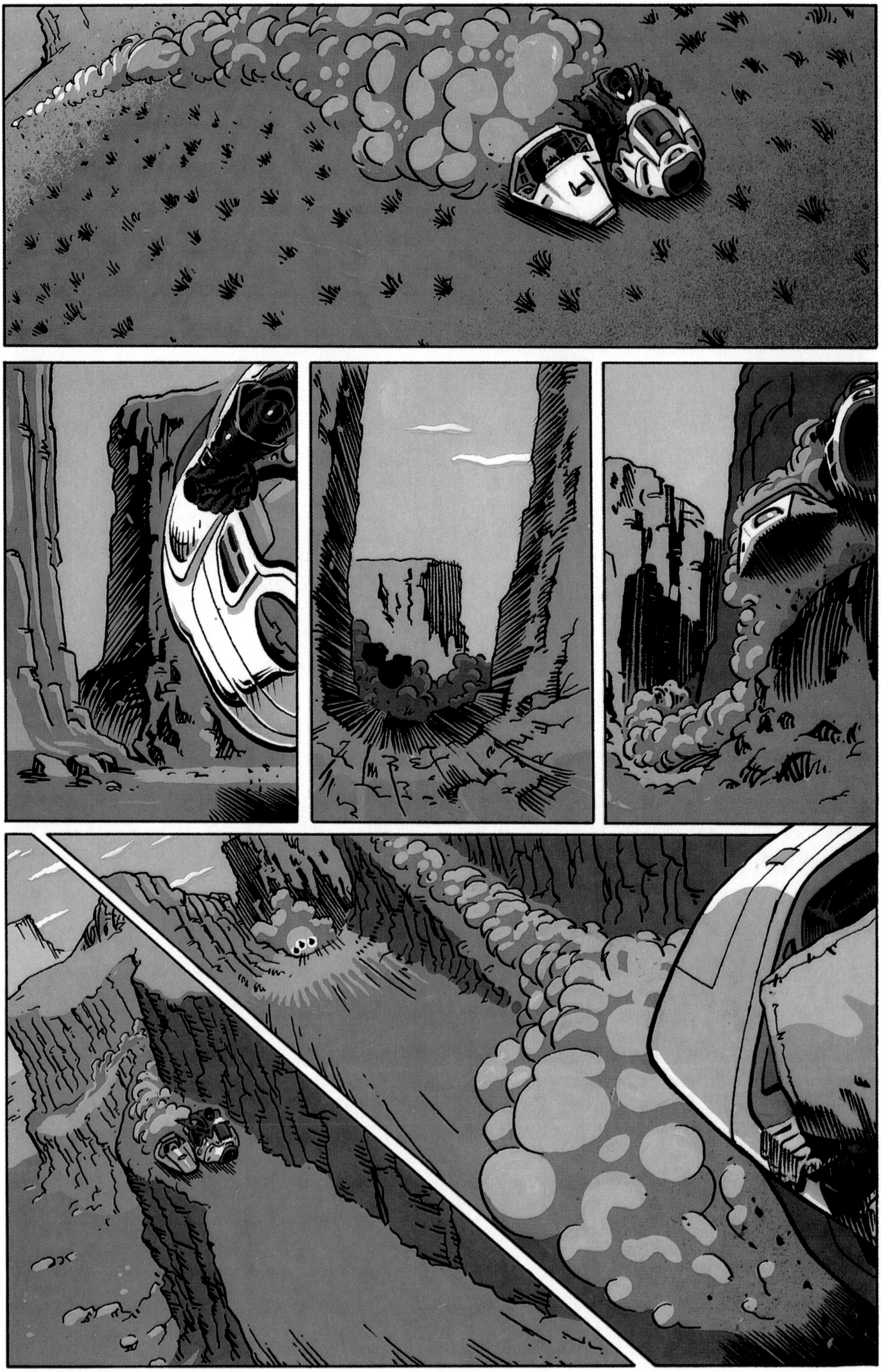

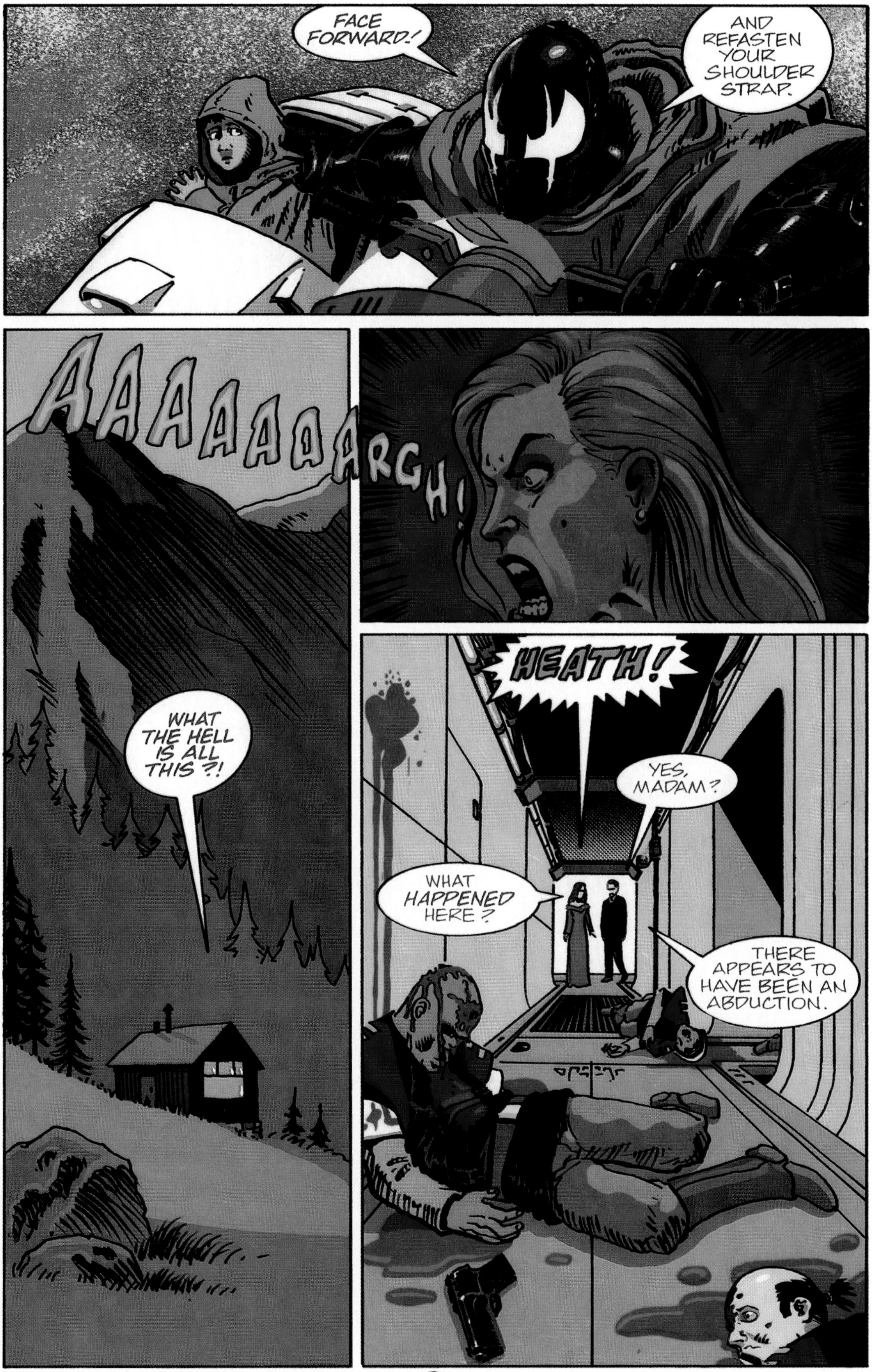
FACE FORWARD!
AND REFASTEN YOUR SHOULDER STRAP.
AAAAAAAARGH!
WHAT THE HELL IS ALL THIS ?!
HEATH!
YES, MADAM?
WHAT HAPPENED HERE?
THERE APPEARS TO HAVE BEEN AN ABDUCTION.

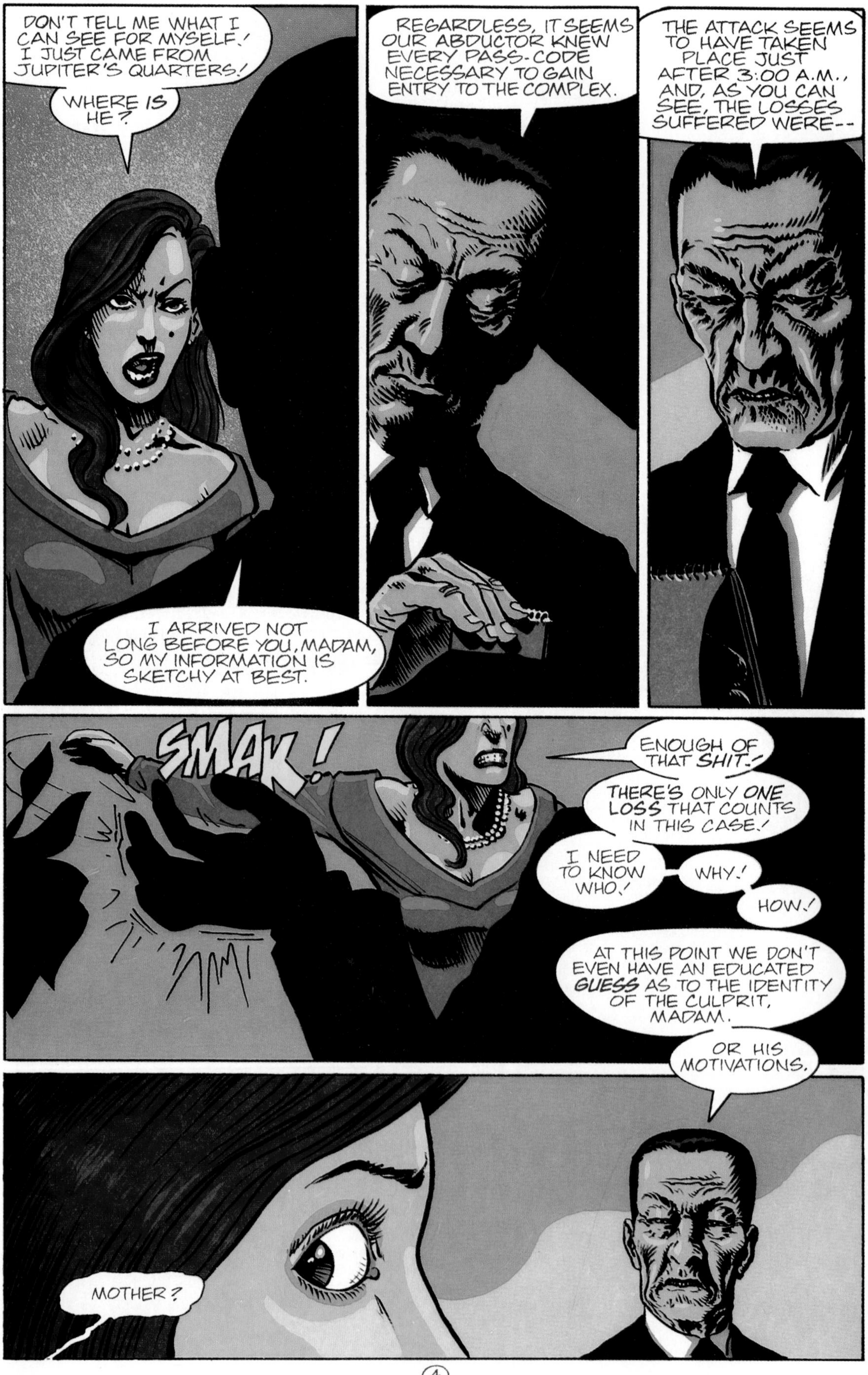
DON'T TELL ME WHAT I CAN SEE FOR MYSELF! I JUST CAME FROM JUPITER'S QUARTERS!
WHERE IS HE?
I ARRIVED NOT LONG BEFORE YOU, MADAM, SO MY INFORMATION IS SKETCHY AT BEST.
REGARDLESS, IT SEEMS OUR ABDUCTOR KNEW EVERY PASS-CODE NECESSARY TO GAIN ENTRY TO THE COMPLEX.
THE ATTACK SEEMS TO HAVE TAKEN PLACE JUST AFTER 3:00 A.M., AND, AS YOU CAN SEE, THE LOSSES SUFFERED WERE--
SMAK!
ENOUGH OF THAT SHIT!
THERE'S ONLY ONE LOSS THAT COUNTS IN THIS CASE!
I NEED TO KNOW WHO!
WHY!
HOW!
AT THIS POINT WE DON'T EVEN HAVE AN EDUCATED GUESS AS TO THE IDENTITY OF THE CULPRIT, MADAM.
OR HIS MOTIVATIONS.
MOTHER?

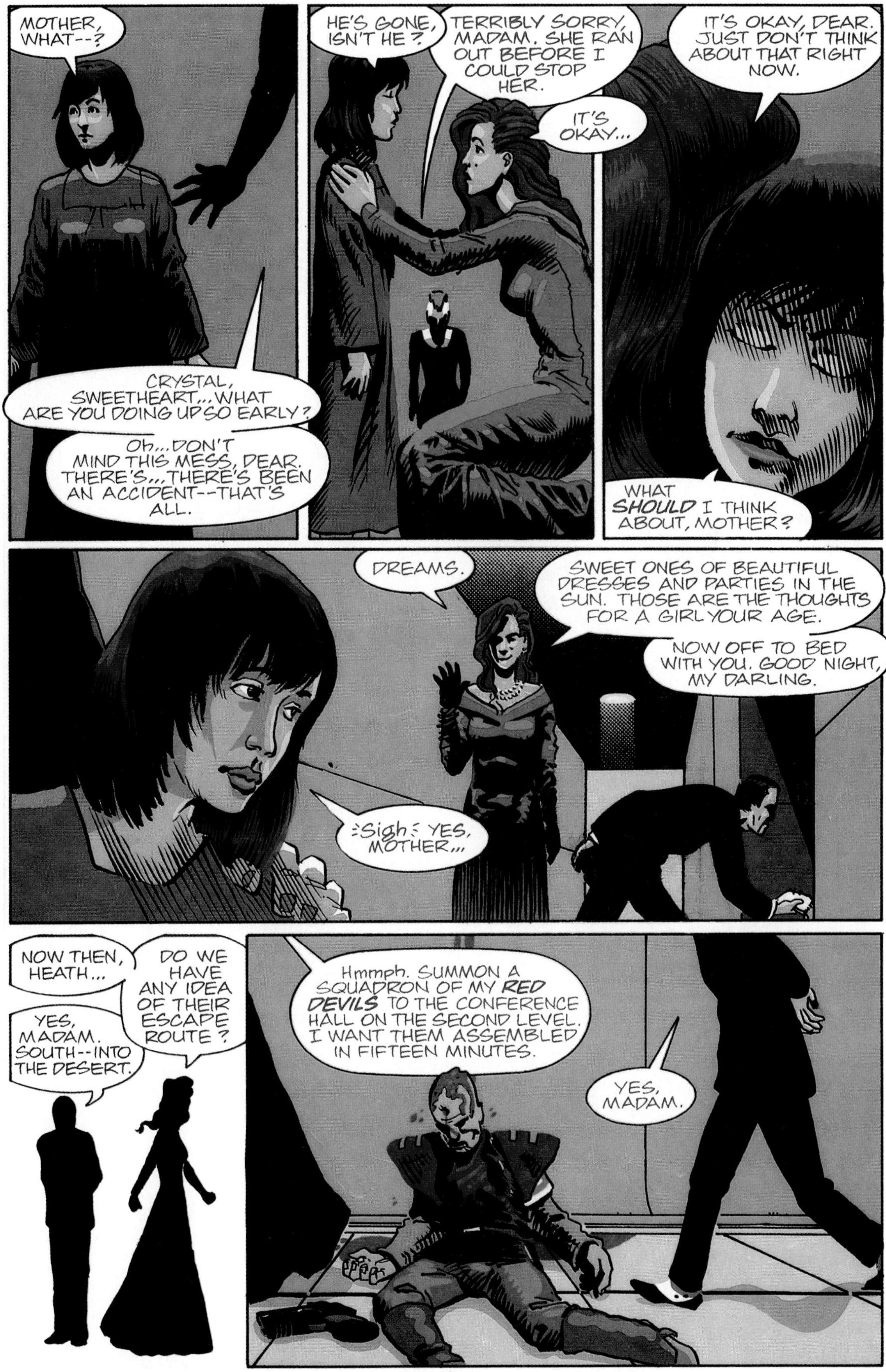
MOTHER, WHAT--?
CRYSTAL, SWEETHEART... WHAT ARE YOU DOING UP SO EARLY?
Oh... DON'T MIND THIS MESS, DEAR. THERE'S... THERE'S BEEN AN ACCIDENT--THAT'S ALL.
HE'S GONE, ISN'T HE?
TERRIBLY SORRY, MADAM. SHE RAN OUT BEFORE I COULD STOP HER.
IT'S OKAY...
IT'S OKAY, DEAR. JUST DON'T THINK ABOUT THAT RIGHT NOW.
WHAT SHOULD I THINK ABOUT, MOTHER?
DREAMS.
SWEET ONES OF BEAUTIFUL DRESSES AND PARTIES IN THE SUN. THOSE ARE THE THOUGHTS FOR A GIRL YOUR AGE.
NOW OFF TO BED WITH YOU. GOOD NIGHT, MY DARLING.
:Sigh: YES, MOTHER...
NOW THEN, HEATH...
DO WE HAVE ANY IDEA OF THEIR ESCAPE ROUTE?
YES, MADAM. SOUTH--INTO THE DESERT.
Hmmph. SUMMON A SQUADRON OF MY RED DEVILS TO THE CONFERENCE HALL ON THE SECOND LEVEL. I WANT THEM ASSEMBLED IN FIFTEEN MINUTES.
YES, MADAM.

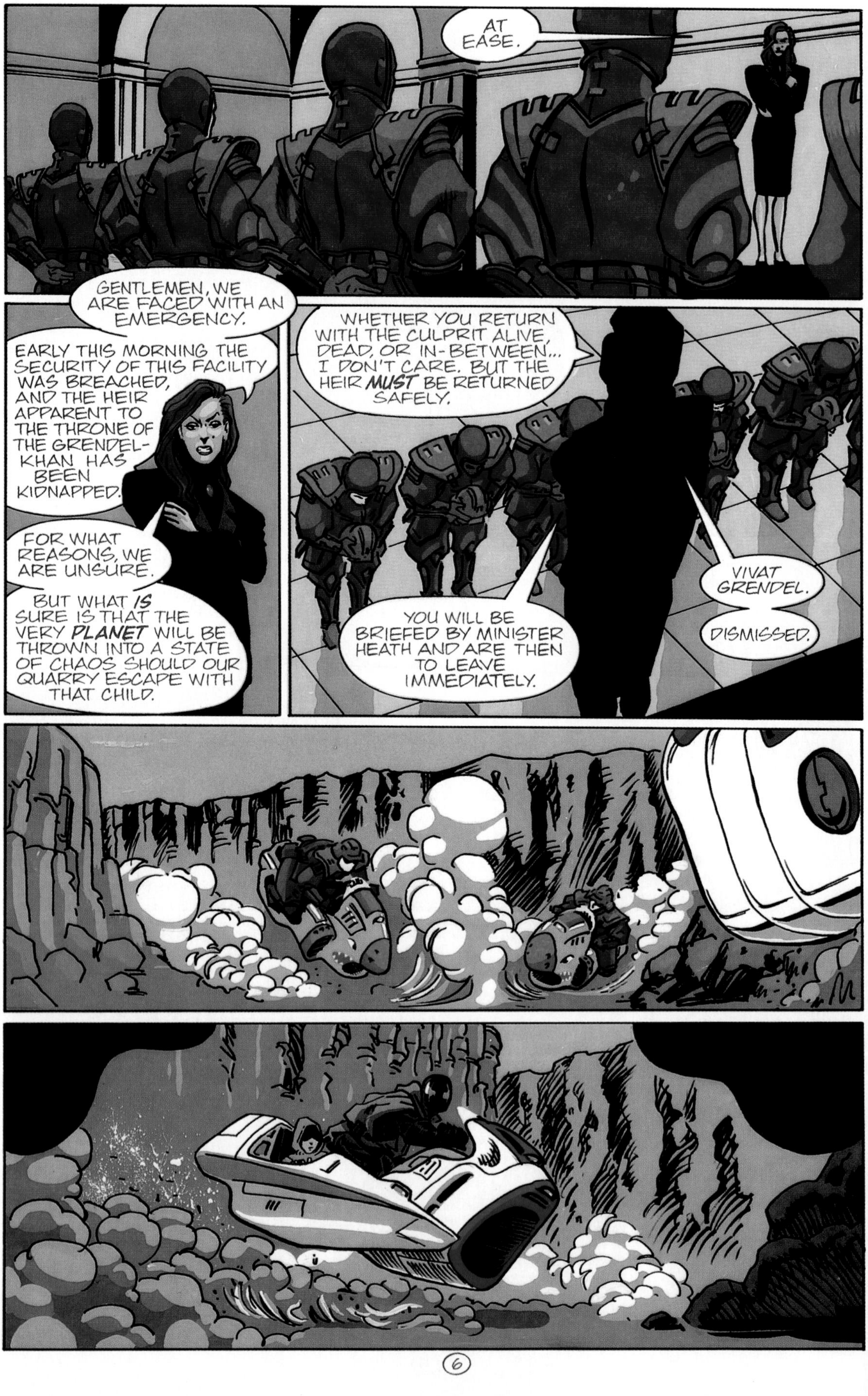
AT EASE.
GENTLEMEN, WE ARE FACED WITH AN EMERGENCY.
EARLY THIS MORNING THE SECURITY OF THIS FACILITY WAS BREACHED, AND THE HEIR APPARENT TO THE THRONE OF THE GRENDEL-KHAN HAS BEEN KIDNAPPED.
FOR WHAT REASONS, WE ARE UNSURE.
BUT WHAT *IS* SURE IS THAT THE VERY *PLANET* WILL BE THROWN INTO A STATE OF CHAOS SHOULD OUR QUARRY ESCAPE WITH THAT CHILD.
WHETHER YOU RETURN WITH THE CULPRIT ALIVE, DEAD, OR IN-BETWEEN... I DON'T CARE. BUT THE HEIR *MUST* BE RETURNED SAFELY.
YOU WILL BE BRIEFED BY MINISTER HEATH AND ARE THEN TO LEAVE IMMEDIATELY.
VIVAT GRENDEL.
DISMISSED.

BZZZ... WHIRR...

SHAK

CLICK!

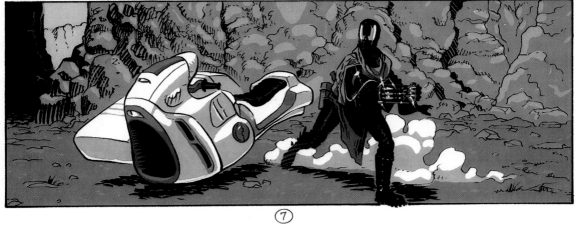

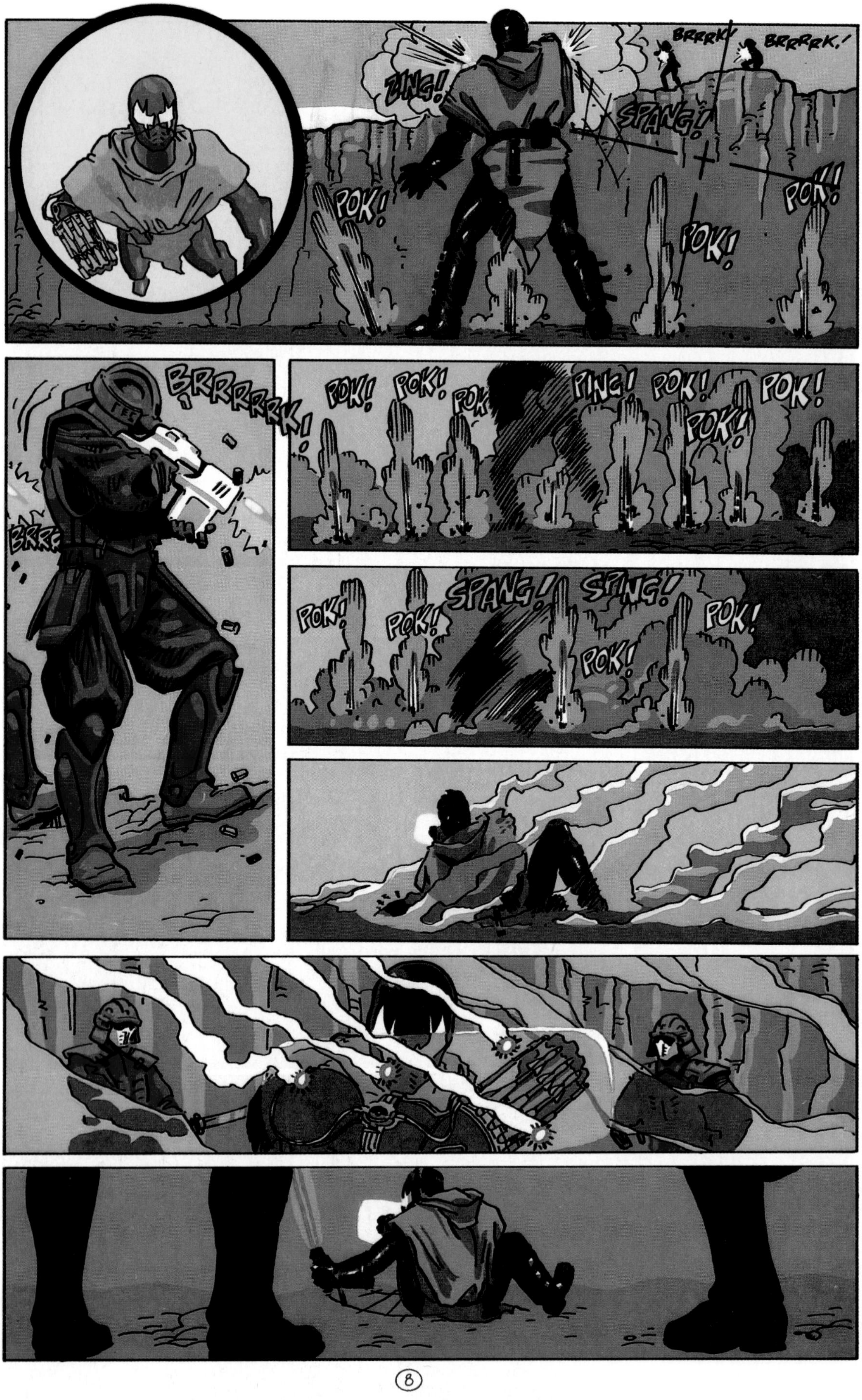
ZING!
BRRRRK!
BRRRRK.!
SPANG!
POK!
POK!
POK!
BRRRRRRRK!
POK!
POK!
PING!
POK!
POK!
POK!
POK!
POK!
SPANG!
SPING!
POK!
POK!

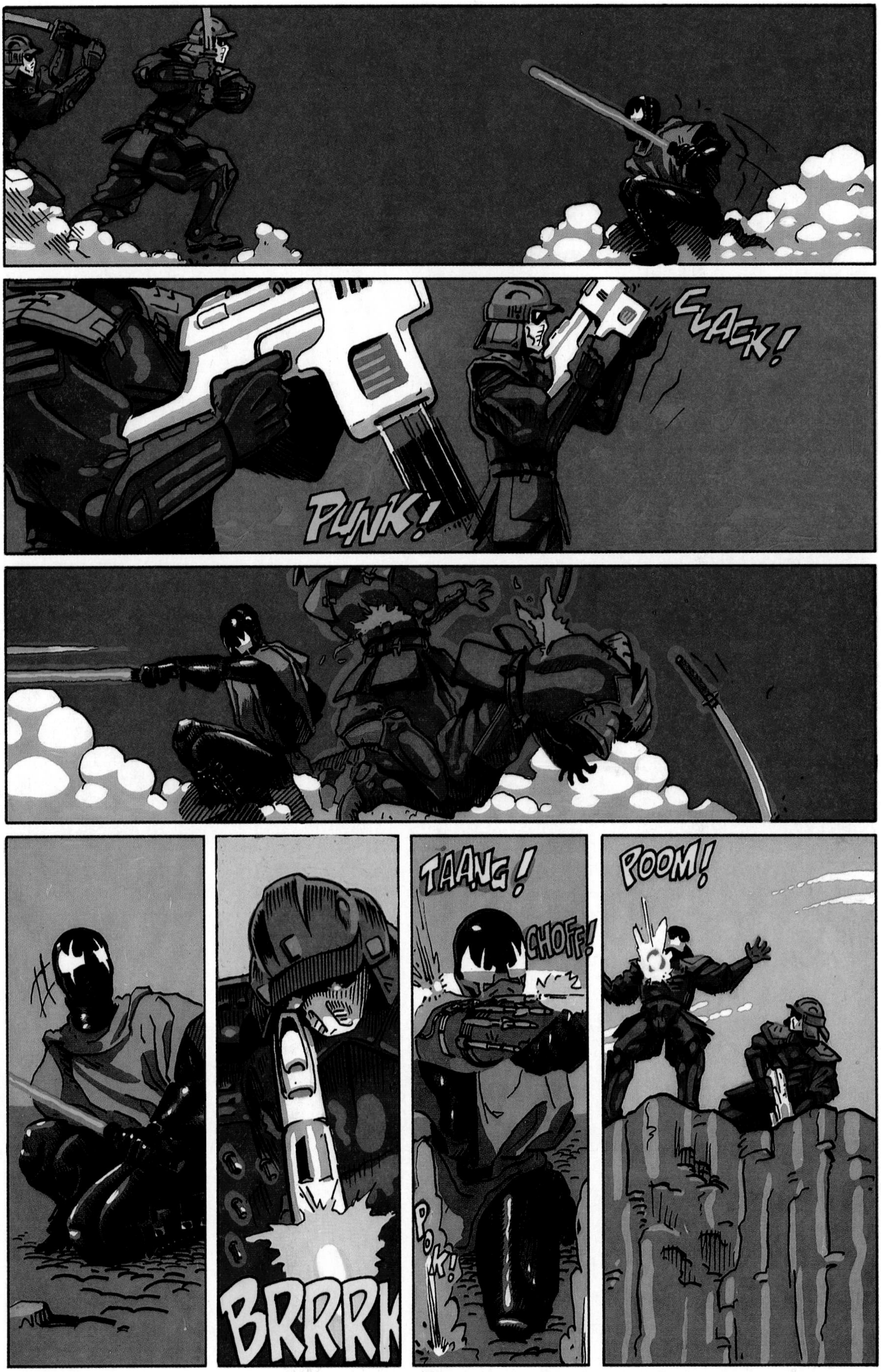
CLACK!
PUNK!
BRRRK
TAANG!
CHOFF!
POK!
POOM!

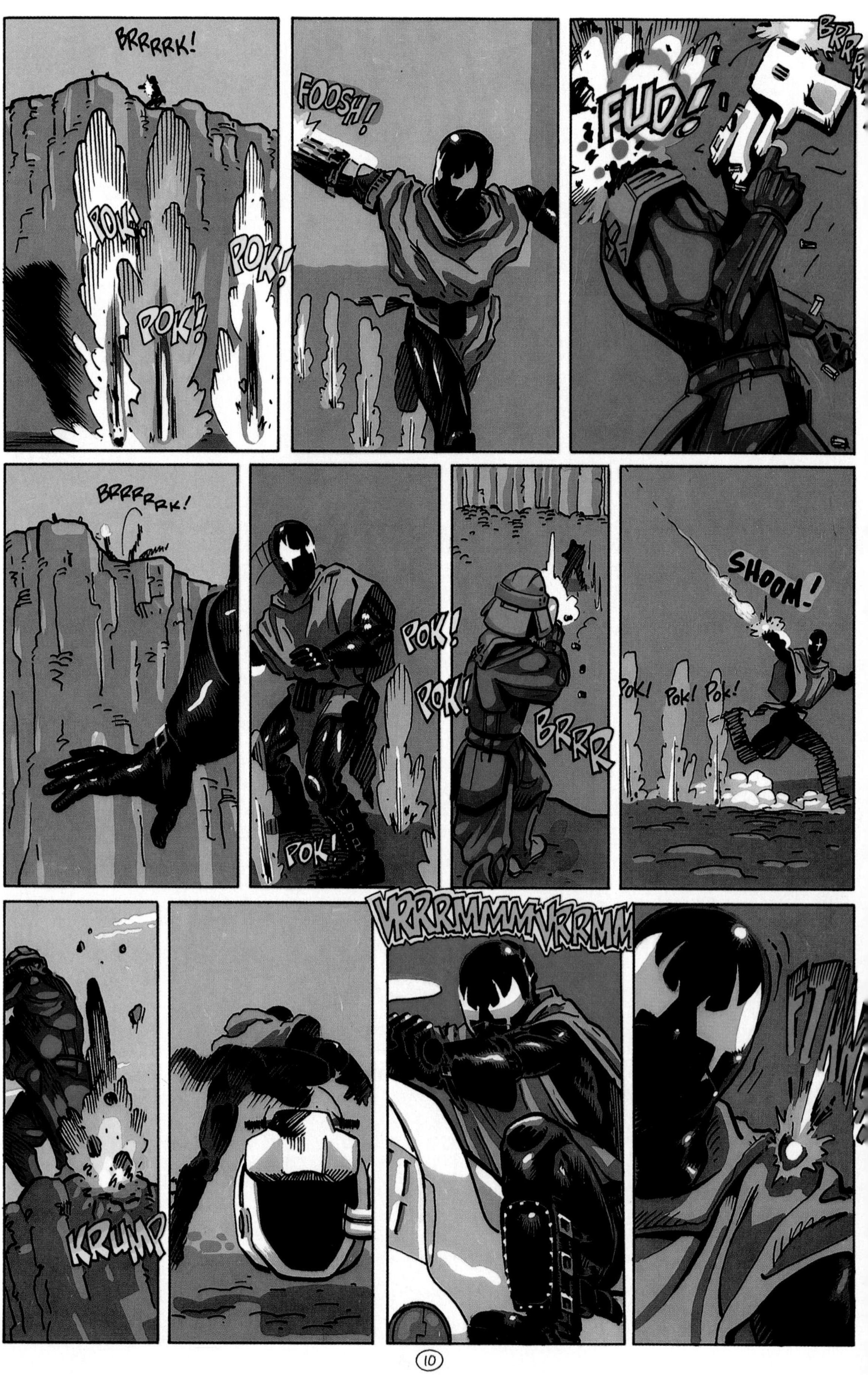
BRRRRK!
POK!
POK!
POK!
FOOSH!
FUD!
BRRRRRK!
POK!
POK!
POK!
BRRR
SHOOM!
POK! POK! POK!
KRUMP
VRRRMMMVRRMM

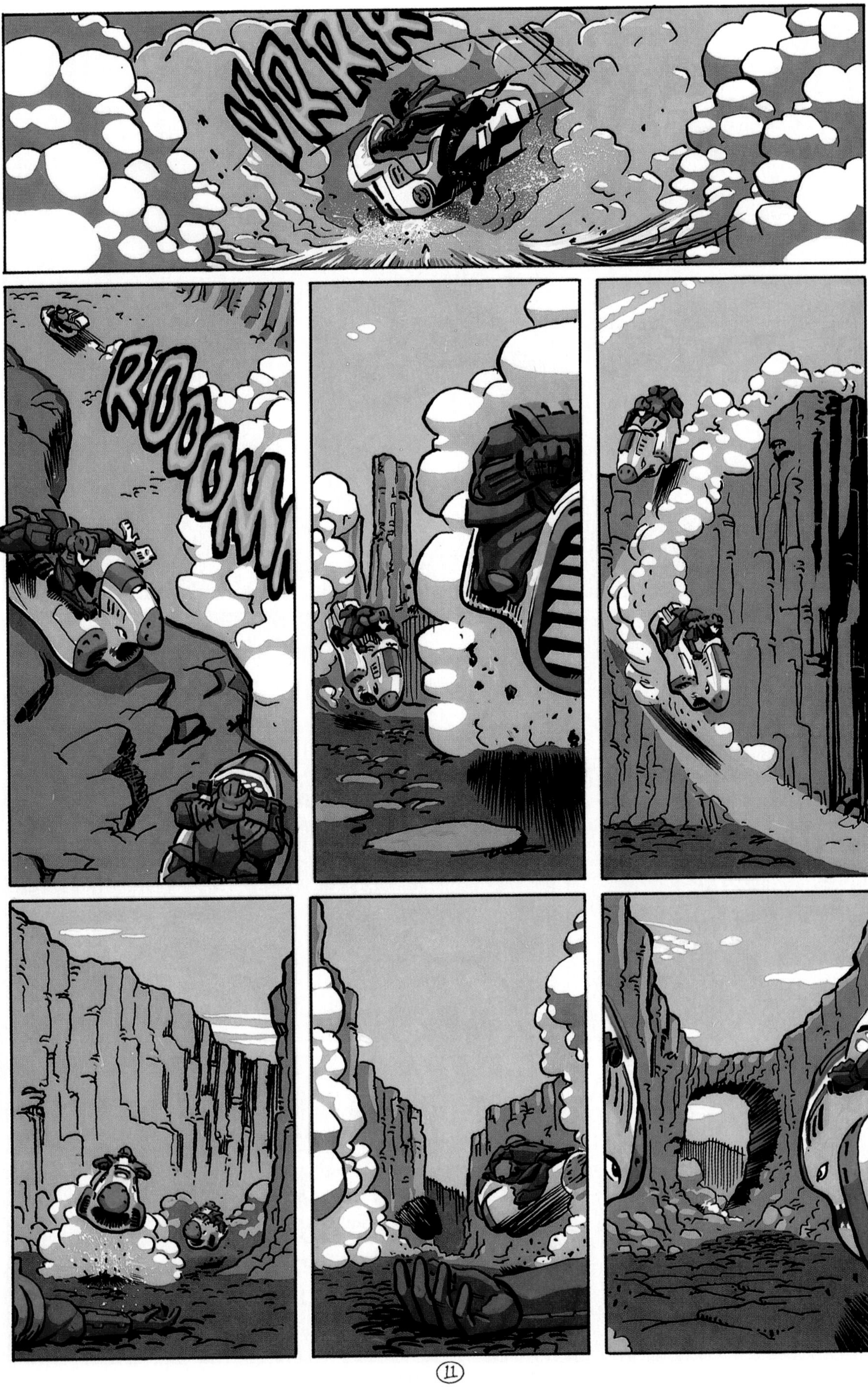
VRRR
ROOOM

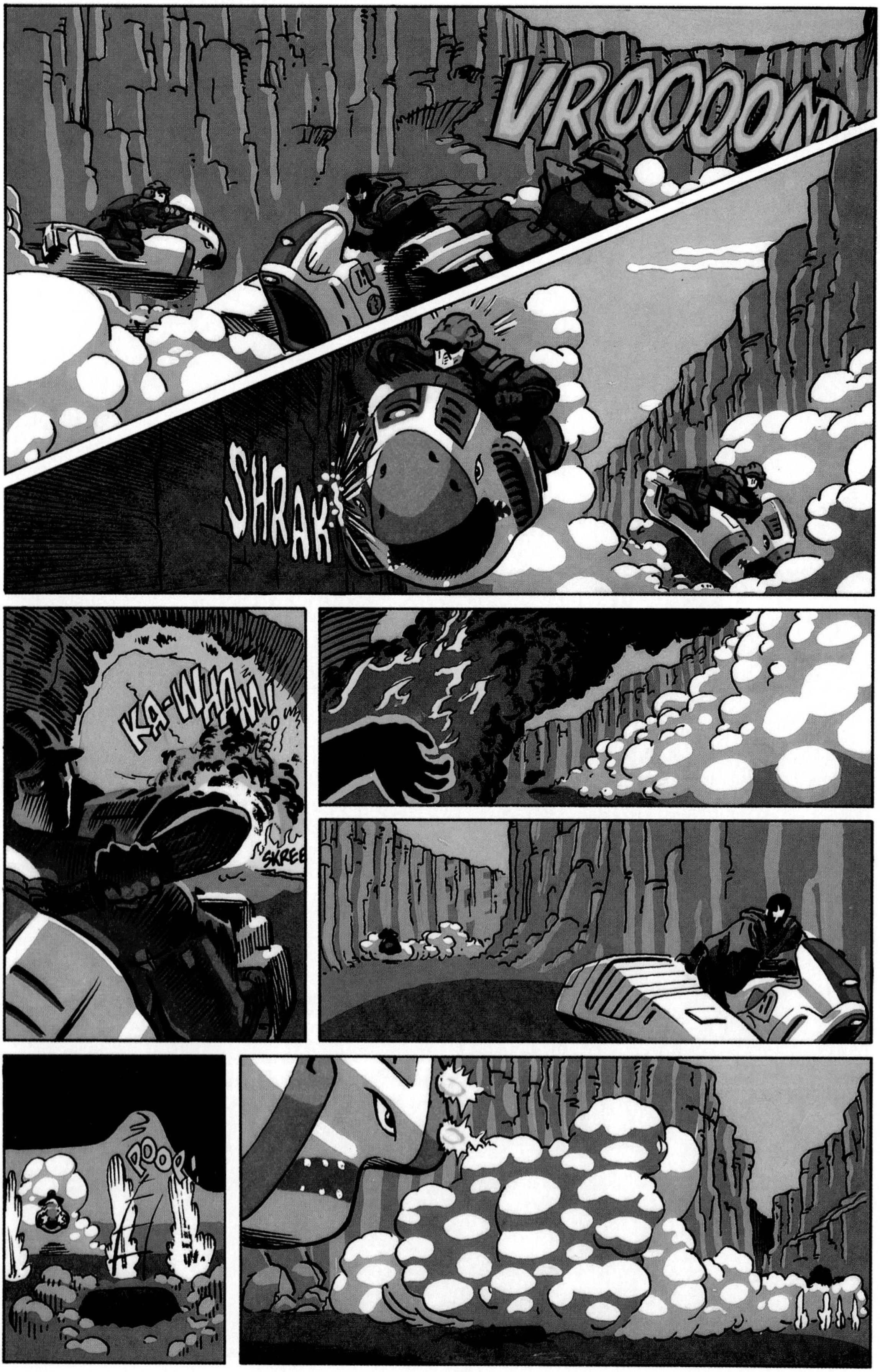
VROOOOOM
SHRAK
KA-WHAM!
SKREE
POOP

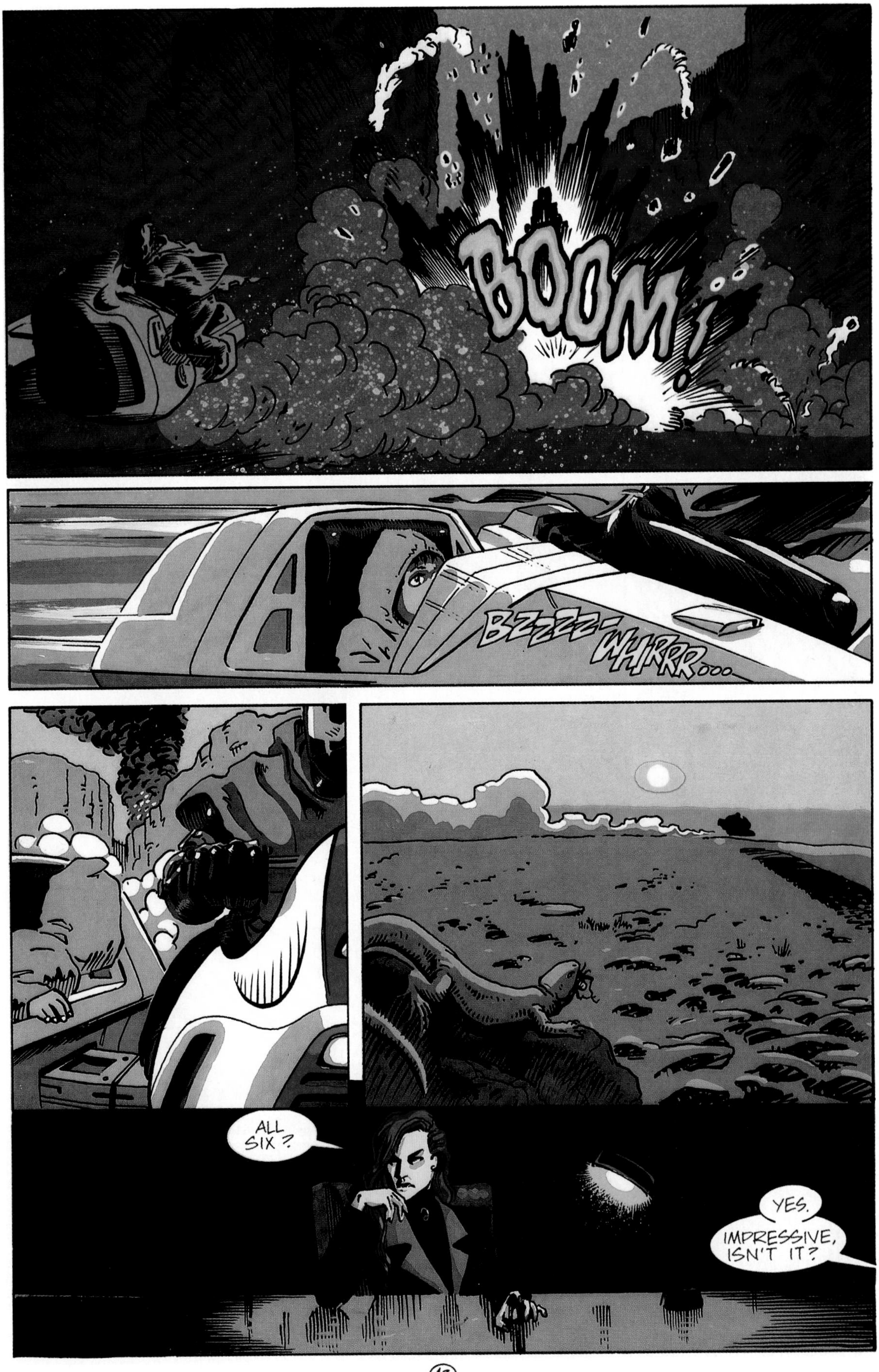
BOOM!
BZZZZ-WHRRR...
ALL SIX?
YES.
IMPRESSIVE, ISN'T IT?

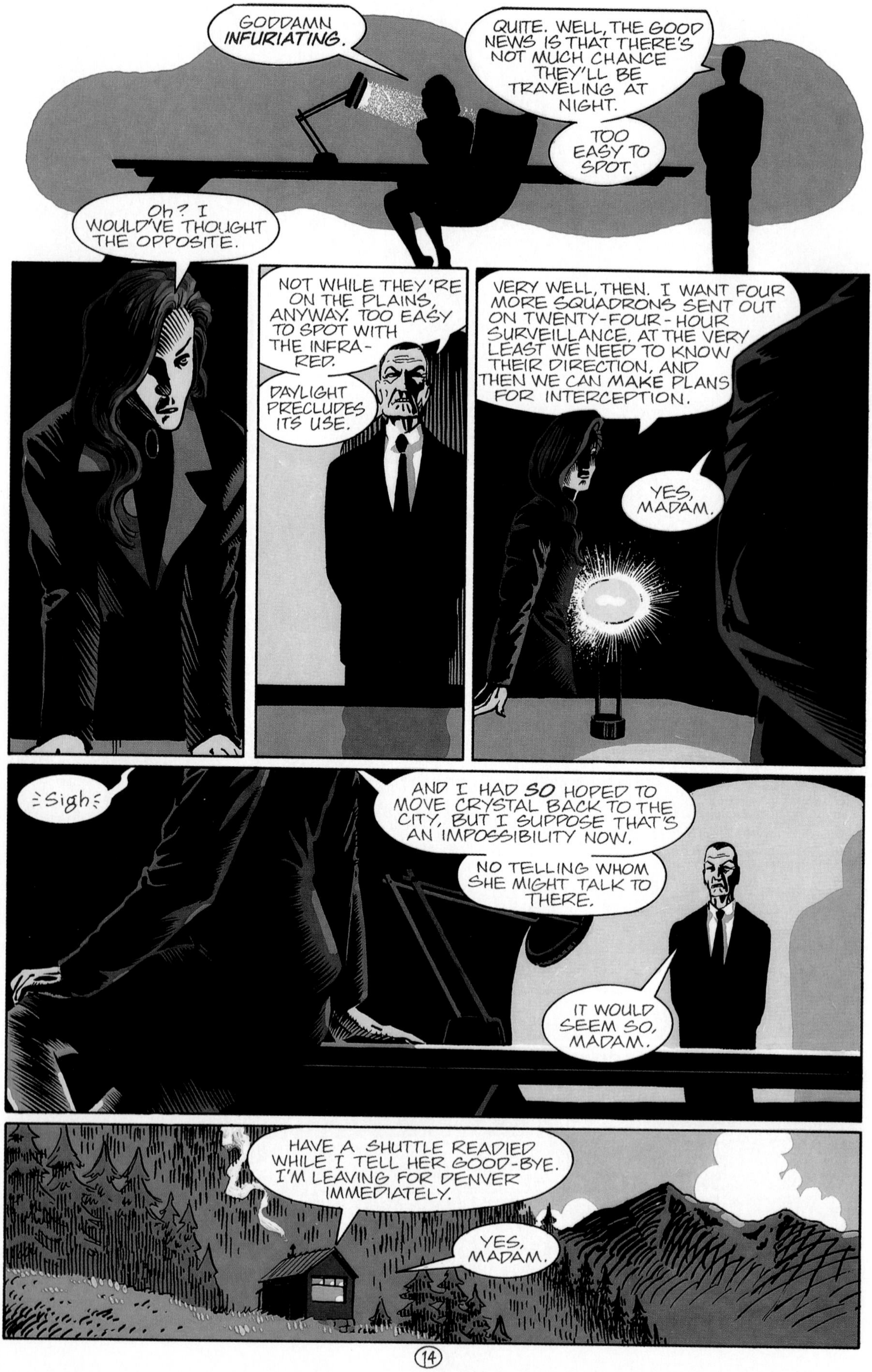
GODDAMN INFURIATING.
QUITE. WELL, THE GOOD NEWS IS THAT THERE'S NOT MUCH CHANCE THEY'LL BE TRAVELING AT NIGHT.
TOO EASY TO SPOT.
Oh? I WOULD'VE THOUGHT THE OPPOSITE.
NOT WHILE THEY'RE ON THE PLAINS, ANYWAY. TOO EASY TO SPOT WITH THE INFRA-RED.
DAYLIGHT PRECLUDES ITS USE.
VERY WELL, THEN. I WANT FOUR MORE SQUADRONS SENT OUT ON TWENTY-FOUR-HOUR SURVEILLANCE. AT THE VERY LEAST WE NEED TO KNOW THEIR DIRECTION, AND THEN WE CAN MAKE PLANS FOR INTERCEPTION.
YES, MADAM.
Sigh
AND I HAD SO HOPED TO MOVE CRYSTAL BACK TO THE CITY, BUT I SUPPOSE THAT'S AN IMPOSSIBILITY NOW.
NO TELLING WHOM SHE MIGHT TALK TO THERE.
IT WOULD SEEM SO, MADAM.
HAVE A SHUTTLE READIED WHILE I TELL HER GOOD-BYE. I'M LEAVING FOR DENVER IMMEDIATELY.
YES, MADAM.

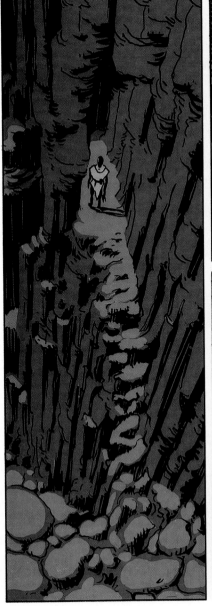

IT'S ME. DON'T BE FRIGHTENED.

I'VE BROUGHT DINNER.

NO MORE WOOD ON THE FIRE. NOT ONLY WILL THE SMOKE ATTRACT THOSE FOLLOWING US, BUT IT WILL EAT THROUGH OUR AIR AS WELL.

COME WATCH AS I PREPARE THIS.

SOON, WE EAT.

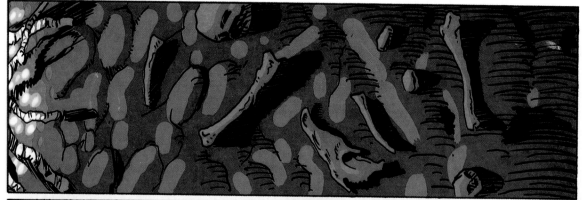

RUSTLE
RUSTLE

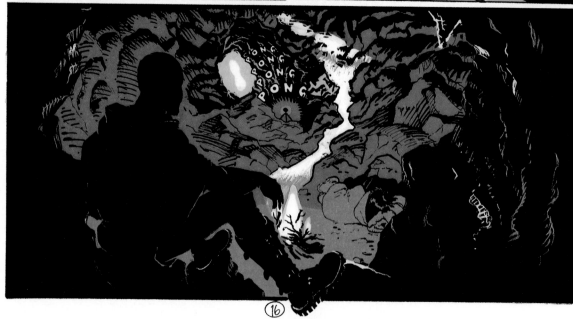

PONG
PONG
PONG
PONG

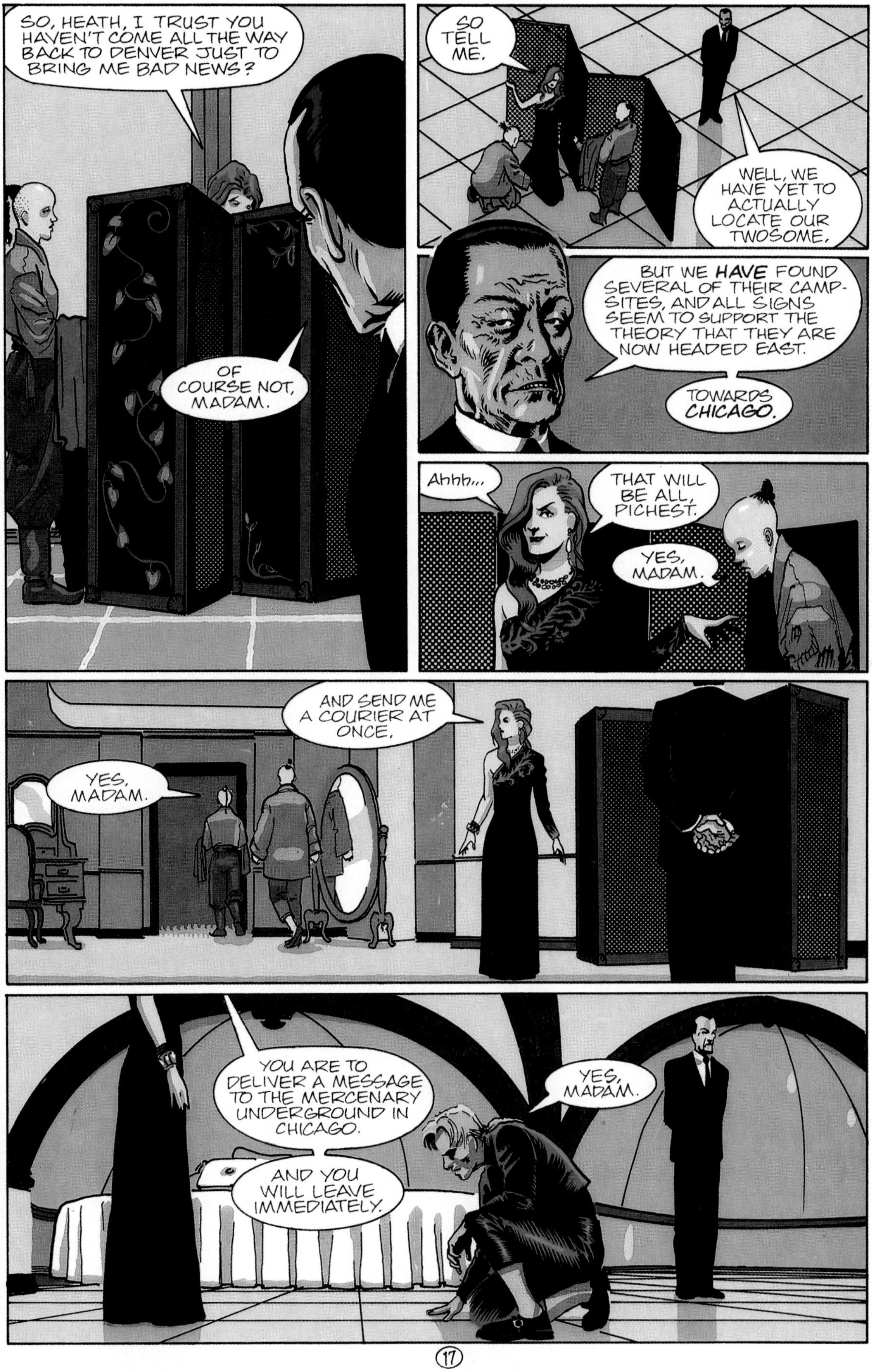
SO, HEATH, I TRUST YOU HAVEN'T COME ALL THE WAY BACK TO DENVER JUST TO BRING ME BAD NEWS?
OF COURSE NOT, MADAM.
SO TELL ME.
WELL, WE HAVE YET TO ACTUALLY LOCATE OUR TWOSOME.
BUT WE **HAVE** FOUND SEVERAL OF THEIR CAMP-SITES, AND ALL SIGNS SEEM TO SUPPORT THE THEORY THAT THEY ARE NOW HEADED EAST.
TOWARDS **CHICAGO.**
Ahhh...
THAT WILL BE ALL, PICHEST.
YES, MADAM.
AND SEND ME A COURIER AT ONCE.
YES, MADAM.
YOU ARE TO DELIVER A MESSAGE TO THE MERCENARY UNDERGROUND IN CHICAGO.
AND YOU WILL LEAVE IMMEDIATELY.
YES, MADAM.

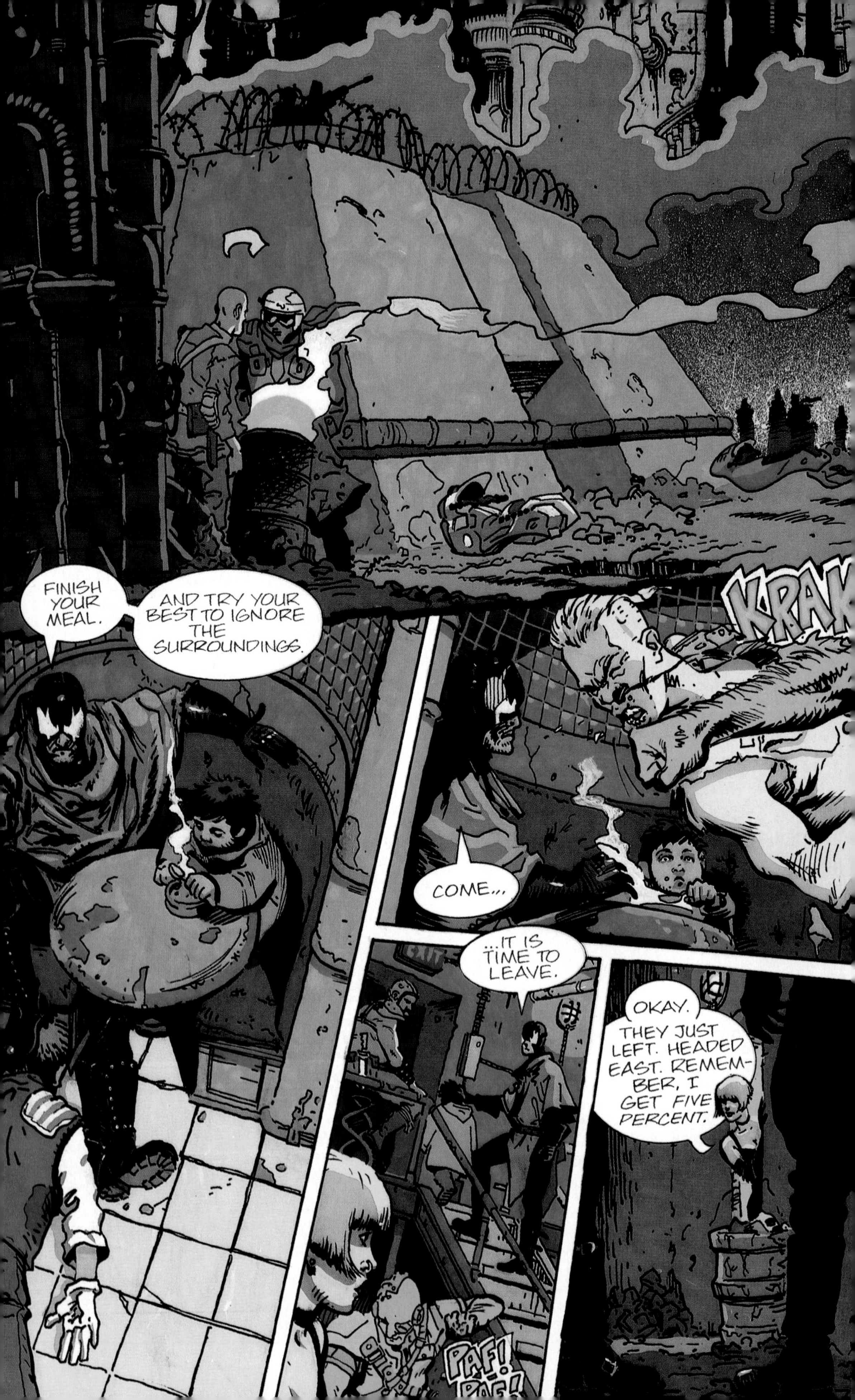
FINISH YOUR MEAL.
AND TRY YOUR BEST TO IGNORE THE SURROUNDINGS.
KRAK
COME...
...IT IS TIME TO LEAVE.
EXIT
OKAY. THEY JUST LEFT. HEADED EAST. REMEMBER, I GET FIVE PERCENT.
PAF!

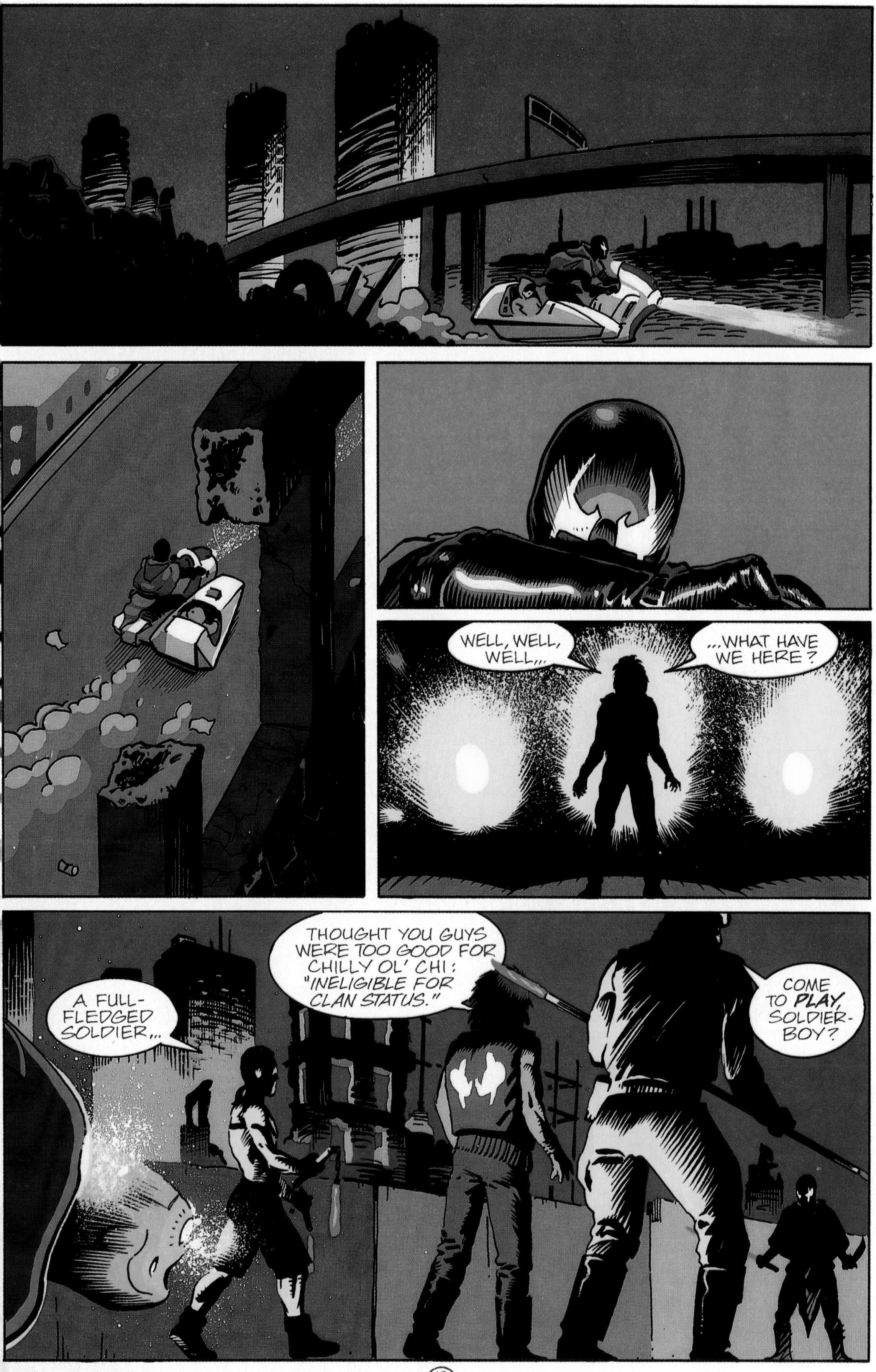
WELL, WELL, WELL...
...WHAT HAVE WE HERE?
A FULL-FLEDGED SOLDIER...
THOUGHT YOU GUYS WERE TOO GOOD FOR CHILLY OL' CHI: "INELIGIBLE FOR CLAN STATUS."
COME TO PLAY, SOLDIER-BOY?

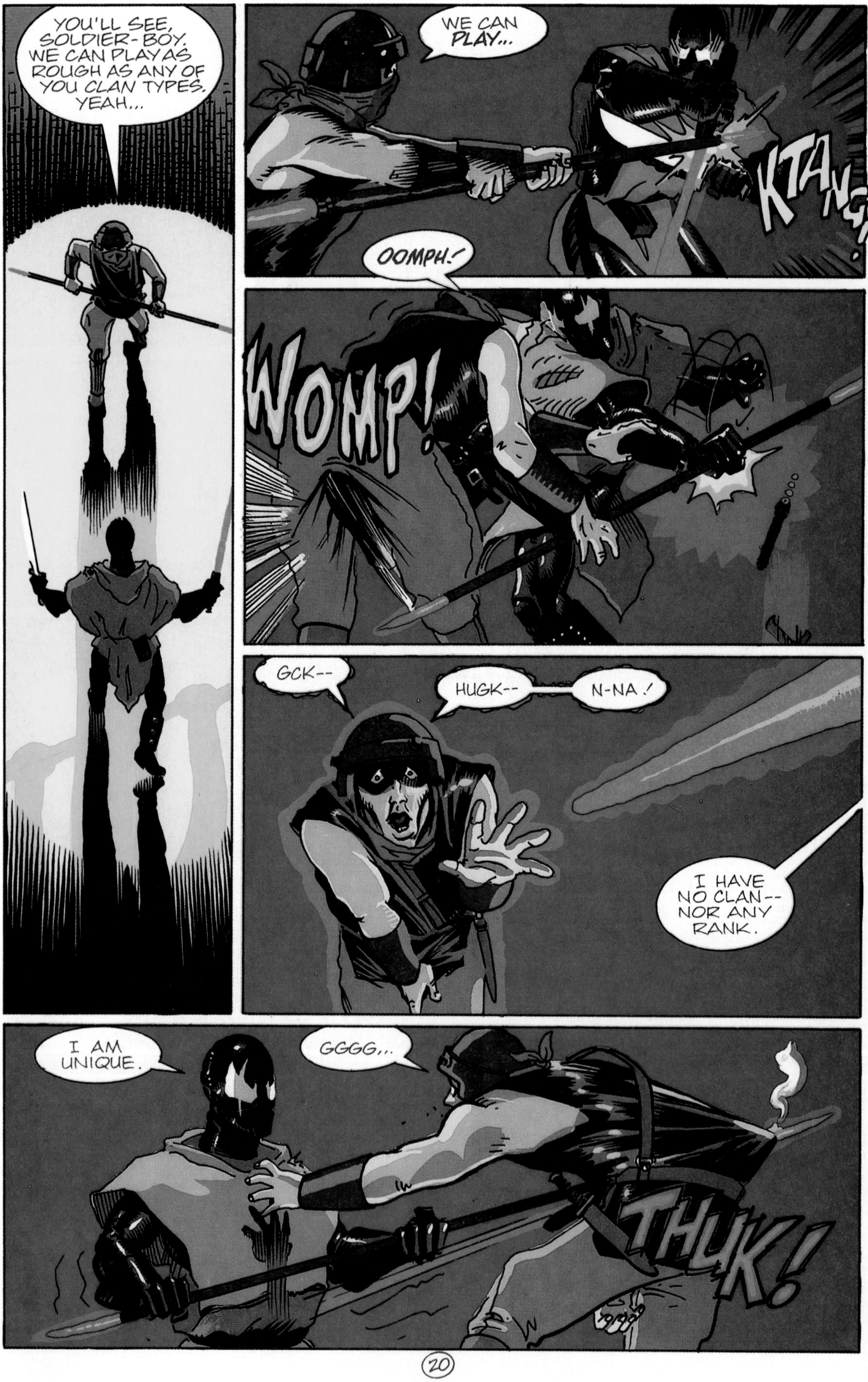

YOU'LL SEE, SOLDIER-BOY. WE CAN PLAY AS ROUGH AS ANY OF YOU CLAN TYPES, YEAH...
WE CAN PLAY...
KTANG!
OOMPH!
WOMP!
GCK--
HUGK--
N-NA!
I HAVE NO CLAN-- NOR ANY RANK.
I AM UNIQUE.
GGGG...
THUK!

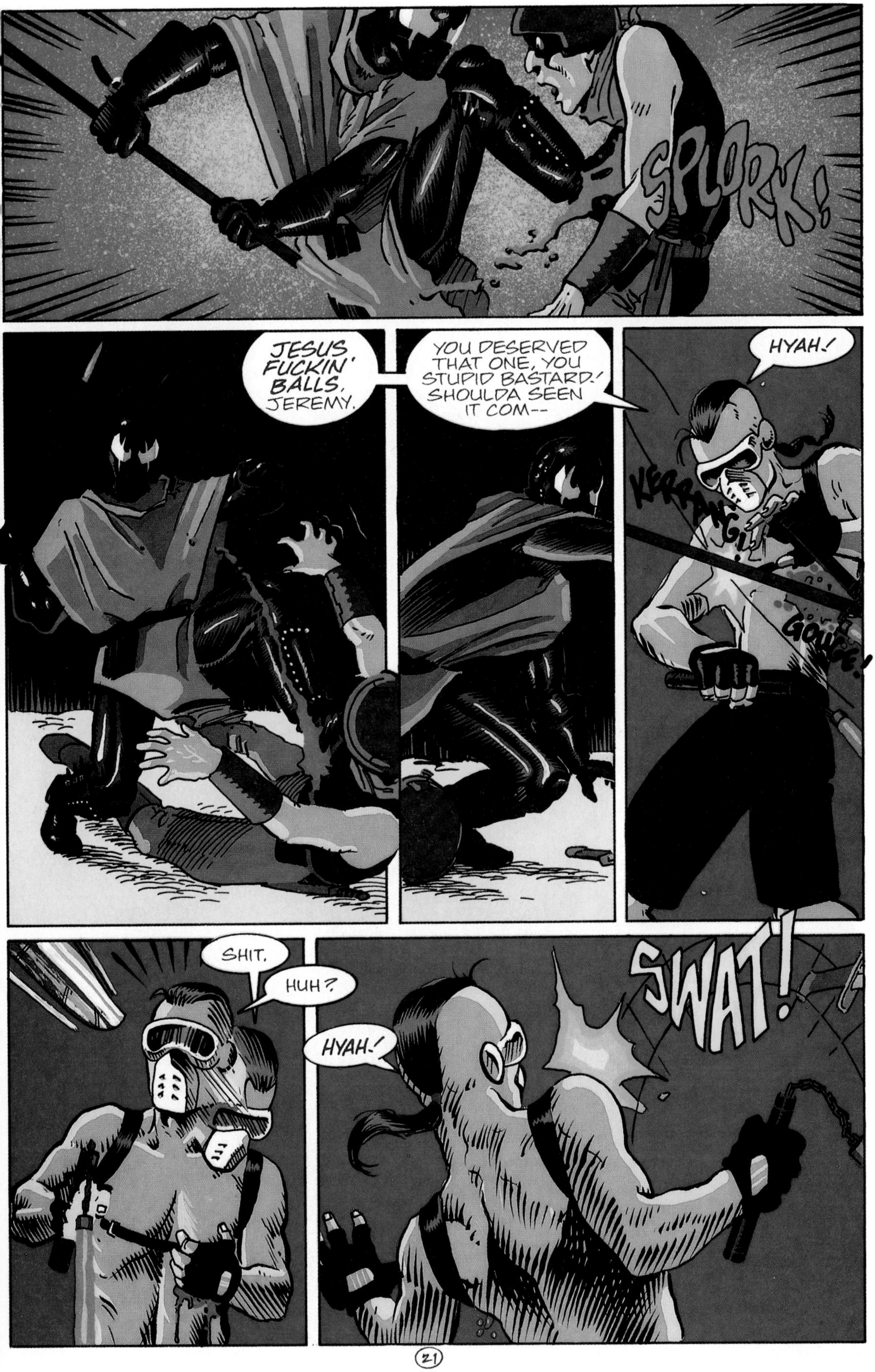
SPLORK!
JESUS. FUCKIN' BALLS, JEREMY.
YOU DESERVED THAT ONE, YOU STUPID BASTARD! SHOULDA SEEN IT COM--
HYAH!
KERRANG!
GOUGE!
SHIT.
HUH?
HYAH!
SWAT!

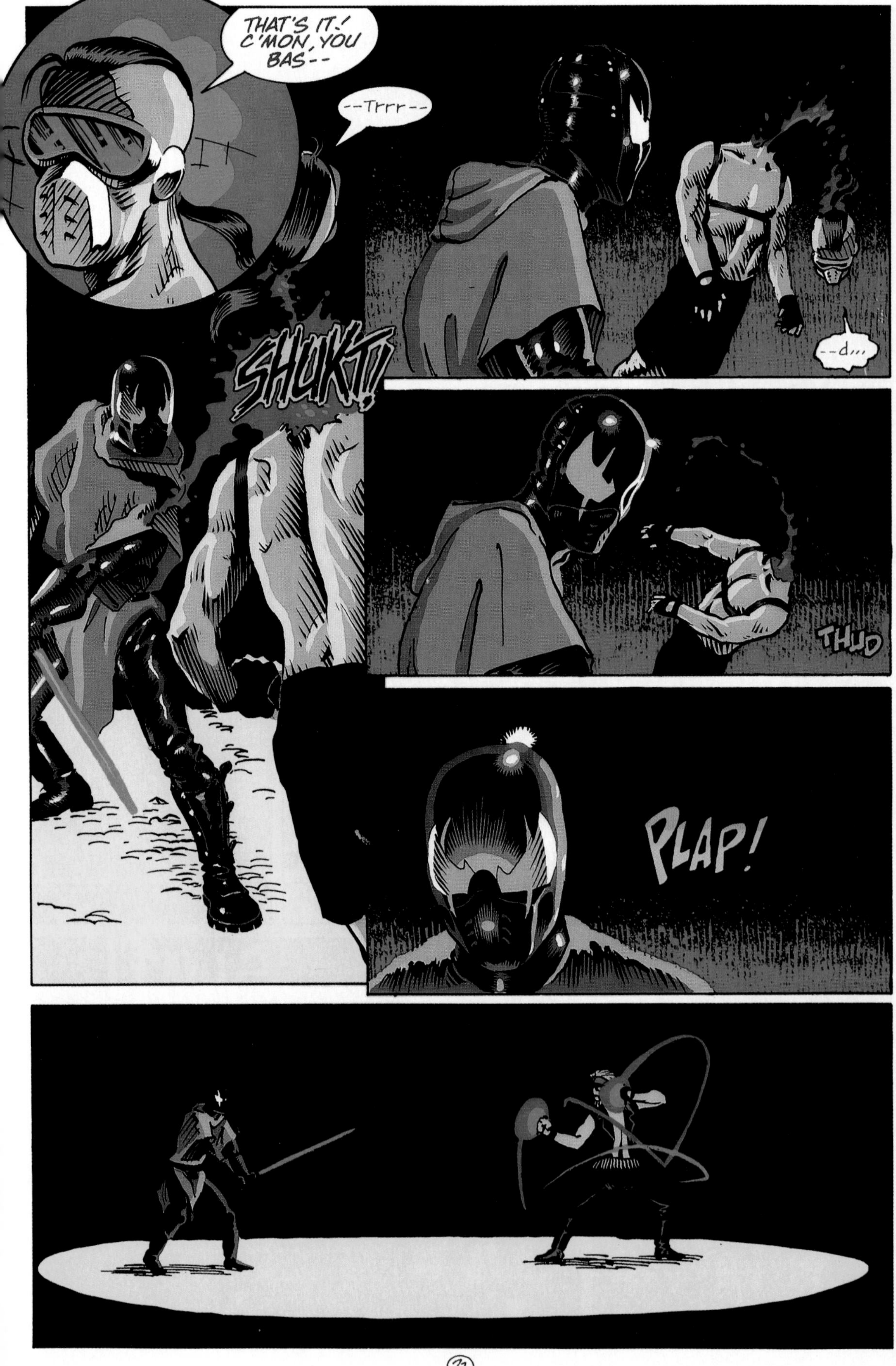
THAT'S IT! C'MON, YOU BAS--
--Trrr--
--d...
SHUKT!
THUD
PLAP!

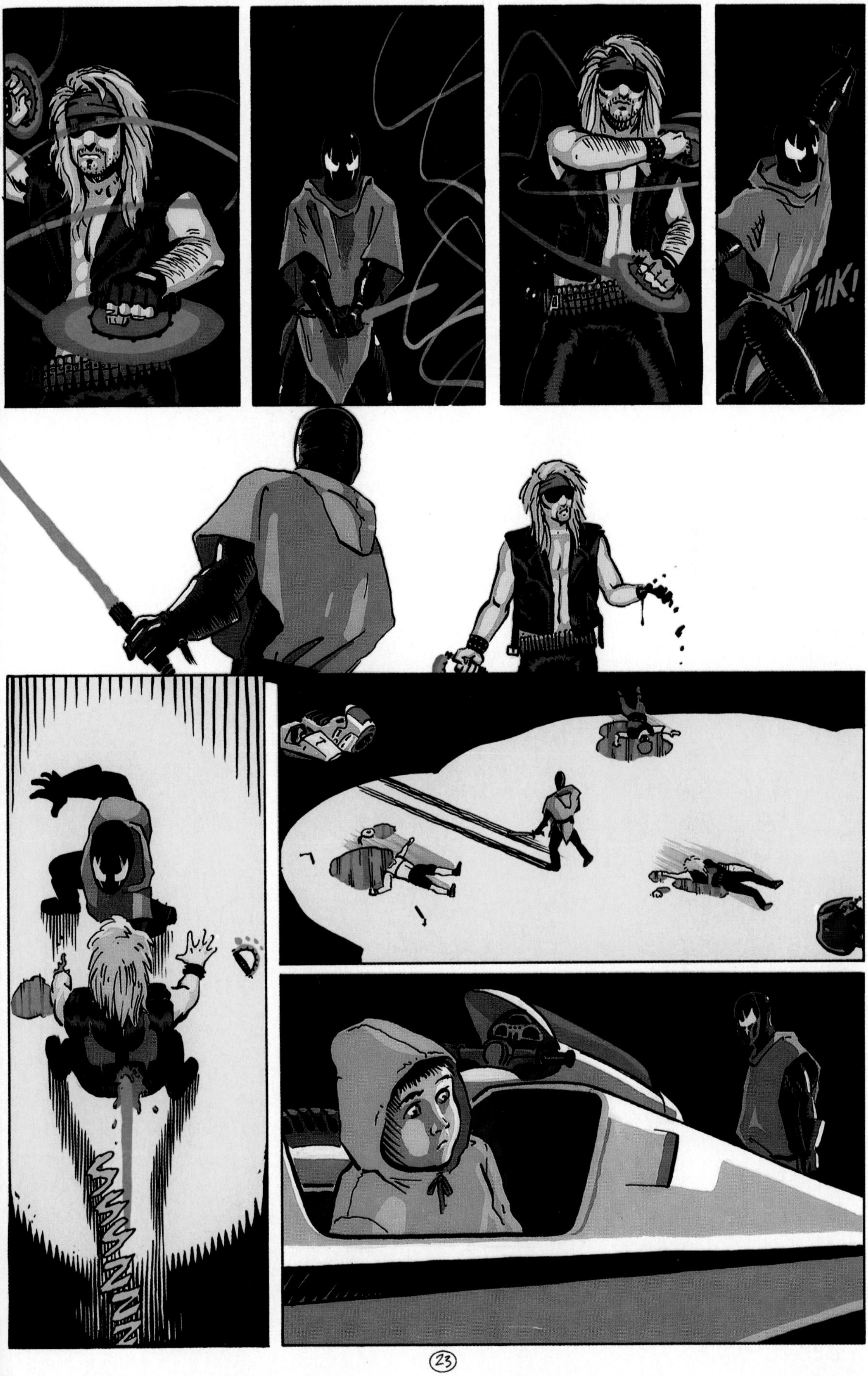
ZIK!

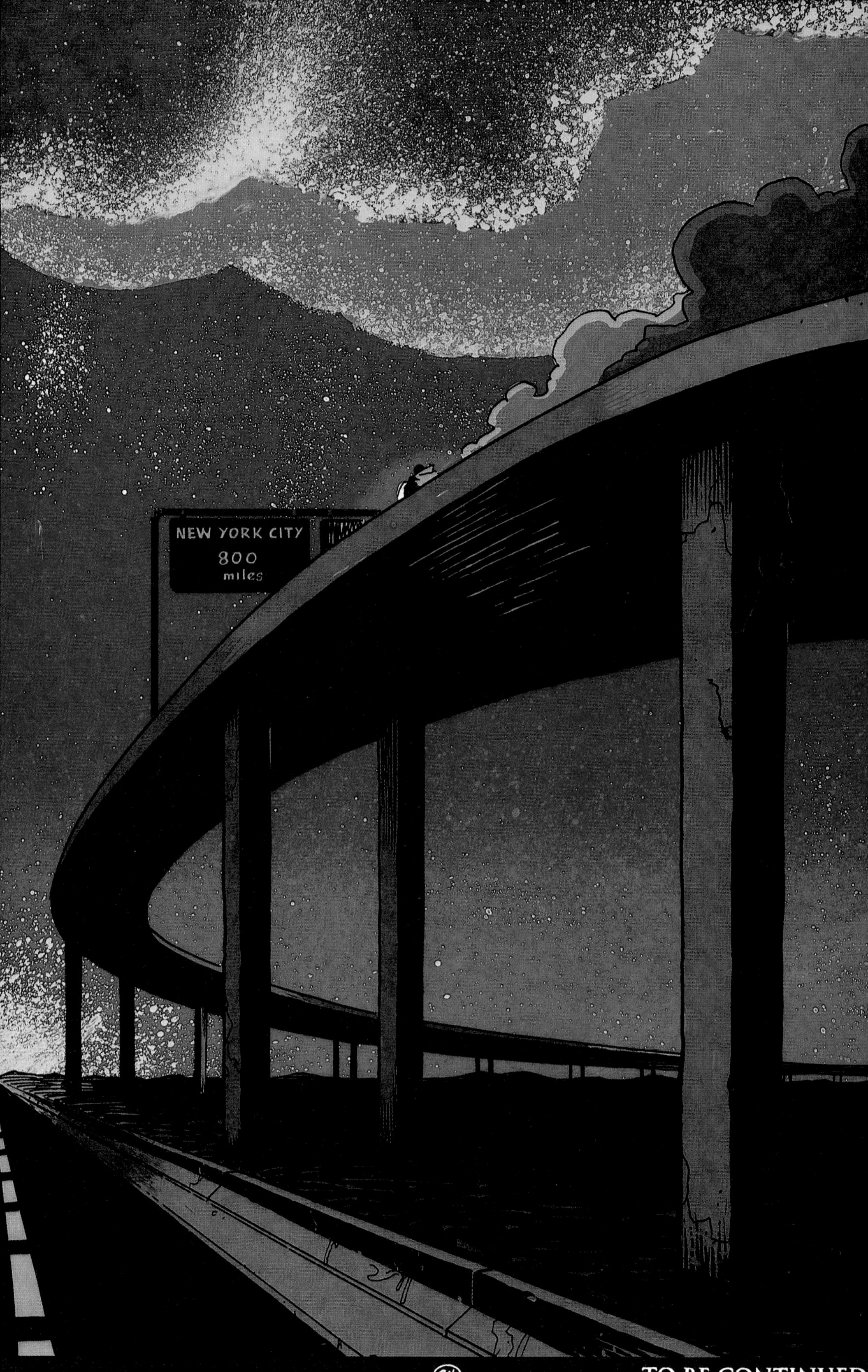
NEW YORK CITY
800
miles



TO BE CONTINUED

# CHAPTER 2
# DEVIL
## *in the city*

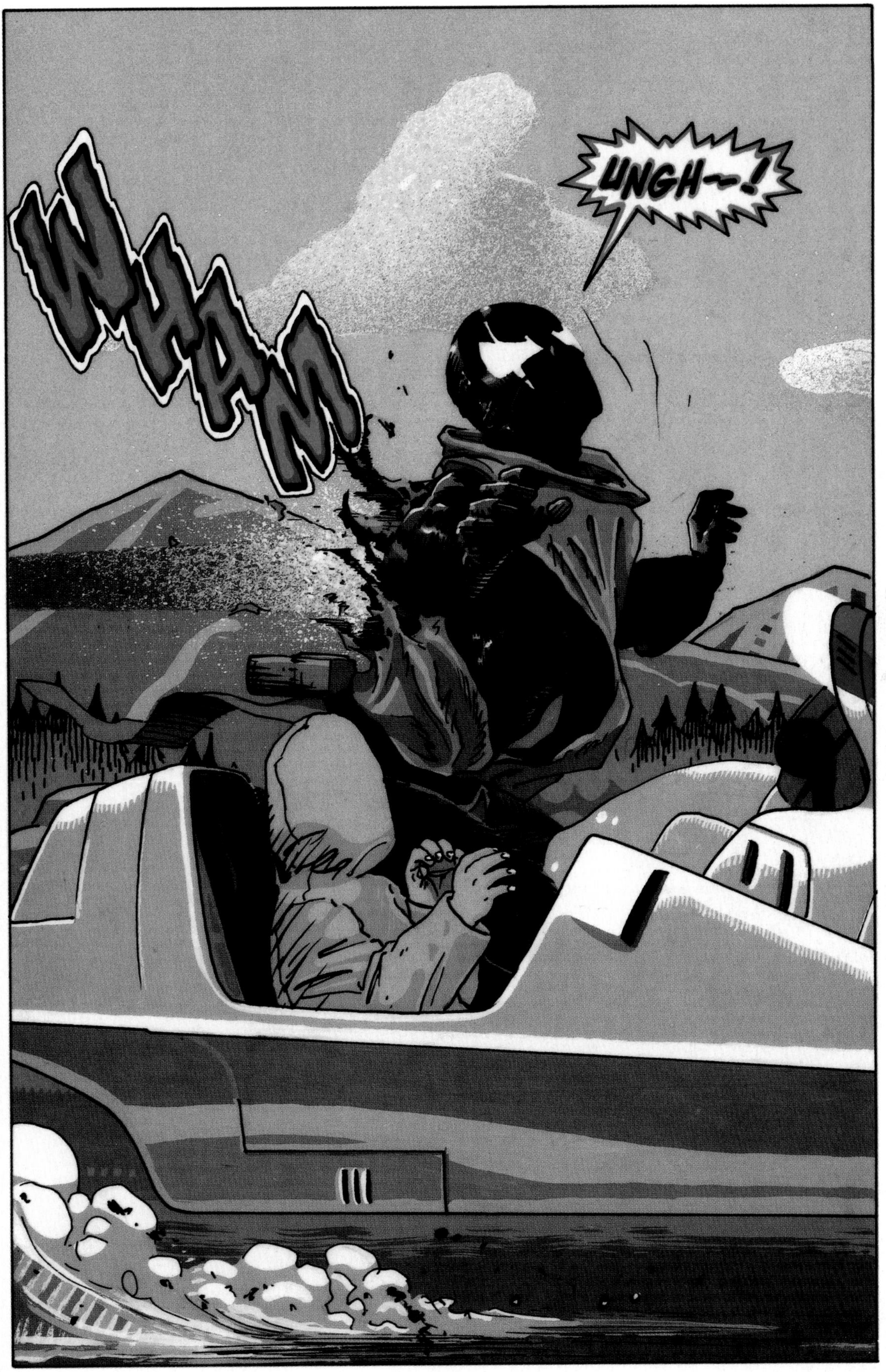
WHAM
UNGH--!

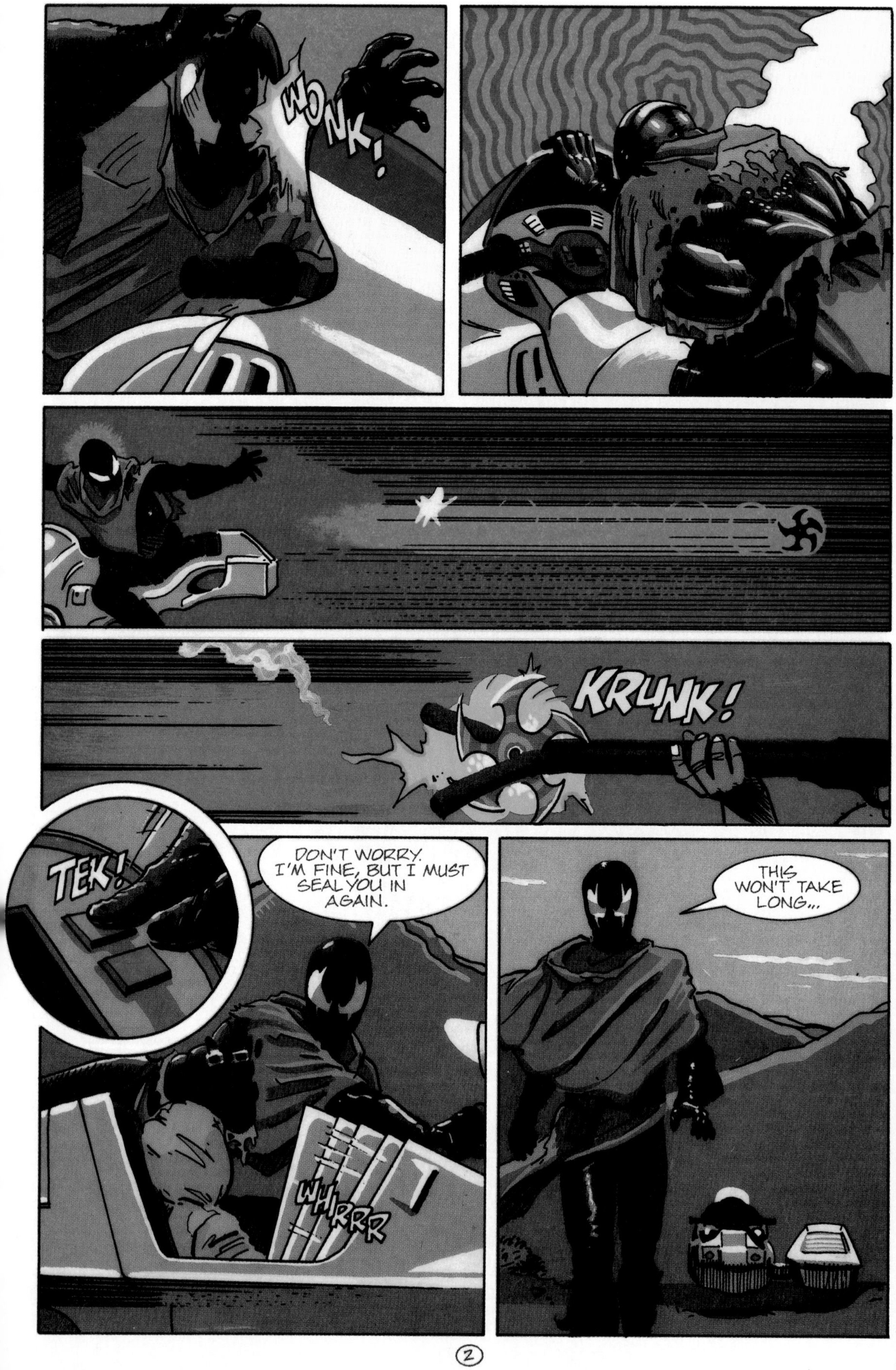
WONK!
KRUNK!
TEK!
DON'T WORRY. I'M FINE, BUT I MUST SEAL YOU IN AGAIN.
WHIRRR
THIS WON'T TAKE LONG...

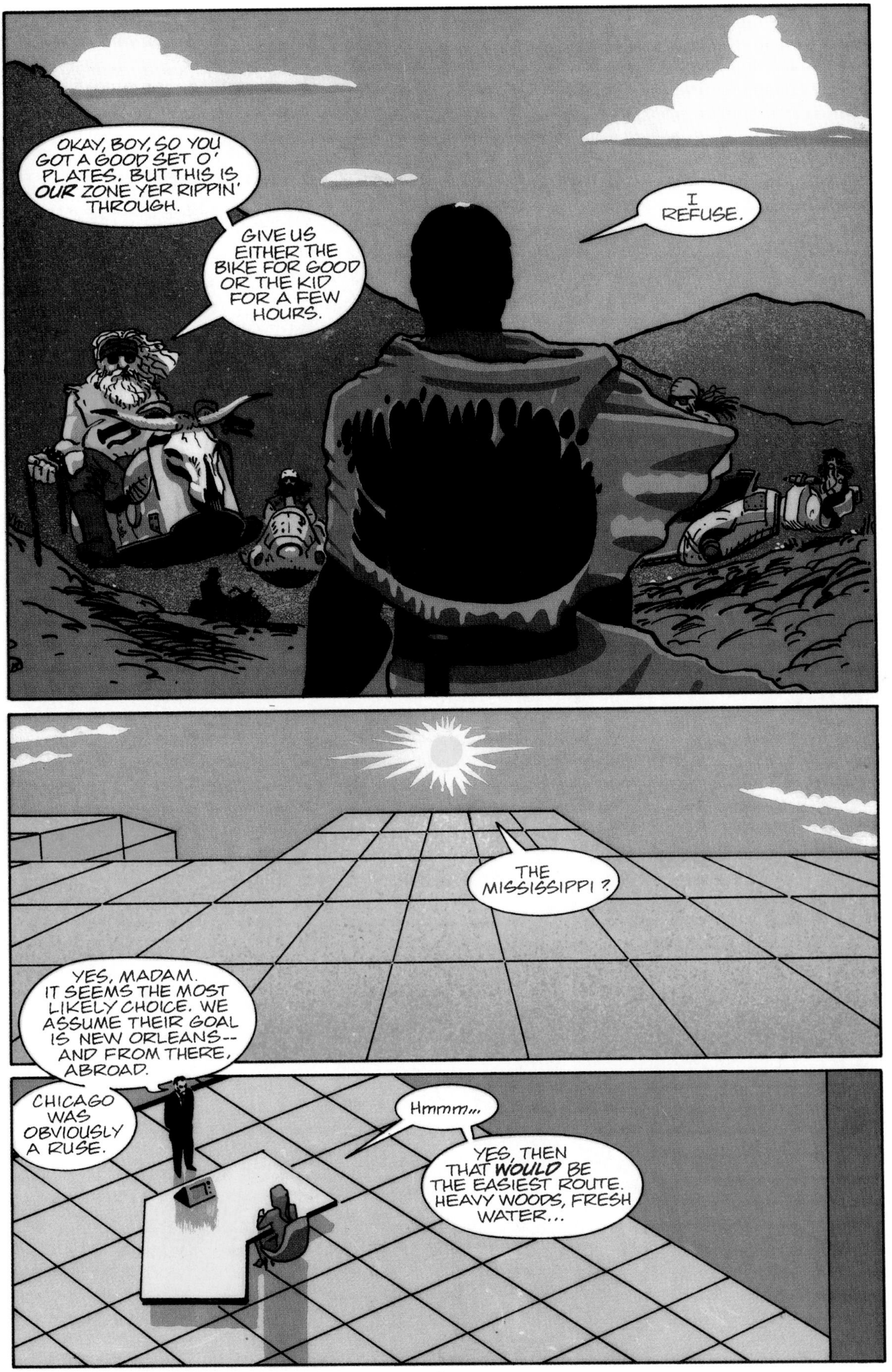
OKAY, BOY, SO YOU GOT A GOOD SET O' PLATES. BUT THIS IS OUR ZONE YER RIPPIN' THROUGH.
GIVE US EITHER THE BIKE FOR GOOD OR THE KID FOR A FEW HOURS.
I REFUSE.
THE MISSISSIPPI?
YES, MADAM. IT SEEMS THE MOST LIKELY CHOICE. WE ASSUME THEIR GOAL IS NEW ORLEANS-- AND FROM THERE, ABROAD.
CHICAGO WAS OBVIOUSLY A RUSE.
Hmmm...
YES, THEN THAT WOULD BE THE EASIEST ROUTE. HEAVY WOODS, FRESH WATER...

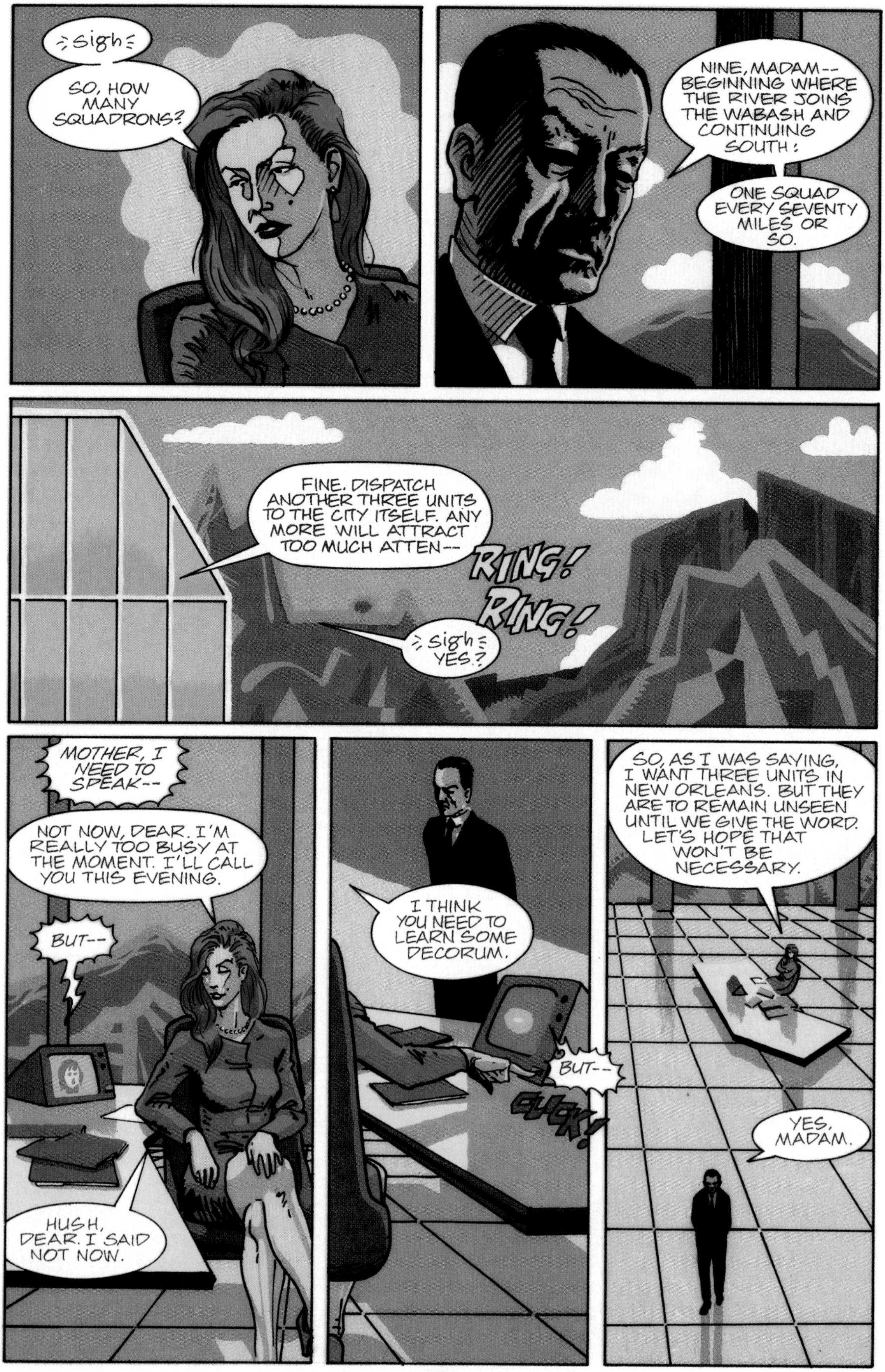
sigh
SO, HOW MANY SQUADRONS?
NINE, MADAM-- BEGINNING WHERE THE RIVER JOINS THE WABASH AND CONTINUING SOUTH:
ONE SQUAD EVERY SEVENTY MILES OR SO.
FINE. DISPATCH ANOTHER THREE UNITS TO THE CITY ITSELF. ANY MORE WILL ATTRACT TOO MUCH ATTEN--
RING!
RING!
sigh YES?
MOTHER, I NEED TO SPEAK--
NOT NOW, DEAR. I'M REALLY TOO BUSY AT THE MOMENT. I'LL CALL YOU THIS EVENING.
BUT--
HUSH, DEAR. I SAID NOT NOW.
I THINK YOU NEED TO LEARN SOME DECORUM.
BUT--
CLICK!
SO, AS I WAS SAYING, I WANT THREE UNITS IN NEW ORLEANS. BUT THEY ARE TO REMAIN UNSEEN UNTIL WE GIVE THE WORD. LET'S HOPE THAT WON'T BE NECESSARY.
YES, MADAM.

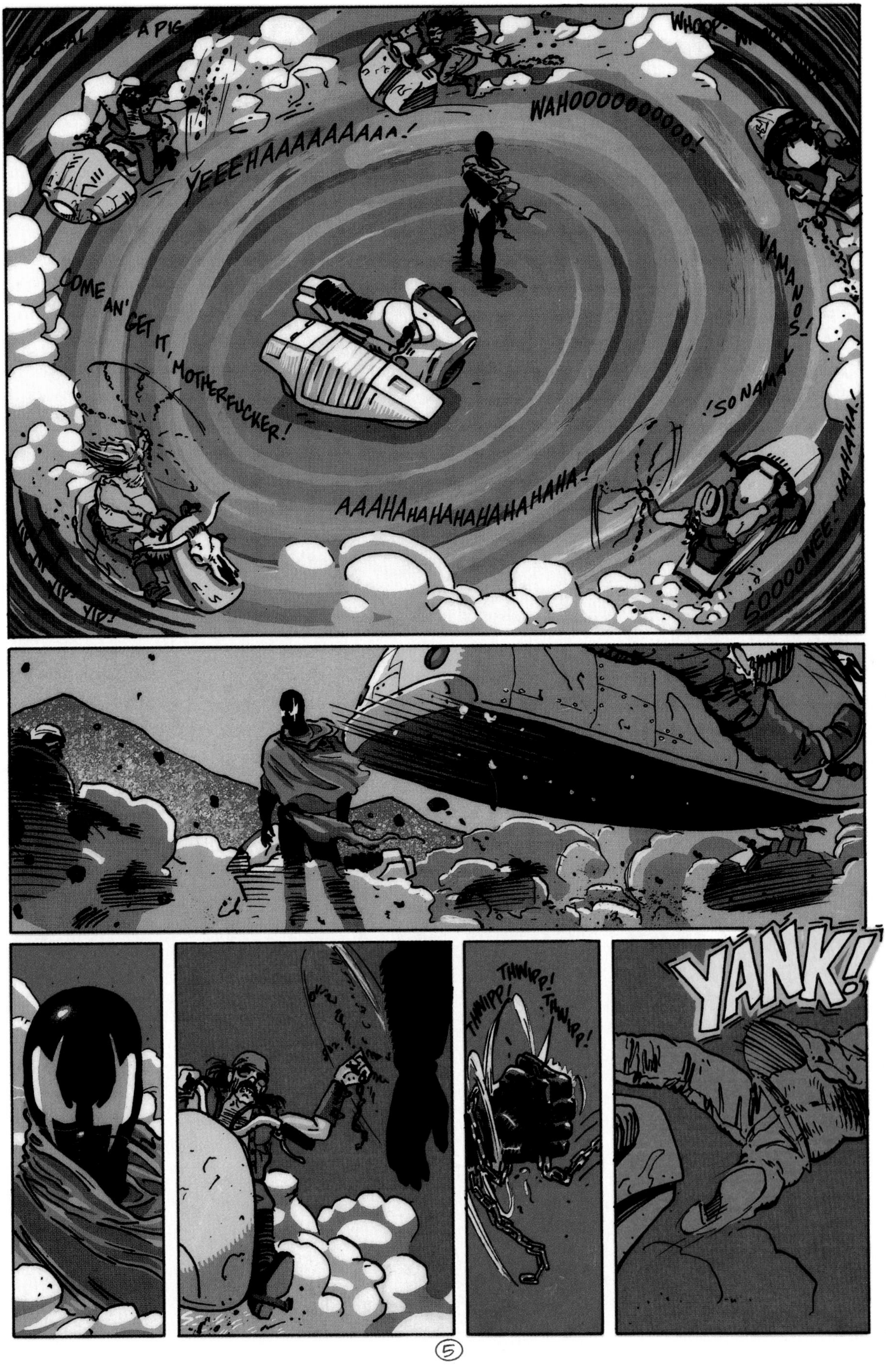
YEEEHAAAAAAAAA!
WAHOOOOOOOOOOO!
VAMANOS!
COME AN' GET IT, MOTHERFUCKER!
AAAHAHAHAHAHAHAHAHA!
SOOOOWEE! HAHAHA!
THWIPP! THWIPP! THWIPP!
YANK!

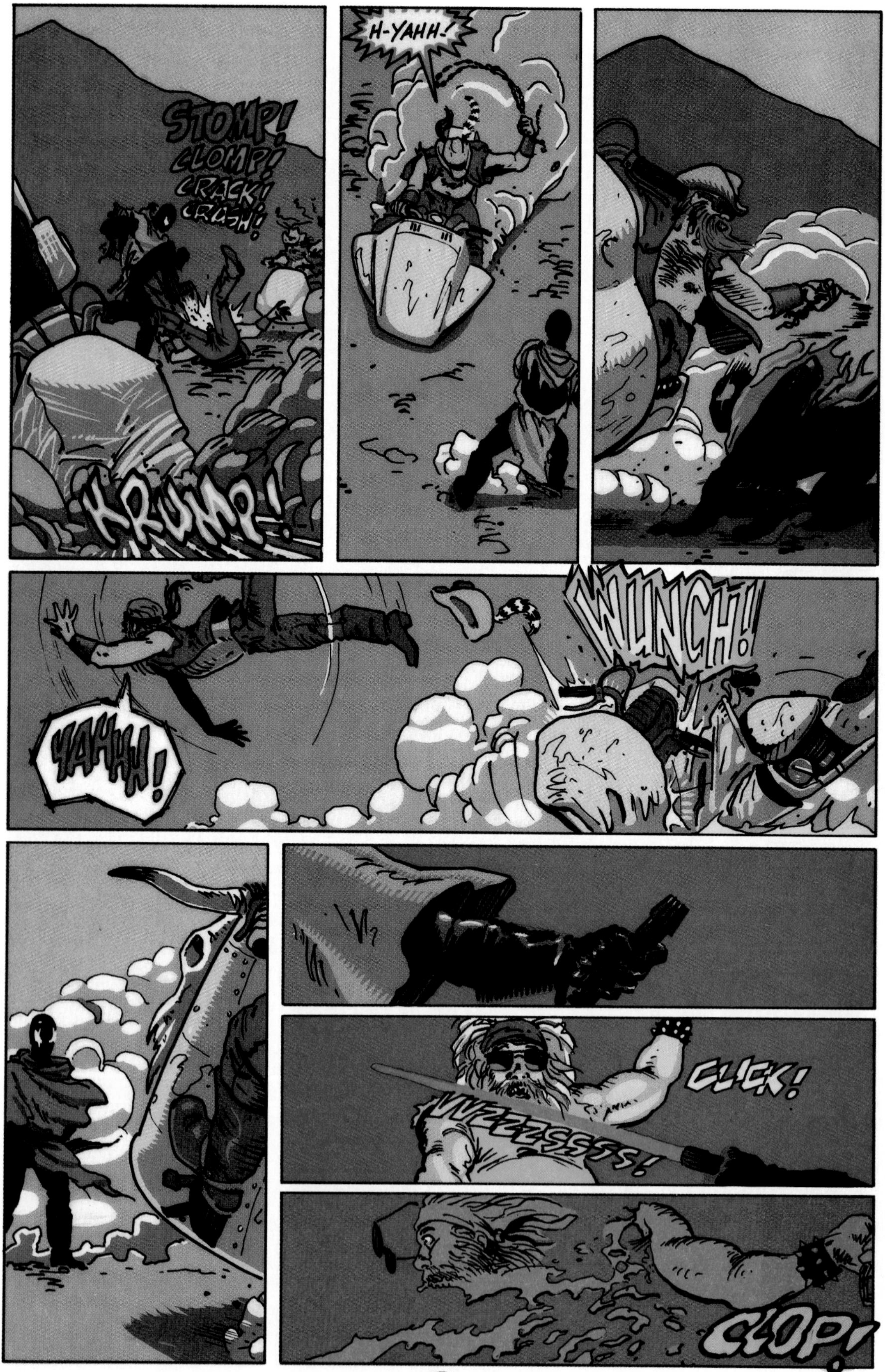
STOMP!
CLOMP!
CRACK!
CRASH!
KRUMP!
H-YAHH!
WUNCH!
YAHHH!
CLICK!
VVZZZSSSSS!
CLOP!

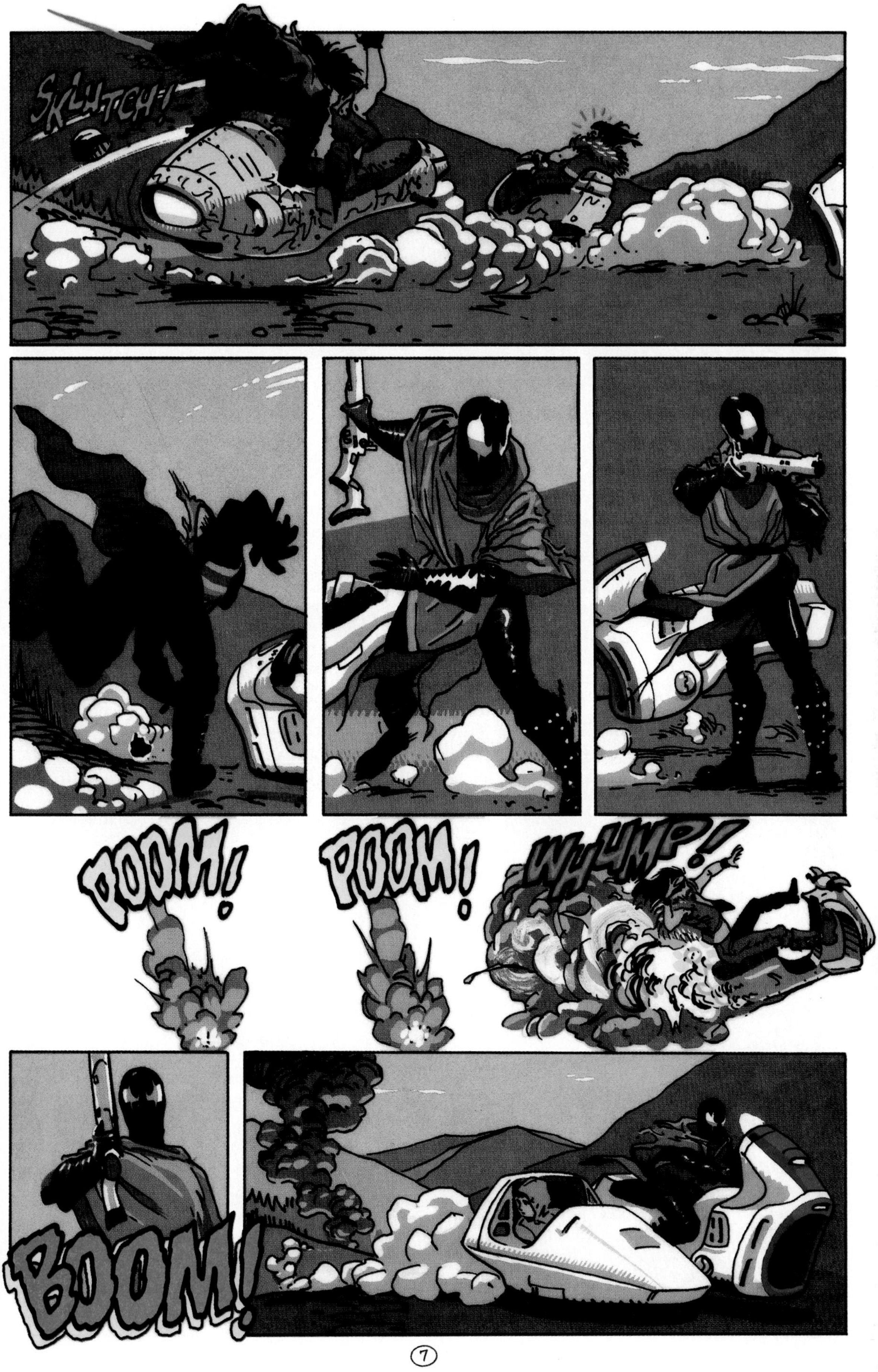
SKLUTCH!
POOM!
POOM!
WHUMP!
BOOM!

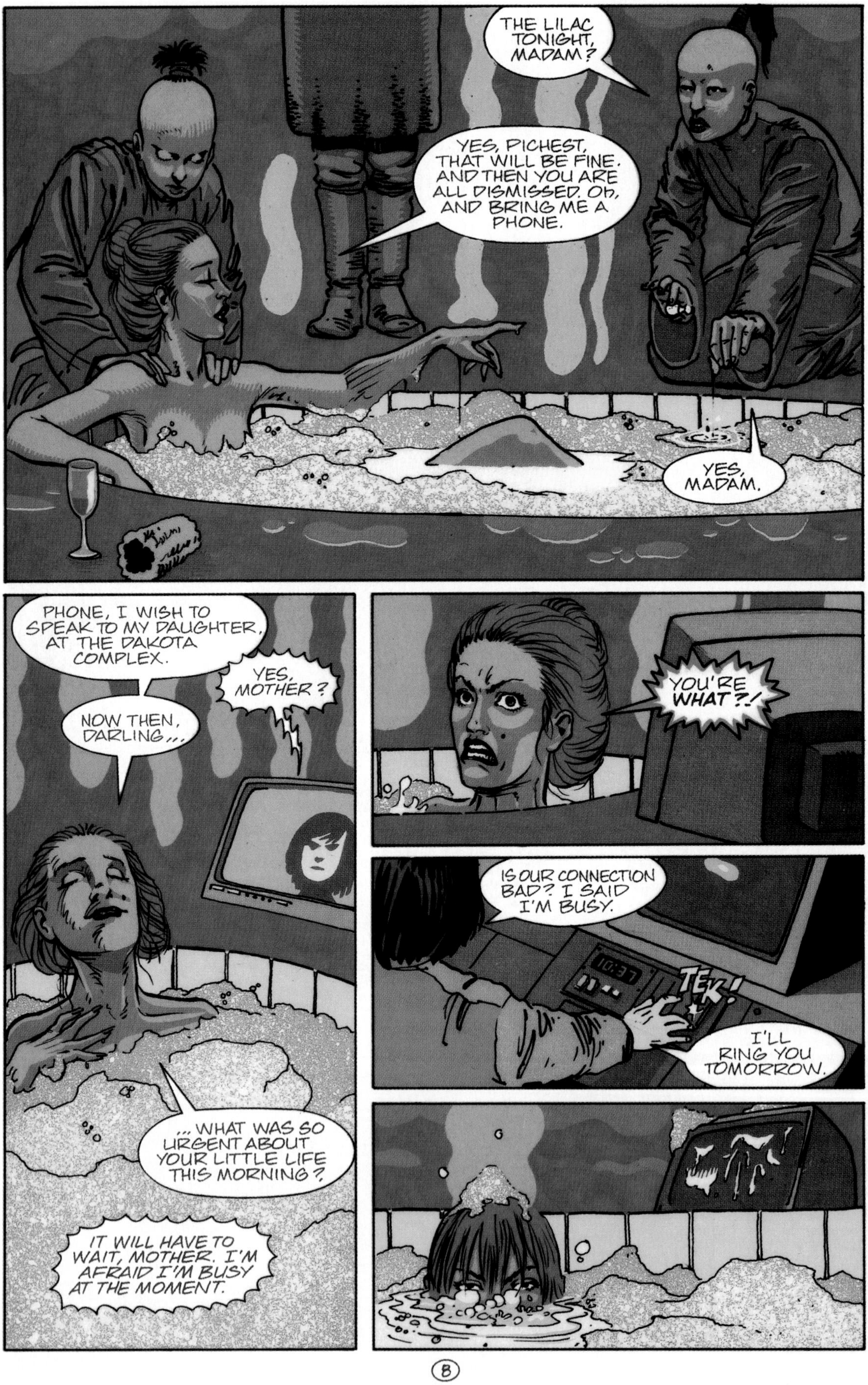
THE LILAC TONIGHT, MADAM?
YES, PICHEST, THAT WILL BE FINE. AND THEN YOU ARE ALL DISMISSED. Oh, AND BRING ME A PHONE.
YES, MADAM.
PHONE, I WISH TO SPEAK TO MY DAUGHTER, AT THE DAKOTA COMPLEX.
YES, MOTHER?
NOW THEN, DARLING...
...WHAT WAS SO URGENT ABOUT YOUR LITTLE LIFE THIS MORNING?
IT WILL HAVE TO WAIT, MOTHER. I'M AFRAID I'M BUSY AT THE MOMENT.
YOU'RE WHAT?!
IS OUR CONNECTION BAD? I SAID I'M BUSY.
TEK!
I'LL RING YOU TOMORROW.

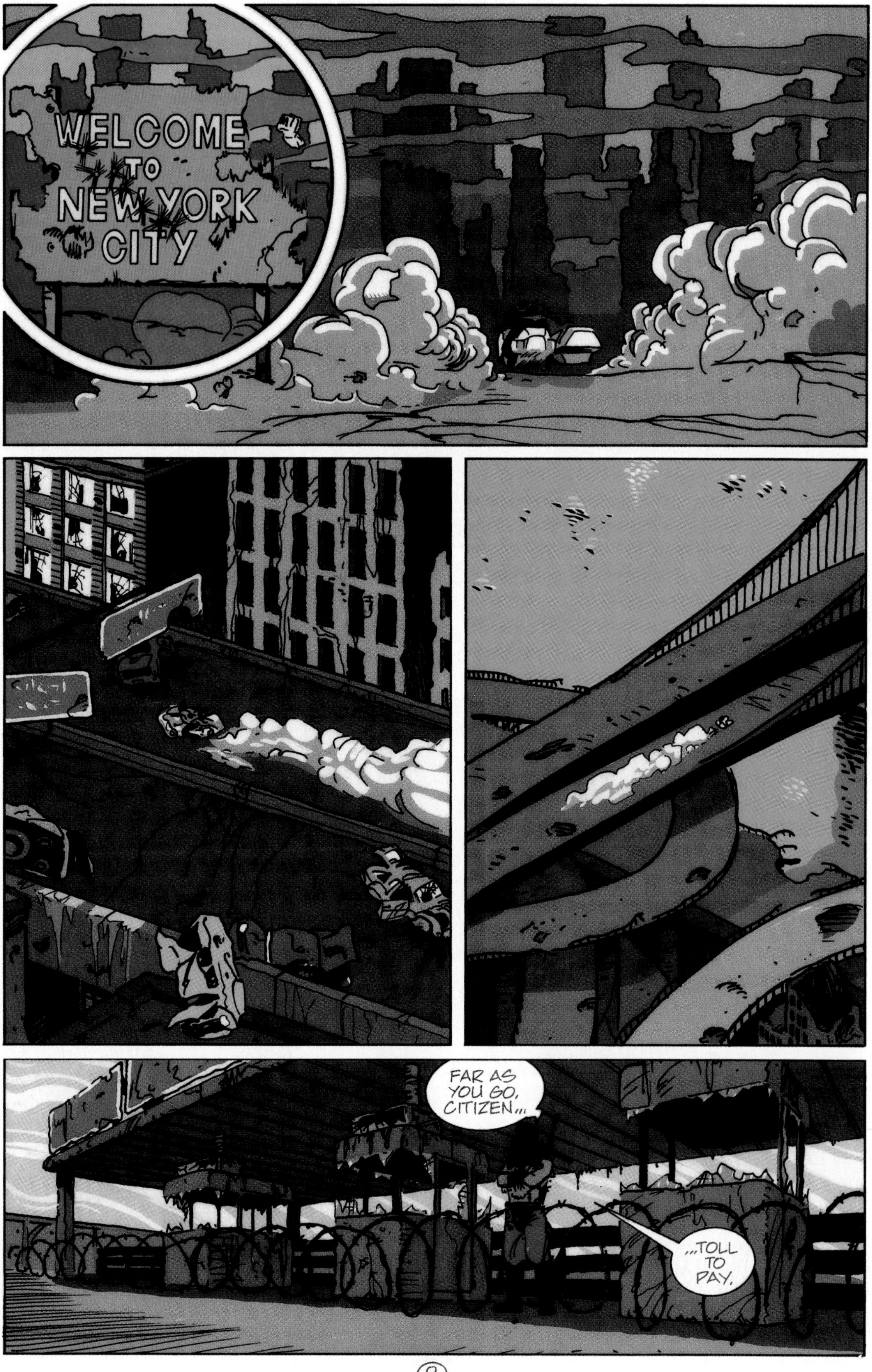
WELCOME TO NEW YORK CITY
FAR AS YOU GO, CITIZEN...
...TOLL TO PAY.

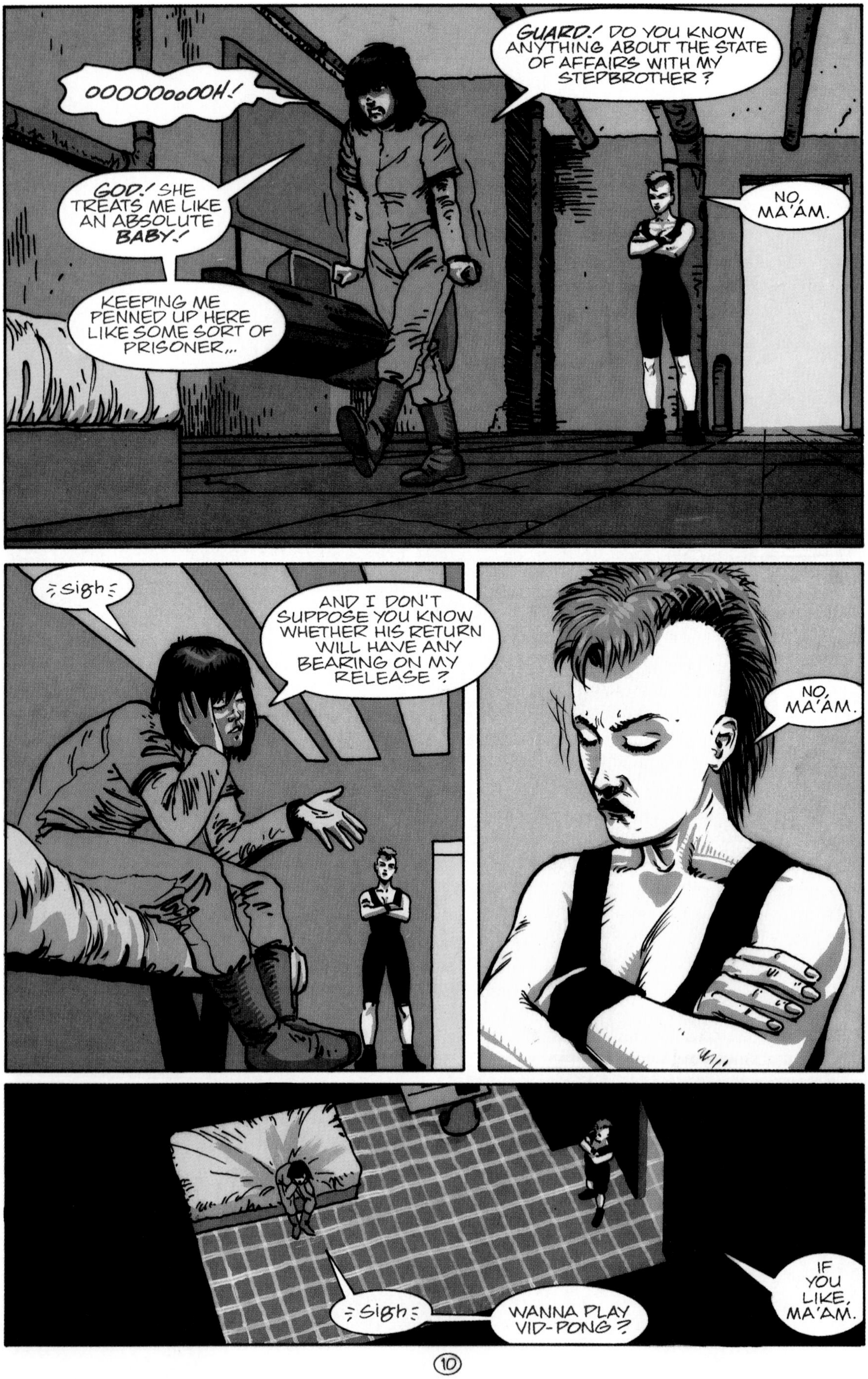
OOOOOOooOOH!
GUARD! DO YOU KNOW ANYTHING ABOUT THE STATE OF AFFAIRS WITH MY STEPBROTHER?
GOD! SHE TREATS ME LIKE AN ABSOLUTE BABY!
KEEPING ME PENNED UP HERE LIKE SOME SORT OF PRISONER...
NO, MA'AM.
sigh
AND I DON'T SUPPOSE YOU KNOW WHETHER HIS RETURN WILL HAVE ANY BEARING ON MY RELEASE?
NO, MA'AM.
sigh
WANNA PLAY VID-PONG?
IF YOU LIKE, MA'AM.

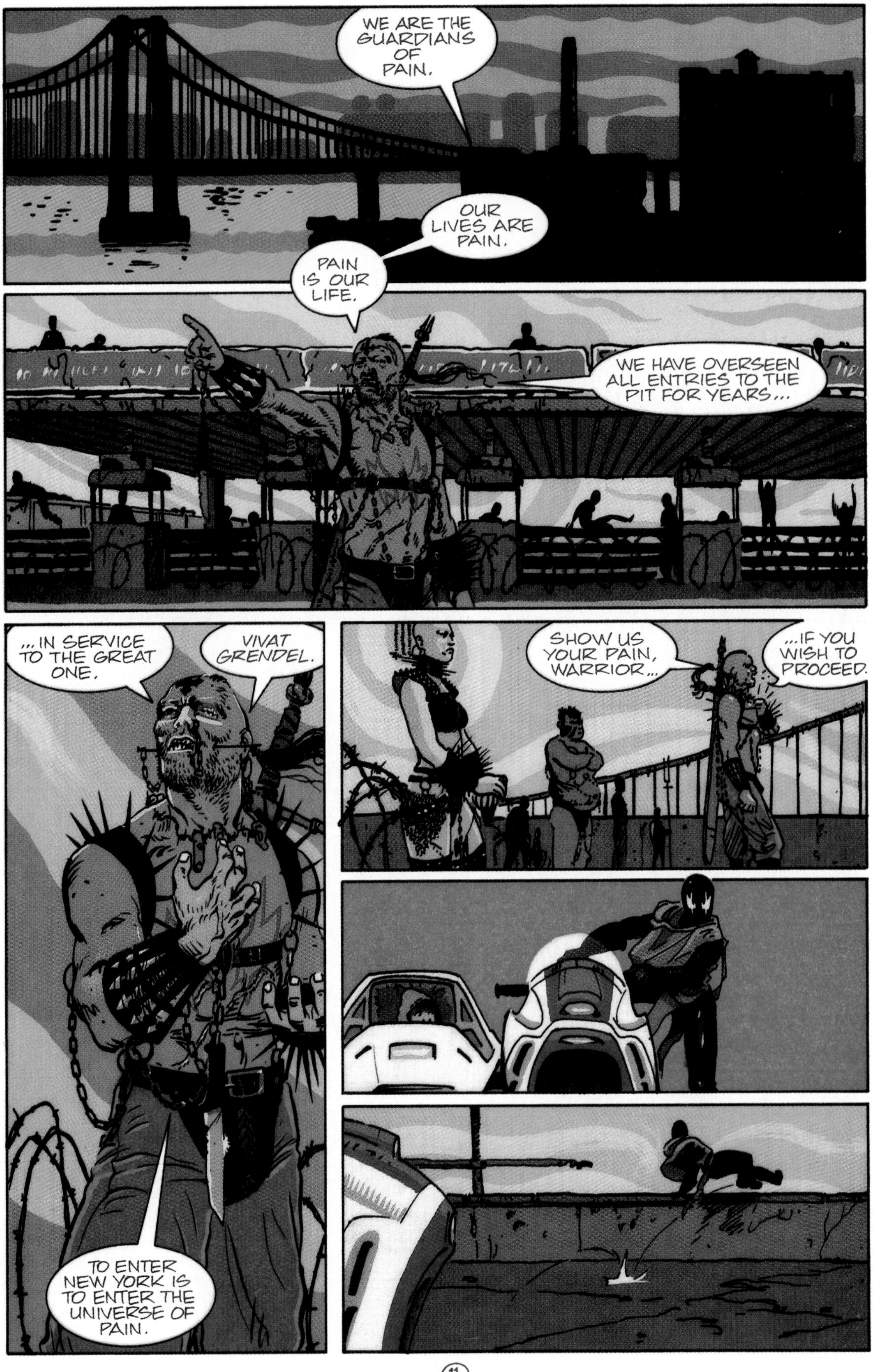
WE ARE THE GUARDIANS OF PAIN.
OUR LIVES ARE PAIN.
PAIN IS OUR LIFE.
WE HAVE OVERSEEN ALL ENTRIES TO THE PIT FOR YEARS...
...IN SERVICE TO THE GREAT ONE.
VIVAT GRENDEL.
TO ENTER NEW YORK IS TO ENTER THE UNIVERSE OF PAIN.
SHOW US YOUR PAIN, WARRIOR...
...IF YOU WISH TO PROCEED.

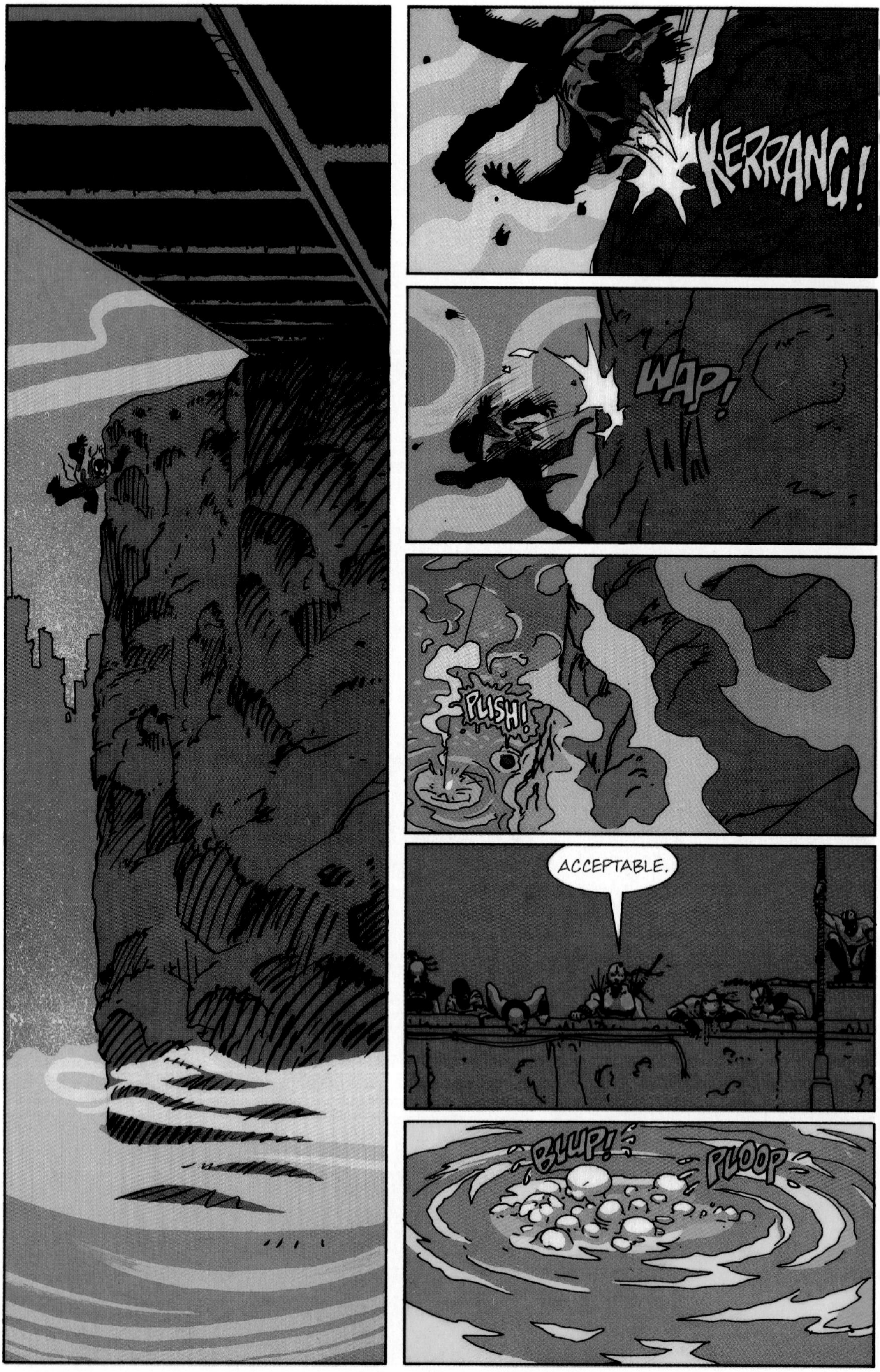
K-ERRANG!
WAP!
PLISH!
ACCEPTABLE.
BLUP!
PLOOP

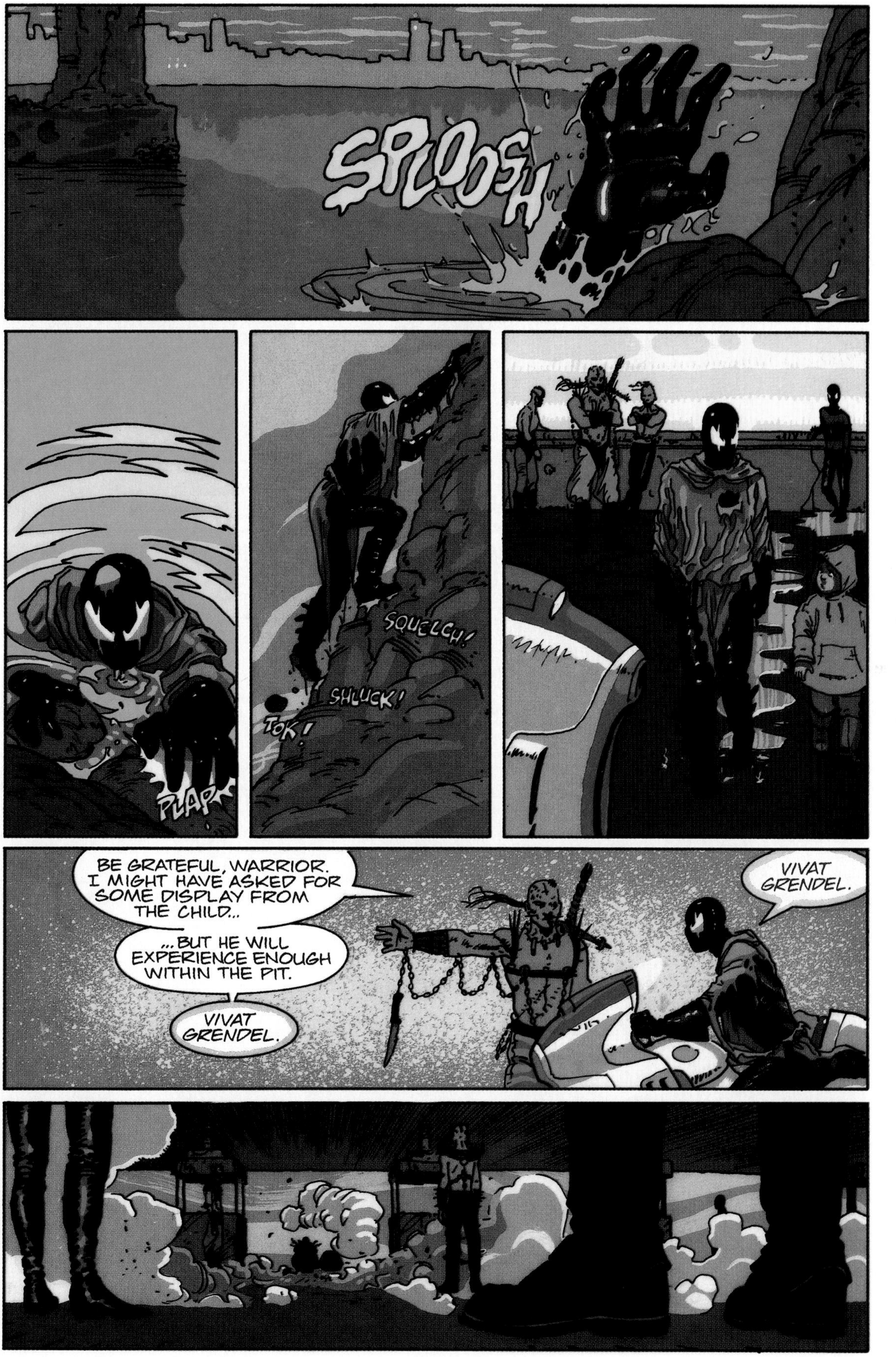
SPLOOSH
PLAP
SQUELCH!
SHLUCK!
TOK!
BE GRATEFUL, WARRIOR. I MIGHT HAVE ASKED FOR SOME DISPLAY FROM THE CHILD...
...BUT HE WILL EXPERIENCE ENOUGH WITHIN THE PIT.
VIVAT GRENDEL.
VIVAT GRENDEL.

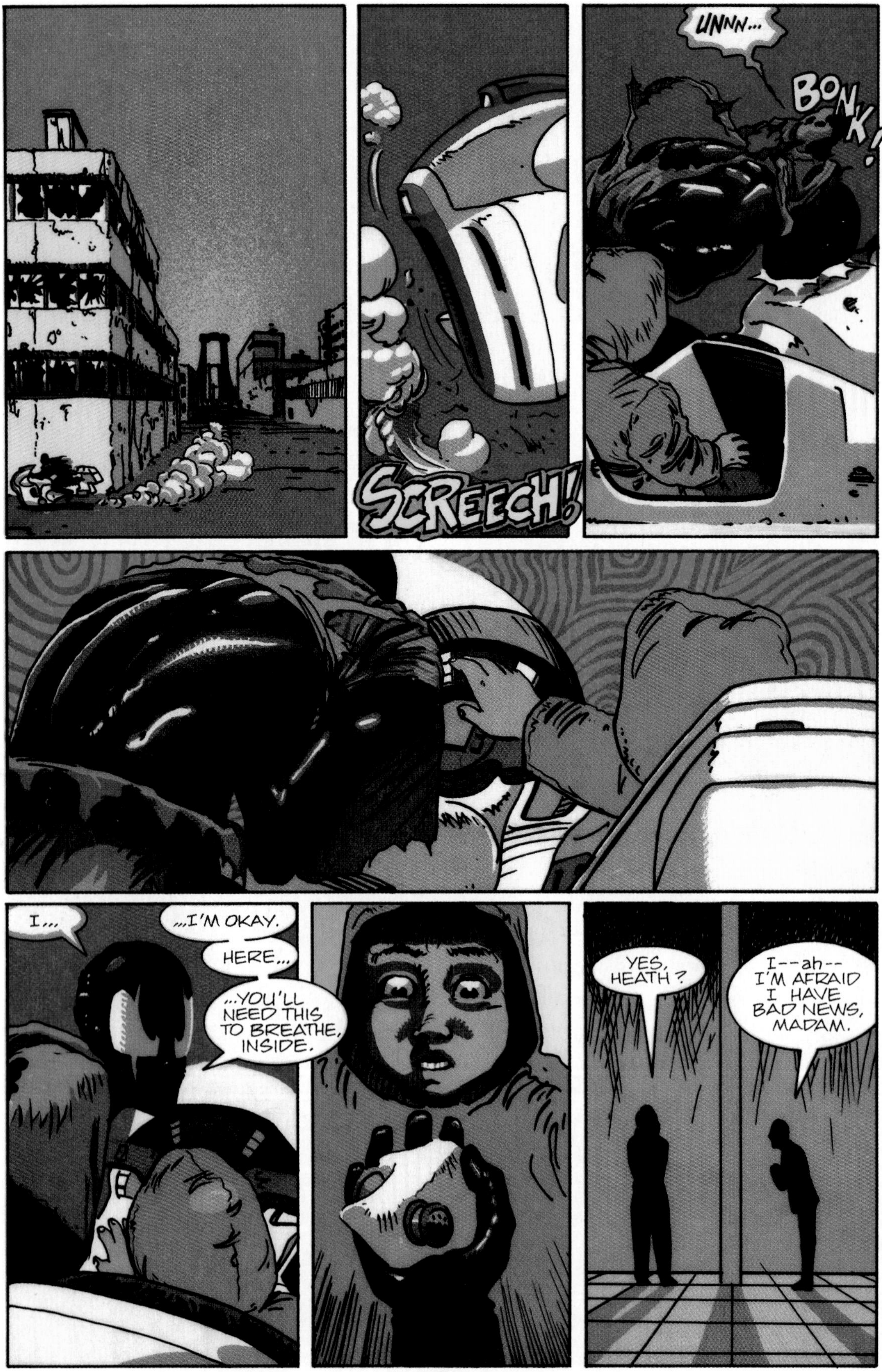
SCREECH!
UNNN...
BONK!
I...
...I'M OKAY.
HERE...
...YOU'LL NEED THIS TO BREATHE, INSIDE.
YES, HEATH?
I--ah-- I'M AFRAID I HAVE BAD NEWS, MADAM.

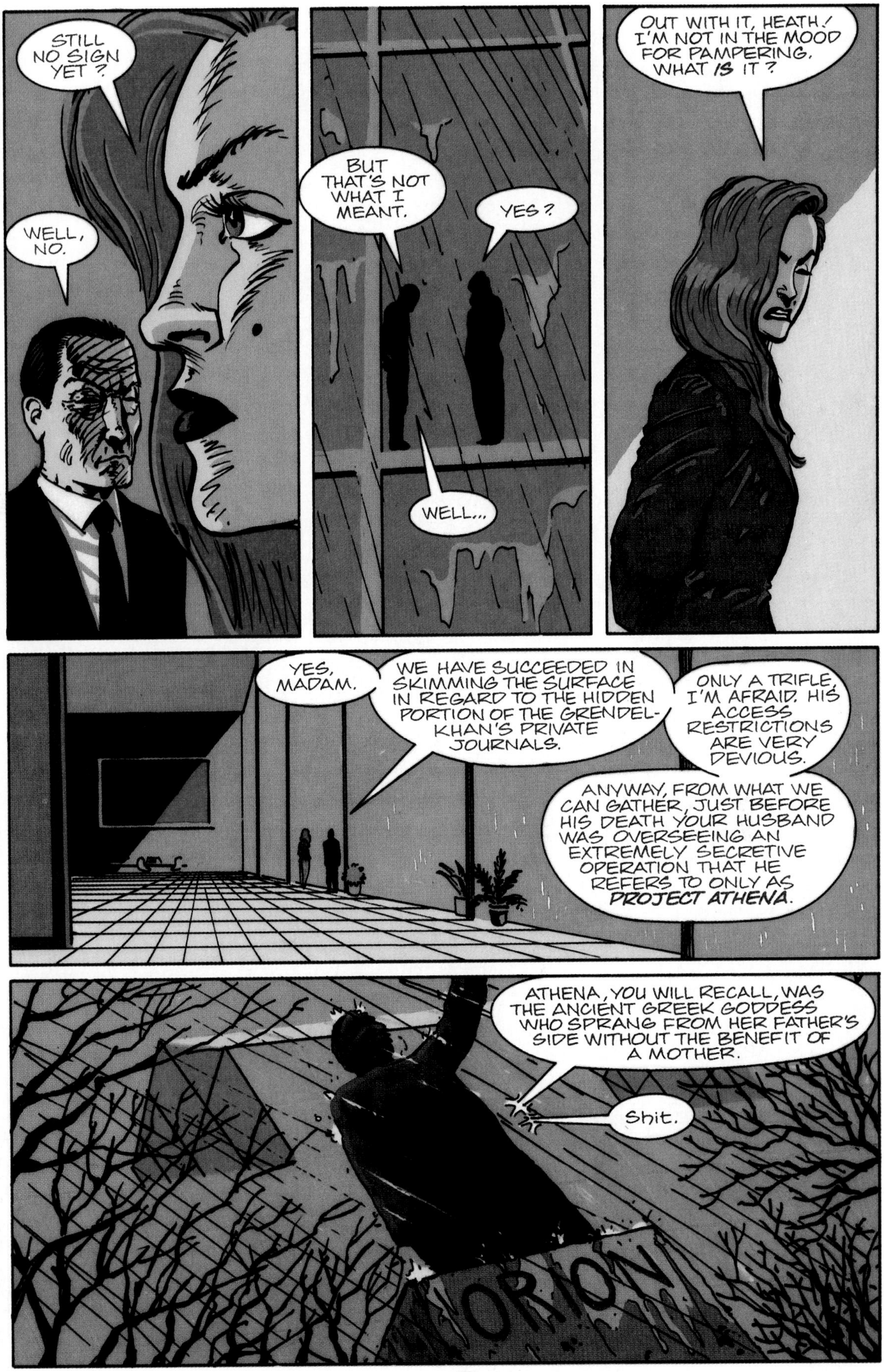
STILL NO SIGN YET ?
WELL, NO.
BUT THAT'S NOT WHAT I MEANT.
YES ?
WELL...
OUT WITH IT, HEATH! I'M NOT IN THE MOOD FOR PAMPERING. WHAT IS IT ?
YES, MADAM.
WE HAVE SUCCEEDED IN SKIMMING THE SURFACE IN REGARD TO THE HIDDEN PORTION OF THE GRENDEL-KHAN'S PRIVATE JOURNALS.
ONLY A TRIFLE, I'M AFRAID. HIS ACCESS RESTRICTIONS ARE VERY DEVIOUS.
ANYWAY, FROM WHAT WE CAN GATHER, JUST BEFORE HIS DEATH YOUR HUSBAND WAS OVERSEEING AN EXTREMELY SECRETIVE OPERATION THAT HE REFERS TO ONLY AS PROJECT ATHENA.
ATHENA, YOU WILL RECALL, WAS THE ANCIENT GREEK GODDESS WHO SPRANG FROM HER FATHER'S SIDE WITHOUT THE BENEFIT OF A MOTHER.
Shit.
ORION

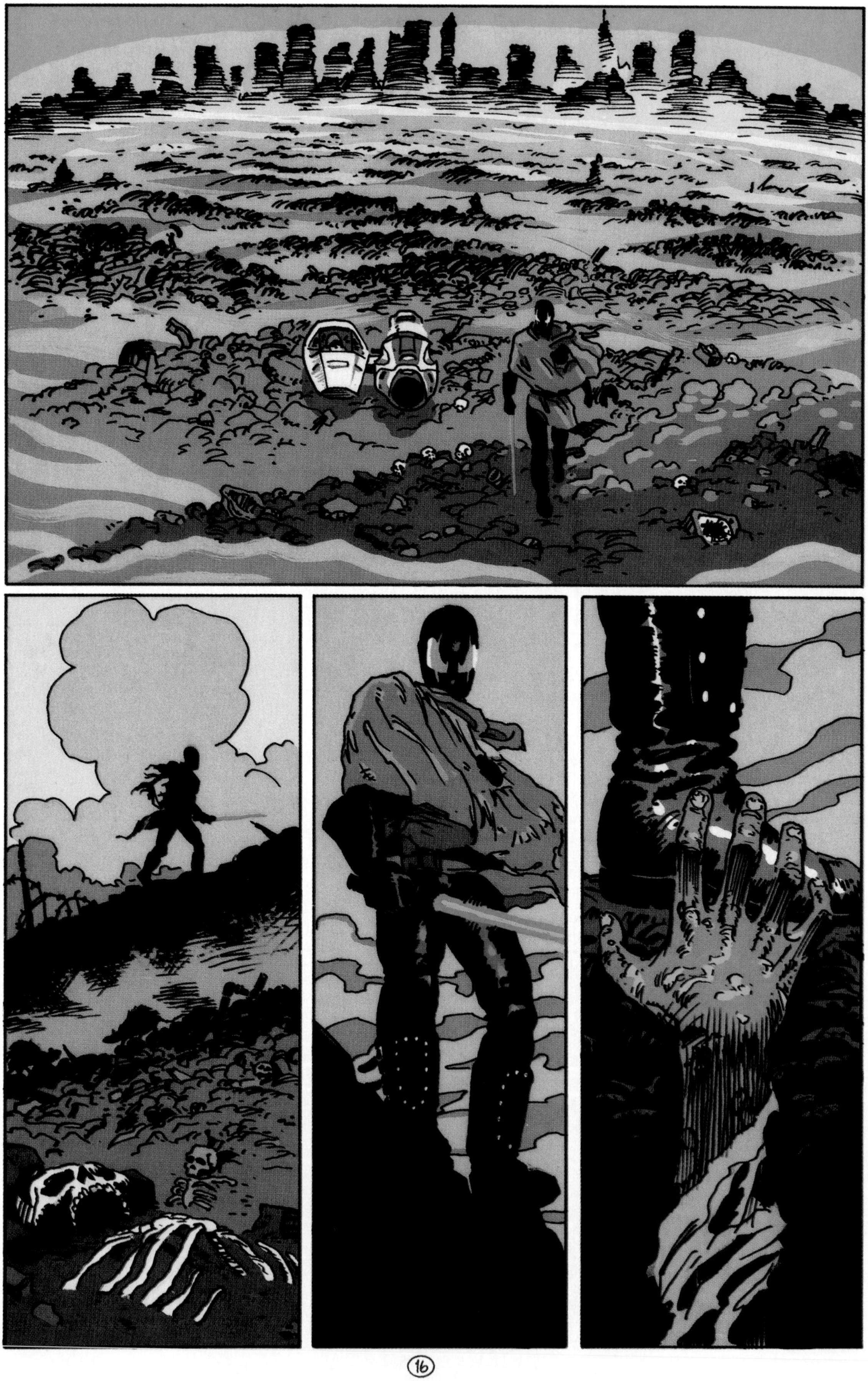

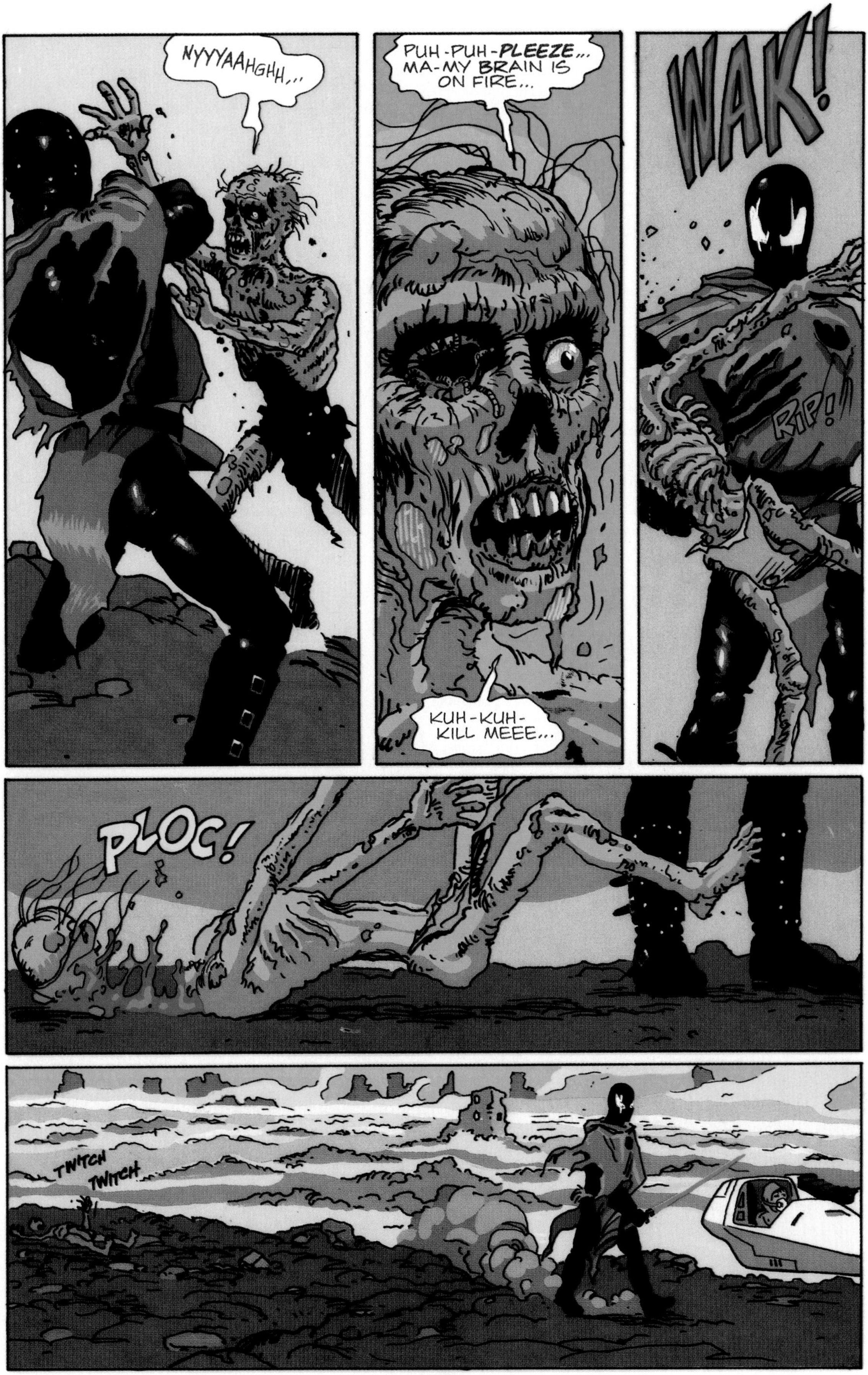
NYYYAAHGHH,,,
PUH-PUH-PLEEZE... MA-MY BRAIN IS ON FIRE...
KUH-KUH-KILL MEEE...
WAK!
RIP!
PLOC!
TWITCH TWITCH

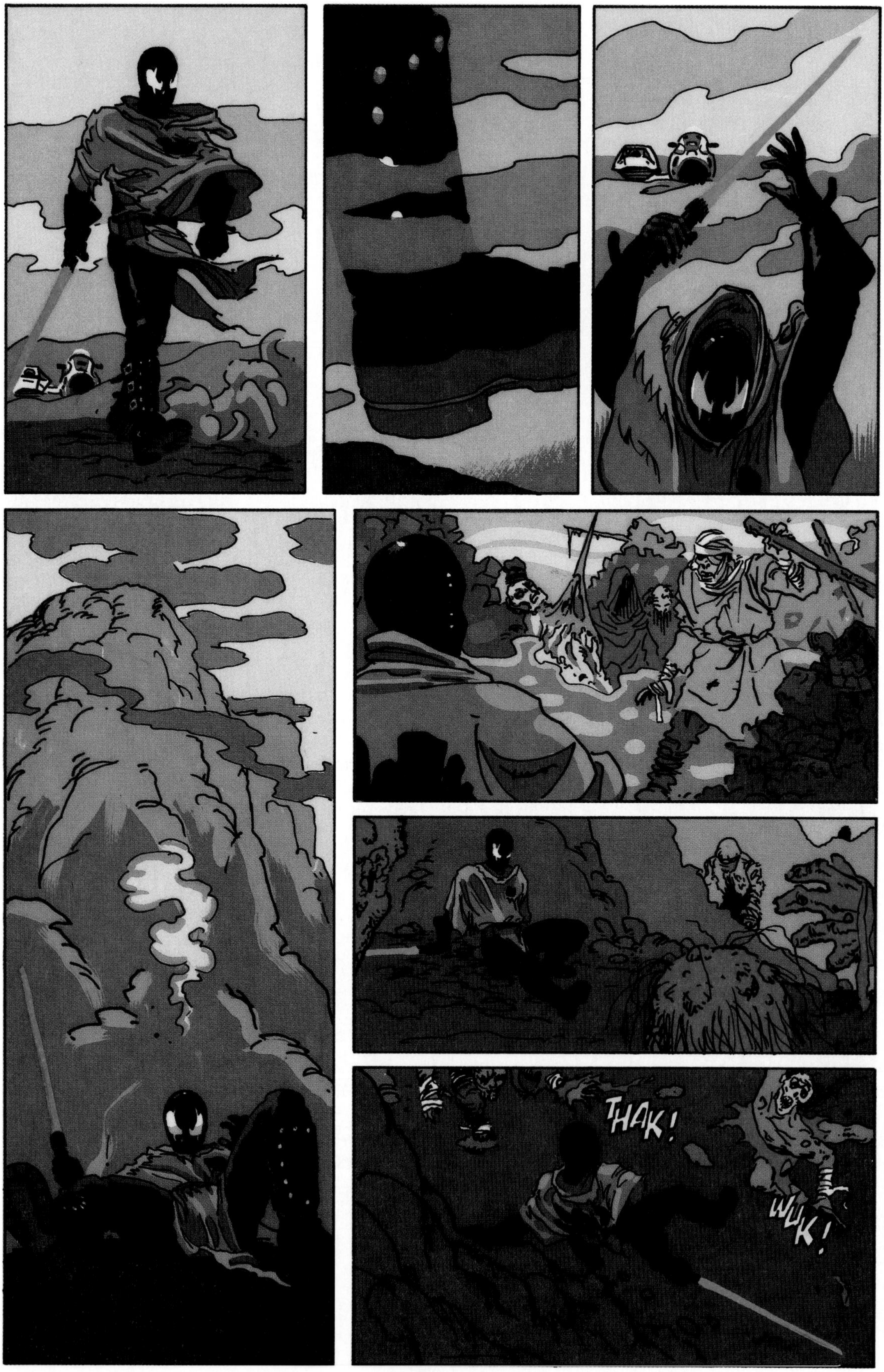
THAK!
WUK!

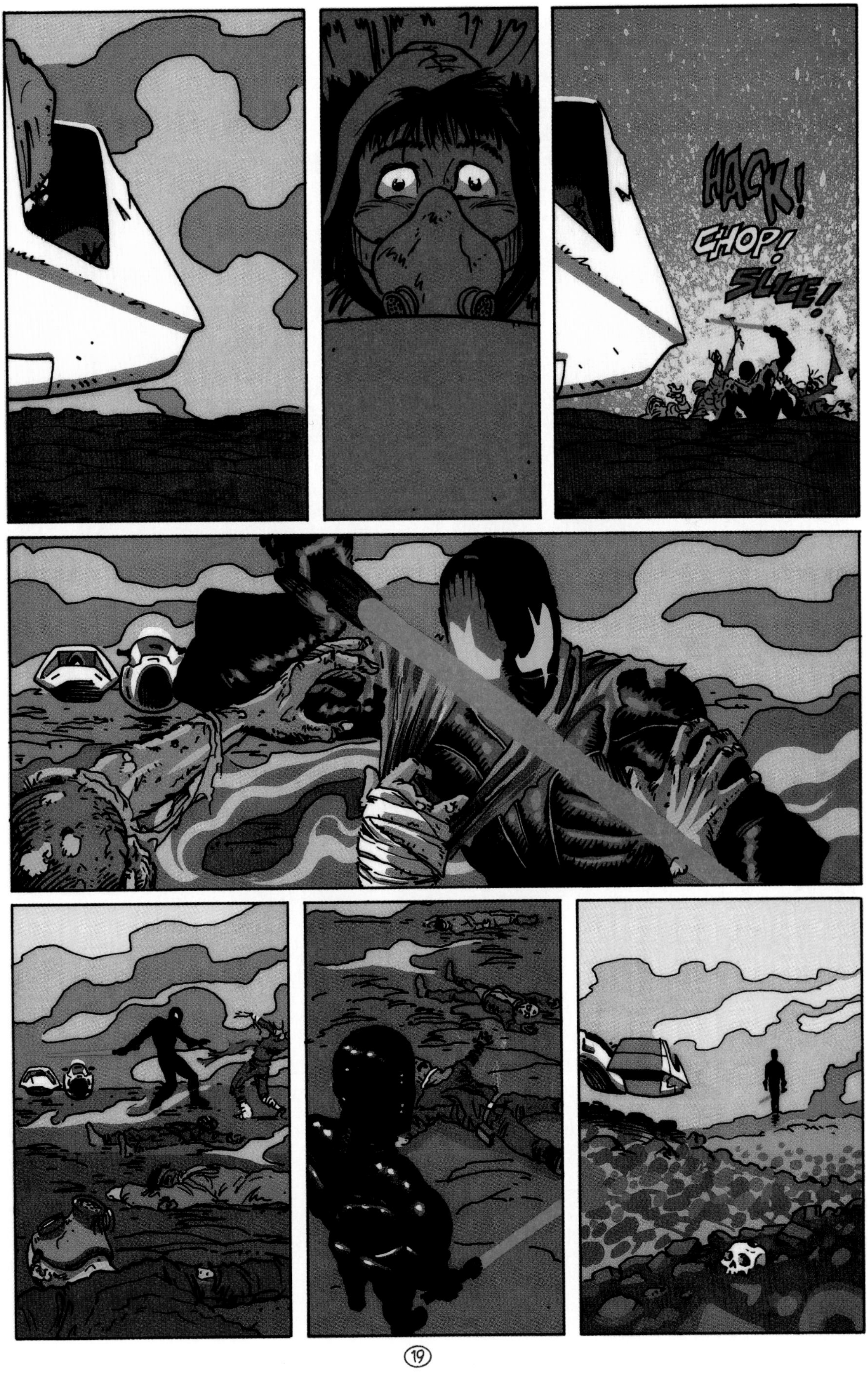
HACK!
CHOP!
SLICE!

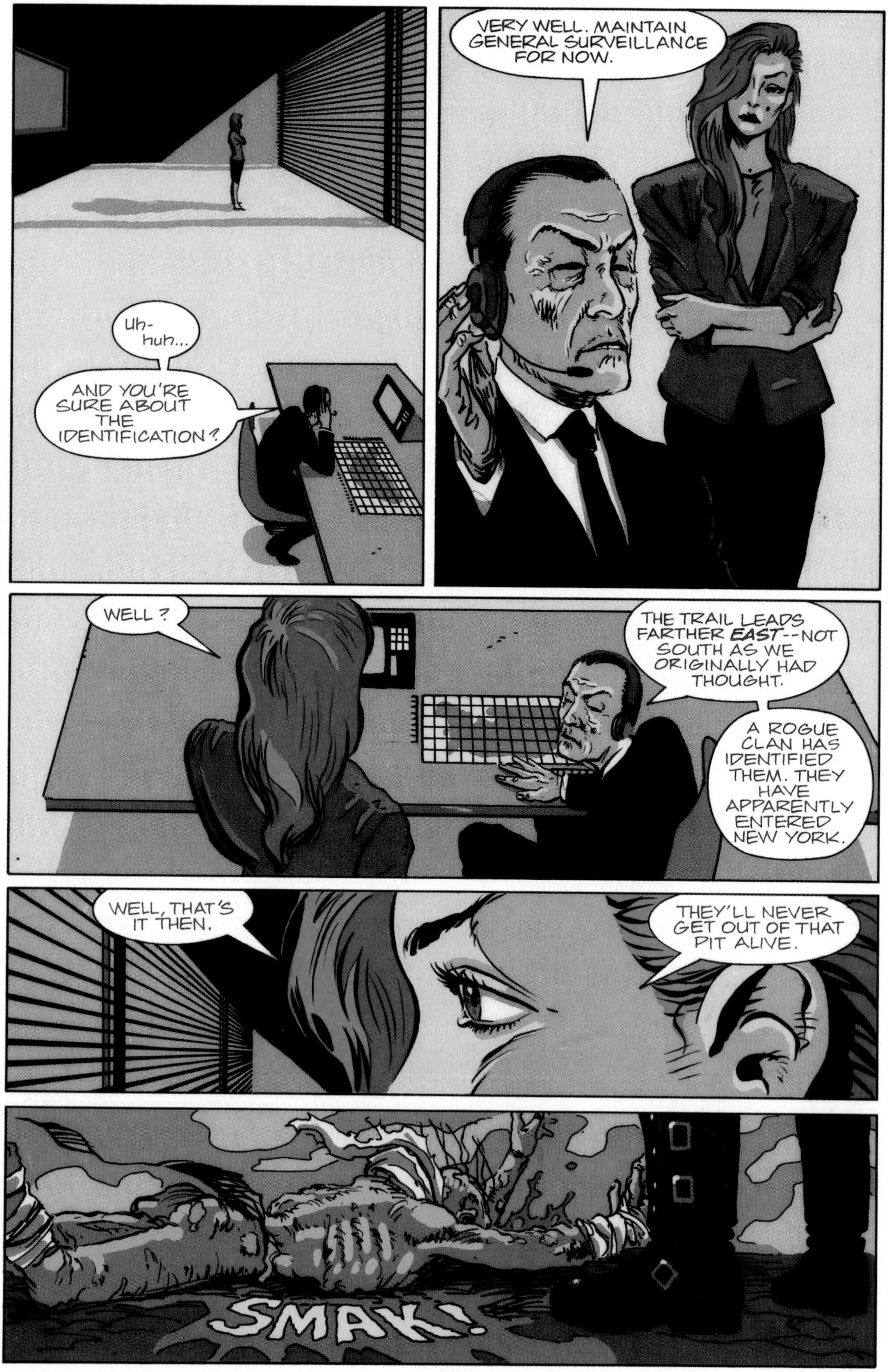
Uh-huh...
AND YOU'RE SURE ABOUT THE IDENTIFICATION?
VERY WELL. MAINTAIN GENERAL SURVEILLANCE FOR NOW.
WELL?
THE TRAIL LEADS FARTHER EAST--NOT SOUTH AS WE ORIGINALLY HAD THOUGHT.
A ROGUE CLAN HAS IDENTIFIED THEM. THEY HAVE APPARENTLY ENTERED NEW YORK.
WELL, THAT'S IT THEN.
THEY'LL NEVER GET OUT OF THAT PIT ALIVE.
SMAK!

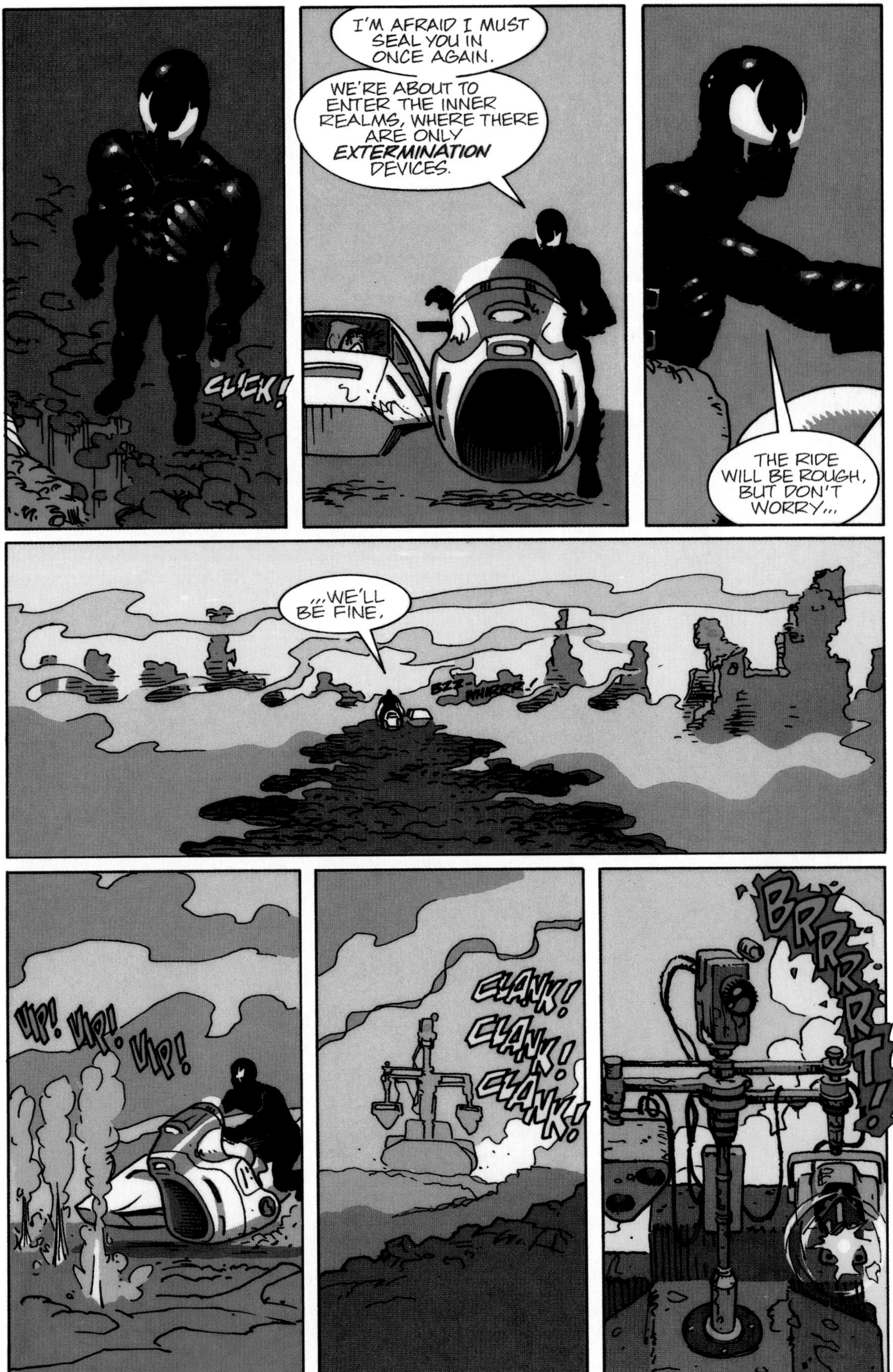
CLICK!
I'M AFRAID I MUST SEAL YOU IN ONCE AGAIN.
WE'RE ABOUT TO ENTER THE INNER REALMS, WHERE THERE ARE ONLY **EXTERMINATION** DEVICES.
THE RIDE WILL BE ROUGH, BUT DON'T WORRY...
...WE'LL BE FINE.
BZZ-WHIRRR!
VIP! VIP! VIP!
CLANK! CLANK! CLANK!
BRRRRT!

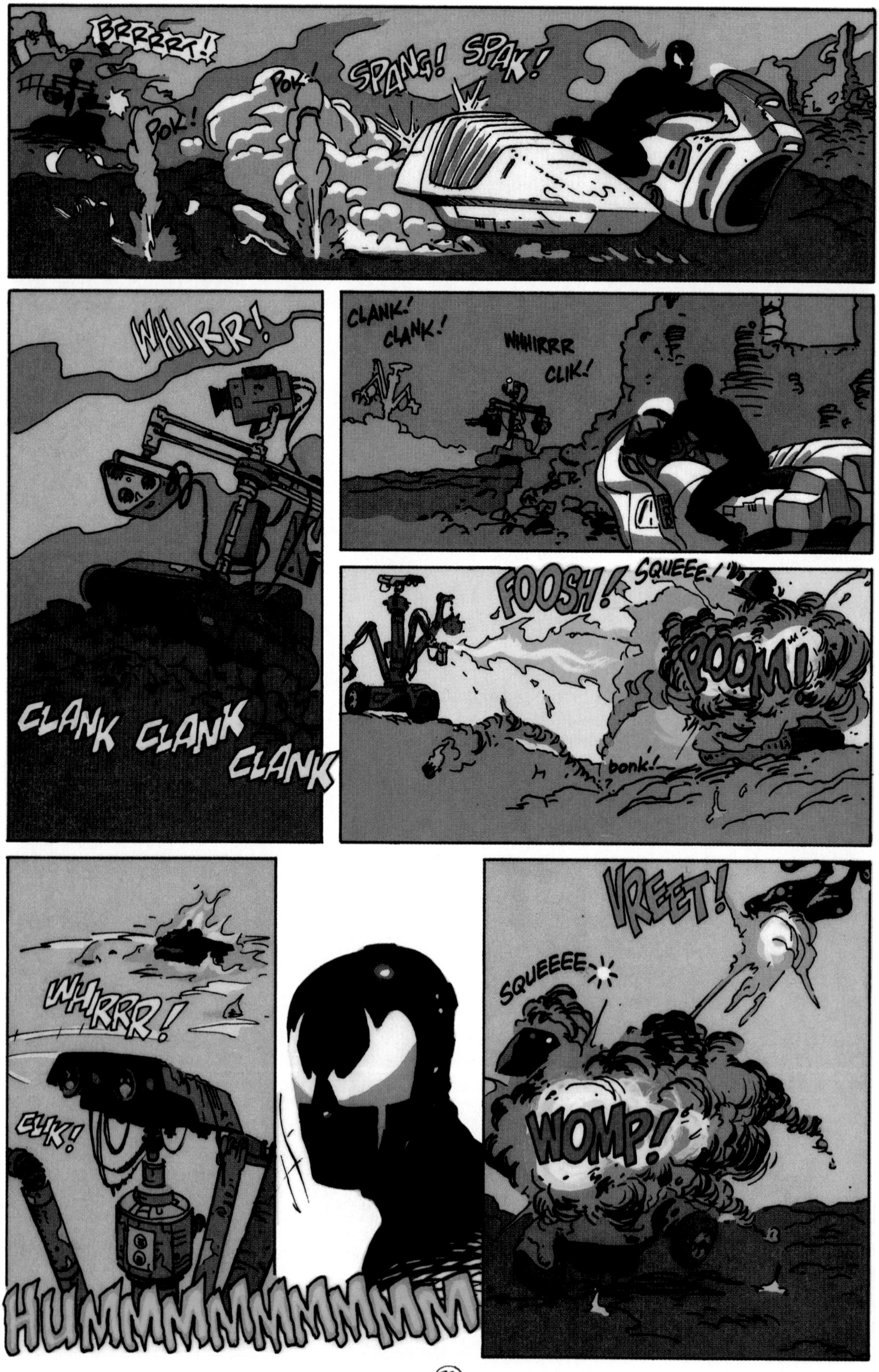
BRRRRRT!!
POK!
POK!
SPANG! SPAK!
WHIRR!
CLANK CLANK
CLANK
CLANK!
CLANK!
WHHIRRR
CLIK!
FOOSH!
SQUEEE!
POOM!
bonk!
WHIRRR!
CLIK!
HUMMMMMMMMMM
VREET!
SQUEEEE
WOMP!

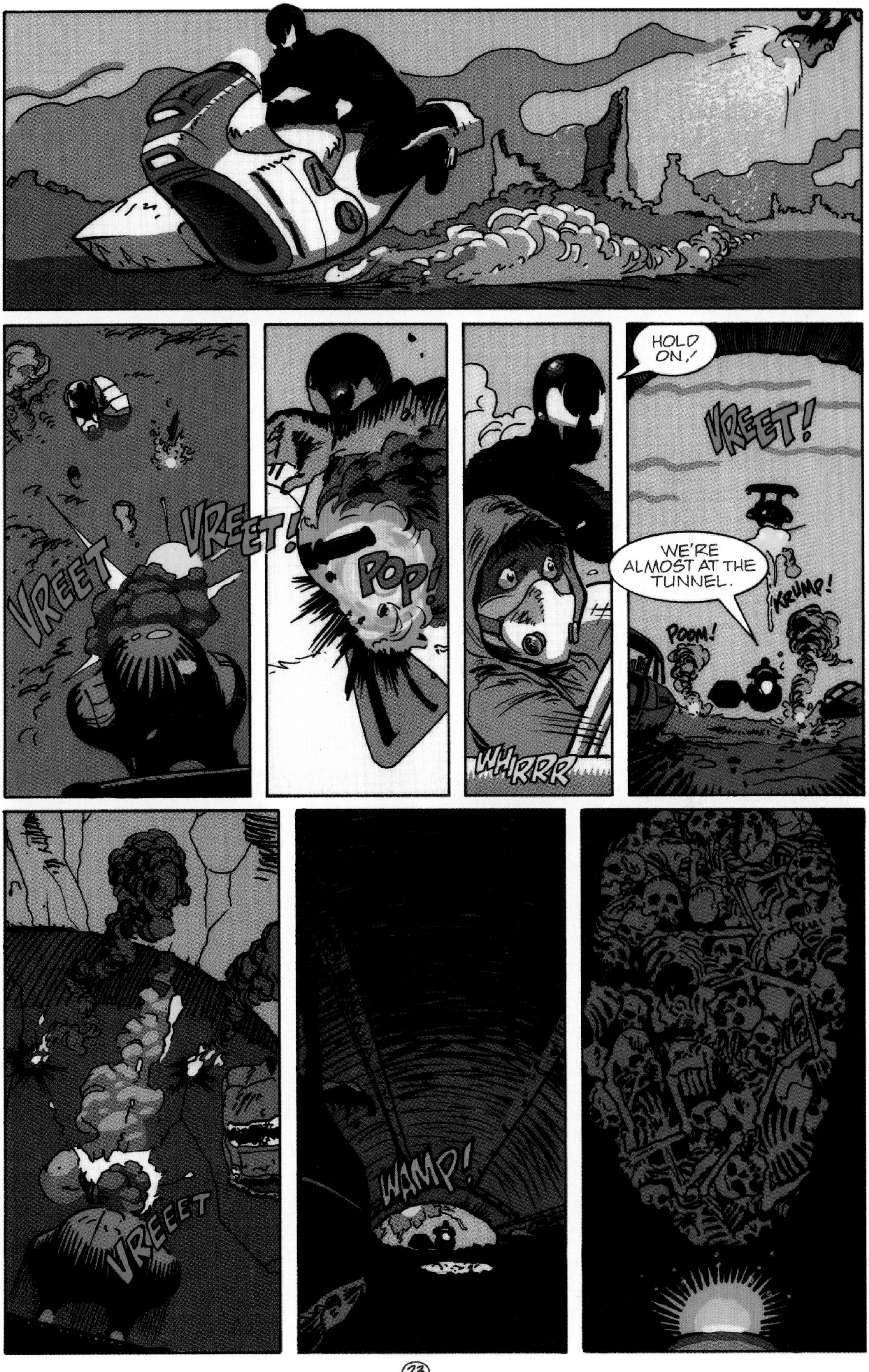
VREEET
VREET!
POP!
WHRRR
HOLD ON!
VREET!
WE'RE ALMOST AT THE TUNNEL.
KRUMP!
POOM!
VREEET
WAMP!

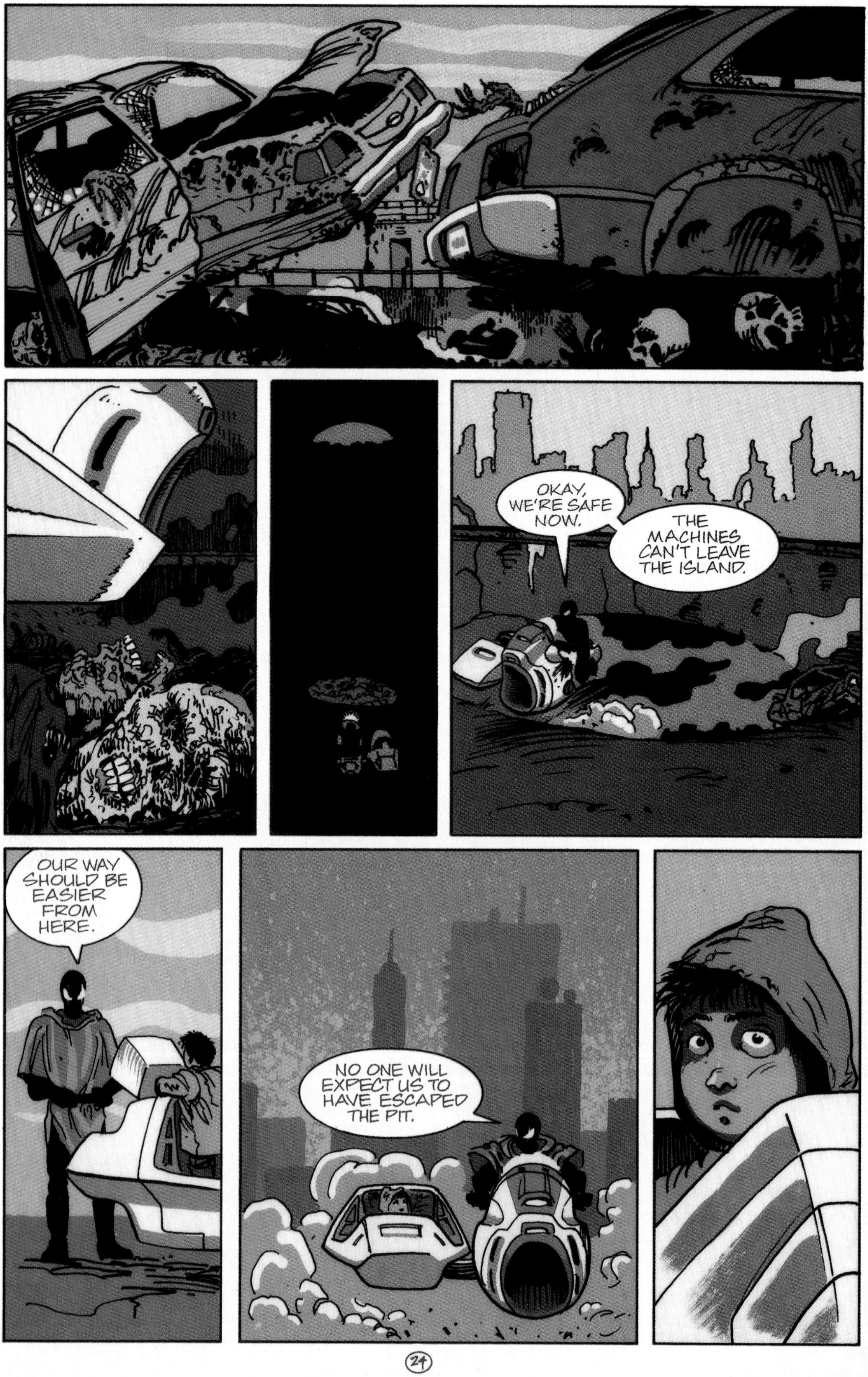
OKAY, WE'RE SAFE NOW.
THE MACHINES CAN'T LEAVE THE ISLAND.
OUR WAY SHOULD BE EASIER FROM HERE.
NO ONE WILL EXPECT US TO HAVE ESCAPED THE PIT.

# DEVIL *in the bayou*

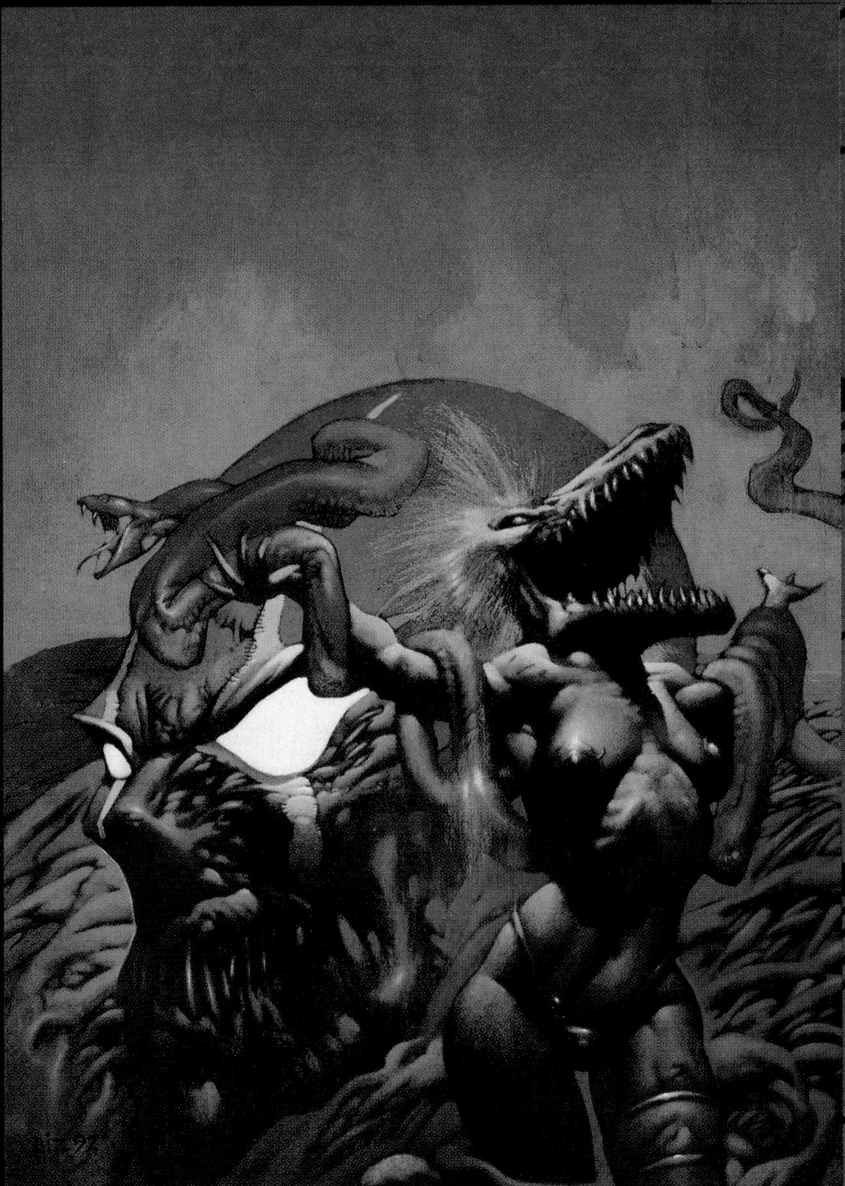

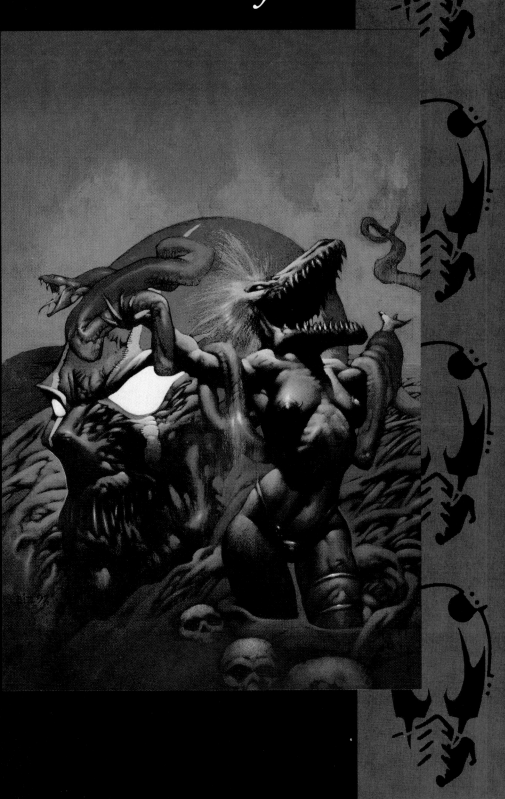

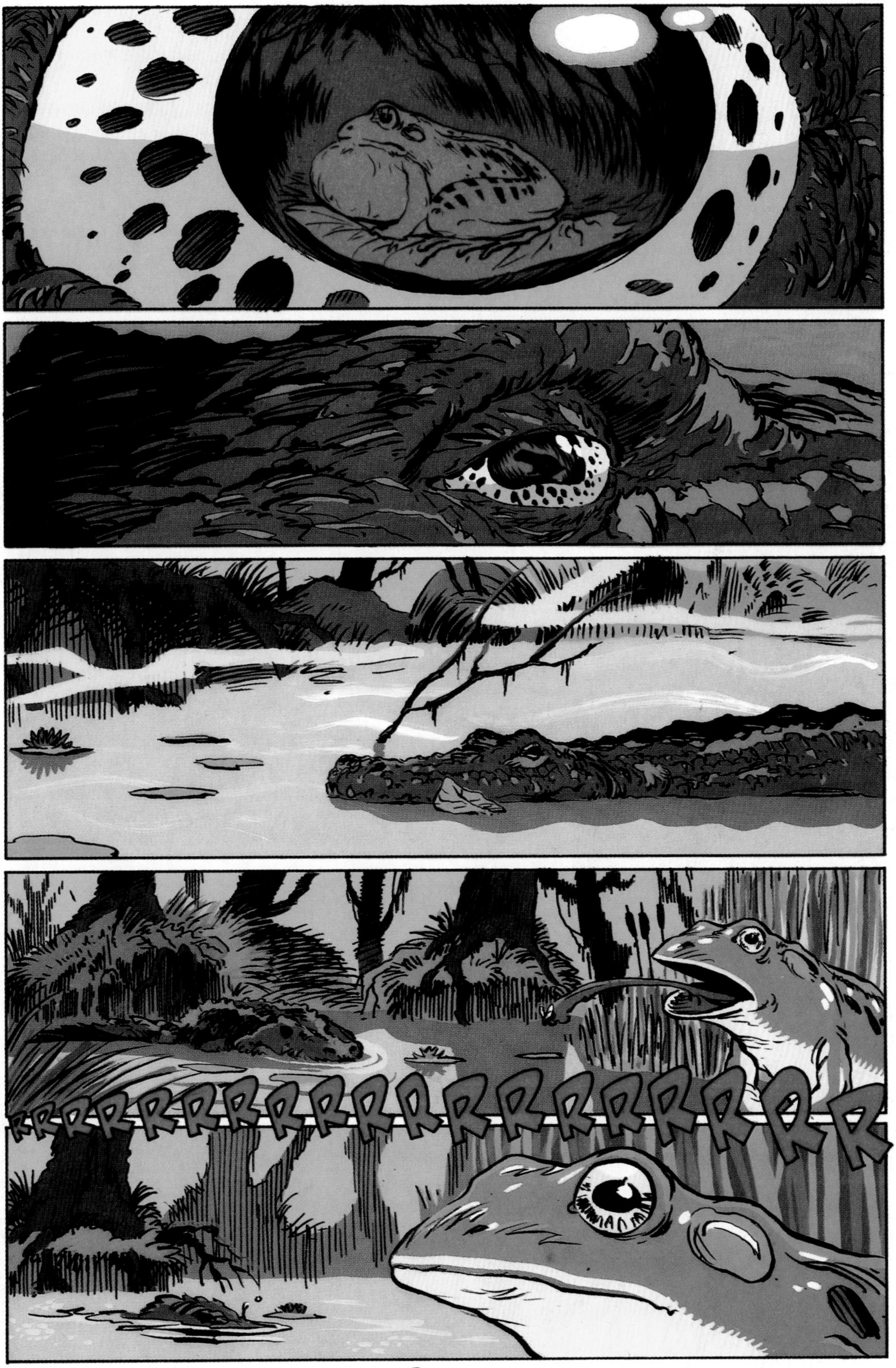
RRRRRRRRRRRRRRRRRRR

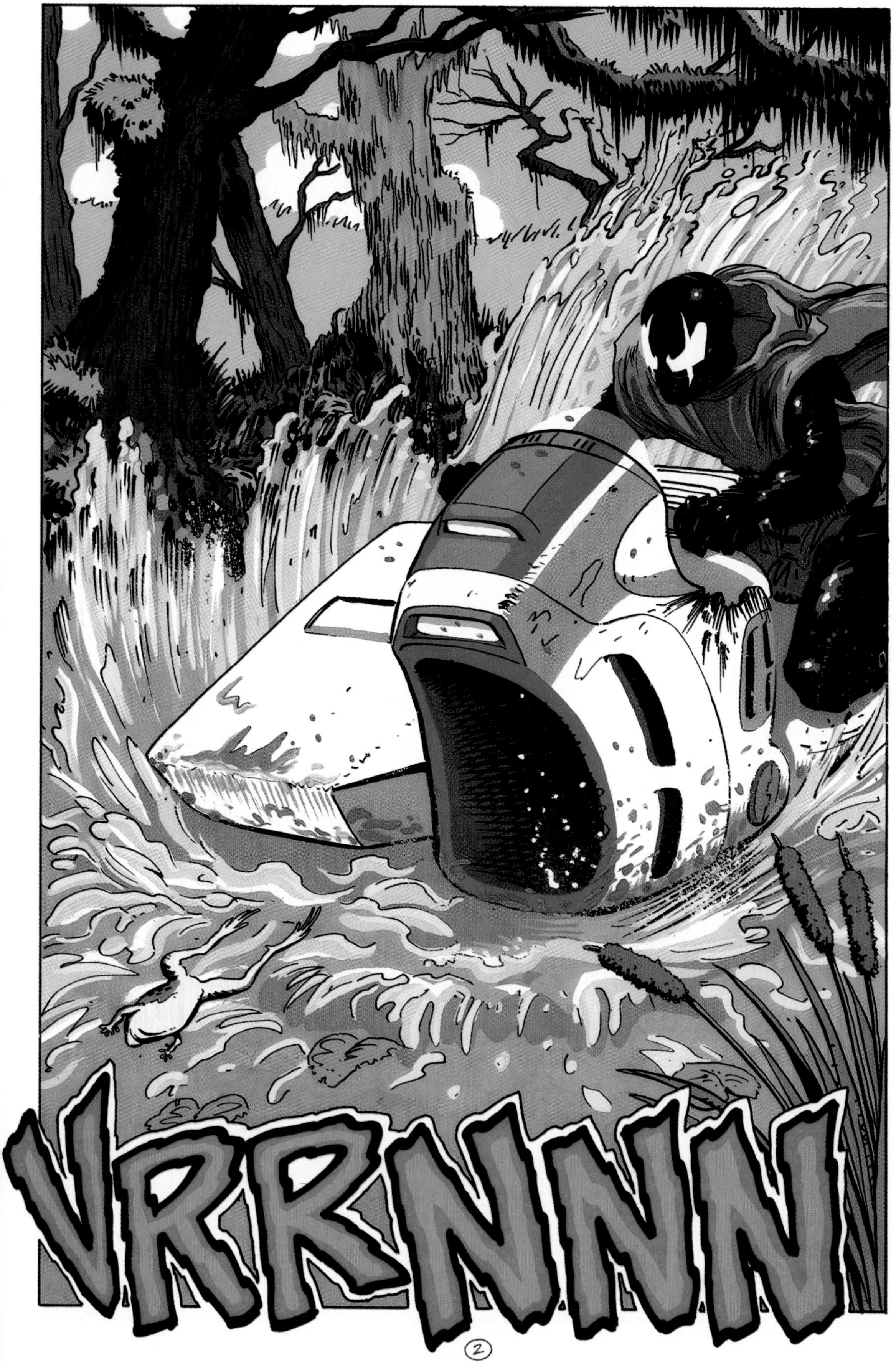
VRRNNN

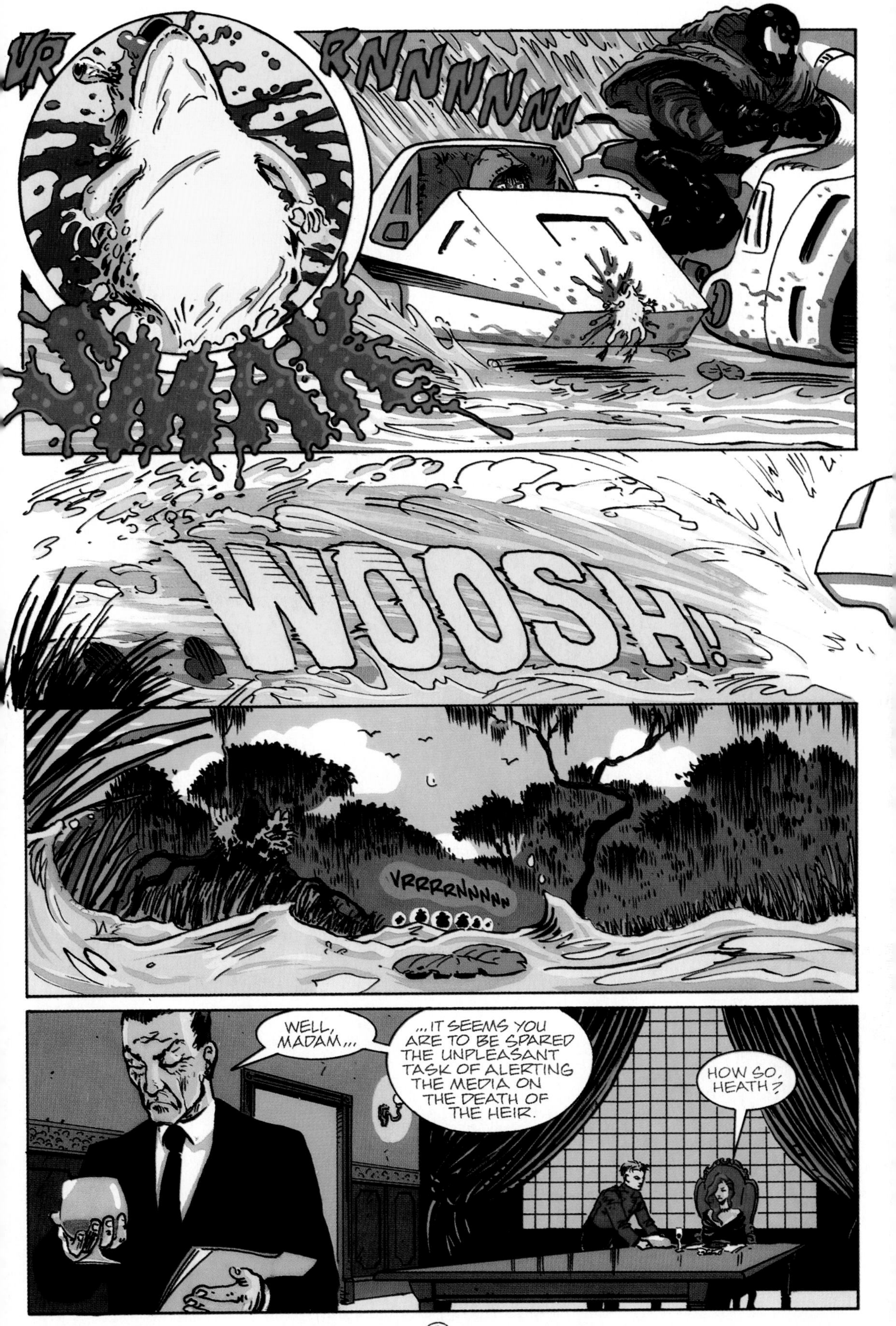
VRRNNNNNNnn
SMAK
WOOSH!
VRRRRNNNNN
WELL, MADAM,...
...IT SEEMS YOU ARE TO BE SPARED THE UNPLEASANT TASK OF ALERTING THE MEDIA ON THE DEATH OF THE HEIR.
HOW SO, HEATH?

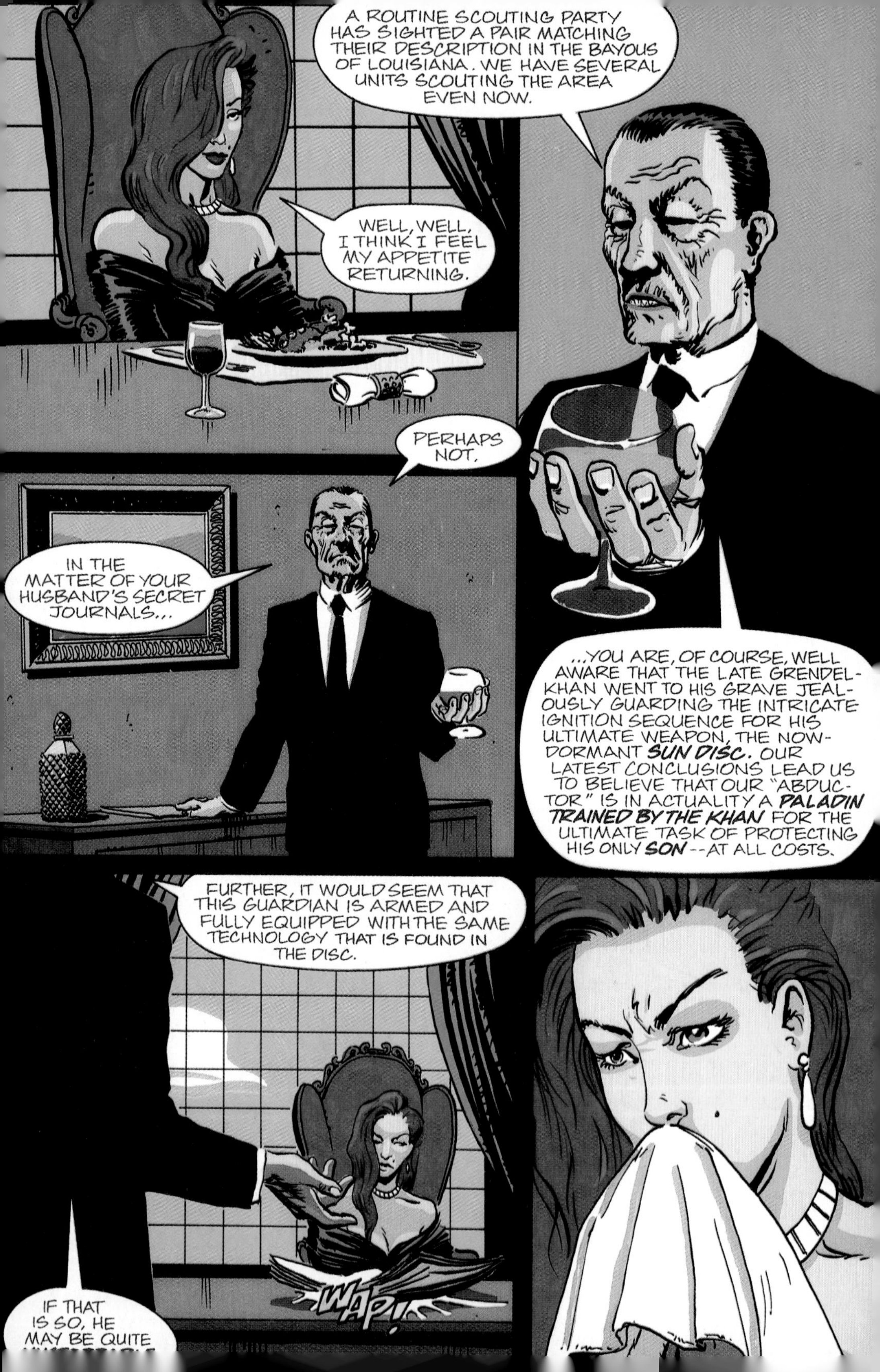
A ROUTINE SCOUTING PARTY HAS SIGHTED A PAIR MATCHING THEIR DESCRIPTION IN THE BAYOUS OF LOUISIANA. WE HAVE SEVERAL UNITS SCOUTING THE AREA EVEN NOW.
WELL, WELL, I THINK I FEEL MY APPETITE RETURNING.
PERHAPS NOT.
IN THE MATTER OF YOUR HUSBAND'S SECRET JOURNALS...
...YOU ARE, OF COURSE, WELL AWARE THAT THE LATE GRENDEL-KHAN WENT TO HIS GRAVE JEALOUSLY GUARDING THE INTRICATE IGNITION SEQUENCE FOR HIS ULTIMATE WEAPON, THE NOW-DORMANT SUN DISC. OUR LATEST CONCLUSIONS LEAD US TO BELIEVE THAT OUR "ABDUCTOR" IS IN ACTUALITY A PALADIN TRAINED BY THE KHAN FOR THE ULTIMATE TASK OF PROTECTING HIS ONLY SON--AT ALL COSTS.
FURTHER, IT WOULD SEEM THAT THIS GUARDIAN IS ARMED AND FULLY EQUIPPED WITH THE SAME TECHNOLOGY THAT IS FOUND IN THE DISC.
WAP!
IF THAT IS SO, HE MAY BE QUITE

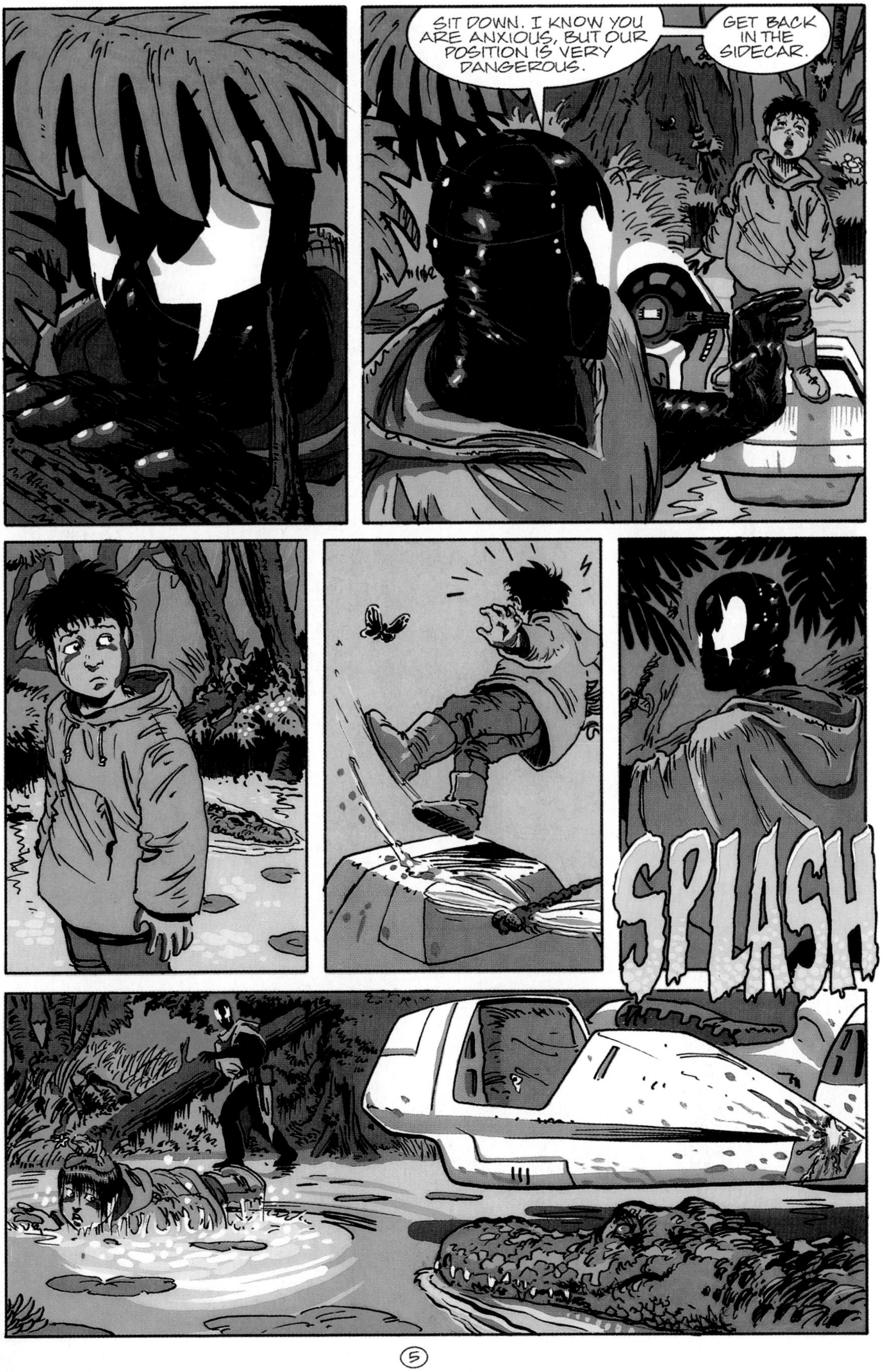
SIT DOWN. I KNOW YOU ARE ANXIOUS, BUT OUR POSITION IS VERY DANGEROUS.
GET BACK IN THE SIDECAR.
SPLASH

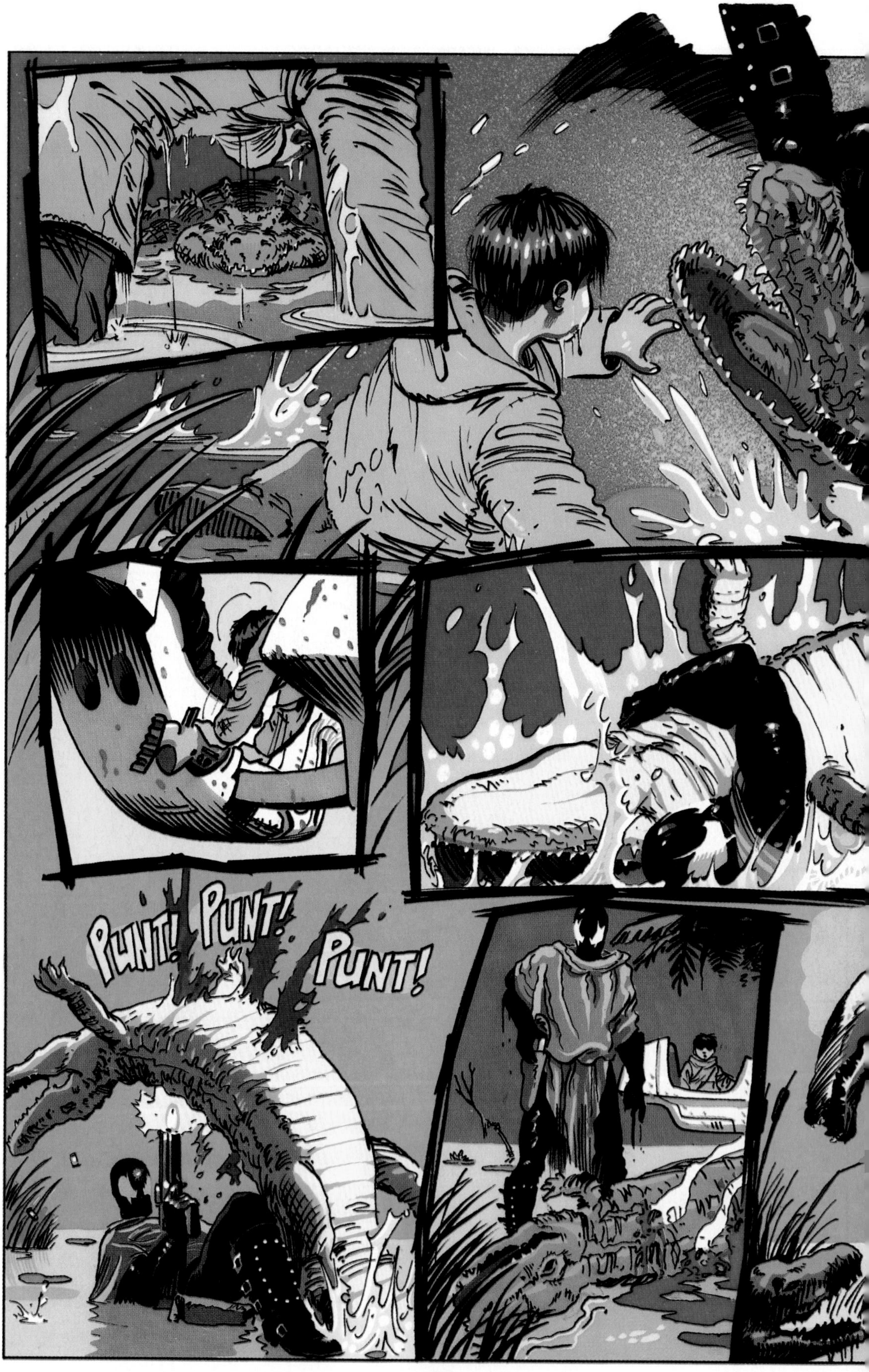
PUNT! PUNT! PUNT!

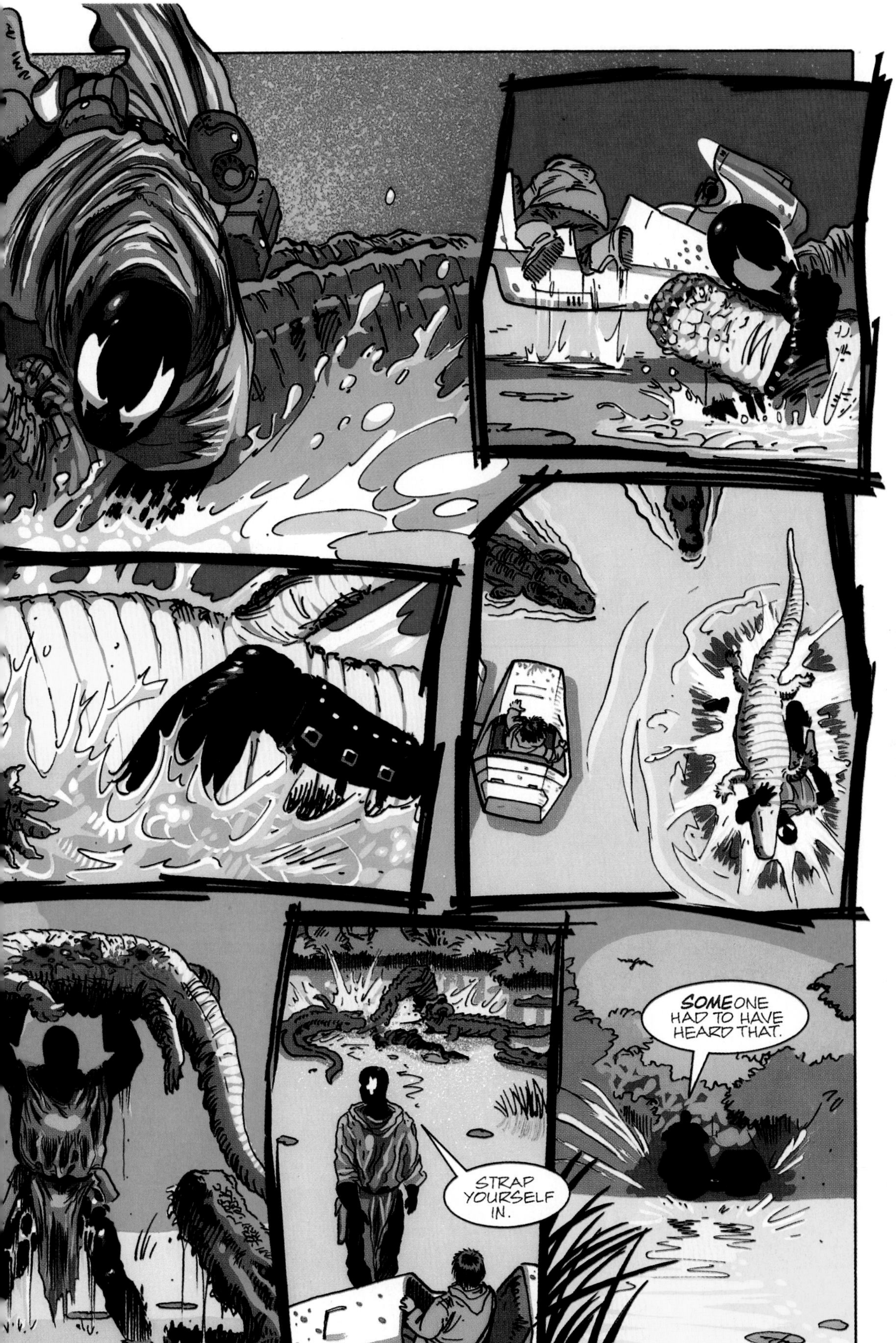
SOMEONE HAD TO HAVE HEARD THAT.
STRAP YOURSELF IN.

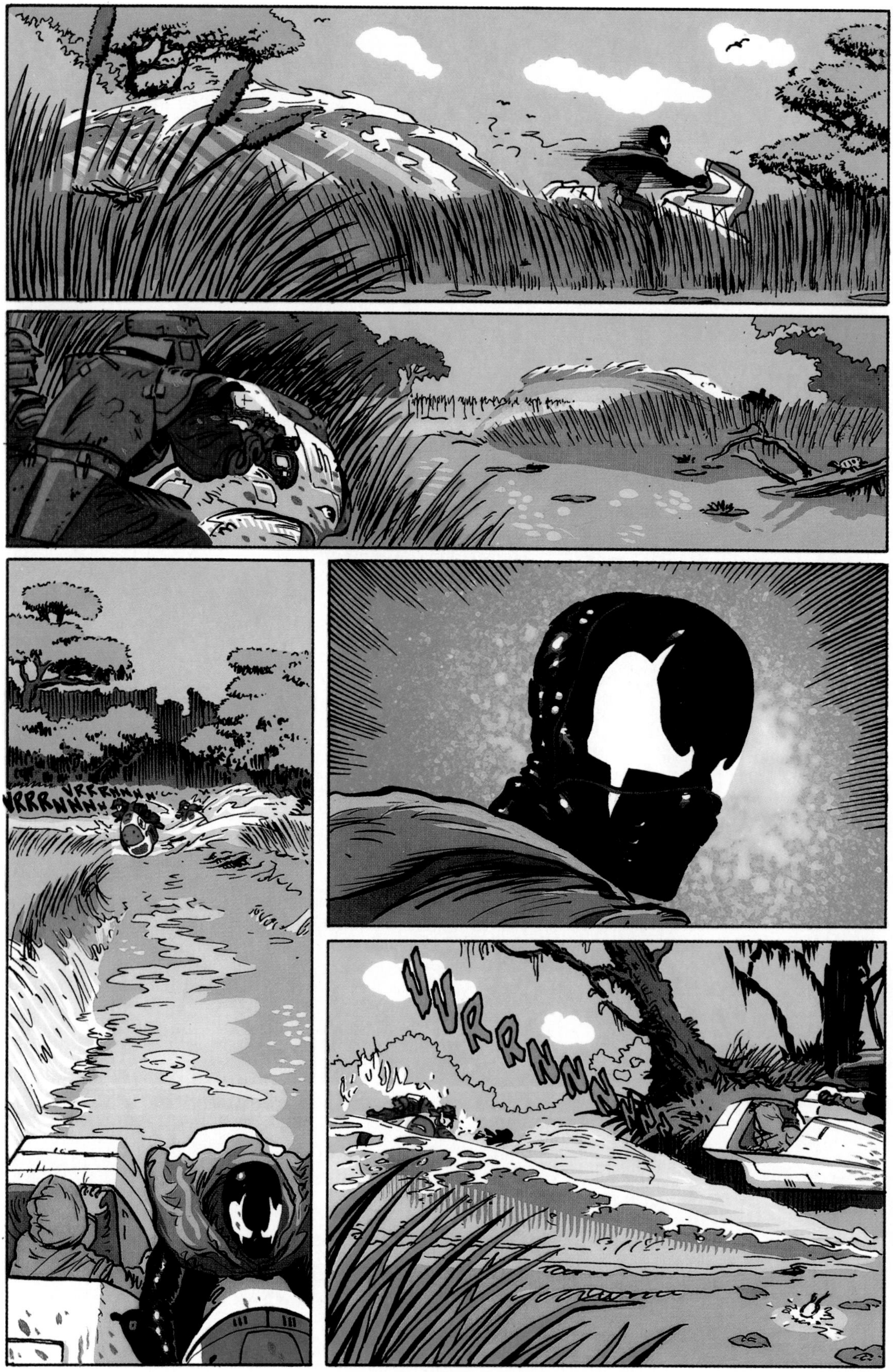
VRRRNNNN
VRRRNNNNN
VVRRNNNN

UVRRR
RRR

RNNNNN

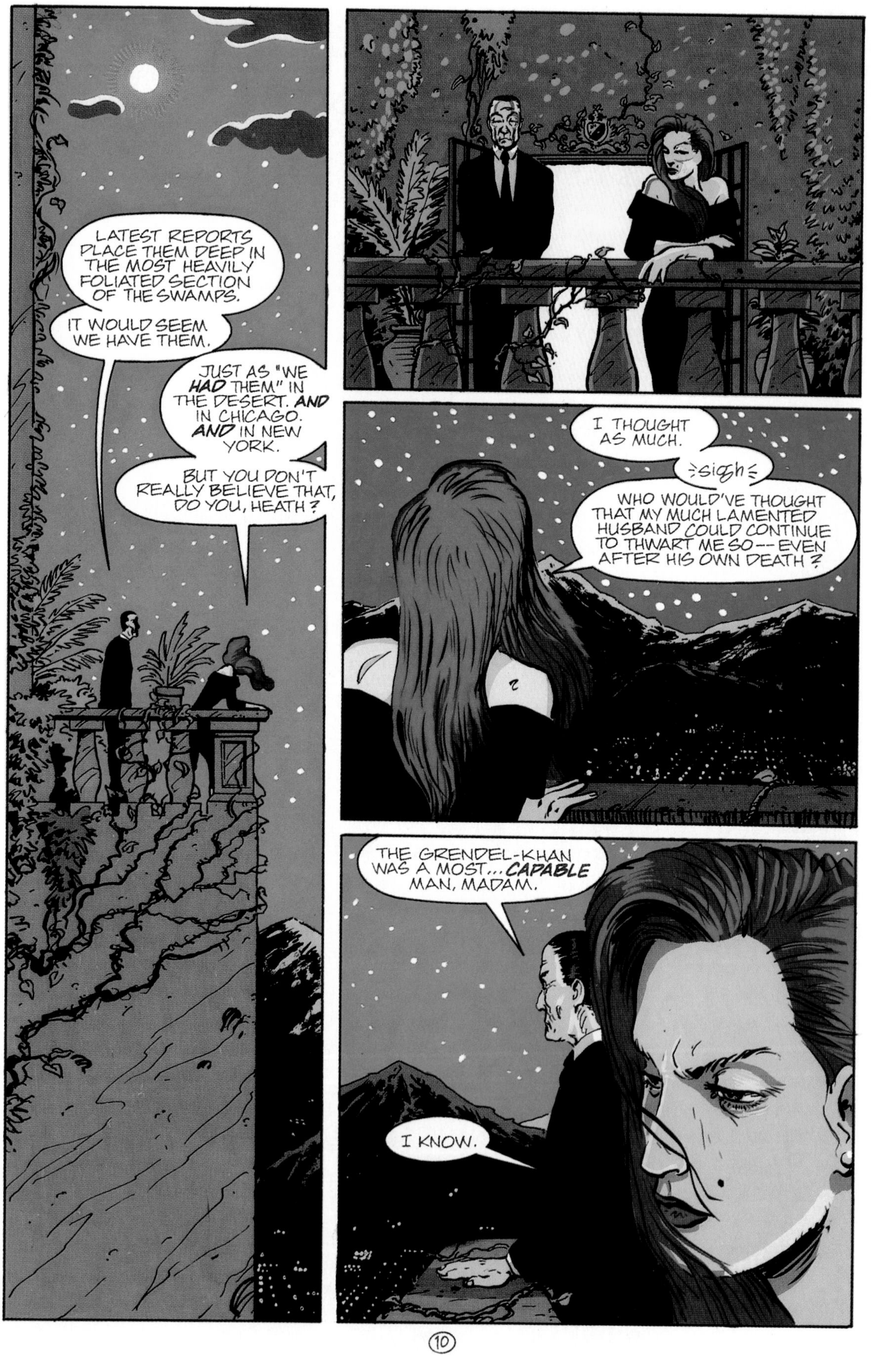
LATEST REPORTS PLACE THEM DEEP IN THE MOST HEAVILY FOLIATED SECTION OF THE SWAMPS.
IT WOULD SEEM WE HAVE THEM.
JUST AS "WE **HAD** THEM" IN THE DESERT. **AND** IN CHICAGO. **AND** IN NEW YORK.
BUT YOU DON'T REALLY BELIEVE THAT, DO YOU, HEATH?
I THOUGHT AS MUCH.
sigh
WHO WOULD'VE THOUGHT THAT MY MUCH LAMENTED HUSBAND COULD CONTINUE TO THWART ME SO--EVEN AFTER HIS OWN DEATH?
THE GRENDEL-KHAN WAS A MOST... **CAPABLE** MAN, MADAM.
I KNOW.

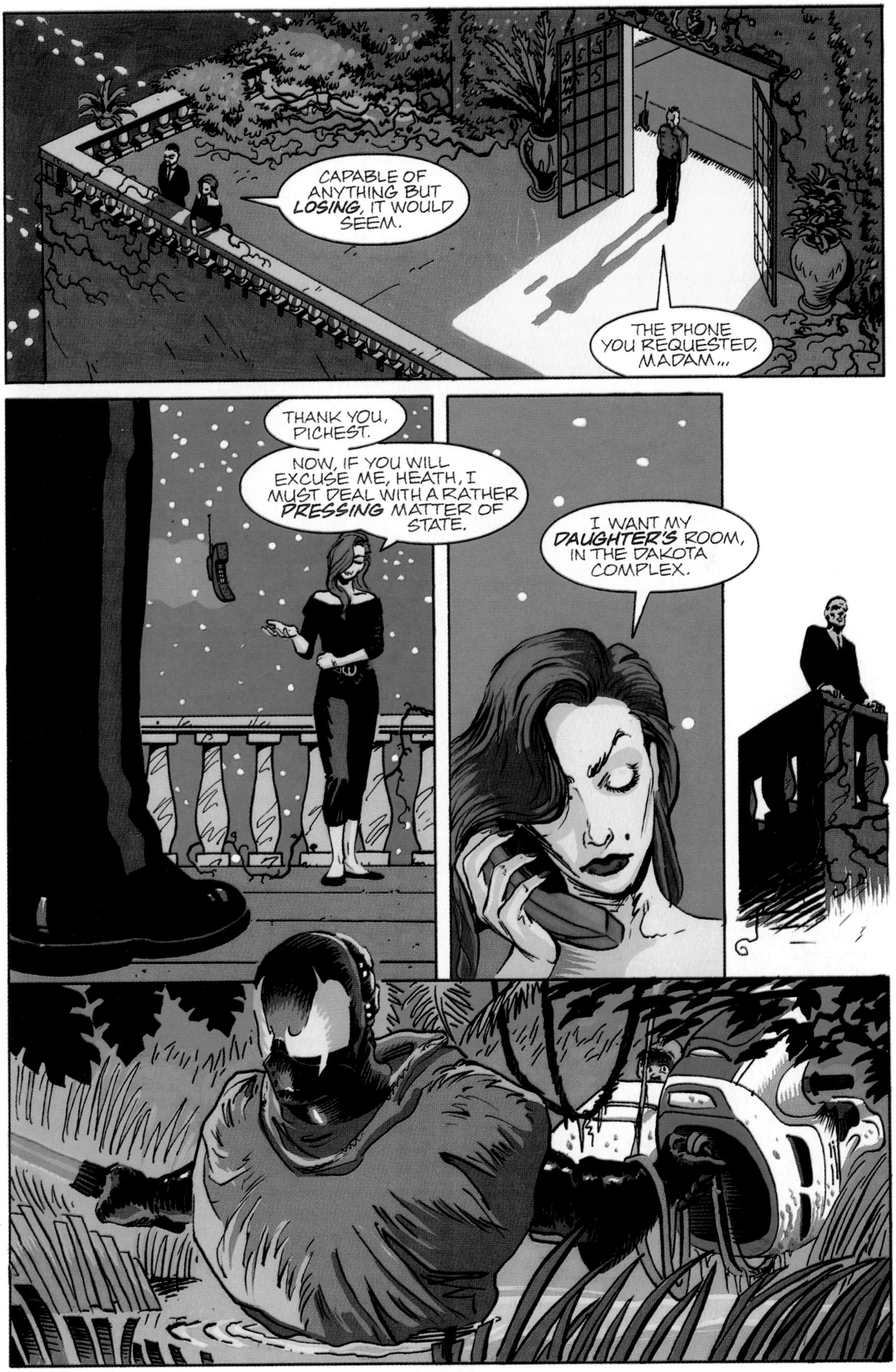
CAPABLE OF ANYTHING BUT LOSING, IT WOULD SEEM.
THE PHONE YOU REQUESTED, MADAM...
THANK YOU, PICHEST.
NOW, IF YOU WILL EXCUSE ME, HEATH, I MUST DEAL WITH A RATHER PRESSING MATTER OF STATE.
I WANT MY DAUGHTER'S ROOM, IN THE DAKOTA COMPLEX.

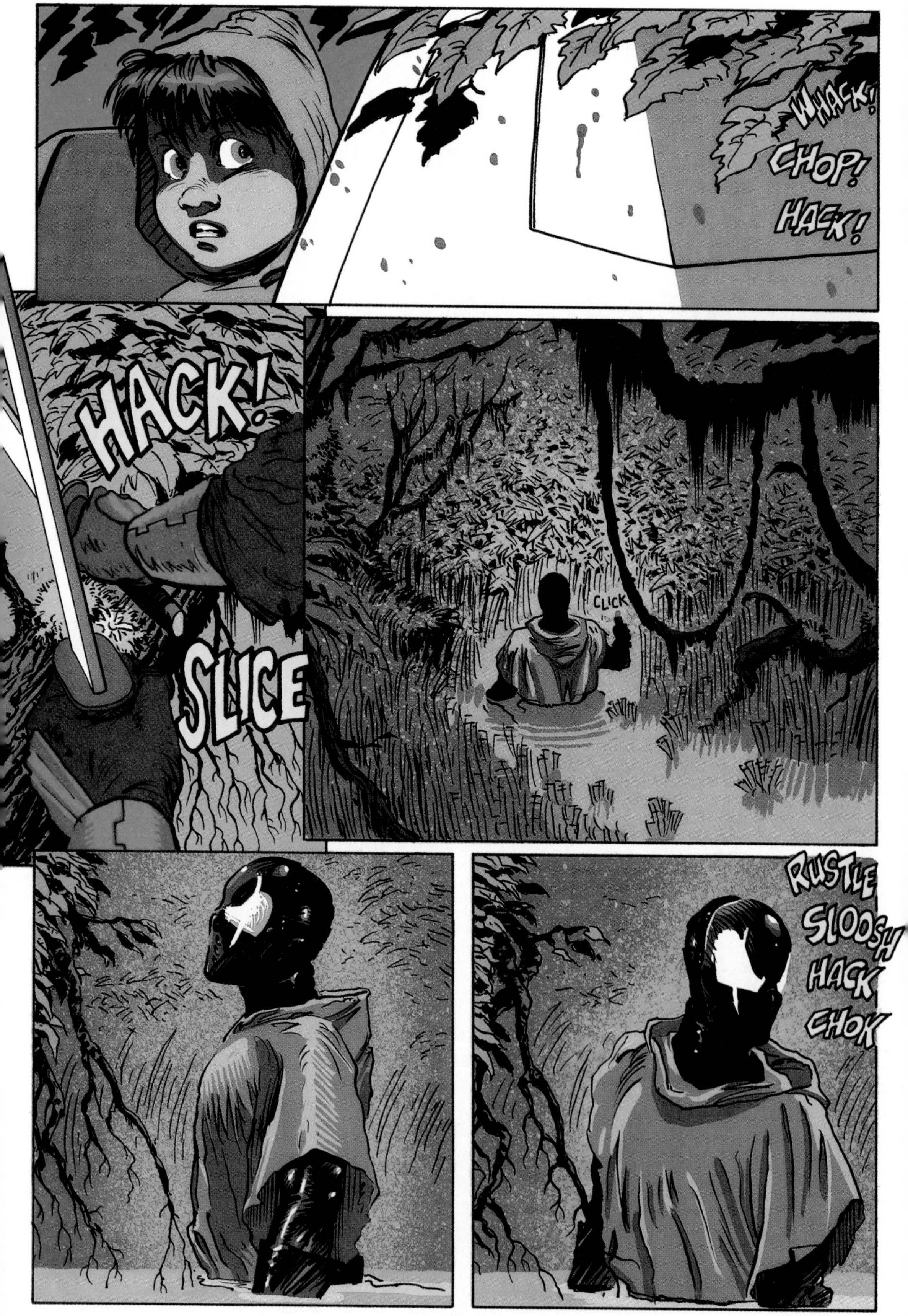
WHACK!
CHOP!
HACK!
HACK!
SLICE
CLICK
RUSTLE
SLOOSH
HACK
CHOK

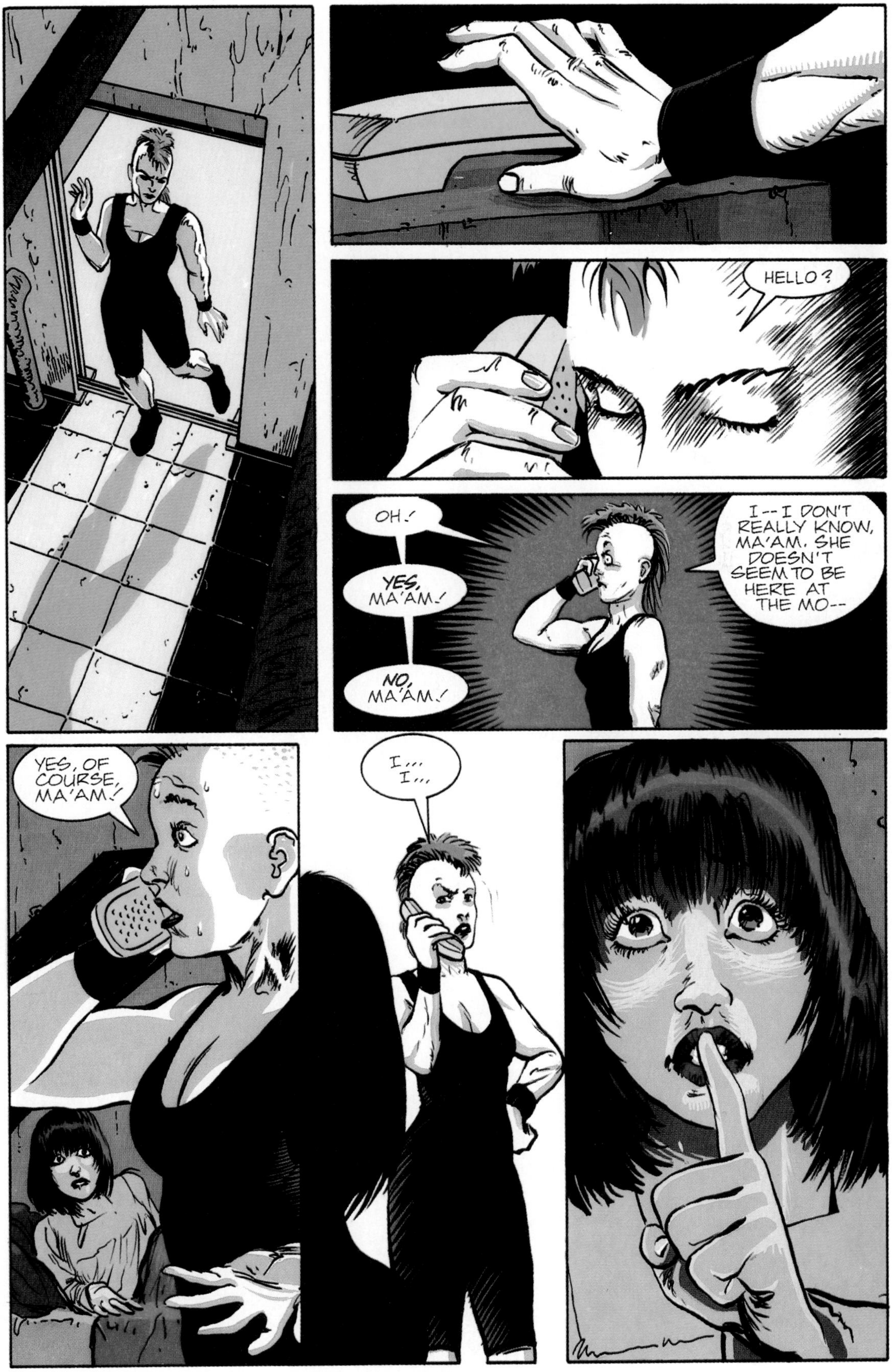
HELLO?
OH!
YES, MA'AM!
NO, MA'AM!
I--I DON'T REALLY KNOW, MA'AM. SHE DOESN'T SEEM TO BE HERE AT THE MO--
YES, OF COURSE, MA'AM!
I... I...

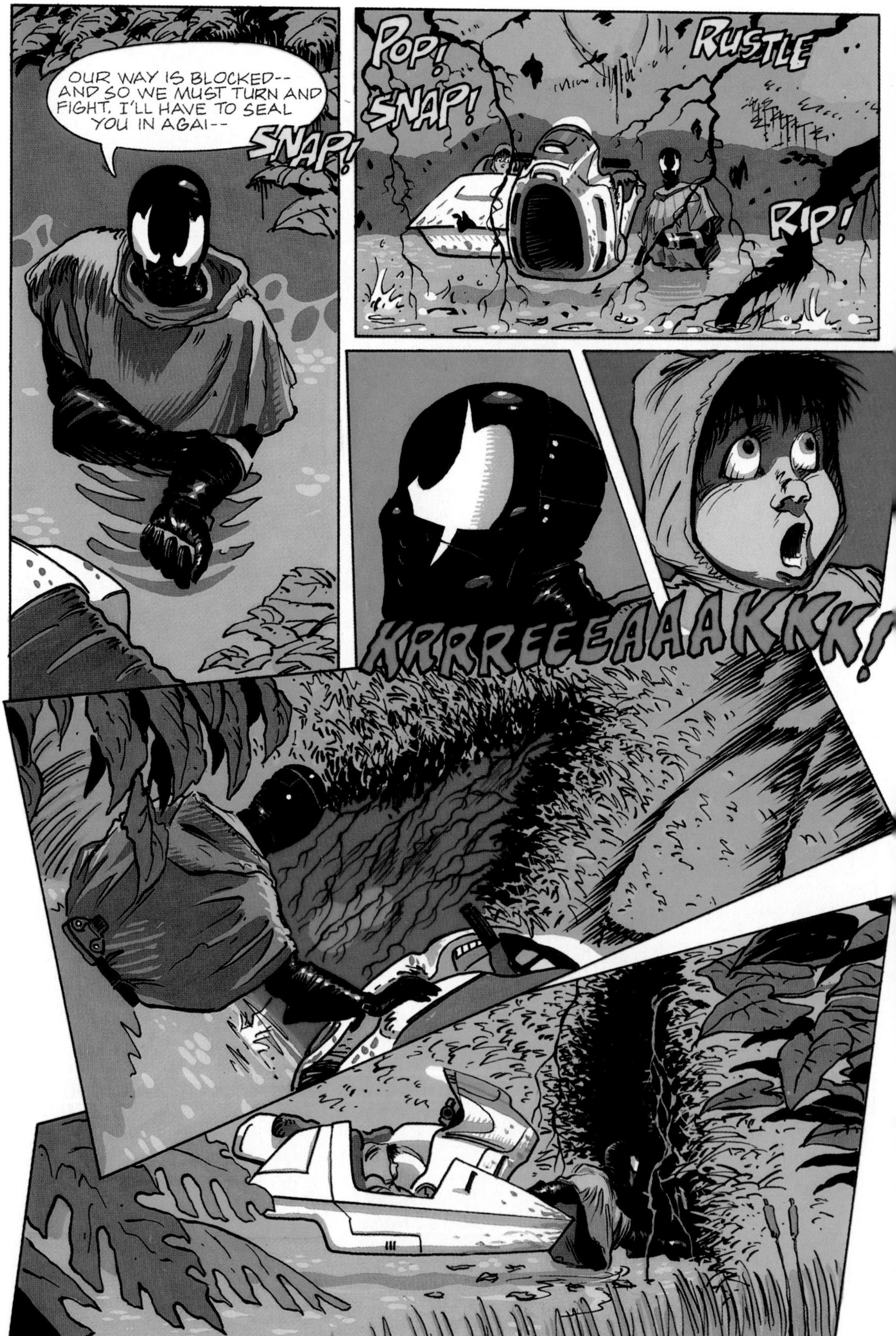
OUR WAY IS BLOCKED-- AND SO WE MUST TURN AND FIGHT. I'LL HAVE TO SEAL YOU IN AGAI--
SNAP!
POP!
SNAP!
RUSTLE
RIP!
KRRREEEAAAKKK!

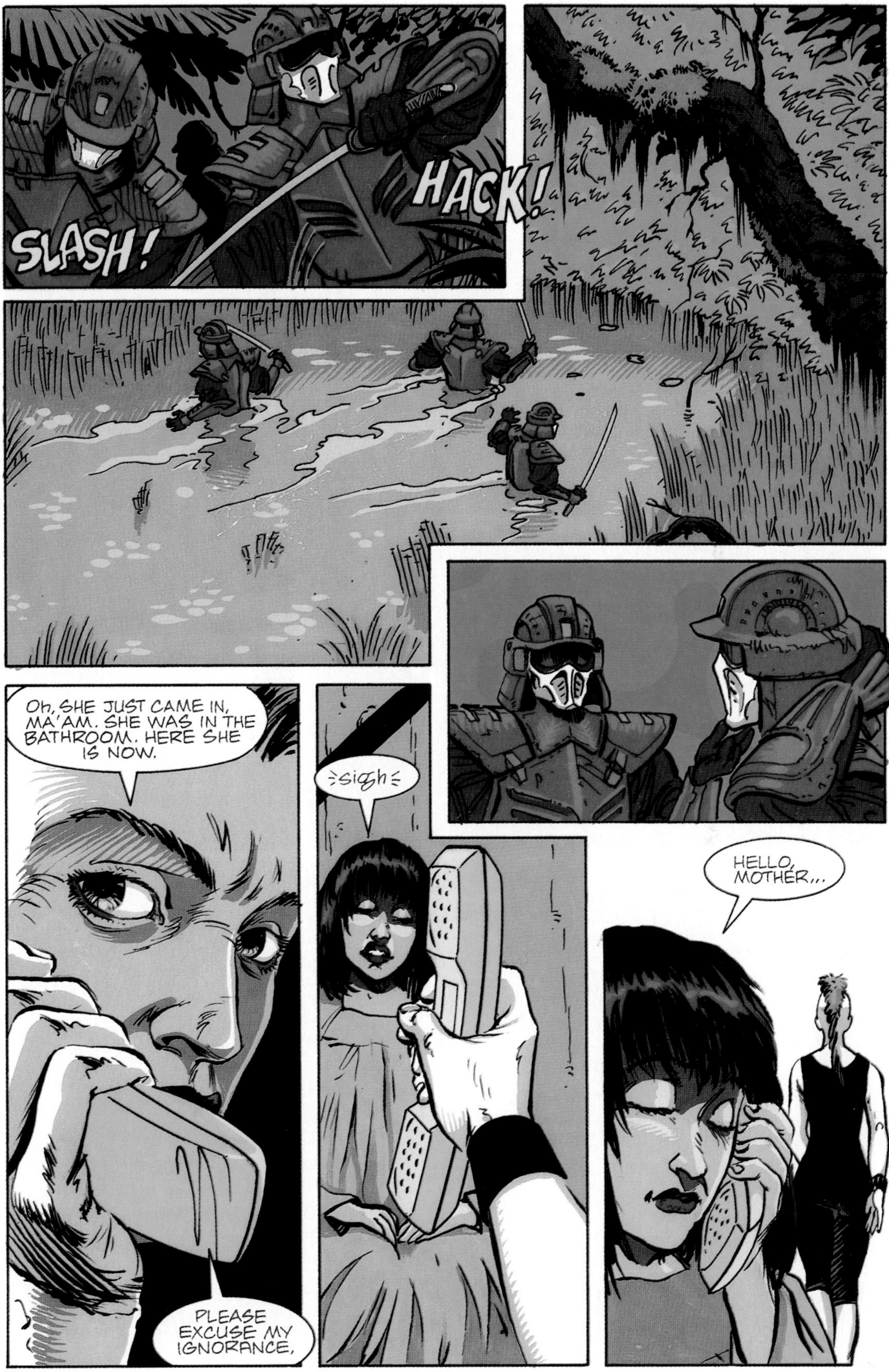
SLASH!
HACK!
Oh, SHE JUST CAME IN, MA'AM. SHE WAS IN THE BATHROOM. HERE SHE IS NOW.
PLEASE EXCUSE MY IGNORANCE.
sigh
HELLO, MOTHER...

SQUISHSQUELCHSQUISHSQUELCHSQUISHSQUELCHSQUISHSQUELCHSQUISH

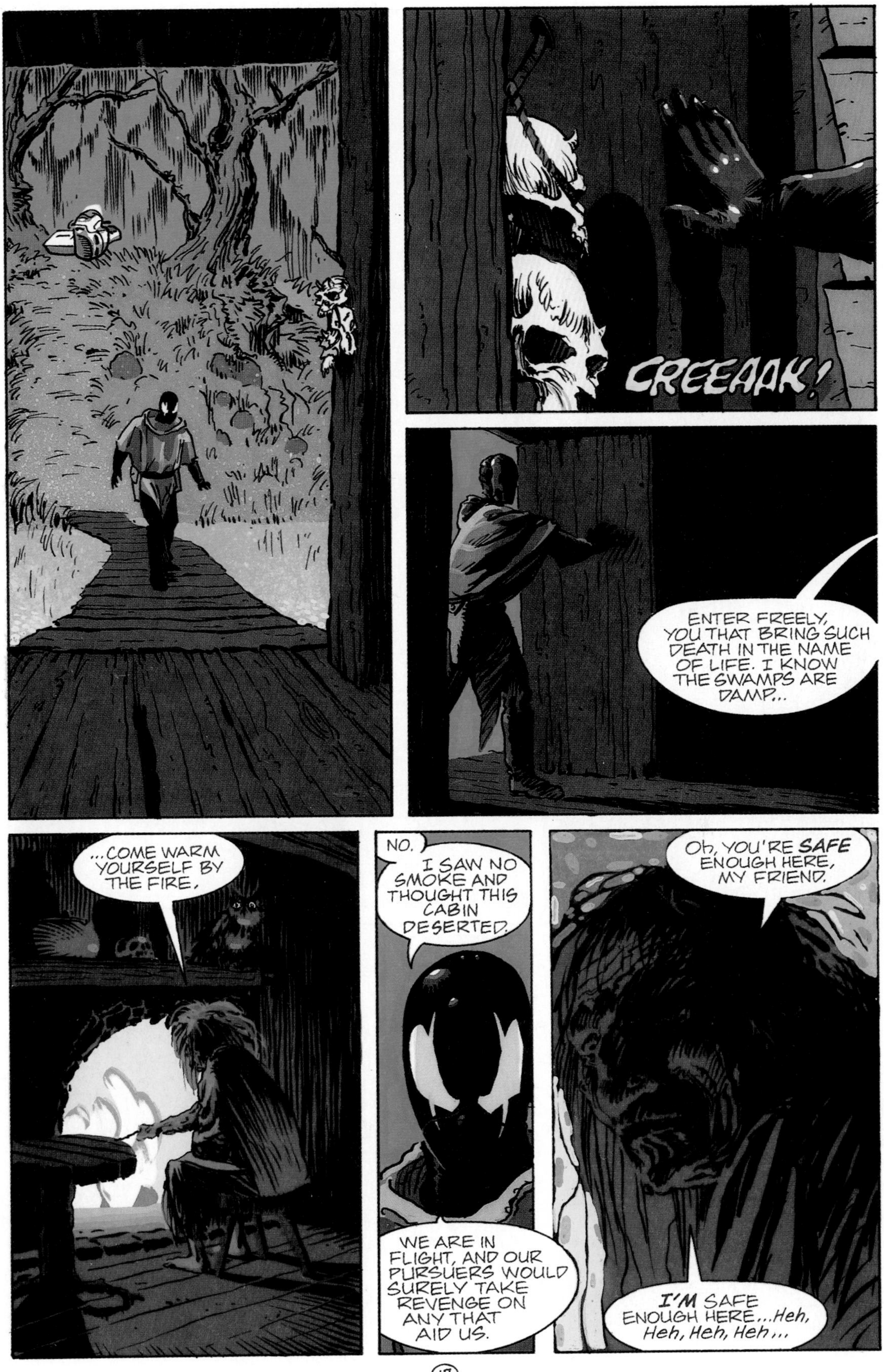
CREEAAK!
ENTER FREELY, YOU THAT BRING SUCH DEATH IN THE NAME OF LIFE. I KNOW THE SWAMPS ARE DAMP...
...COME WARM YOURSELF BY THE FIRE,
NO.
I SAW NO SMOKE AND THOUGHT THIS CABIN DESERTED.
WE ARE IN FLIGHT, AND OUR PURSUERS WOULD SURELY TAKE REVENGE ON ANY THAT AID US.
Oh, YOU'RE SAFE ENOUGH HERE, MY FRIEND.
I'M SAFE ENOUGH HERE...Heh, Heh, Heh, Heh...

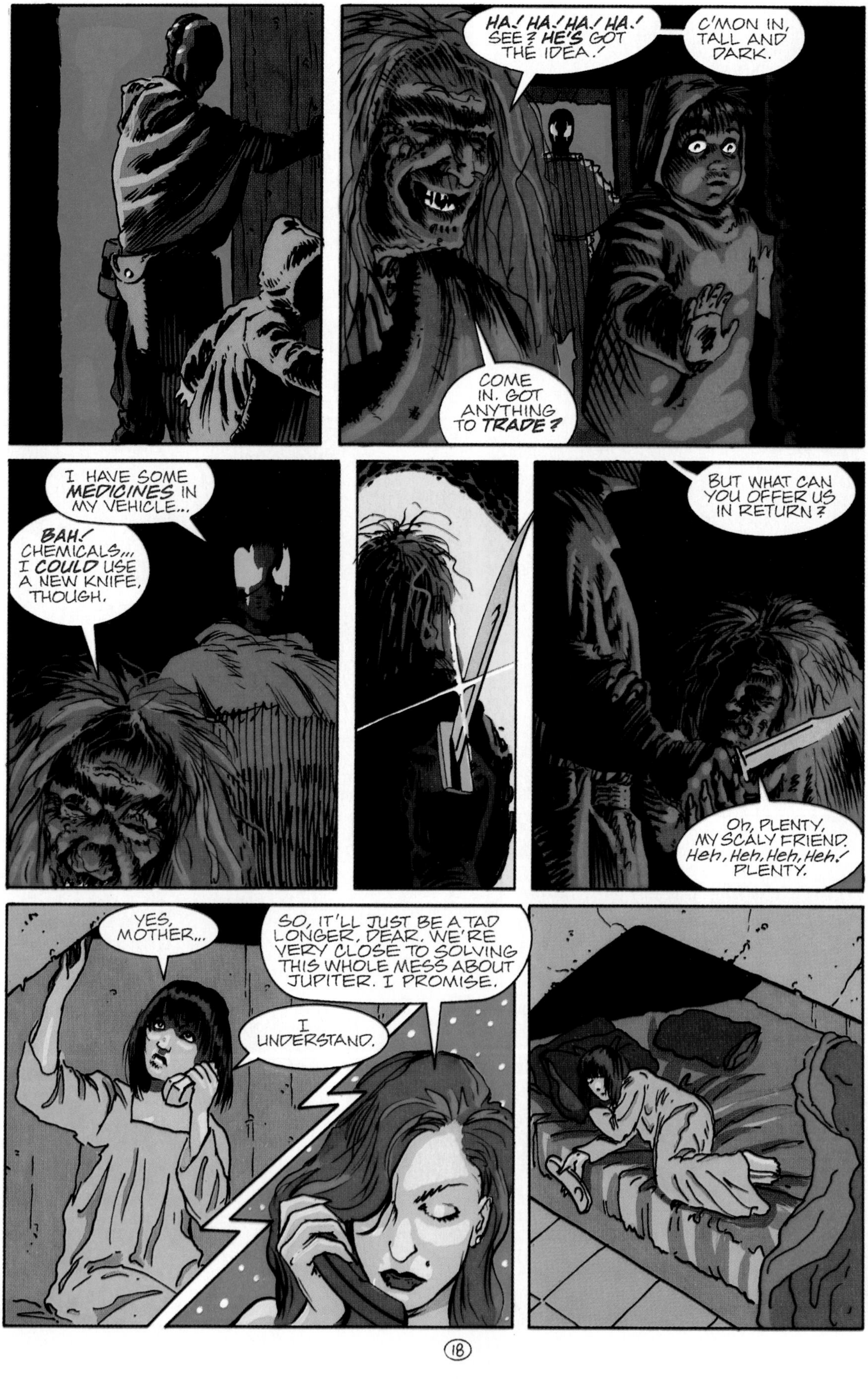
HA! HA! HA! HA! SEE? HE'S GOT THE IDEA!
C'MON IN, TALL AND DARK.
COME IN. GOT ANYTHING TO TRADE?
I HAVE SOME MEDICINES IN MY VEHICLE...
BAH! CHEMICALS... I COULD USE A NEW KNIFE, THOUGH.
BUT WHAT CAN YOU OFFER US IN RETURN?
Oh, PLENTY, MY SCALY FRIEND. Heh, Heh, Heh, Heh! PLENTY.
YES, MOTHER...
SO, IT'LL JUST BE A TAD LONGER, DEAR. WE'RE VERY CLOSE TO SOLVING THIS WHOLE MESS ABOUT JUPITER. I PROMISE.
I UNDERSTAND.

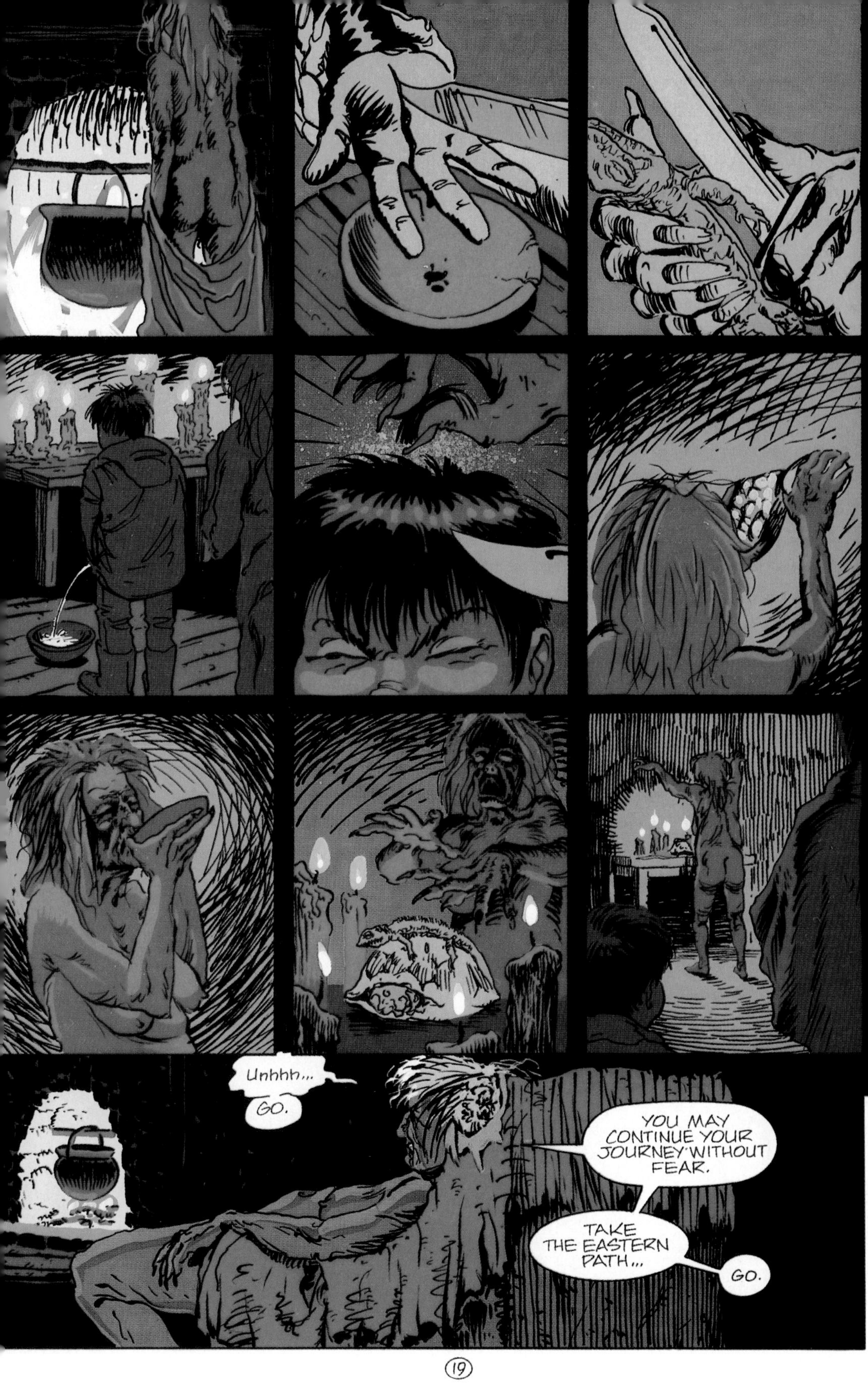
Unhhh...
GO.
YOU MAY CONTINUE YOUR JOURNEY WITHOUT FEAR.
TAKE THE EASTERN PATH...
GO.

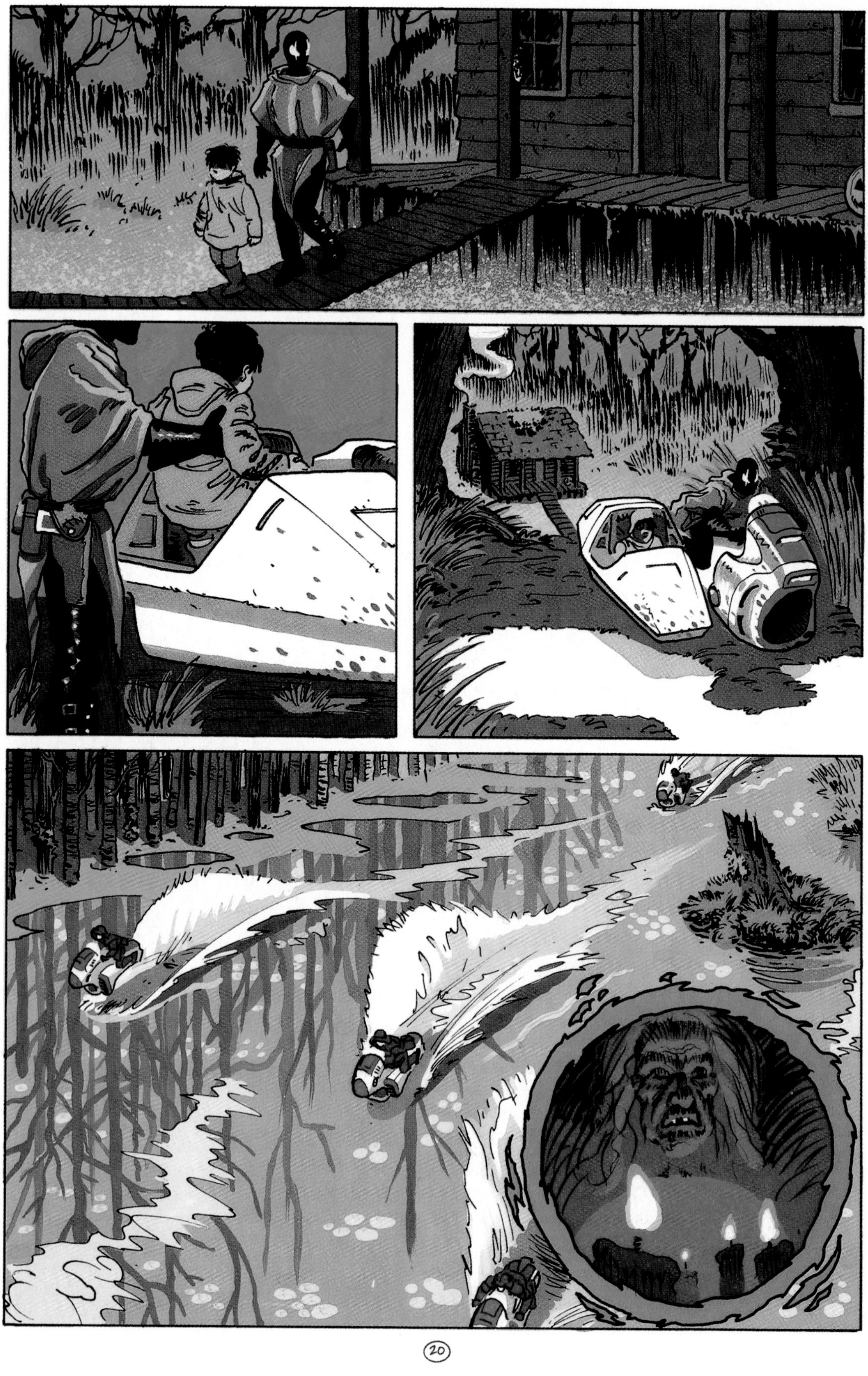

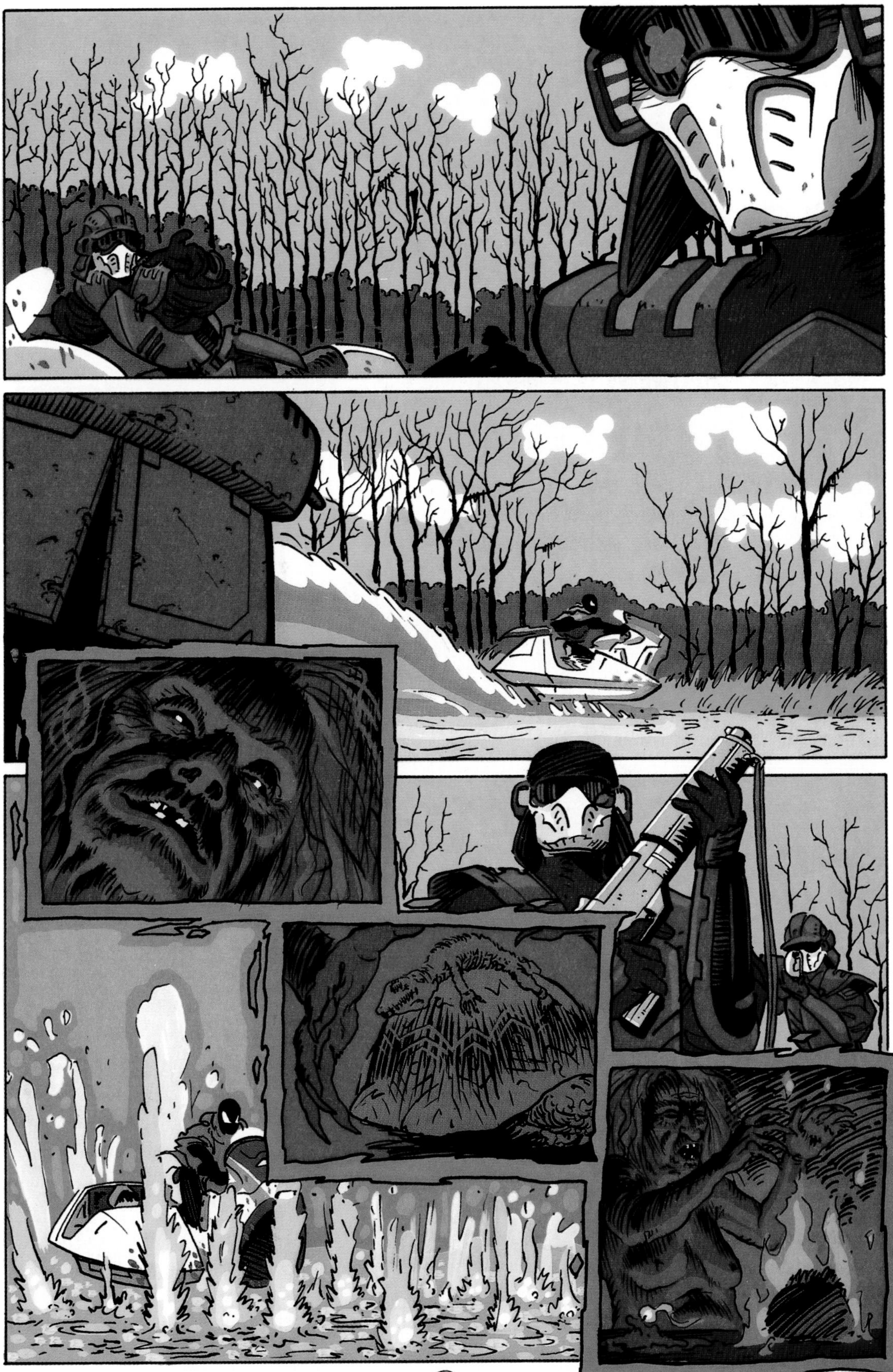

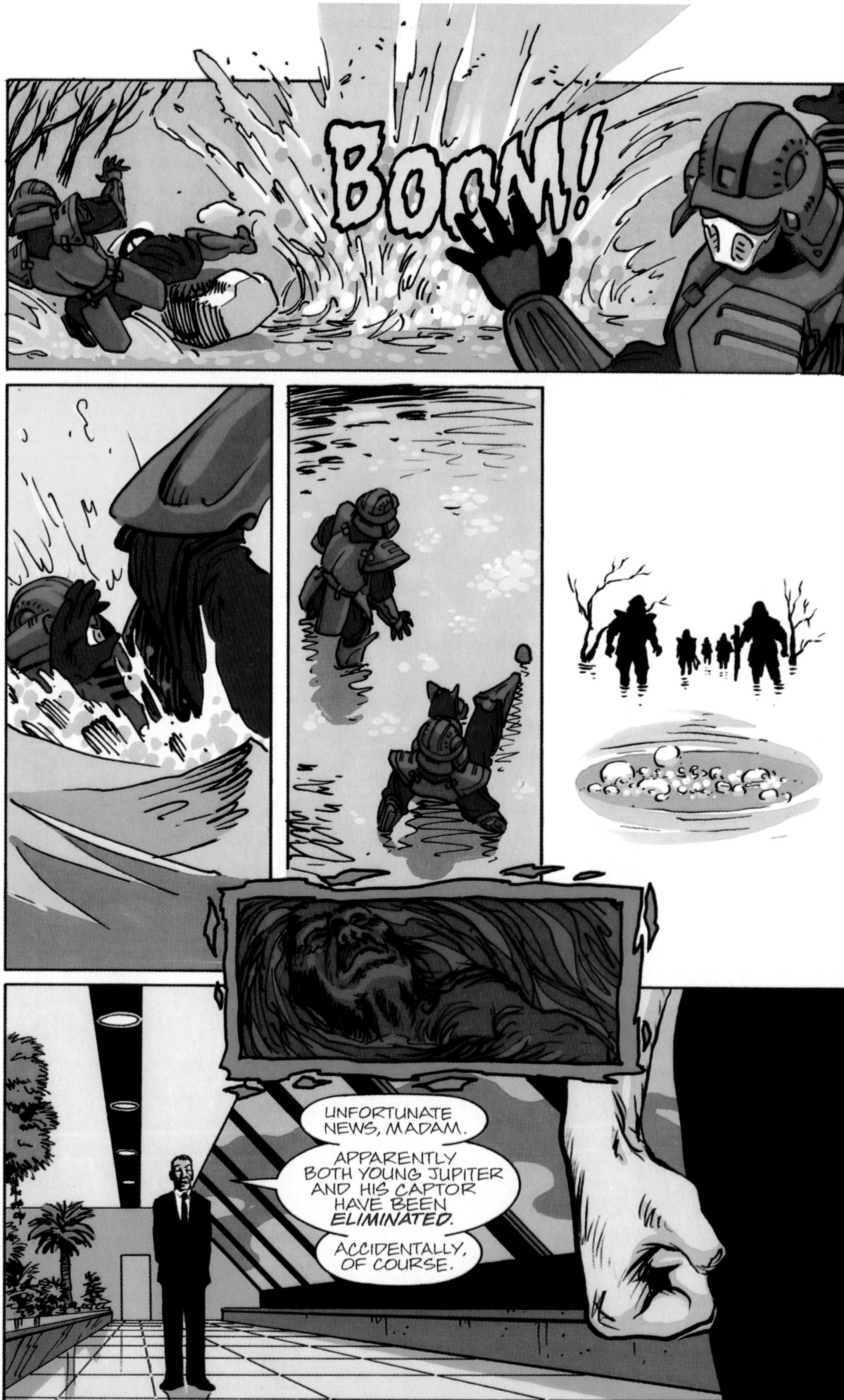
BOOM!
UNFORTUNATE NEWS, MADAM.
APPARENTLY BOTH YOUNG JUPITER AND HIS CAPTOR HAVE BEEN *ELIMINATED*.
ACCIDENTALLY, OF COURSE.

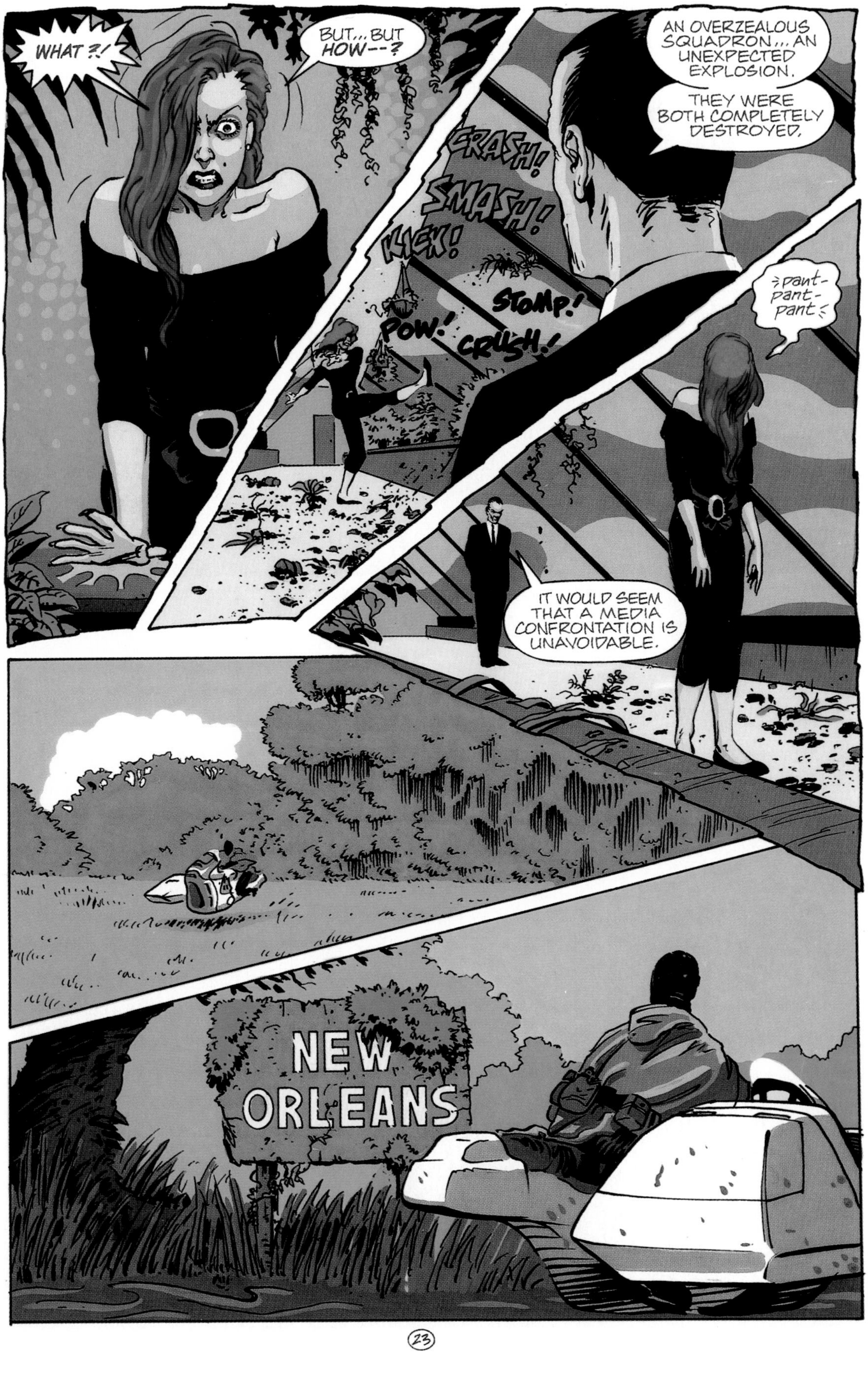
WHAT ?!
BUT... BUT HOW--?
AN OVERZEALOUS SQUADRON... AN UNEXPECTED EXPLOSION.
THEY WERE BOTH COMPLETELY DESTROYED.
CRASH!
SMASH!
KICK!
STOMP!
POW!
CRUSH!
pant-pant-pant
IT WOULD SEEM THAT A MEDIA CONFRONTATION IS UNAVOIDABLE.
NEW ORLEANS

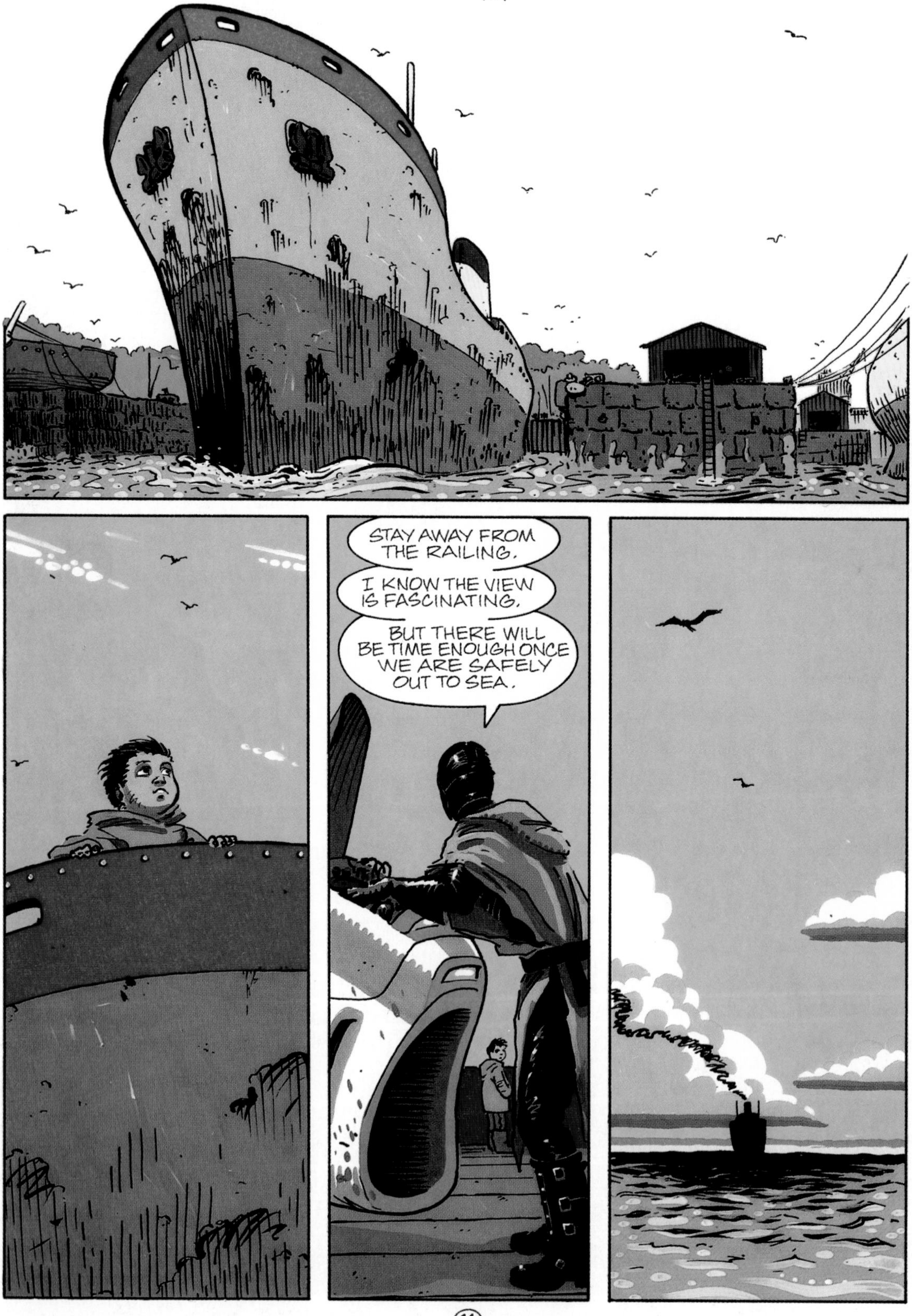
STAY AWAY FROM THE RAILING.
I KNOW THE VIEW IS FASCINATING.
BUT THERE WILL BE TIME ENOUGH ONCE WE ARE SAFELY OUT TO SEA.

CHAPTER 4

# DEVIL *and the deep blue sea*

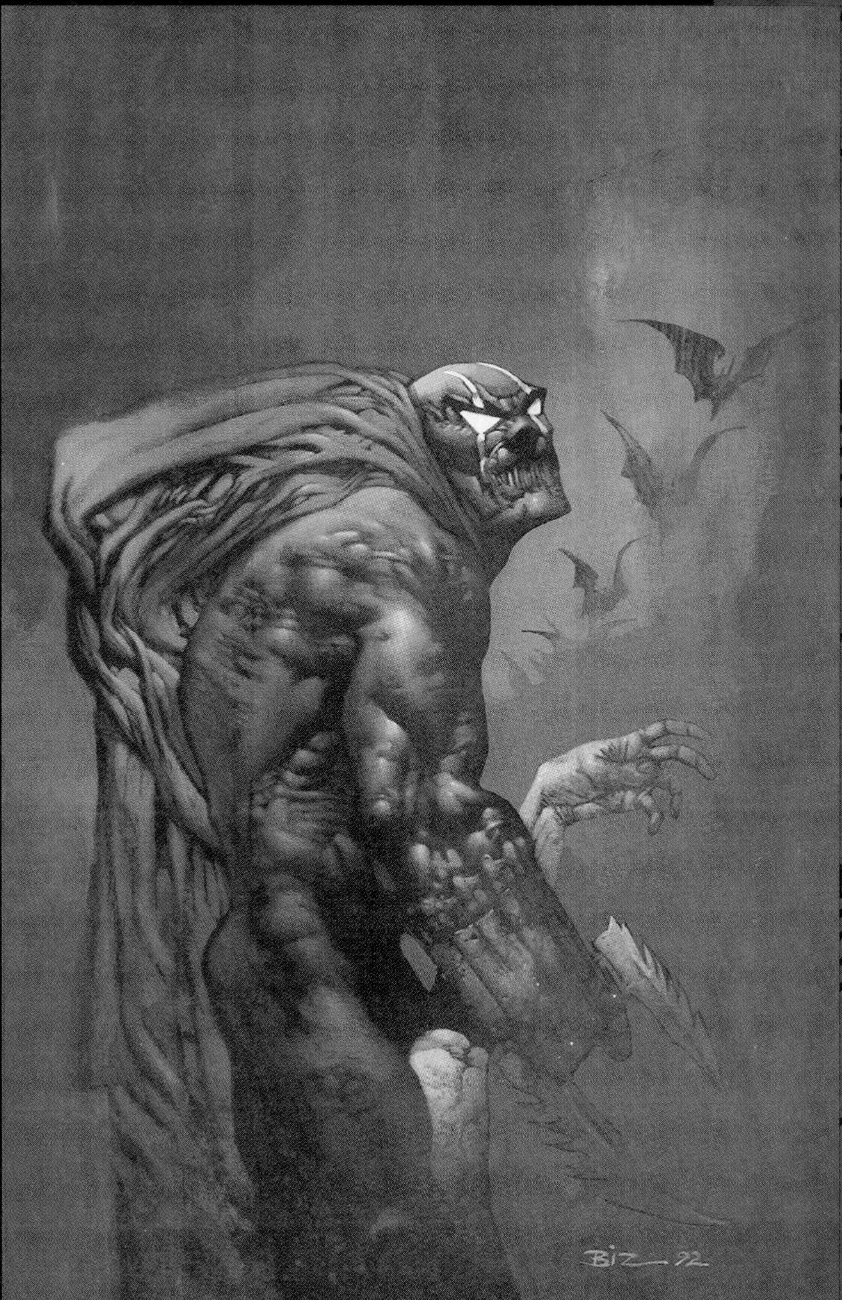
BIZ 92

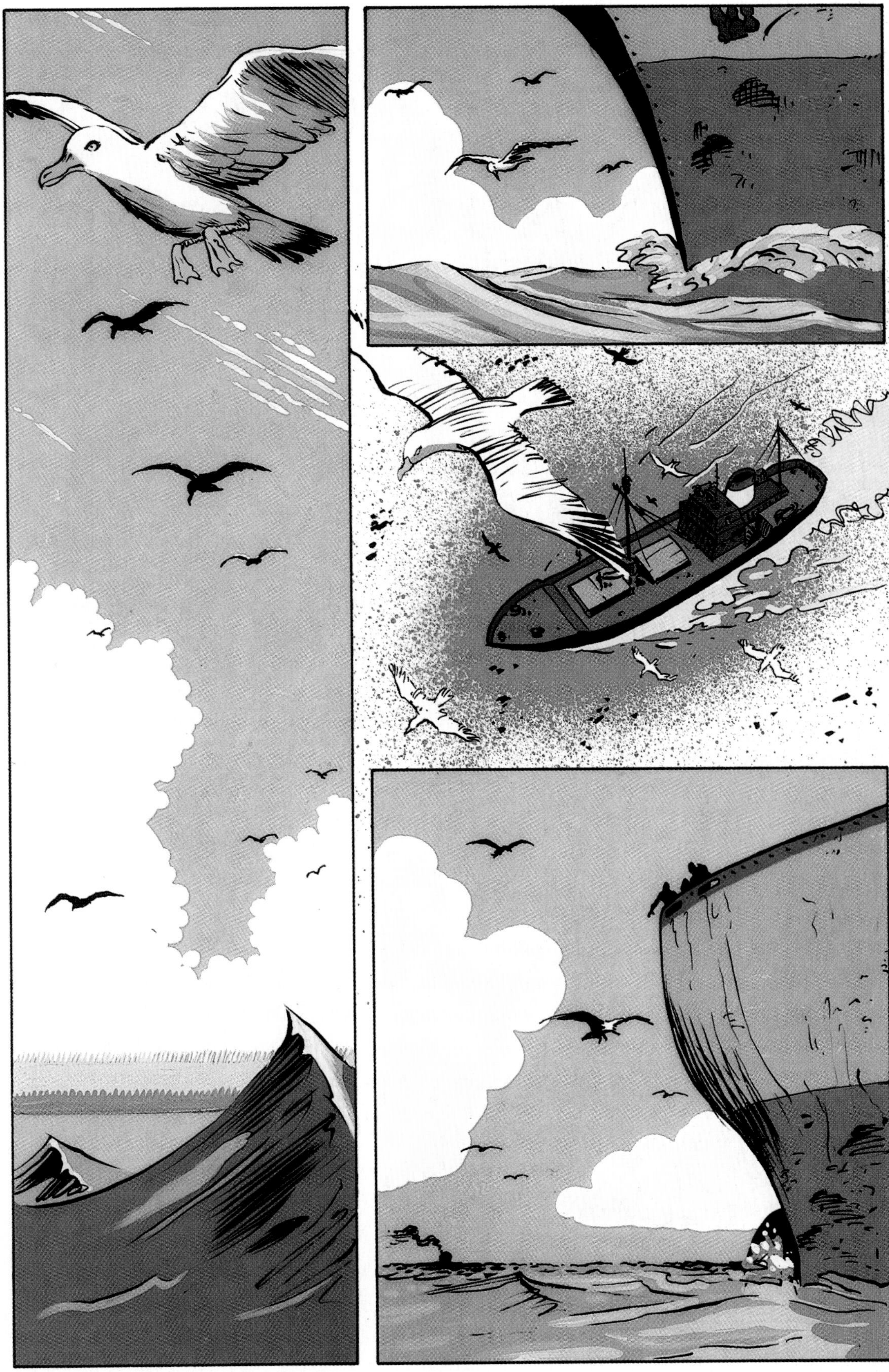

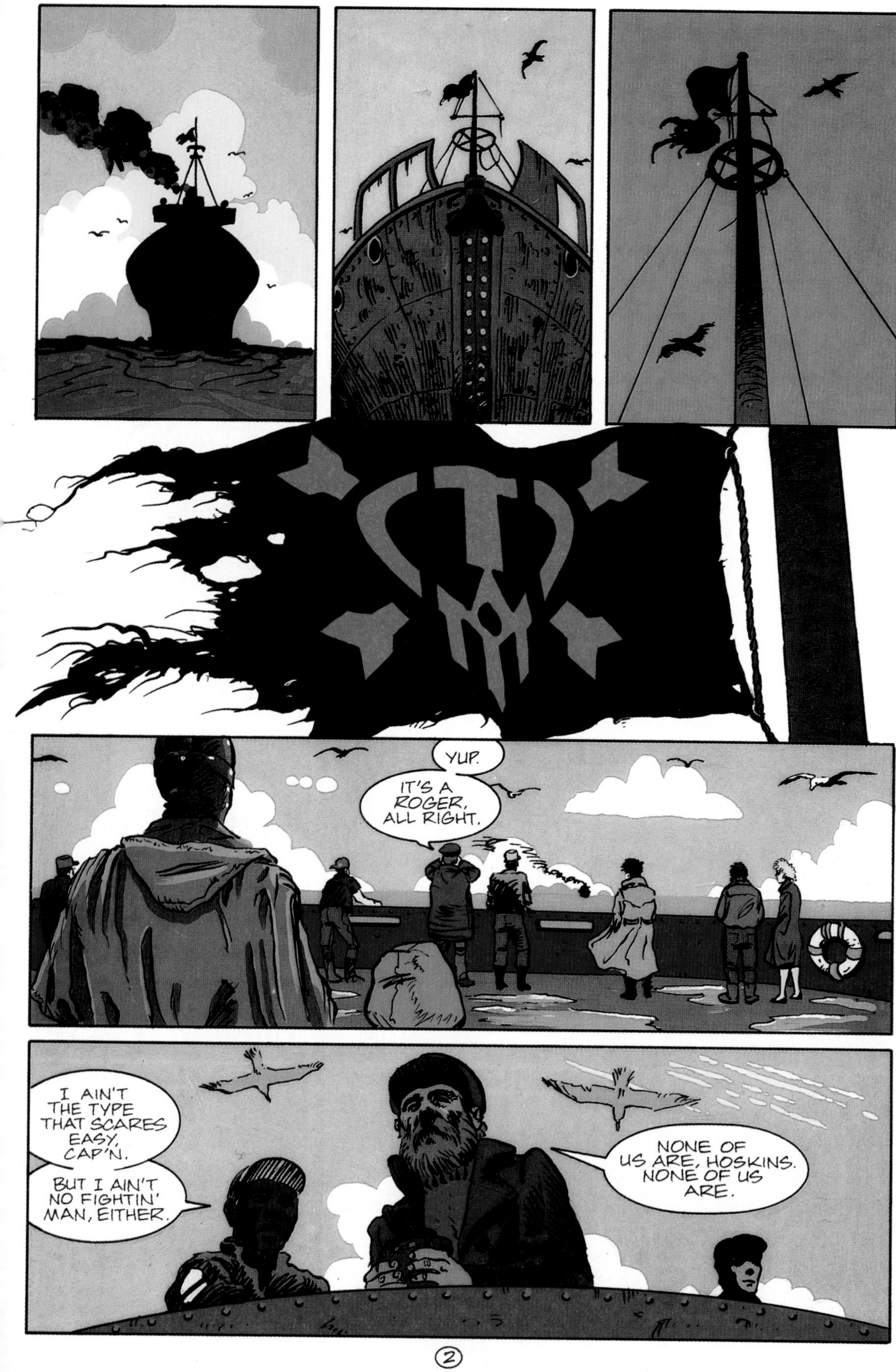

YUP.
IT'S A ROGER, ALL RIGHT.
I AIN'T THE TYPE THAT SCARES EASY, CAP'N.
BUT I AIN'T NO FIGHTIN' MAN, EITHER.
NONE OF US ARE, HOSKINS. NONE OF US ARE.

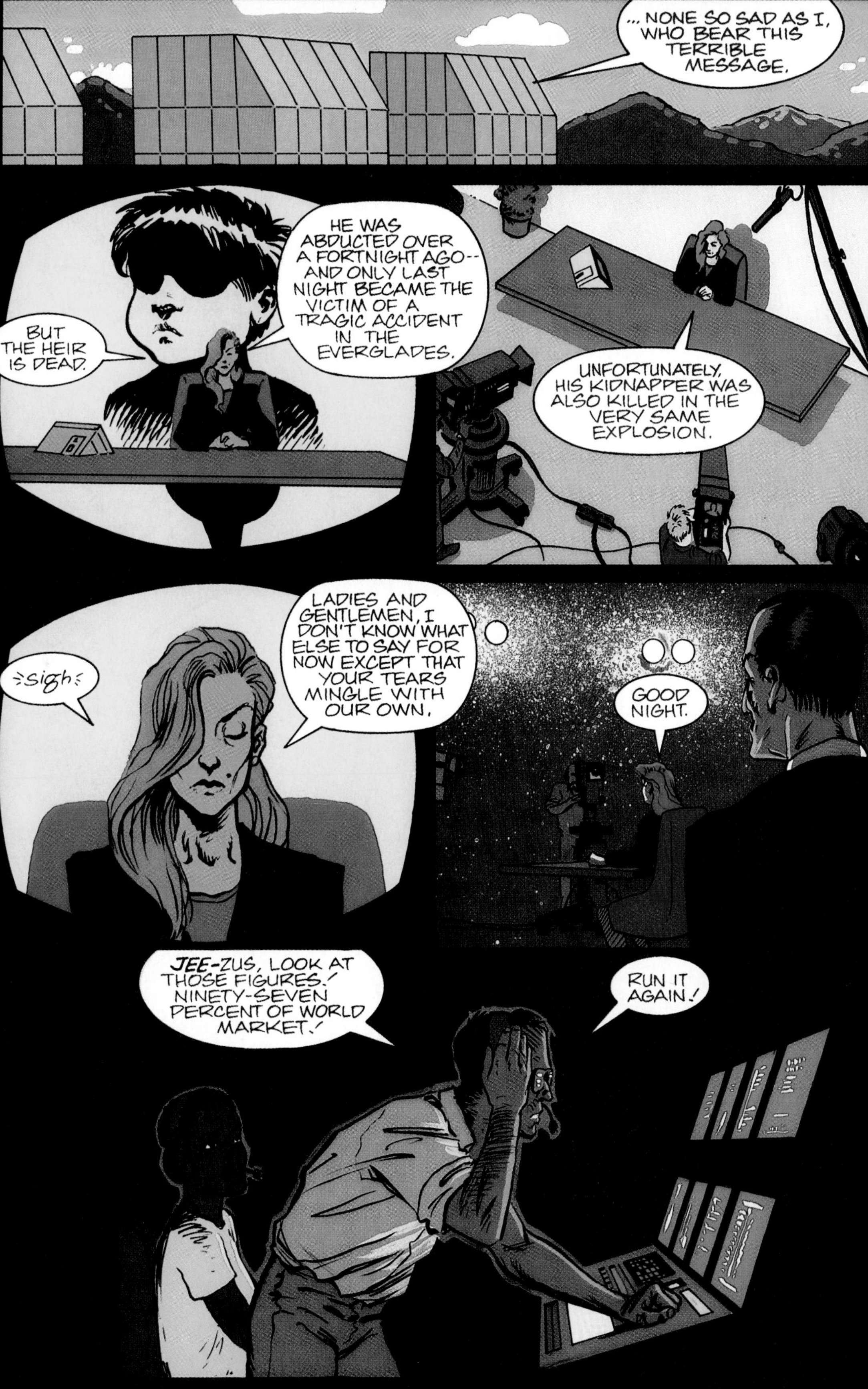

...NONE SO SAD AS I, WHO BEAR THIS TERRIBLE MESSAGE.
BUT THE HEIR IS DEAD.
HE WAS ABDUCTED OVER A FORTNIGHT AGO-- AND ONLY LAST NIGHT BECAME THE VICTIM OF A TRAGIC ACCIDENT IN THE EVERGLADES.
UNFORTUNATELY, HIS KIDNAPPER WAS ALSO KILLED IN THE VERY SAME EXPLOSION.
sigh
LADIES AND GENTLEMEN, I DON'T KNOW WHAT ELSE TO SAY FOR NOW EXCEPT THAT YOUR TEARS MINGLE WITH OUR OWN.
GOOD NIGHT.
JEE-ZUS, LOOK AT THOSE FIGURES! NINETY-SEVEN PERCENT OF WORLD MARKET!
RUN IT AGAIN!

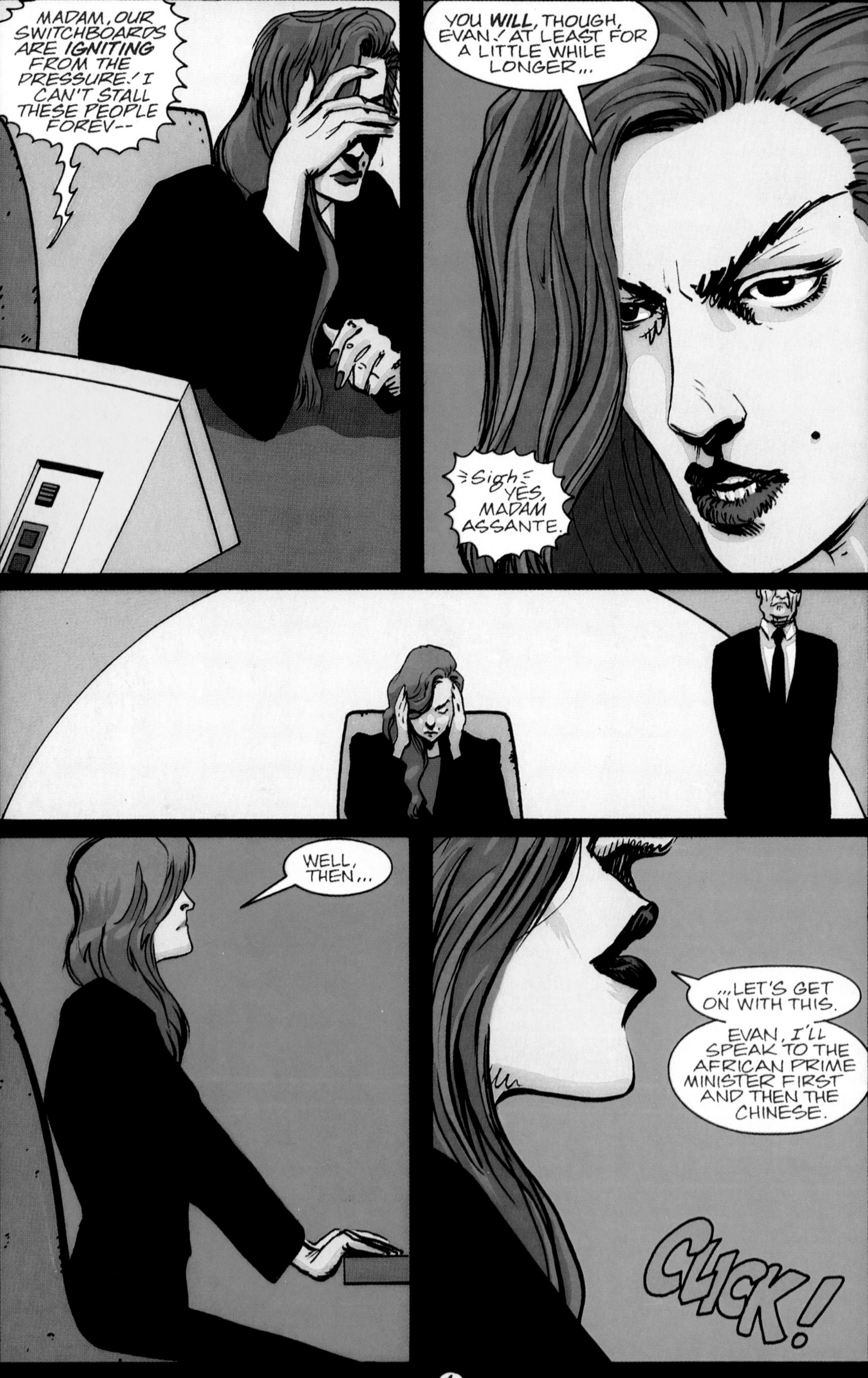

MADAM, OUR SWITCHBOARDS ARE **IGNITING** FROM THE PRESSURE! I CAN'T STALL THESE PEOPLE FOREV--
YOU **WILL**, THOUGH, EVAN! AT LEAST FOR A LITTLE WHILE LONGER...
*Sigh* YES, MADAM ASSANTE.
WELL, THEN...
...LET'S GET ON WITH THIS.
EVAN, *I'LL* SPEAK TO THE AFRICAN PRIME MINISTER FIRST AND THEN THE CHINESE.
CLICK!

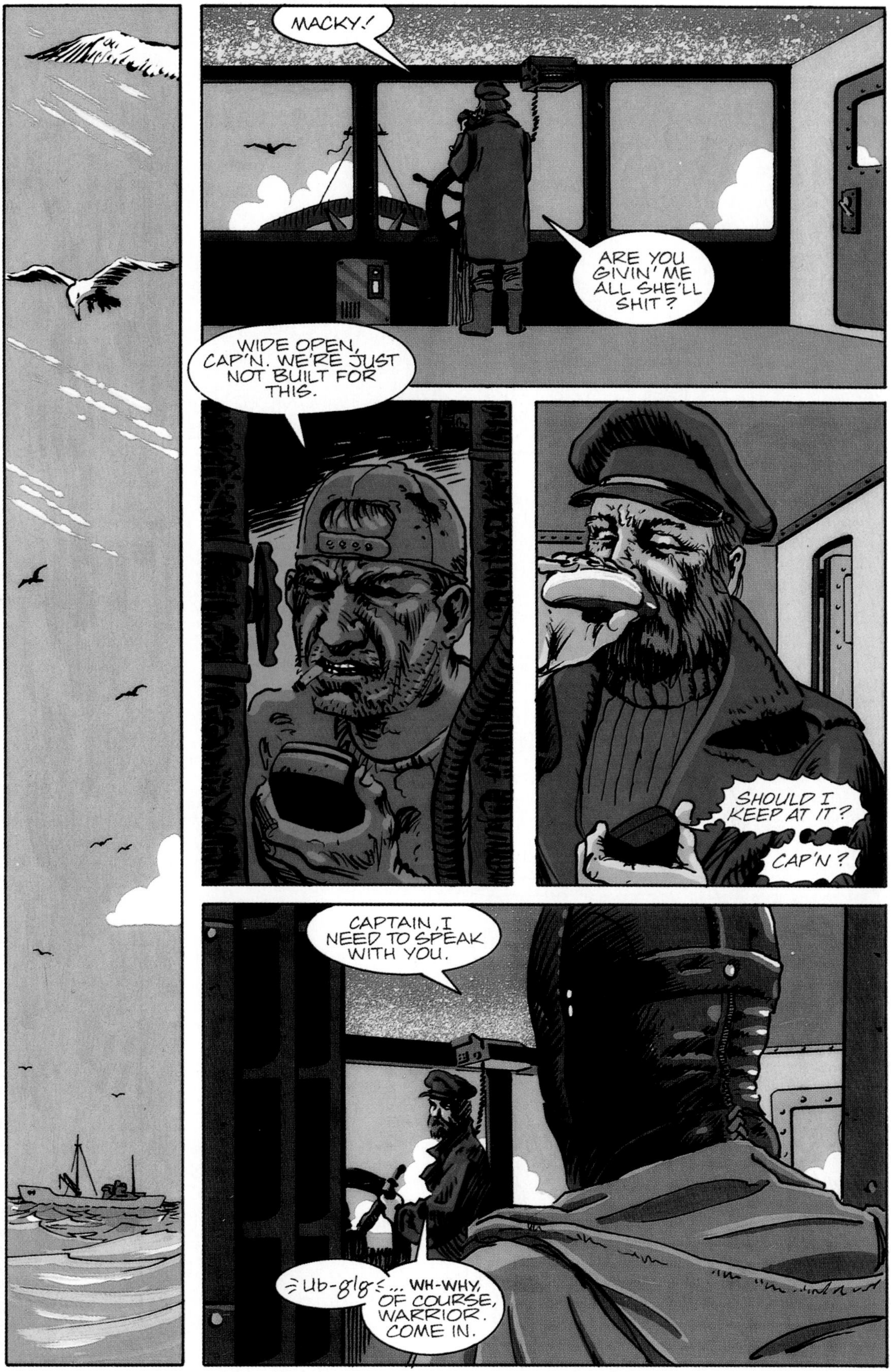
MACKY!
ARE YOU GIVIN' ME ALL SHE'LL SHIT?
WIDE OPEN, CAP'N. WE'RE JUST NOT BUILT FOR THIS.
SHOULD I KEEP AT IT?
CAP'N?
CAPTAIN, I NEED TO SPEAK WITH YOU.
ub-glg... WH-WHY, OF COURSE, WARRIOR. COME IN.

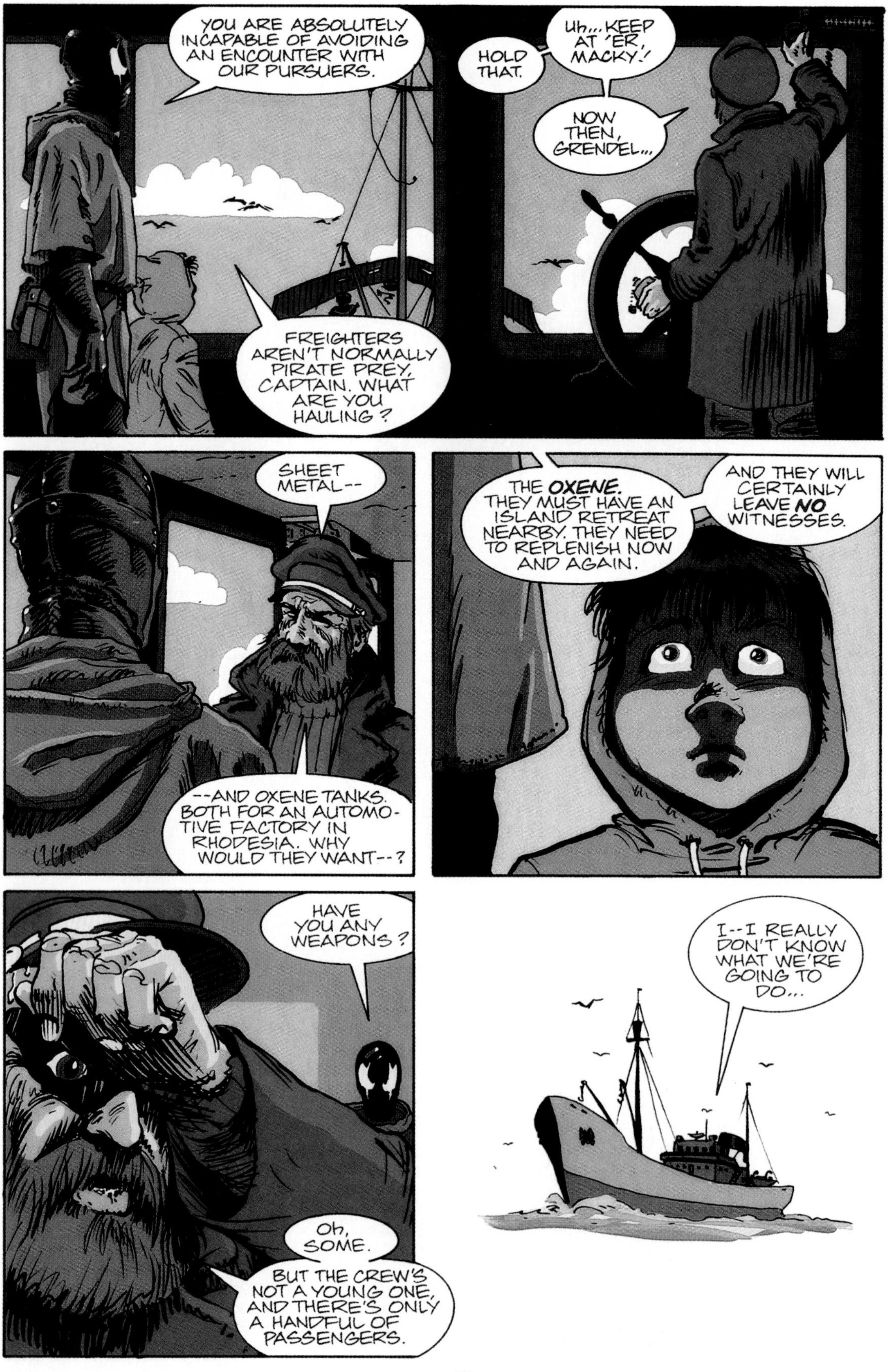
YOU ARE ABSOLUTELY INCAPABLE OF AVOIDING AN ENCOUNTER WITH OUR PURSUERS.
FREIGHTERS AREN'T NORMALLY PIRATE PREY, CAPTAIN. WHAT ARE YOU HAULING?
HOLD THAT.
Uh... KEEP AT 'ER, MACKY!
NOW THEN, GRENDEL...
SHEET METAL--
--AND OXENE TANKS. BOTH FOR AN AUTOMOTIVE FACTORY IN RHODESIA. WHY WOULD THEY WANT--?
THE OXENE. THEY MUST HAVE AN ISLAND RETREAT NEARBY. THEY NEED TO REPLENISH NOW AND AGAIN.
AND THEY WILL CERTAINLY LEAVE NO WITNESSES.
HAVE YOU ANY WEAPONS?
Oh, SOME.
BUT THE CREW'S NOT A YOUNG ONE, AND THERE'S ONLY A HANDFUL OF PASSENGERS.
I--I REALLY DON'T KNOW WHAT WE'RE GOING TO DO...

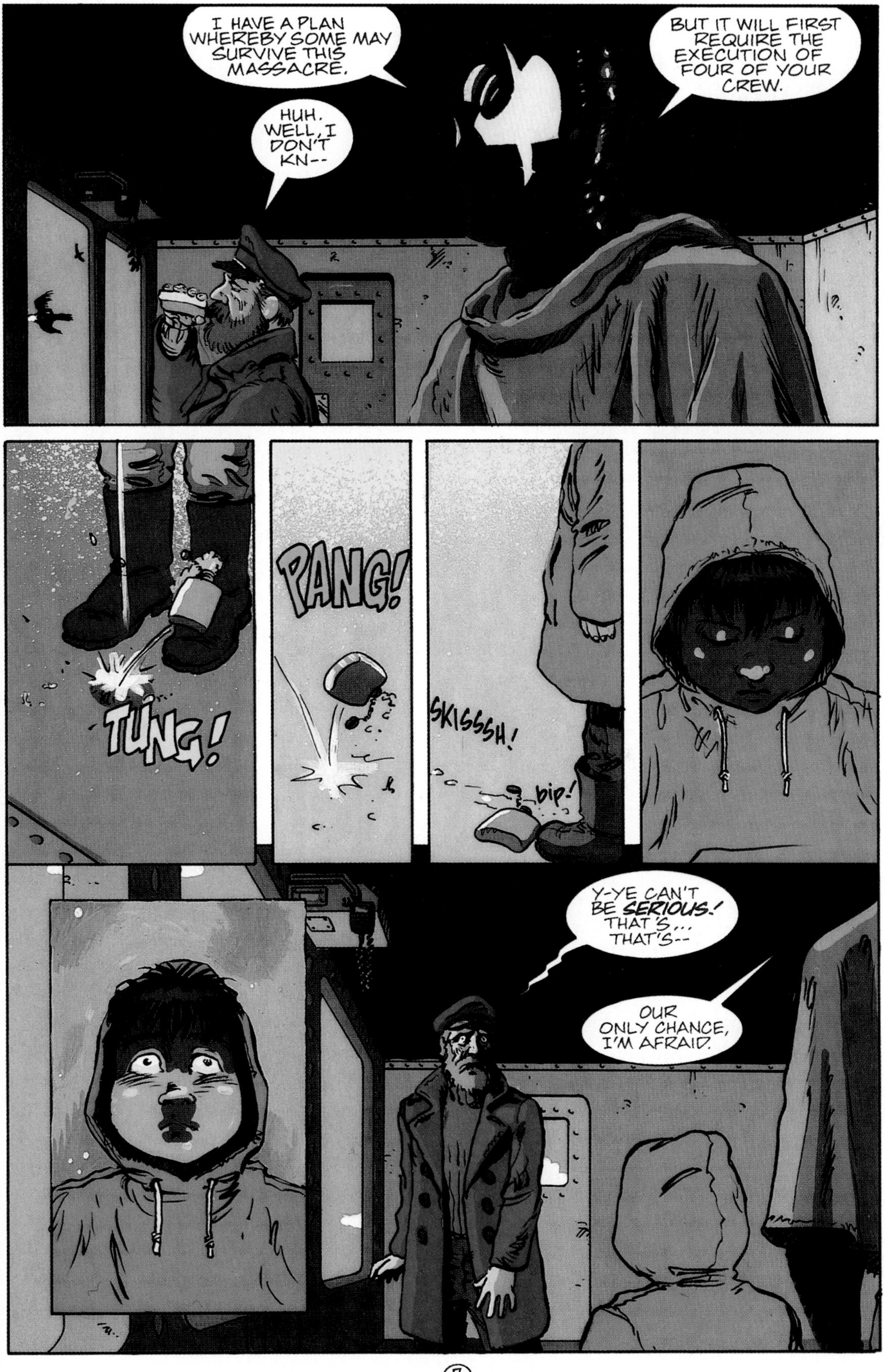
I HAVE A PLAN WHEREBY SOME MAY SURVIVE THIS MASSACRE.
BUT IT WILL FIRST REQUIRE THE EXECUTION OF FOUR OF YOUR CREW.
HUH. WELL, I DON'T KN--
TUNG!
PANG!
SKISSSH!
bip!
Y-YE CAN'T BE SERIOUS! THAT'S... THAT'S--
OUR ONLY CHANCE, I'M AFRAID.

"...AND ONLY LAST NIGHT BECAME THE VICTIM OF A TRAGIC ACCIDENT IN THE EVERGLADES."

"UNFORTUNATELY, HIS KIDNAPPER WAS ALSO KILLED IN THE VERY SAME EXPLOSION."

≥sigh≤

LADIES AND GENTLEMEN, I DON'T KNOW WHAT ELSE TO SAY FOR NOW EXCEPT THAT YOUR TEARS MING

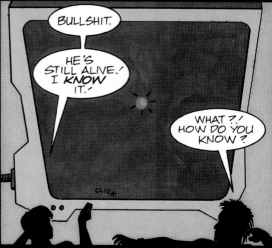

BULLSHIT.

HE'S STILL ALIVE! I *KNOW* IT!

WHAT?! HOW DO YOU KNOW?

CLICK

Skritch Skritch

I JUST DO.

BUT... JUST FROM A TELECAST?

NO. IT'S MORE THAN THAT. I DON'T KNOW...

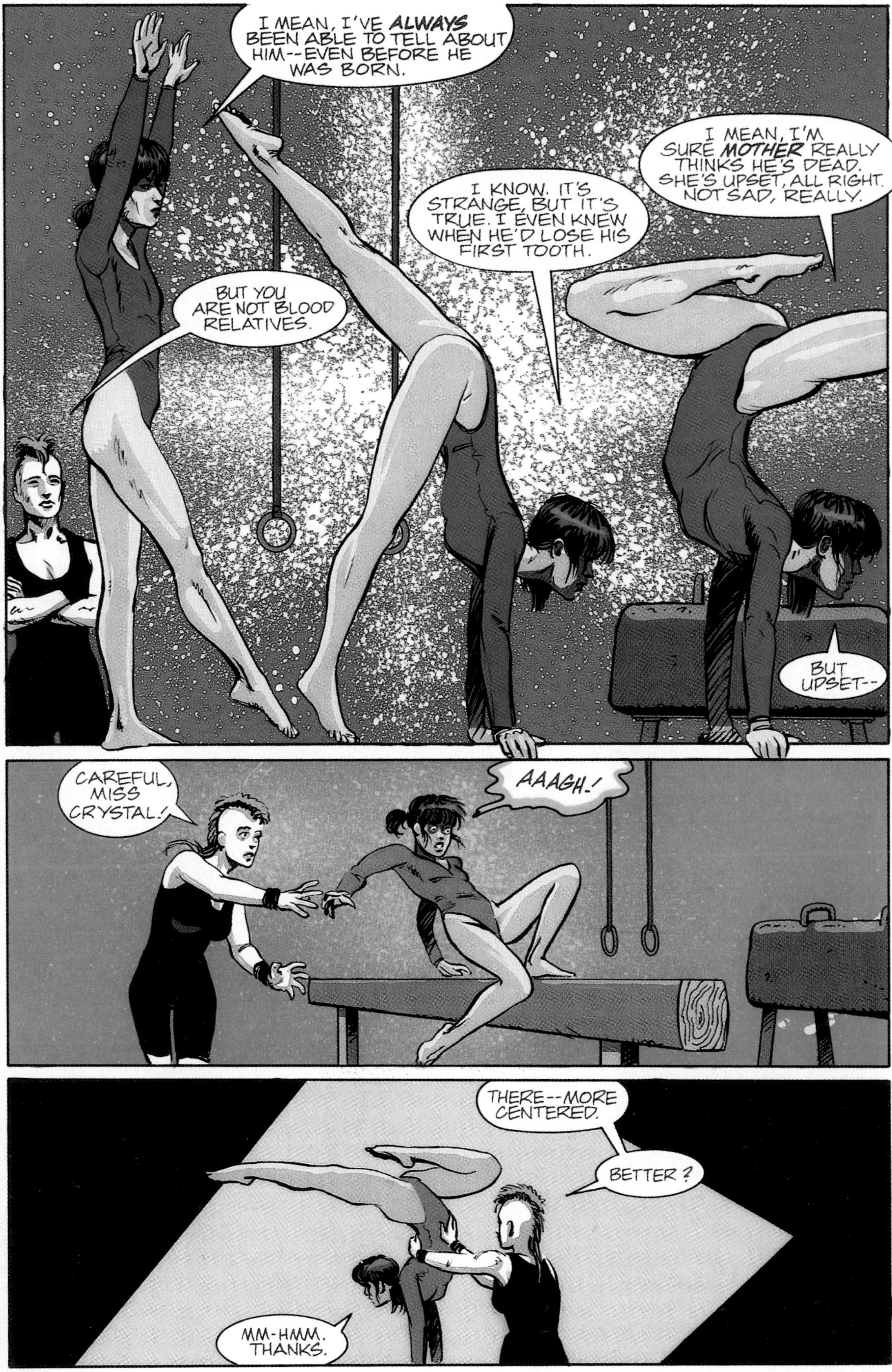
I MEAN, I'VE ALWAYS BEEN ABLE TO TELL ABOUT HIM--EVEN BEFORE HE WAS BORN.
BUT YOU ARE NOT BLOOD RELATIVES.
I KNOW. IT'S STRANGE, BUT IT'S TRUE. I EVEN KNEW WHEN HE'D LOSE HIS FIRST TOOTH.
I MEAN, I'M SURE MOTHER REALLY THINKS HE'S DEAD. SHE'S UPSET, ALL RIGHT. NOT SAD, REALLY.
BUT UPSET--
CAREFUL, MISS CRYSTAL!
AAAGH!
THERE--MORE CENTERED.
BETTER?
MM-HMM. THANKS.

B-BUT I CAN'T...

THEY ARE VICIOUS, HABITUAL KILLERS.

WE HAVE NO HOPE WITHOUT THE ELEMENT OF SURPRISE.

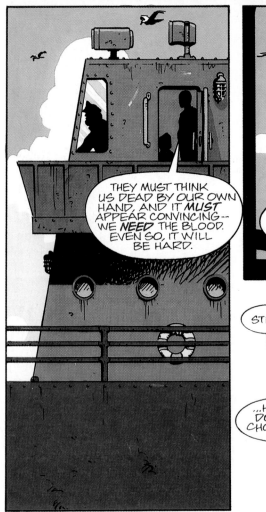

THEY MUST THINK US DEAD BY OUR OWN HAND, AND IT *MUST* APPEAR CONVINCING-- WE *NEED* THE BLOOD. EVEN SO, IT WILL BE HARD.

BETTER THAN SURRENDERIN', I GUESS.

STILL...

...HOW DO WE CHOOSE?

IT MUST BE THOSE WHOSE DEATHS WILL HAVE THE LEAST EFFECT.

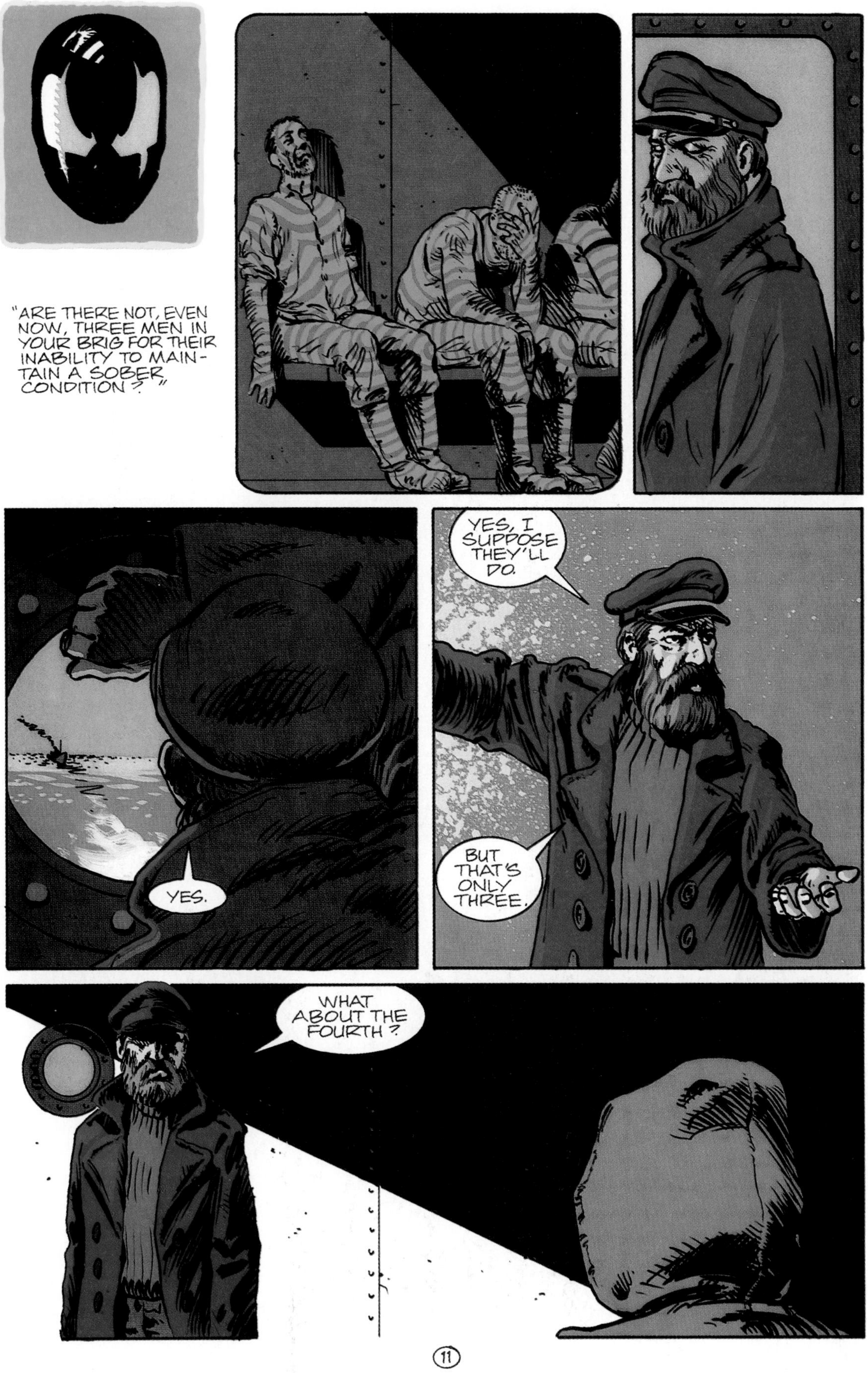
"ARE THERE NOT, EVEN NOW, THREE MEN IN YOUR BRIG FOR THEIR INABILITY TO MAIN-TAIN A SOBER CONDITION ? "
YES.
YES, I SUPPOSE THEY'LL DO.
BUT THAT'S ONLY THREE.
WHAT ABOUT THE FOURTH ?

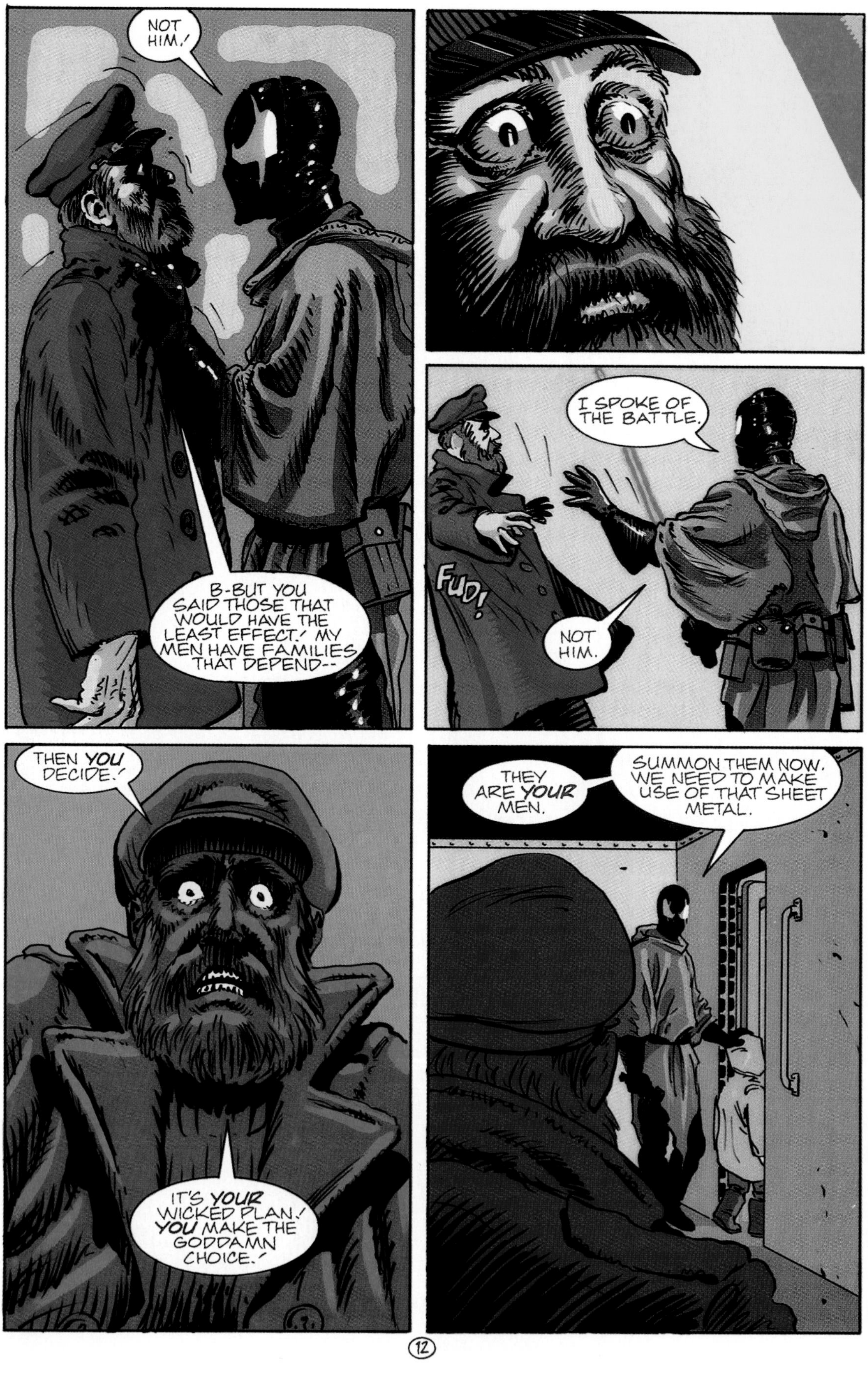
NOT HIM.!
B-BUT YOU SAID THOSE THAT WOULD HAVE THE LEAST EFFECT! MY MEN HAVE FAMILIES THAT DEPEND--
I SPOKE OF THE BATTLE.
FUD!
NOT HIM.
THEN YOU DECIDE!
IT'S YOUR WICKED PLAN! YOU MAKE THE GODDAMN CHOICE!
THEY ARE YOUR MEN.
SUMMON THEM NOW. WE NEED TO MAKE USE OF THAT SHEET METAL.

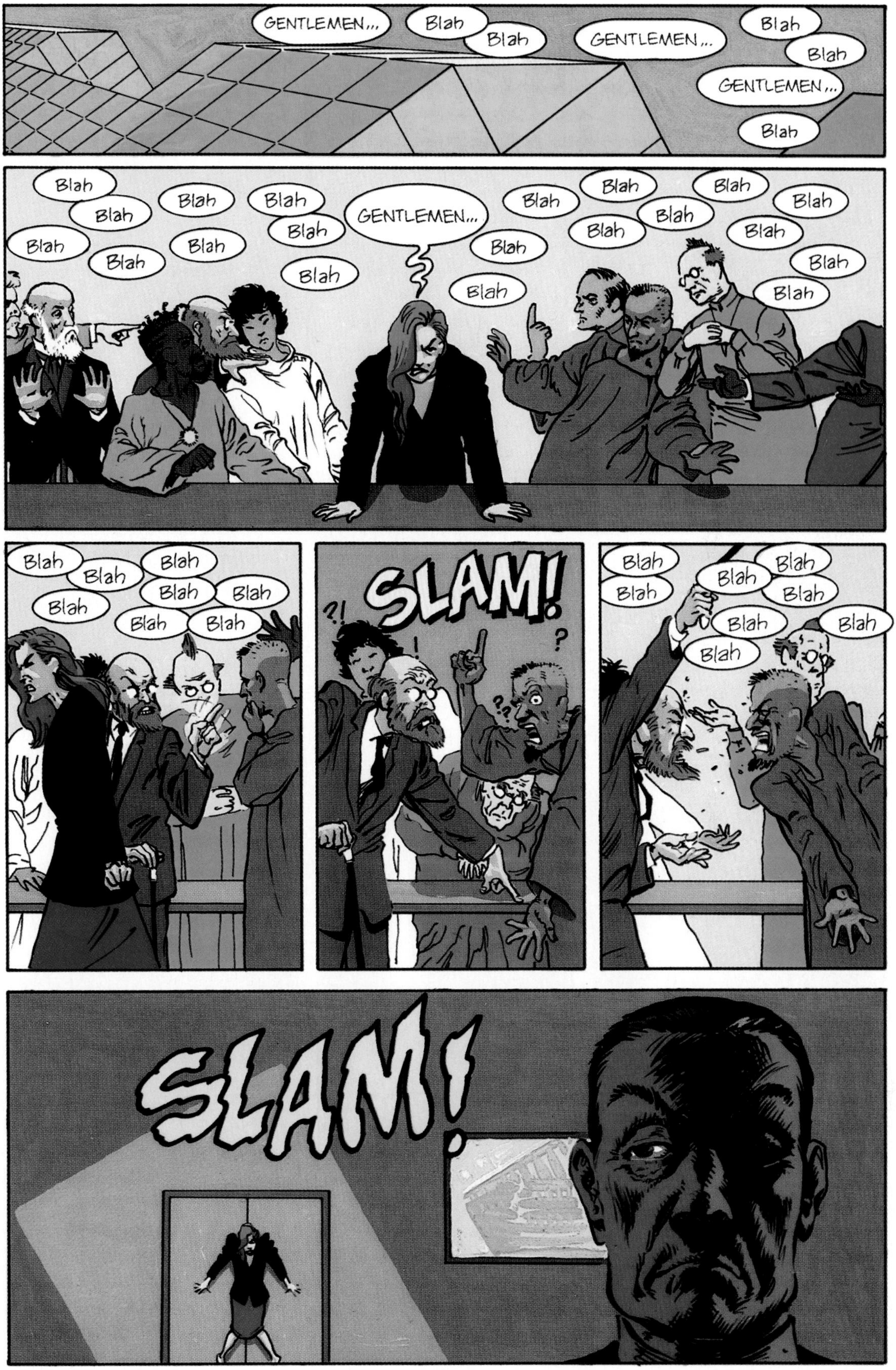
GENTLEMEN...
Blah
Blah
GENTLEMEN...
Blah
Blah
GENTLEMEN...
Blah
Blah
Blah
Blah
Blah
Blah
Blah
Blah
Blah
Blah
GENTLEMEN...
Blah
Blah
Blah
Blah
Blah
Blah
Blah
Blah
Blah
Blah
Blah
Blah
Blah
Blah
Blah
Blah
Blah
Blah
Blah
SLAM!
?!
!
?
??
Blah
Blah
Blah
Blah
Blah
Blah
Blah
Blah
Blah
SLAM!

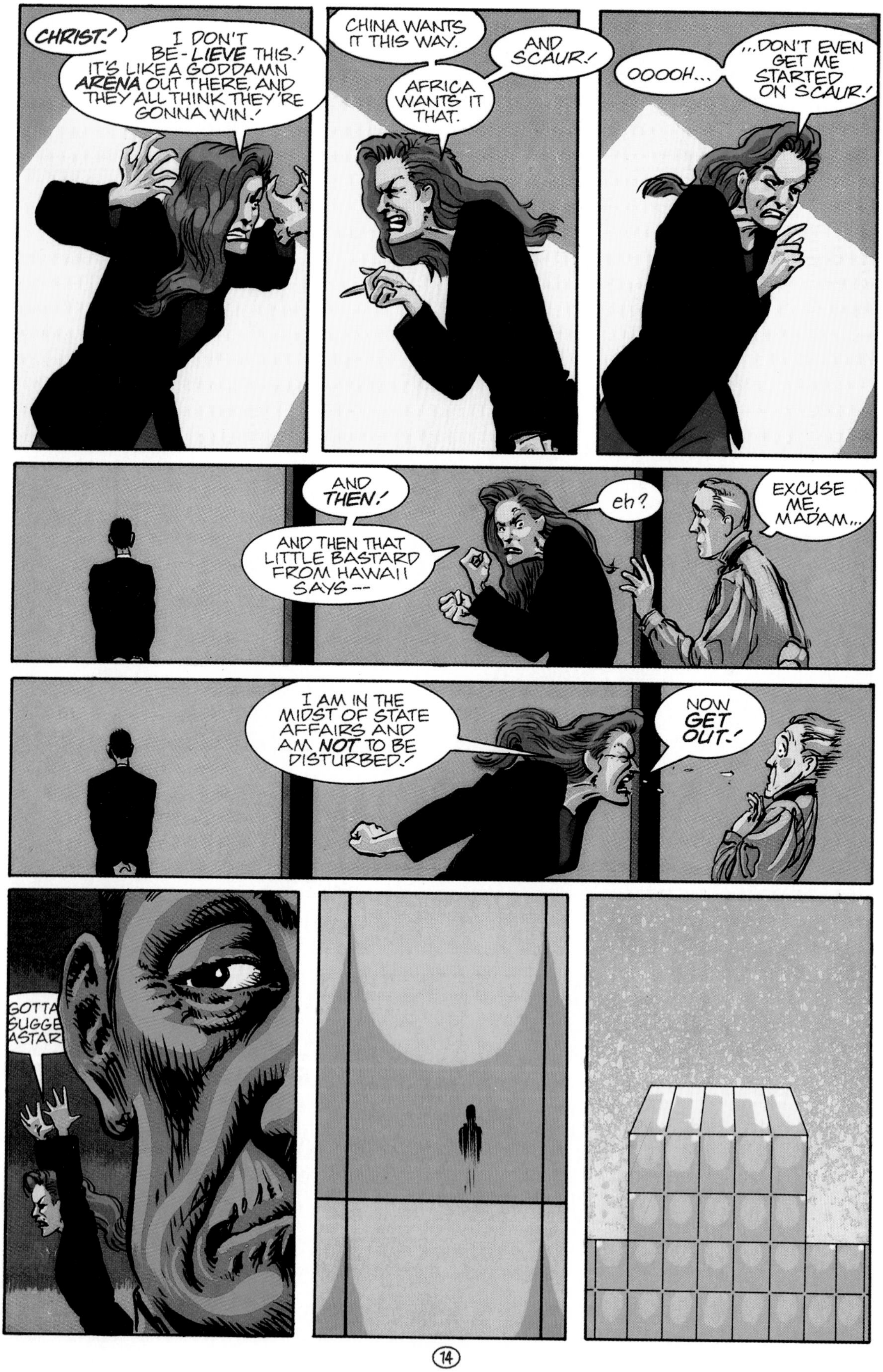
CHRIST!
I DON'T BE-LIEVE THIS! IT'S LIKE A GODDAMN ARENA OUT THERE, AND THEY ALL THINK THEY'RE GONNA WIN!
CHINA WANTS IT THIS WAY.
AFRICA WANTS IT THAT.
AND SCAUR!
OOOOH...
...DON'T EVEN GET ME STARTED ON SCAUR!
AND THEN!
AND THEN THAT LITTLE BASTARD FROM HAWAII SAYS --
eh?
EXCUSE ME, MADAM...
I AM IN THE MIDST OF STATE AFFAIRS AND AM NOT TO BE DISTURBED!
NOW GET OUT!
GOTTA
SUGGE
ASTAR

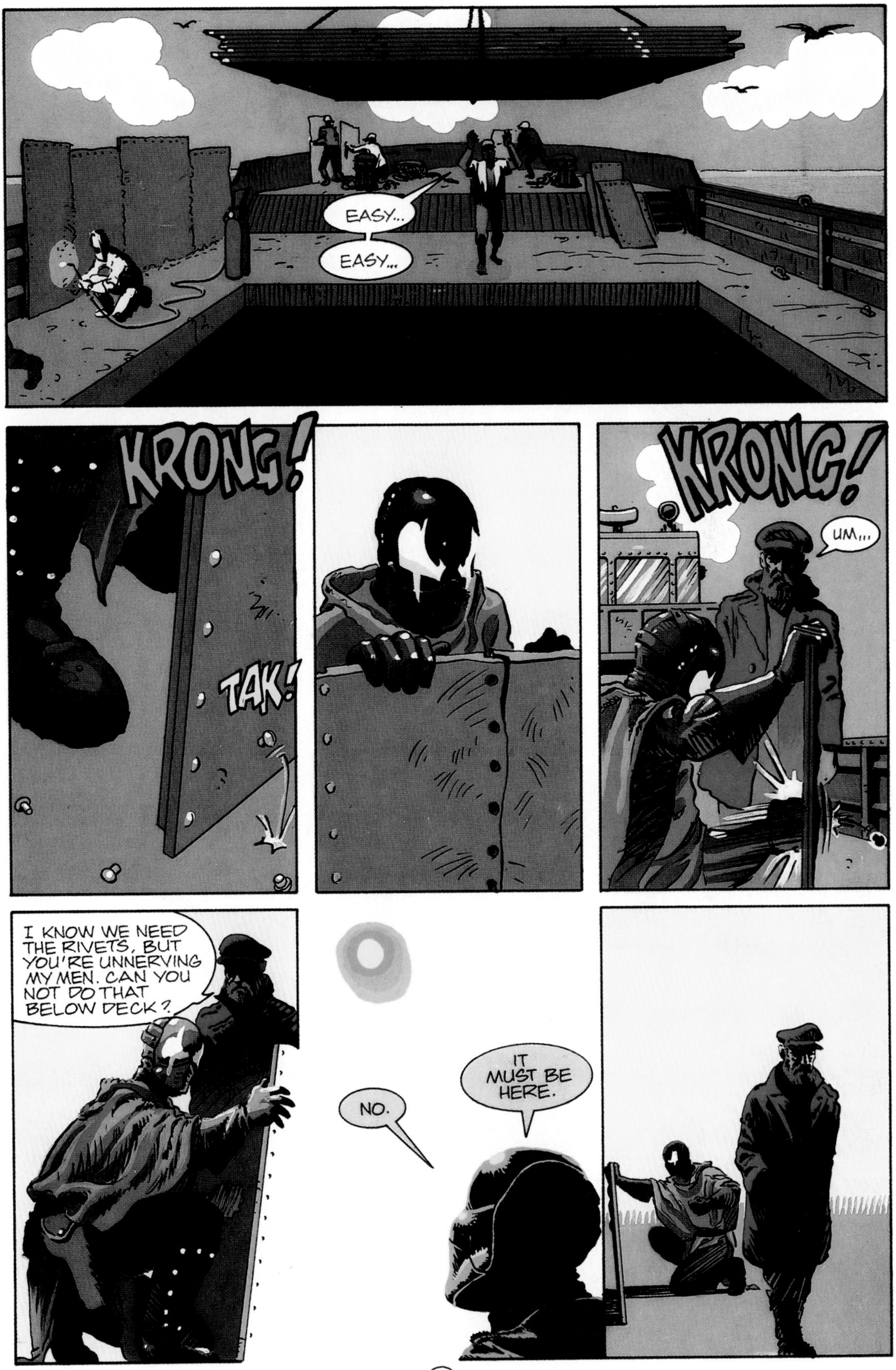
EASY...
EASY...
KRONG!
TAK!
KRONG!
UM...
I KNOW WE NEED THE RIVETS, BUT YOU'RE UNNERVING MY MEN. CAN YOU NOT DO THAT BELOW DECK?
NO.
IT MUST BE HERE.

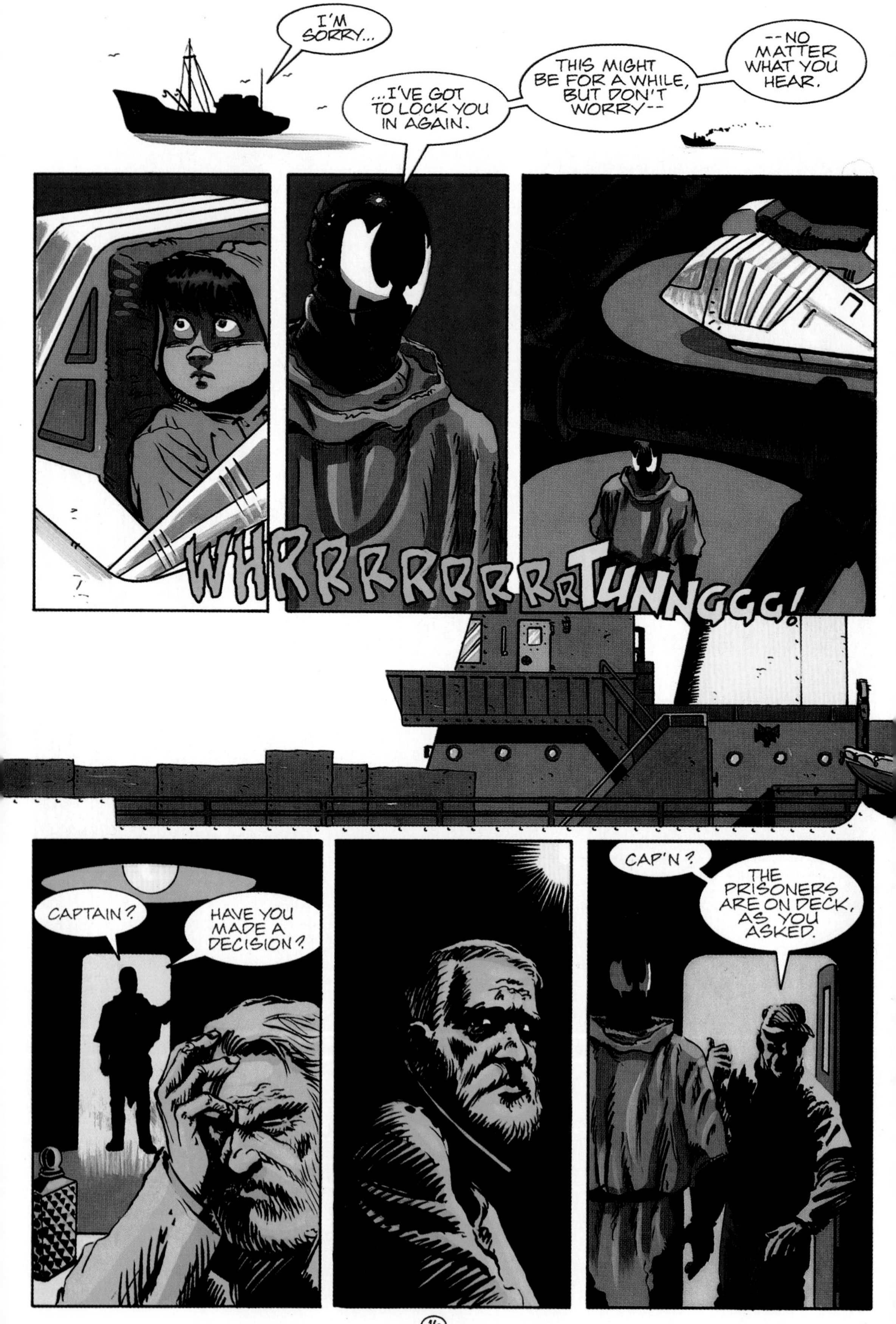
I'M SORRY...
...I'VE GOT TO LOCK YOU IN AGAIN.
THIS MIGHT BE FOR A WHILE, BUT DON'T WORRY--
--NO MATTER WHAT YOU HEAR.
WHRRRRRRRRRTUNNGGG!
CAPTAIN?
HAVE YOU MADE A DECISION?
CAP'N?
THE PRISONERS ARE ON DECK, AS YOU ASKED.

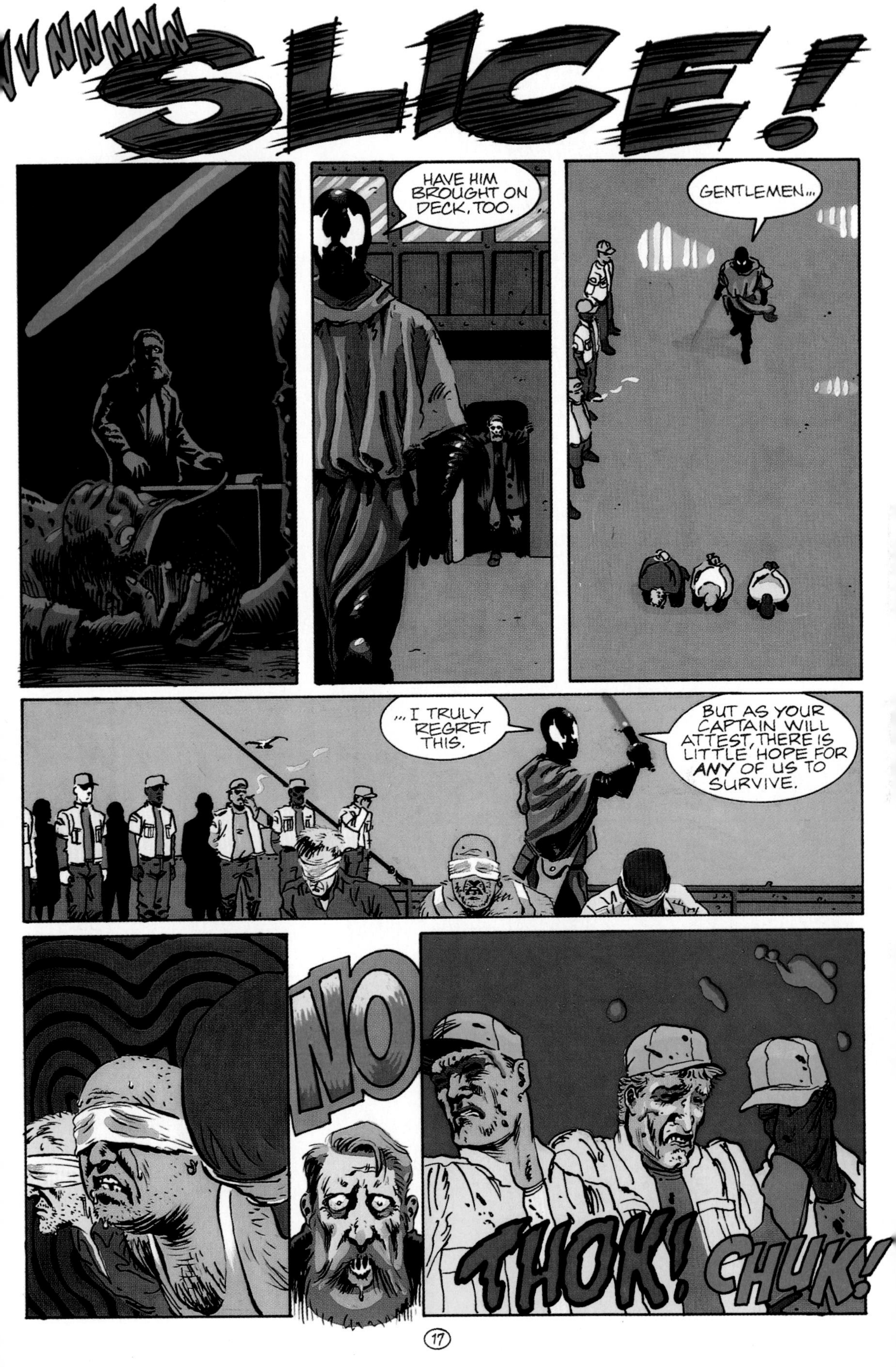
VVNNNNN
SLICE!
HAVE HIM BROUGHT ON DECK, TOO.
GENTLEMEN...
...I TRULY REGRET THIS.
BUT AS YOUR CAPTAIN WILL ATTEST, THERE IS LITTLE HOPE FOR ANY OF US TO SURVIVE.
NO
THOK! CHUK!

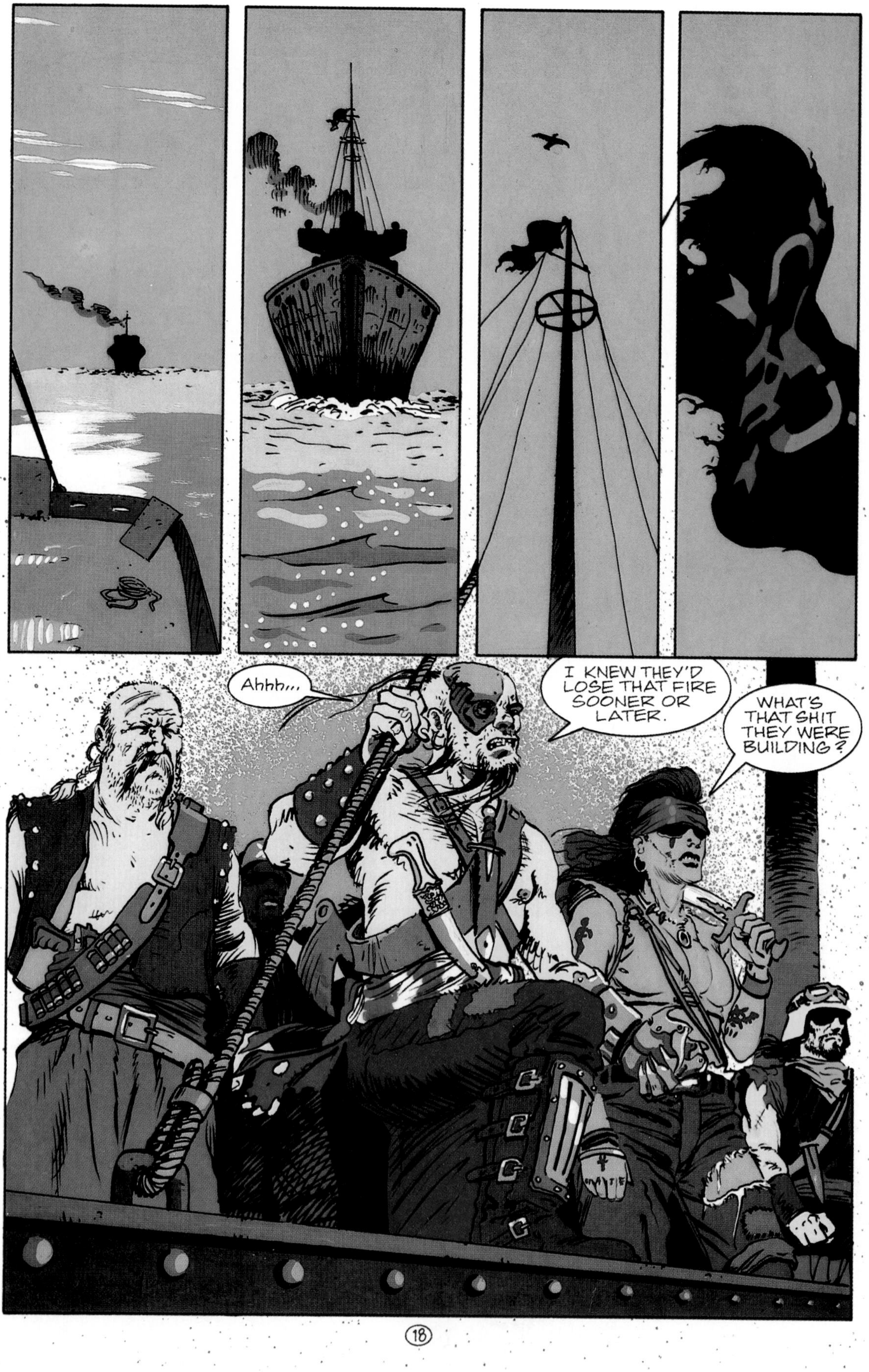
Ahhh...
I KNEW THEY'D LOSE THAT FIRE SOONER OR LATER.
WHAT'S THAT SHIT THEY WERE BUILDING?

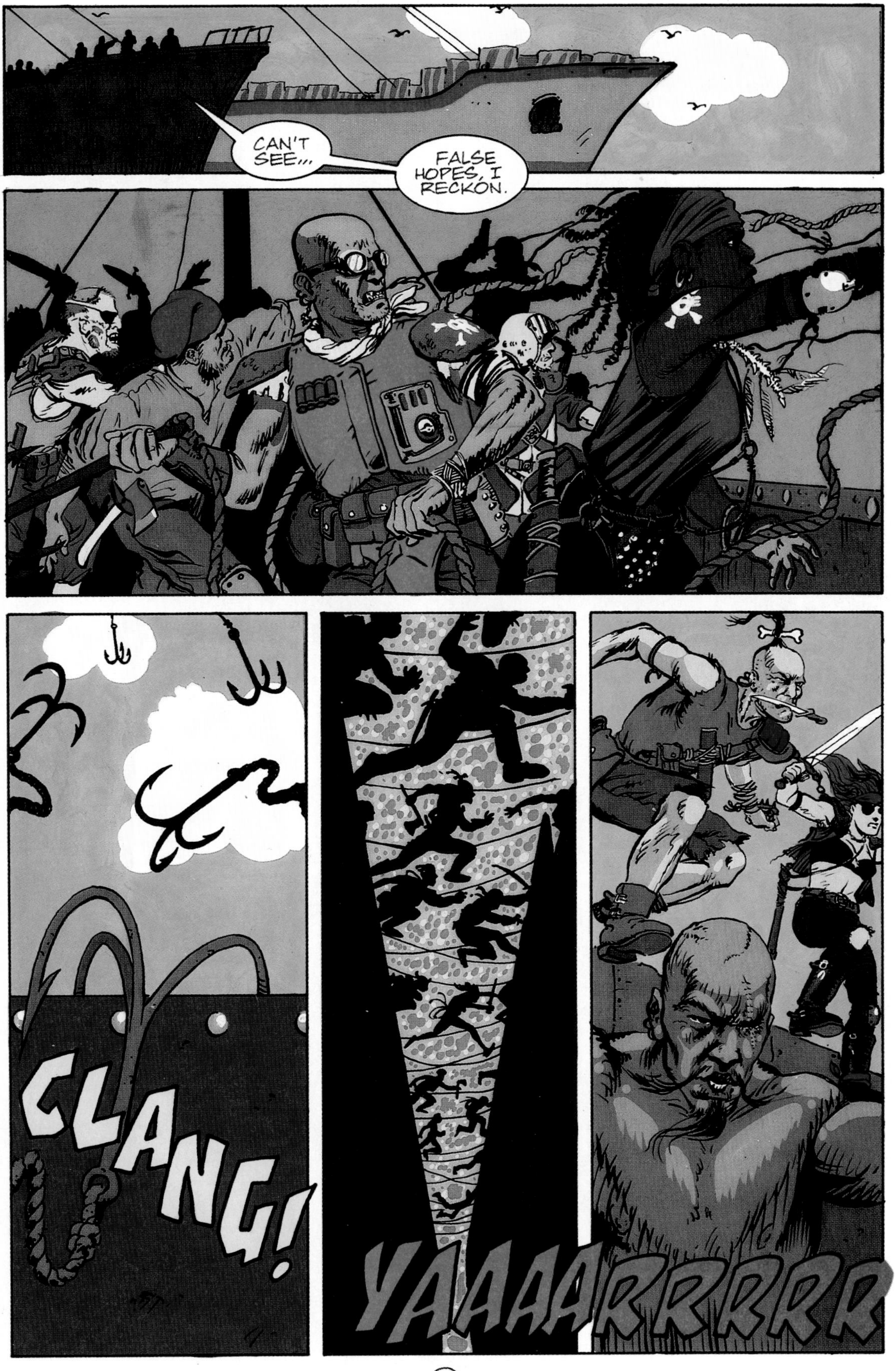

CAN'T SEE...
FALSE HOPES, I RECKON.
CLANG!
YAAAARRRRR

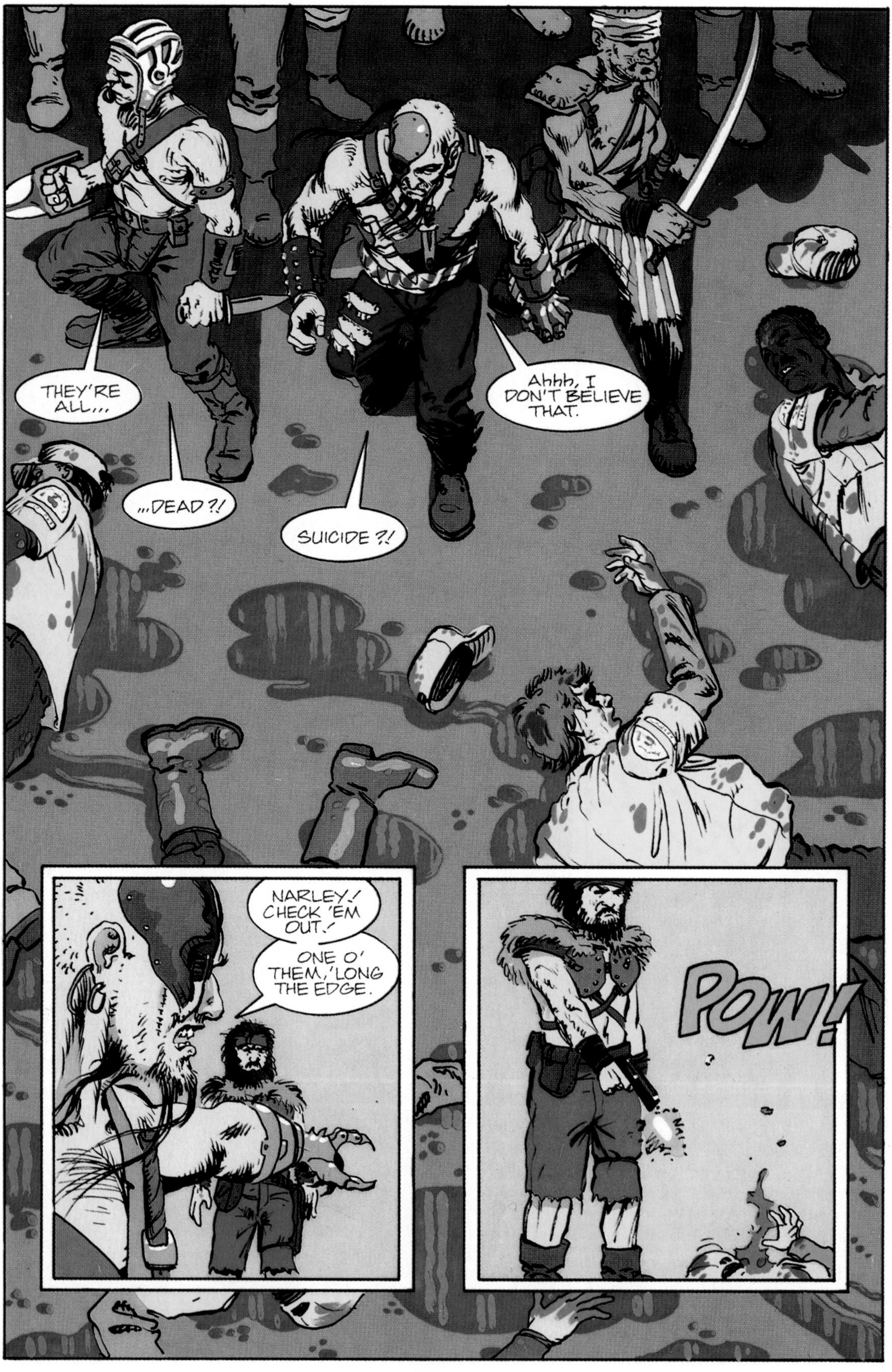
THEY'RE ALL...
...DEAD?!
SUICIDE?!
Ahhh, I DON'T BELIEVE THAT.
NARLEY! CHECK 'EM OUT!
ONE O' THEM, 'LONG THE EDGE.
POW!

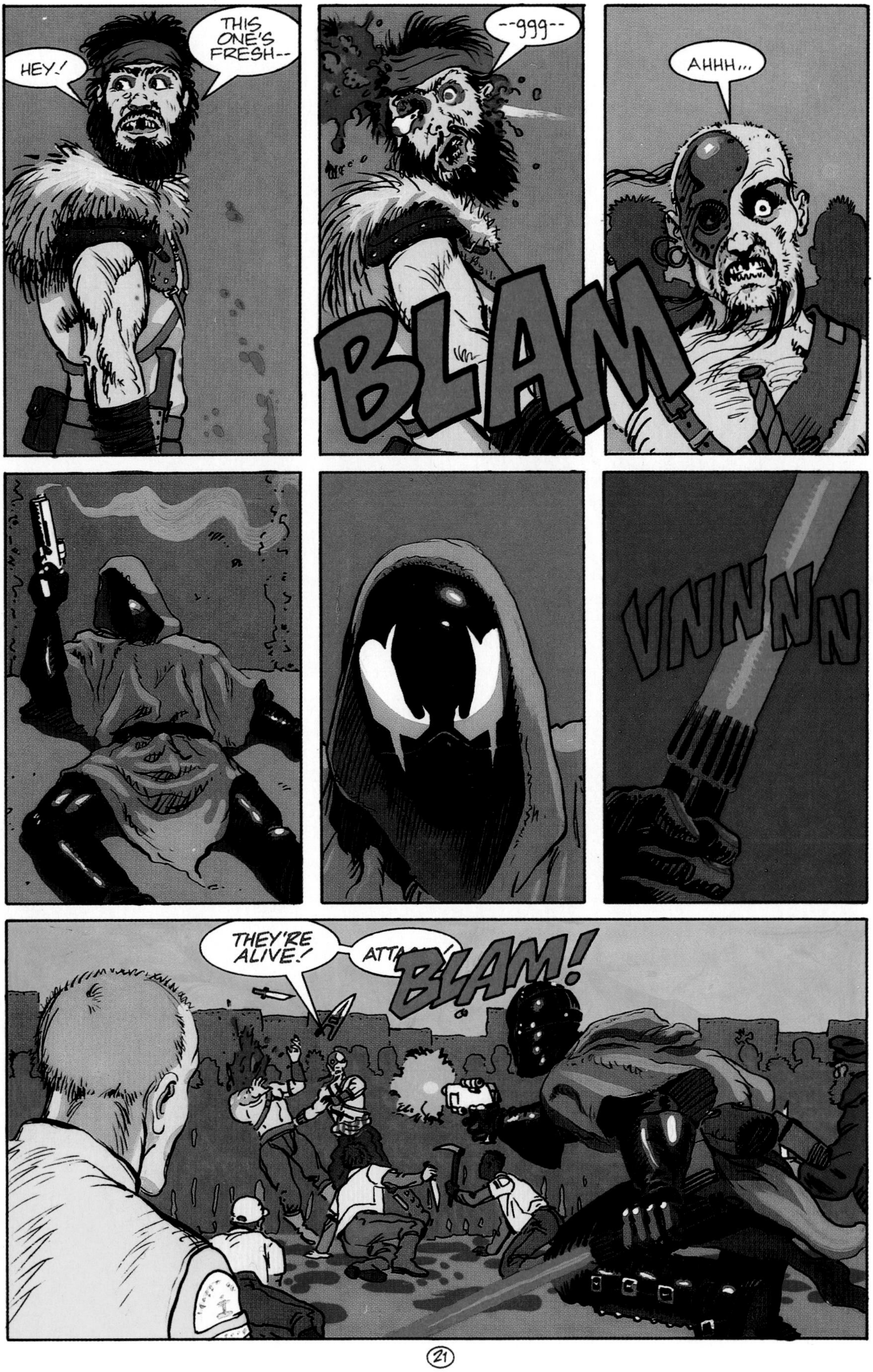
HEY!
THIS ONE'S FRESH--
--ggg--
BLAM
AHHH...
VNNNN
THEY'RE ALIVE!
ATTA
BLAM!

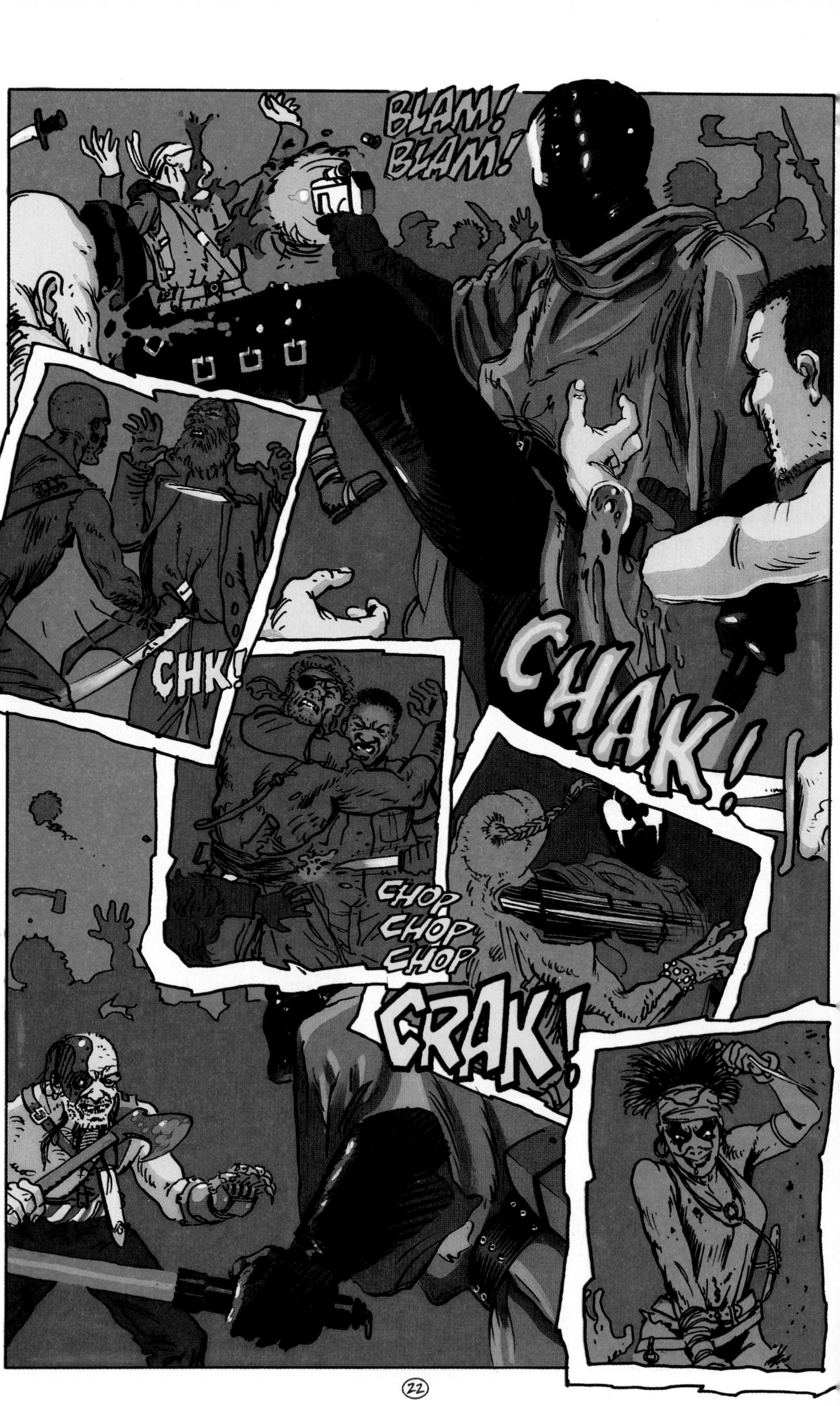
BLAM!
BLAM!
CHK!
CHAK!
CHOP
CHOP
CHOP
CRAK!

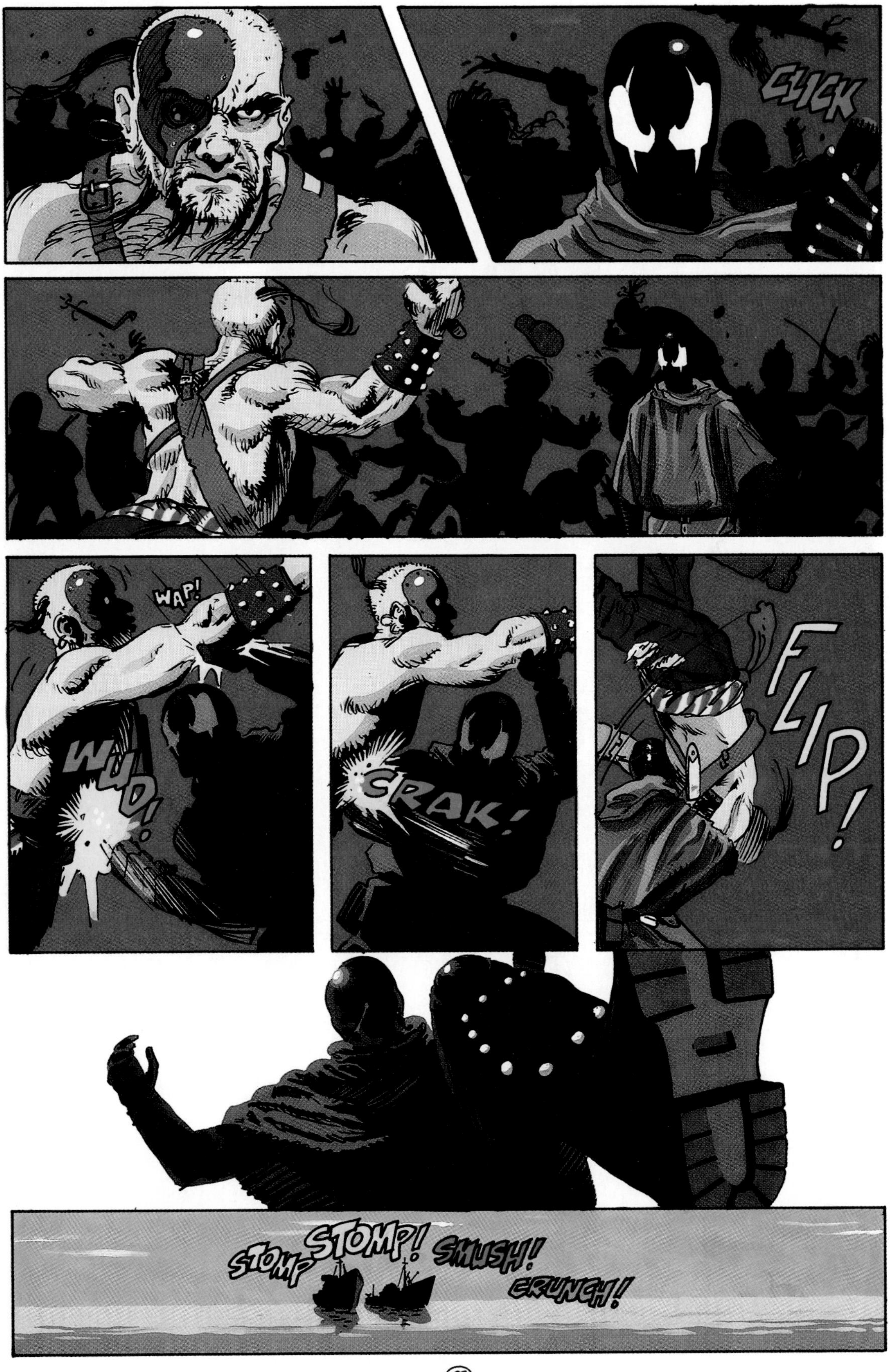
CLICK
WAP!
WUD!
CRAK!
FLIP!
STOMP STOMP! SMUSH!
CRUNCH!

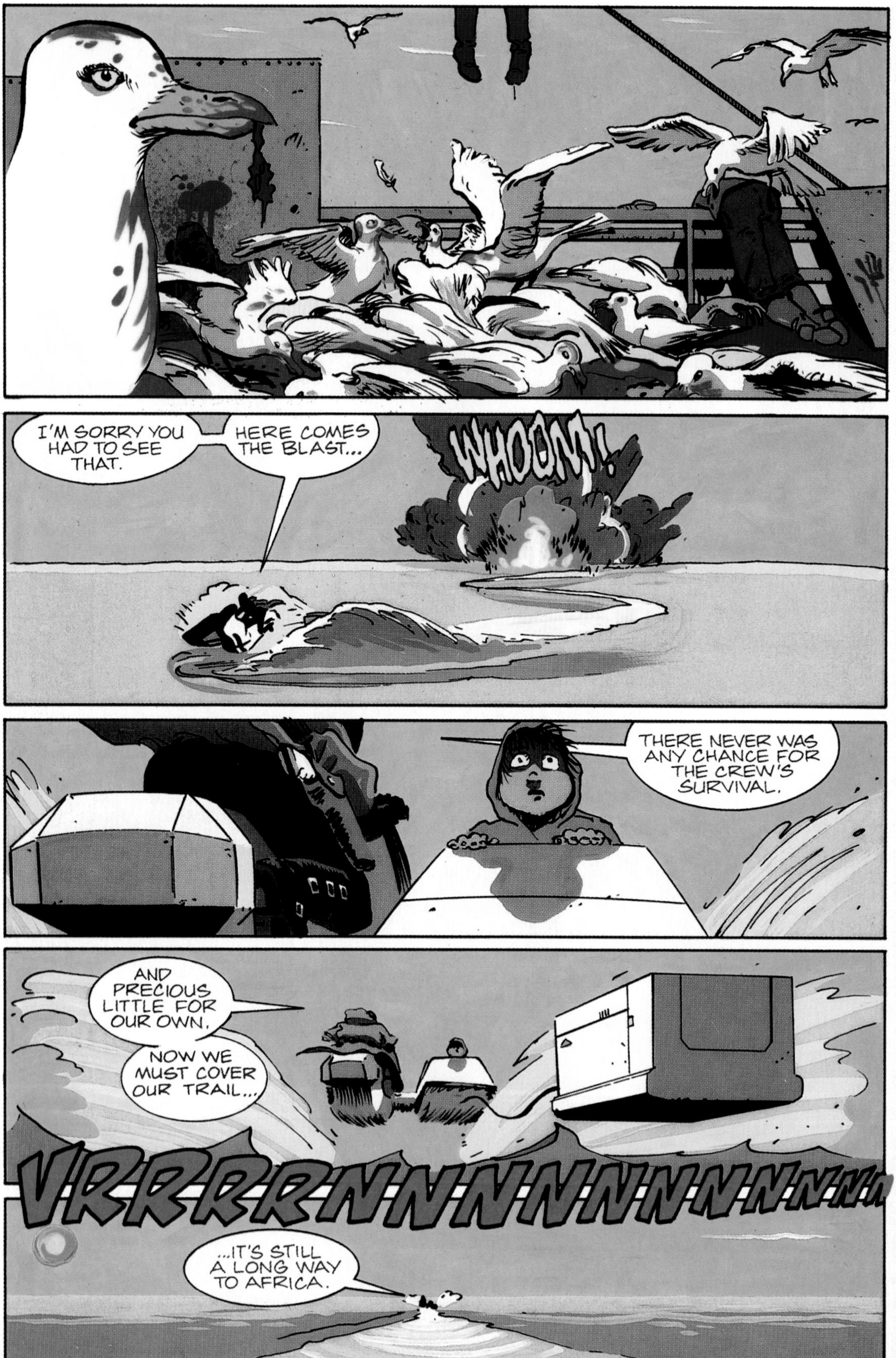

I'M SORRY YOU HAD TO SEE THAT.
HERE COMES THE BLAST...
WHOOM!
THERE NEVER WAS ANY CHANCE FOR THE CREW'S SURVIVAL.
AND PRECIOUS LITTLE FOR OUR OWN.
NOW WE MUST COVER OUR TRAIL...
VRRRRNNNNNNNNNNNN
...IT'S STILL A LONG WAY TO AFRICA.

CHAPTER 5

# DEVIL *on the veldt*

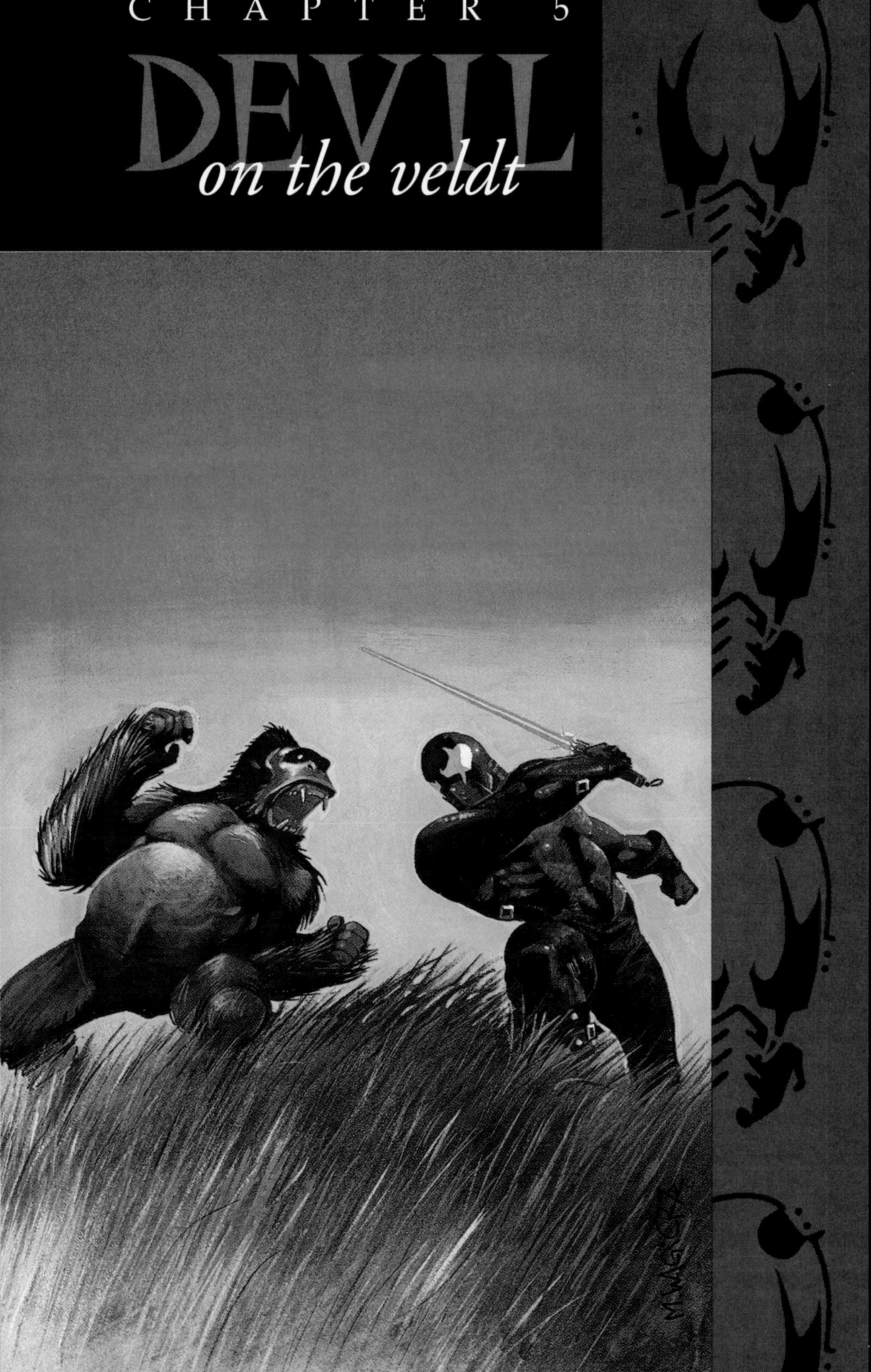

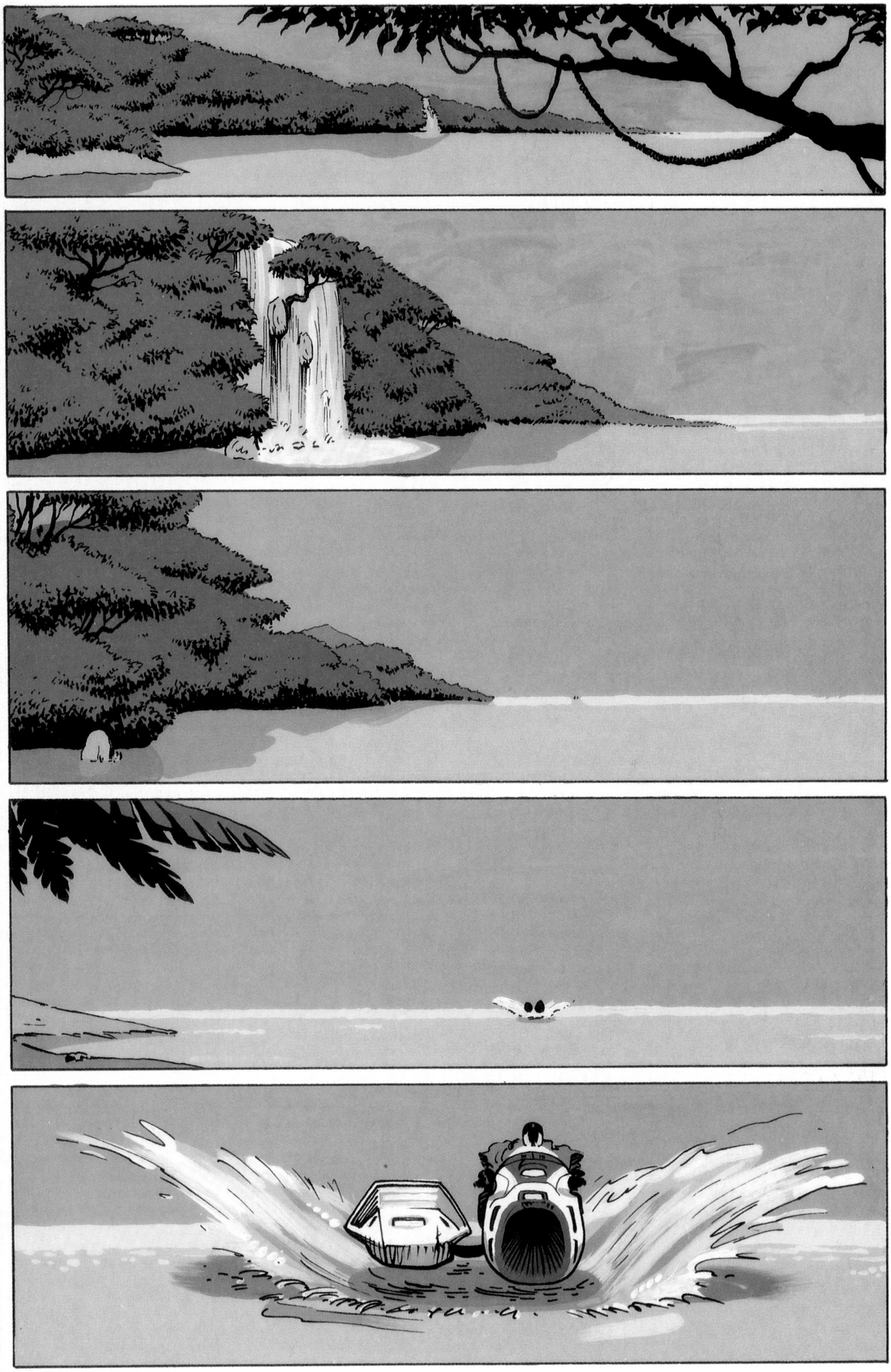

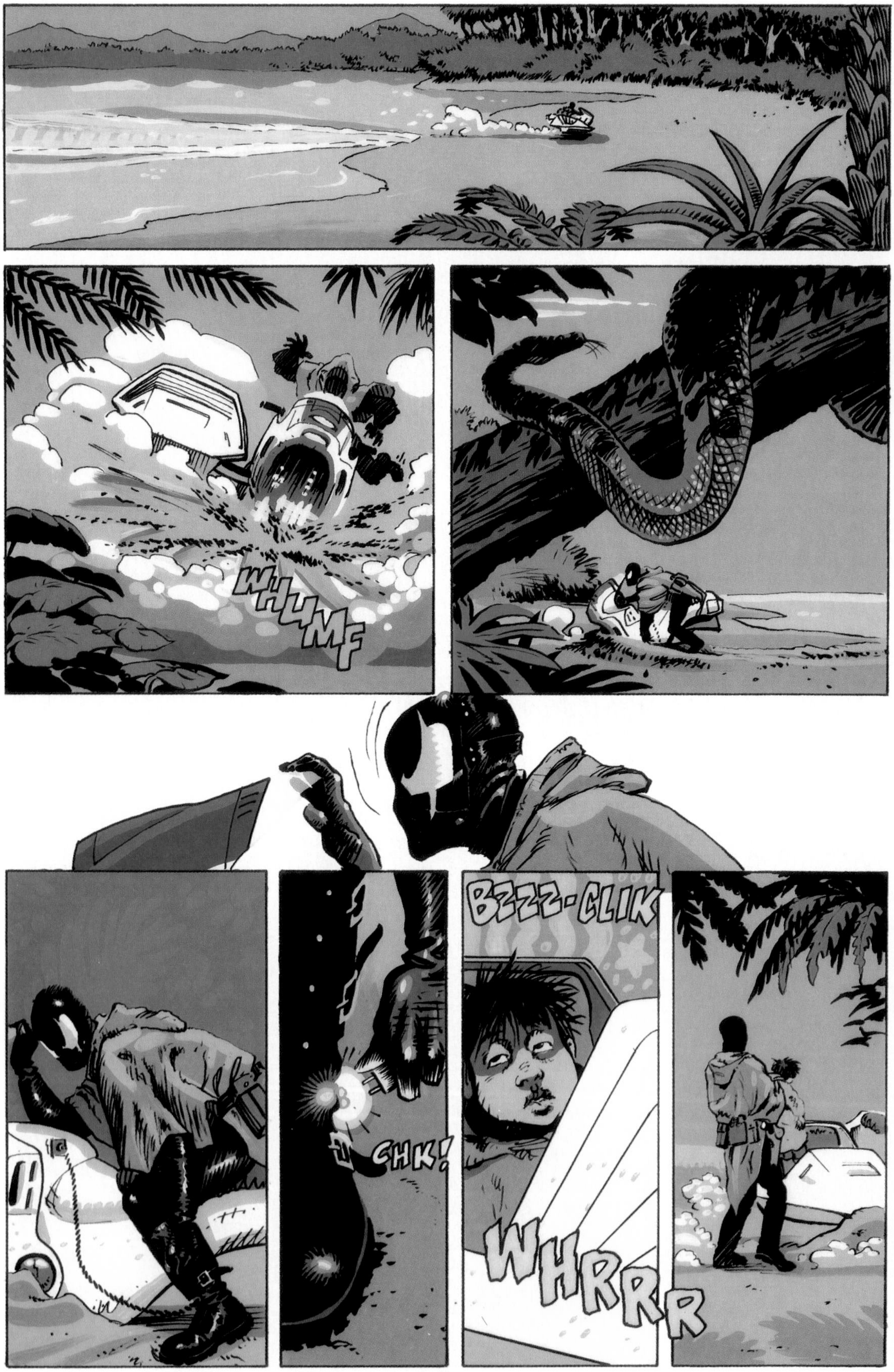
WHUMF
CHK!
BZZZ-CLIK
WHRRR

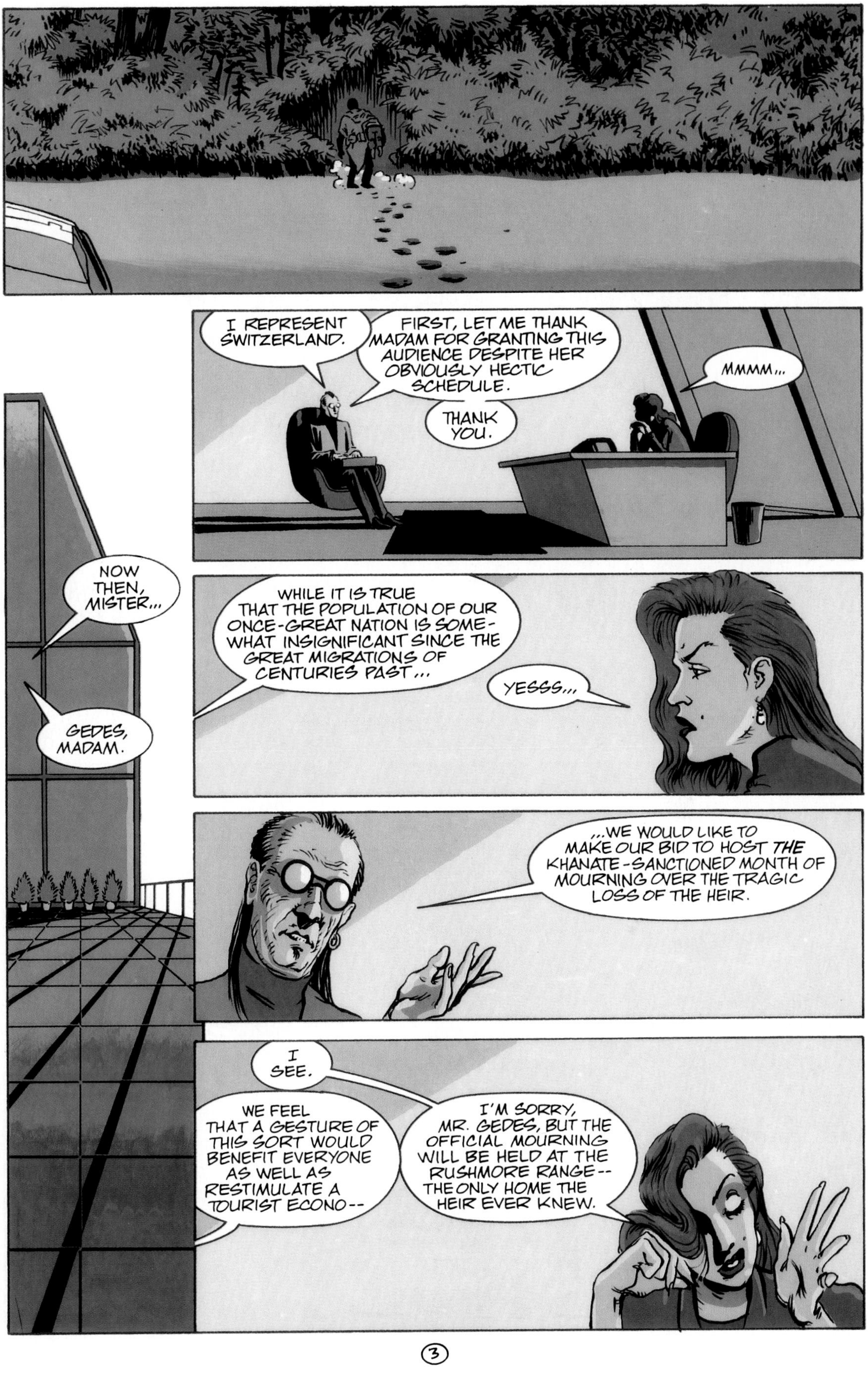
I REPRESENT SWITZERLAND.
FIRST, LET ME THANK MADAM FOR GRANTING THIS AUDIENCE DESPITE HER OBVIOUSLY HECTIC SCHEDULE.
THANK YOU.
MMMM...
NOW THEN, MISTER...
GEDES, MADAM.
WHILE IT IS TRUE THAT THE POPULATION OF OUR ONCE-GREAT NATION IS SOME-WHAT INSIGNIFICANT SINCE THE GREAT MIGRATIONS OF CENTURIES PAST...
YESSS...
...WE WOULD LIKE TO MAKE OUR BID TO HOST THE KHANATE-SANCTIONED MONTH OF MOURNING OVER THE TRAGIC LOSS OF THE HEIR.
I SEE.
WE FEEL THAT A GESTURE OF THIS SORT WOULD BENEFIT EVERYONE AS WELL AS RESTIMULATE A TOURIST ECONO--
I'M SORRY, MR. GEDES, BUT THE OFFICIAL MOURNING WILL BE HELD AT THE RUSHMORE RANGE-- THE ONLY HOME THE HEIR EVER KNEW.

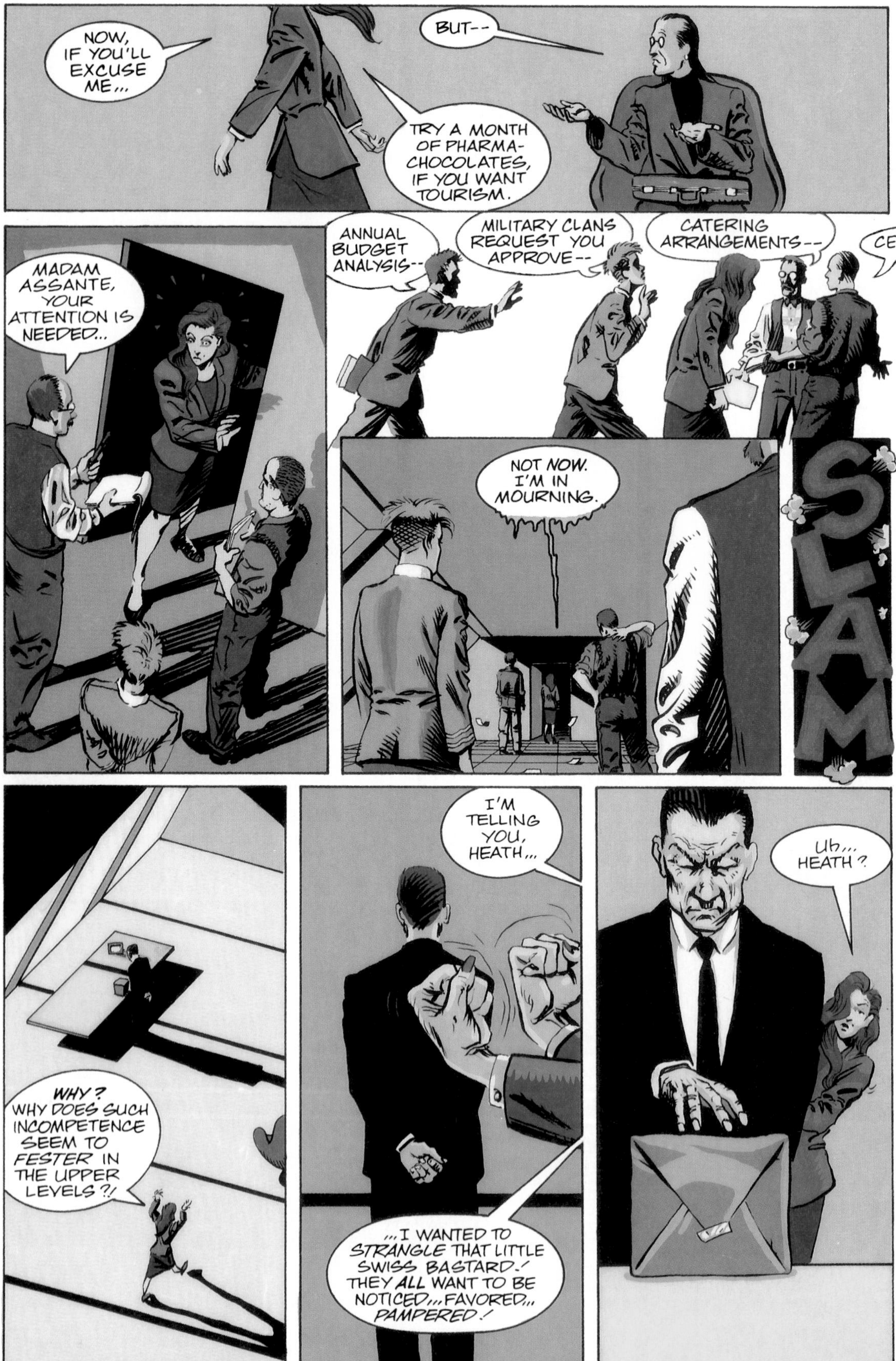
NOW, IF YOU'LL EXCUSE ME...
BUT--
TRY A MONTH OF PHARMA-CHOCOLATES, IF YOU WANT TOURISM.
MADAM ASSANTE, YOUR ATTENTION IS NEEDED...
ANNUAL BUDGET ANALYSIS--
MILITARY CLANS REQUEST YOU APPROVE--
CATERING ARRANGEMENTS--
CEN
NOT NOW. I'M IN MOURNING.
SLAM
WHY? WHY DOES SUCH INCOMPETENCE SEEM TO FESTER IN THE UPPER LEVELS?!
I'M TELLING YOU, HEATH...
...I WANTED TO STRANGLE THAT LITTLE SWISS BASTARD! THEY ALL WANT TO BE NOTICED...FAVORED... PAMPERED!
Uh... HEATH?

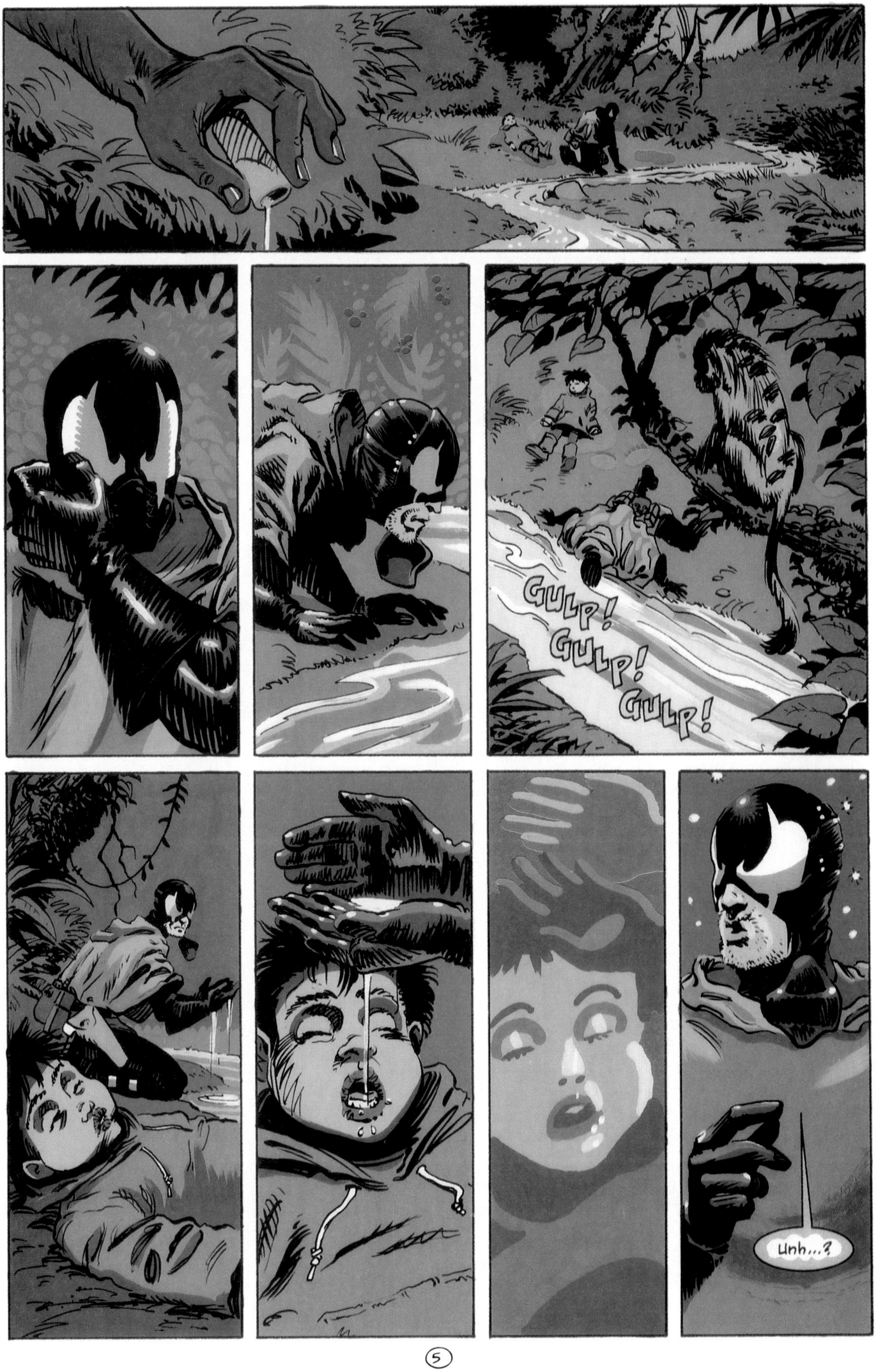
GULP! GULP! GULP!
Unh...?

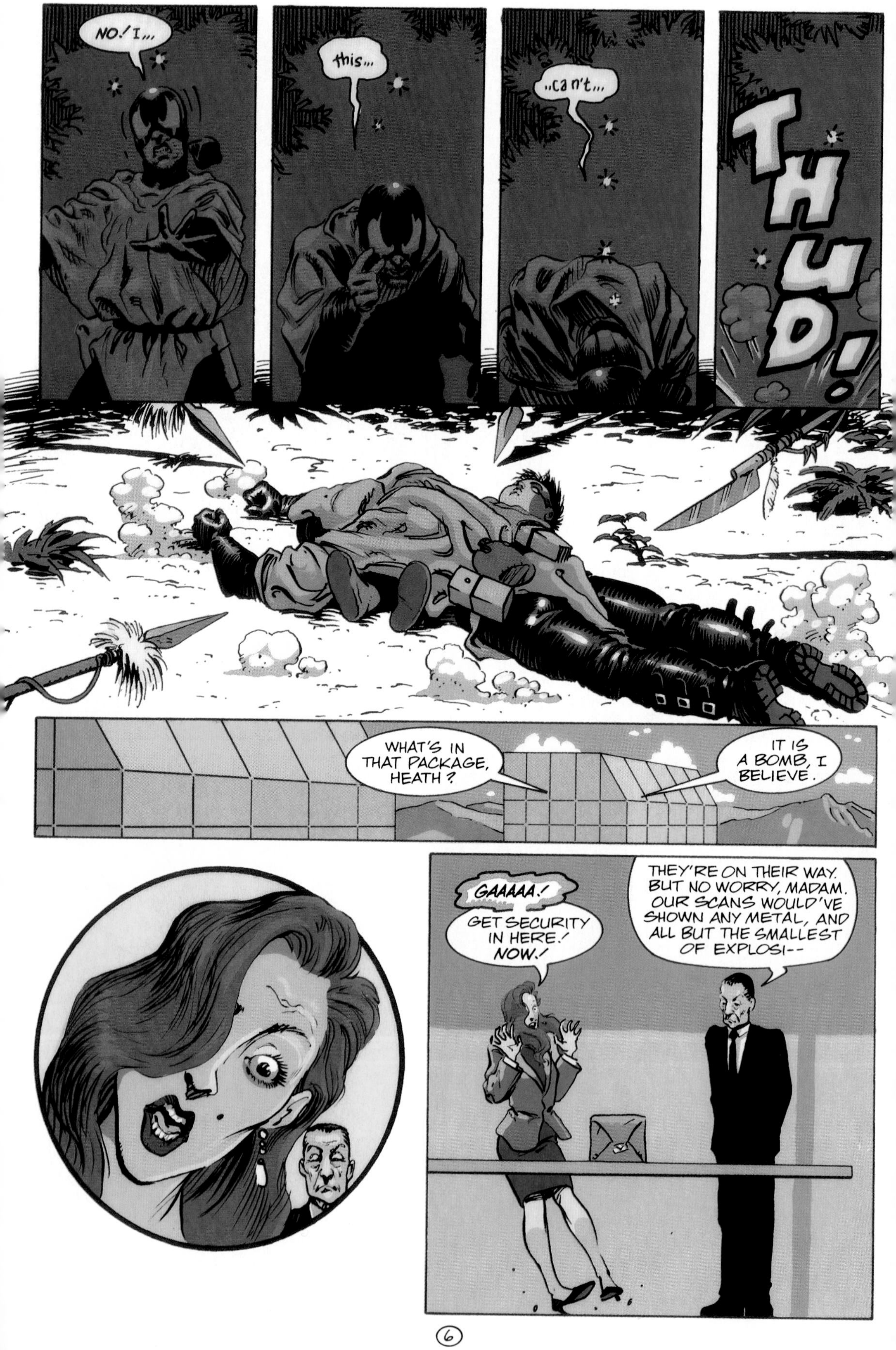
NO! I...
this...
...can't...
THUD!
WHAT'S IN THAT PACKAGE, HEATH?
IT IS A BOMB, I BELIEVE.
GAAAAA!
GET SECURITY IN HERE! NOW!
THEY'RE ON THEIR WAY. BUT NO WORRY, MADAM. OUR SCANS WOULD'VE SHOWN ANY METAL, AND ALL BUT THE SMALLEST OF EXPLOSI--

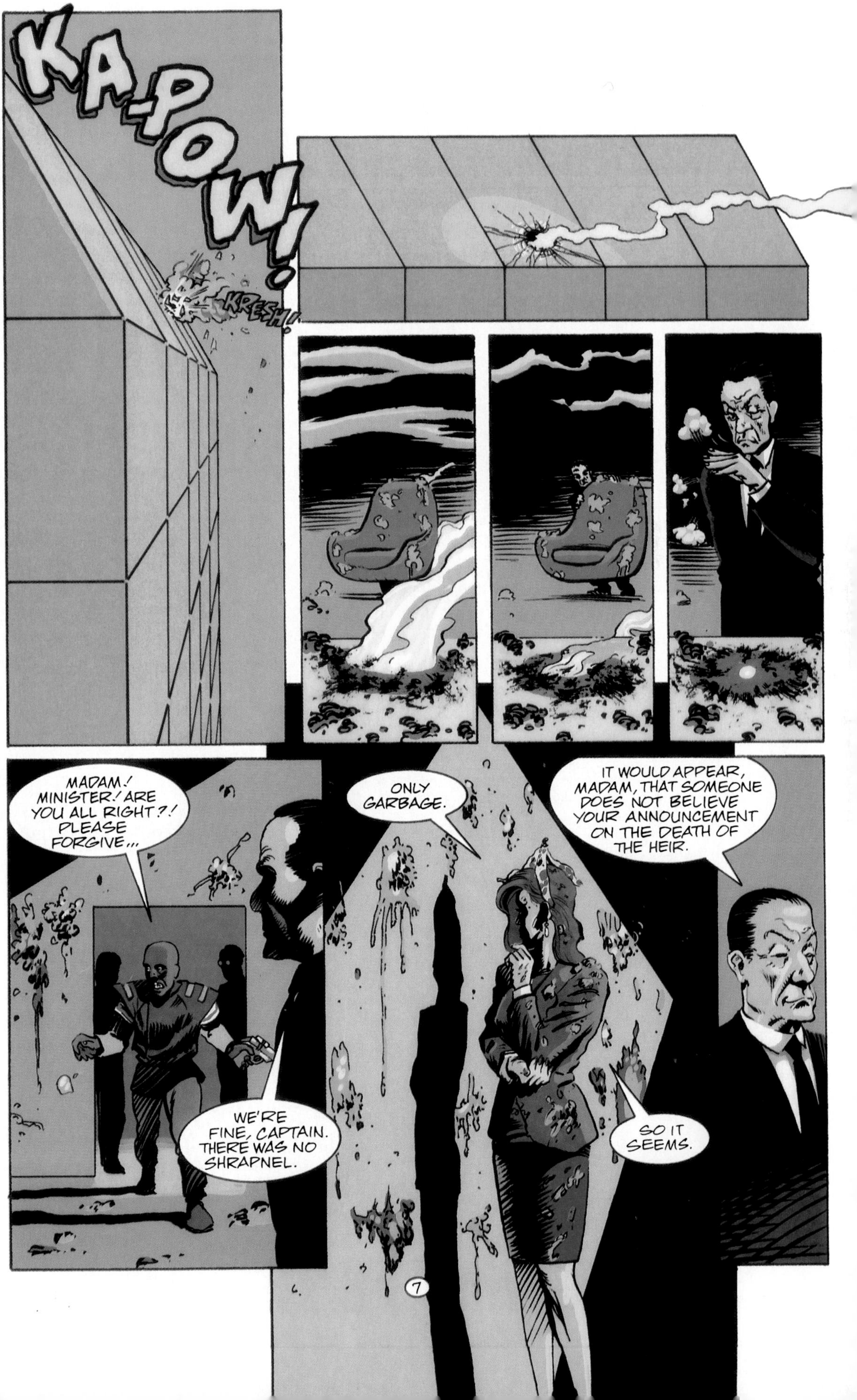
KA-POW!
KRESH!
MADAM! MINISTER! ARE YOU ALL RIGHT?! PLEASE FORGIVE...
WE'RE FINE, CAPTAIN. THERE WAS NO SHRAPNEL.
ONLY GARBAGE.
IT WOULD APPEAR, MADAM, THAT SOMEONE DOES NOT BELIEVE YOUR ANNOUNCEMENT ON THE DEATH OF THE HEIR.
SO IT SEEMS.

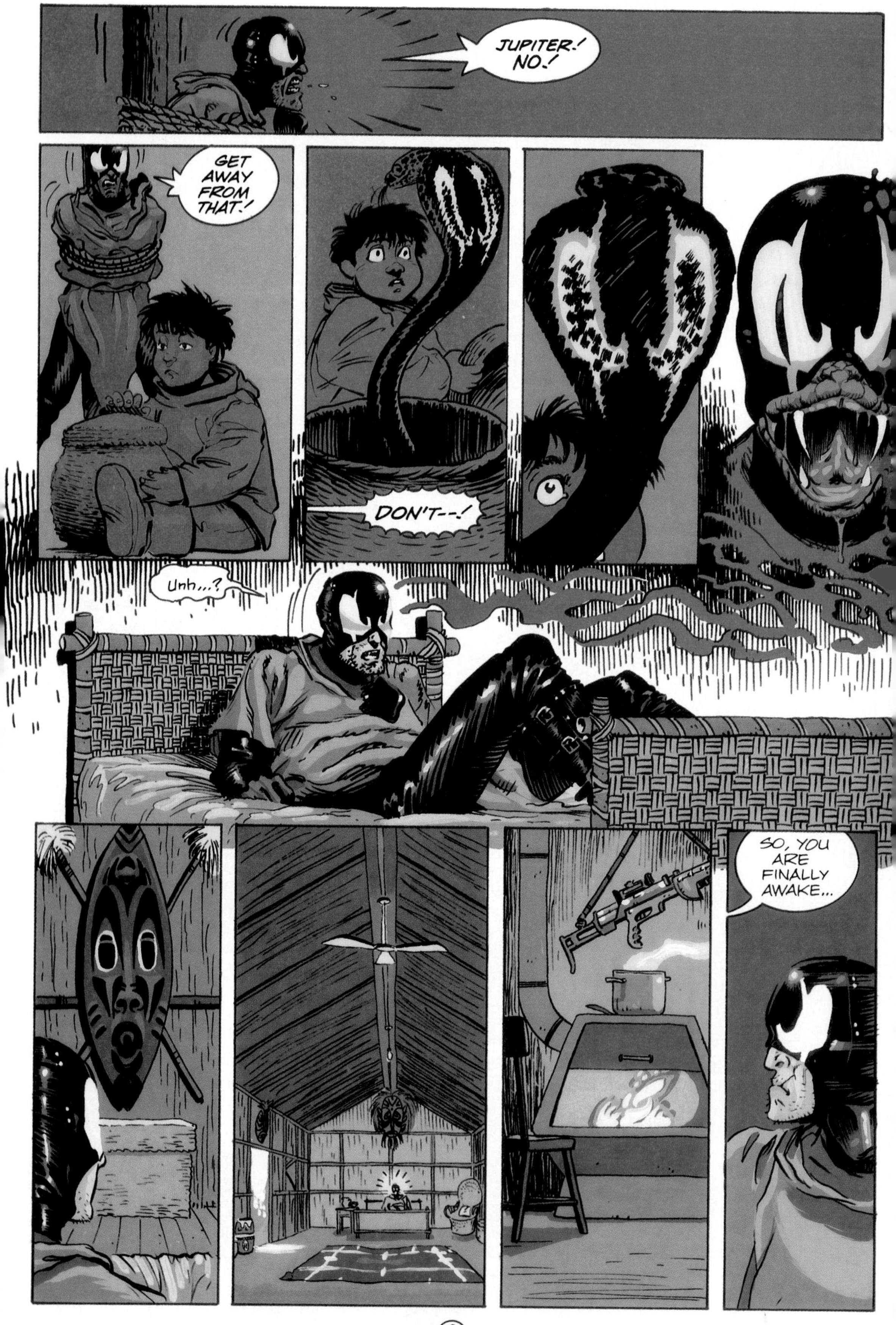
JUPITER! NO!
GET AWAY FROM THAT!
DON'T--!
Unh...?
SO, YOU ARE FINALLY AWAKE...

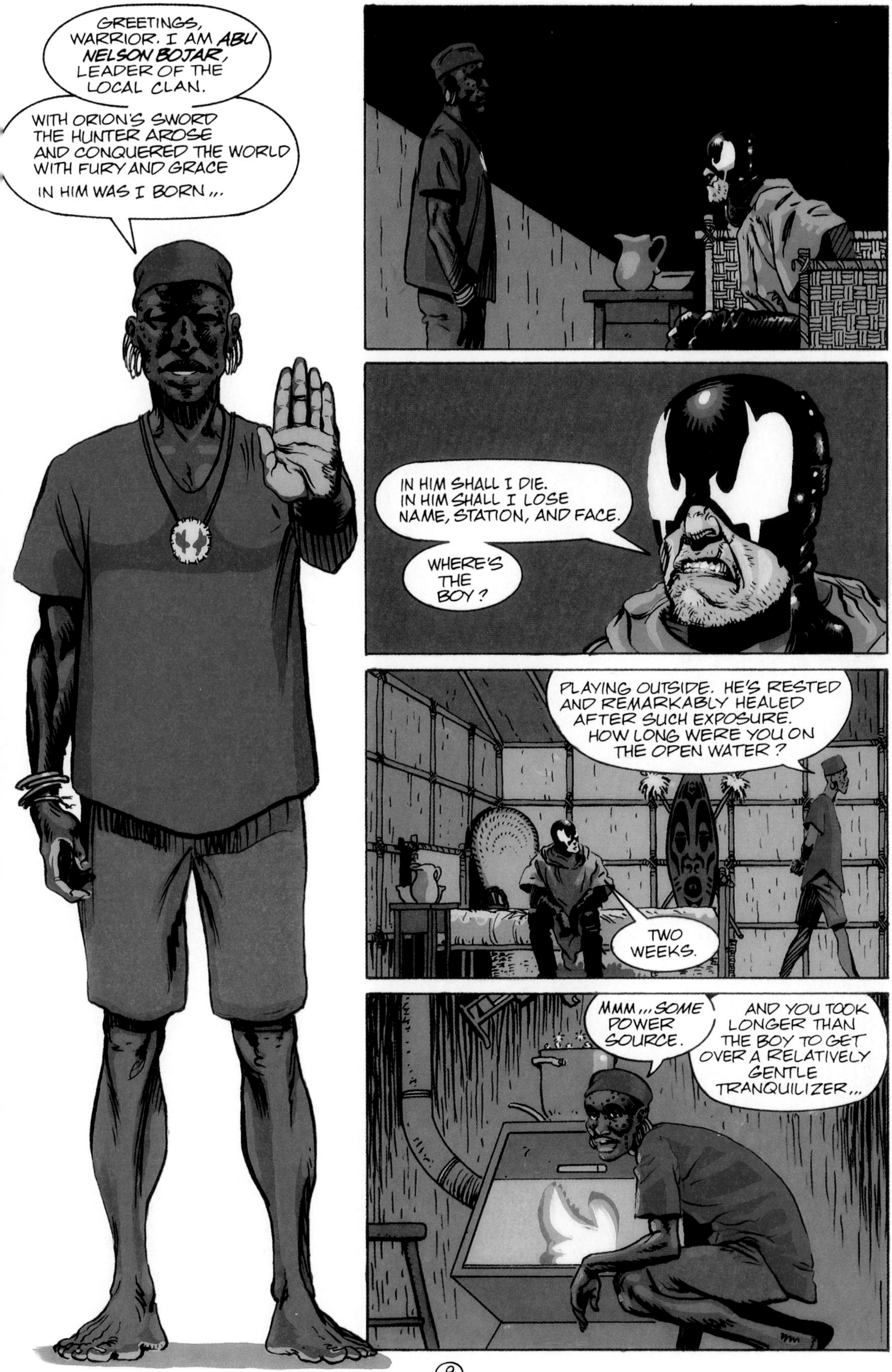
GREETINGS, WARRIOR. I AM ABU NELSON BOJAR, LEADER OF THE LOCAL CLAN.
WITH ORION'S SWORD THE HUNTER AROSE AND CONQUERED THE WORLD WITH FURY AND GRACE
IN HIM WAS I BORN...
IN HIM SHALL I DIE. IN HIM SHALL I LOSE NAME, STATION, AND FACE.
WHERE'S THE BOY?
PLAYING OUTSIDE. HE'S RESTED AND REMARKABLY HEALED AFTER SUCH EXPOSURE. HOW LONG WERE YOU ON THE OPEN WATER?
TWO WEEKS.
MMM... SOME POWER SOURCE.
AND YOU TOOK LONGER THAN THE BOY TO GET OVER A RELATIVELY GENTLE TRANQUILIZER...

I WAS EXHAUSTED... DELIRIOUS. OR I WOULD'VE FILTERED THE WATER FIRST.

AND SO WE EXAMINED YOU AS BEST WE COULD. I WAS A NUCLEAR-SLAVE BEFORE THE GREAT KHAN CAME. YOU'RE NO ORDINARY KIDNAPPER...

...AND THAT BOY IS NO ORDINARY HOSTAGE.

I AM SWORN TO PROTECT HIM--AGAINST POLITICAL MANIPULATORS-- 'TIL HE IS OF AGE. I AM CHARGED BY THE WILL OF THE GREAT KHAN HIMSELF.

THE OFFICIAL WORD IS THAT THE HEIR'S DEAD. AND THEY DO SEEM TO BELIEVE THAT.

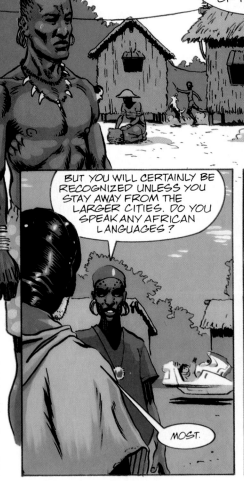

AS I SAID, I REMEMBER MY LIFE BEFORE THE RULE OF THE KHAN.

AND I THINK THINGS WOULD BE FOR THE BEST IN THE HANDS OF HIS CHOSEN.

BUT YOU WILL CERTAINLY BE RECOGNIZED UNLESS YOU STAY AWAY FROM THE LARGER CITIES. DO YOU SPEAK ANY AFRICAN LANGUAGES?

MOST.

GOOD. BUT BEST TO DISGUISE THE BOY AS A LOCAL. THERE IS A MARKETPLACE HALF A DAY FROM HERE THAT SHOULD BE SAFE ENOUGH.

THANK YOU.

VIVAT GRENDEL!

VIVAT GRENDEL!

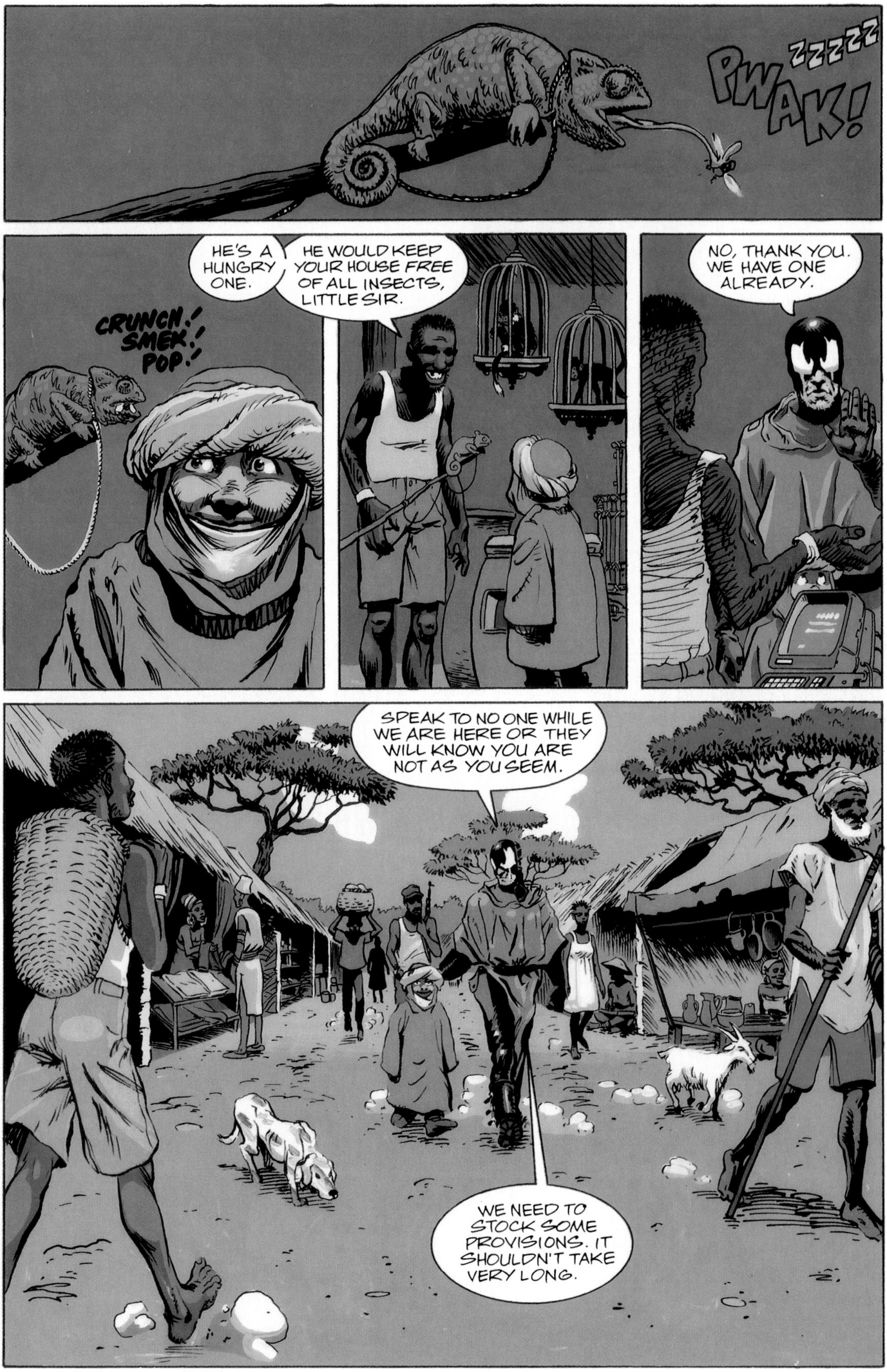
PWAK!
ZZZZZ
CRUNCH! SMEK! POP!
HE'S A HUNGRY ONE.
HE WOULD KEEP YOUR HOUSE FREE OF ALL INSECTS, LITTLE SIR.
NO, THANK YOU. WE HAVE ONE ALREADY.
SPEAK TO NO ONE WHILE WE ARE HERE OR THEY WILL KNOW YOU ARE NOT AS YOU SEEM.
WE NEED TO STOCK SOME PROVISIONS. IT SHOULDN'T TAKE VERY LONG.

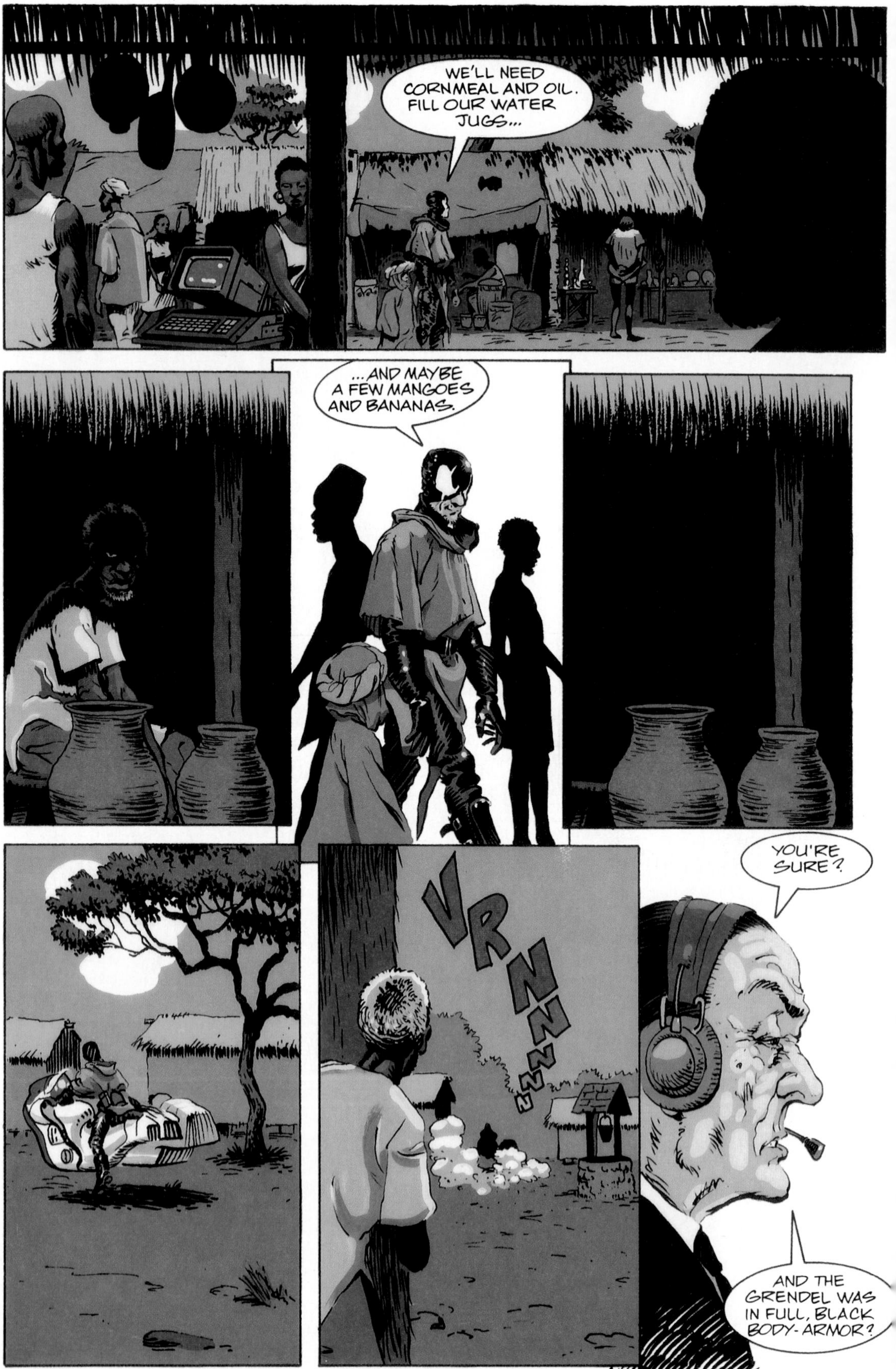
WE'LL NEED CORNMEAL AND OIL. FILL OUR WATER JUGS...
...AND MAYBE A FEW MANGOES AND BANANAS.
VRNNNN
YOU'RE SURE?
AND THE GRENDEL WAS IN FULL, BLACK BODY-ARMOR?

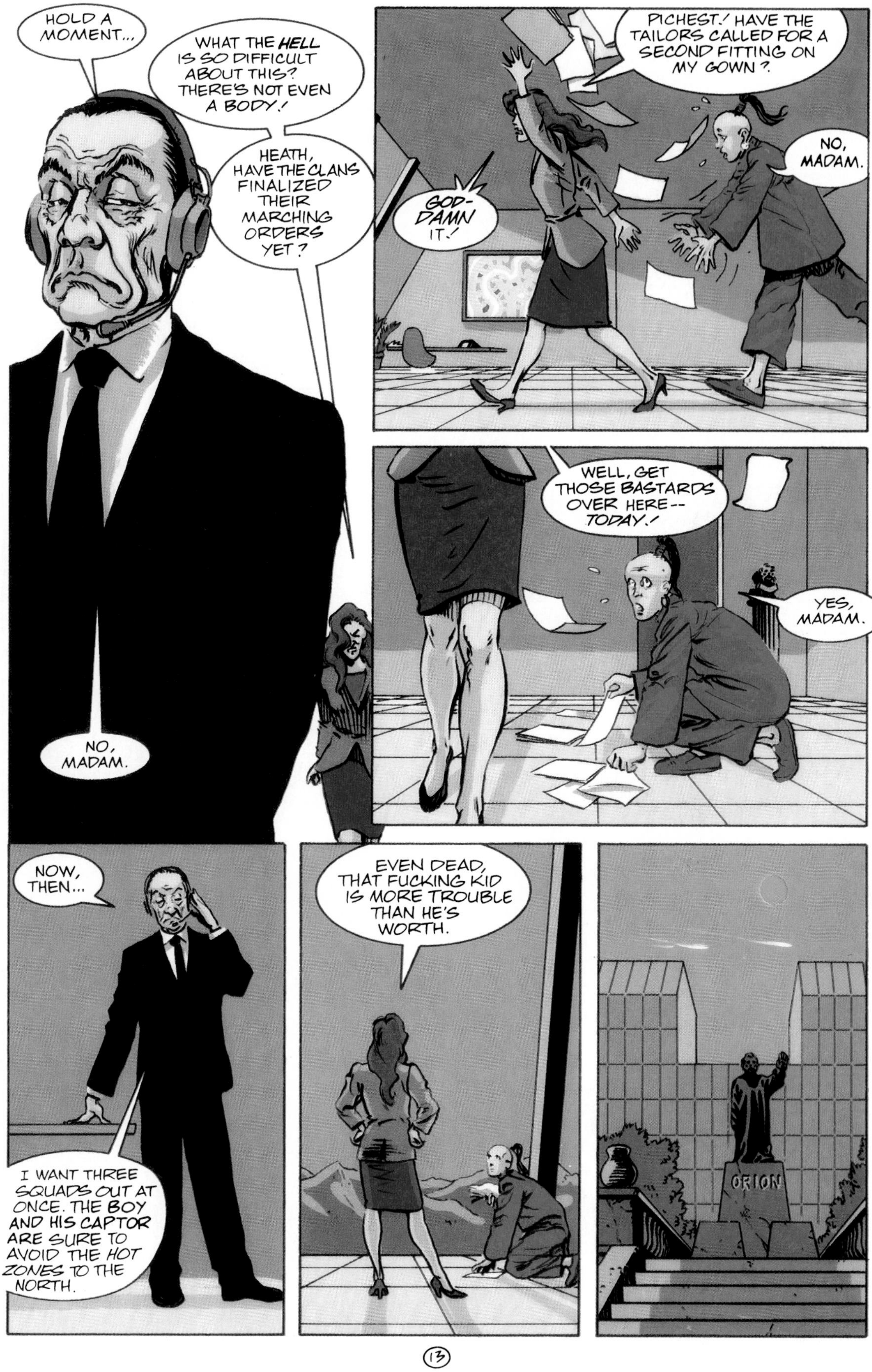
HOLD A MOMENT...
WHAT THE HELL IS SO DIFFICULT ABOUT THIS? THERE'S NOT EVEN A BODY!
HEATH, HAVE THE CLANS FINALIZED THEIR MARCHING ORDERS YET?
NO, MADAM.
PICHEST! HAVE THE TAILORS CALLED FOR A SECOND FITTING ON MY GOWN?
GOD-DAMN IT!
NO, MADAM.
WELL, GET THOSE BASTARDS OVER HERE-- TODAY!
YES, MADAM.
NOW, THEN...
I WANT THREE SQUADS OUT AT ONCE. THE BOY AND HIS CAPTOR ARE SURE TO AVOID THE HOT ZONES TO THE NORTH.
EVEN DEAD, THAT FUCKING KID IS MORE TROUBLE THAN HE'S WORTH.
ORION

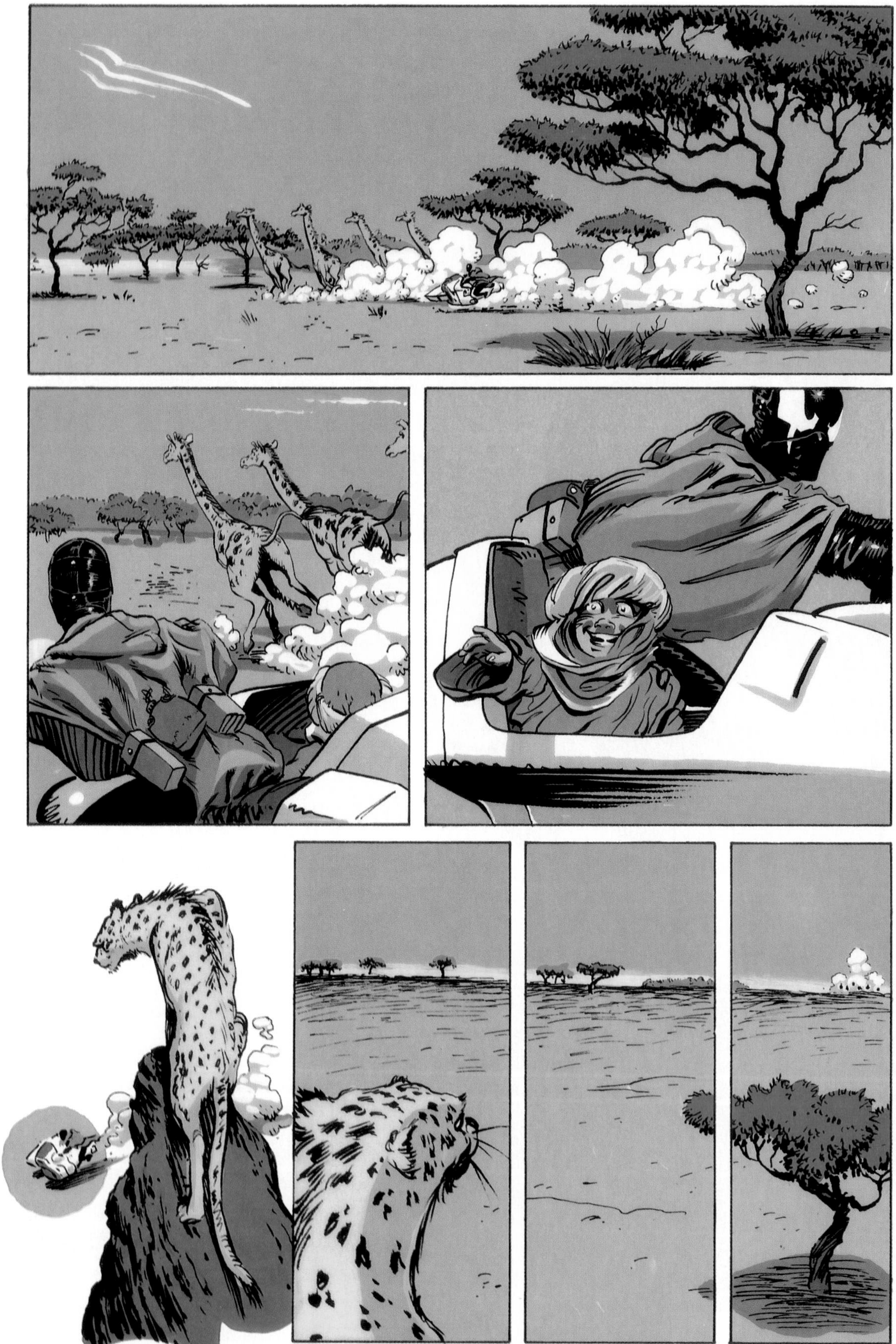

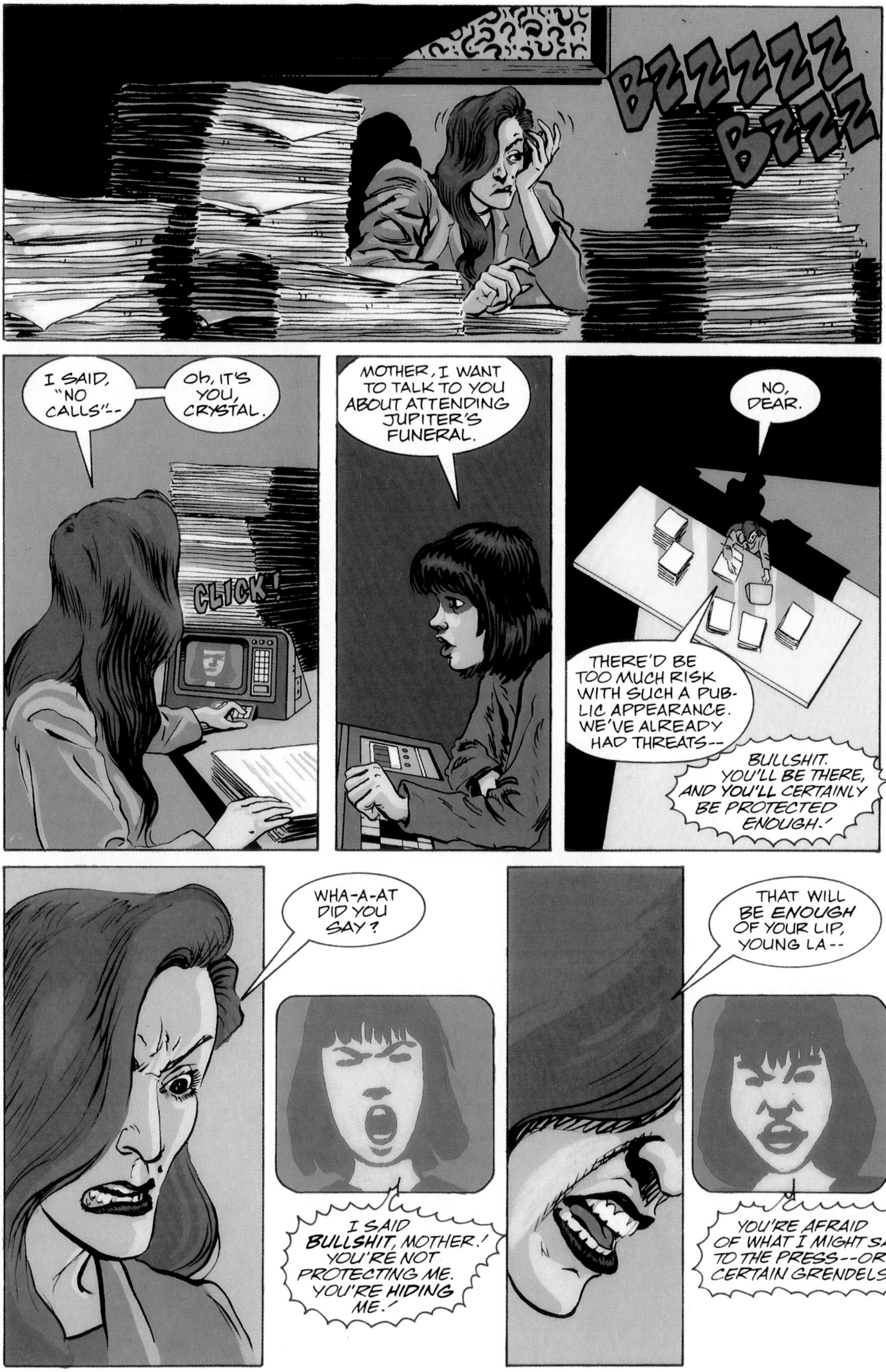
BZZZZZZ BZZZ
I SAID, "NO CALLS"--
Oh, IT'S YOU, CRYSTAL.
CLICK!
MOTHER, I WANT TO TALK TO YOU ABOUT ATTENDING JUPITER'S FUNERAL.
NO, DEAR.
THERE'D BE TOO MUCH RISK WITH SUCH A PUBLIC APPEARANCE. WE'VE ALREADY HAD THREATS--
BULLSHIT. YOU'LL BE THERE, AND YOU'LL CERTAINLY BE PROTECTED ENOUGH!
WHA-A-AT DID YOU SAY?
I SAID BULLSHIT, MOTHER! YOU'RE NOT PROTECTING ME. YOU'RE HIDING ME!
THAT WILL BE ENOUGH OF YOUR LIP, YOUNG LA--
YOU'RE AFRAID OF WHAT I MIGHT SAY TO THE PRESS--OR TO CERTAIN GRENDELS...

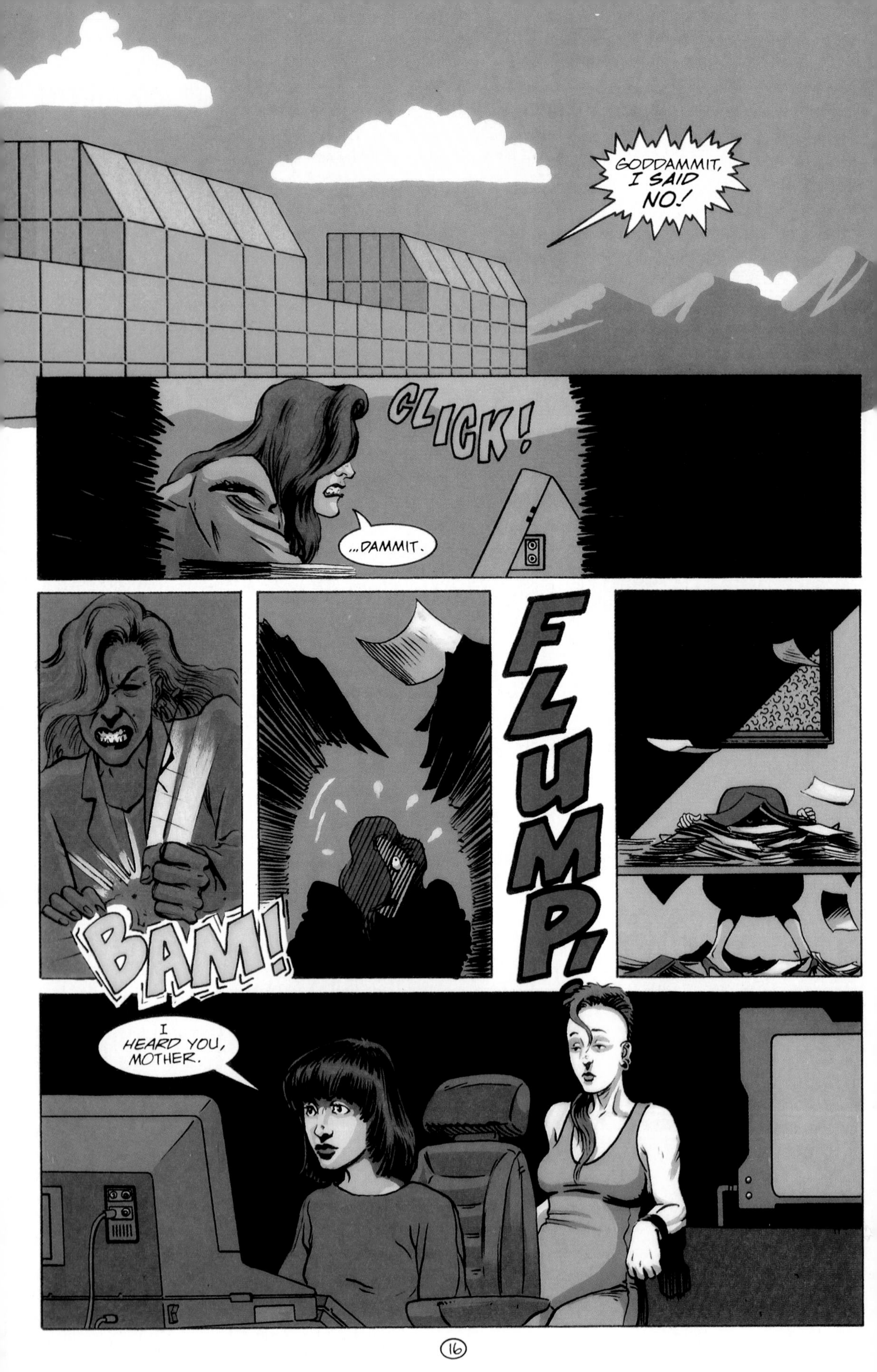

GODDAMMIT, I SAID NO!
CLICK!
...DAMMIT.
BAM!
FLUMP!
I HEARD YOU, MOTHER.

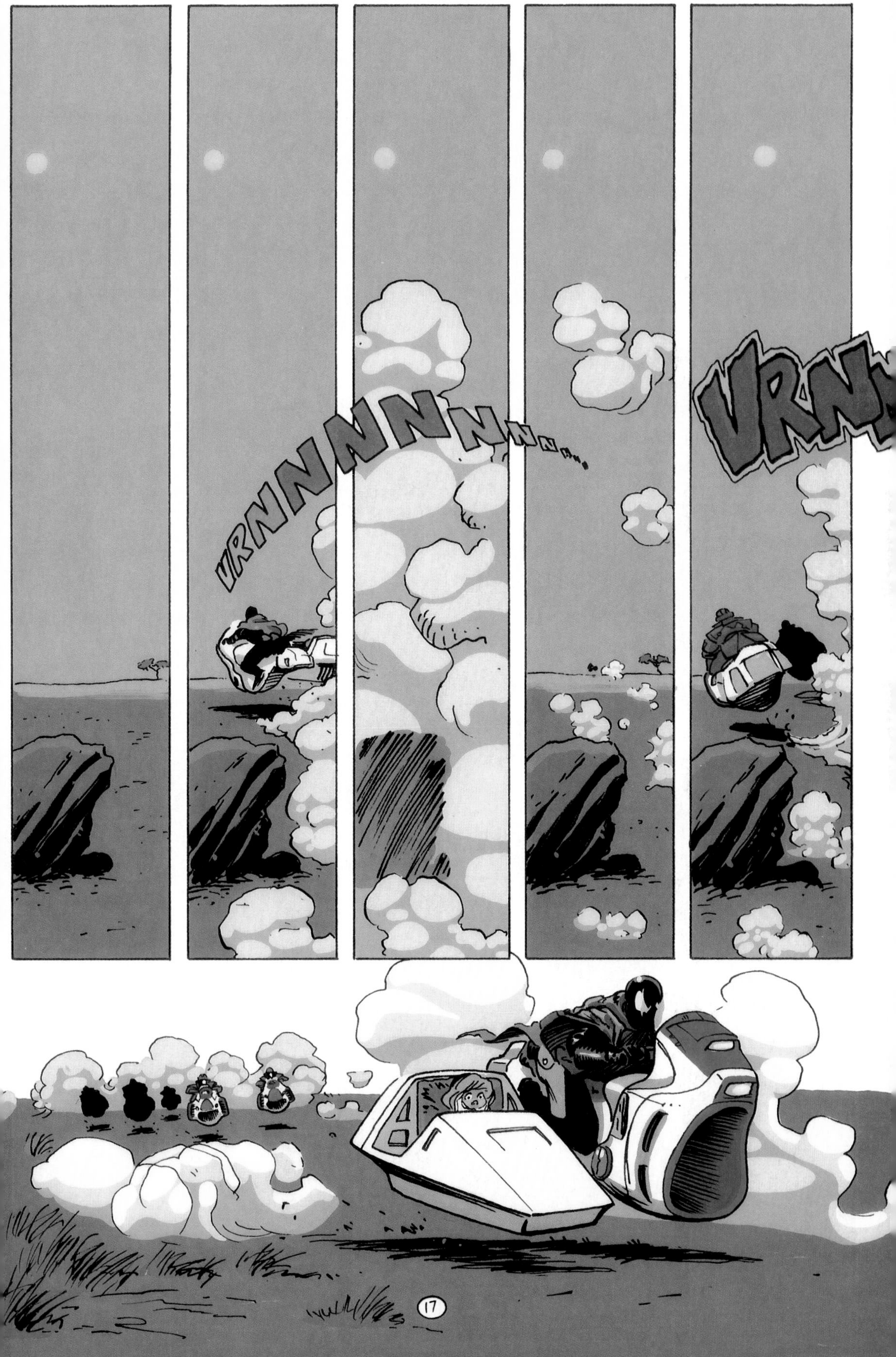
VRNNNNNnnn...
VRN

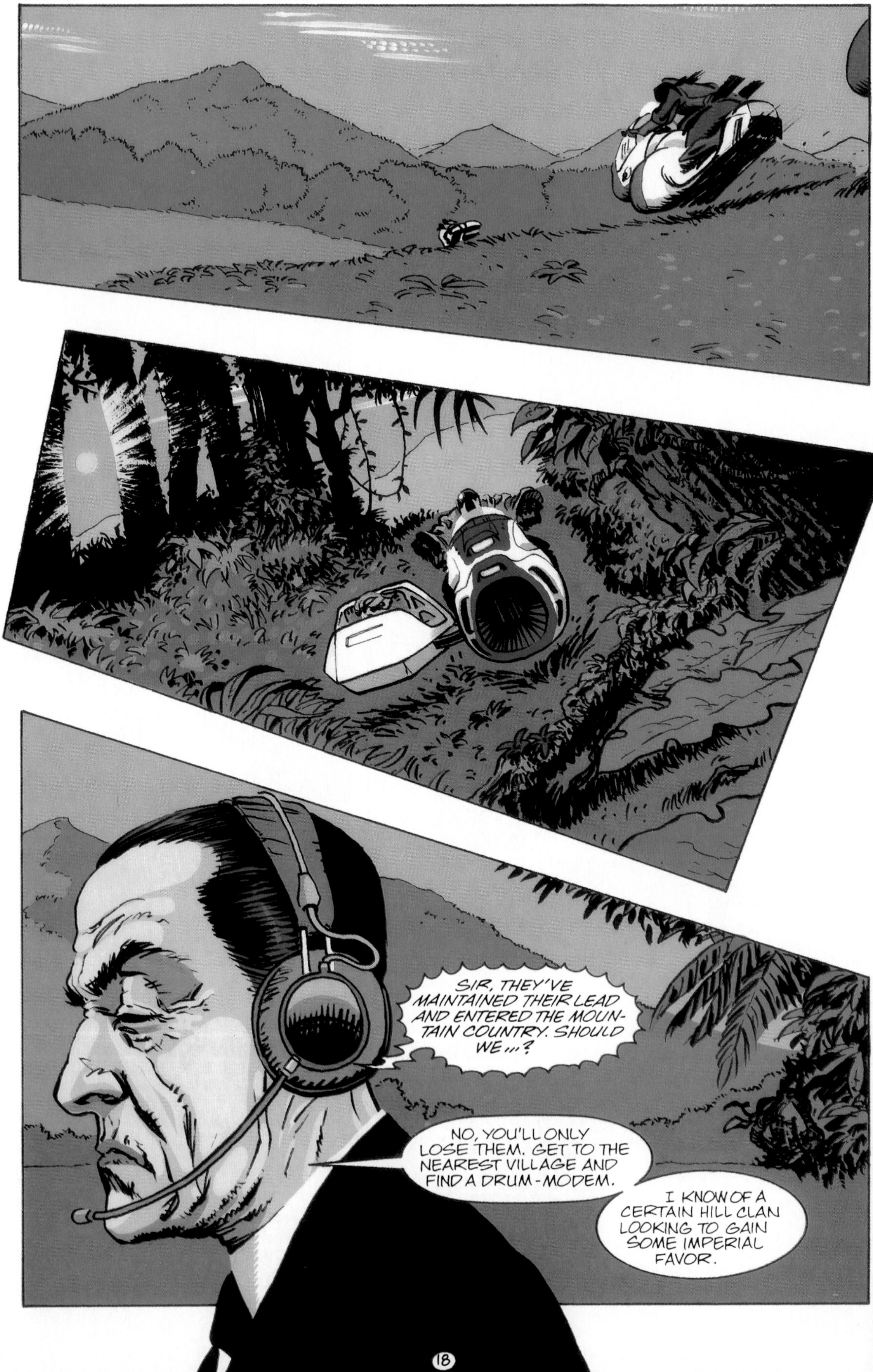
SIR, THEY'VE MAINTAINED THEIR LEAD AND ENTERED THE MOUNTAIN COUNTRY. SHOULD WE...?
NO, YOU'LL ONLY LOSE THEM. GET TO THE NEAREST VILLAGE AND FIND A DRUM-MODEM.
I KNOW OF A CERTAIN HILL CLAN LOOKING TO GAIN SOME IMPERIAL FAVOR.

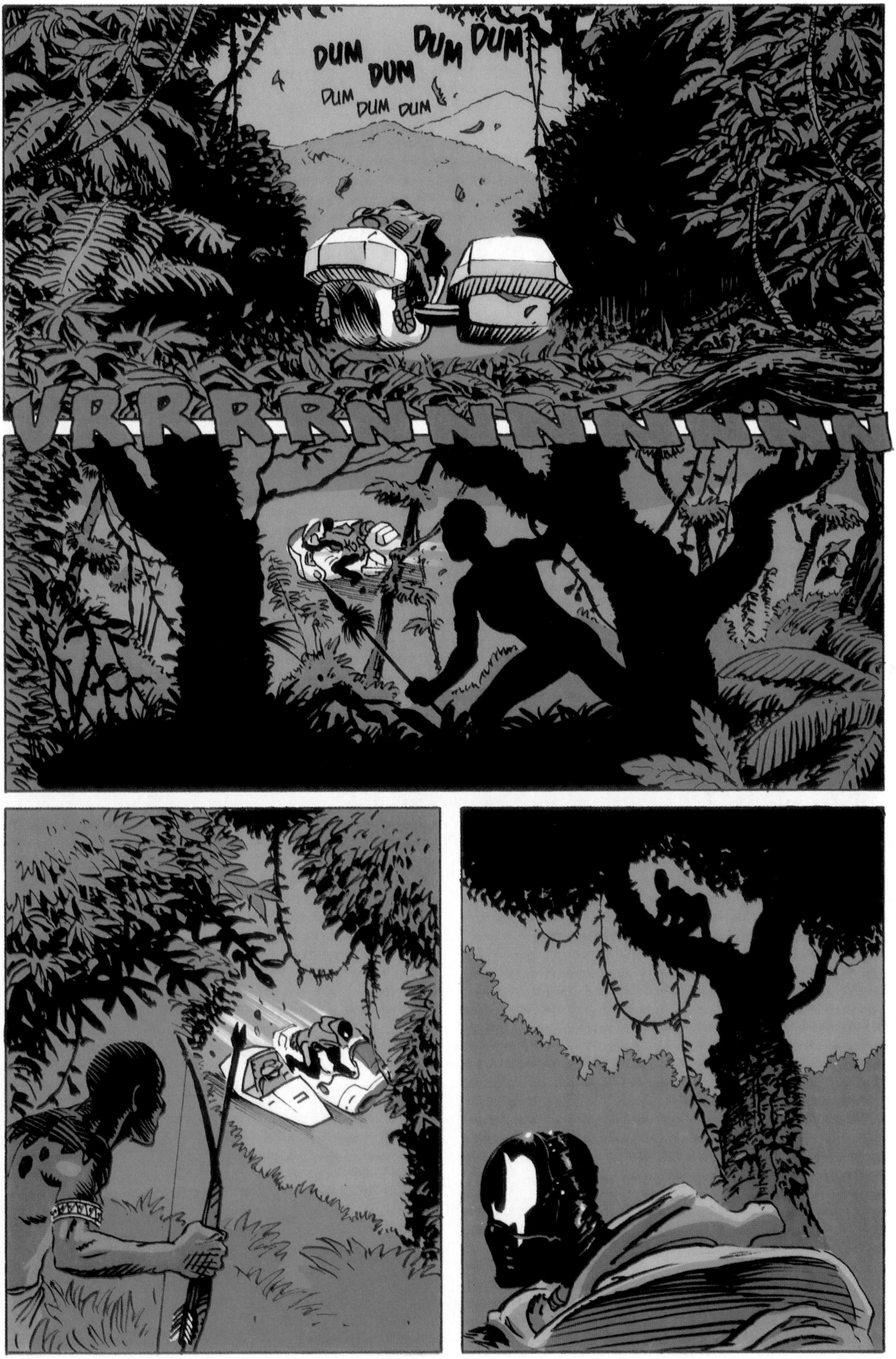
DUM DUM DUM DUM
DUM DUM DUM
VRRRRNNNNNNN

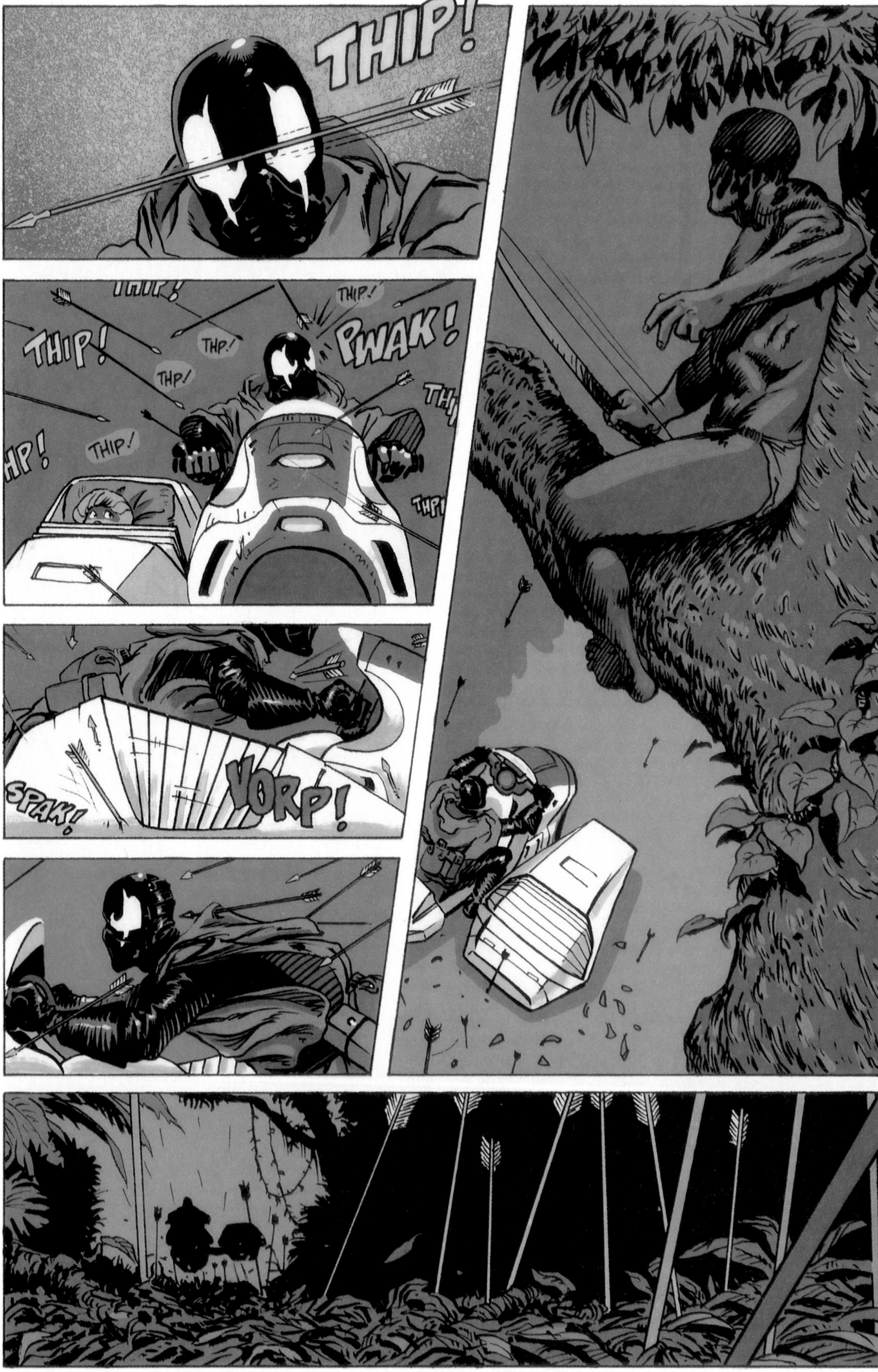
THIP!
THIP!
THP!
THP!
THIP!
PWAK!
THIP!
THIP!
SPAK!
VORP!

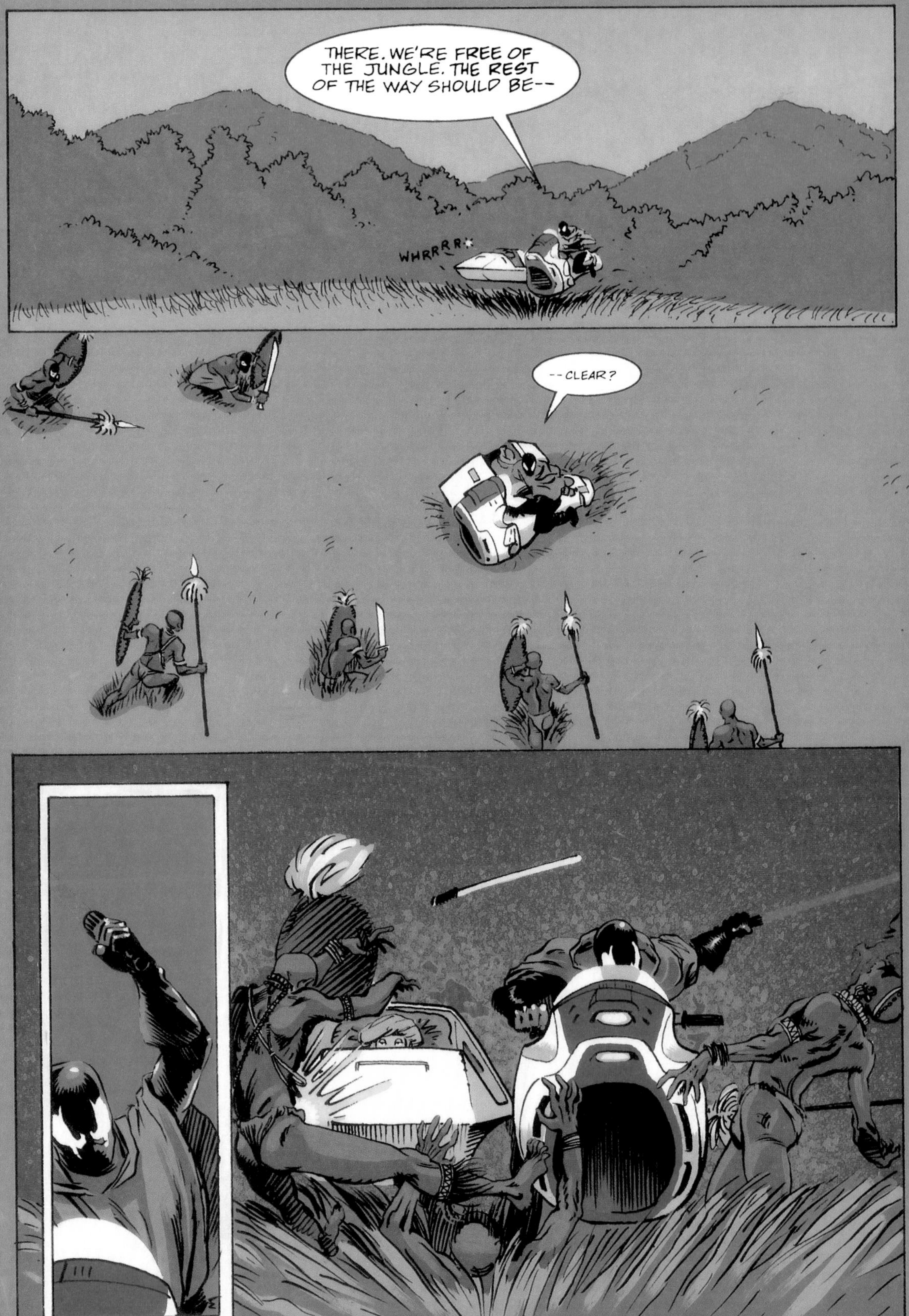
THERE. WE'RE FREE OF THE JUNGLE. THE REST OF THE WAY SHOULD BE--
WHRRRR
--CLEAR?

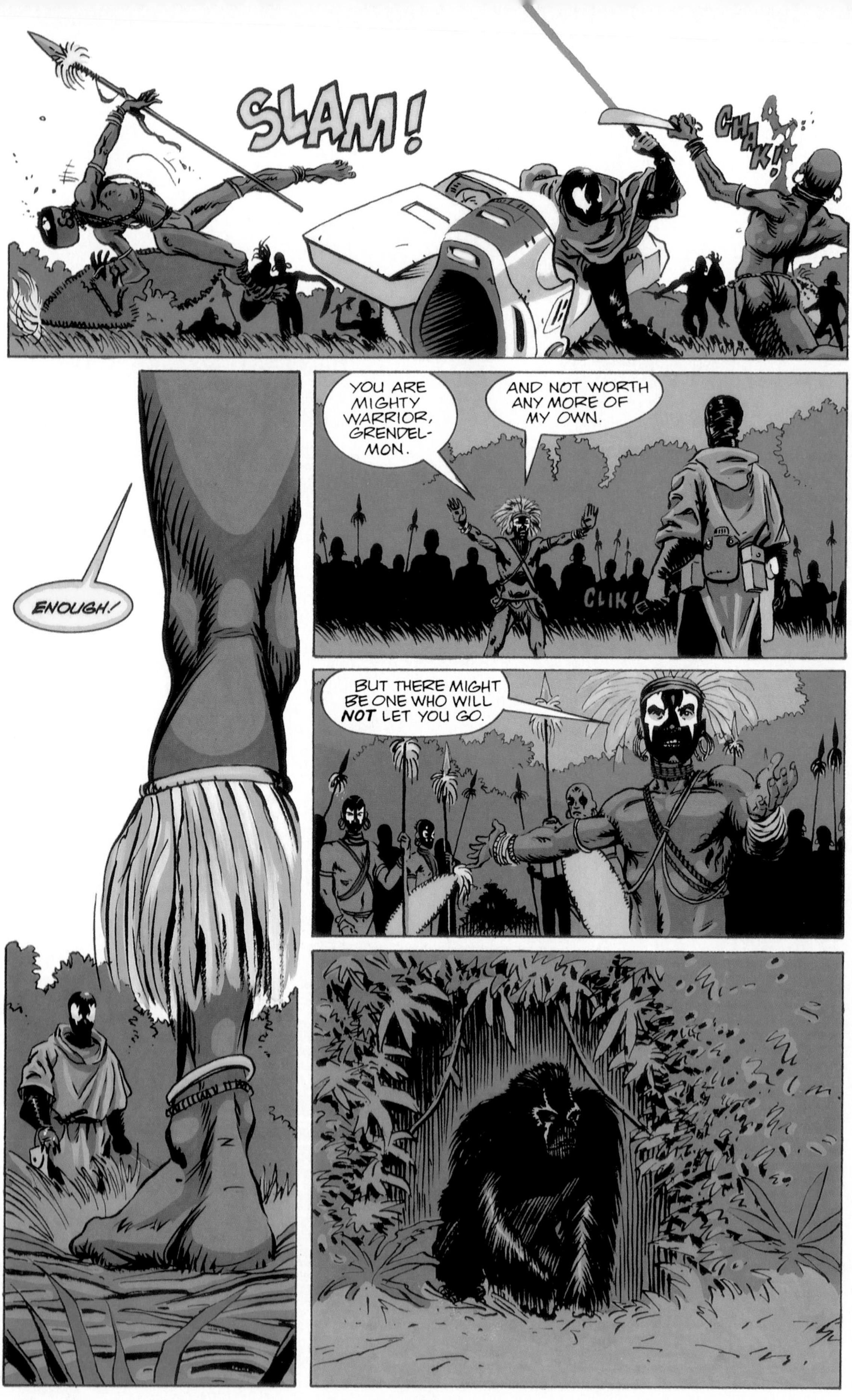
SLAM!
CHAK!
ENOUGH!
YOU ARE MIGHTY WARRIOR, GRENDEL-MON.
AND NOT WORTH ANY MORE OF MY OWN.
CLIK!
BUT THERE MIGHT BE ONE WHO WILL NOT LET YOU GO.

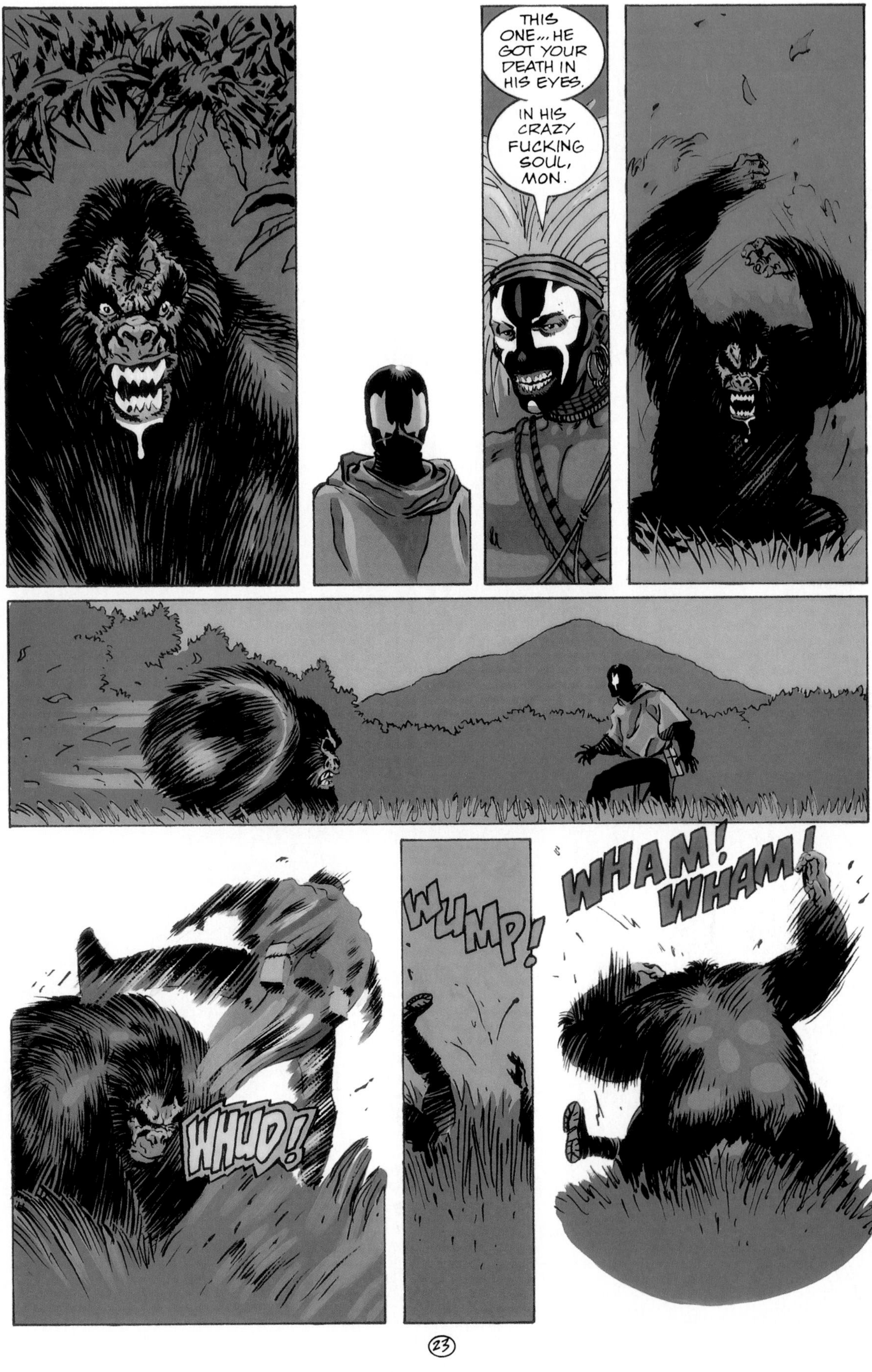
THIS ONE... HE GOT YOUR DEATH IN HIS EYES.
IN HIS CRAZY FUCKING SOUL, MON.
WHUD!
WUMP!
WHAM! WHAM!

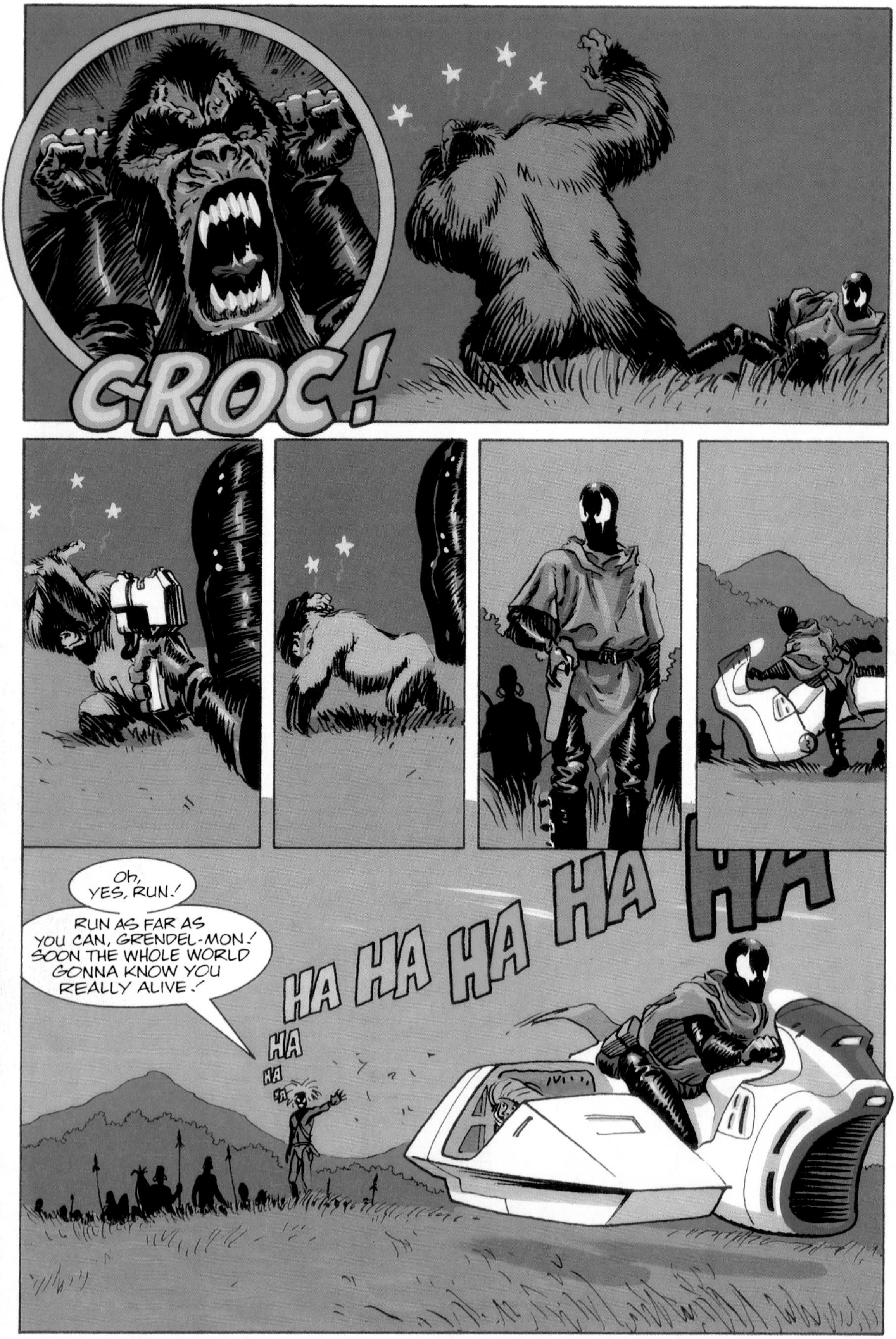
CROC!
Oh, YES, RUN!
RUN AS FAR AS YOU CAN, GRENDEL-MON! SOON THE WHOLE WORLD GONNA KNOW YOU REALLY ALIVE!
HA HA HA HA HA
HA
HA

CHAPTER 6

# DEVIL *in hell*

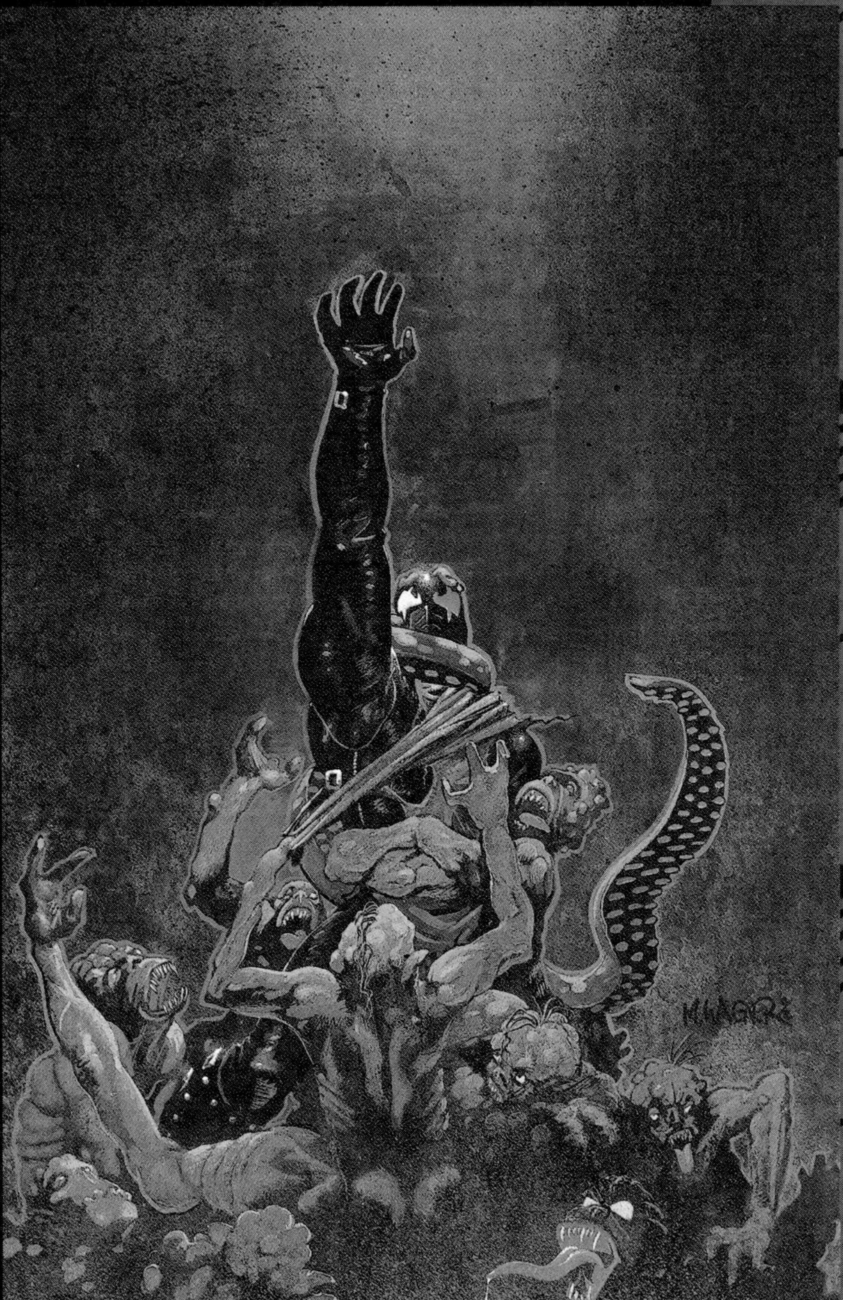

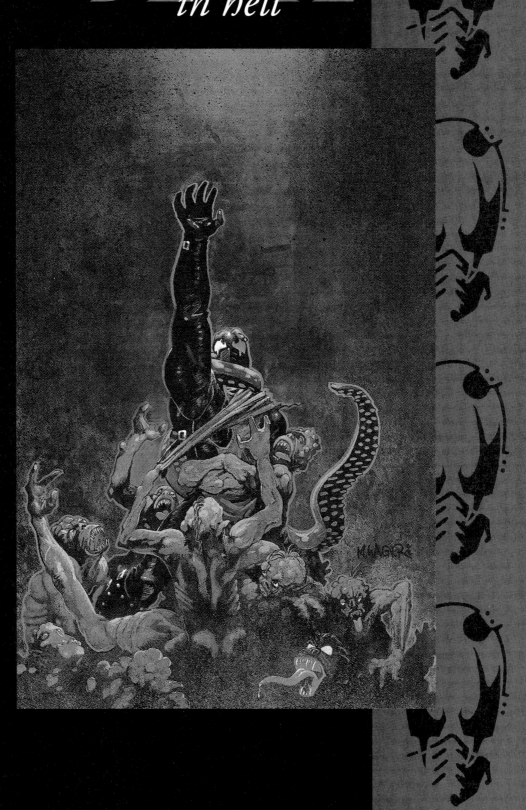

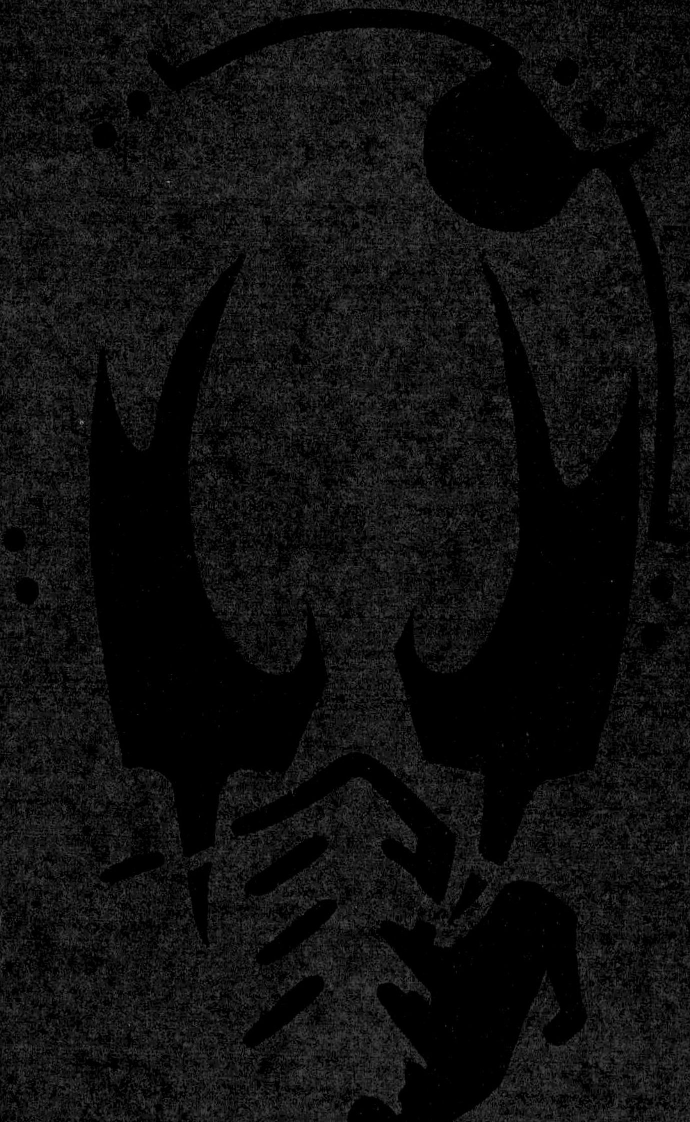

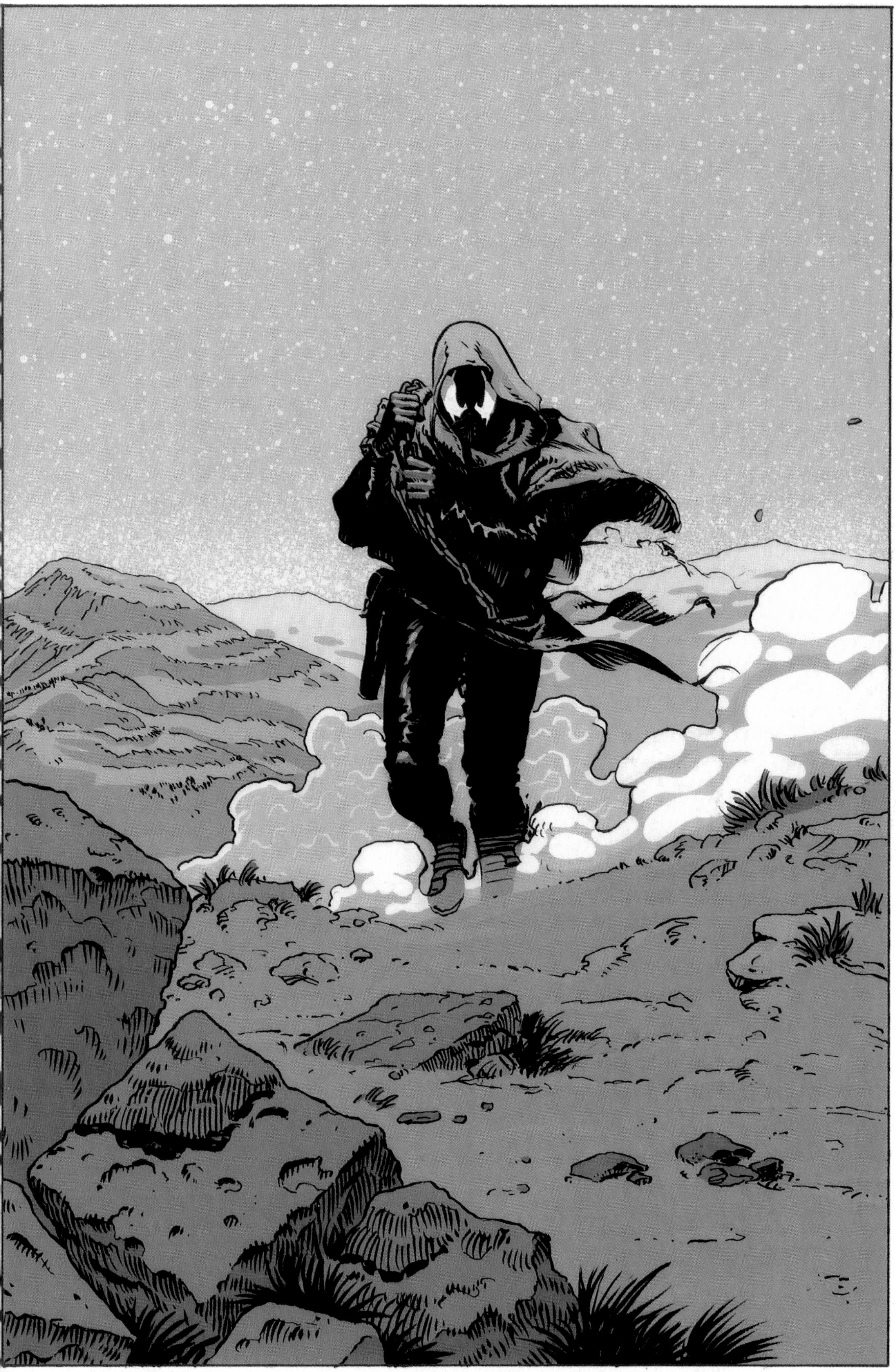

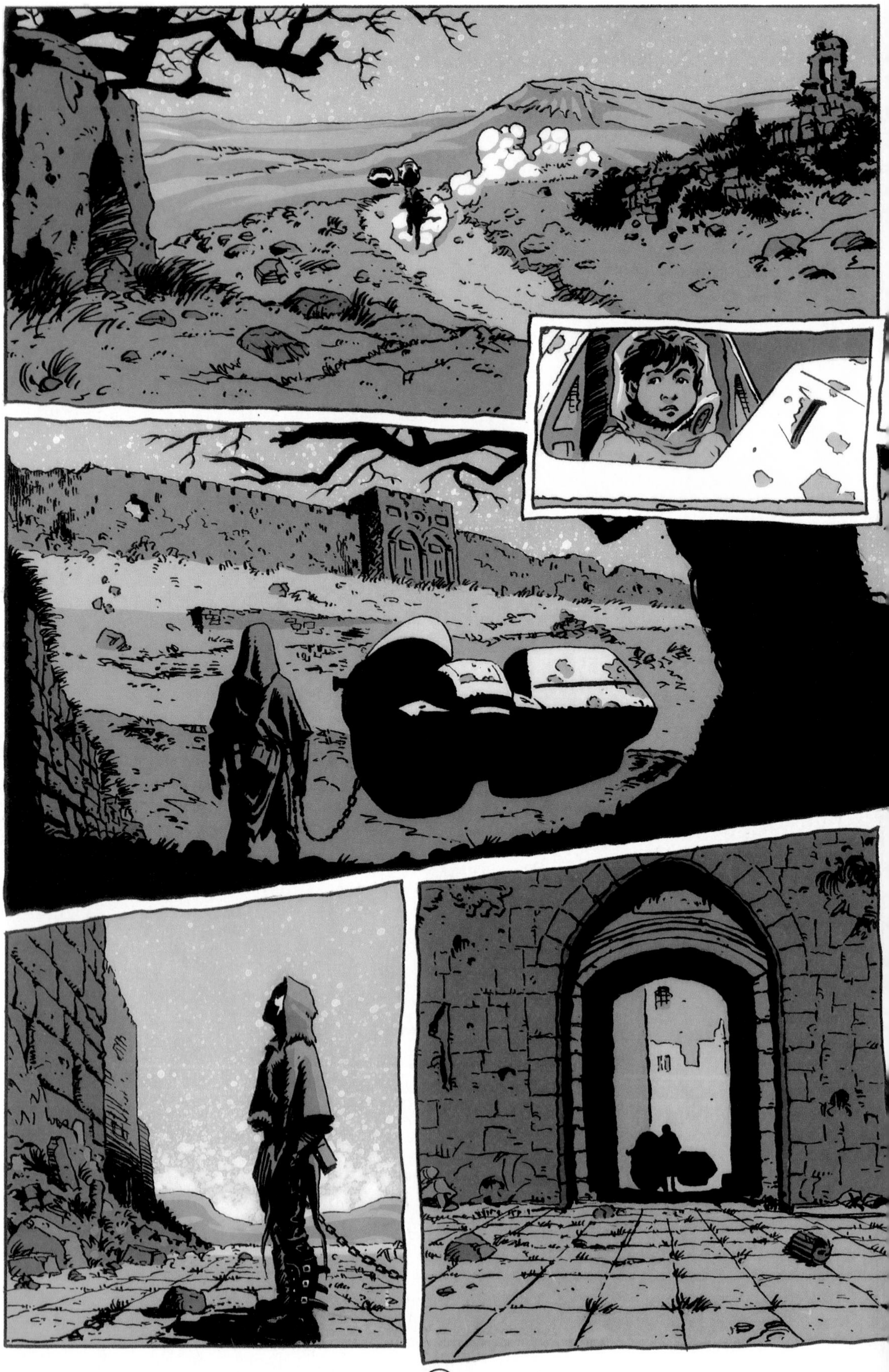

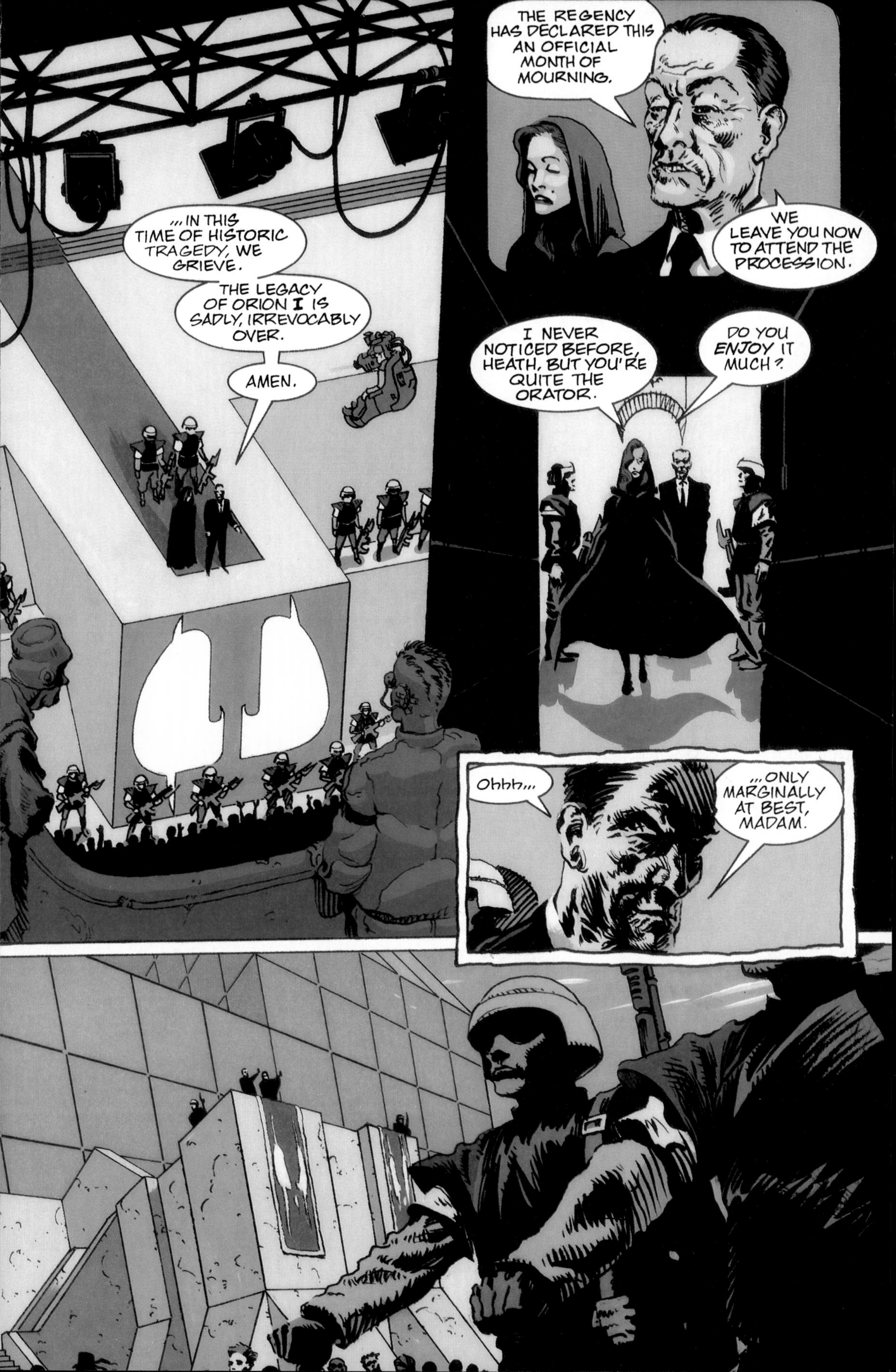
...IN THIS TIME OF HISTORIC TRAGEDY, WE GRIEVE.
THE LEGACY OF ORION I IS SADLY, IRREVOCABLY OVER.
AMEN.
THE REGENCY HAS DECLARED THIS AN OFFICIAL MONTH OF MOURNING.
WE LEAVE YOU NOW TO ATTEND THE PROCESSION.
I NEVER NOTICED BEFORE, HEATH, BUT YOU'RE QUITE THE ORATOR.
DO YOU ENJOY IT MUCH?
Ohhh...
...ONLY MARGINALLY AT BEST, MADAM.

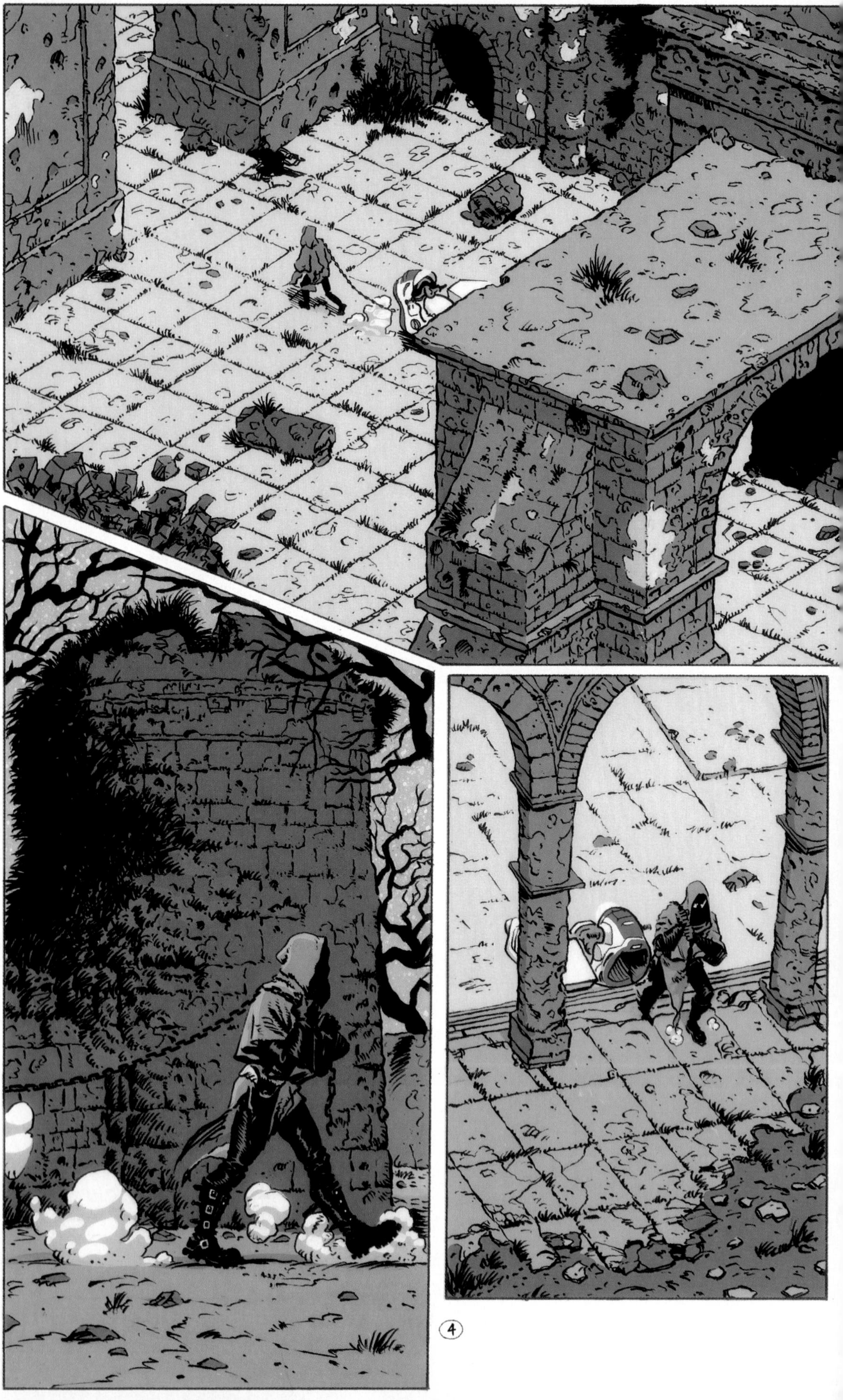

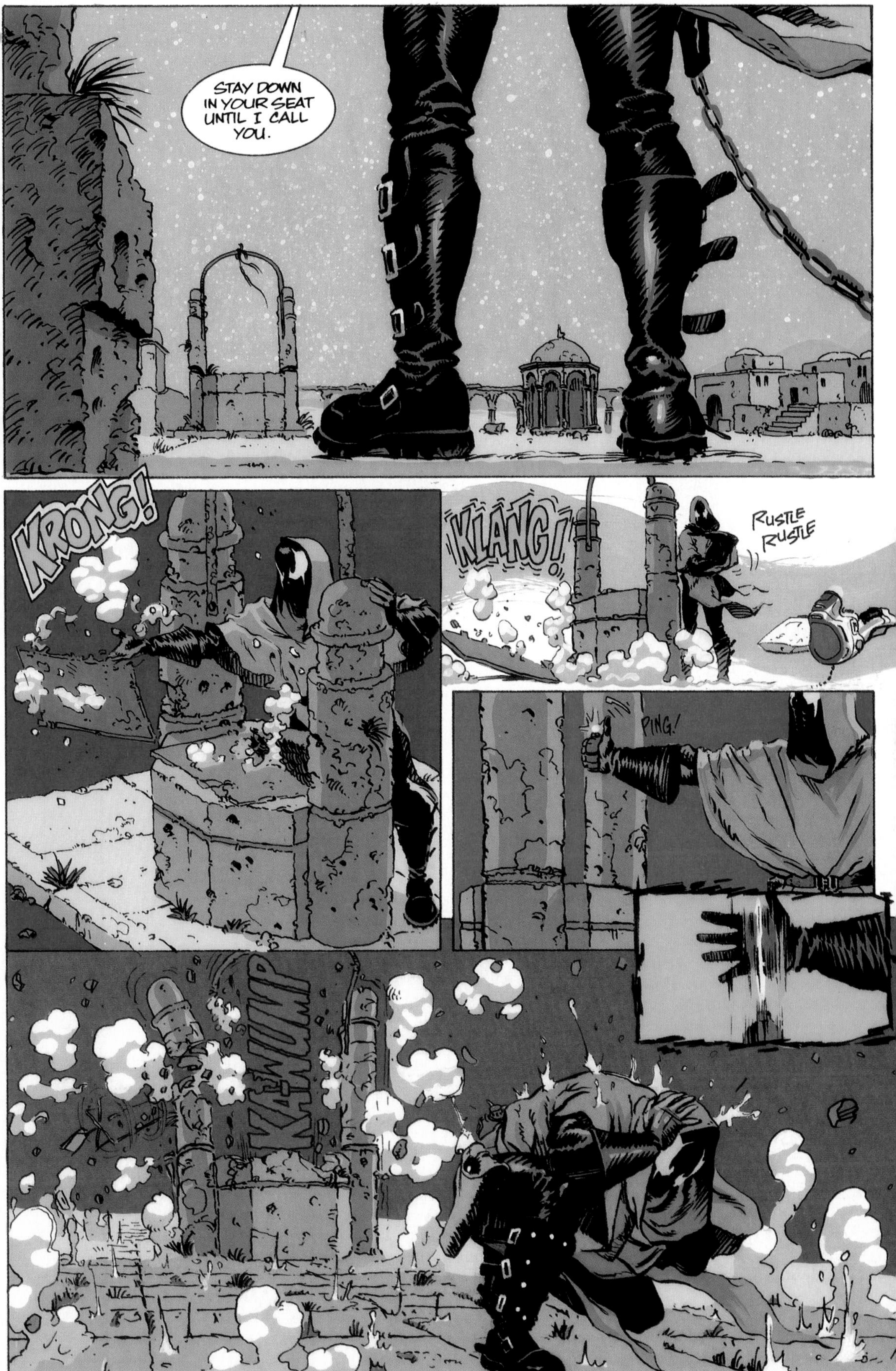
STAY DOWN IN YOUR SEAT UNTIL I CALL YOU.
KRONG!
KLANG!
RUSTLE RUSTLE
PING!
KA-WUMP

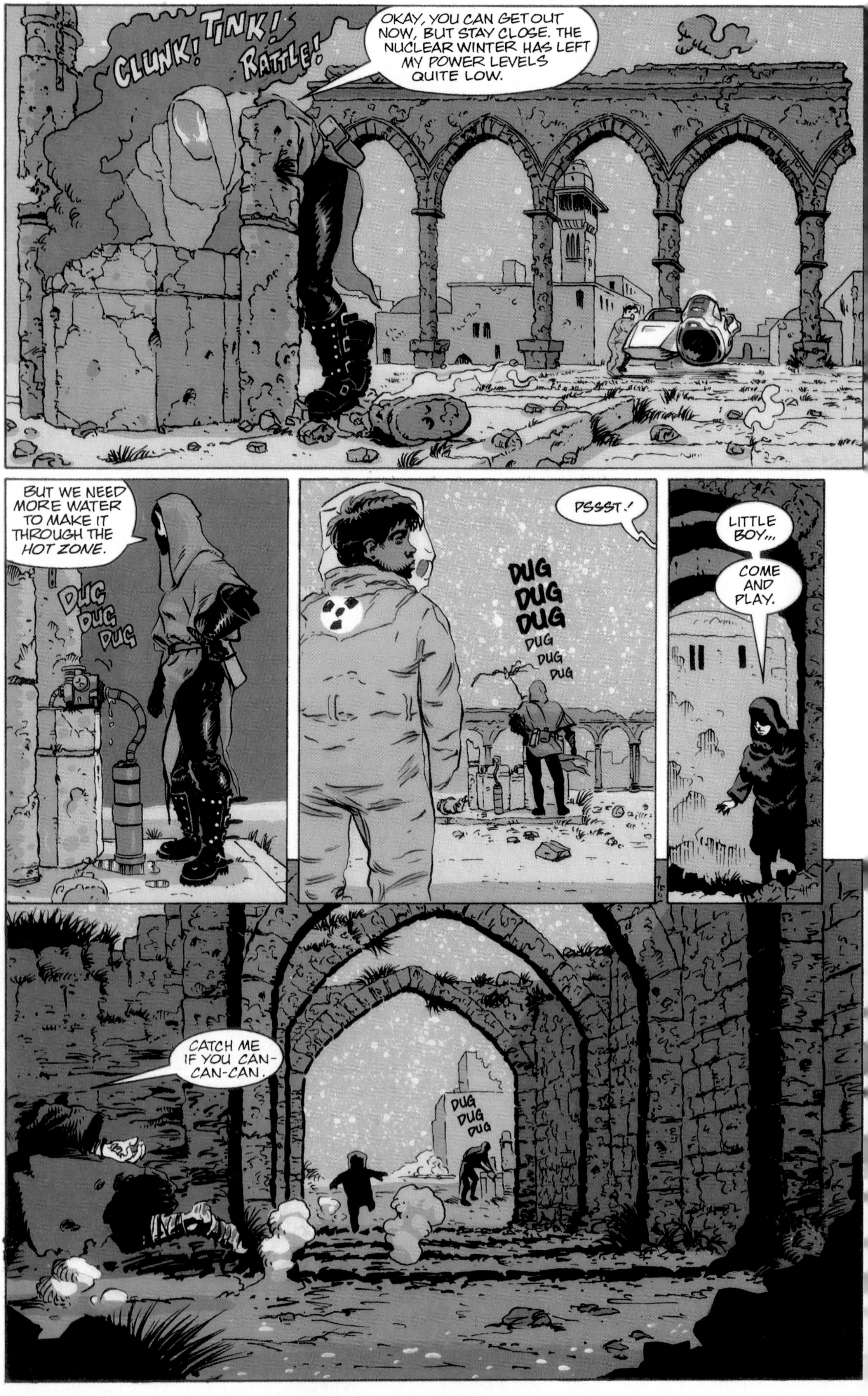
CLUNK! TINK! RATTLE!
OKAY, YOU CAN GET OUT NOW, BUT STAY CLOSE. THE NUCLEAR WINTER HAS LEFT MY POWER LEVELS QUITE LOW.
BUT WE NEED MORE WATER TO MAKE IT THROUGH THE HOT ZONE.
DUG DUG DUG
PSSST.!
DUG DUG DUG DUG DUG DUG
LITTLE BOY...
COME AND PLAY.
CATCH ME IF YOU CAN-CAN-CAN.
DUG DUG DUG

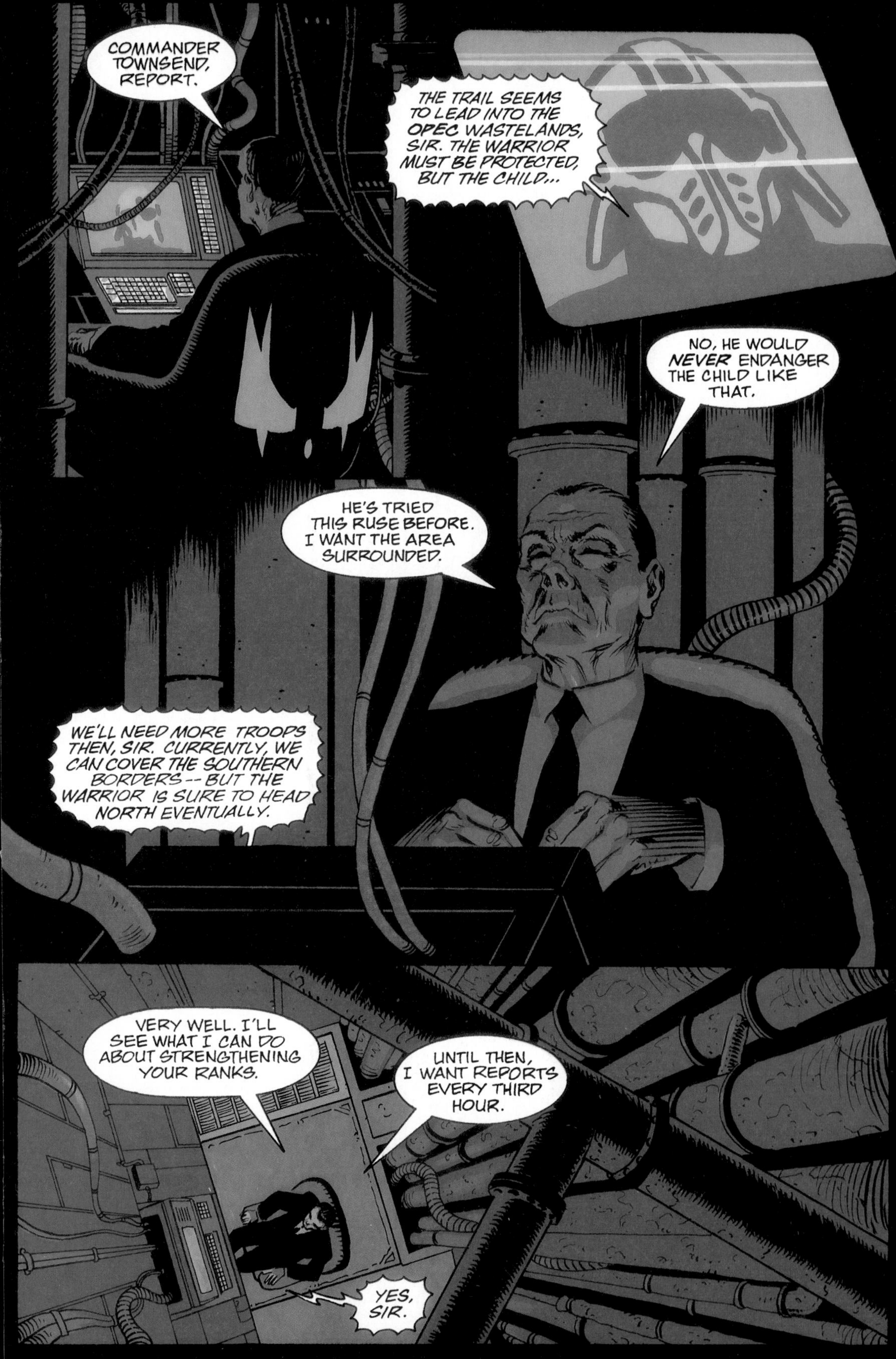
COMMANDER TOWNSEND, REPORT.
THE TRAIL SEEMS TO LEAD INTO THE OPEC WASTELANDS, SIR. THE WARRIOR MUST BE PROTECTED, BUT THE CHILD...
NO, HE WOULD NEVER ENDANGER THE CHILD LIKE THAT.
HE'S TRIED THIS RUSE BEFORE. I WANT THE AREA SURROUNDED.
WE'LL NEED MORE TROOPS THEN, SIR. CURRENTLY, WE CAN COVER THE SOUTHERN BORDERS-- BUT THE WARRIOR IS SURE TO HEAD NORTH EVENTUALLY.
VERY WELL. I'LL SEE WHAT I CAN DO ABOUT STRENGTHENING YOUR RANKS.
UNTIL THEN, I WANT REPORTS EVERY THIRD HOUR.
YES, SIR.

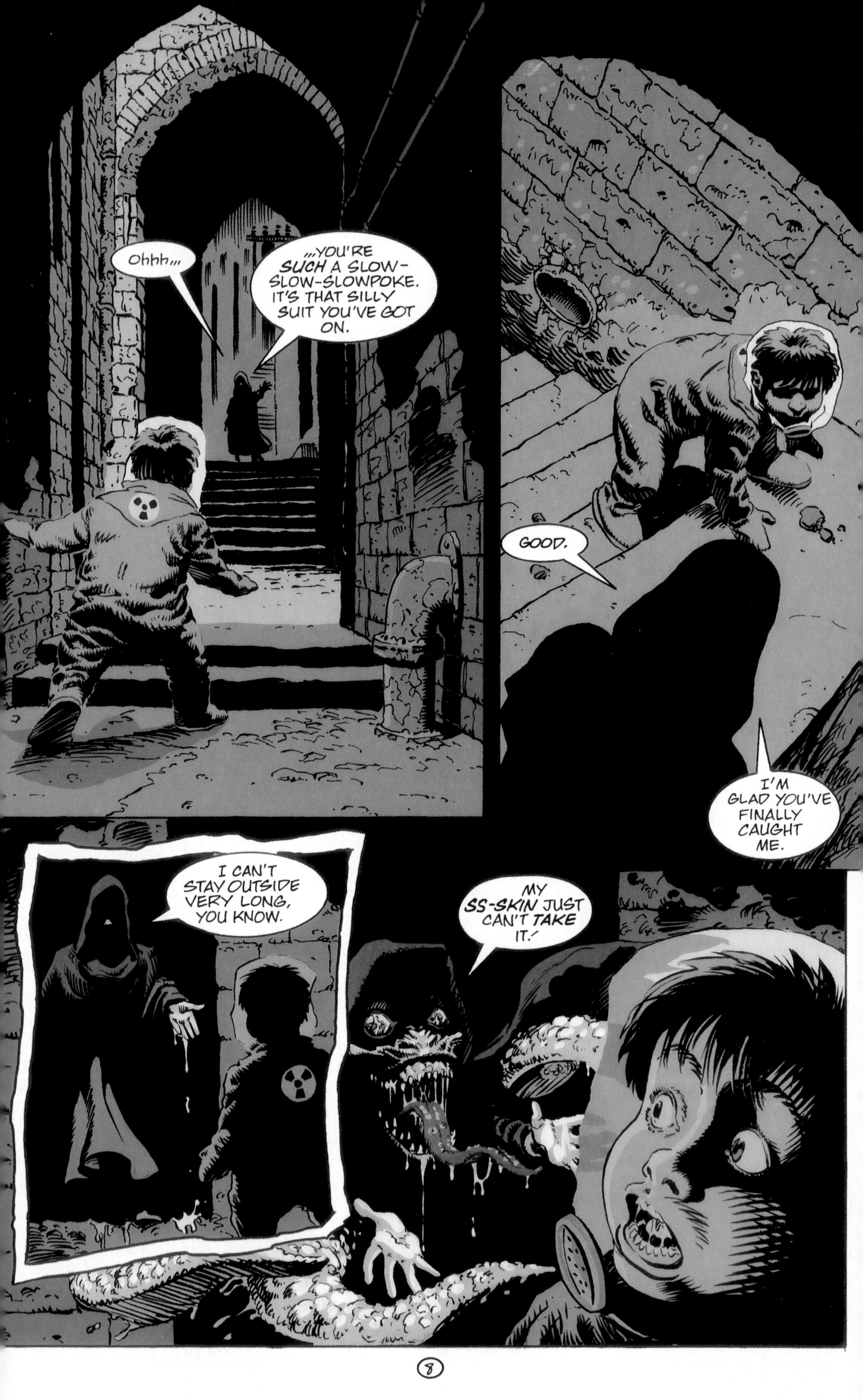
Ohhh...
...YOU'RE SUCH A SLOW-SLOW-SLOWPOKE. IT'S THAT SILLY SUIT YOU'VE GOT ON.
GOOD.
I'M GLAD YOU'VE FINALLY CAUGHT ME.
I CAN'T STAY OUTSIDE VERY LONG, YOU KNOW.
MY SS-SKIN JUST CAN'T TAKE IT.!

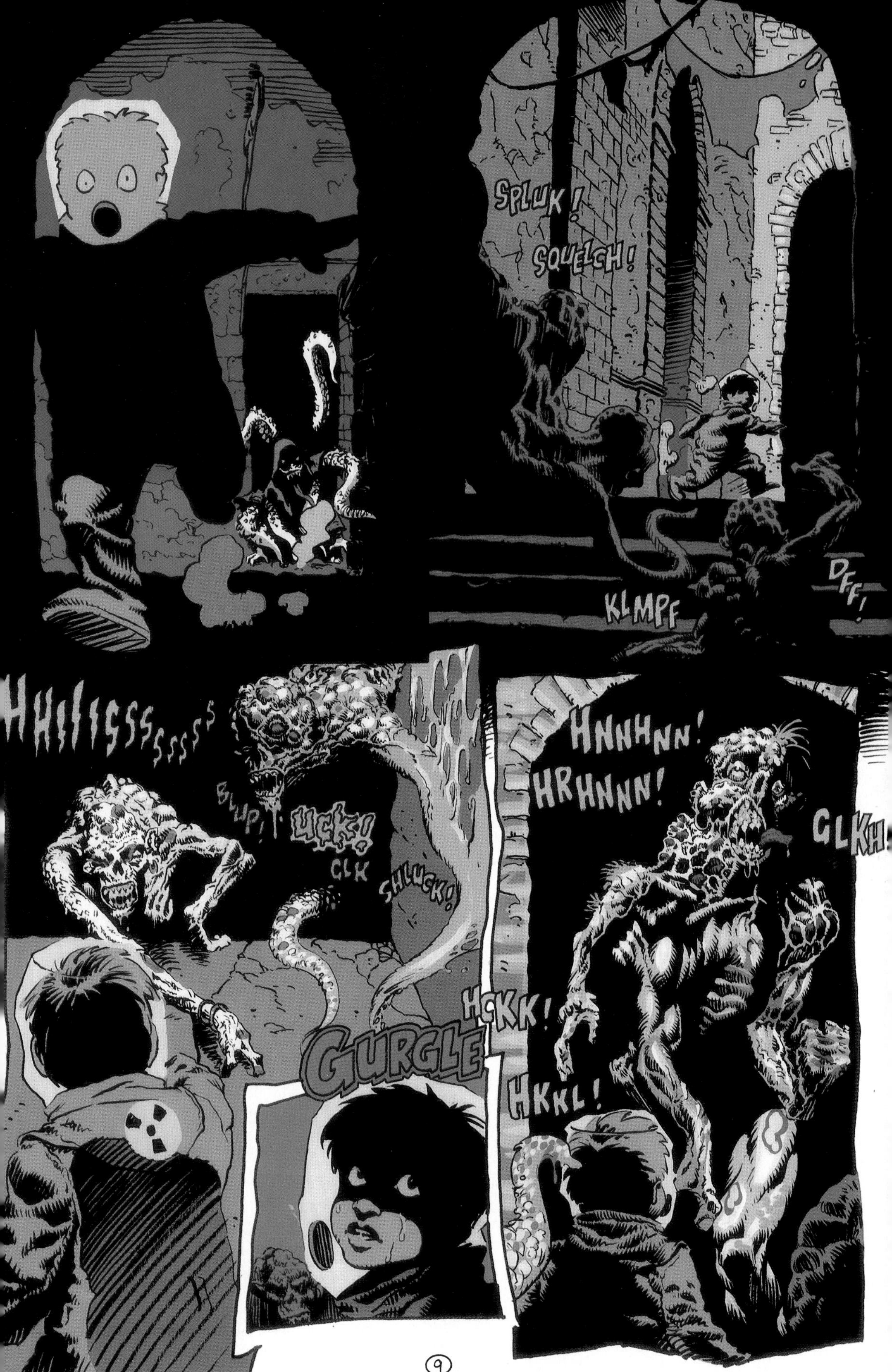
SPLUK!
SQUELCH!
KLMPF
DFF!
HHISSSSSSSSSS
BLUP!
UCK!
CLK
SHLUCK!
GURGLE
HCKK!
HNNHNN!
HRHNNN!
GLKH!
HKKL!

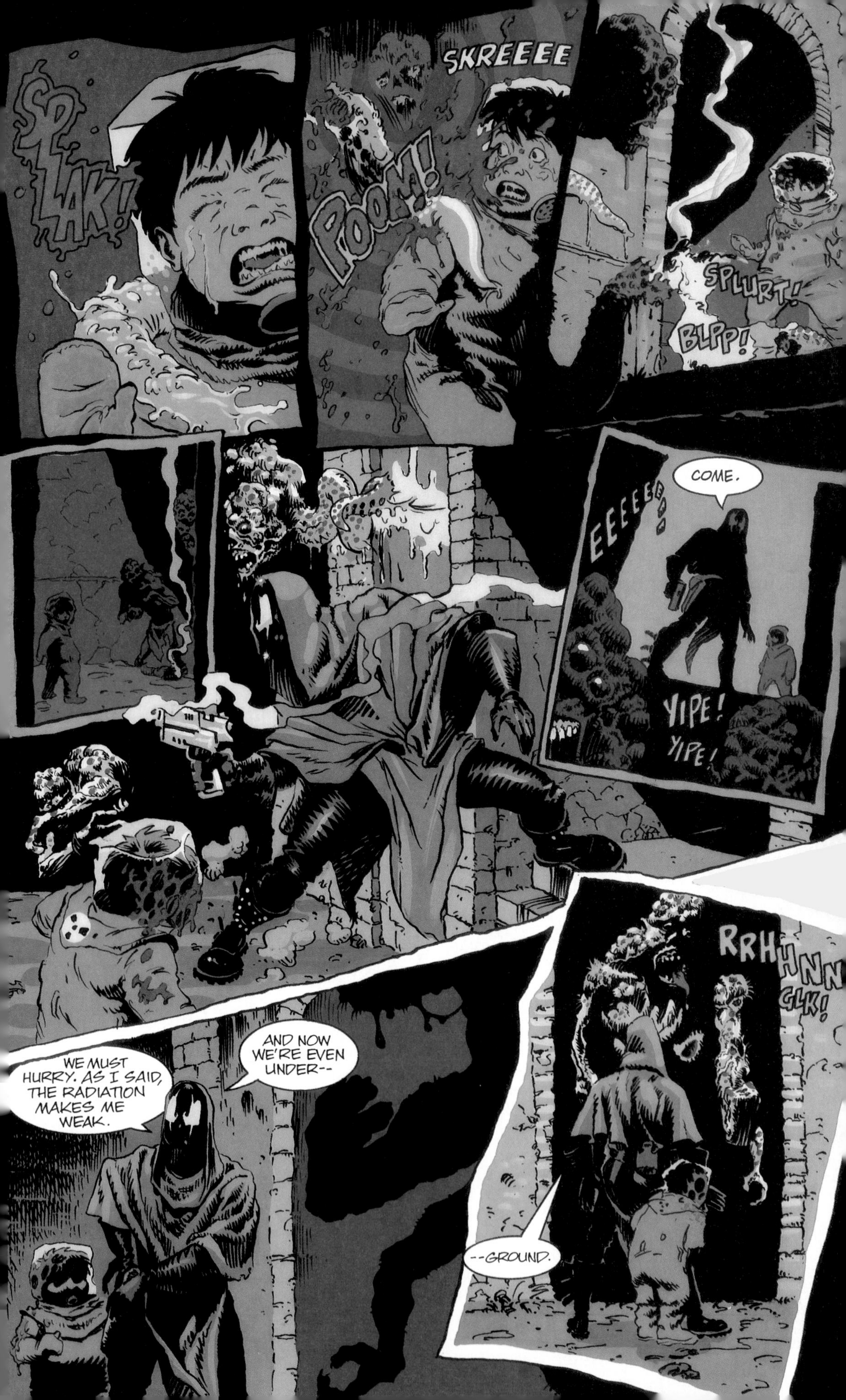
SPLAK!
SKREEEEE
POOM!
SPLURT!
BLPP!
EEEEEE
COME.
YIPE!
YIPE!
RRHHNN
GLK!
WE MUST HURRY. AS I SAID, THE RADIATION MAKES ME WEAK.
AND NOW WE'RE EVEN UNDER--
--GROUND.

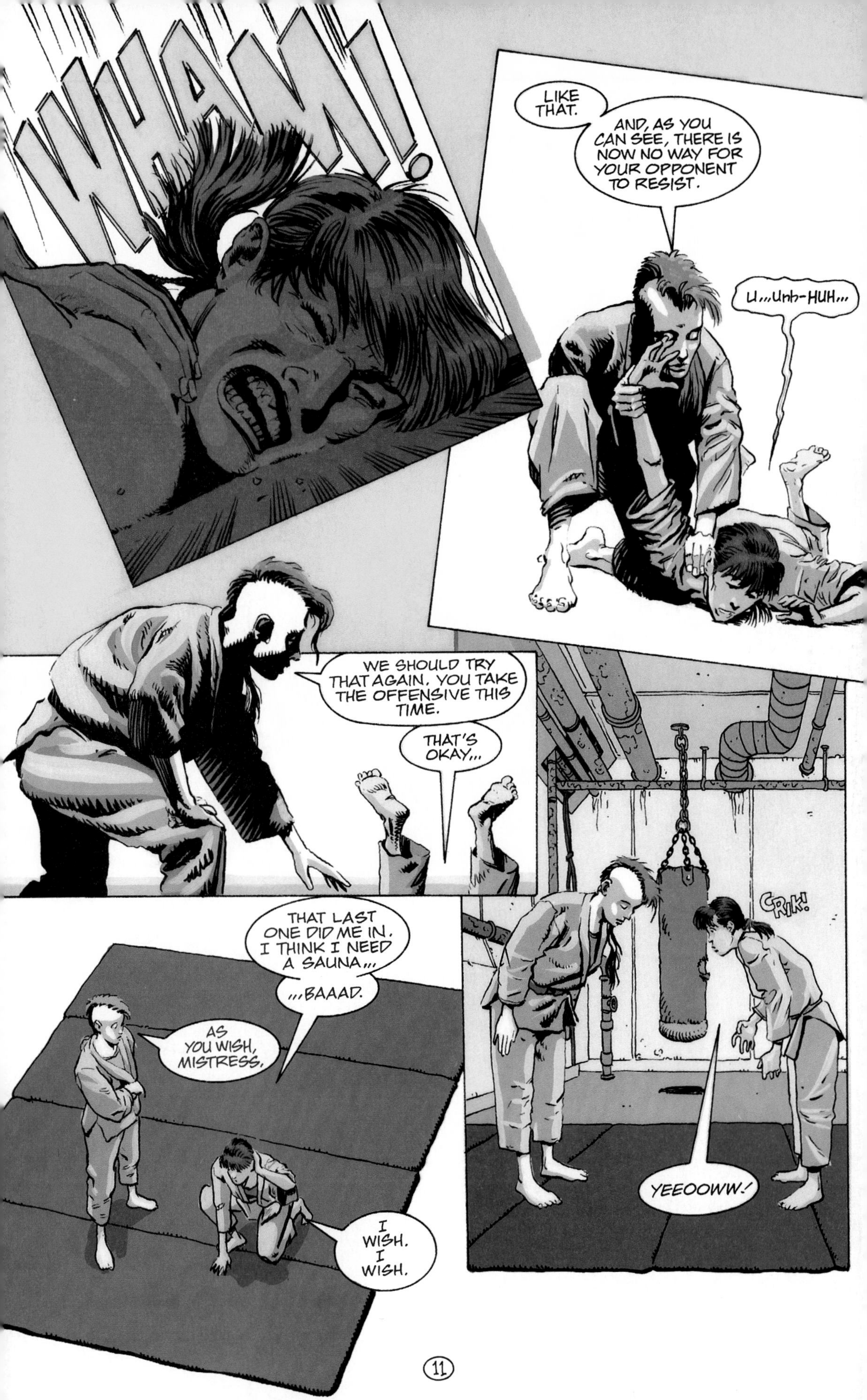
WHAM!
LIKE THAT.
AND, AS YOU CAN SEE, THERE IS NOW NO WAY FOR YOUR OPPONENT TO RESIST.
U,,,Unh-HUH,,,
WE SHOULD TRY THAT AGAIN. YOU TAKE THE OFFENSIVE THIS TIME.
THAT'S OKAY,,,
CRIK!
YEEOOWW!
THAT LAST ONE DID ME IN. I THINK I NEED A SAUNA,,,
,,,BAAAD.
AS YOU WISH, MISTRESS.
I WISH. I WISH.

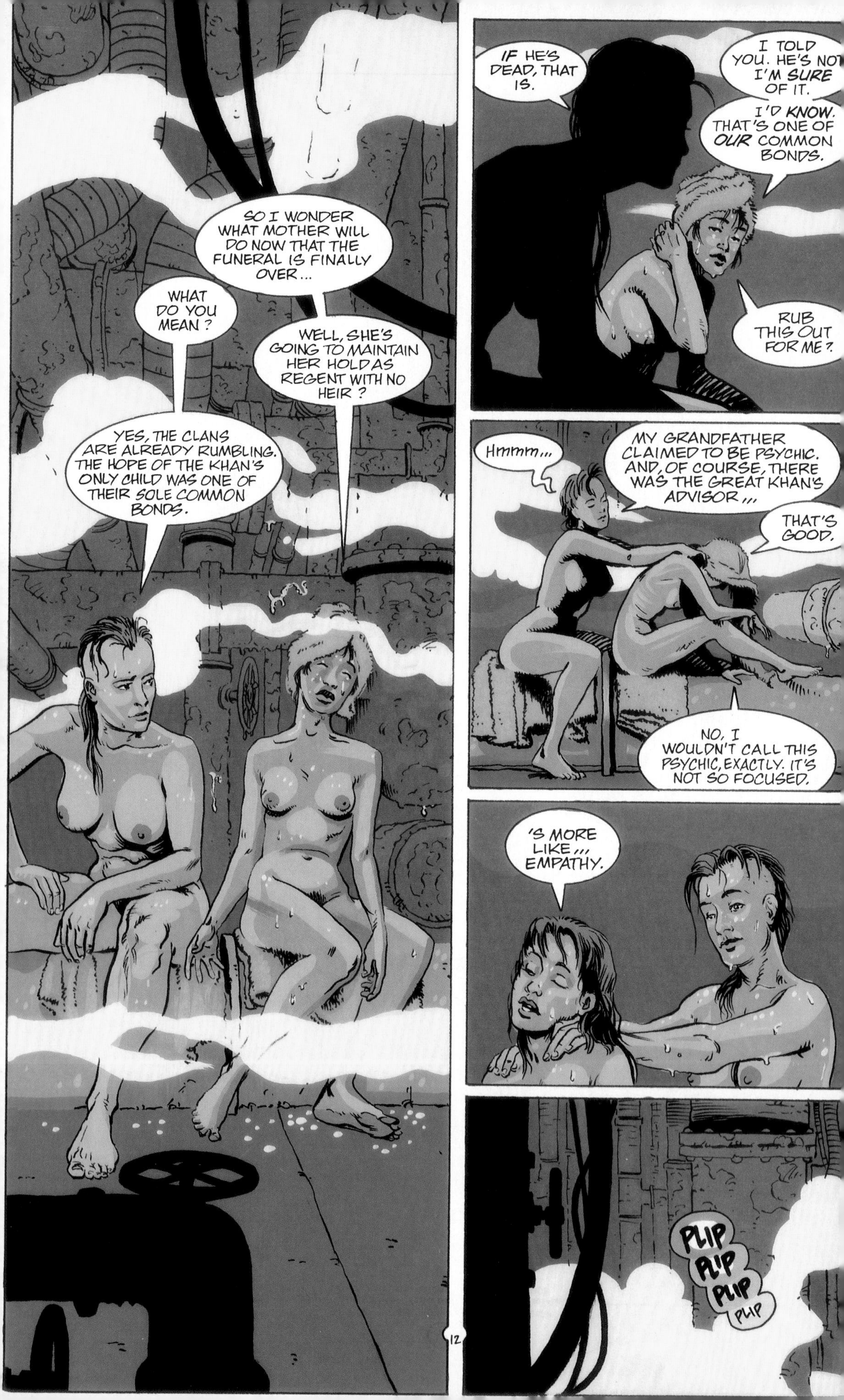
SO I WONDER WHAT MOTHER WILL DO NOW THAT THE FUNERAL IS FINALLY OVER...
WHAT DO YOU MEAN ?
WELL, SHE'S GOING TO MAINTAIN HER HOLD AS REGENT WITH NO HEIR ?
YES, THE CLANS ARE ALREADY RUMBLING. THE HOPE OF THE KHAN'S ONLY CHILD WAS ONE OF THEIR SOLE COMMON BONDS.
IF HE'S DEAD, THAT IS.
I TOLD YOU. HE'S NOT. I'M SURE OF IT.
I'D KNOW. THAT'S ONE OF OUR COMMON BONDS.
RUB THIS OUT FOR ME ?
Hmmm,,,
MY GRANDFATHER CLAIMED TO BE PSYCHIC. AND, OF COURSE, THERE WAS THE GREAT KHAN'S ADVISOR,,,
THAT'S GOOD.
NO, I WOULDN'T CALL THIS PSYCHIC, EXACTLY. IT'S NOT SO FOCUSED.
'S MORE LIKE,,, EMPATHY.
PLIP
PLIP
PLIP
PLIP

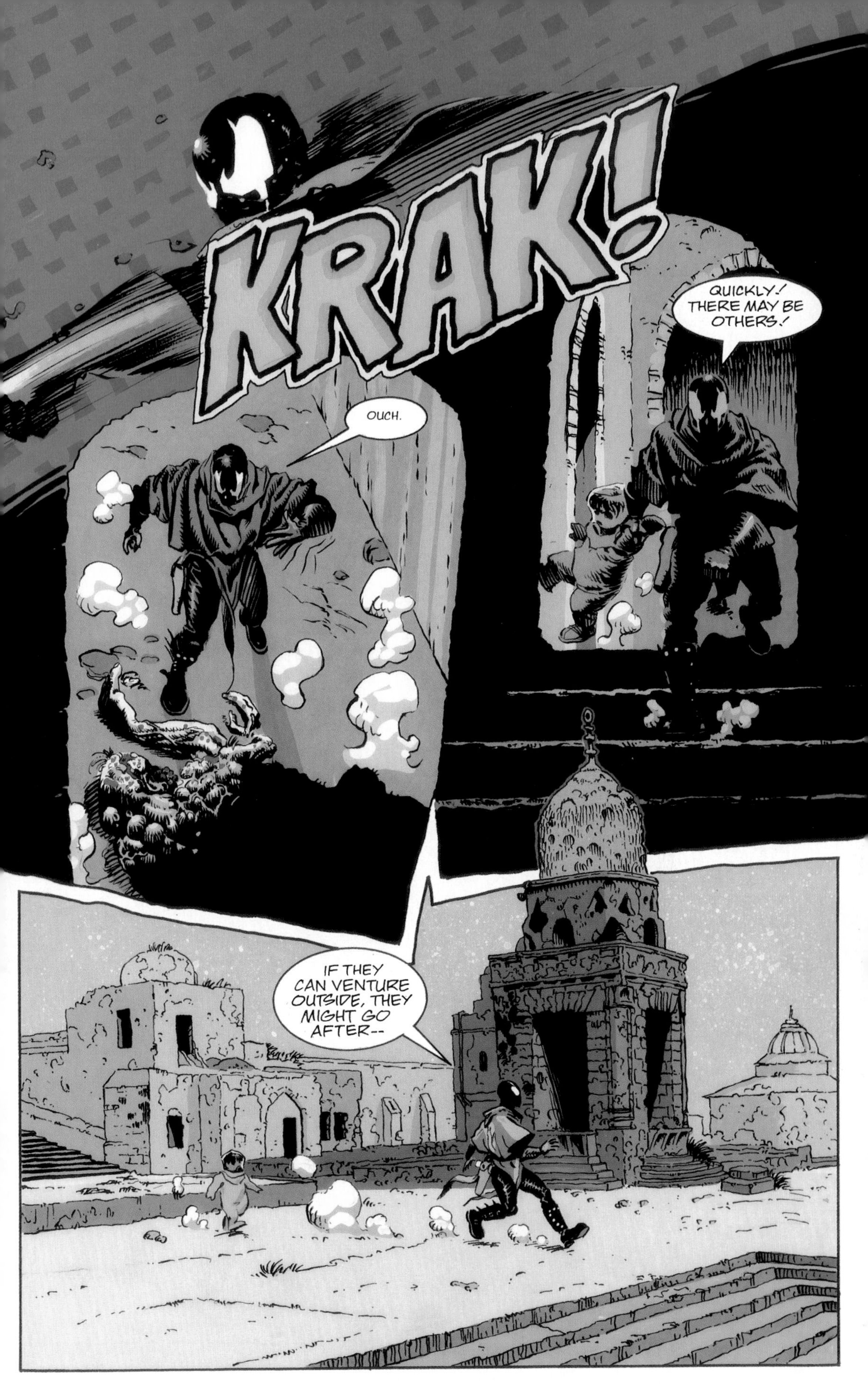
KRAK!
OUCH.
QUICKLY! THERE MAY BE OTHERS!
IF THEY CAN VENTURE OUTSIDE, THEY MIGHT GO AFTER--

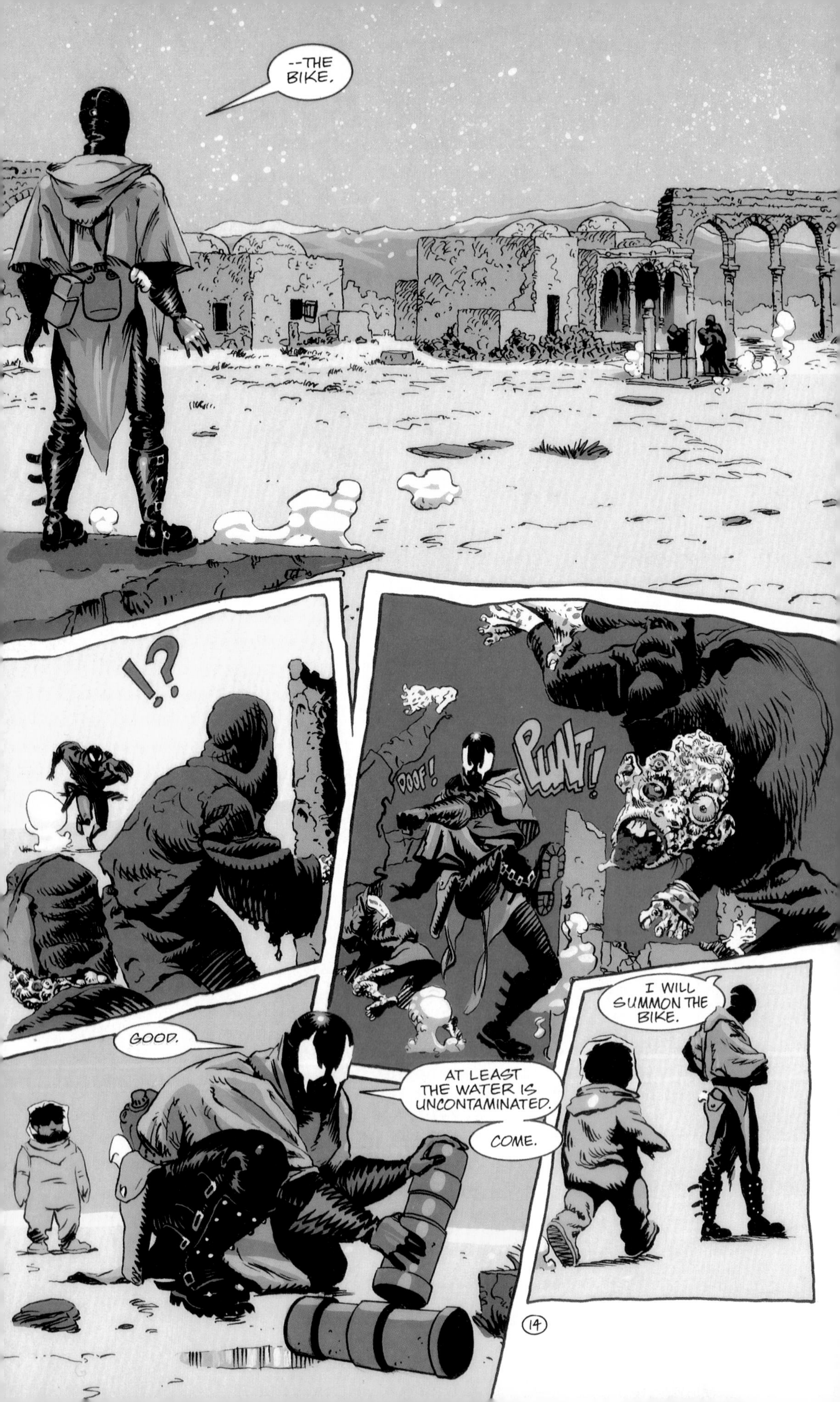

--THE BIKE.
!?
DOOF!
PUNT!
GOOD.
AT LEAST THE WATER IS UNCONTAMINATED.
COME.
I WILL SUMMON THE BIKE.

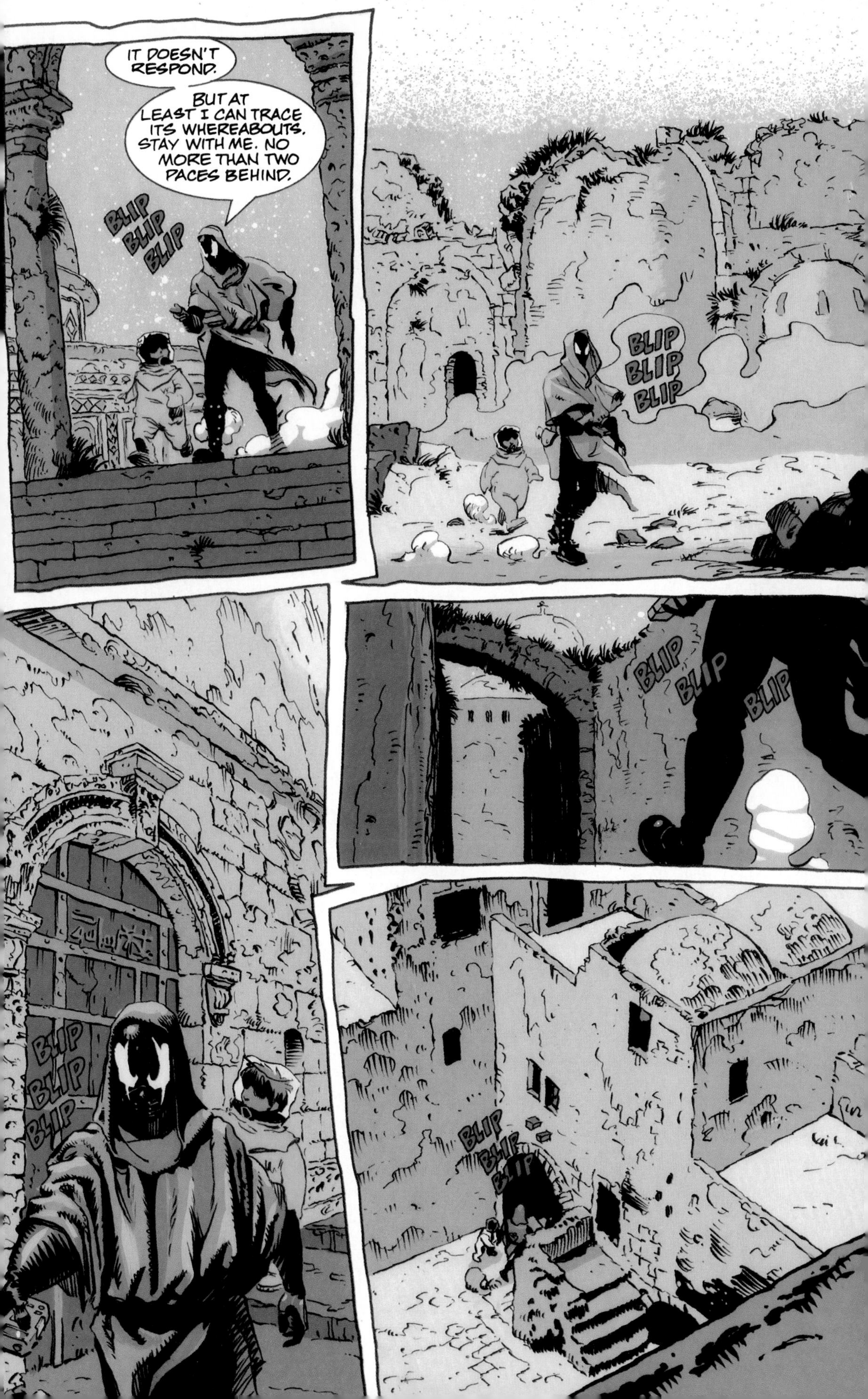
IT DOESN'T RESPOND.
BUT AT LEAST I CAN TRACE ITS WHEREABOUTS. STAY WITH ME. NO MORE THAN TWO PACES BEHIND.
BLIP BLIP BLIP
BLIP BLIP BLIP
BLIP BLIP BLIP
BLIP BLIP BLIP
BLIP BLIP BLIP

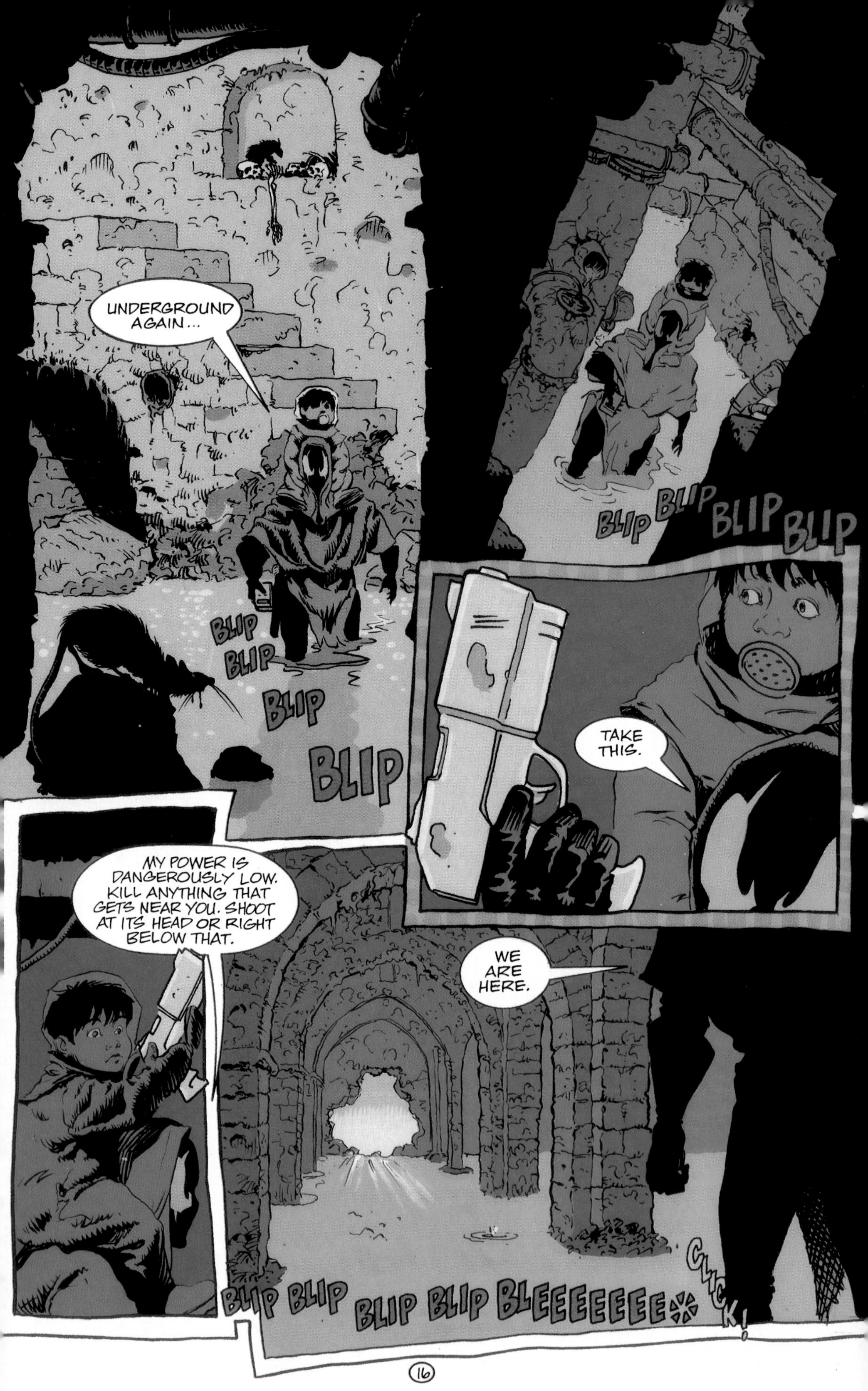
UNDERGROUND AGAIN...
BLIP
BLIP
BLIP
BLIP
BLIP BLIP BLIP BLIP
TAKE THIS.
MY POWER IS DANGEROUSLY LOW. KILL ANYTHING THAT GETS NEAR YOU. SHOOT AT ITS HEAD OR RIGHT BELOW THAT.
WE ARE HERE.
BLIP BLIP BLIP BLIP BLEEEEEEEE
CWICK!

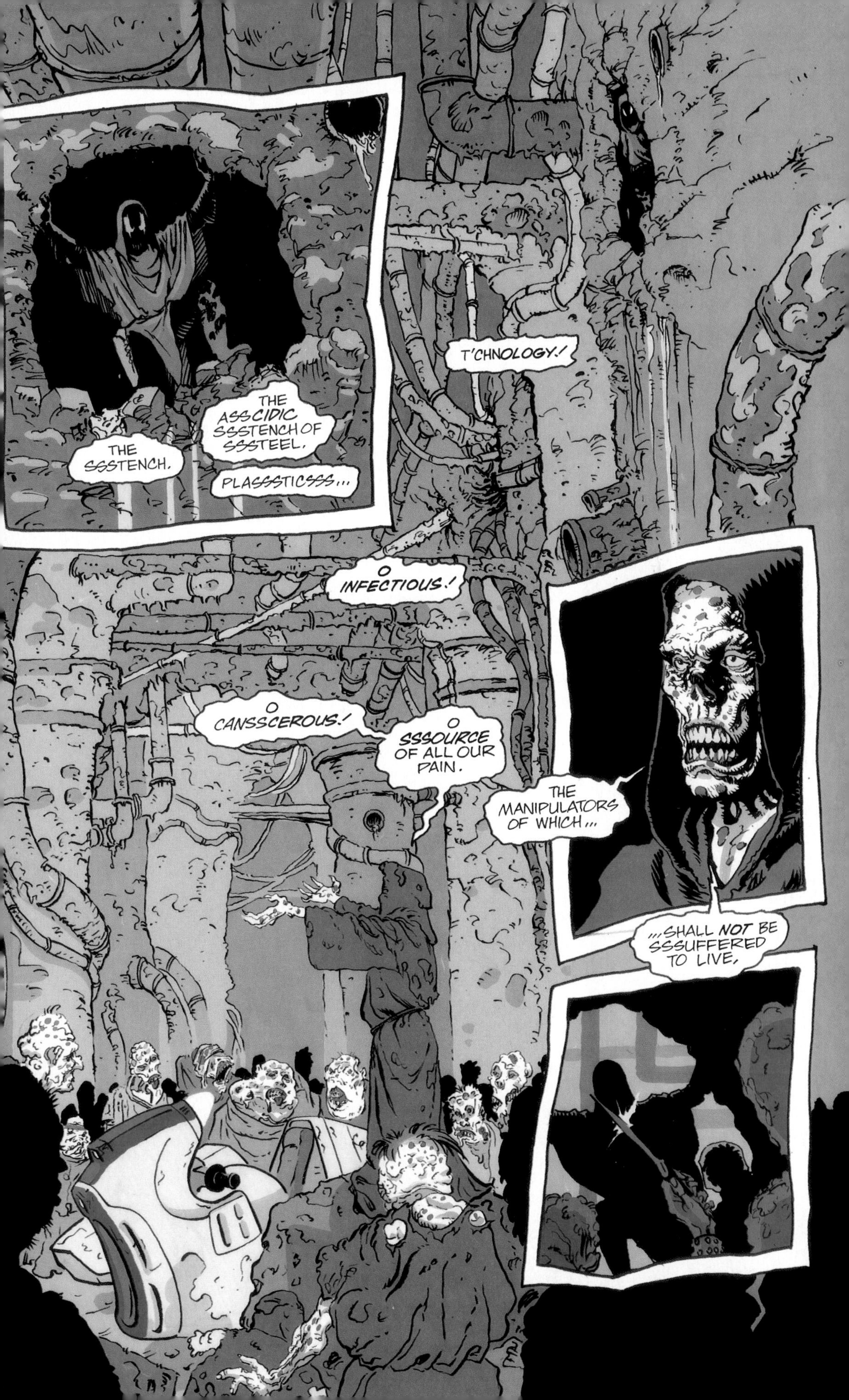
THE SSSTENCH.
THE ASSCIDIC SSSTENCH OF SSSTEEL,
PLASSSTICSSS...
T'CHNOLOGY!
O INFECTIOUS!
O CANSSCEROUS!
O SSSOURCE OF ALL OUR PAIN.
THE MANIPULATORS OF WHICH...
...SHALL NOT BE SSSUFFERED TO LIVE.

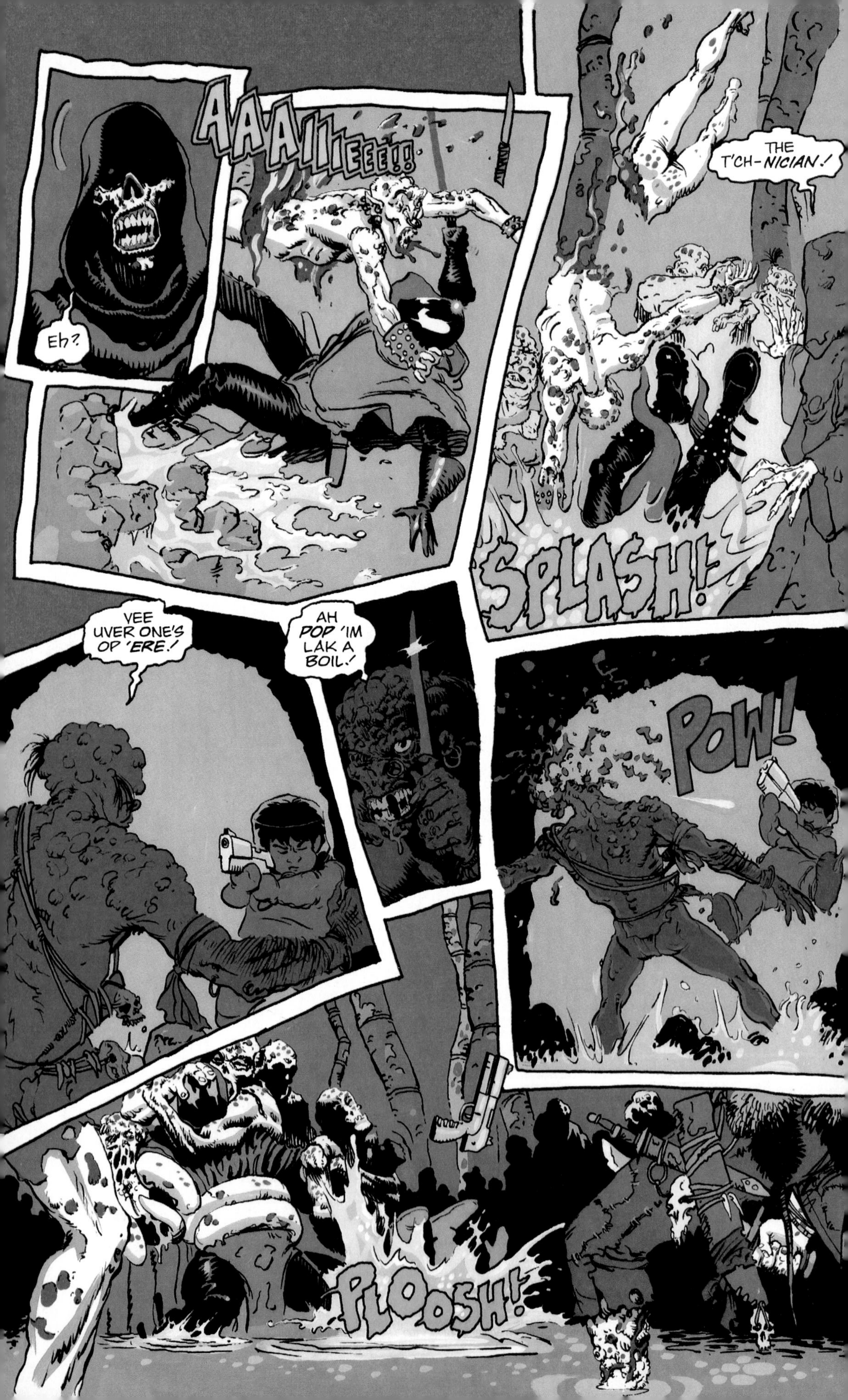
AAAIIIEEE!!
Eh?
THE T'CH-NICIAN!
SPLASH!
VEE UVER ONE'S OP 'ERE!
AH POP 'IM LAK A BOIL!
POW!
PLOOSH!

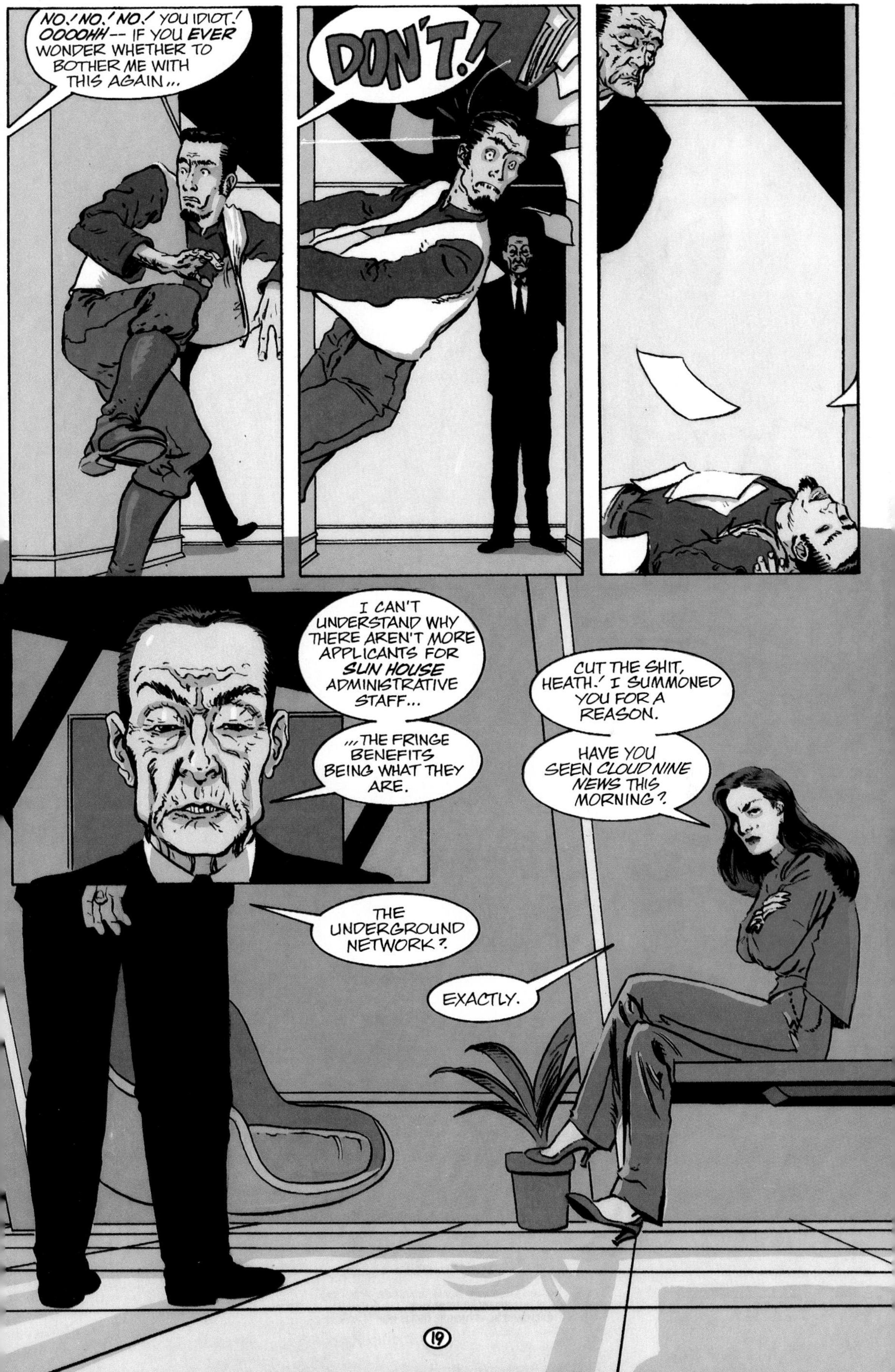
NO! NO! NO! YOU IDIOT! OOOOHH -- IF YOU EVER WONDER WHETHER TO BOTHER ME WITH THIS AGAIN...
DON'T!
I CAN'T UNDERSTAND WHY THERE AREN'T MORE APPLICANTS FOR SUN HOUSE ADMINISTRATIVE STAFF...
...THE FRINGE BENEFITS BEING WHAT THEY ARE.
CUT THE SHIT, HEATH! I SUMMONED YOU FOR A REASON.
HAVE YOU SEEN CLOUD NINE NEWS THIS MORNING?
THE UNDERGROUND NETWORK?
EXACTLY.

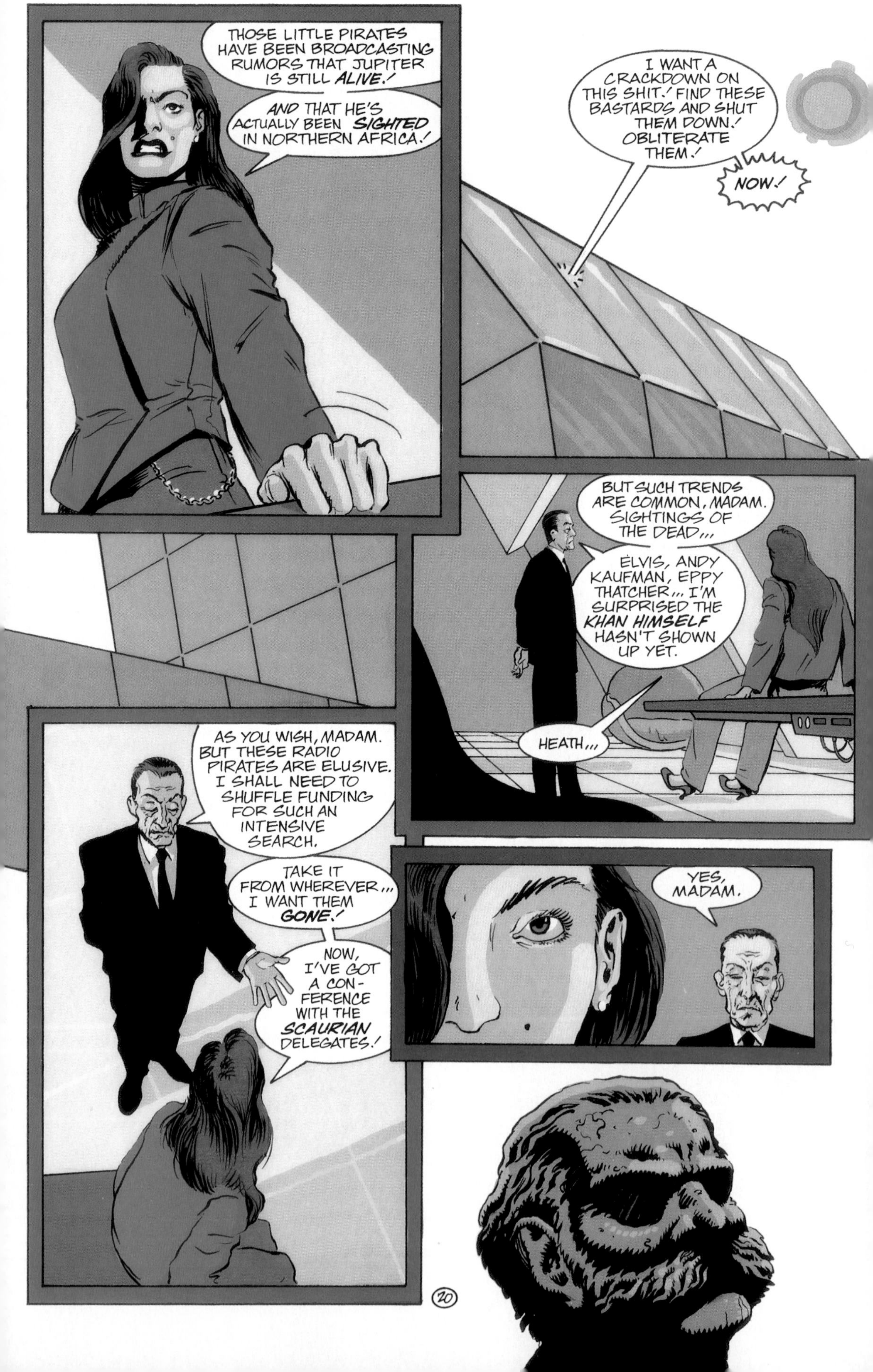

THOSE LITTLE PIRATES HAVE BEEN BROADCASTING RUMORS THAT JUPITER IS STILL ALIVE!
AND THAT HE'S ACTUALLY BEEN SIGHTED IN NORTHERN AFRICA!
I WANT A CRACKDOWN ON THIS SHIT! FIND THESE BASTARDS AND SHUT THEM DOWN! OBLITERATE THEM!
NOW!
BUT SUCH TRENDS ARE COMMON, MADAM. SIGHTINGS OF THE DEAD...
ELVIS, ANDY KAUFMAN, EPPY THATCHER... I'M SURPRISED THE KHAN HIMSELF HASN'T SHOWN UP YET.
HEATH...
AS YOU WISH, MADAM. BUT THESE RADIO PIRATES ARE ELUSIVE. I SHALL NEED TO SHUFFLE FUNDING FOR SUCH AN INTENSIVE SEARCH.
TAKE IT FROM WHEREVER... I WANT THEM GONE!
NOW, I'VE GOT A CON-FERENCE WITH THE SCAURIAN DELEGATES!
YES, MADAM.

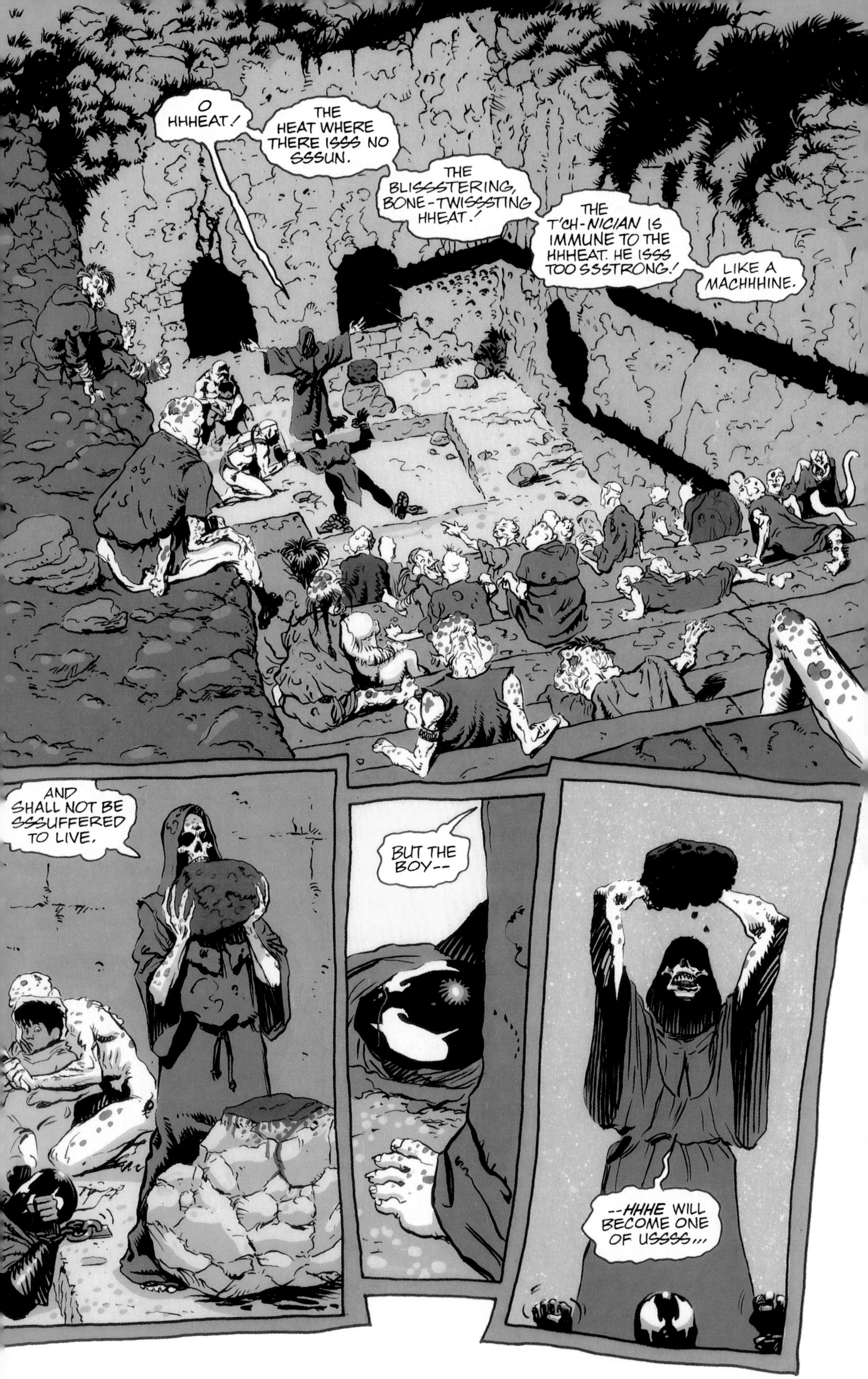
O HHHEAT!
THE HEAT WHERE THERE ISSS NO SSSUN.
THE BLISSSTERING, BONE-TWISSSTING HHEAT!
THE T'CH-NICIAN IS IMMUNE TO THE HHHEAT. HE ISSS TOO SSSTRONG!
LIKE A MACHHHINE.
AND SHALL NOT BE SSSUFFERED TO LIVE.
BUT THE BOY--
--HHHE WILL BECOME ONE OF USSSS...

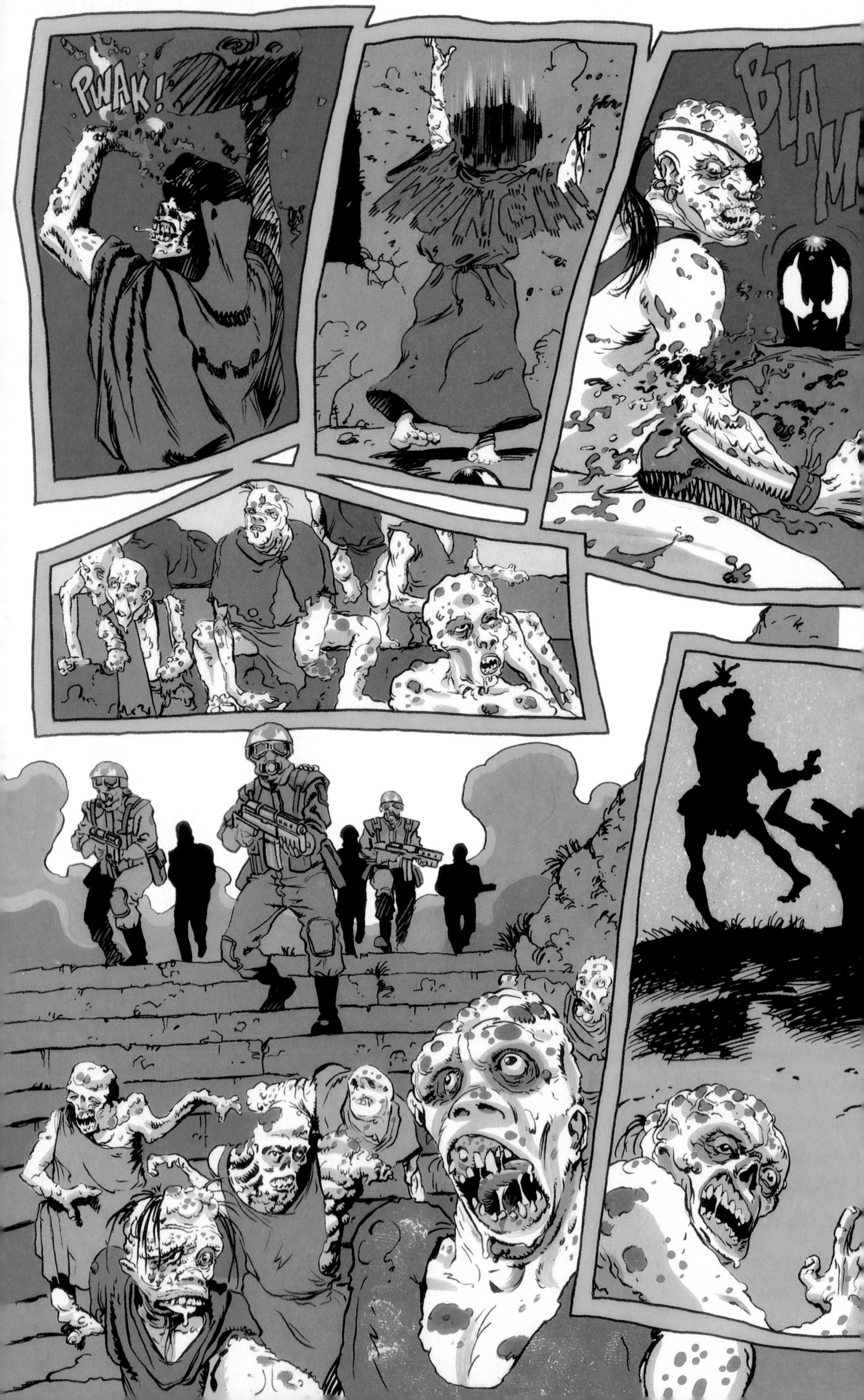

PWAK!
WUNGH!
BLAM

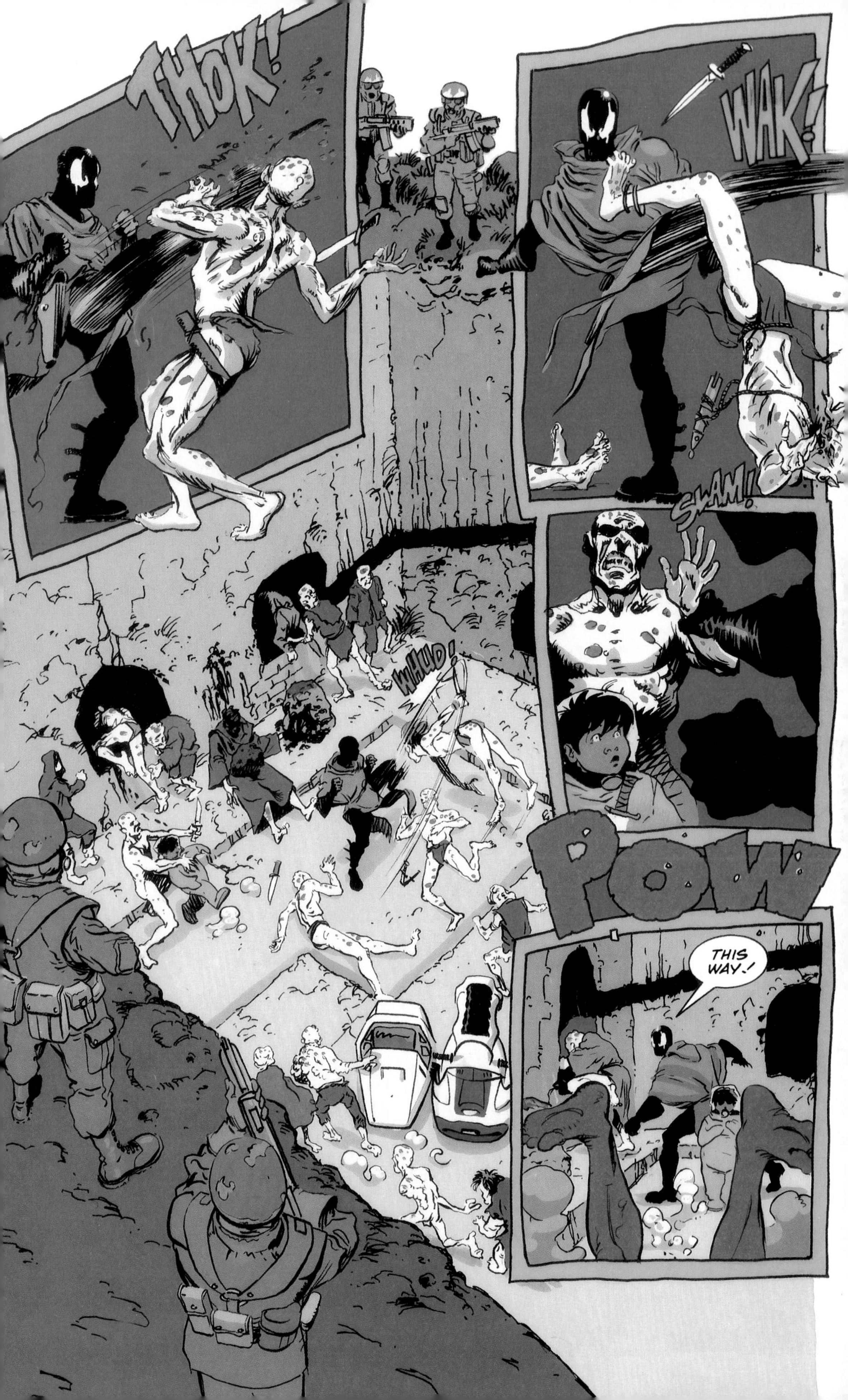
THOK!
WAK!
SLAM!
WHUD!
POW!
THIS WAY.!

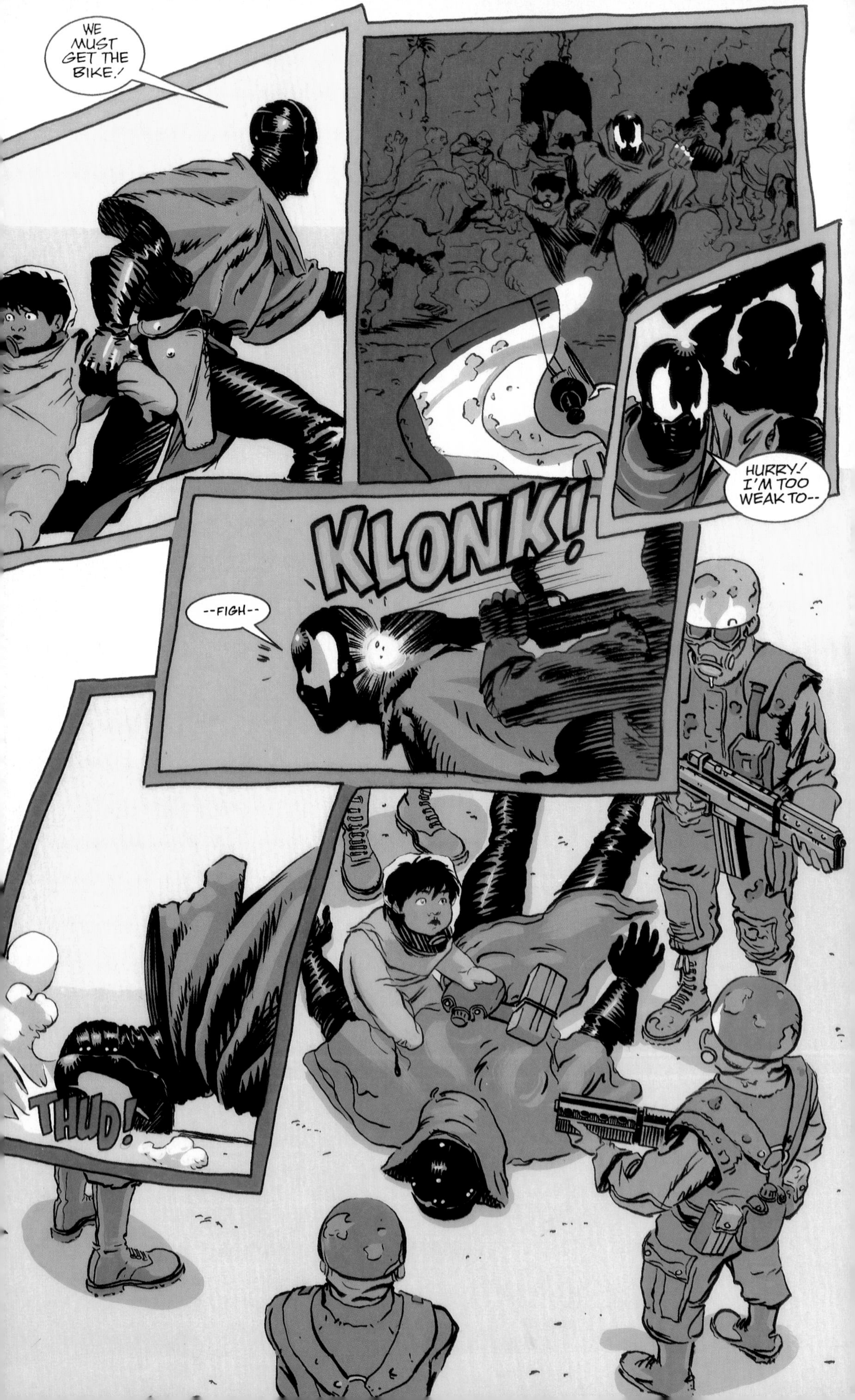
WE MUST GET THE BIKE.!
HURRY.! I'M TOO WEAK TO--
KLONK!
--FIGH--
THUD!

# CHAPTER 7
# DEVIL *in chains*

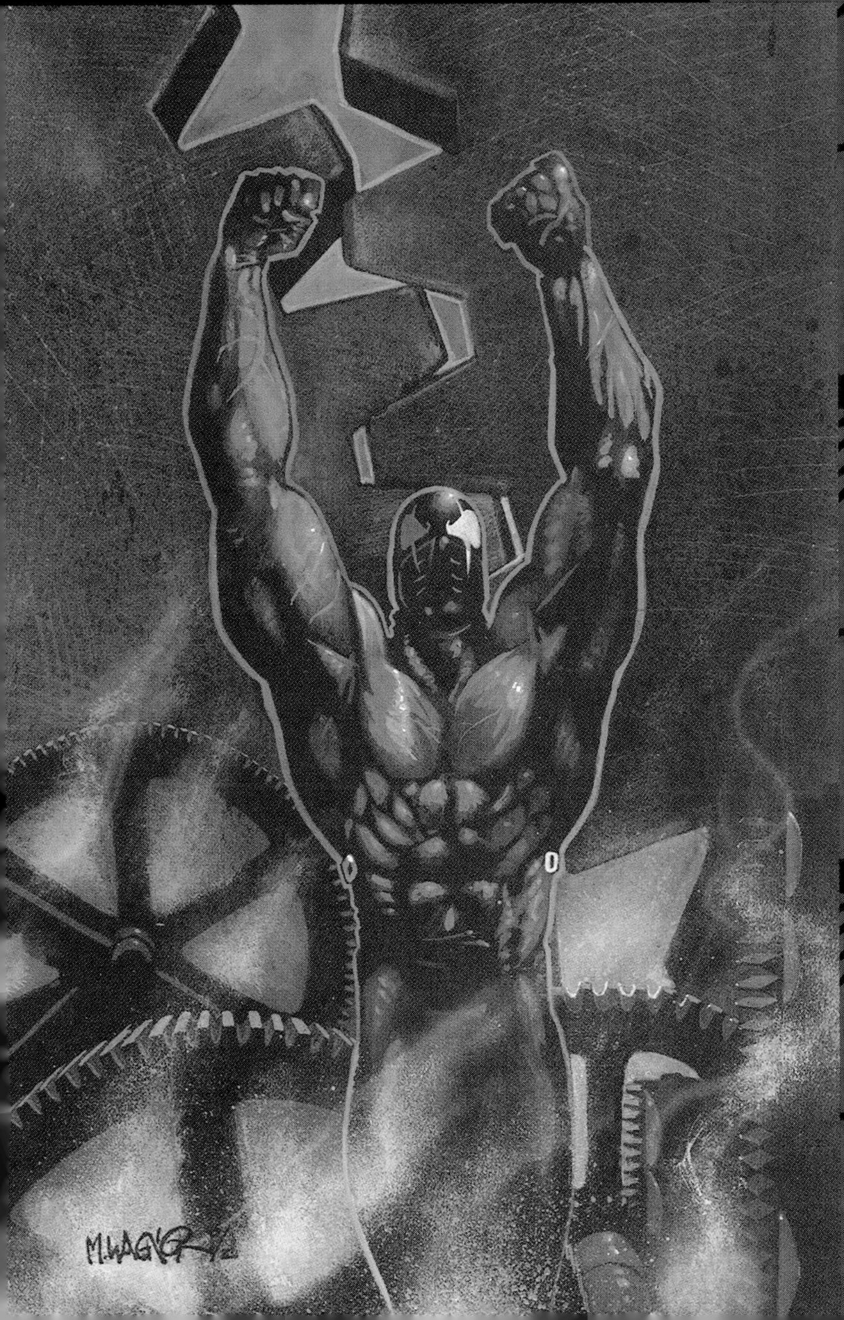

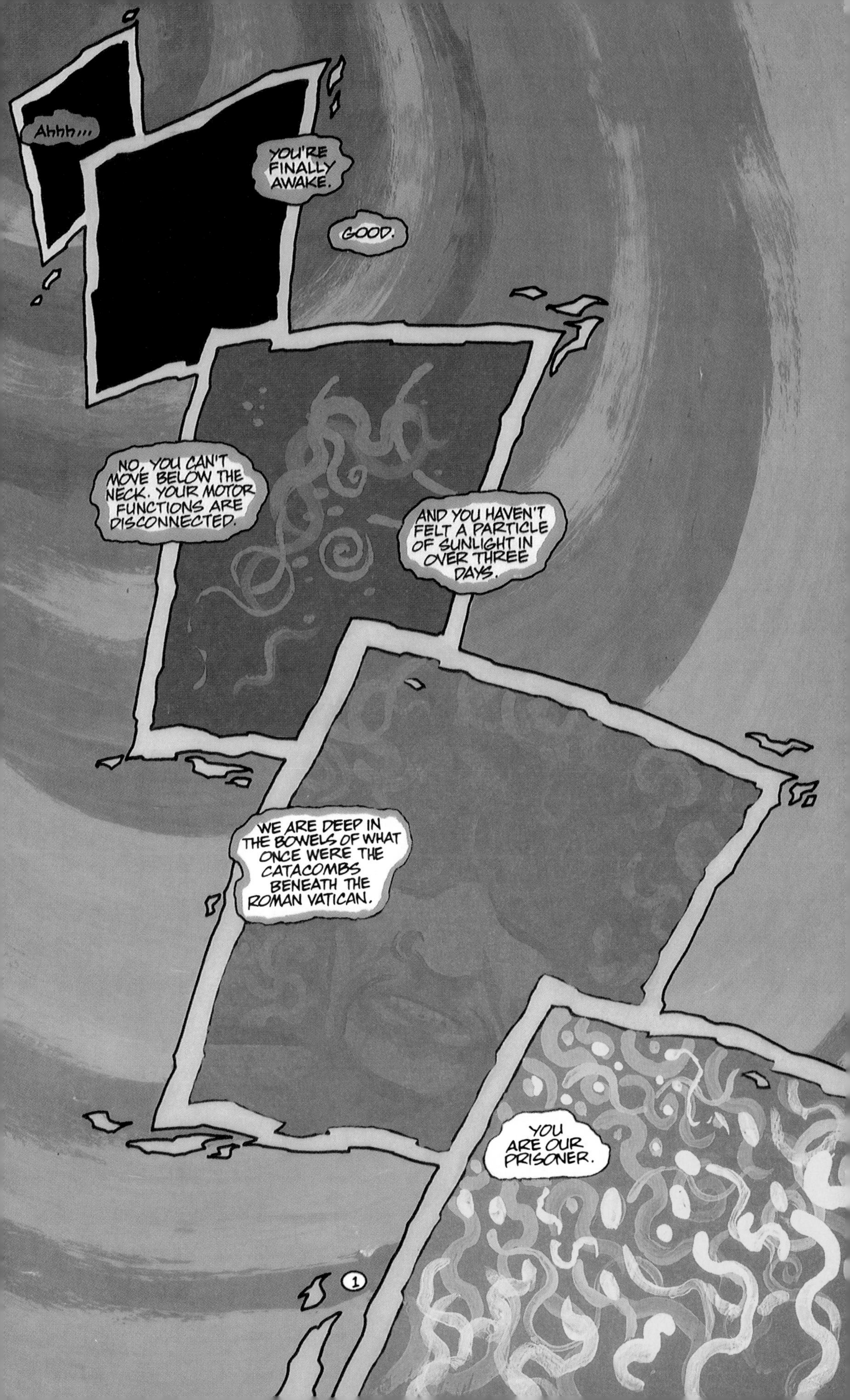
Ahhh...
YOU'RE FINALLY AWAKE.
GOOD.
NO, YOU CAN'T MOVE BELOW THE NECK. YOUR MOTOR FUNCTIONS ARE DISCONNECTED.
AND YOU HAVEN'T FELT A PARTICLE OF SUNLIGHT IN OVER THREE DAYS.
WE ARE DEEP IN THE BOWELS OF WHAT ONCE WERE THE CATACOMBS BENEATH THE ROMAN VATICAN.
YOU ARE OUR PRISONER.
1

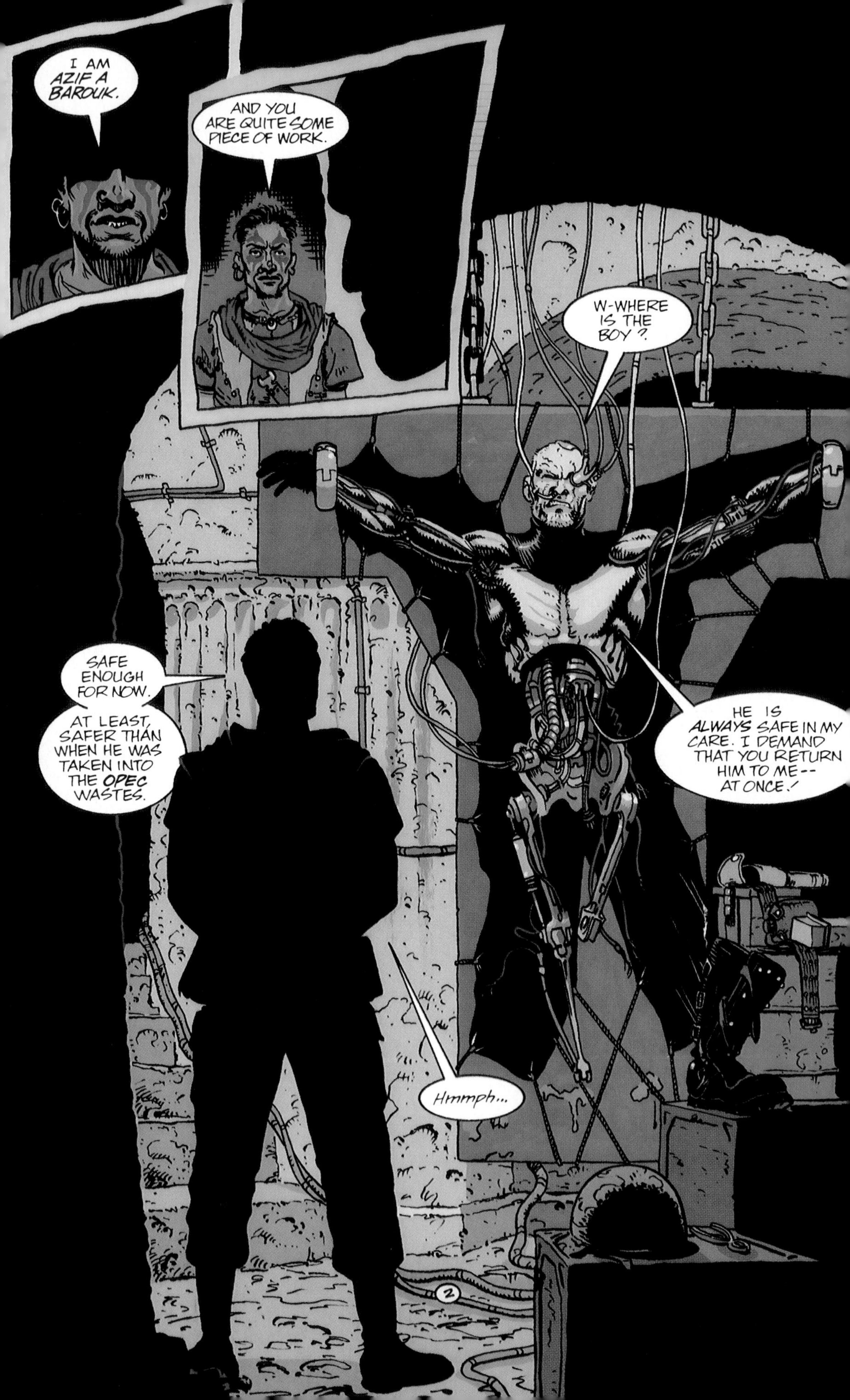
I AM AZIF A BAROUK.
AND YOU ARE QUITE SOME PIECE OF WORK.
W-WHERE IS THE BOY ?
SAFE ENOUGH FOR NOW.
AT LEAST, SAFER THAN WHEN HE WAS TAKEN INTO THE OPEC WASTES.
HE IS ALWAYS SAFE IN MY CARE. I DEMAND THAT YOU RETURN HIM TO ME-- AT ONCE!
Hmmph...
2

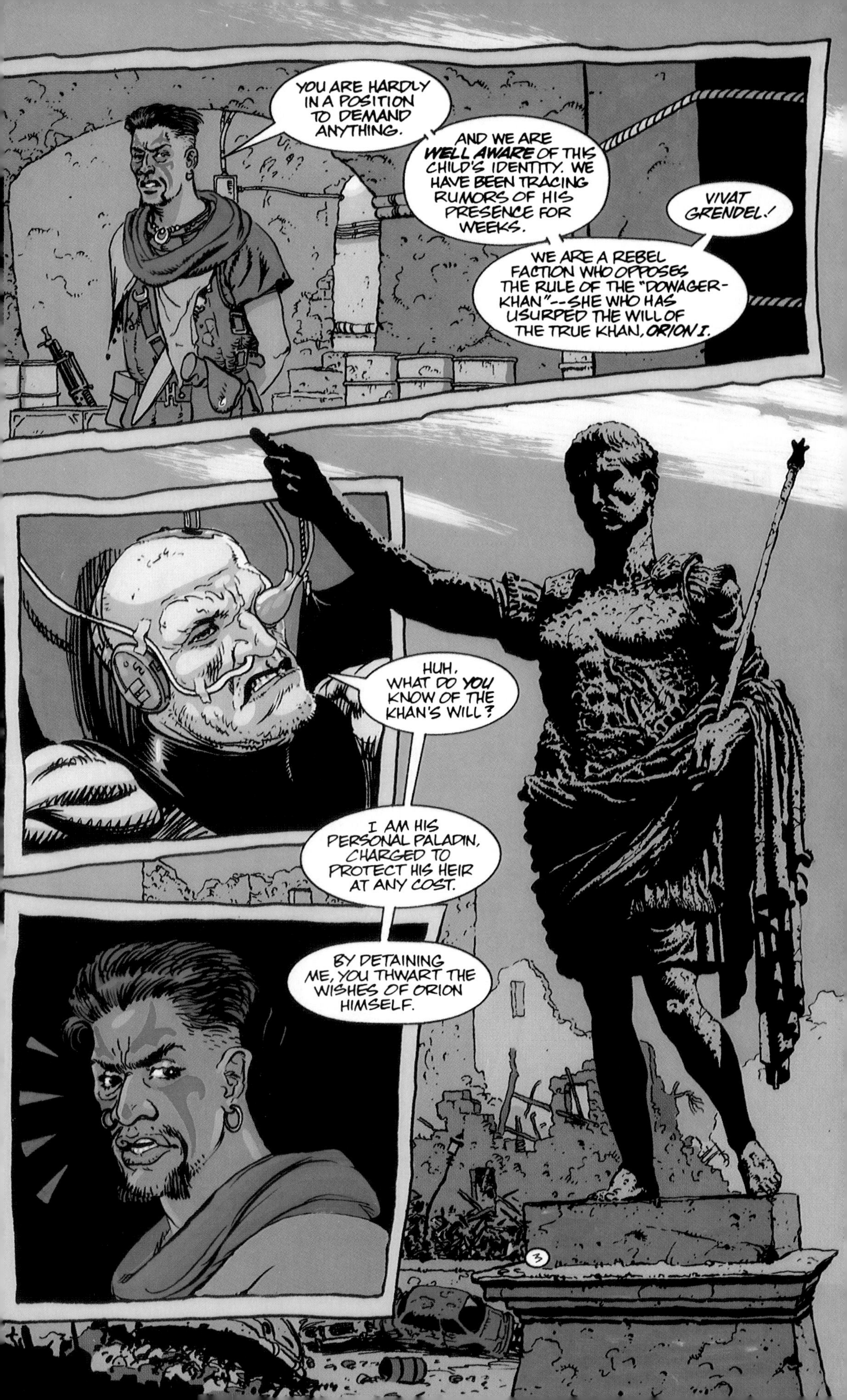
YOU ARE HARDLY IN A POSITION TO DEMAND ANYTHING.
AND WE ARE WELL AWARE OF THIS CHILD'S IDENTITY. WE HAVE BEEN TRACING RUMORS OF HIS PRESENCE FOR WEEKS.
VIVAT GRENDEL!
WE ARE A REBEL FACTION WHO OPPOSES THE RULE OF THE "DOWAGER-KHAN"--SHE WHO HAS USURPED THE WILL OF THE TRUE KHAN, ORION I.
HUH, WHAT DO YOU KNOW OF THE KHAN'S WILL?
I AM HIS PERSONAL PALADIN, CHARGED TO PROTECT HIS HEIR AT ANY COST.
BY DETAINING ME, YOU THWART THE WISHES OF ORION HIMSELF.
3

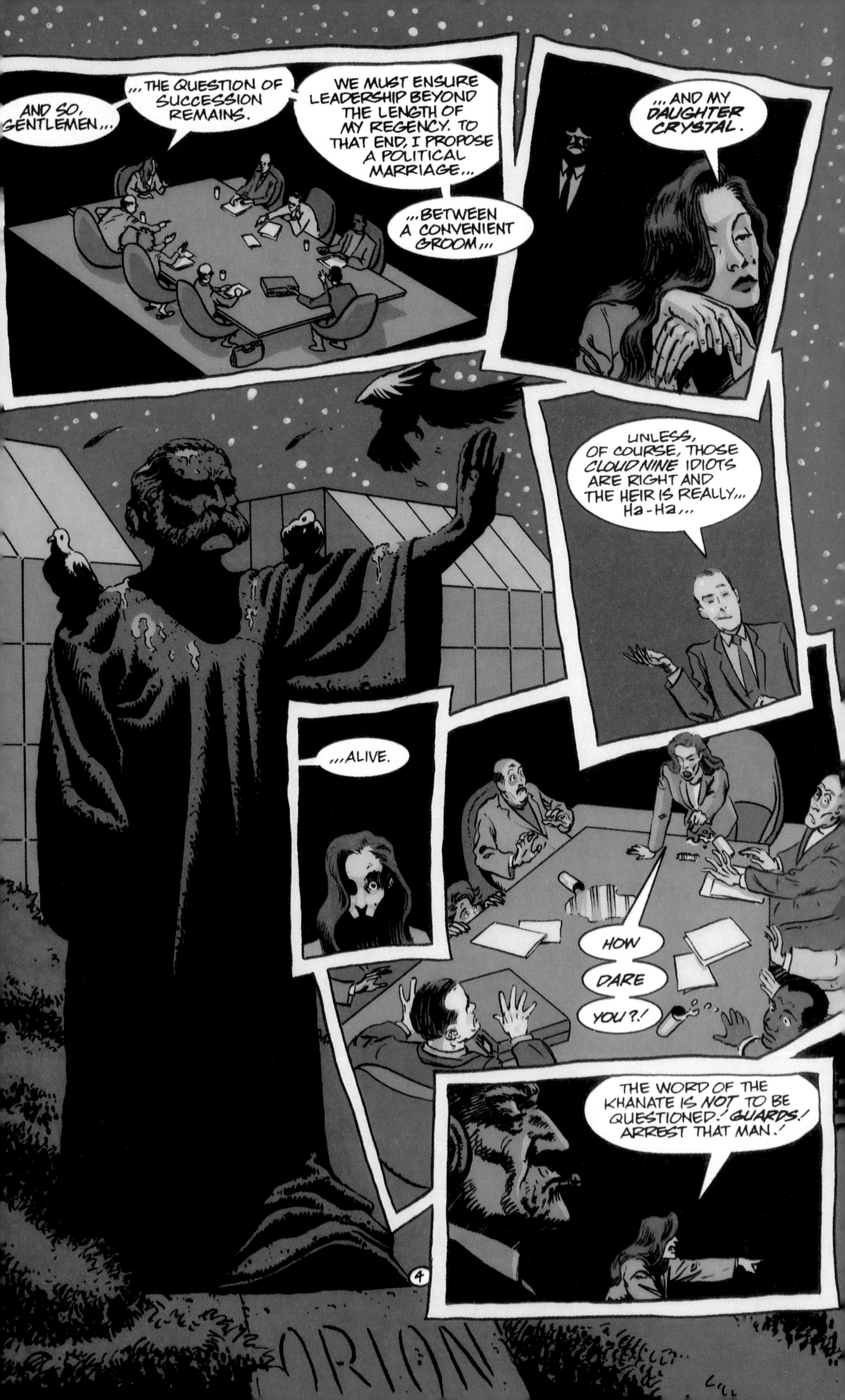
AND SO, GENTLEMEN...
...THE QUESTION OF SUCCESSION REMAINS.
WE MUST ENSURE LEADERSHIP BEYOND THE LENGTH OF MY REGENCY. TO THAT END, I PROPOSE A POLITICAL MARRIAGE...
...BETWEEN A CONVENIENT GROOM...
...AND MY DAUGHTER CRYSTAL.
UNLESS, OF COURSE, THOSE CLOUD NINE IDIOTS ARE RIGHT AND THE HEIR IS REALLY... Ha-Ha...
...ALIVE.
HOW
DARE
YOU?!
THE WORD OF THE KHANATE IS NOT TO BE QUESTIONED! GUARDS! ARREST THAT MAN!
4
ORION

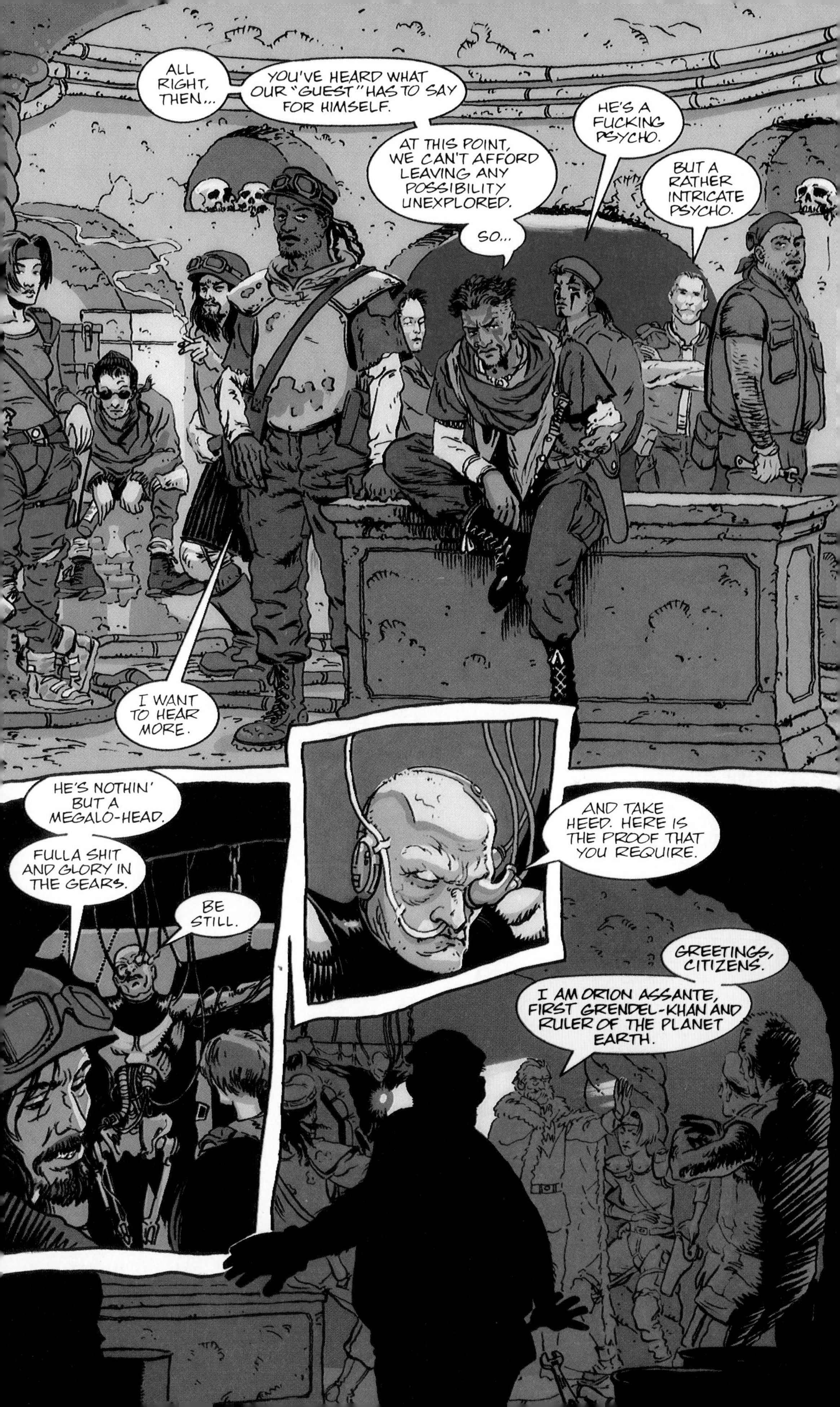
ALL RIGHT, THEN...
YOU'VE HEARD WHAT OUR "GUEST" HAS TO SAY FOR HIMSELF.
AT THIS POINT, WE CAN'T AFFORD LEAVING ANY POSSIBILITY UNEXPLORED.
SO...
HE'S A FUCKING PSYCHO.
BUT A RATHER INTRICATE PSYCHO.
I WANT TO HEAR MORE.
HE'S NOTHIN' BUT A MEGALO-HEAD.
FULLA SHIT AND GLORY IN THE GEARS.
BE STILL.
AND TAKE HEED. HERE IS THE PROOF THAT YOU REQUIRE.
GREETINGS, CITIZENS.
I AM ORION ASSANTE, FIRST GRENDEL-KHAN AND RULER OF THE PLANET EARTH.

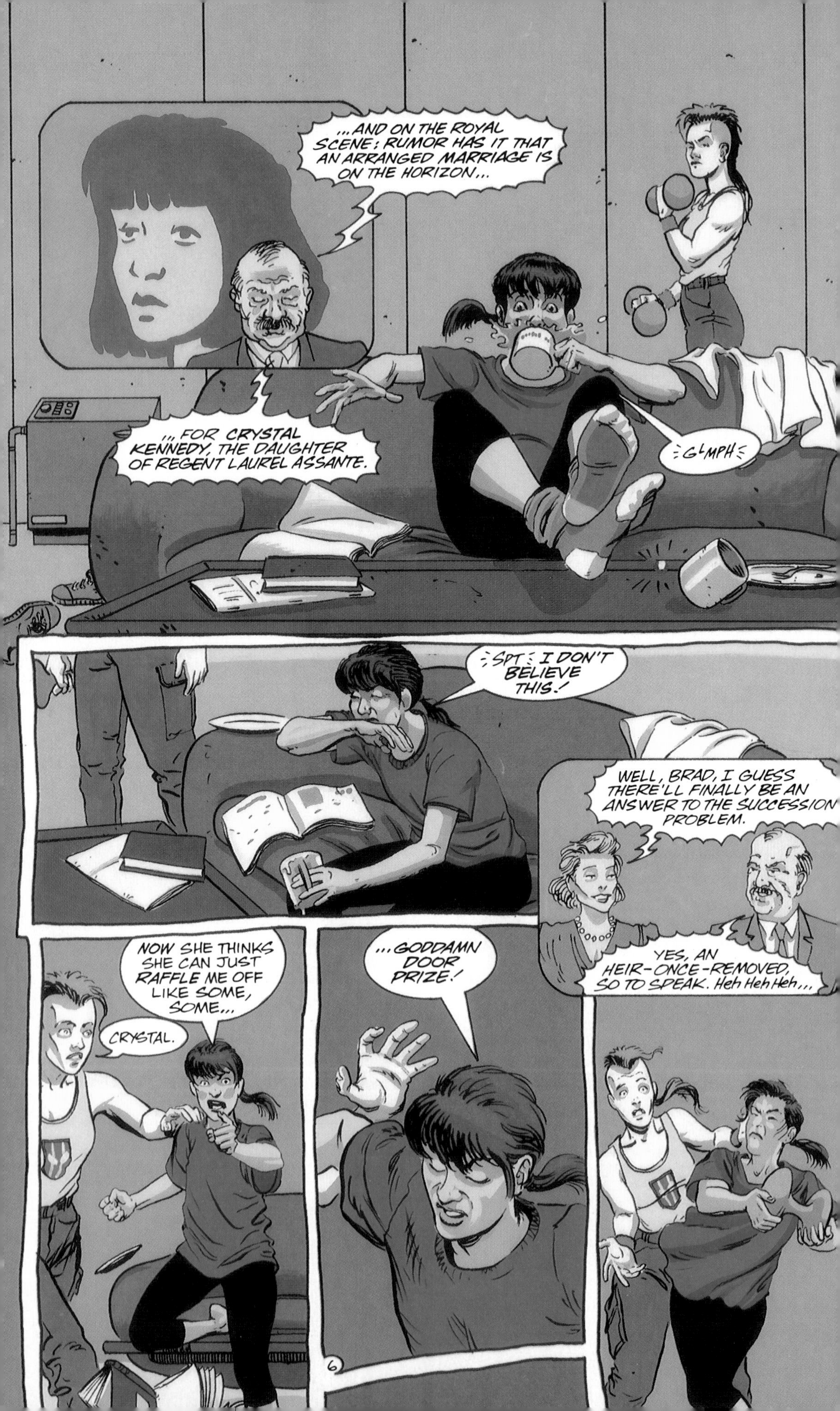
...AND ON THE ROYAL SCENE: RUMOR HAS IT THAT AN ARRANGED MARRIAGE IS ON THE HORIZON...
...FOR CRYSTAL KENNEDY, THE DAUGHTER OF REGENT LAUREL ASSANTE.
GLMPH
SPT I DON'T BELIEVE THIS!
WELL, BRAD, I GUESS THERE'LL FINALLY BE AN ANSWER TO THE SUCCESSION PROBLEM.
YES, AN HEIR-ONCE-REMOVED, SO TO SPEAK. Heh Heh Heh...
NOW SHE THINKS SHE CAN JUST RAFFLE ME OFF LIKE SOME, SOME...
CRYSTAL.
...GODDAMN DOOR PRIZE!

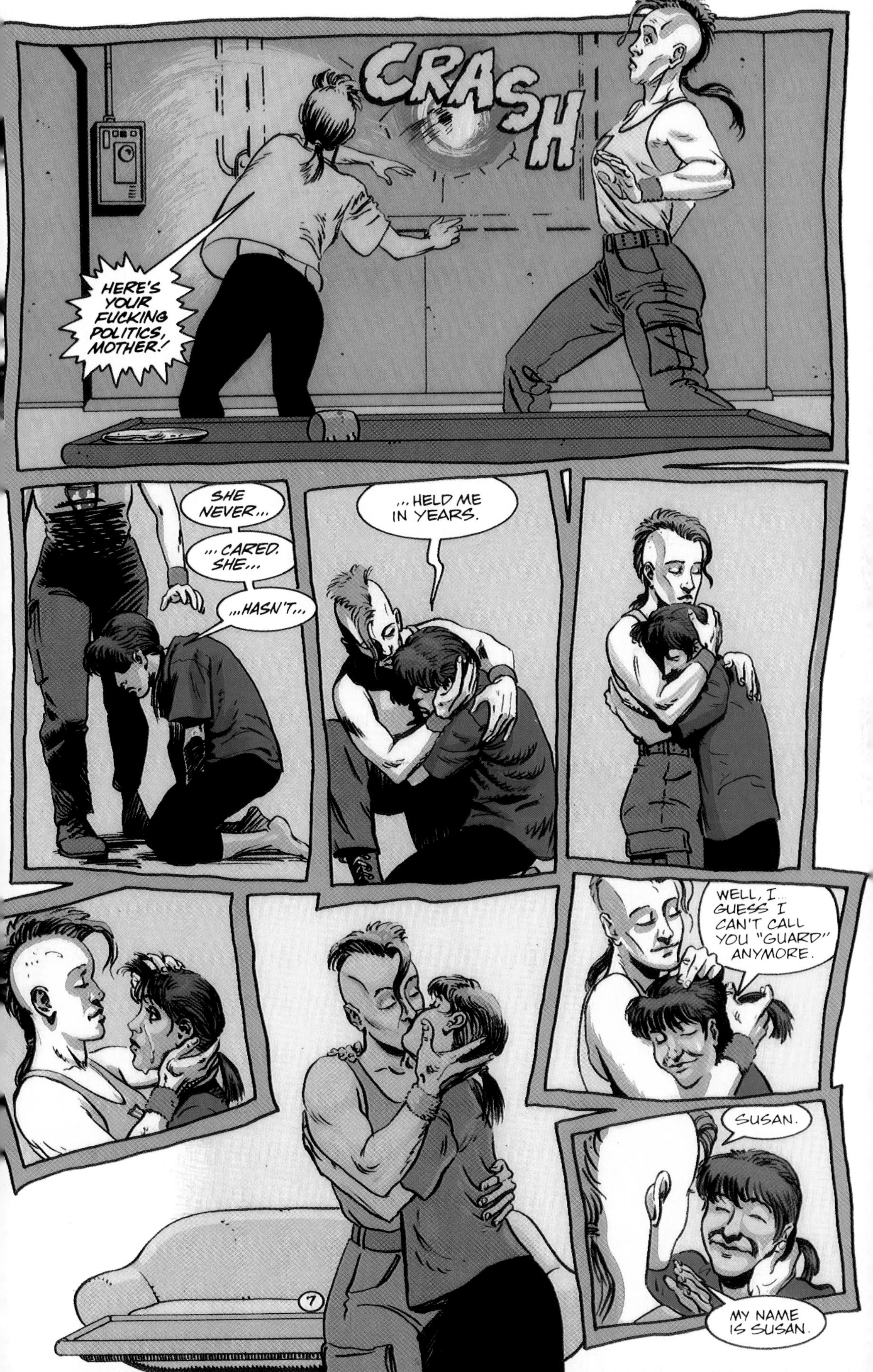
CRASH
HERE'S YOUR FUCKING POLITICS, MOTHER!
SHE NEVER...
...CARED. SHE...
...HASN'T...
...HELD ME IN YEARS.
WELL, I... GUESS I CAN'T CALL YOU "GUARD" ANYMORE.
SUSAN.
MY NAME IS SUSAN.

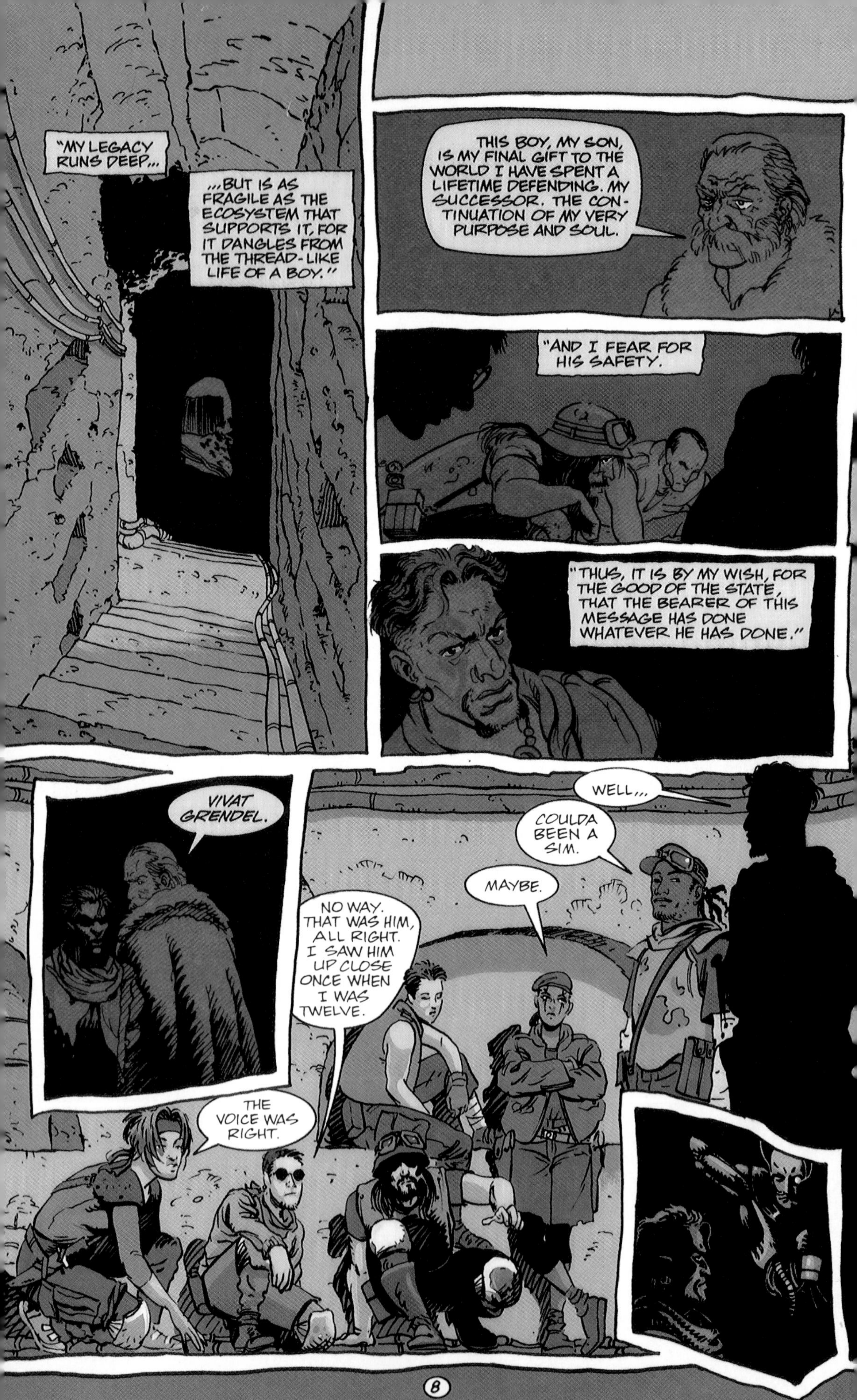
"MY LEGACY RUNS DEEP...
...BUT IS AS FRAGILE AS THE ECOSYSTEM THAT SUPPORTS IT, FOR IT DANGLES FROM THE THREAD-LIKE LIFE OF A BOY."
THIS BOY, MY SON, IS MY FINAL GIFT TO THE WORLD I HAVE SPENT A LIFETIME DEFENDING. MY SUCCESSOR. THE CONTINUATION OF MY VERY PURPOSE AND SOUL.
"AND I FEAR FOR HIS SAFETY.
"THUS, IT IS BY MY WISH, FOR THE GOOD OF THE STATE, THAT THE BEARER OF THIS MESSAGE HAS DONE WHATEVER HE HAS DONE."
VIVAT GRENDEL.
WELL...
COULDA BEEN A SIM.
MAYBE.
NO WAY. THAT WAS HIM, ALL RIGHT. I SAW HIM UP CLOSE ONCE WHEN I WAS TWELVE.
THE VOICE WAS RIGHT.

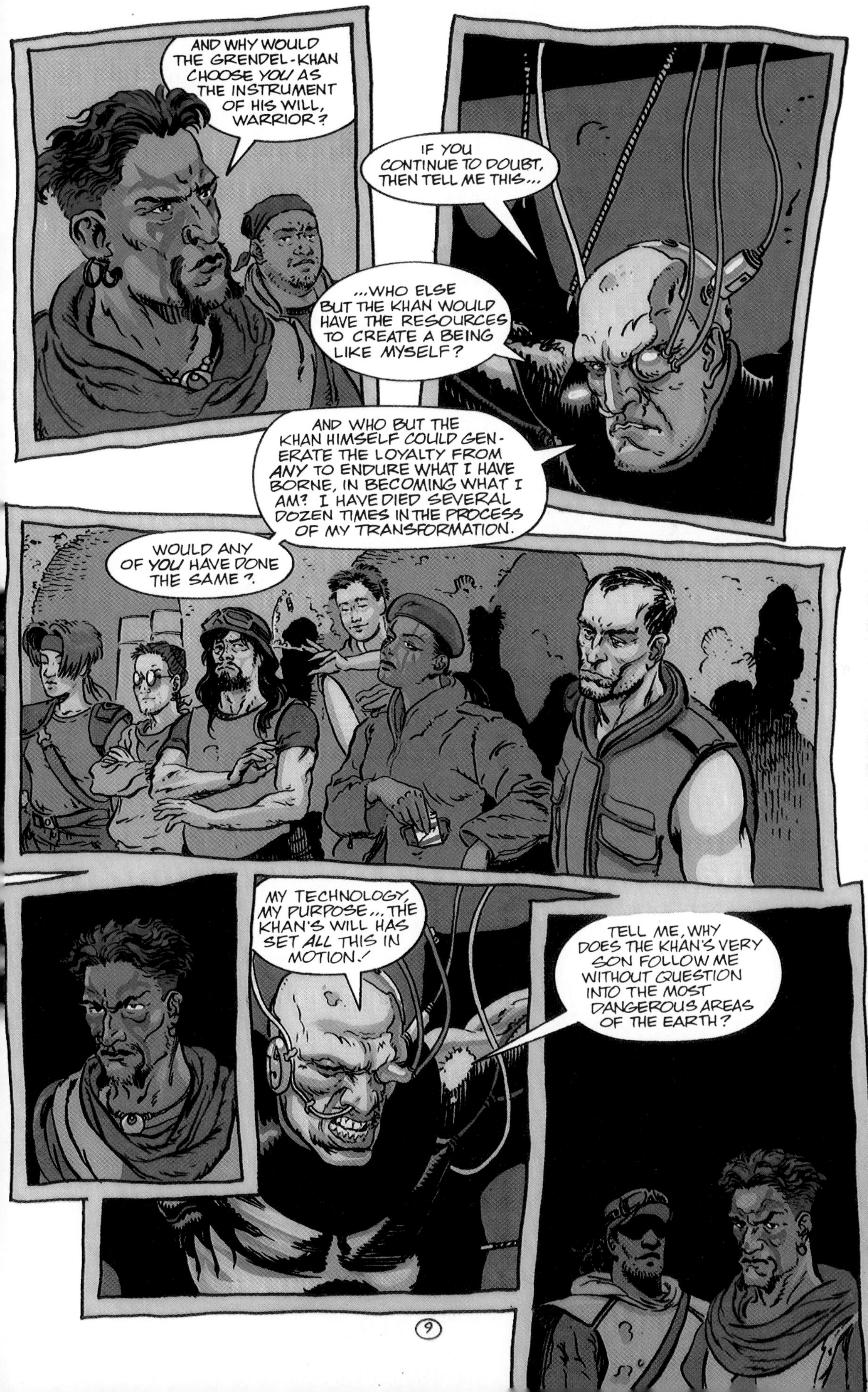
AND WHY WOULD THE GRENDEL-KHAN CHOOSE YOU AS THE INSTRUMENT OF HIS WILL, WARRIOR?
IF YOU CONTINUE TO DOUBT, THEN TELL ME THIS...
...WHO ELSE BUT THE KHAN WOULD HAVE THE RESOURCES TO CREATE A BEING LIKE MYSELF?
AND WHO BUT THE KHAN HIMSELF COULD GENERATE THE LOYALTY FROM ANY TO ENDURE WHAT I HAVE BORNE, IN BECOMING WHAT I AM? I HAVE DIED SEVERAL DOZEN TIMES IN THE PROCESS OF MY TRANSFORMATION.
WOULD ANY OF YOU HAVE DONE THE SAME?
MY TECHNOLOGY, MY PURPOSE... THE KHAN'S WILL HAS SET ALL THIS IN MOTION!
TELL ME, WHY DOES THE KHAN'S VERY SON FOLLOW ME WITHOUT QUESTION INTO THE MOST DANGEROUS AREAS OF THE EARTH?

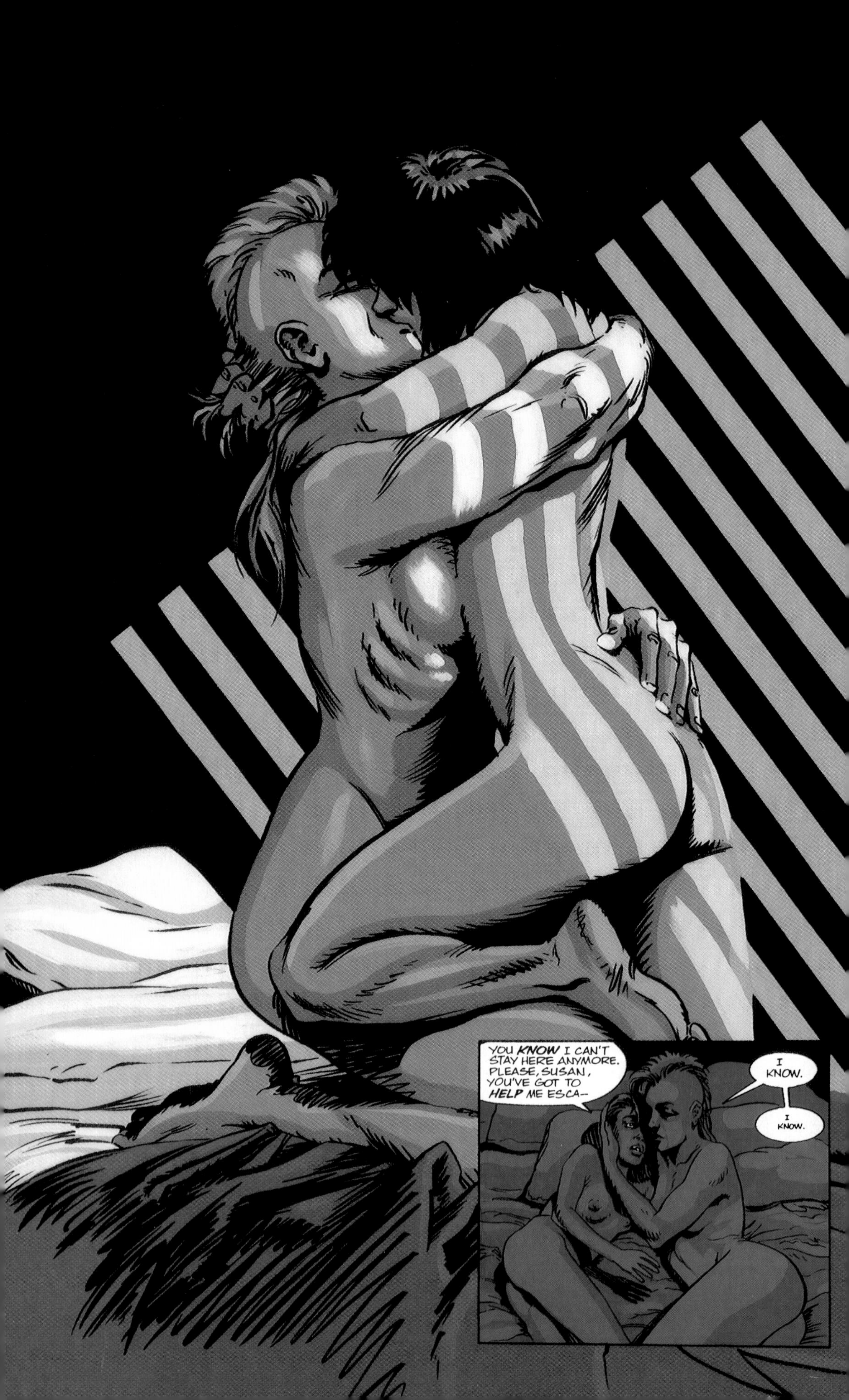

YOU KNOW I CAN'T STAY HERE ANYMORE. PLEASE, SUSAN, YOU'VE GOT TO HELP ME ESCA–
I KNOW.
I KNOW.

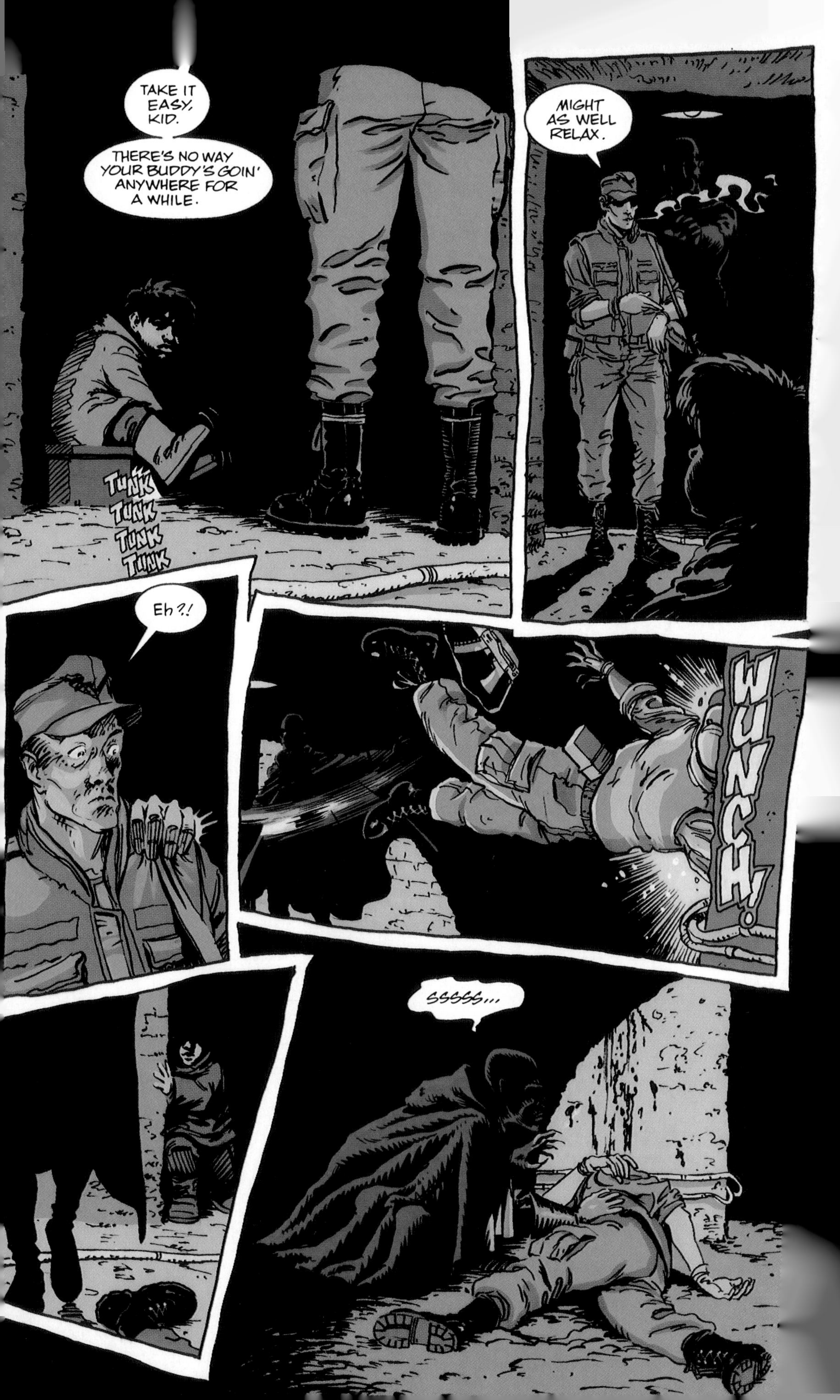
TAKE IT EASY, KID.
THERE'S NO WAY YOUR BUDDY'S GOIN' ANYWHERE FOR A WHILE.
TUNK TUNK TUNK TUNK
MIGHT AS WELL RELAX.
Eh?!
WUNCH!
SSSSS...

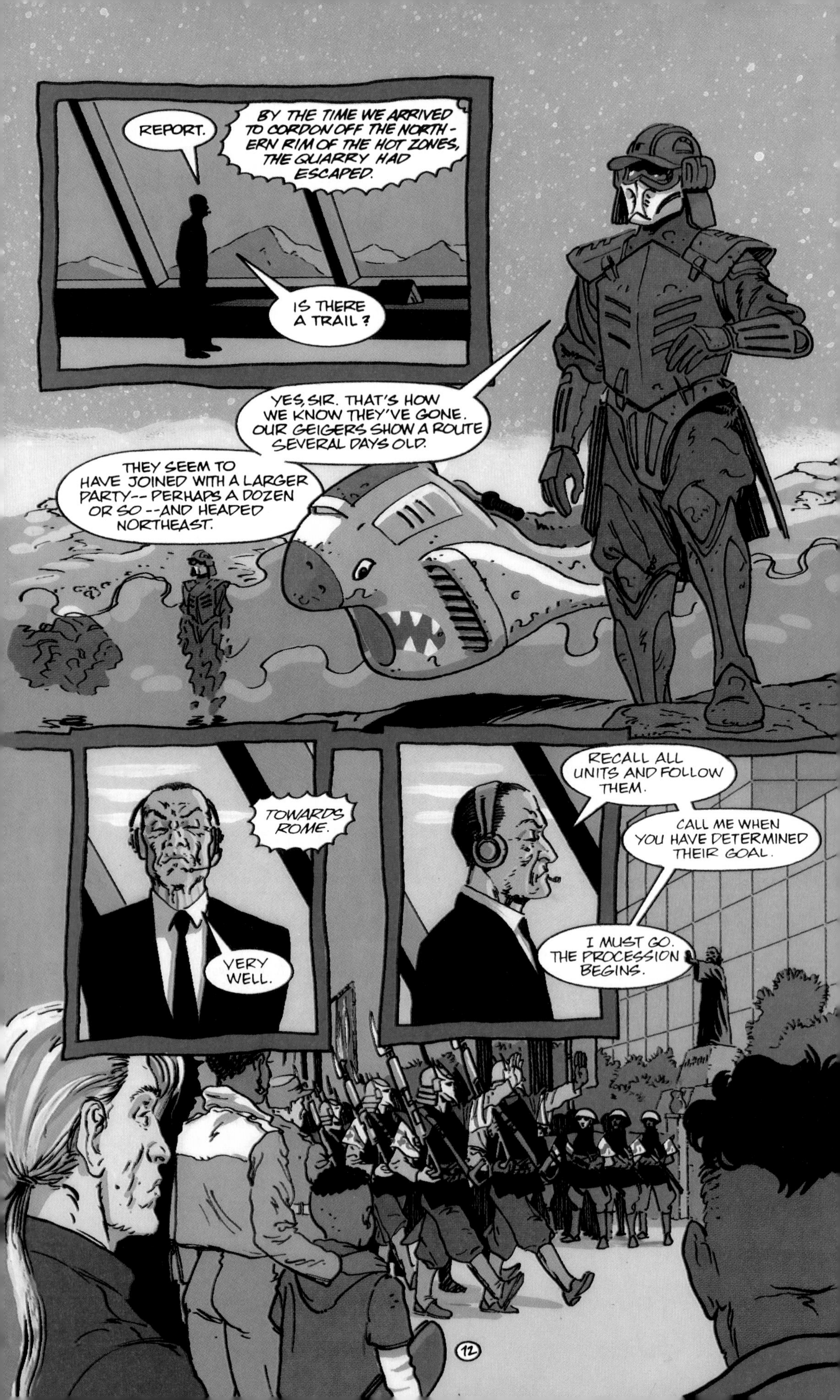
REPORT.
BY THE TIME WE ARRIVED TO CORDON OFF THE NORTH-ERN RIM OF THE HOT ZONES, THE QUARRY HAD ESCAPED.
IS THERE A TRAIL?
YES, SIR. THAT'S HOW WE KNOW THEY'VE GONE. OUR GEIGERS SHOW A ROUTE SEVERAL DAYS OLD.
THEY SEEM TO HAVE JOINED WITH A LARGER PARTY-- PERHAPS A DOZEN OR SO --AND HEADED NORTHEAST.
TOWARDS ROME.
VERY WELL.
RECALL ALL UNITS AND FOLLOW THEM.
CALL ME WHEN YOU HAVE DETERMINED THEIR GOAL.
I MUST GO. THE PROCESSION BEGINS.

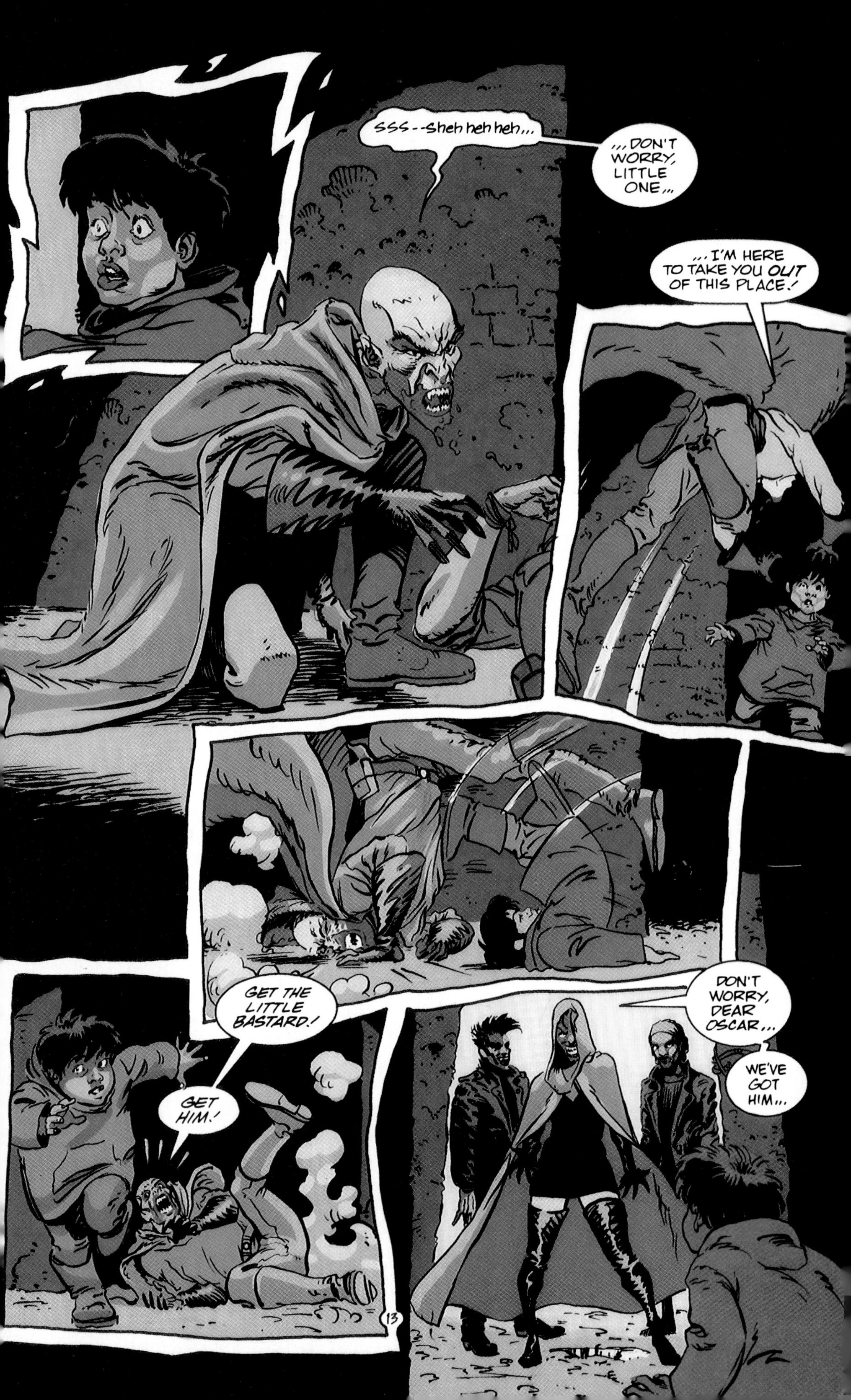
SSS--sheh heh heh...
...DON'T WORRY, LITTLE ONE...
...I'M HERE TO TAKE YOU OUT OF THIS PLACE.!
GET THE LITTLE BASTARD.!
GET HIM.!
DON'T WORRY, DEAR OSCAR...
WE'VE GOT HIM...
13

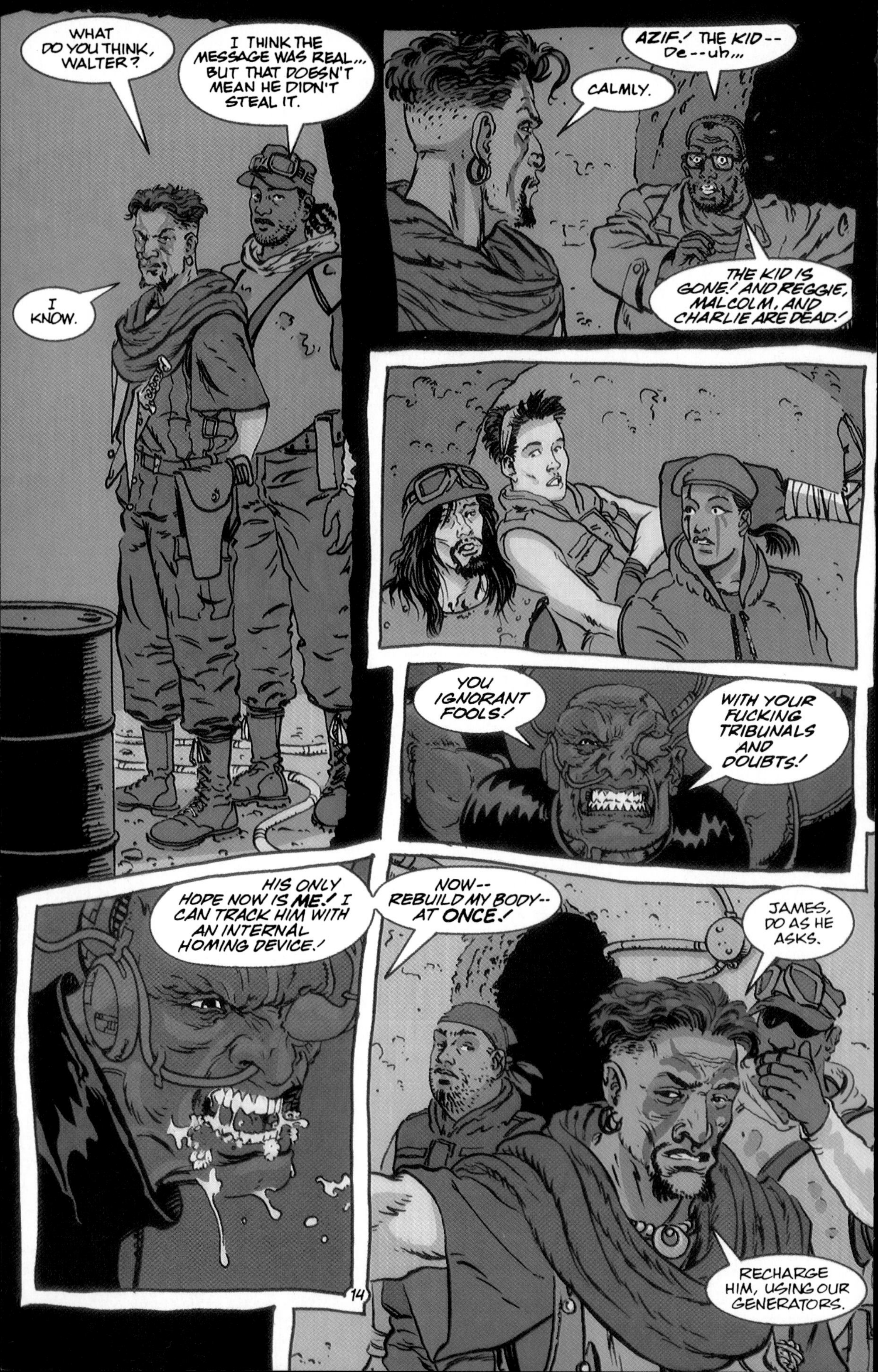
WHAT DO YOU THINK, WALTER?
I THINK THE MESSAGE WAS REAL... BUT THAT DOESN'T MEAN HE DIDN'T STEAL IT.
I KNOW.
CALMLY.
AZIF! THE KID-- De--uh...
THE KID IS GONE! AND REGGIE, MALCOLM, AND CHARLIE ARE DEAD!
YOU IGNORANT FOOLS!
WITH YOUR FUCKING TRIBUNALS AND DOUBTS!
HIS ONLY HOPE NOW IS ME! I CAN TRACK HIM WITH AN INTERNAL HOMING DEVICE!
NOW-- REBUILD MY BODY-- AT ONCE!
JAMES, DO AS HE ASKS.
RECHARGE HIM, USING OUR GENERATORS.

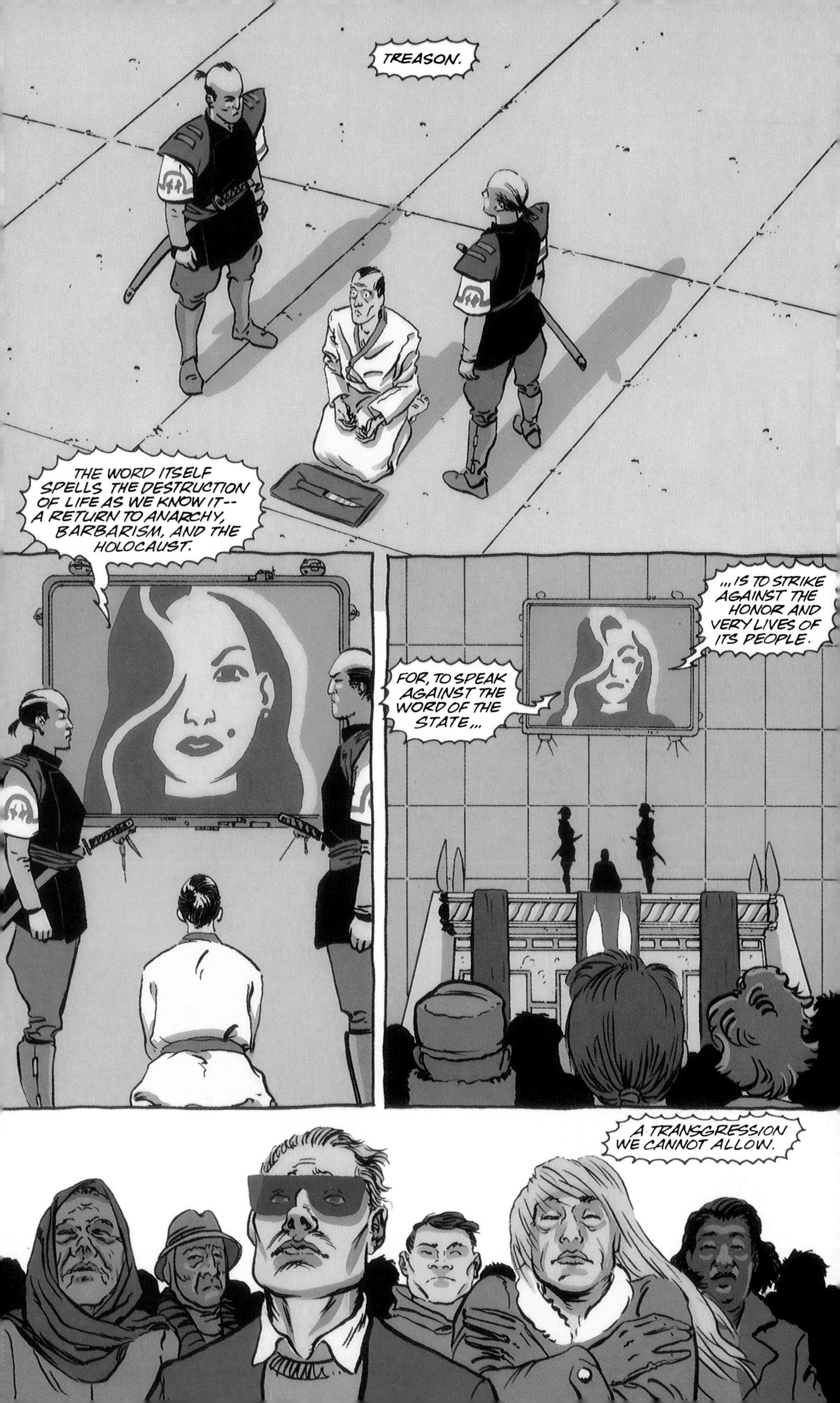
TREASON.
THE WORD ITSELF SPELLS THE DESTRUCTION OF LIFE AS WE KNOW IT-- A RETURN TO ANARCHY, BARBARISM, AND THE HOLOCAUST.
FOR, TO SPEAK AGAINST THE WORD OF THE STATE,...
...IS TO STRIKE AGAINST THE HONOR AND VERY LIVES OF ITS PEOPLE.
A TRANSGRESSION WE CANNOT ALLOW.

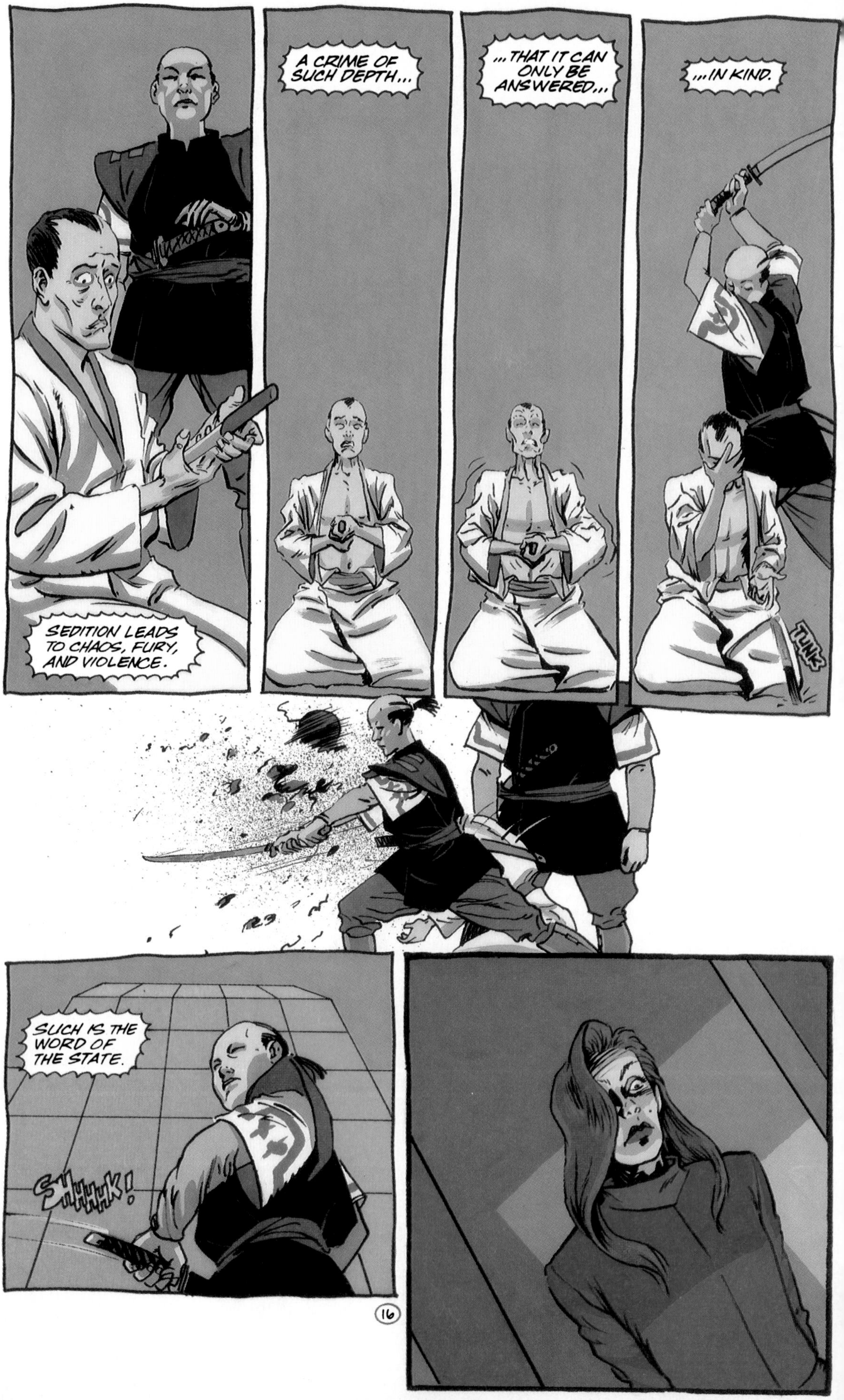
SEDITION LEADS TO CHAOS, FURY, AND VIOLENCE.
A CRIME OF SUCH DEPTH...
...THAT IT CAN ONLY BE ANSWERED...
...IN KIND.
TUNK
SUCH IS THE WORD OF THE STATE.
SHHUK!

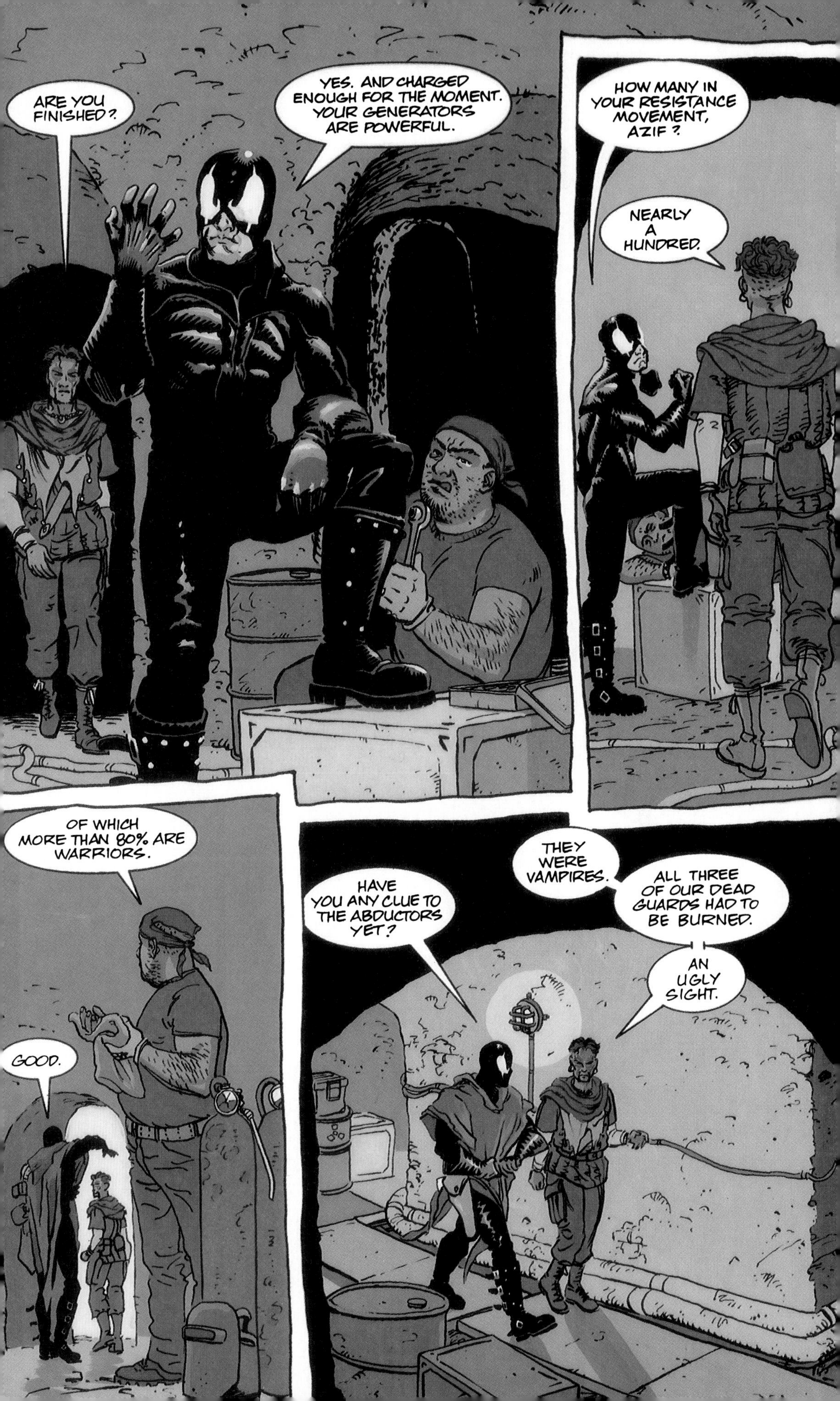
ARE YOU FINISHED?
YES. AND CHARGED ENOUGH FOR THE MOMENT. YOUR GENERATORS ARE POWERFUL.
HOW MANY IN YOUR RESISTANCE MOVEMENT, AZIF?
NEARLY A HUNDRED.
OF WHICH MORE THAN 80% ARE WARRIORS.
GOOD.
HAVE YOU ANY CLUE TO THE ABDUCTORS YET?
THEY WERE VAMPIRES.
ALL THREE OF OUR DEAD GUARDS HAD TO BE BURNED.
AN UGLY SIGHT.

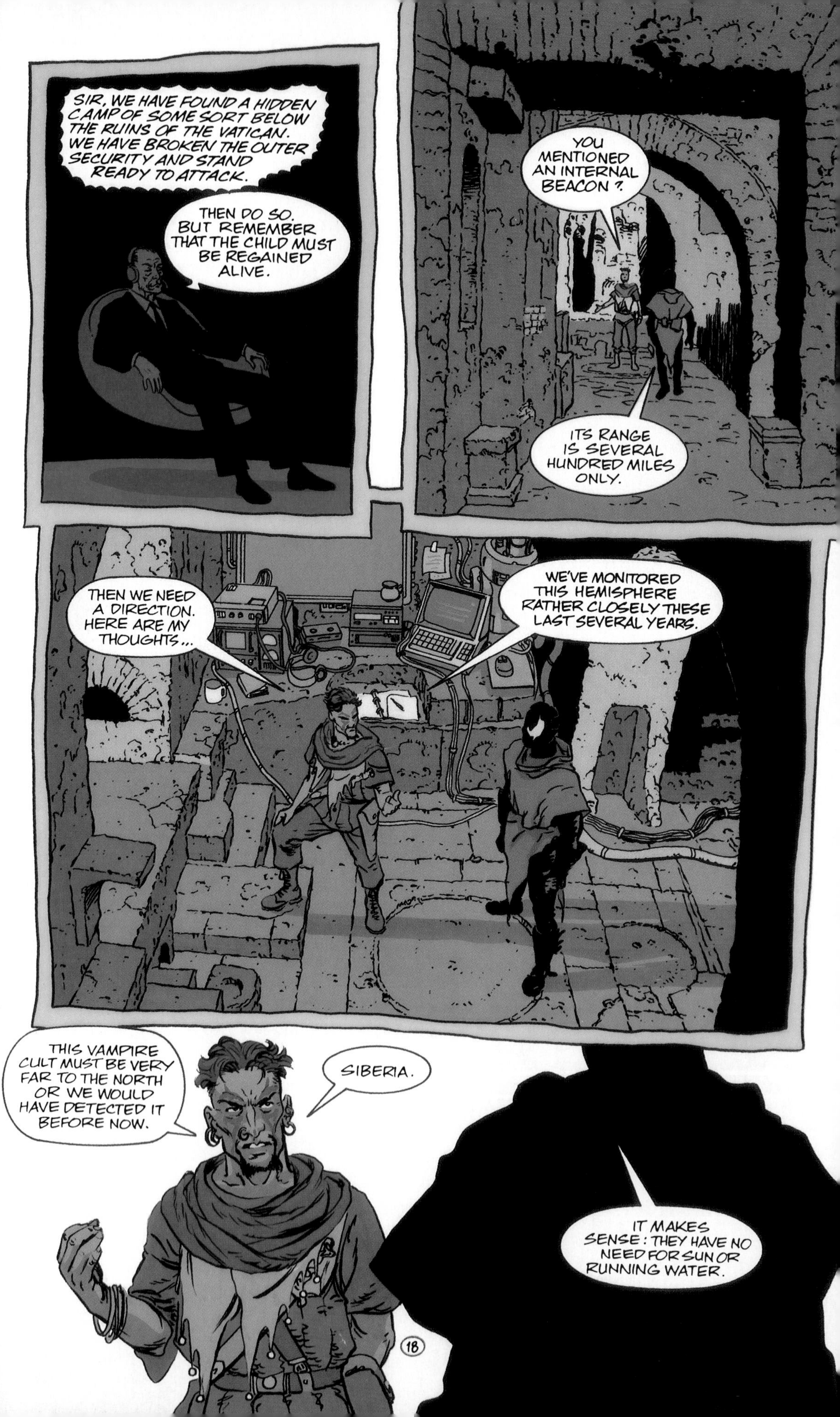

SIR, WE HAVE FOUND A HIDDEN CAMP OF SOME SORT BELOW THE RUINS OF THE VATICAN. WE HAVE BROKEN THE OUTER SECURITY AND STAND READY TO ATTACK.
THEN DO SO. BUT REMEMBER THAT THE CHILD MUST BE REGAINED ALIVE.
YOU MENTIONED AN INTERNAL BEACON ?
ITS RANGE IS SEVERAL HUNDRED MILES ONLY.
THEN WE NEED A DIRECTION. HERE ARE MY THOUGHTS...
WE'VE MONITORED THIS HEMISPHERE RATHER CLOSELY THESE LAST SEVERAL YEARS.
THIS VAMPIRE CULT MUST BE VERY FAR TO THE NORTH OR WE WOULD HAVE DETECTED IT BEFORE NOW.
SIBERIA.
IT MAKES SENSE: THEY HAVE NO NEED FOR SUN OR RUNNING WATER.
18

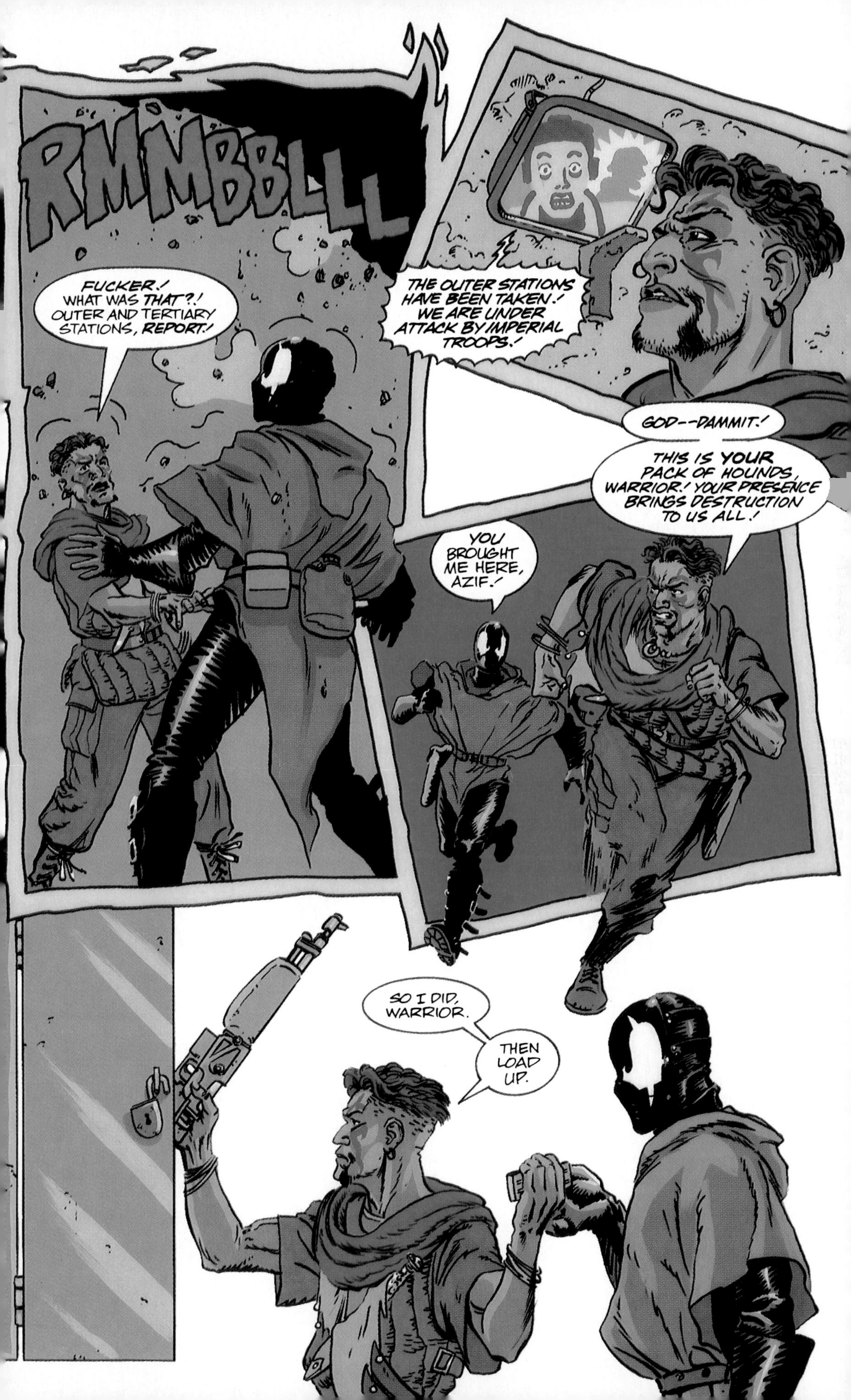
RMMBBLLL
FUCKER! WHAT WAS THAT?! OUTER AND TERTIARY STATIONS, REPORT!
THE OUTER STATIONS HAVE BEEN TAKEN! WE ARE UNDER ATTACK BY IMPERIAL TROOPS!
GOD--DAMMIT!
THIS IS YOUR PACK OF HOUNDS, WARRIOR! YOUR PRESENCE BRINGS DESTRUCTION TO US ALL!
YOU BROUGHT ME HERE, AZIF!
SO I DID, WARRIOR.
THEN LOAD UP.

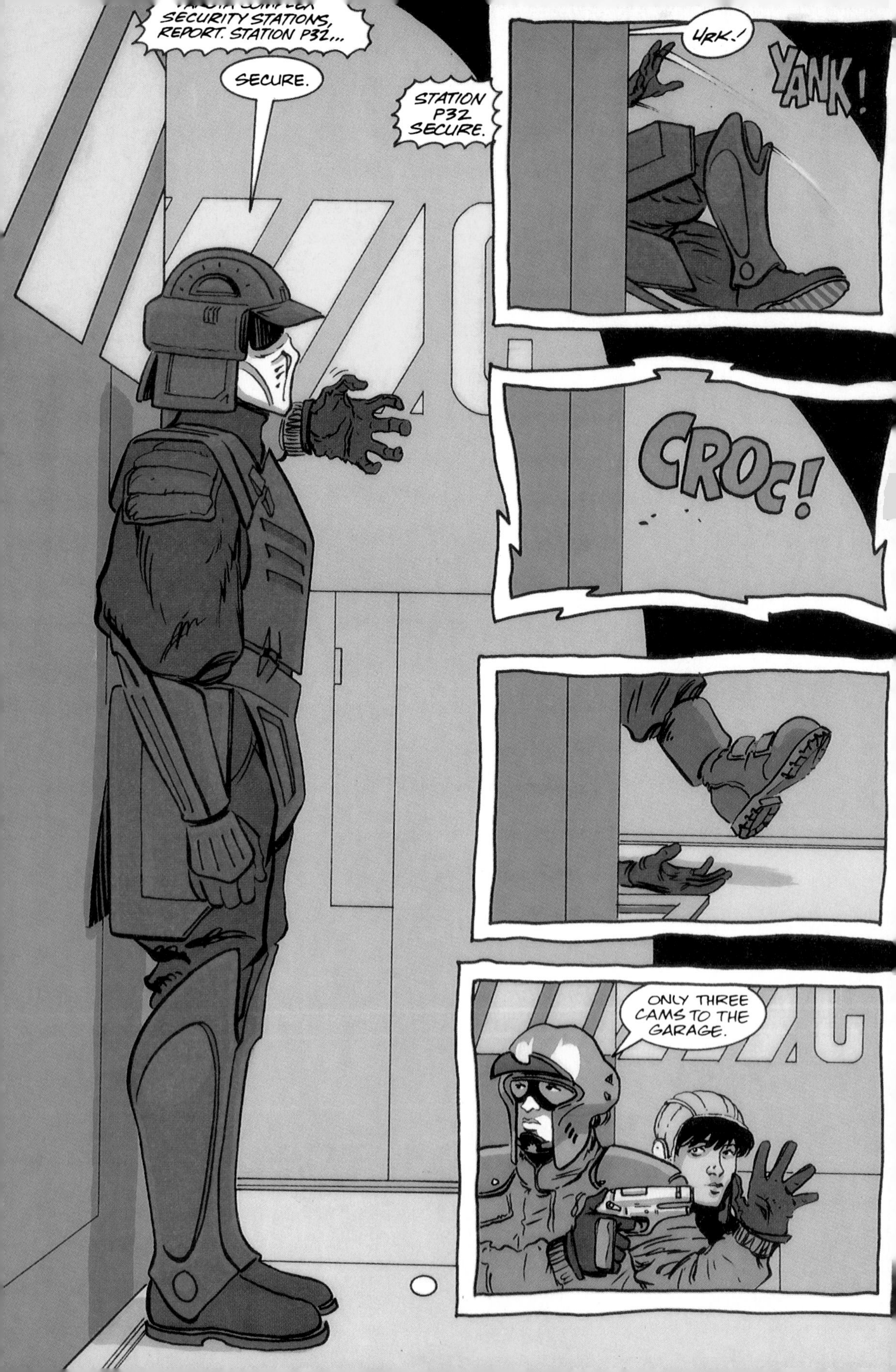
SECURITY STATIONS, REPORT. STATION P32...
SECURE.
STATION P32 SECURE.
URK!
YANK!
CROC!
ONLY THREE CAMS TO THE GARAGE.

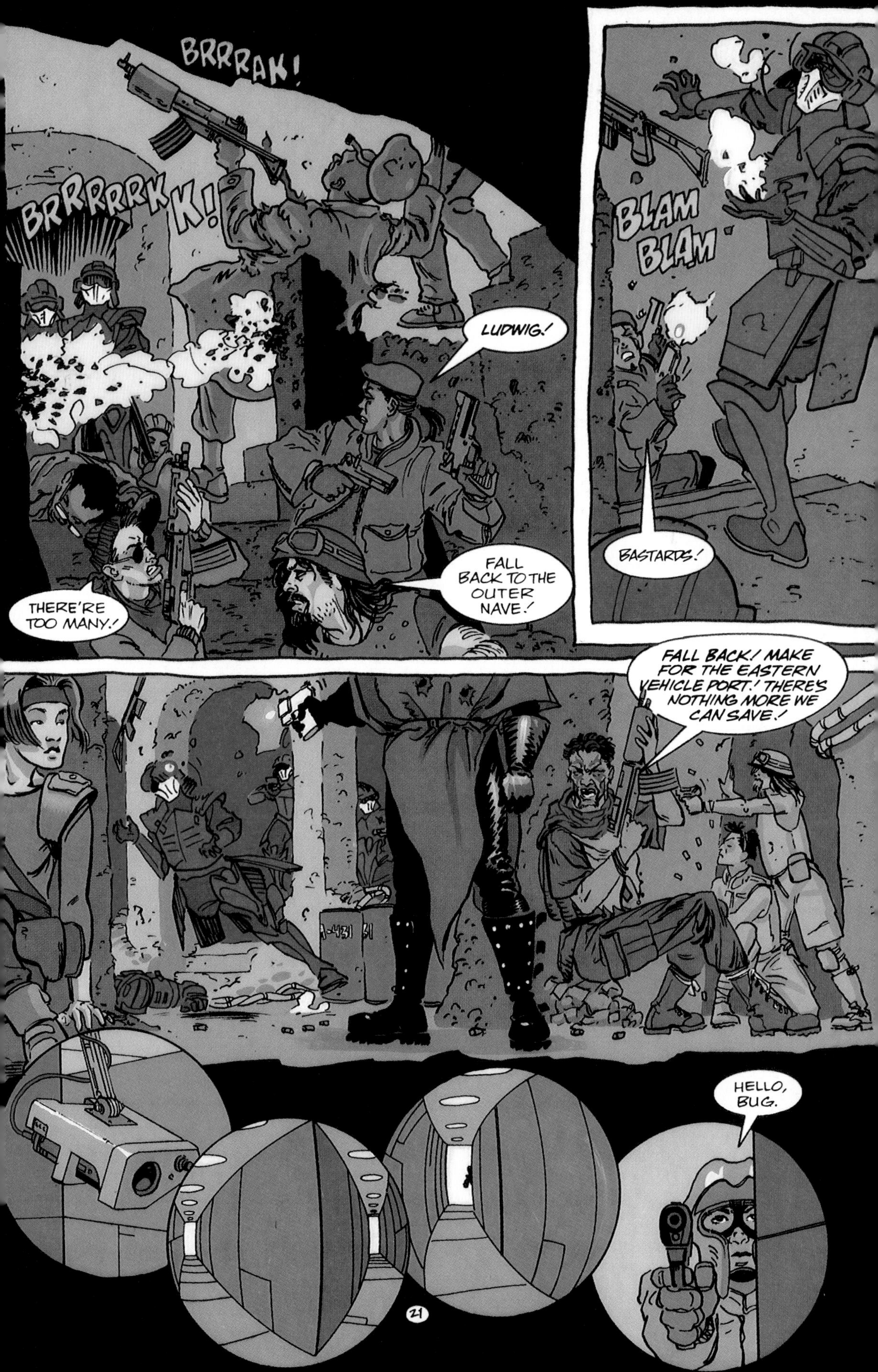
BRRRAK!
BRRRRRK K!
LUDWIG!
THERE'RE TOO MANY!
FALL BACK TO THE OUTER NAVE!
BLAM BLAM
BASTARDS!
FALL BACK! MAKE FOR THE EASTERN VEHICLE PORT! THERE'S NOTHING MORE WE CAN SAVE!
A-431
HELLO, BUG.

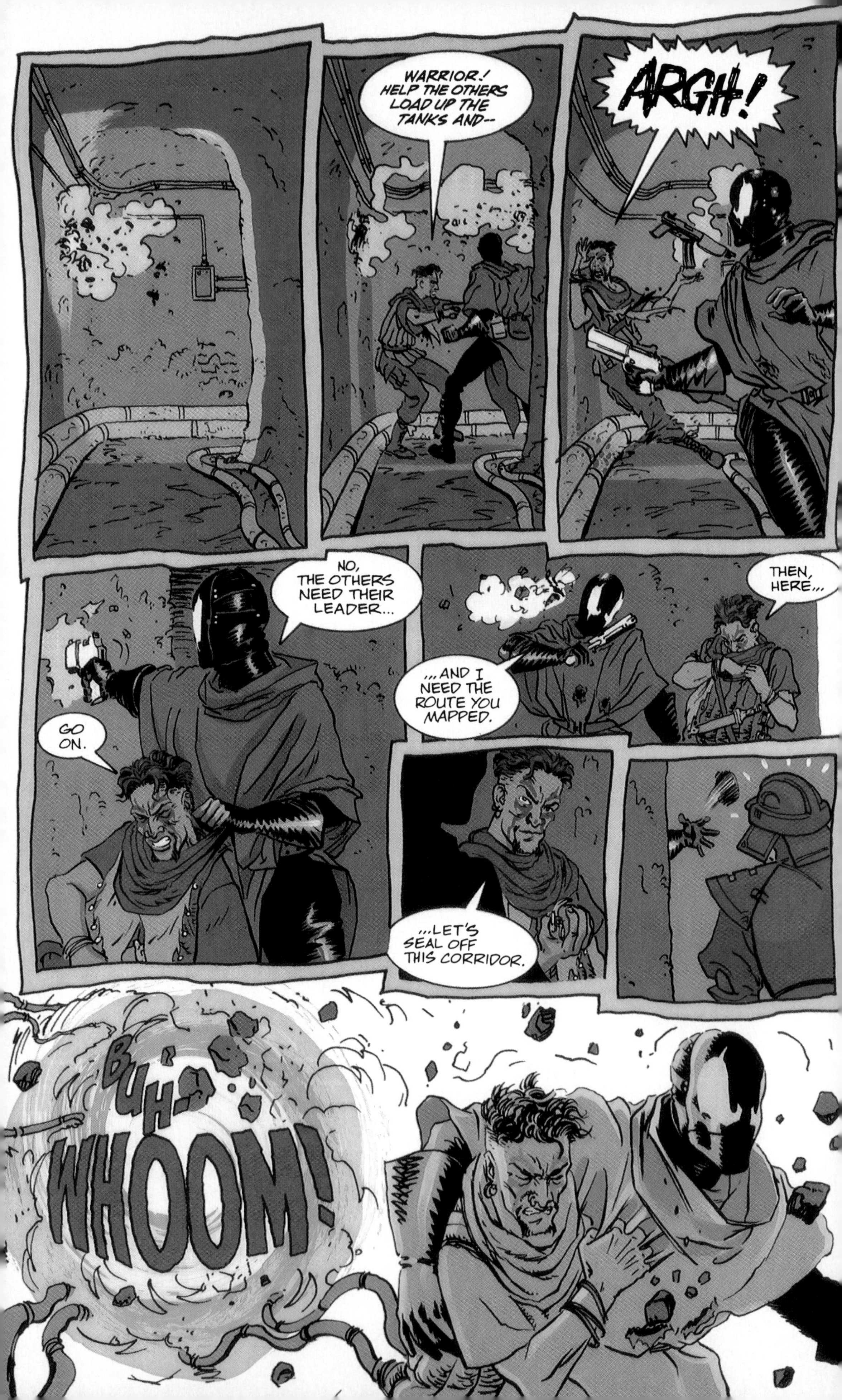
WARRIOR! HELP THE OTHERS LOAD UP THE TANKS AND--
ARGH!
NO, THE OTHERS NEED THEIR LEADER...
GO ON.
THEN, HERE...
...AND I NEED THE ROUTE YOU MAPPED.
...LET'S SEAL OFF THIS CORRIDOR.
BUH-WHOOM!

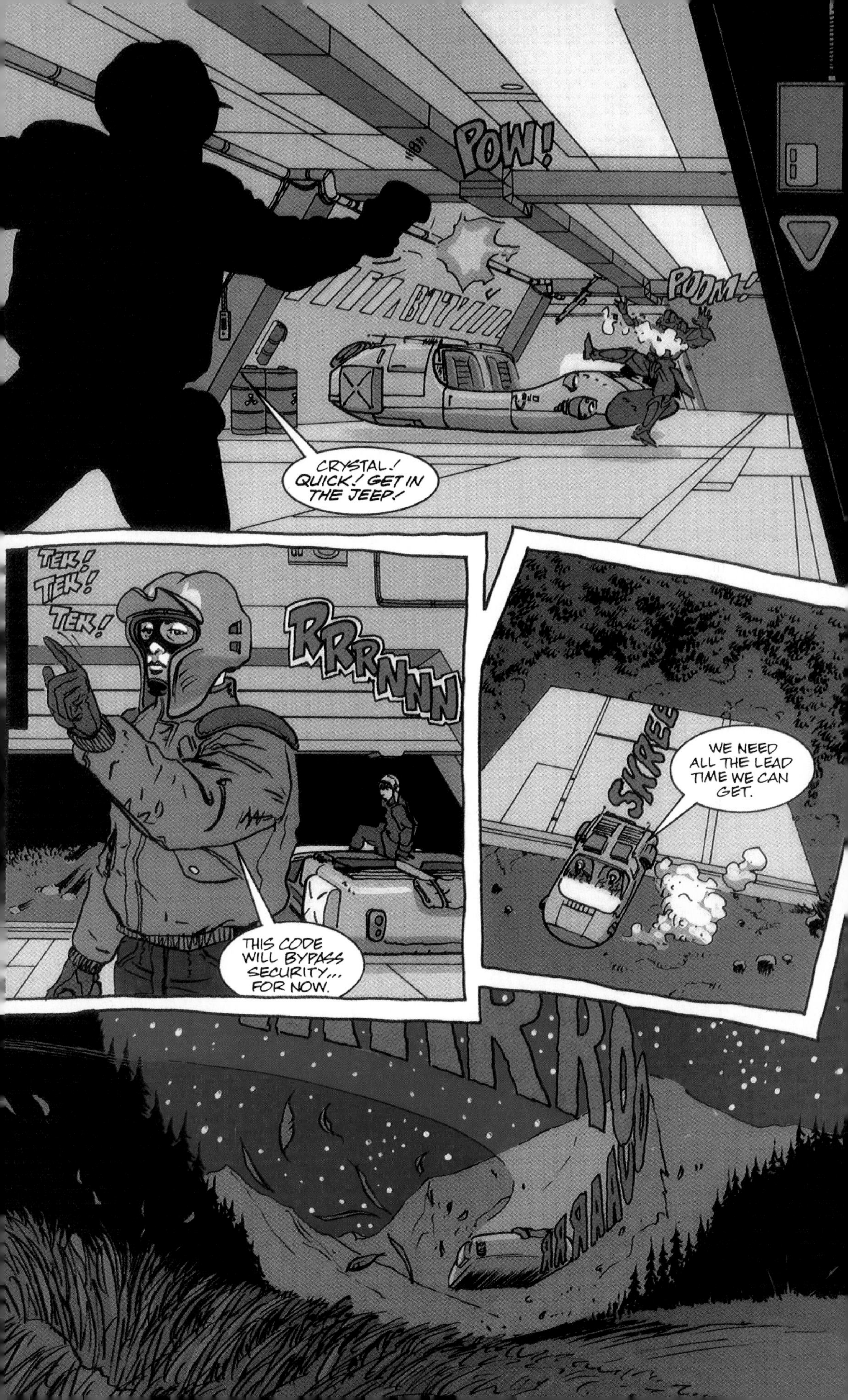
POW!
POOM!
CRYSTAL! QUICK! GET IN THE JEEP!
TEK! TEK! TEK!
RRRNNN
THIS CODE WILL BYPASS SECURITY... FOR NOW.
WE NEED ALL THE LEAD TIME WE CAN GET.

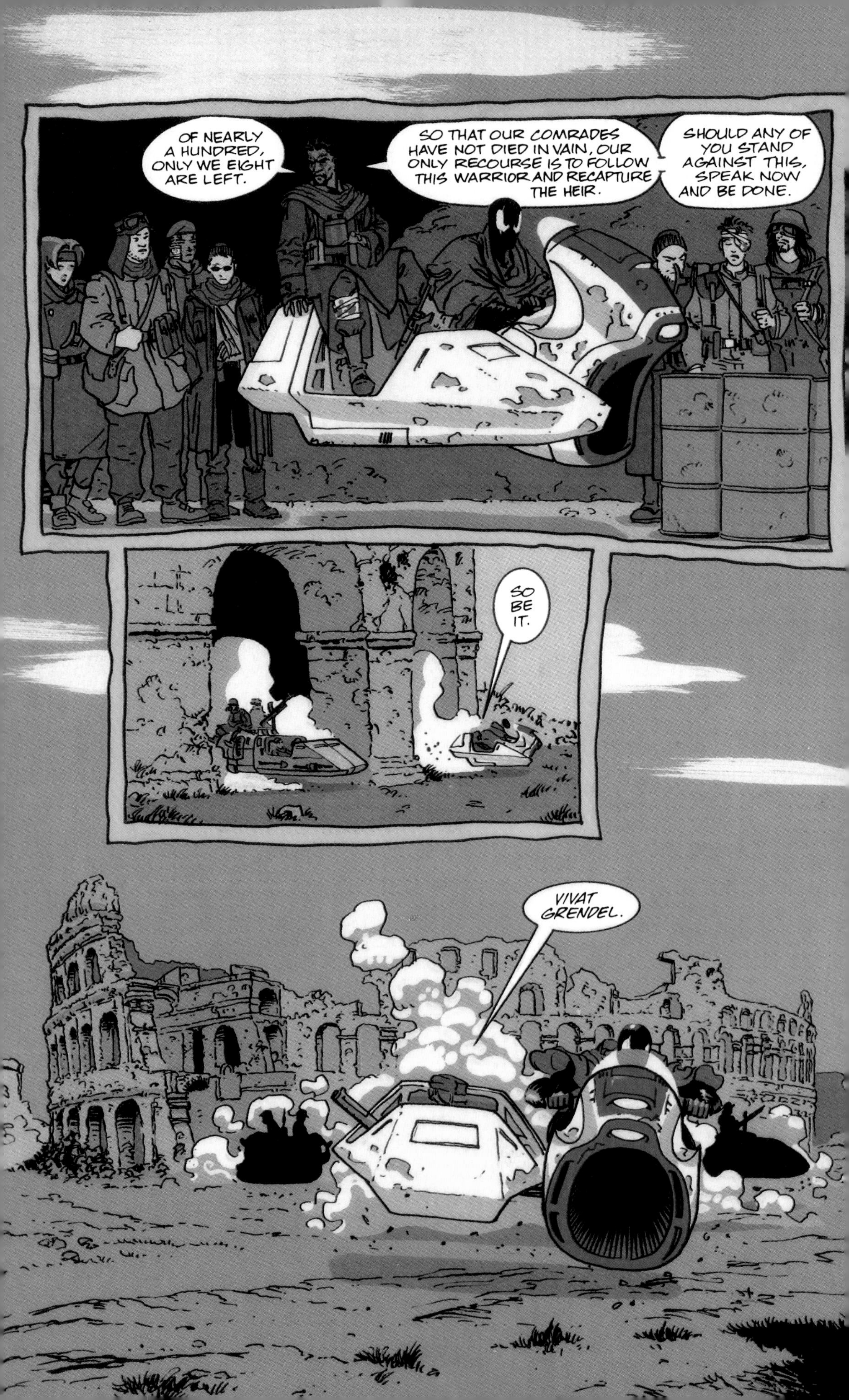
OF NEARLY A HUNDRED, ONLY WE EIGHT ARE LEFT.
SO THAT OUR COMRADES HAVE NOT DIED IN VAIN, OUR ONLY RECOURSE IS TO FOLLOW THIS WARRIOR AND RECAPTURE THE HEIR.
SHOULD ANY OF YOU STAND AGAINST THIS, SPEAK NOW AND BE DONE.
SO BE IT.
VIVAT GRENDEL.

# DEVIL
## *in pursuit*

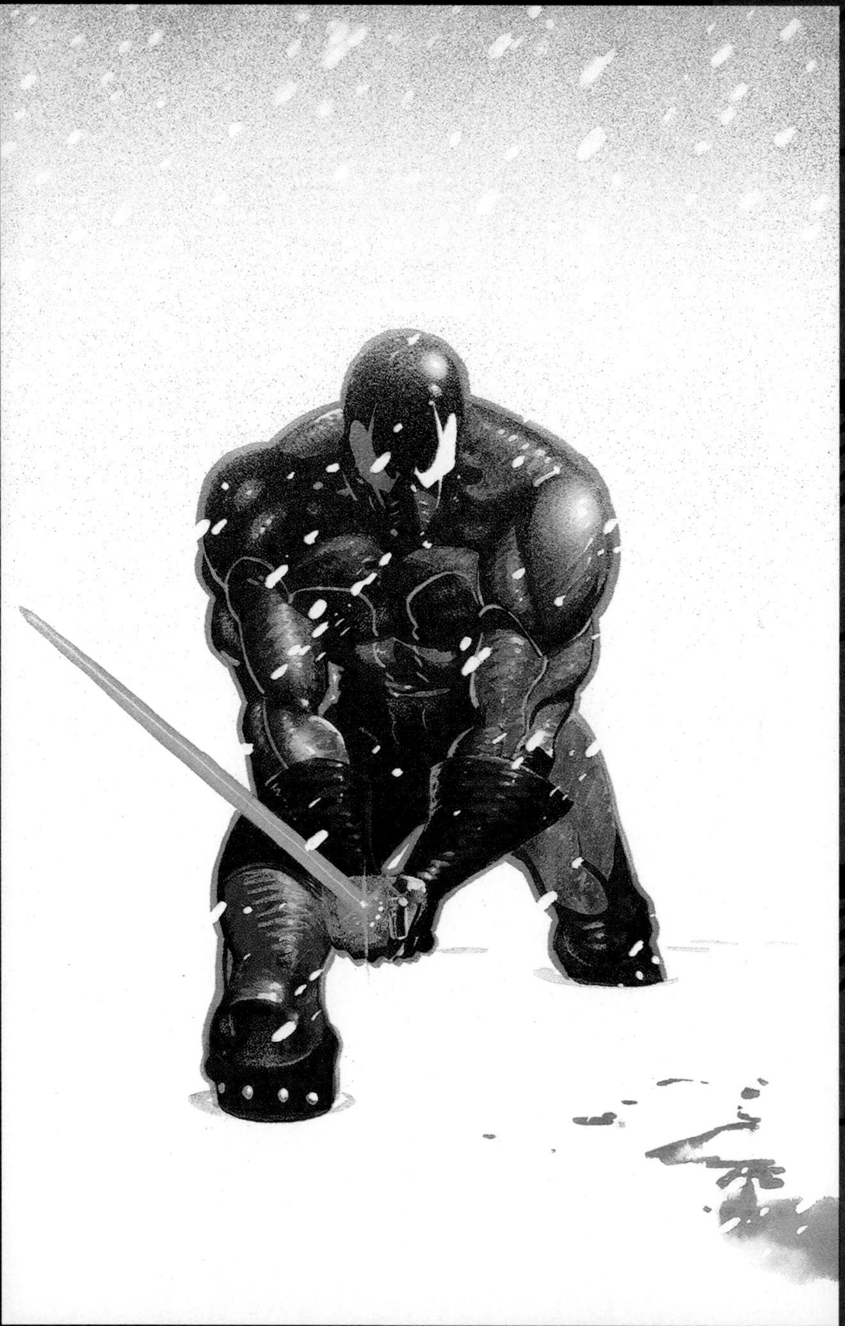

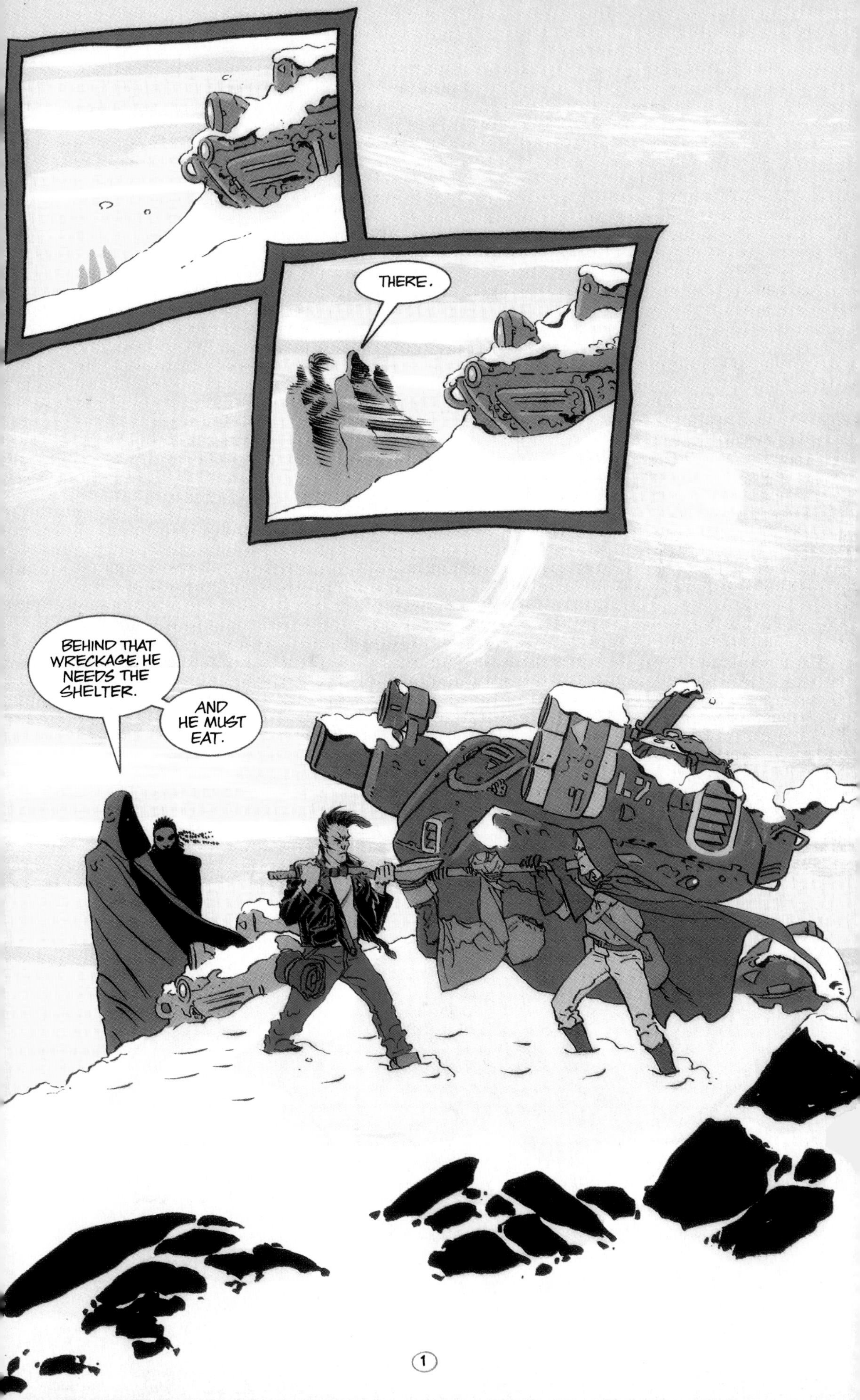
THERE.
BEHIND THAT WRECKAGE. HE NEEDS THE SHELTER.
AND HE MUST EAT.

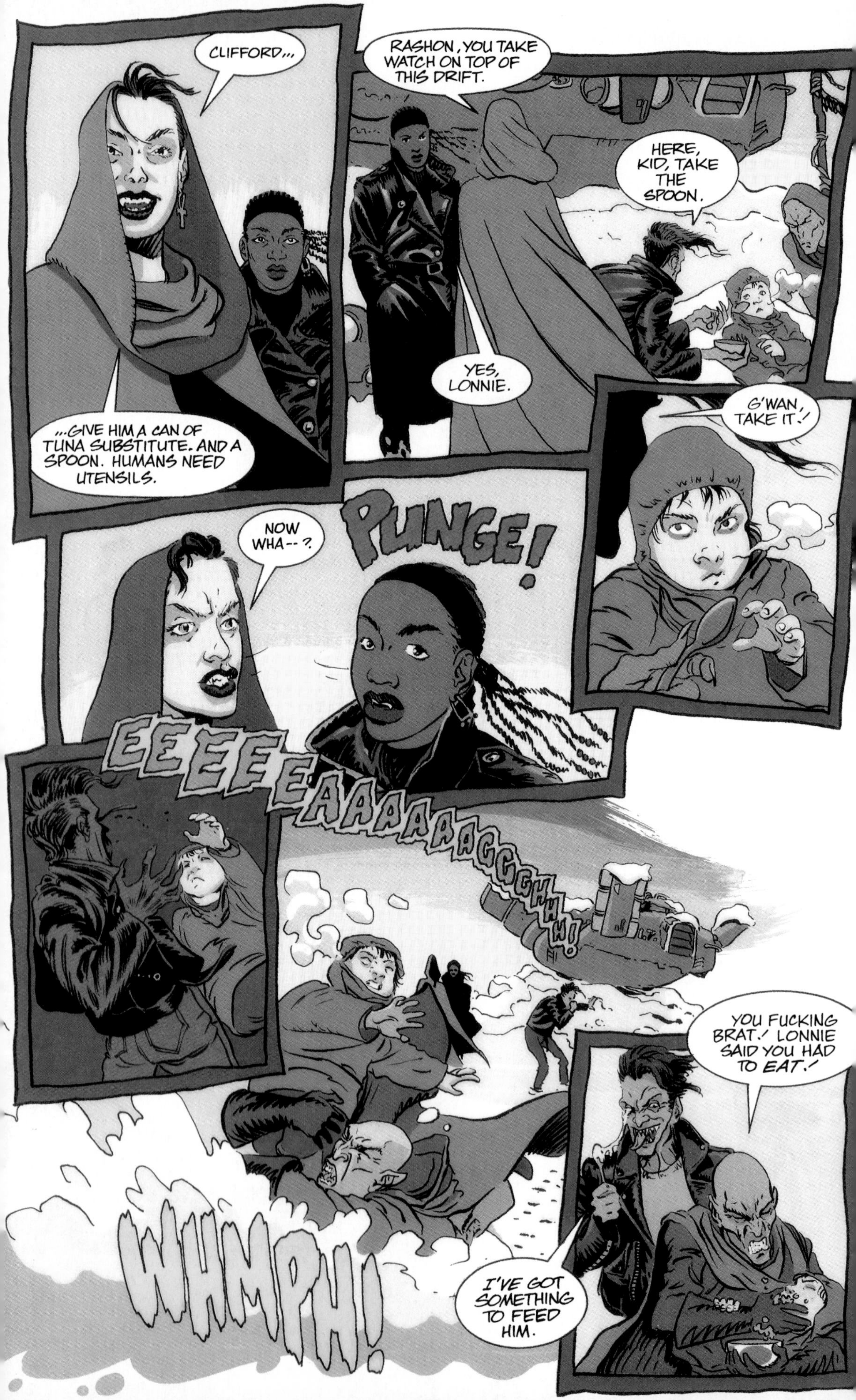
CLIFFORD,,,
...GIVE HIM A CAN OF TUNA SUBSTITUTE. AND A SPOON. HUMANS NEED UTENSILS.
RASHON, YOU TAKE WATCH ON TOP OF THIS DRIFT.
YES, LONNIE.
HERE, KID, TAKE THE SPOON.
G'WAN, TAKE IT!
NOW WHA--?
PLUNGE!
EEEEEEAAAAAAAGGGHHH!
WHMPH!
YOU FUCKING BRAT! LONNIE SAID YOU HAD TO *EAT*!
*I'VE GOT* SOMETHING TO FEED HIM.

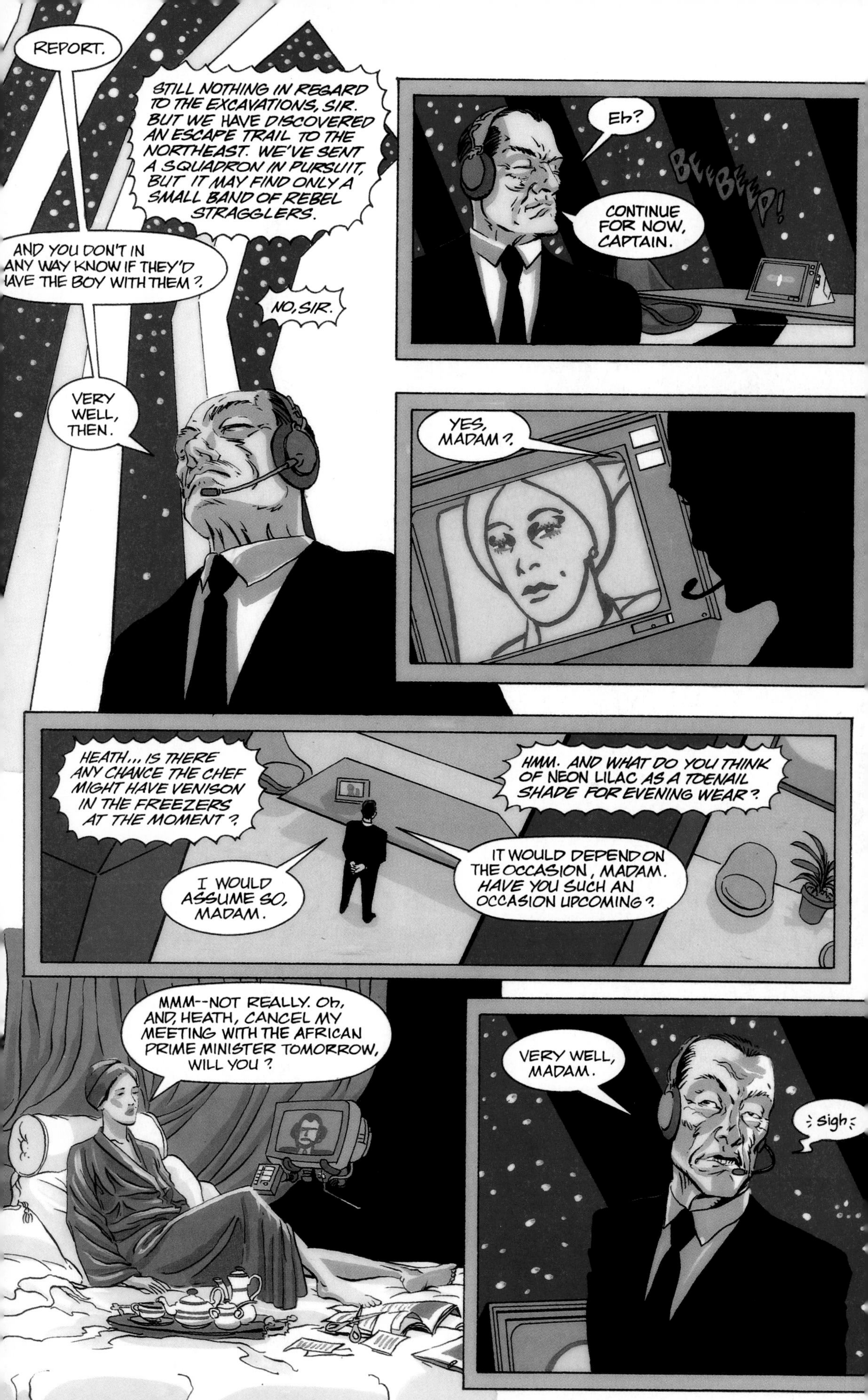
REPORT.
STILL NOTHING IN REGARD TO THE EXCAVATIONS, SIR. BUT WE HAVE DISCOVERED AN ESCAPE TRAIL TO THE NORTHEAST. WE'VE SENT A SQUADRON IN PURSUIT, BUT IT MAY FIND ONLY A SMALL BAND OF REBEL STRAGGLERS.
Eh?
BEEBEEP!
CONTINUE FOR NOW, CAPTAIN.
AND YOU DON'T IN ANY WAY KNOW IF THEY'D HAVE THE BOY WITH THEM?
NO, SIR.
VERY WELL, THEN.
YES, MADAM?
HEATH... IS THERE ANY CHANCE THE CHEF MIGHT HAVE VENISON IN THE FREEZERS AT THE MOMENT?
I WOULD ASSUME SO, MADAM.
HMM. AND WHAT DO YOU THINK OF NEON LILAC AS A TOENAIL SHADE FOR EVENING WEAR?
IT WOULD DEPEND ON THE OCCASION, MADAM. HAVE YOU SUCH AN OCCASION UPCOMING?
MMM--NOT REALLY. Oh, AND, HEATH, CANCEL MY MEETING WITH THE AFRICAN PRIME MINISTER TOMORROW, WILL YOU?
VERY WELL, MADAM.
sigh

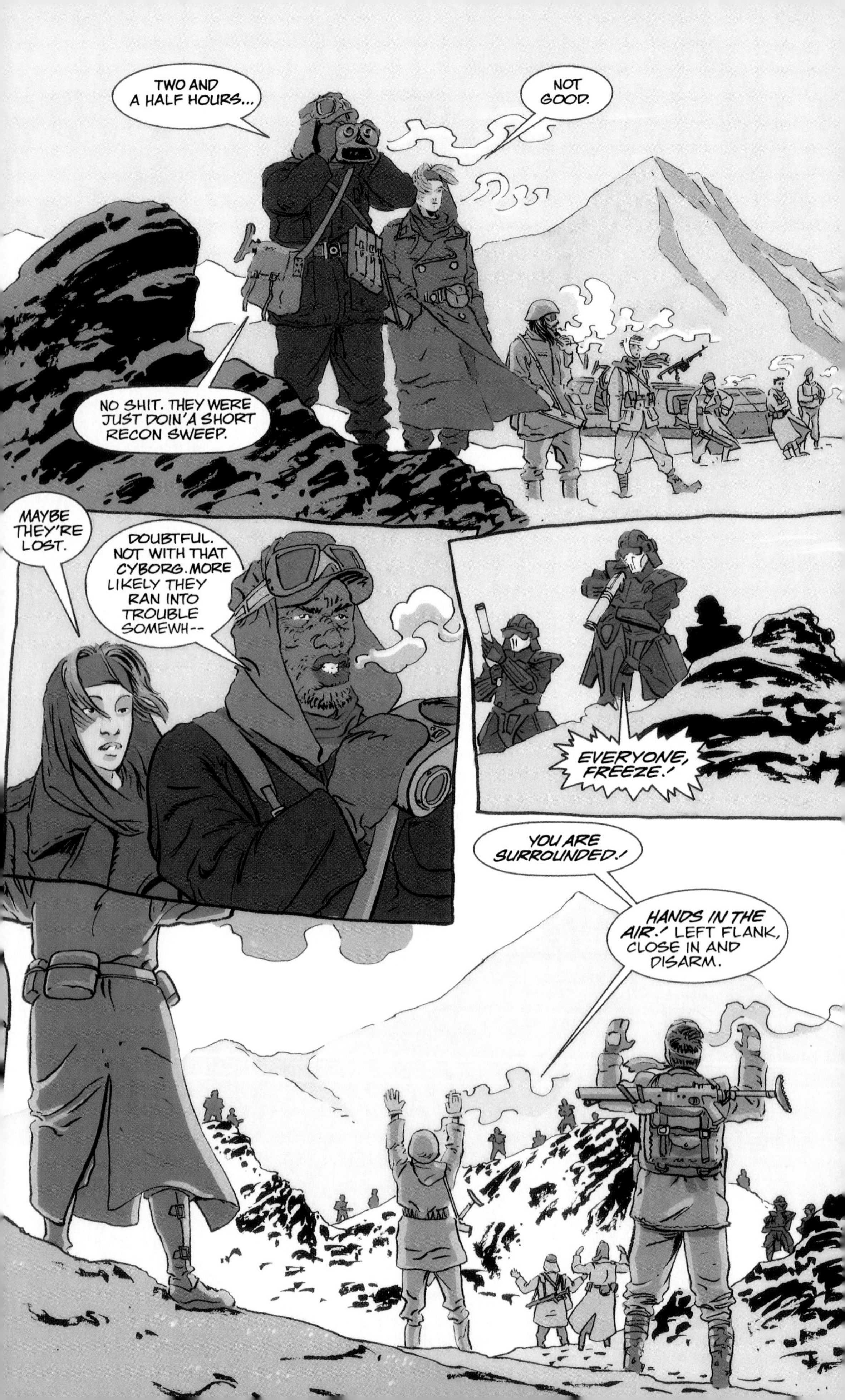
TWO AND A HALF HOURS...
NOT GOOD.
NO SHIT. THEY WERE JUST DOIN'A SHORT RECON SWEEP.
MAYBE THEY'RE LOST.
DOUBTFUL. NOT WITH THAT CYBORG. MORE LIKELY THEY RAN INTO TROUBLE SOMEWH--
EVERYONE, FREEZE!
YOU ARE SURROUNDED!
HANDS IN THE AIR! LEFT FLANK, CLOSE IN AND DISARM.

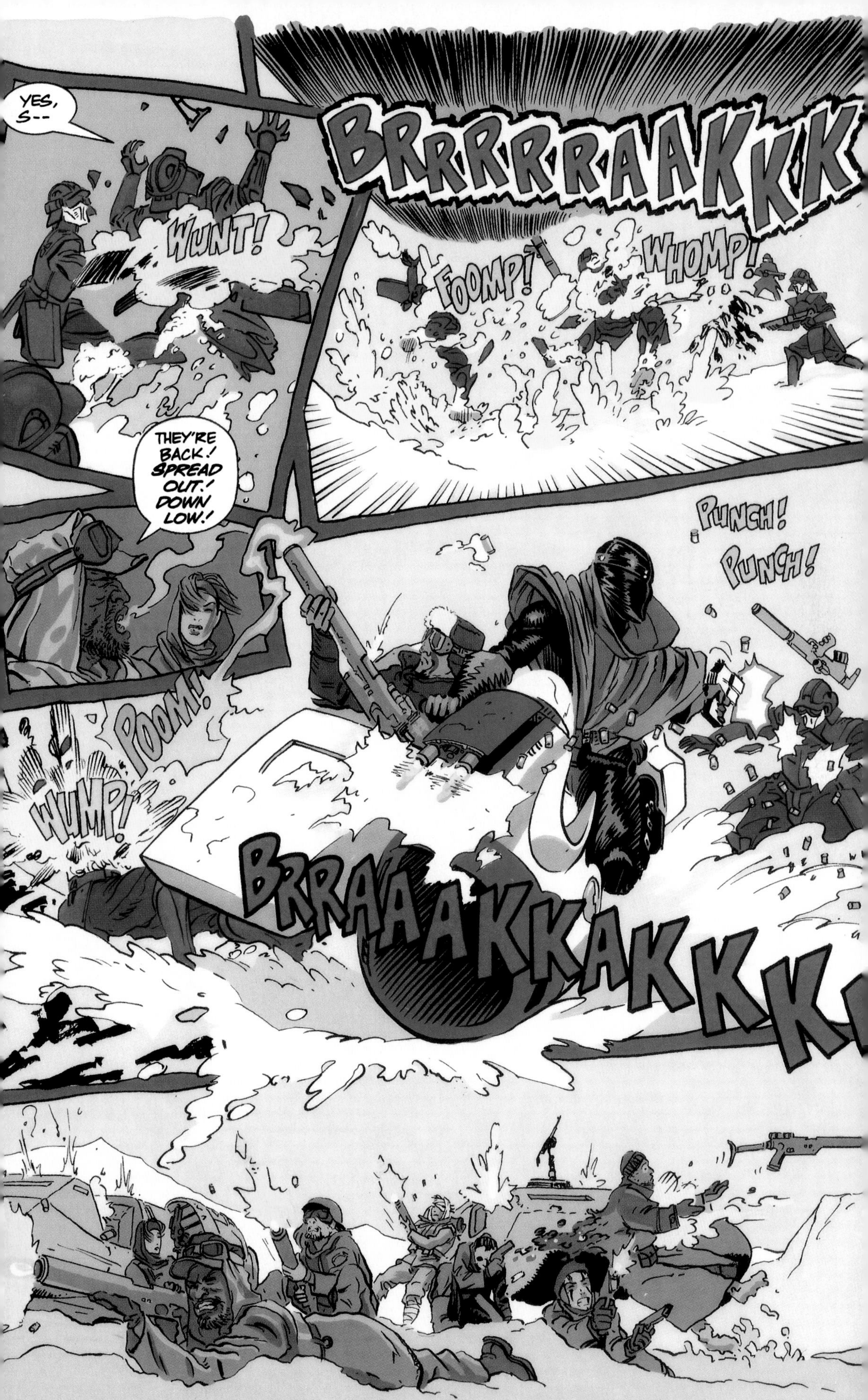
YES, S--
BRRRRRRAAKKK
WUNT!
FOOMP!
WHOMP!
THEY'RE BACK! SPREAD OUT! DOWN LOW!
PUNCH!
PUNCH!
POOM!
WUMP!
BRRAAAKKAKKK

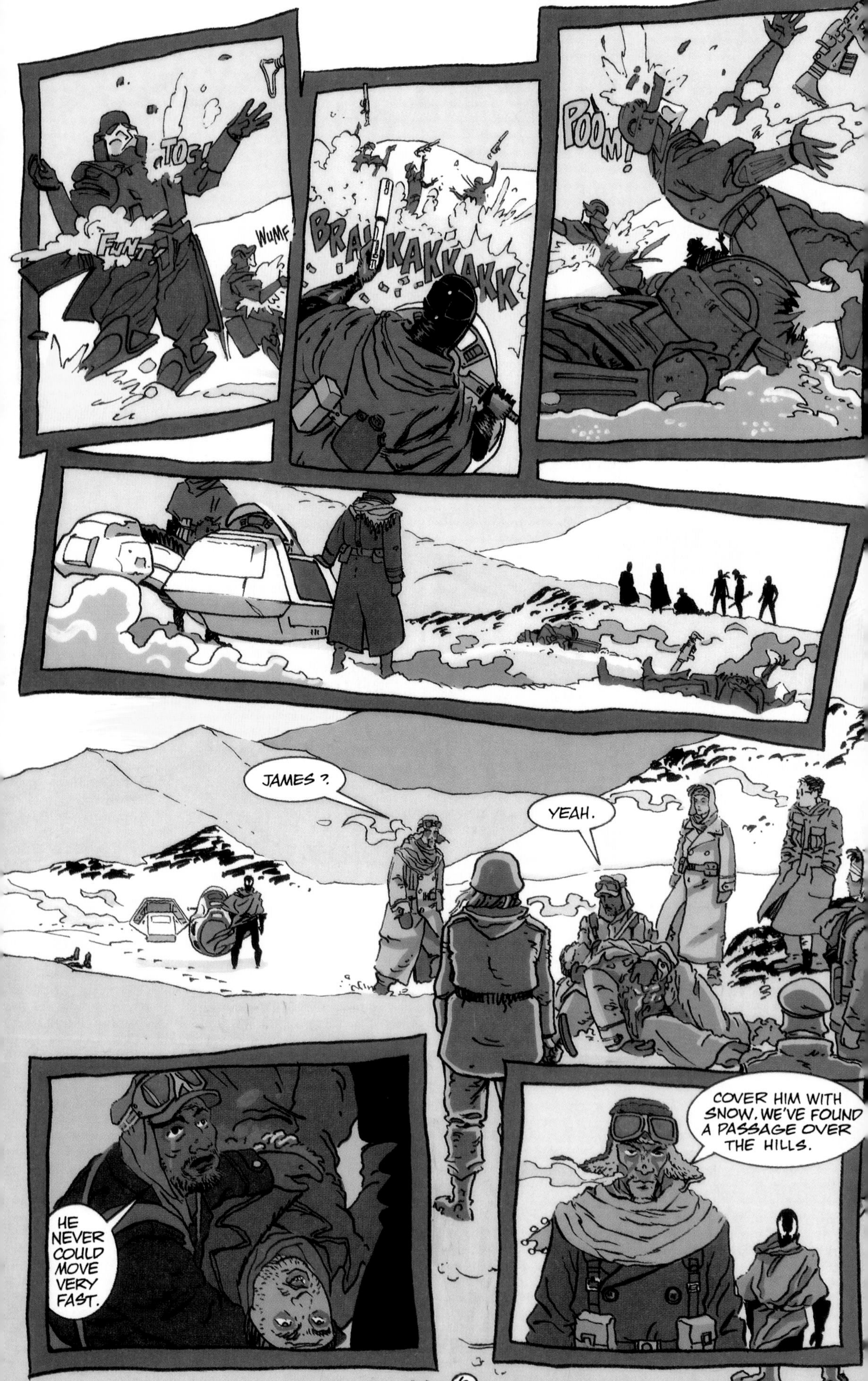
TOC!
FUNT
WUMF
BRAKAKAKKAKK
POOM!
JAMES ?.
YEAH.
HE NEVER COULD MOVE VERY FAST.
COVER HIM WITH SNOW. WE'VE FOUND A PASSAGE OVER THE HILLS.

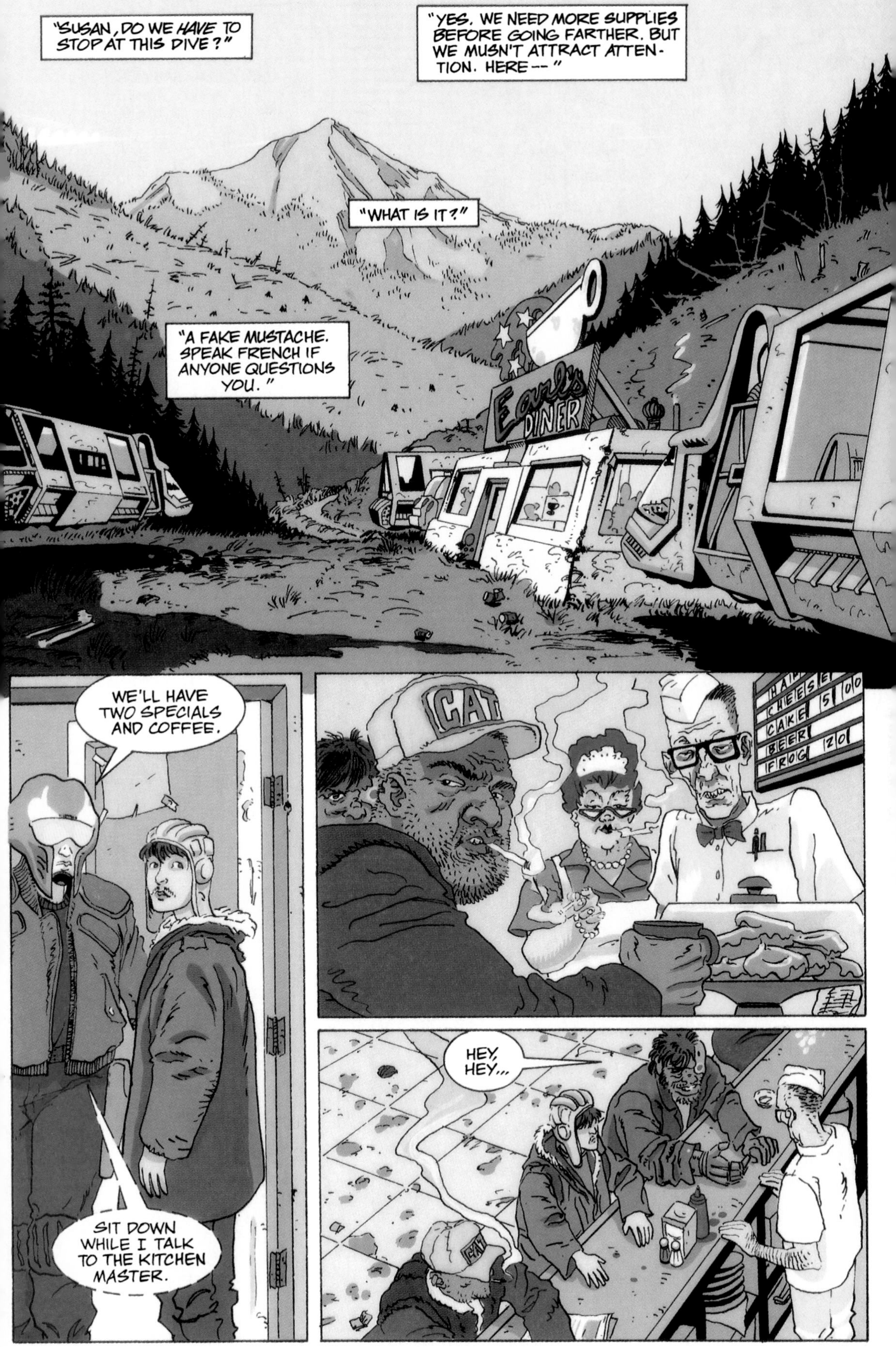
"SUSAN, DO WE *HAVE* TO STOP AT THIS DIVE?"
"YES. WE NEED MORE SUPPLIES BEFORE GOING FARTHER. BUT WE MUSN'T ATTRACT ATTENTION. HERE--"
"WHAT IS IT?"
"A FAKE MUSTACHE. SPEAK FRENCH IF ANYONE QUESTIONS YOU."
Earl's DINER
WE'LL HAVE TWO SPECIALS AND COFFEE.
SIT DOWN WHILE I TALK TO THE KITCHEN MASTER.
CAT
HEY, HEY...

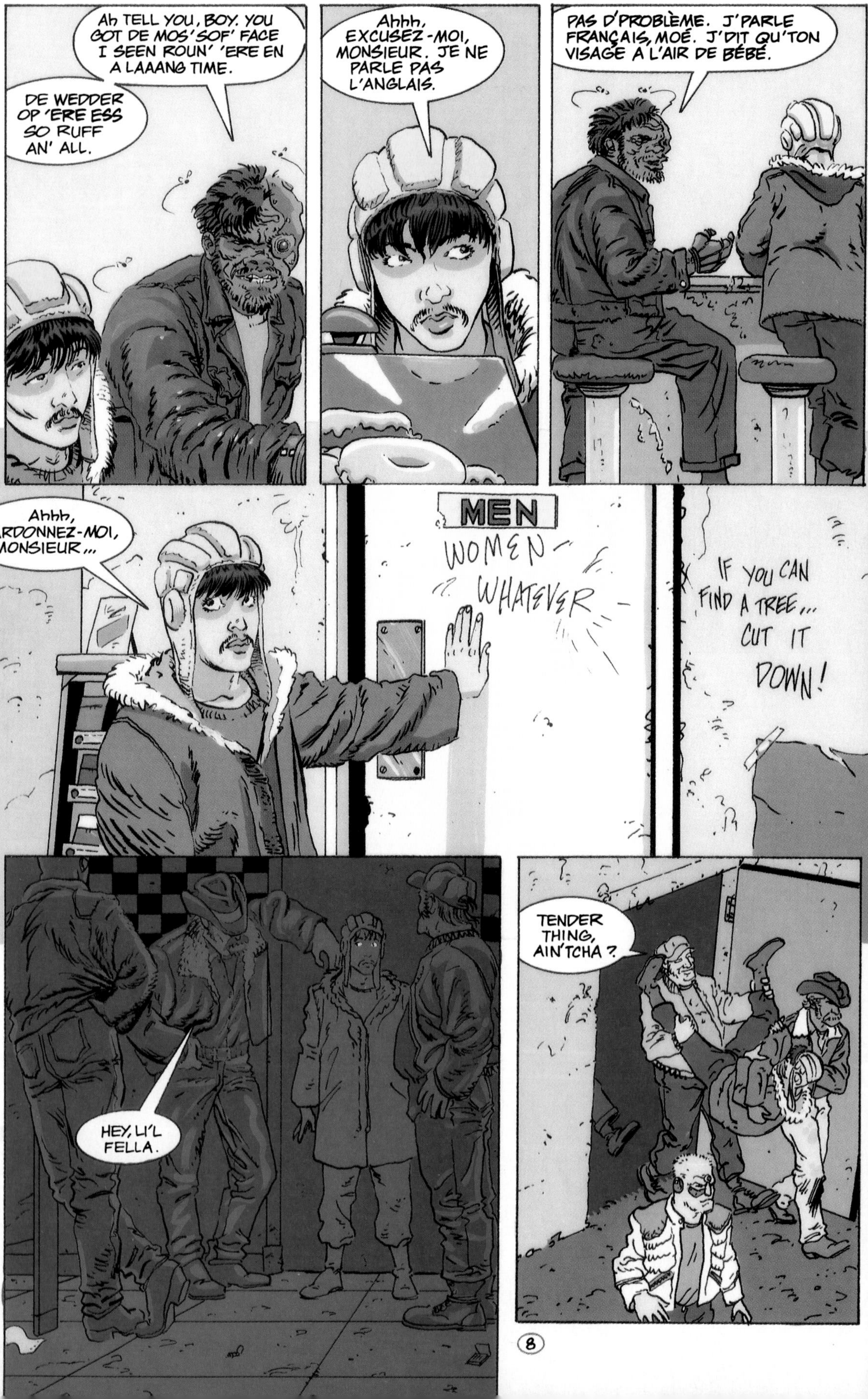
Ah TELL YOU, BOY. YOU GOT DE MOS' 'SOF' FACE I SEEN ROUN' 'ERE EN A LAAANG TIME.
DE WEDDER OP 'ERE ESS SO RUFF AN' ALL.
Ahhh, EXCUSEZ-MOI, MONSIEUR. JE NE PARLE PAS L'ANGLAIS.
PAS D'PROBLÈME. J'PARLE FRANÇAIS, MOÉ. J'DIT QU'TON VISAGE A L'AIR DE BÉBÉ.
Ahhh, PARDONNEZ-MOI, MONSIEUR...
MEN
WOMEN
WHATEVER
IF YOU CAN FIND A TREE... CUT IT DOWN!
HEY, LI'L FELLA.
TENDER THING, AIN'TCHA?

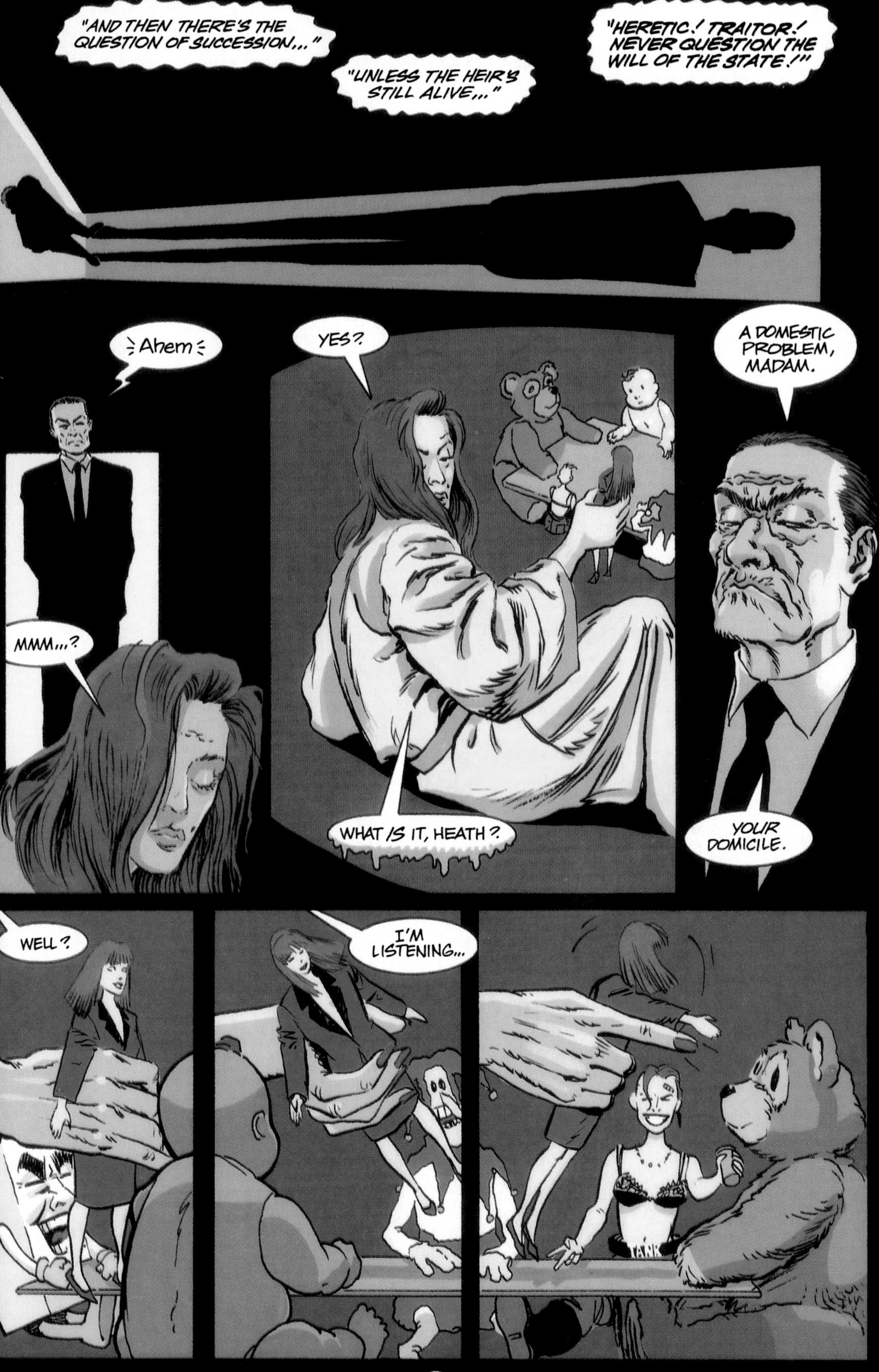
"AND THEN THERE'S THE QUESTION OF SUCCESSION..."
"UNLESS THE HEIR'S STILL ALIVE..."
"HERETIC! TRAITOR! NEVER QUESTION THE WILL OF THE STATE!"
Ahem
MMM...?
YES?
WHAT IS IT, HEATH?
A DOMESTIC PROBLEM, MADAM.
YOUR DOMICILE.
WELL?
I'M LISTENING...
TANK

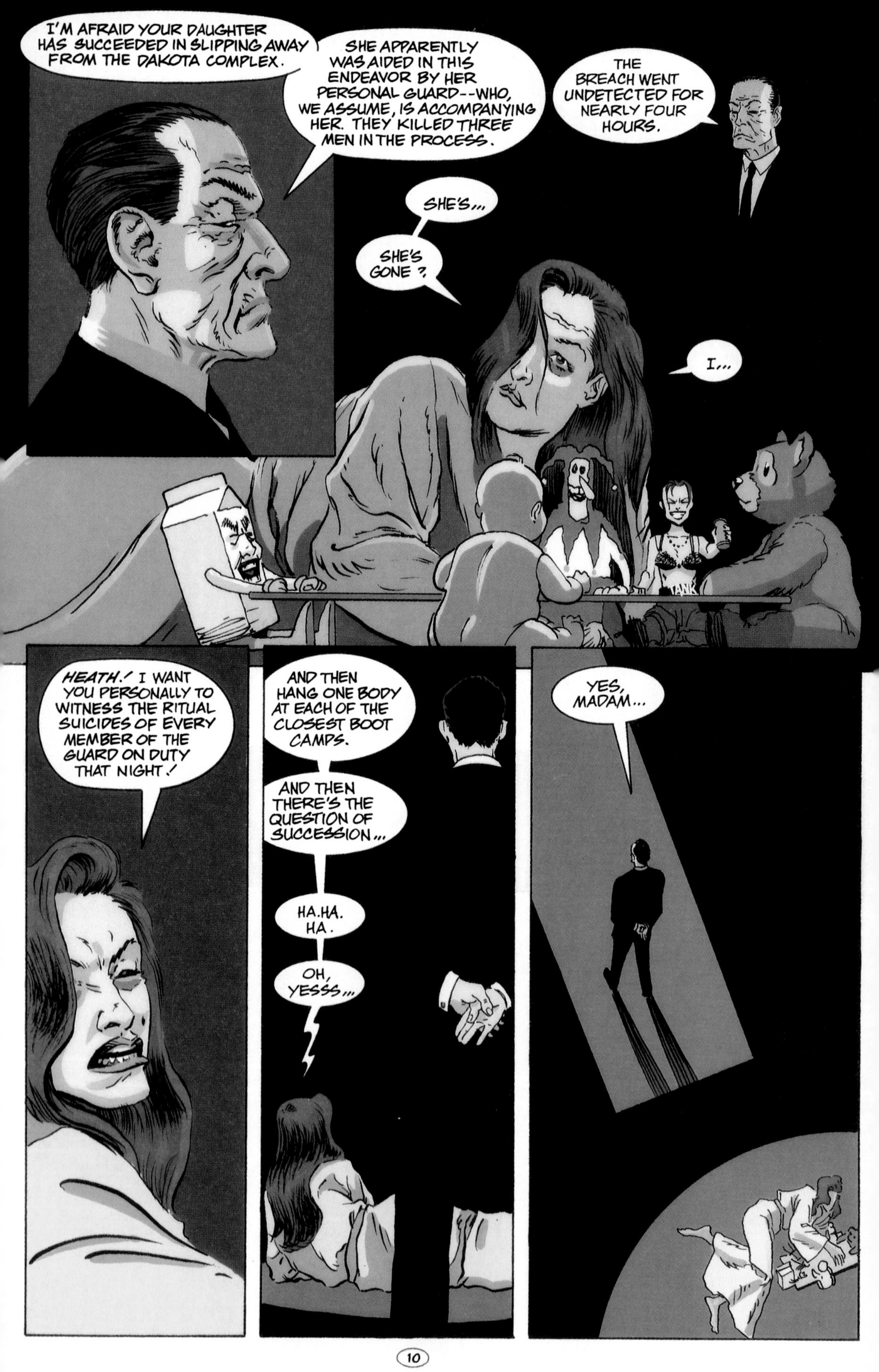
I'M AFRAID YOUR DAUGHTER HAS SUCCEEDED IN SLIPPING AWAY FROM THE DAKOTA COMPLEX.
SHE APPARENTLY WAS AIDED IN THIS ENDEAVOR BY HER PERSONAL GUARD--WHO, WE ASSUME, IS ACCOMPANYING HER. THEY KILLED THREE MEN IN THE PROCESS.
THE BREACH WENT UNDETECTED FOR NEARLY FOUR HOURS.
SHE'S...
SHE'S GONE ?
I...
TANK
HEATH! I WANT YOU PERSONALLY TO WITNESS THE RITUAL SUICIDES OF EVERY MEMBER OF THE GUARD ON DUTY THAT NIGHT!
AND THEN HANG ONE BODY AT EACH OF THE CLOSEST BOOT CAMPS.
AND THEN THERE'S THE QUESTION OF SUCCESSION...
HA.HA. HA.
OH, YESSS...
YES, MADAM...

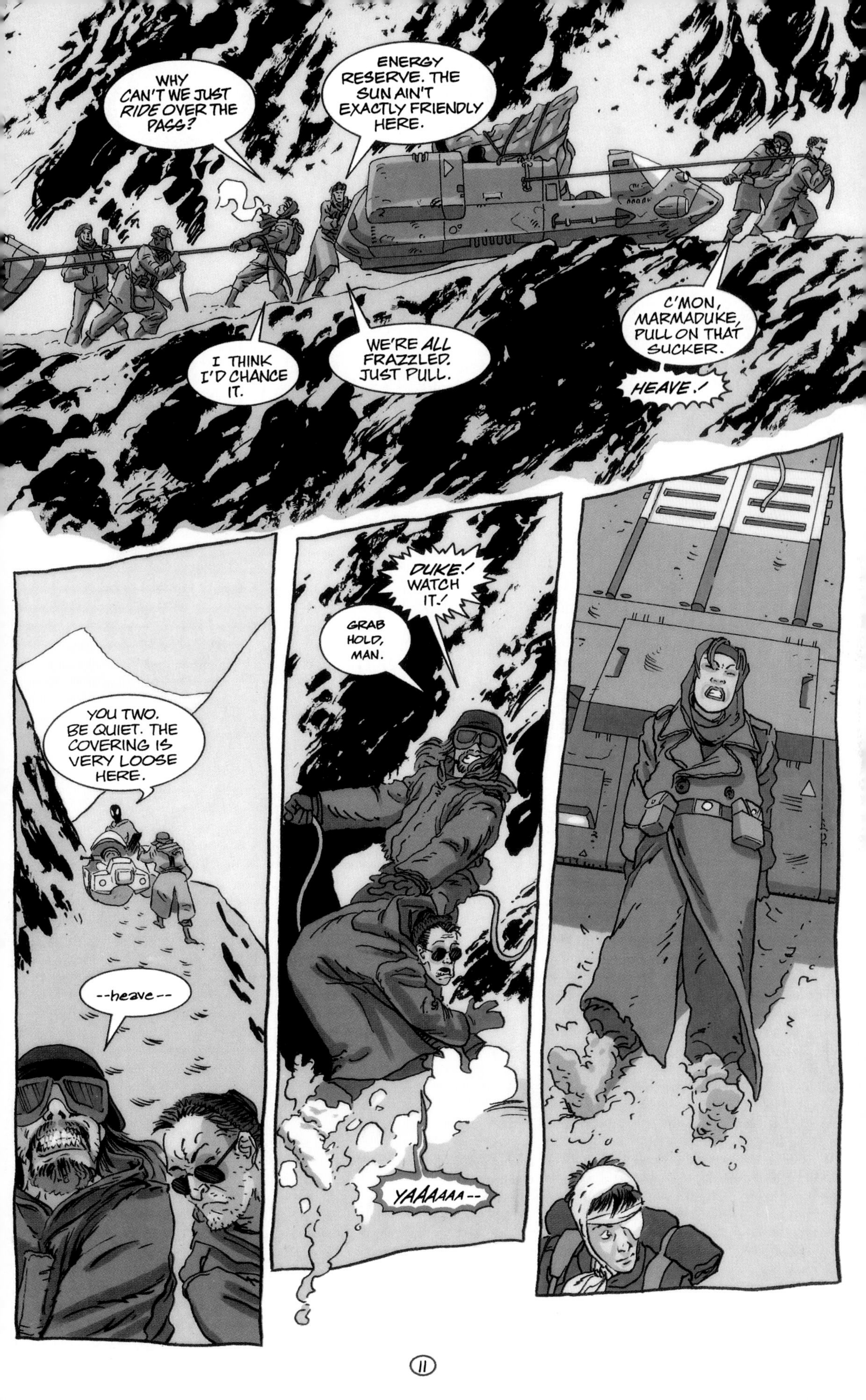
WHY CAN'T WE JUST RIDE OVER THE PASS?
ENERGY RESERVE. THE SUN AIN'T EXACTLY FRIENDLY HERE.
I THINK I'D CHANCE IT.
WE'RE ALL FRAZZLED. JUST PULL.
C'MON, MARMADUKE, PULL ON THAT SUCKER.
HEAVE.!
YOU TWO. BE QUIET. THE COVERING IS VERY LOOSE HERE.
--heave--
DUKE.! WATCH IT.!
GRAB HOLD, MAN.
YAAAAAA--

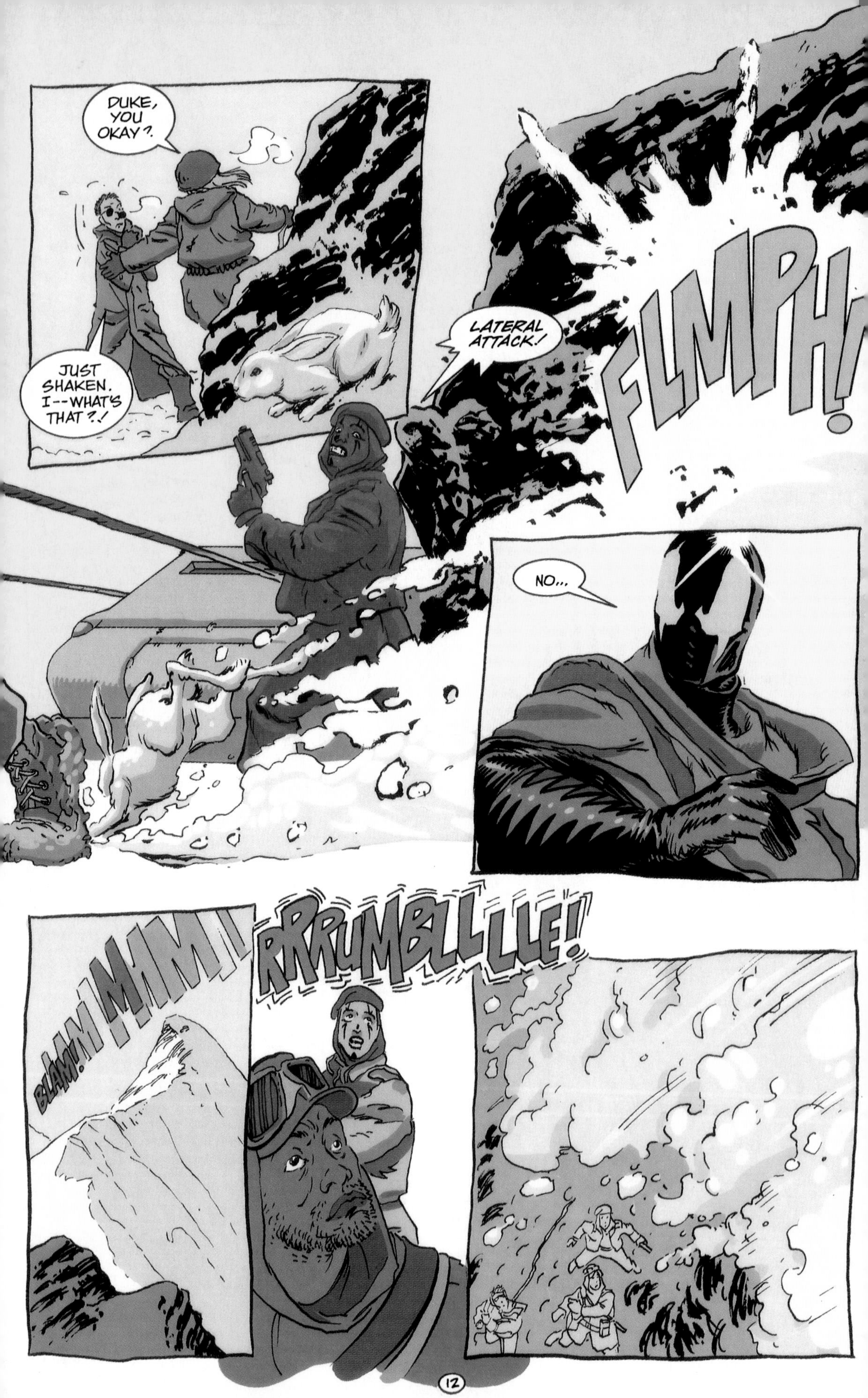

DUKE, YOU OKAY?.
JUST SHAKEN. I--WHAT'S THAT?!
LATERAL ATTACK!
FLMPH!
NO...
BLAMMMM!
RRRUMBLLLE!

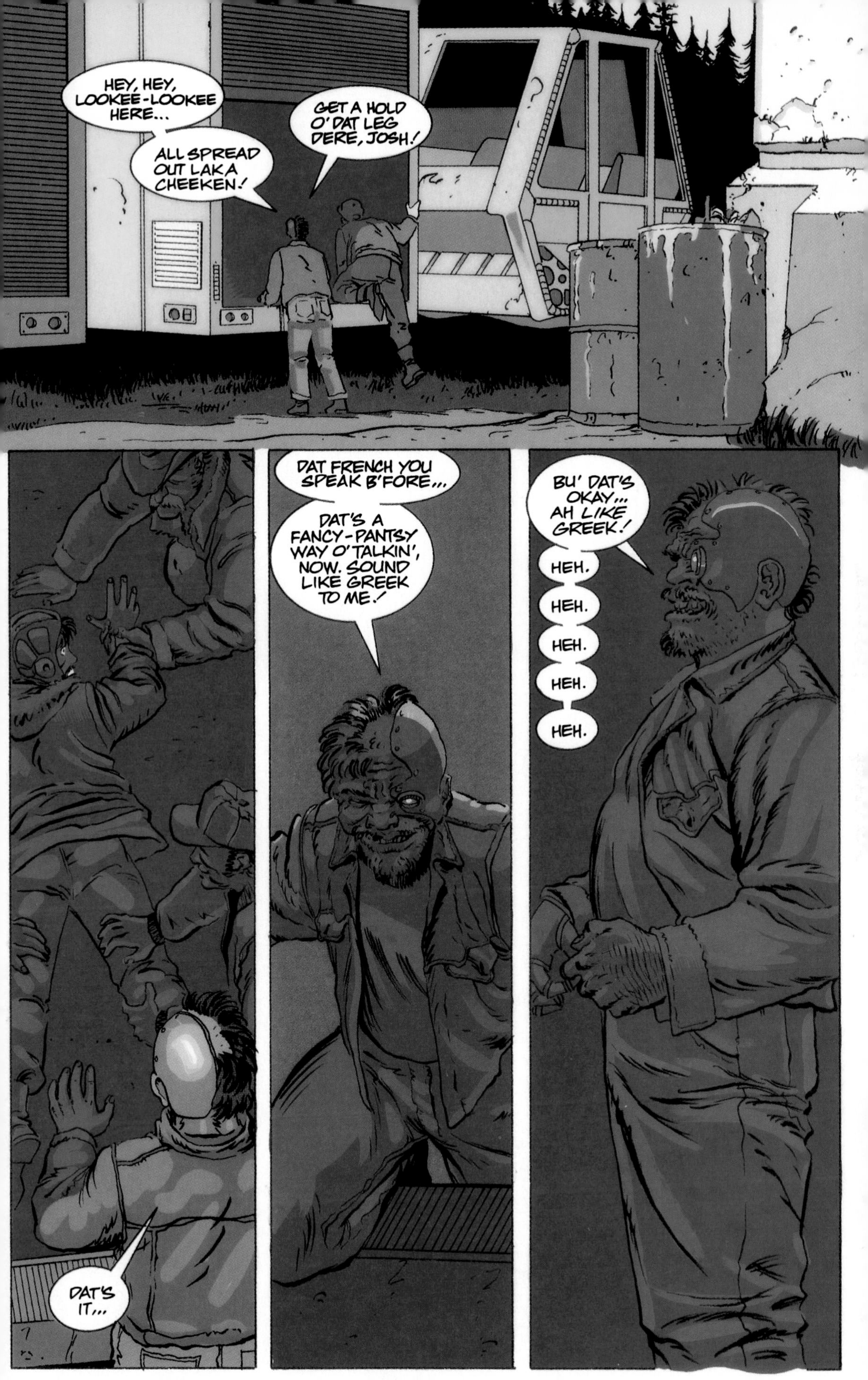
HEY, HEY, LOOKEE-LOOKEE HERE...
ALL SPREAD OUT LAKA CHEEKEN!
GET A HOLD O' DAT LEG DERE, JOSH!
DAT'S IT...
DAT FRENCH YOU SPEAK B'FORE...
DAT'S A FANCY-PANTSY WAY O'TALKIN', NOW. SOUND LIKE GREEK TO ME!
BU' DAT'S OKAY... AH LIKE GREEK!
HEH.
HEH.
HEH.
HEH.
HEH.

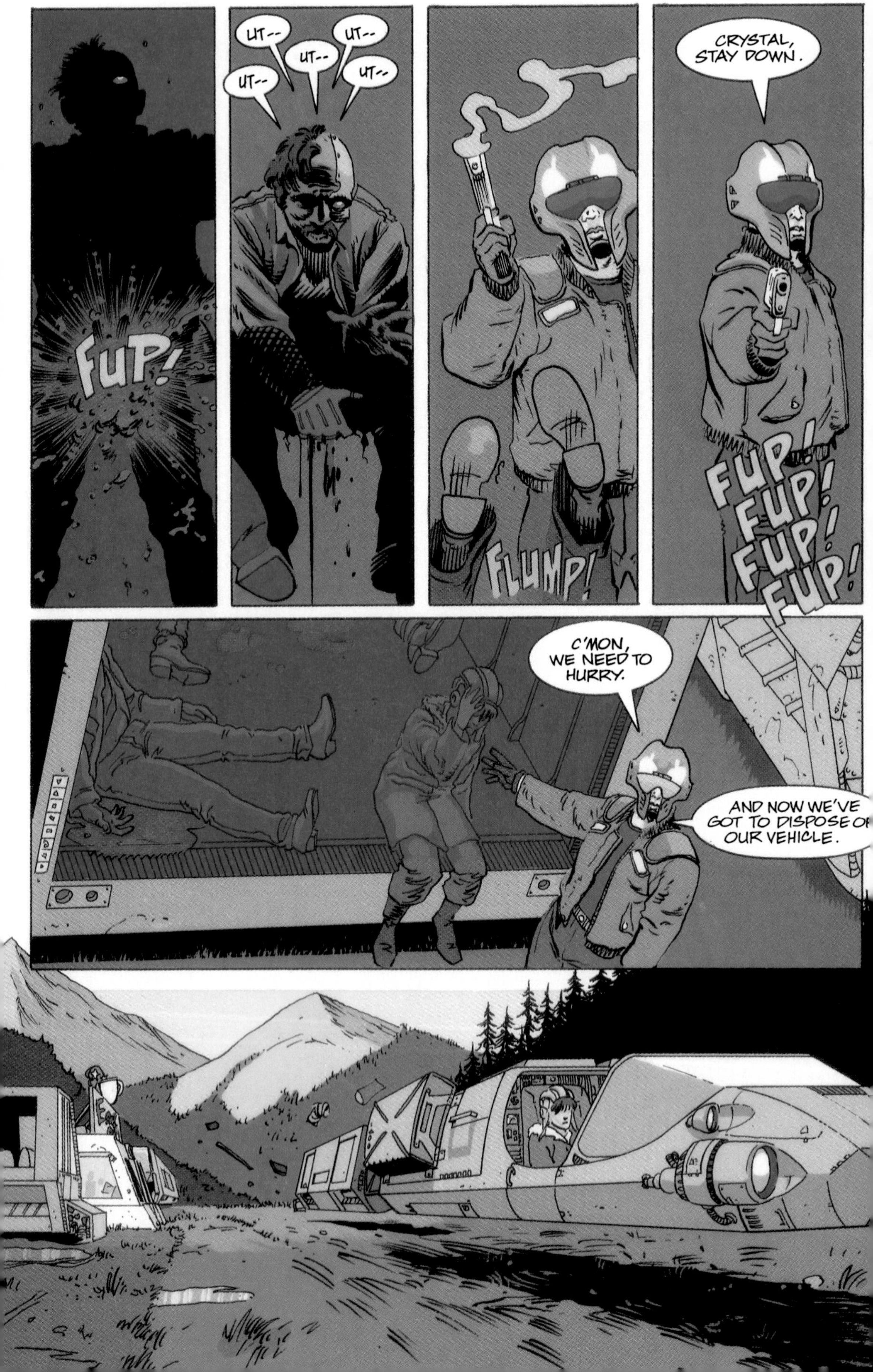
FUP!
UT--
UT--
UT--
UT--
UT--
FLUMP!
CRYSTAL, STAY DOWN.
FUP! FUP! FUP! FUP!
C'MON, WE NEED TO HURRY.
AND NOW WE'VE GOT TO DISPOSE OF OUR VEHICLE.

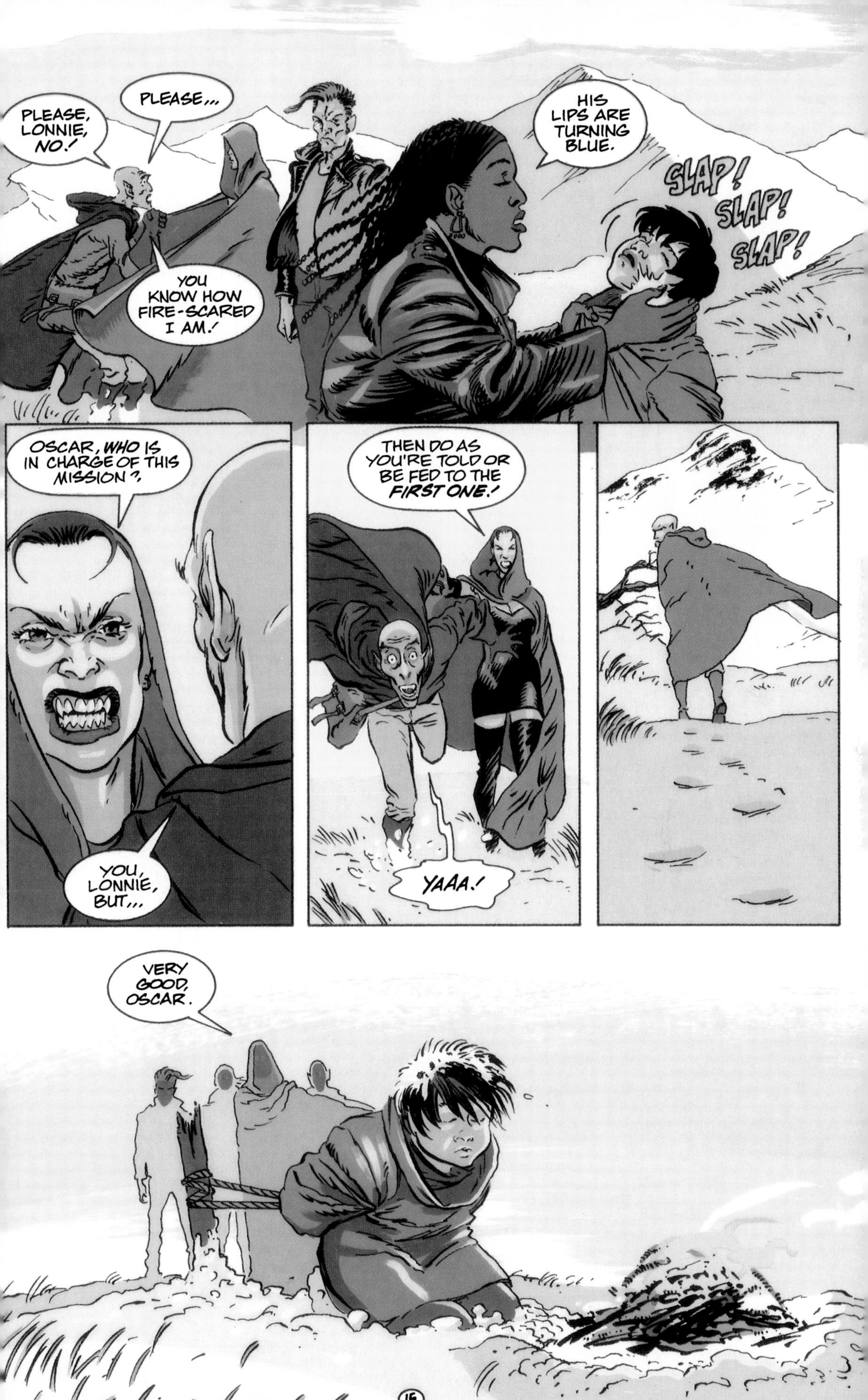
PLEASE, LONNIE, NO.!
PLEASE,,,
YOU KNOW HOW FIRE-SCARED I AM.!
HIS LIPS ARE TURNING BLUE.
SLAP! SLAP! SLAP!
OSCAR, WHO IS IN CHARGE OF THIS MISSION?
YOU, LONNIE, BUT,,,
THEN DO AS YOU'RE TOLD OR BE FED TO THE FIRST ONE.!
YAAA.!
VERY GOOD, OSCAR.

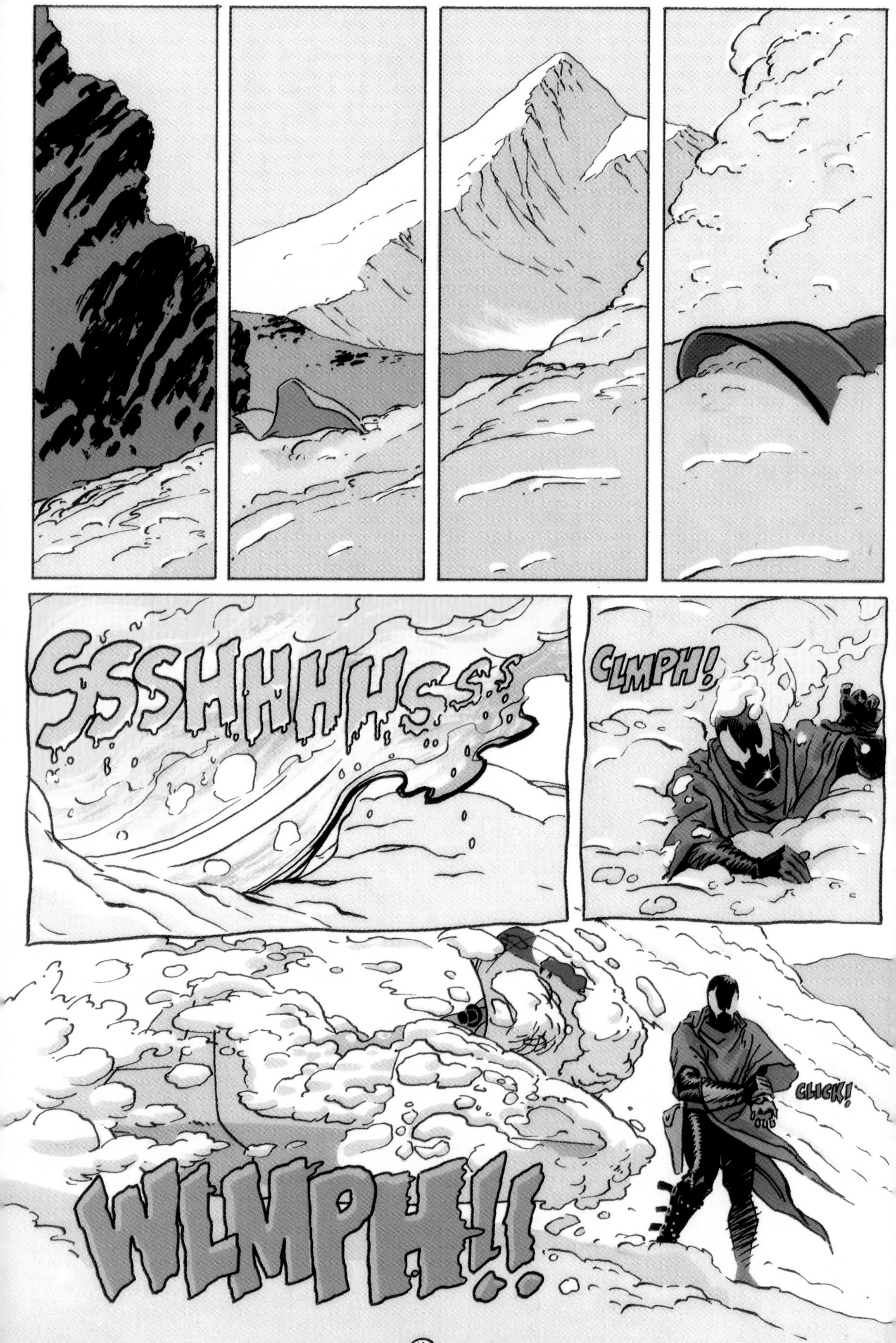
SSSHHHHSSSS
CLMPH!
CLICK!
WLMPH!!

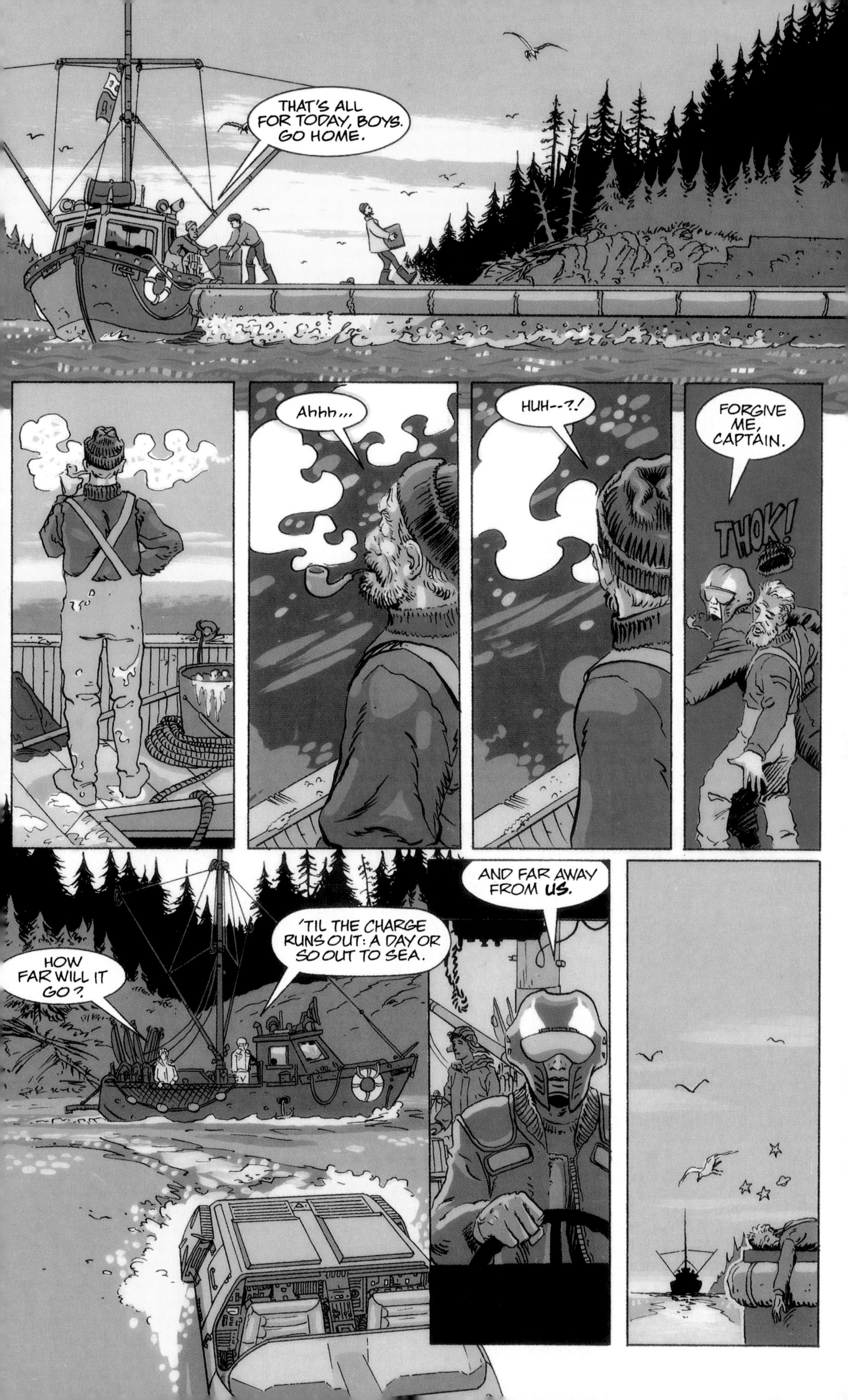
THAT'S ALL FOR TODAY, BOYS. GO HOME.
Ahhh...
HUH--?!
FORGIVE ME, CAPTAIN.
THOK!
HOW FAR WILL IT GO?
'TIL THE CHARGE RUNS OUT: A DAY OR SO OUT TO SEA.
AND FAR AWAY FROM US.

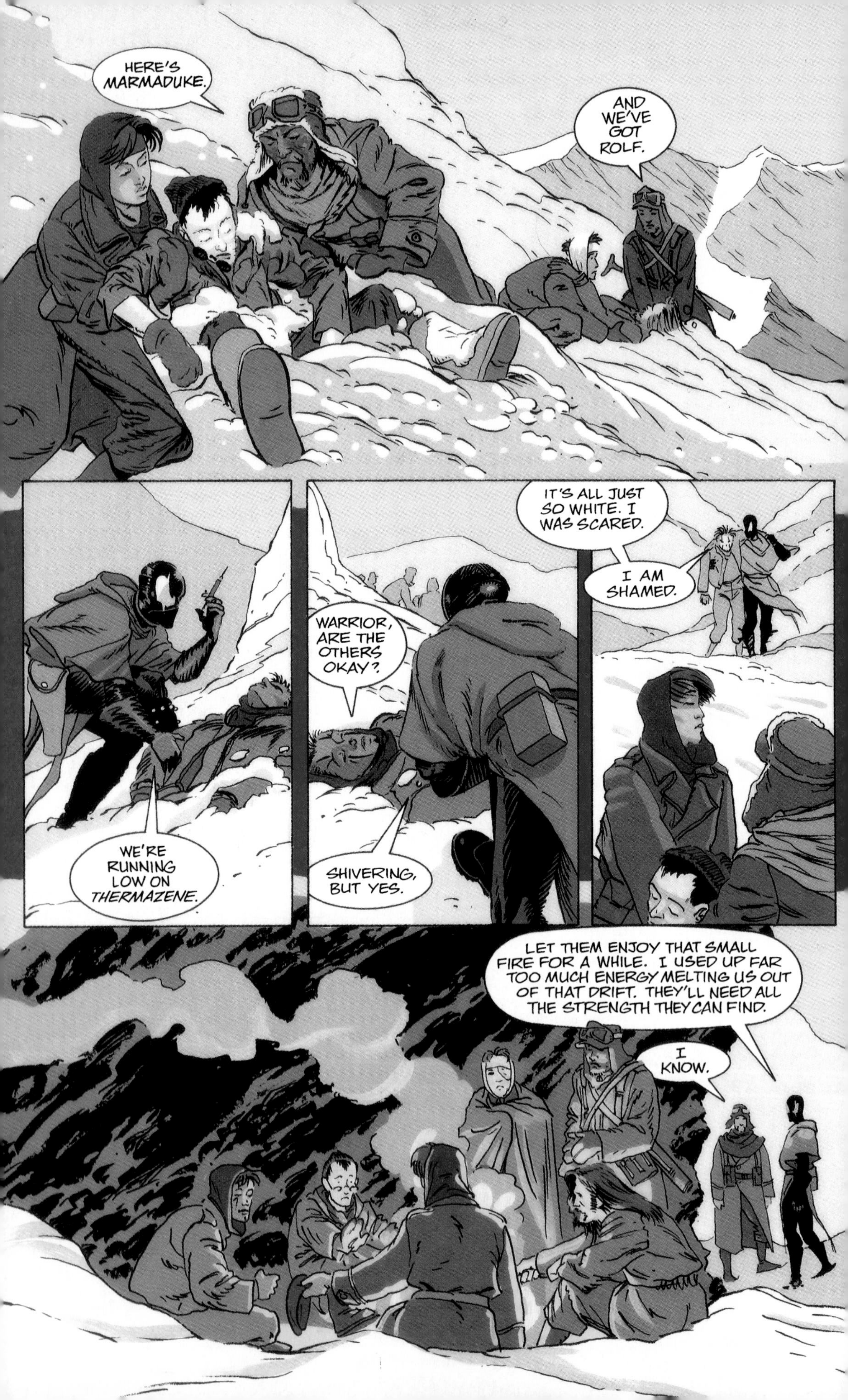
HERE'S MARMADUKE.
AND WE'VE GOT ROLF.
WE'RE RUNNING LOW ON THERMAZENE.
WARRIOR, ARE THE OTHERS OKAY?
SHIVERING, BUT YES.
IT'S ALL JUST SO WHITE. I WAS SCARED.
I AM SHAMED.
LET THEM ENJOY THAT SMALL FIRE FOR A WHILE. I USED UP FAR TOO MUCH ENERGY MELTING US OUT OF THAT DRIFT. THEY'LL NEED ALL THE STRENGTH THEY CAN FIND.
I KNOW.

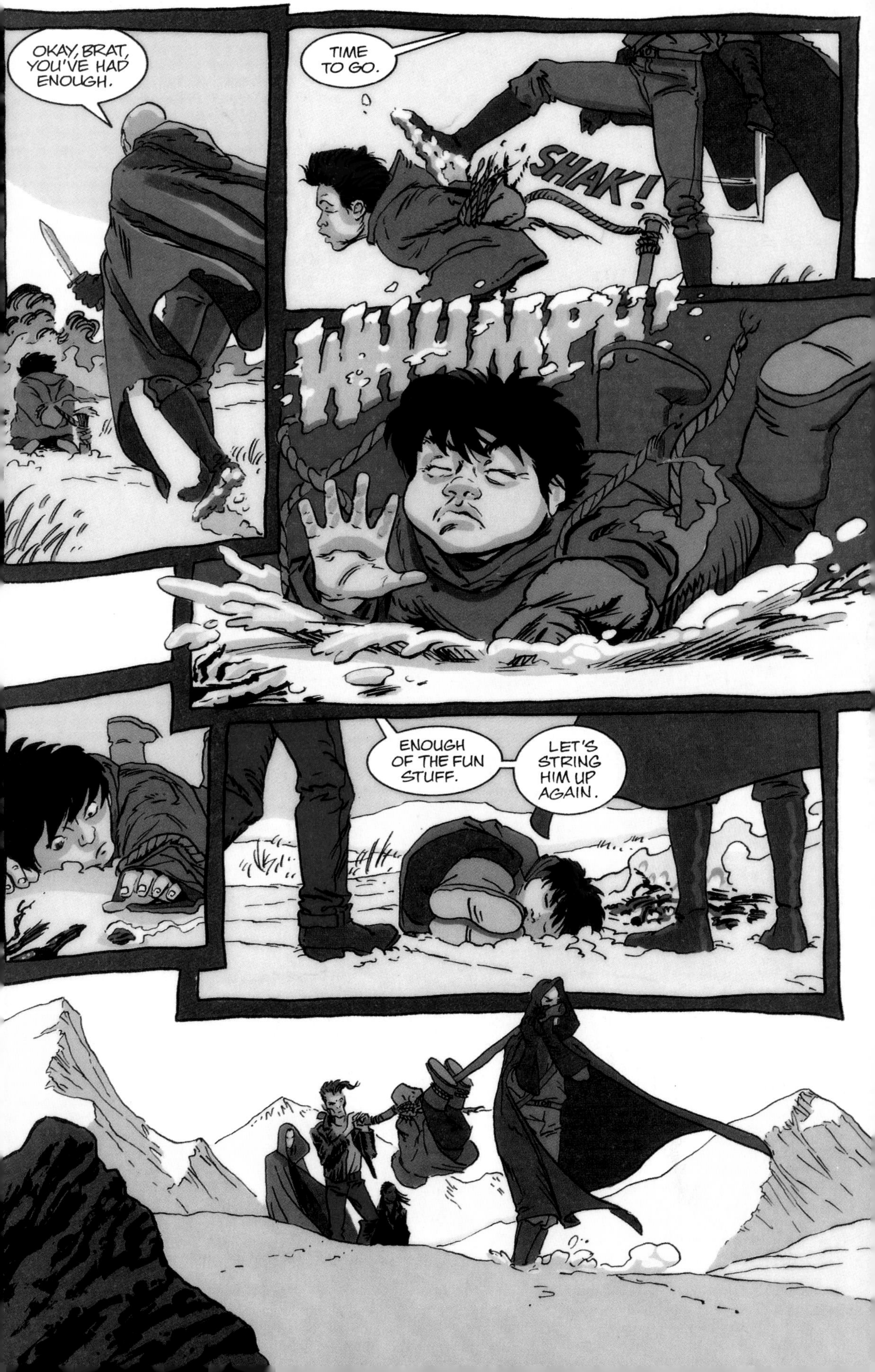
OKAY, BRAT, YOU'VE HAD ENOUGH.
TIME TO GO.
SHAK!
WHUMPH!
ENOUGH OF THE FUN STUFF.
LET'S STRING HIM UP AGAIN.

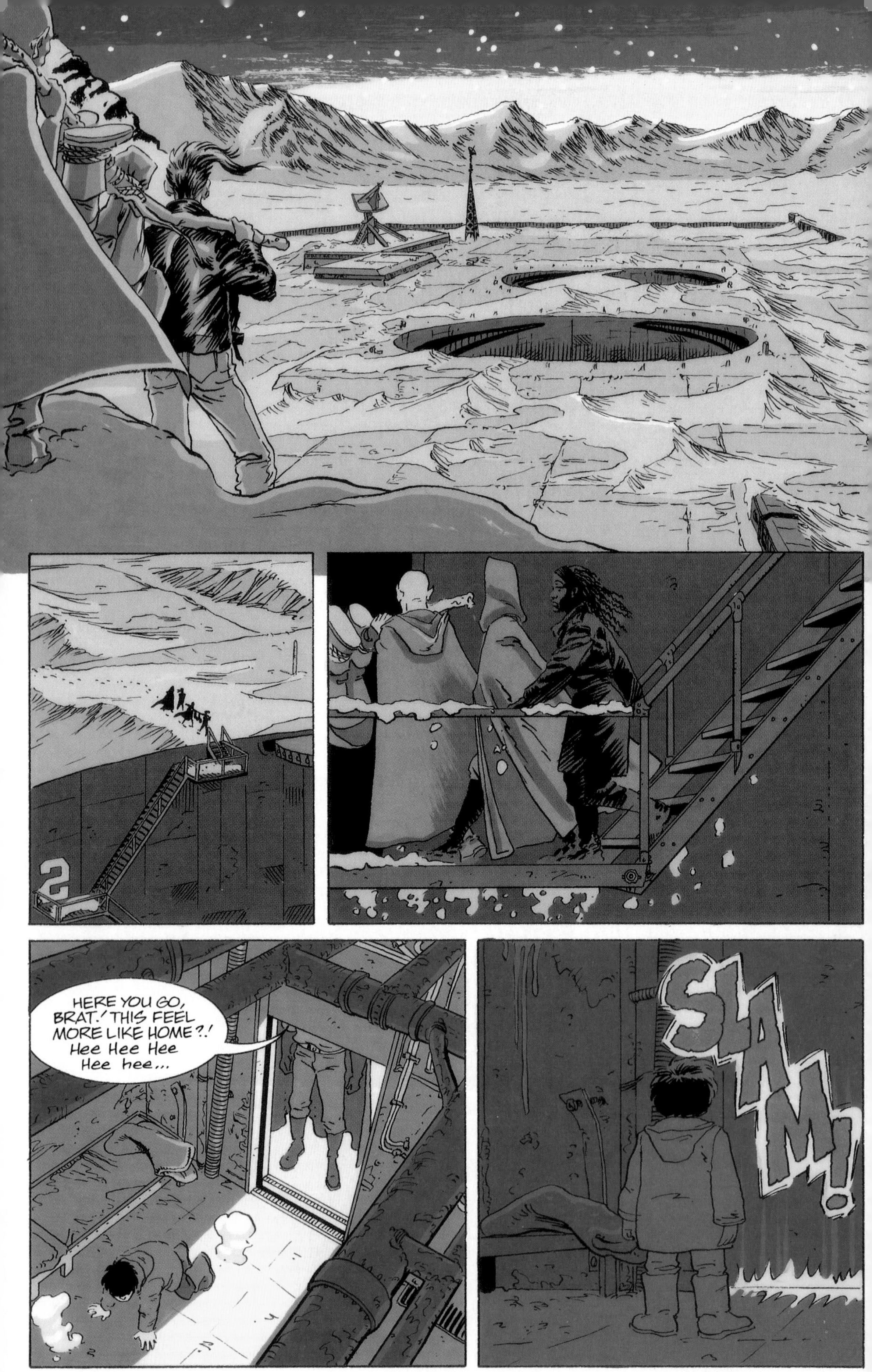
HERE YOU GO,
BRAT.! THIS FEEL
MORE LIKE HOME?!
Hee Hee Hee
Hee hee...
SLAM!

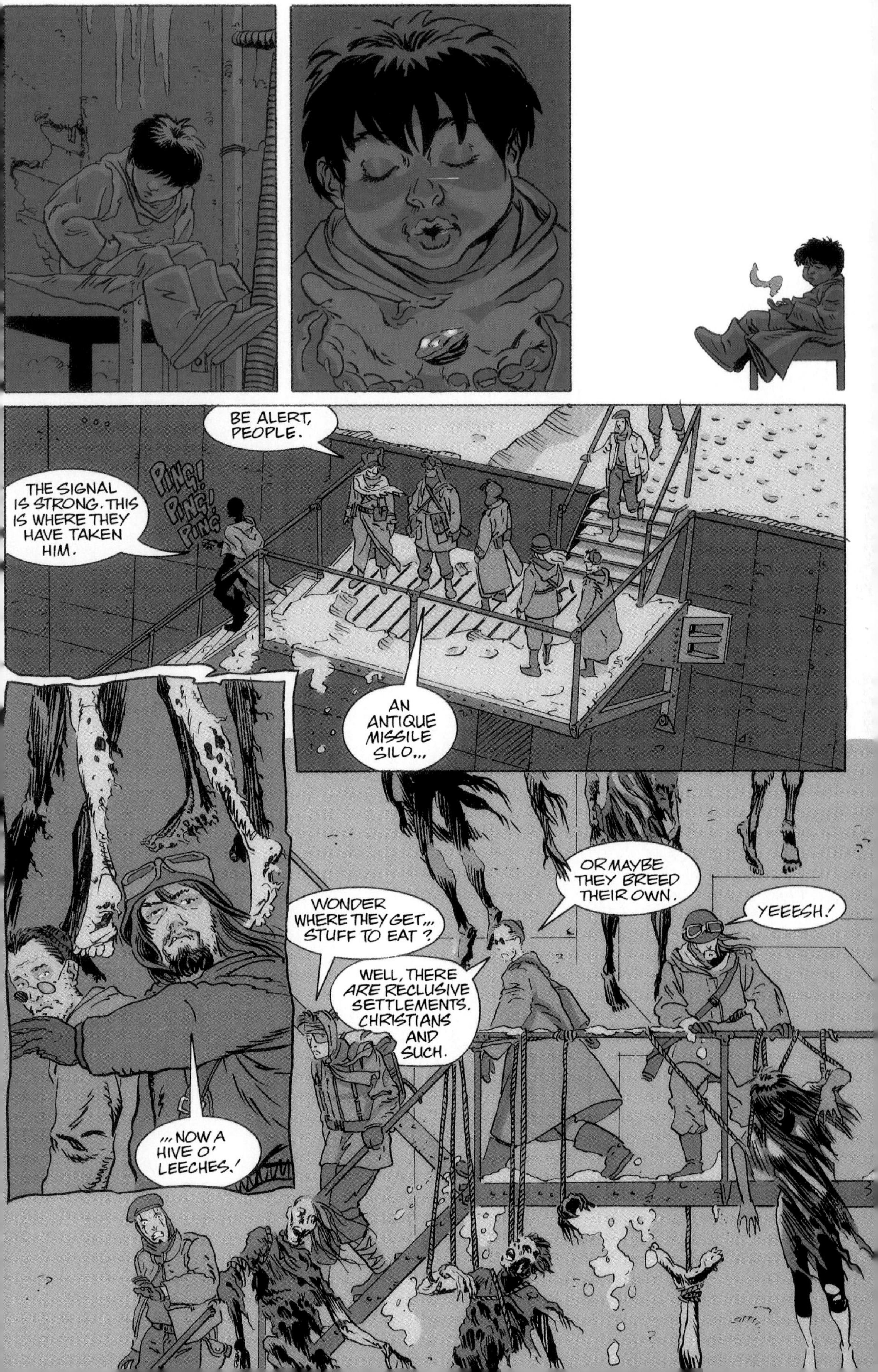
BE ALERT, PEOPLE.
PING! PING! PING
THE SIGNAL IS STRONG. THIS IS WHERE THEY HAVE TAKEN HIM.
AN ANTIQUE MISSILE SILO...
...NOW A HIVE O' LEECHES!
WONDER WHERE THEY GET... STUFF TO EAT ?
WELL, THERE ARE RECLUSIVE SETTLEMENTS. CHRISTIANS AND SUCH.
OR MAYBE THEY BREED THEIR OWN.
YEEESH!

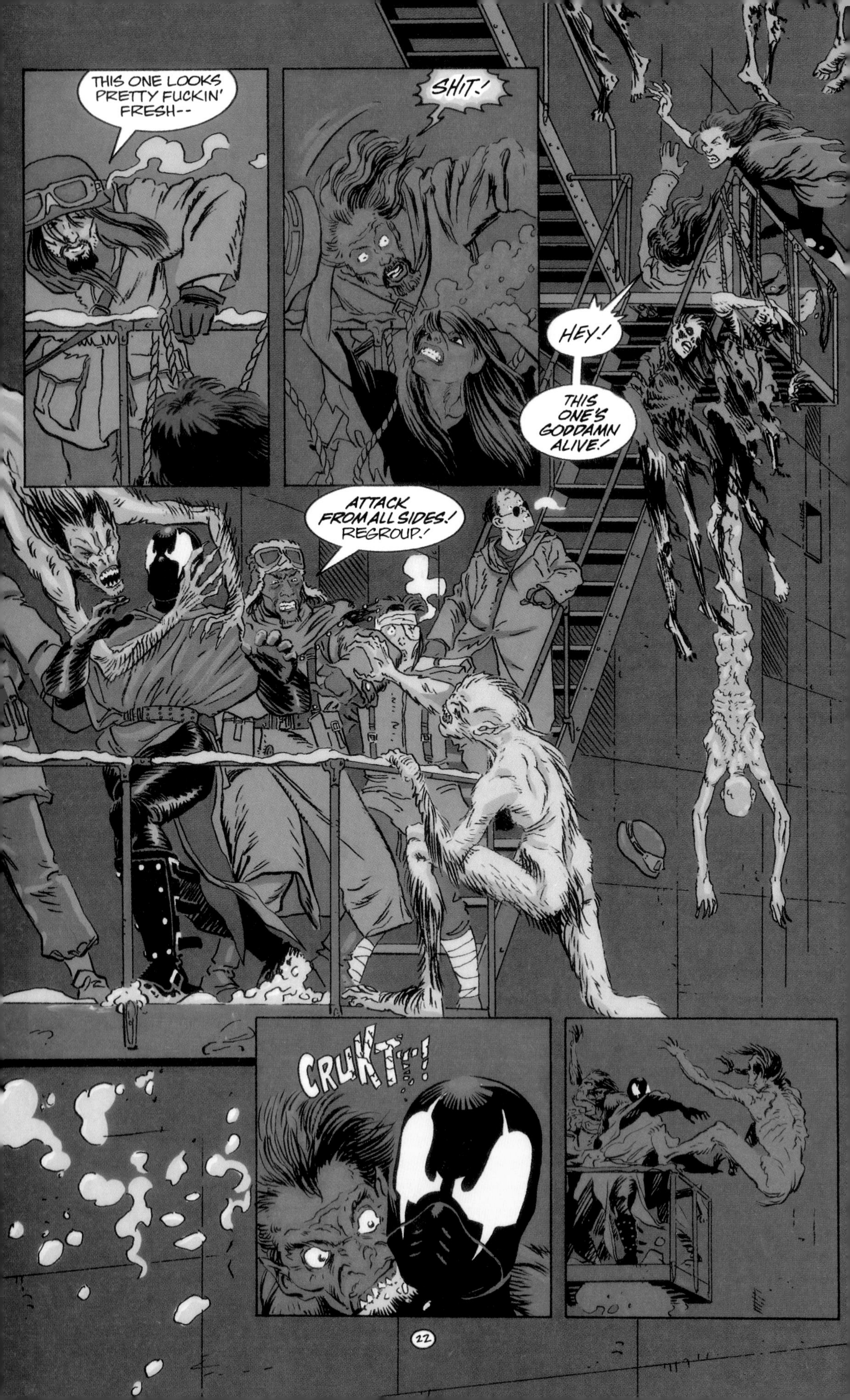
THIS ONE LOOKS PRETTY FUCKIN' FRESH--
SHIT!
HEY!
THIS ONE'S GODDAMN ALIVE!
ATTACK FROM ALL SIDES! REGROUP!
CRUNKT!!!

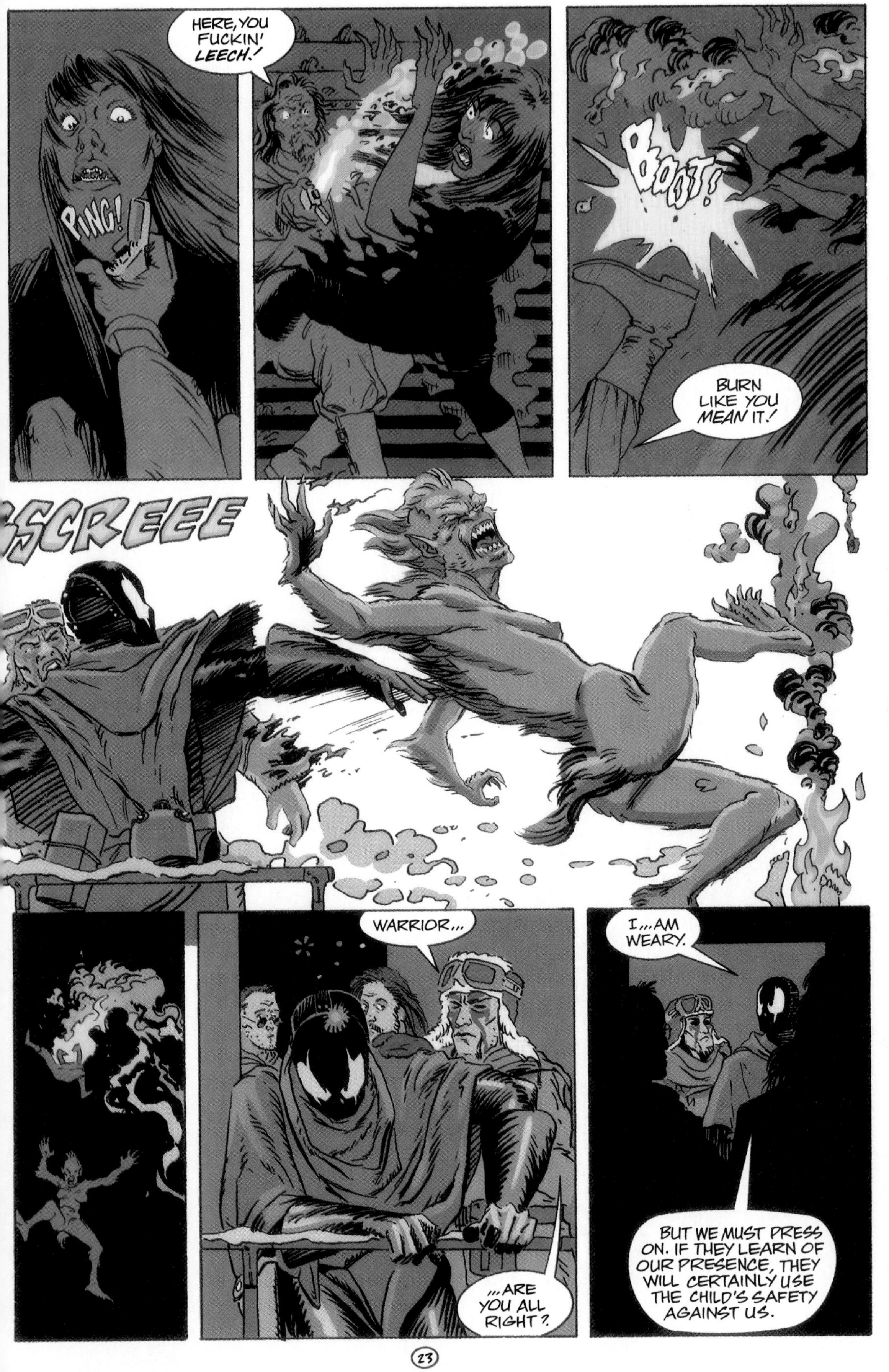
PING!
HERE, YOU FUCKIN' LEECH!
BOOT!
BURN LIKE YOU MEAN IT!
SCREEE
WARRIOR...
...ARE YOU ALL RIGHT?
I...AM WEARY.
BUT WE MUST PRESS ON. IF THEY LEARN OF OUR PRESENCE, THEY WILL CERTAINLY USE THE CHILD'S SAFETY AGAINST US.

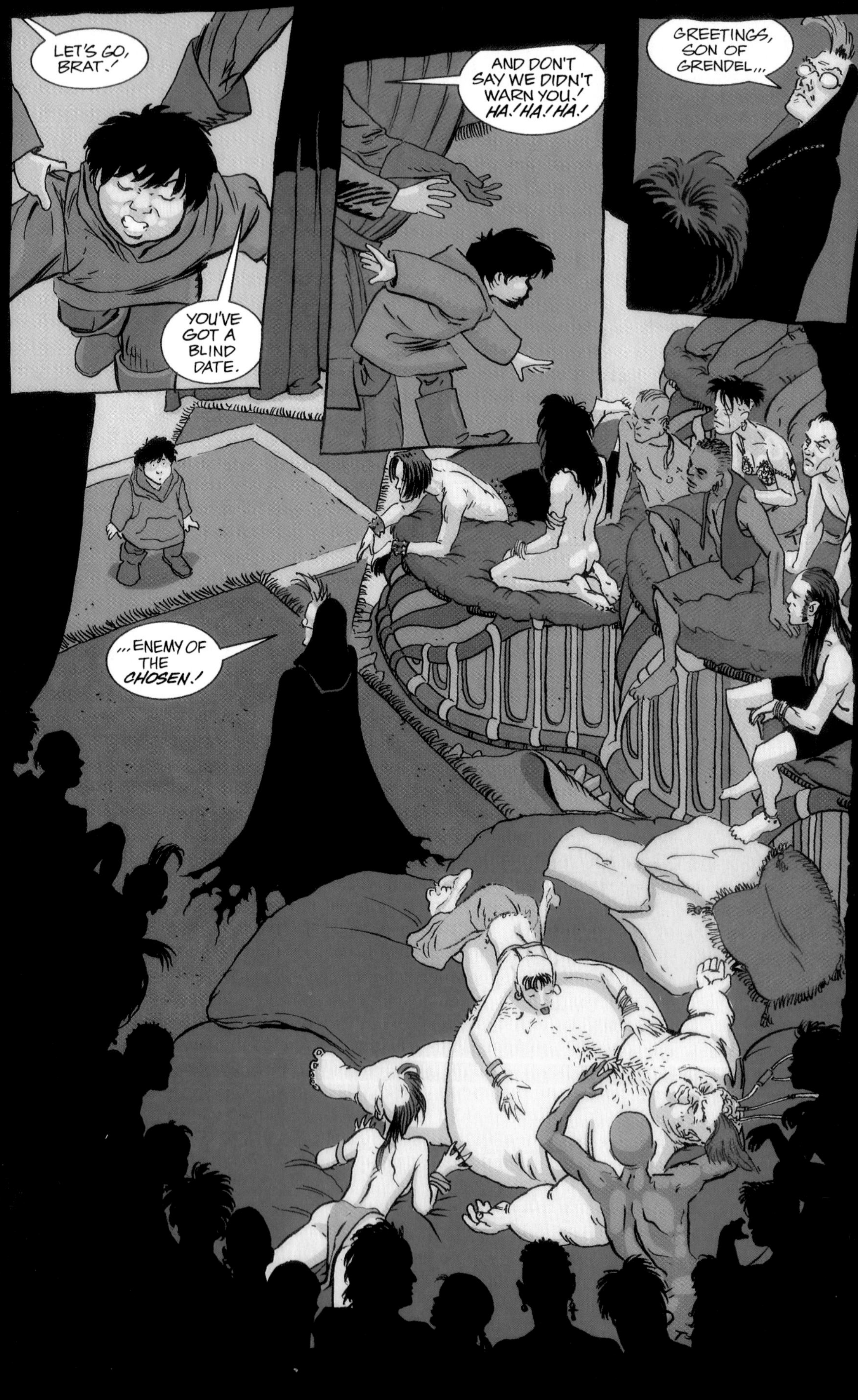
LET'S GO, BRAT.!
YOU'VE GOT A BLIND DATE.
AND DON'T SAY WE DIDN'T WARN YOU.! HA! HA! HA!
GREETINGS, SON OF GRENDEL...
...ENEMY OF THE CHOSEN.!

# CHAPTER 9
# DEVIL
## *to the rescue*

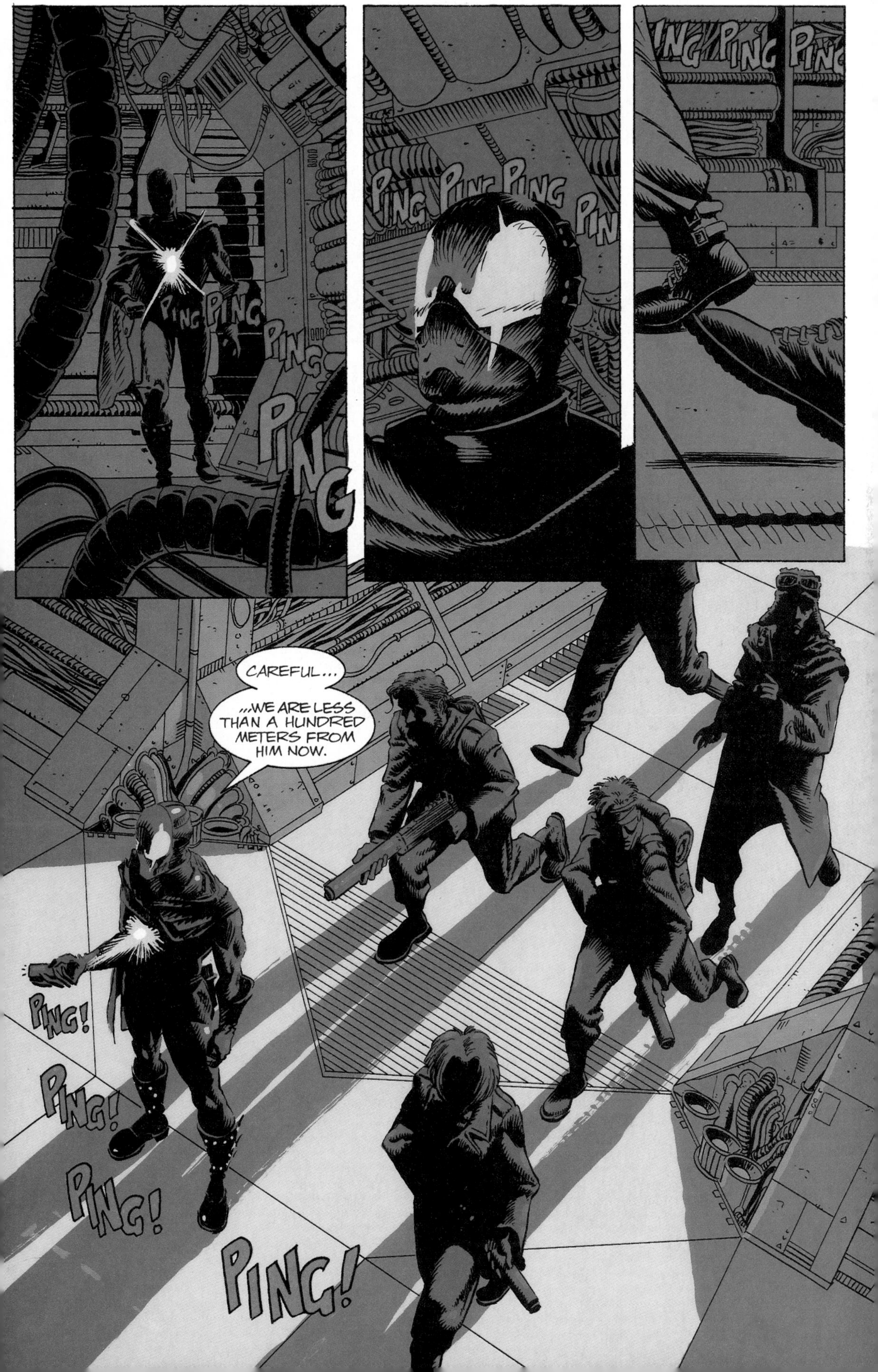
PING PING
PING
PING
PING PING PING PING PING
ING PING PING
CAREFUL...
...WE ARE LESS THAN A HUNDRED METERS FROM HIM NOW.
PING!
PING!
PING!
PING!

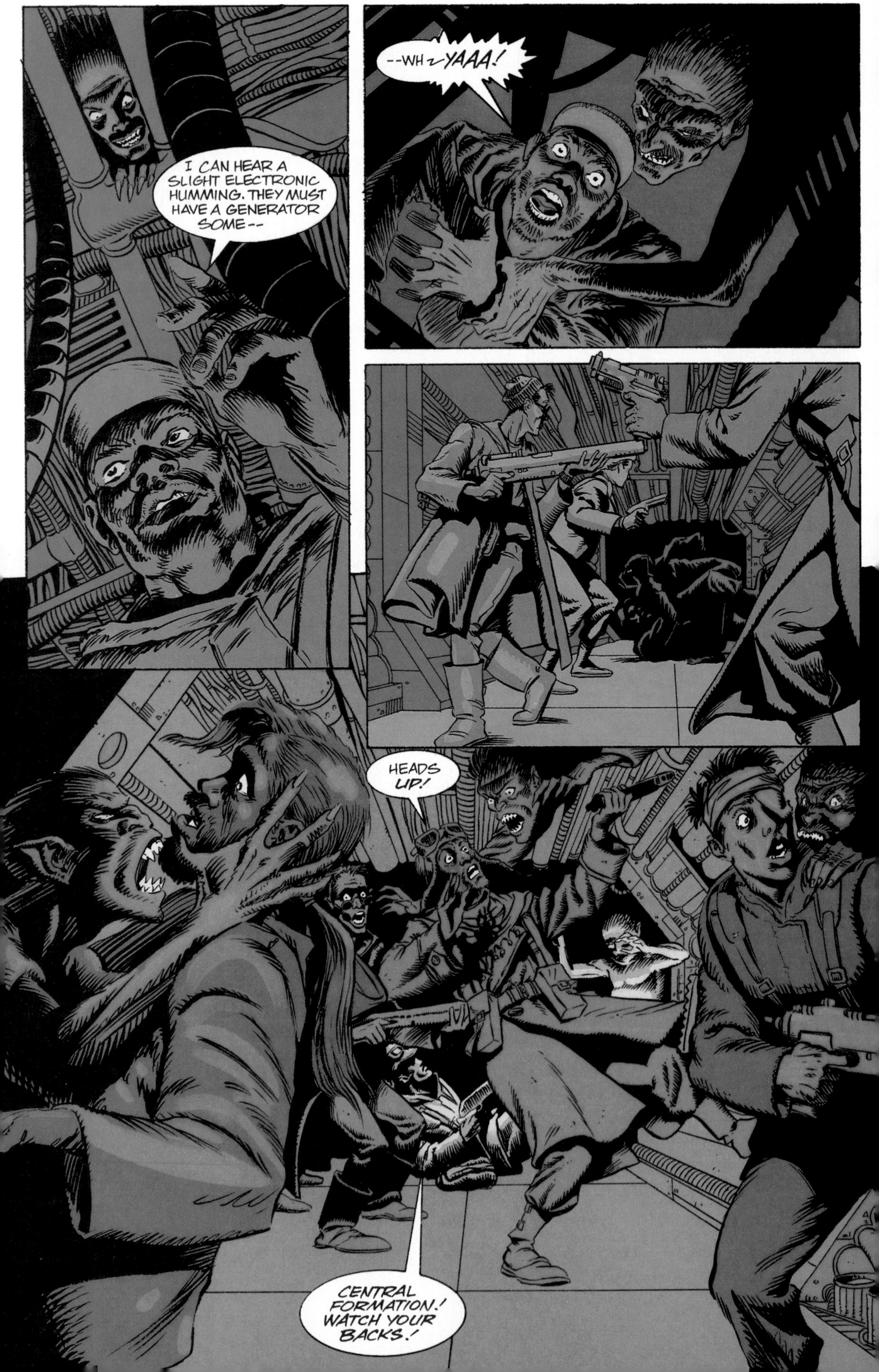
I CAN HEAR A SLIGHT ELECTRONIC HUMMING. THEY MUST HAVE A GENERATOR SOME--
--WH-YAAA!
HEADS UP!
CENTRAL FORMATION! WATCH YOUR BACKS!

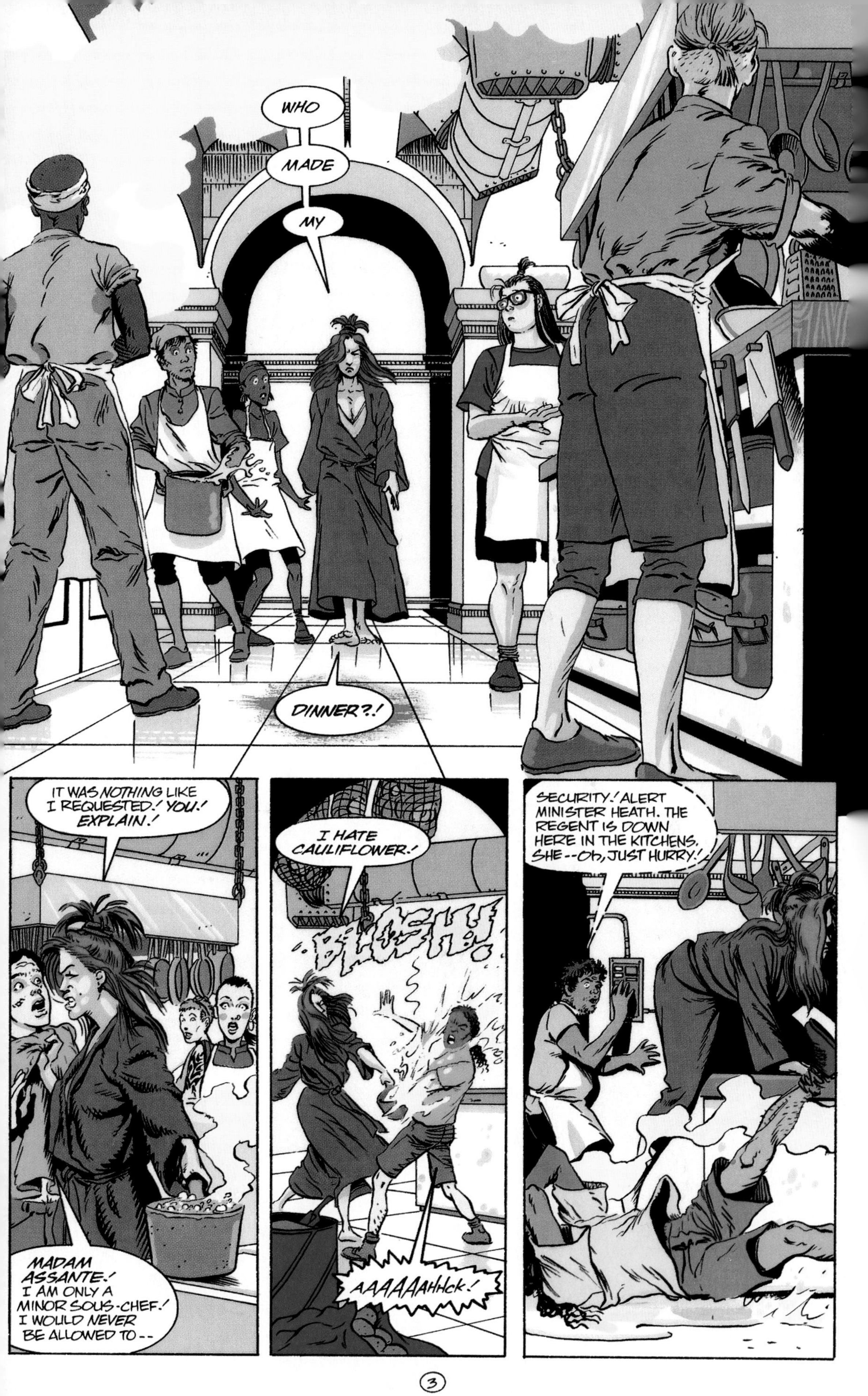
WHO
MADE
MY
DINNER?.!
IT WAS NOTHING LIKE I REQUESTED.! YOU.! EXPLAIN.!
MADAM ASSANTE.! I AM ONLY A MINOR SOUS-CHEF.! I WOULD NEVER BE ALLOWED TO--
I HATE CAULIFLOWER.!
BLOSH!
AAAAAAHHck.!
SECURITY.! ALERT MINISTER HEATH. THE REGENT IS DOWN HERE IN THE KITCHENS. SHE--Oh, JUST HURRY.!

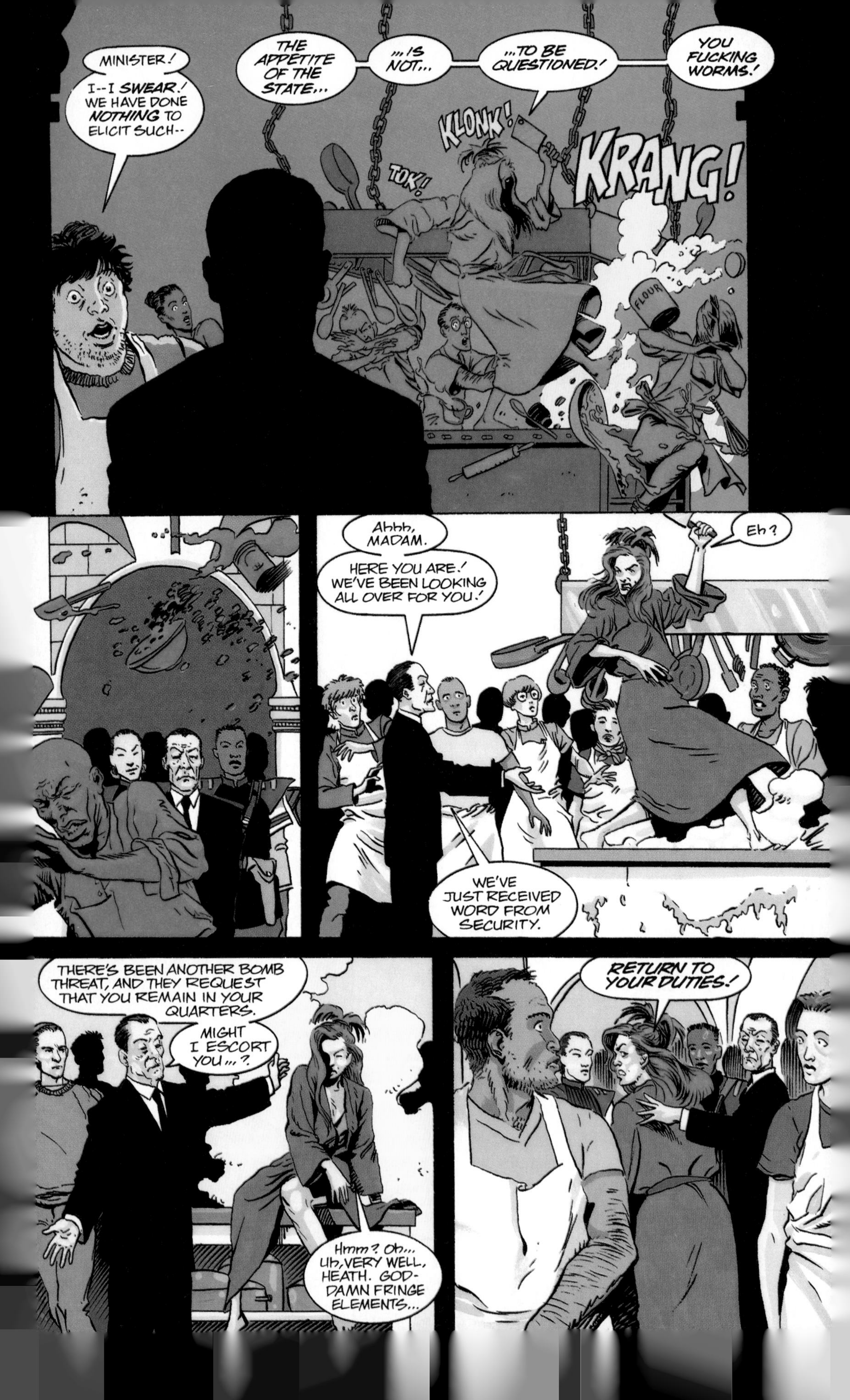
MINISTER! I--I SWEAR! WE HAVE DONE NOTHING TO ELICIT SUCH--
THE APPETITE OF THE STATE...
...IS NOT...
...TO BE QUESTIONED!
YOU FUCKING WORMS!
KLONK!
TOK!
KRANG!
FLOUR
Ahhh, MADAM.
HERE YOU ARE! WE'VE BEEN LOOKING ALL OVER FOR YOU!
Eh?
WE'VE JUST RECEIVED WORD FROM SECURITY.
THERE'S BEEN ANOTHER BOMB THREAT, AND THEY REQUEST THAT YOU REMAIN IN YOUR QUARTERS.
MIGHT I ESCORT YOU...?
Hmm? Oh... Uh, VERY WELL, HEATH. GOD-DAMN FRINGE ELEMENTS...
RETURN TO YOUR DUTIES!

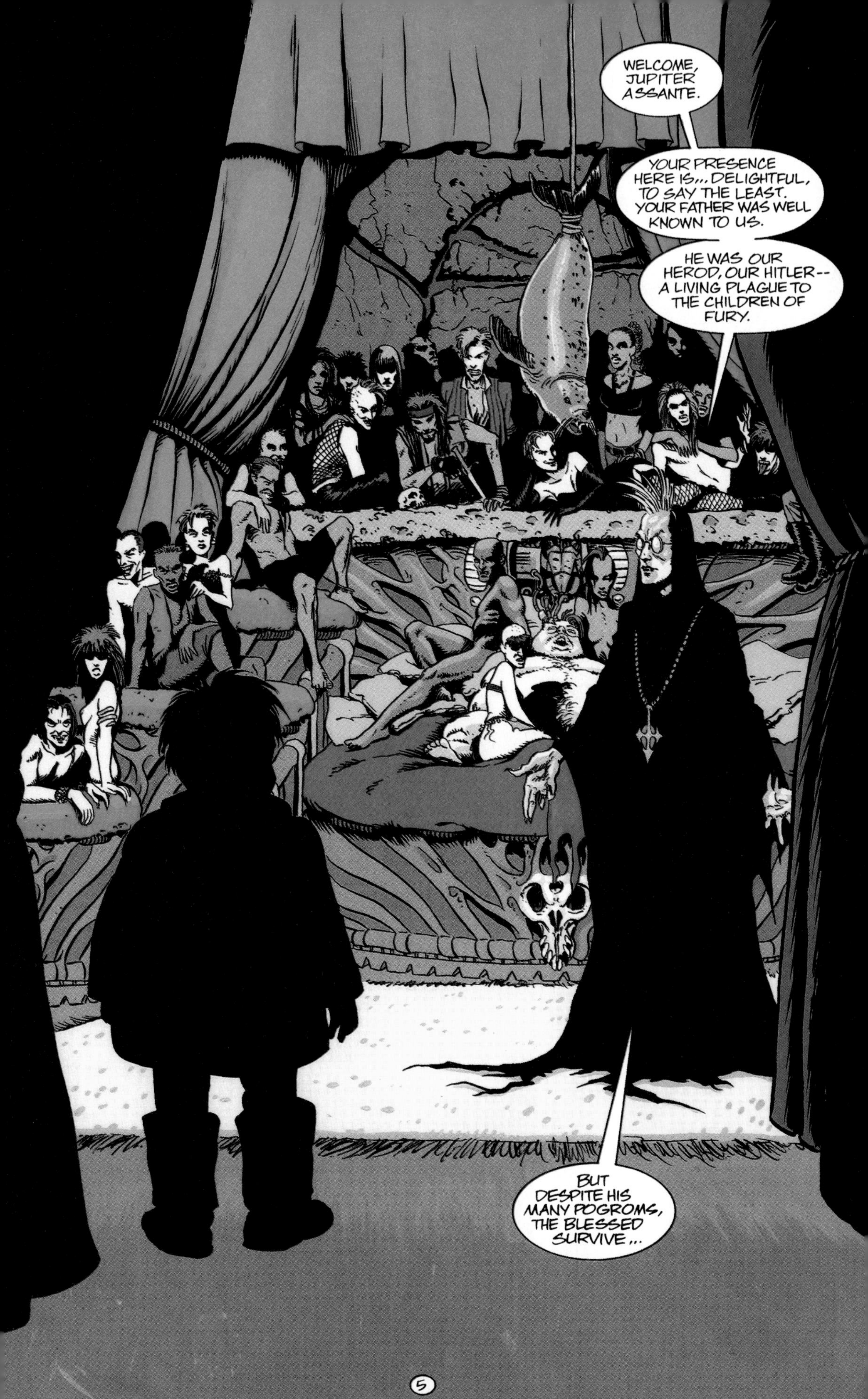
WELCOME, JUPITER ASSANTE.
YOUR PRESENCE HERE IS... DELIGHTFUL, TO SAY THE LEAST. YOUR FATHER WAS WELL KNOWN TO US.
HE WAS OUR HEROD, OUR HITLER-- A LIVING PLAGUE TO THE CHILDREN OF FURY.
BUT DESPITE HIS MANY POGROMS, THE BLESSED SURVIVE...

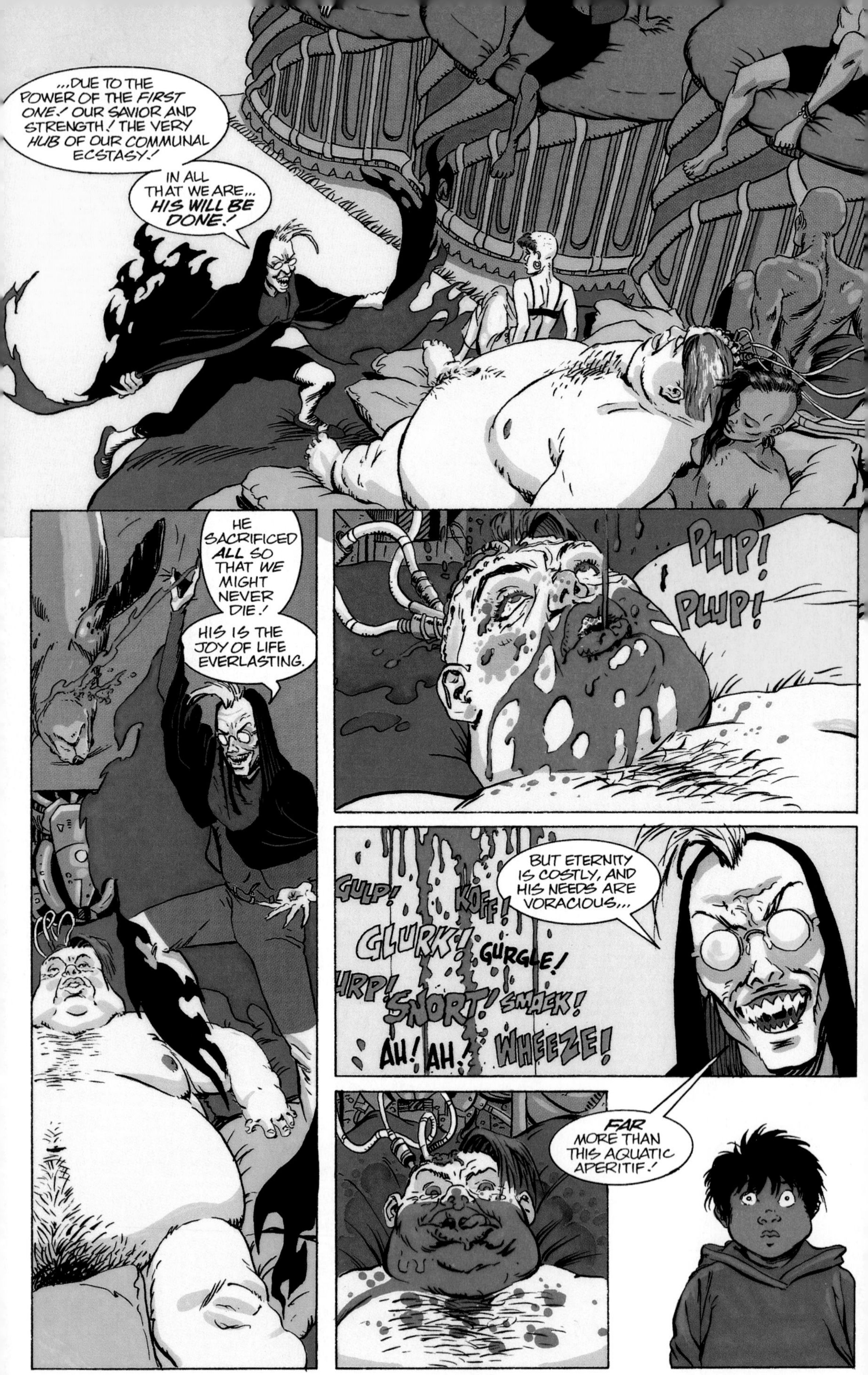
...DUE TO THE POWER OF THE FIRST ONE! OUR SAVIOR AND STRENGTH! THE VERY HUB OF OUR COMMUNAL ECSTASY!
IN ALL THAT WE ARE... HIS WILL BE DONE!
HE SACRIFICED ALL SO THAT WE MIGHT NEVER DIE!
HIS IS THE JOY OF LIFE EVERLASTING.
PLIP! PLUP!
GULP! KOFF! GLURK! GURGLE! HRP! SNORT! SMACK! AH! AH! WHEEZE!
BUT ETERNITY IS COSTLY, AND HIS NEEDS ARE VORACIOUS...
FAR MORE THAN THIS AQUATIC APERITIF!

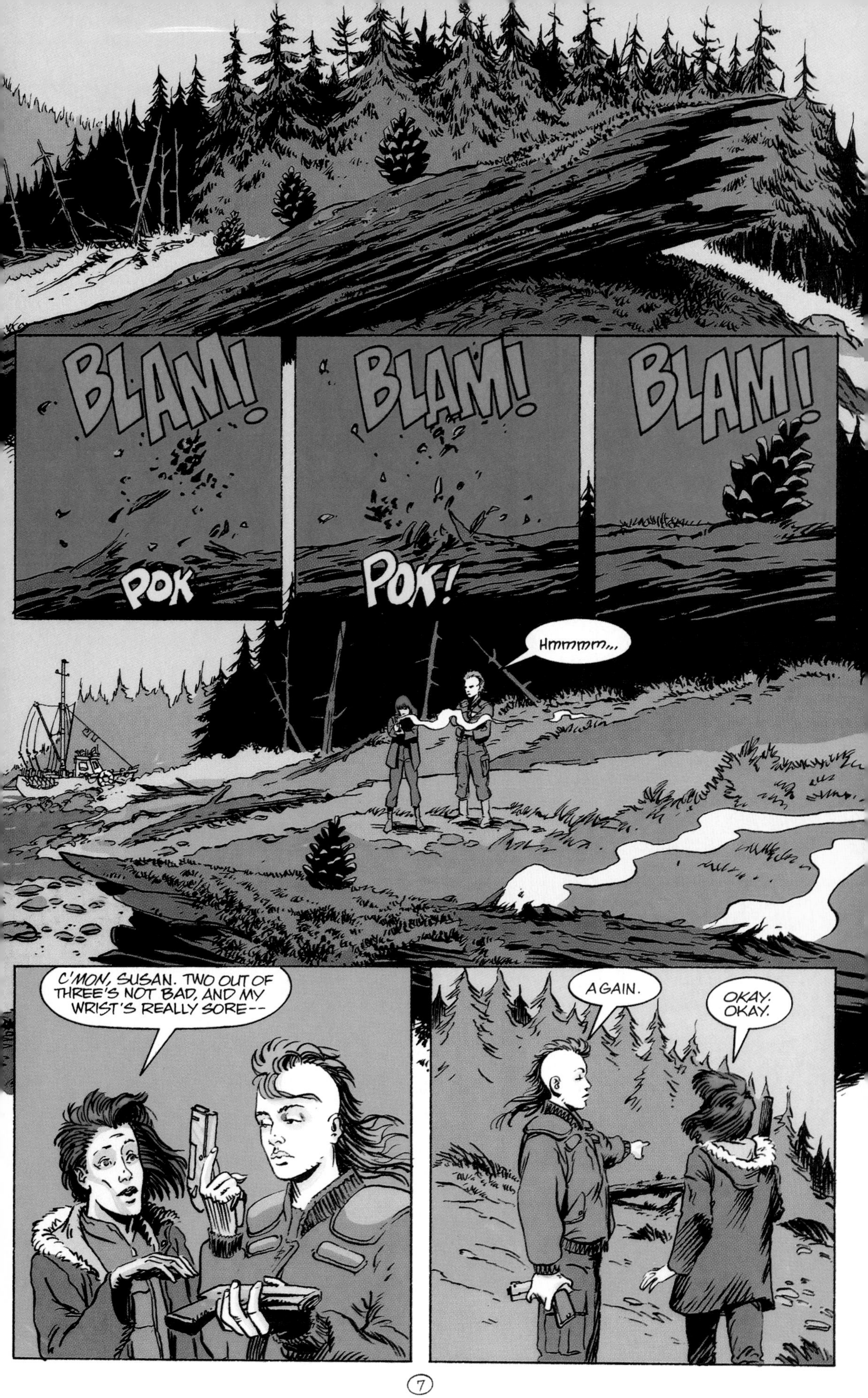
BLAM!
POK
BLAM!
POK!
BLAM!
Hmmmm...
C'MON, SUSAN. TWO OUT OF THREE'S NOT BAD, AND MY WRIST'S REALLY SORE--
AGAIN.
OKAY. OKAY.

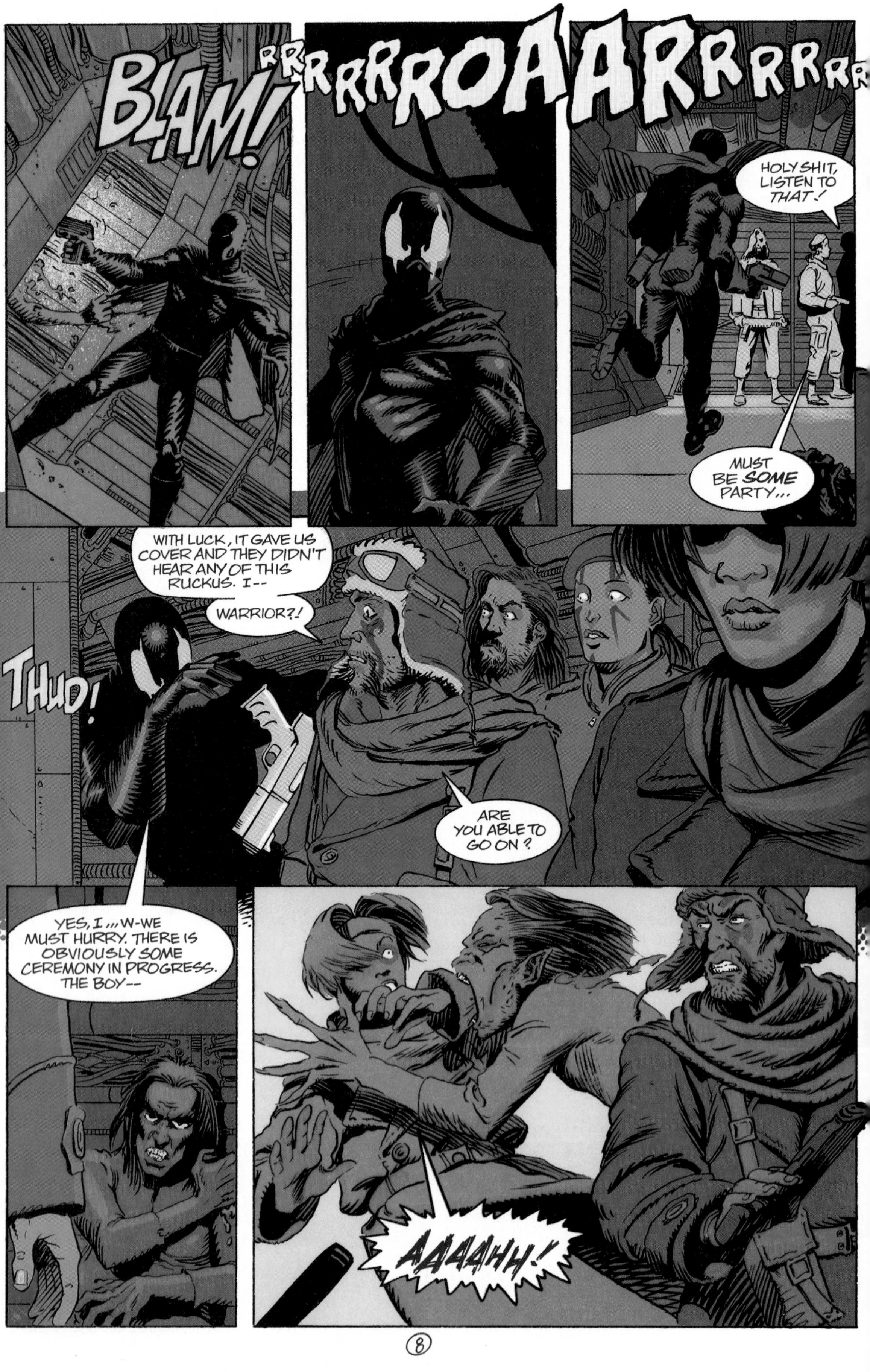

BLAM!
RRRRROAARRRRRR
HOLY SHIT, LISTEN TO THAT!
MUST BE SOME PARTY...
WITH LUCK, IT GAVE US COVER AND THEY DIDN'T HEAR ANY OF THIS RUCKUS. I--
WARRIOR?!
THUD!
ARE YOU ABLE TO GO ON?
YES, I... W-WE MUST HURRY. THERE IS OBVIOUSLY SOME CEREMONY IN PROGRESS. THE BOY--
AAAAHH!

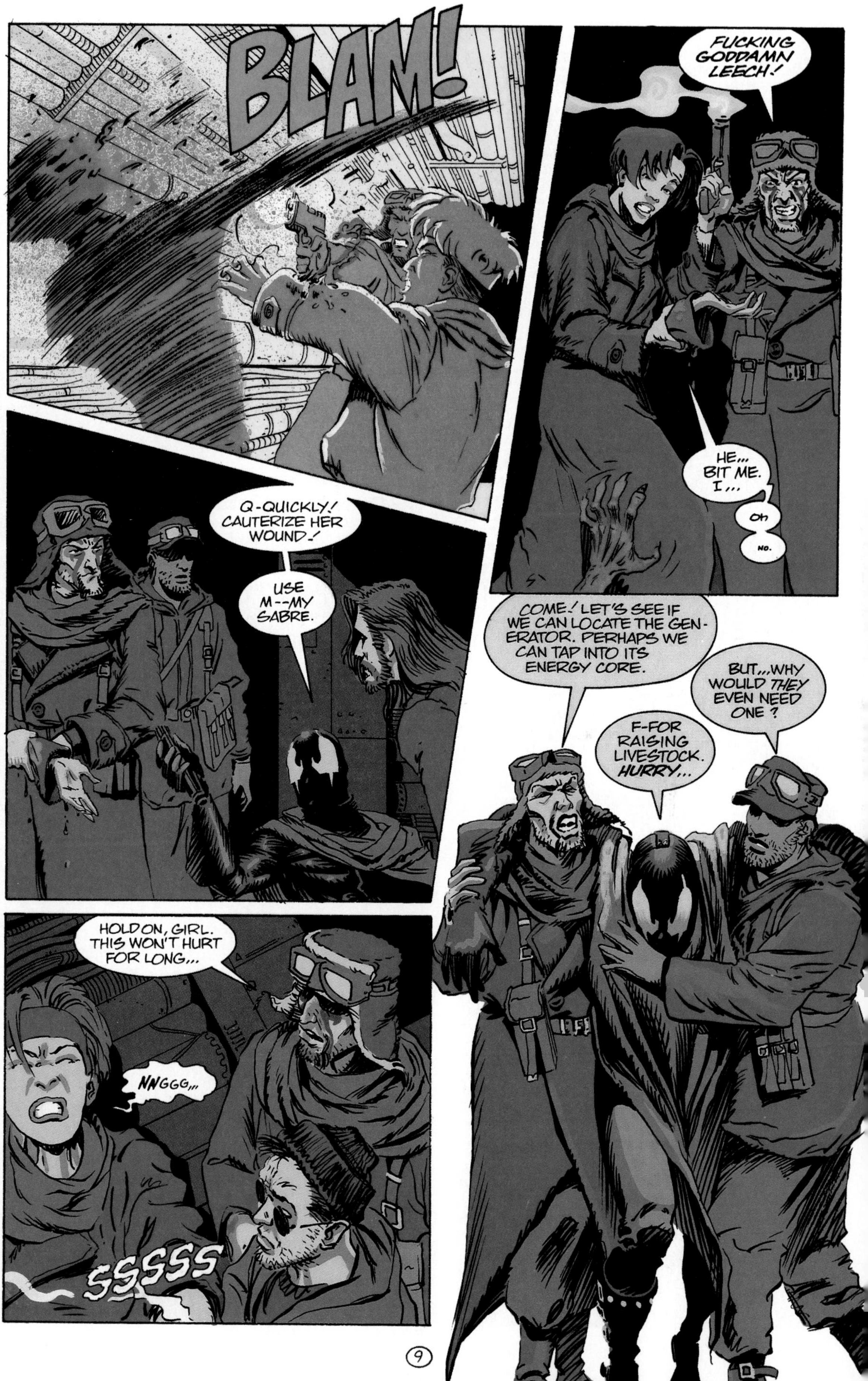
BLAM!
FUCKING GODDAMN LEECH!
HE... BIT ME. I...
Oh
NO.
Q-QUICKLY! CAUTERIZE HER WOUND!
USE M--MY SABRE.
COME! LET'S SEE IF WE CAN LOCATE THE GENERATOR. PERHAPS WE CAN TAP INTO ITS ENERGY CORE.
BUT...WHY WOULD THEY EVEN NEED ONE?
F-FOR RAISING LIVESTOCK. HURRY...
HOLD ON, GIRL. THIS WON'T HURT FOR LONG...
NNGGG...
SSSSS

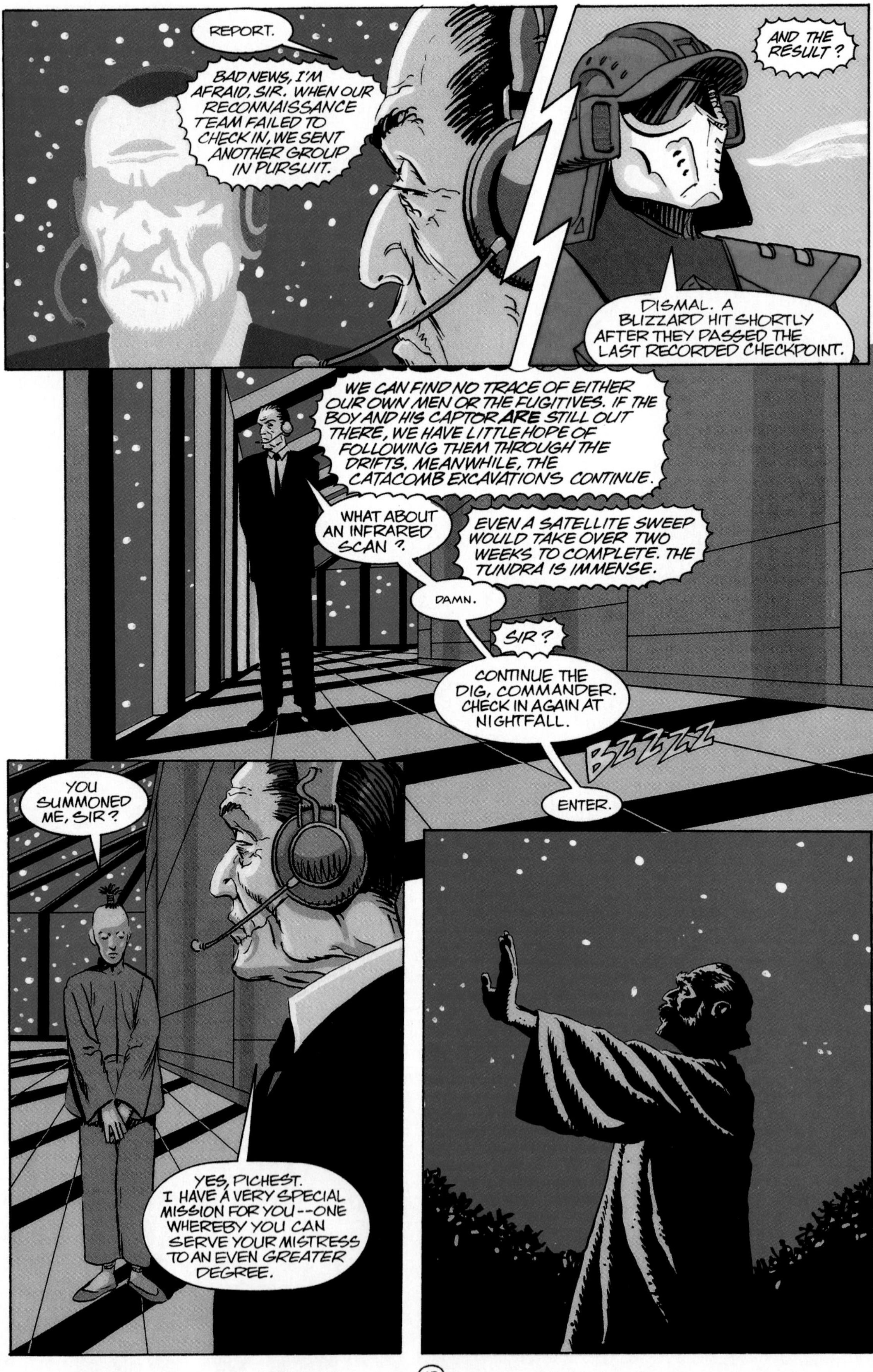
REPORT.
BAD NEWS, I'M AFRAID, SIR. WHEN OUR RECONNAISSANCE TEAM FAILED TO CHECK IN, WE SENT ANOTHER GROUP IN PURSUIT.
AND THE RESULT?
DISMAL. A BLIZZARD HIT SHORTLY AFTER THEY PASSED THE LAST RECORDED CHECKPOINT.
WE CAN FIND NO TRACE OF EITHER OUR OWN MEN OR THE FUGITIVES. IF THE BOY AND HIS CAPTOR ARE STILL OUT THERE, WE HAVE LITTLE HOPE OF FOLLOWING THEM THROUGH THE DRIFTS. MEANWHILE, THE CATACOMB EXCAVATIONS CONTINUE.
WHAT ABOUT AN INFRARED SCAN?
EVEN A SATELLITE SWEEP WOULD TAKE OVER TWO WEEKS TO COMPLETE. THE TUNDRA IS IMMENSE.
DAMN.
SIR?
CONTINUE THE DIG, COMMANDER. CHECK IN AGAIN AT NIGHTFALL.
BZZZZZ
ENTER.
YOU SUMMONED ME, SIR?
YES, PICHEST. I HAVE A VERY SPECIAL MISSION FOR YOU--ONE WHEREBY YOU CAN SERVE YOUR MISTRESS TO AN EVEN GREATER DEGREE.

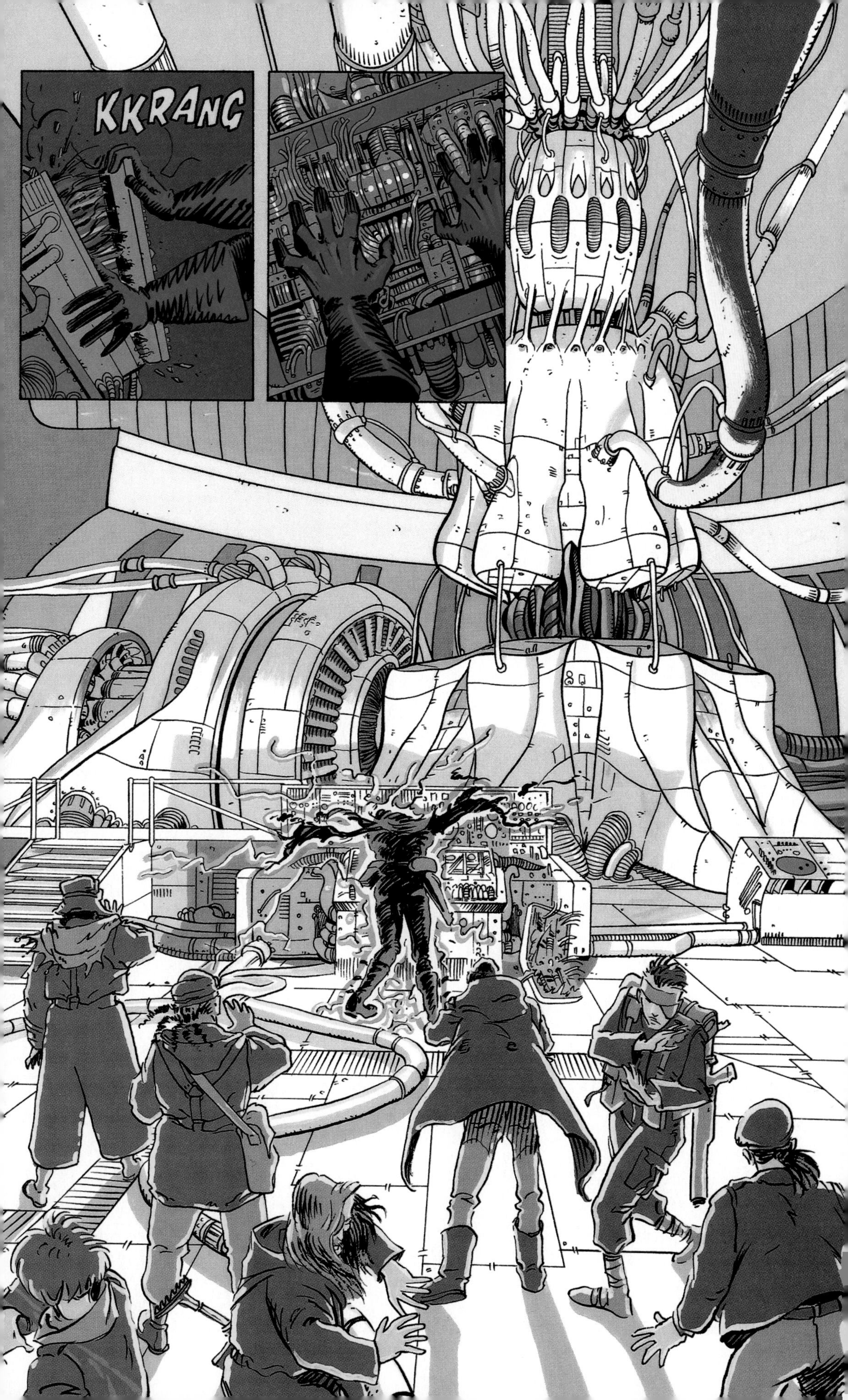
KKRANG

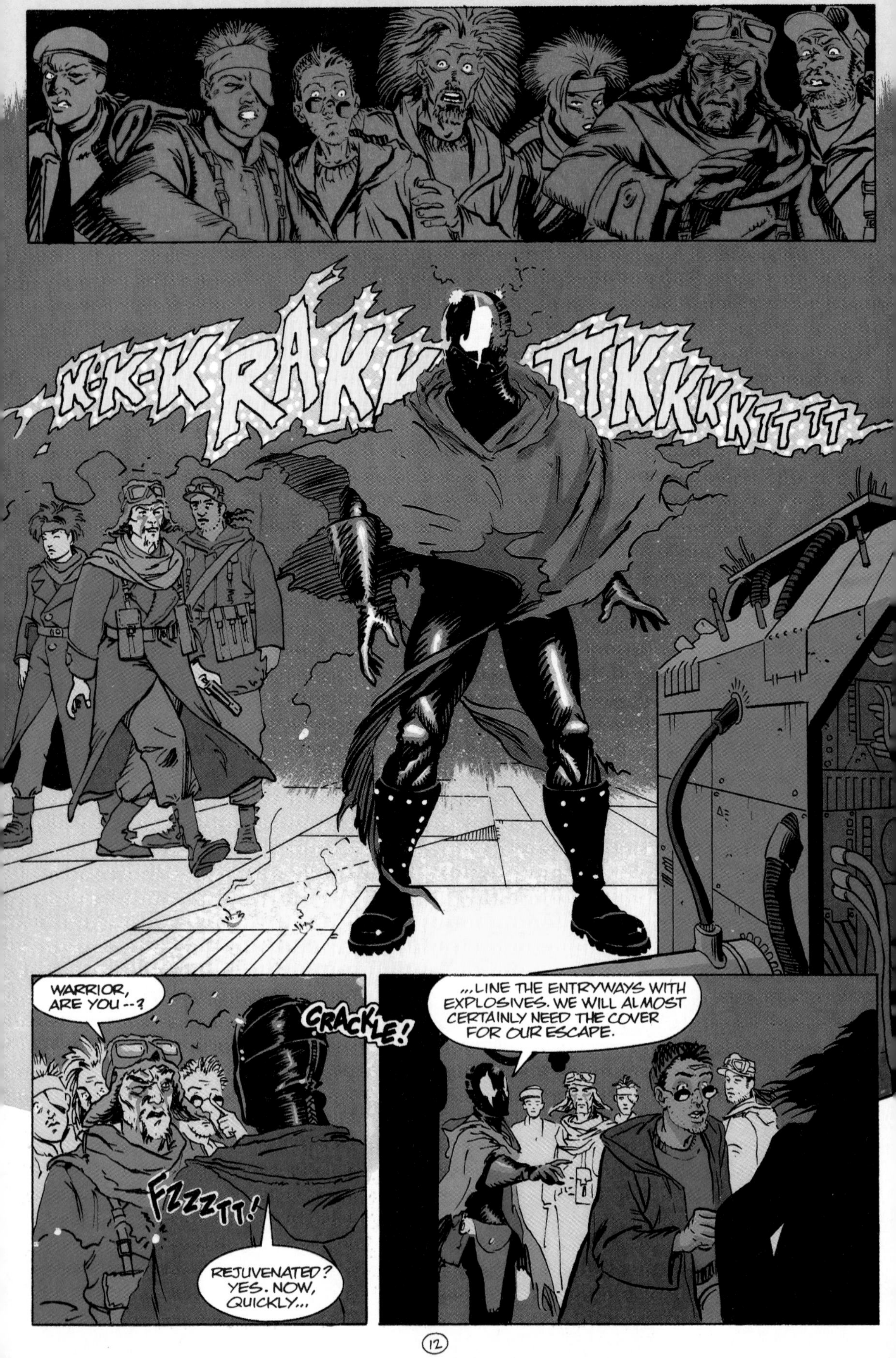
K-K-KRAKK TTKKKKTTTTT
WARRIOR, ARE YOU --?
CRACKLE!
FZZZTT!
REJUVENATED? YES. NOW, QUICKLY...
...LINE THE ENTRYWAYS WITH EXPLOSIVES. WE WILL ALMOST CERTAINLY NEED THE COVER FOR OUR ESCAPE.

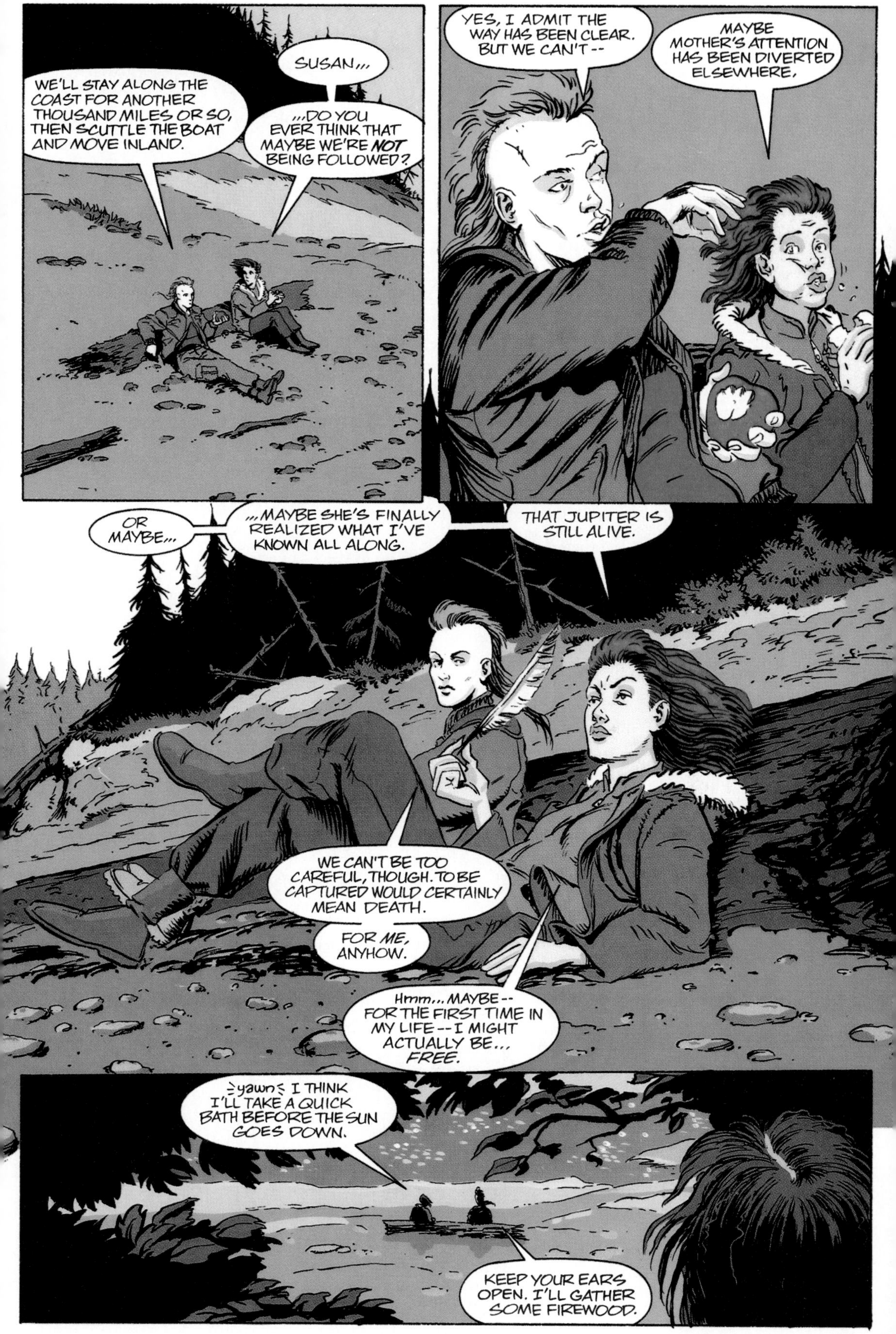
WE'LL STAY ALONG THE COAST FOR ANOTHER THOUSAND MILES OR SO, THEN SCUTTLE THE BOAT AND MOVE INLAND.
SUSAN...
...DO YOU EVER THINK THAT MAYBE WE'RE NOT BEING FOLLOWED?
YES, I ADMIT THE WAY HAS BEEN CLEAR. BUT WE CAN'T --
MAYBE MOTHER'S ATTENTION HAS BEEN DIVERTED ELSEWHERE.
OR MAYBE...
...MAYBE SHE'S FINALLY REALIZED WHAT I'VE KNOWN ALL ALONG.
THAT JUPITER IS STILL ALIVE.
WE CAN'T BE TOO CAREFUL, THOUGH. TO BE CAPTURED WOULD CERTAINLY MEAN DEATH.
FOR ME, ANYHOW.
Hmm... MAYBE -- FOR THE FIRST TIME IN MY LIFE -- I MIGHT ACTUALLY BE... FREE.
yawn I THINK I'LL TAKE A QUICK BATH BEFORE THE SUN GOES DOWN.
KEEP YOUR EARS OPEN. I'LL GATHER SOME FIREWOOD.

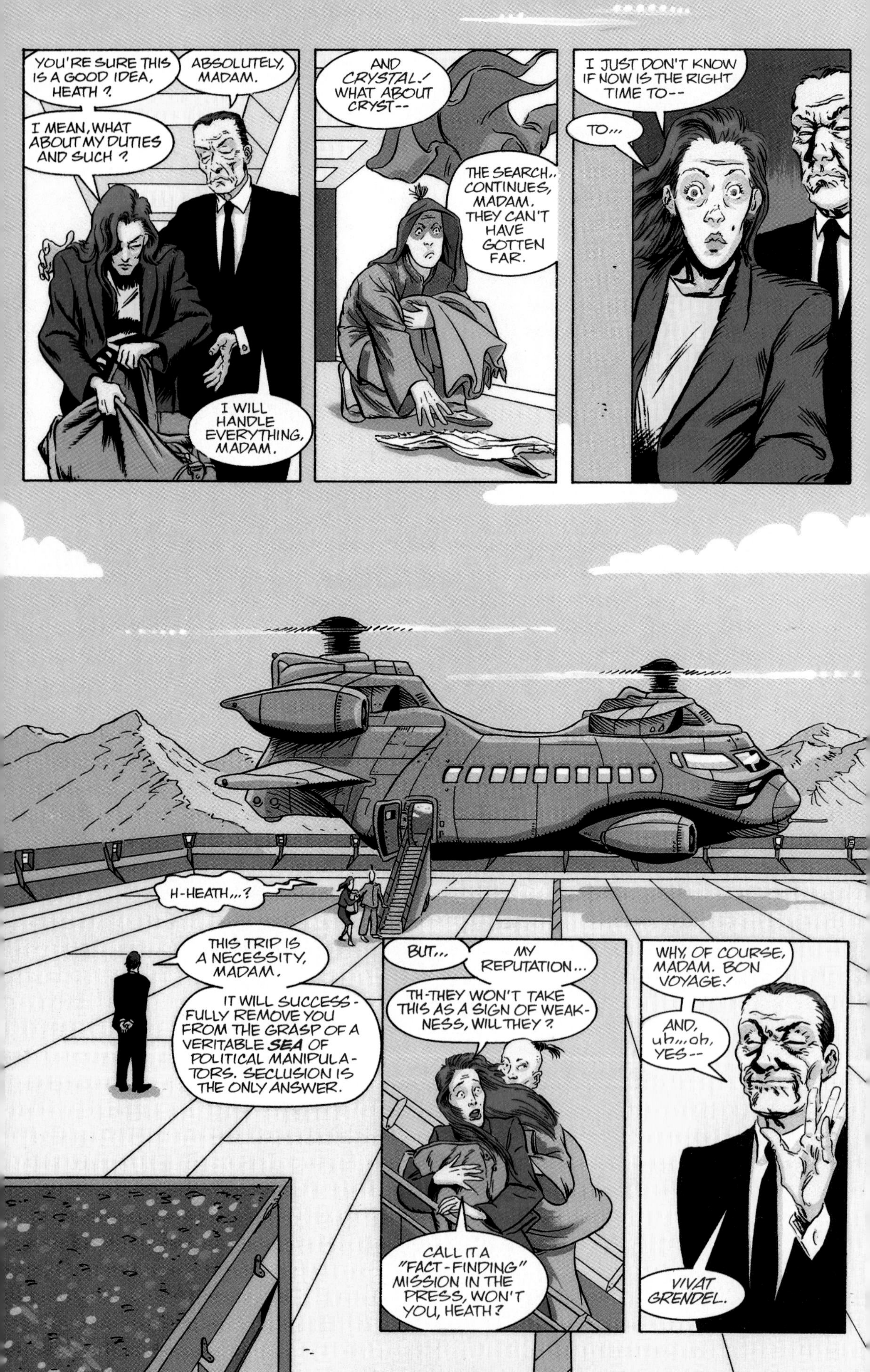
YOU'RE SURE THIS IS A GOOD IDEA, HEATH ?
ABSOLUTELY, MADAM.
I MEAN, WHAT ABOUT MY DUTIES AND SUCH ?
I WILL HANDLE EVERYTHING, MADAM.
AND CRYSTAL! WHAT ABOUT CRYST--
THE SEARCH,, CONTINUES, MADAM. THEY CAN'T HAVE GOTTEN FAR.
I JUST DON'T KNOW IF NOW IS THE RIGHT TIME TO--
TO,,,
H-HEATH,,,?
THIS TRIP IS A NECESSITY, MADAM.
IT WILL SUCCESS-FULLY REMOVE YOU FROM THE GRASP OF A VERITABLE SEA OF POLITICAL MANIPULA-TORS. SECLUSION IS THE ONLY ANSWER.
BUT,,,
MY REPUTATION...
TH-THEY WON'T TAKE THIS AS A SIGN OF WEAK-NESS, WILL THEY ?
CALL IT A "FACT-FINDING" MISSION IN THE PRESS, WON'T YOU, HEATH ?
WHY, OF COURSE, MADAM. BON VOYAGE!
AND, uh,,,oh, YES--
VIVAT GRENDEL.

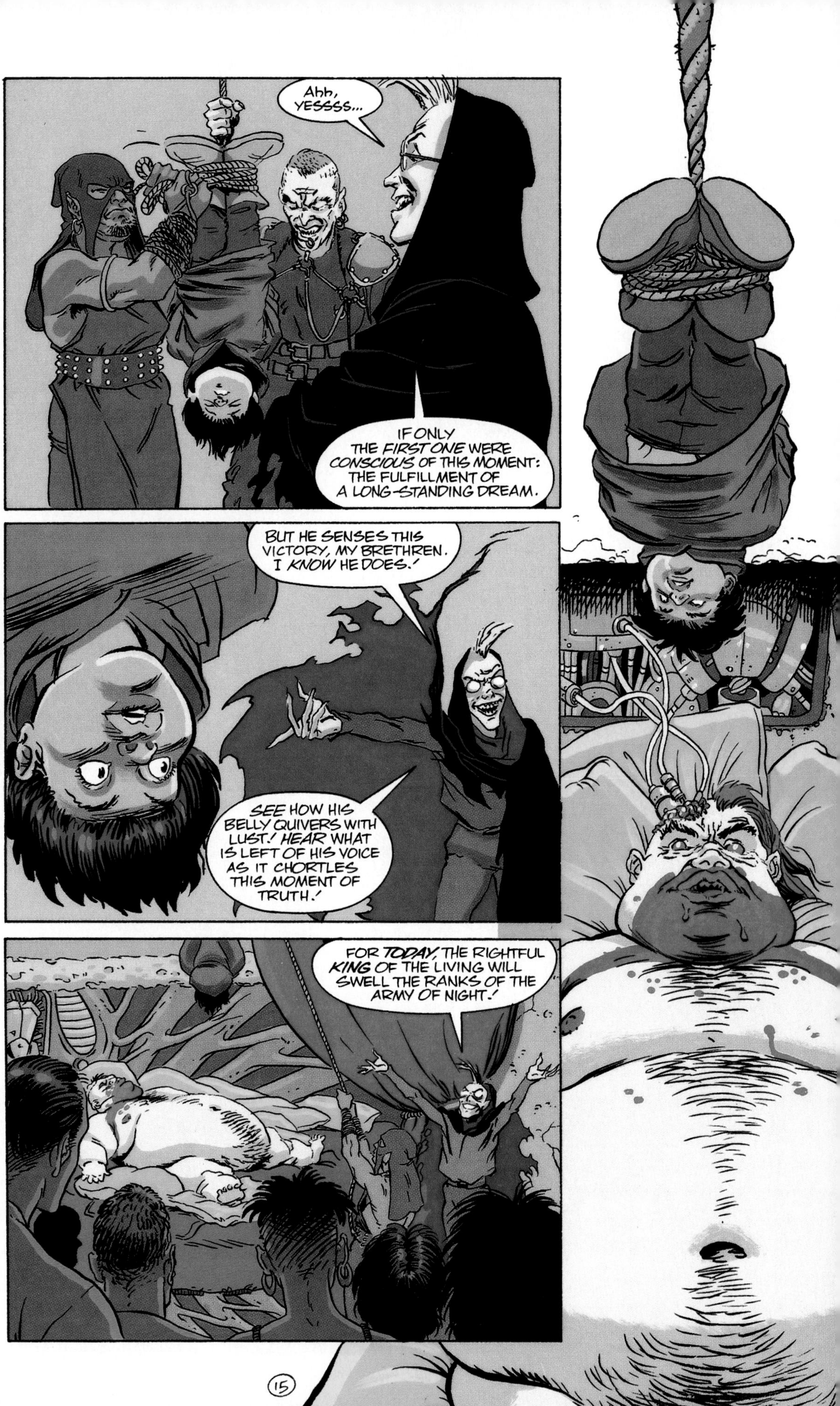
Ahh, YESSSS...
IF ONLY THE FIRST ONE WERE CONSCIOUS OF THIS MOMENT: THE FULFILLMENT OF A LONG-STANDING DREAM.
BUT HE SENSES THIS VICTORY, MY BRETHREN. I KNOW HE DOES.!
SEE HOW HIS BELLY QUIVERS WITH LUST! HEAR WHAT IS LEFT OF HIS VOICE AS IT CHORTLES THIS MOMENT OF TRUTH.!
FOR TODAY, THE RIGHTFUL KING OF THE LIVING WILL SWELL THE RANKS OF THE ARMY OF NIGHT.!

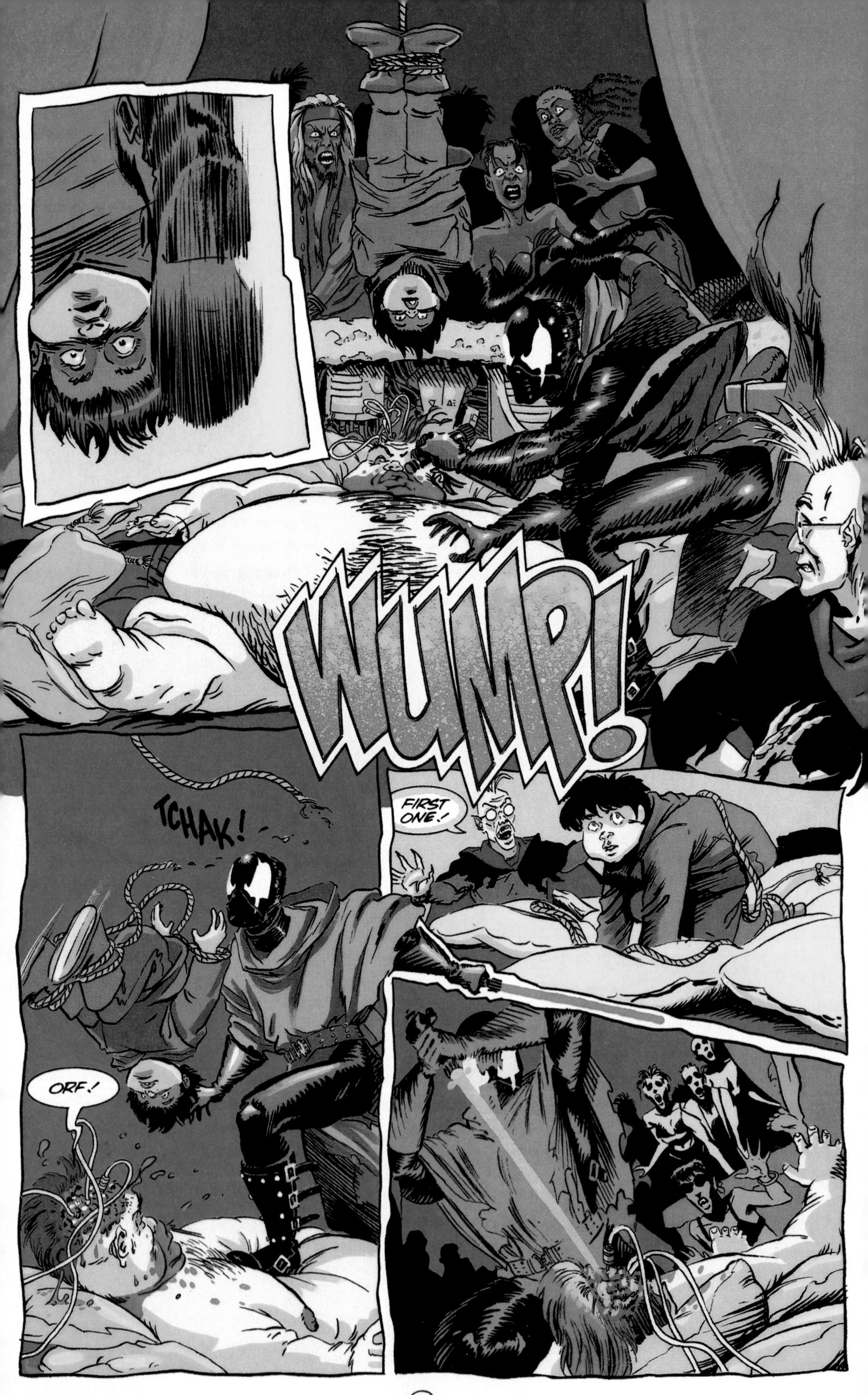
WUMP!
TCHAK!
FIRST ONE.!
ORF!

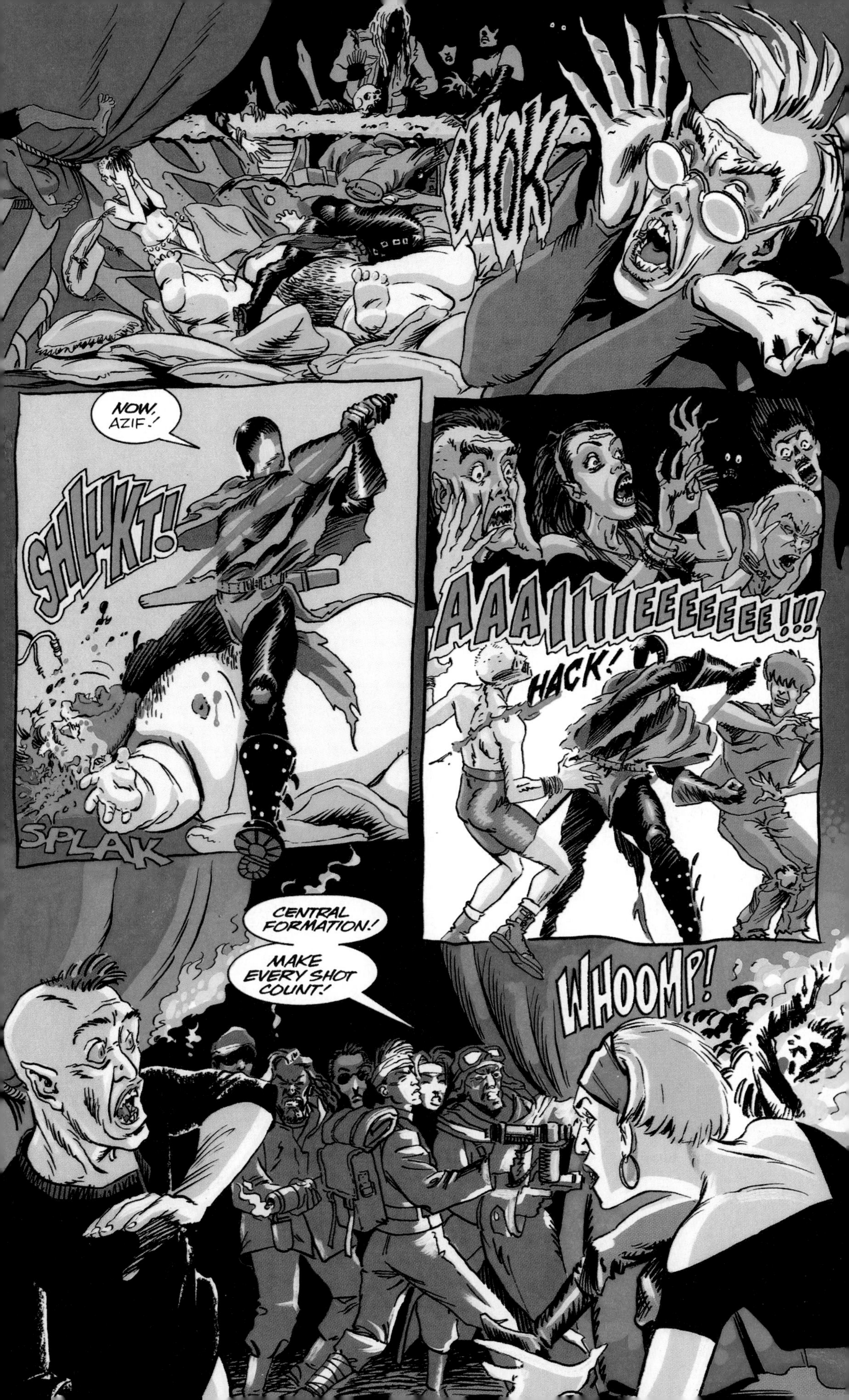
CHOK!
NOW, AZIF.!
SHLUKT!
SPLAK
AAAIIIIEEEEEEEE!!!
HACK!
CENTRAL FORMATION.!
MAKE EVERY SHOT COUNT.!
WHOOMP!

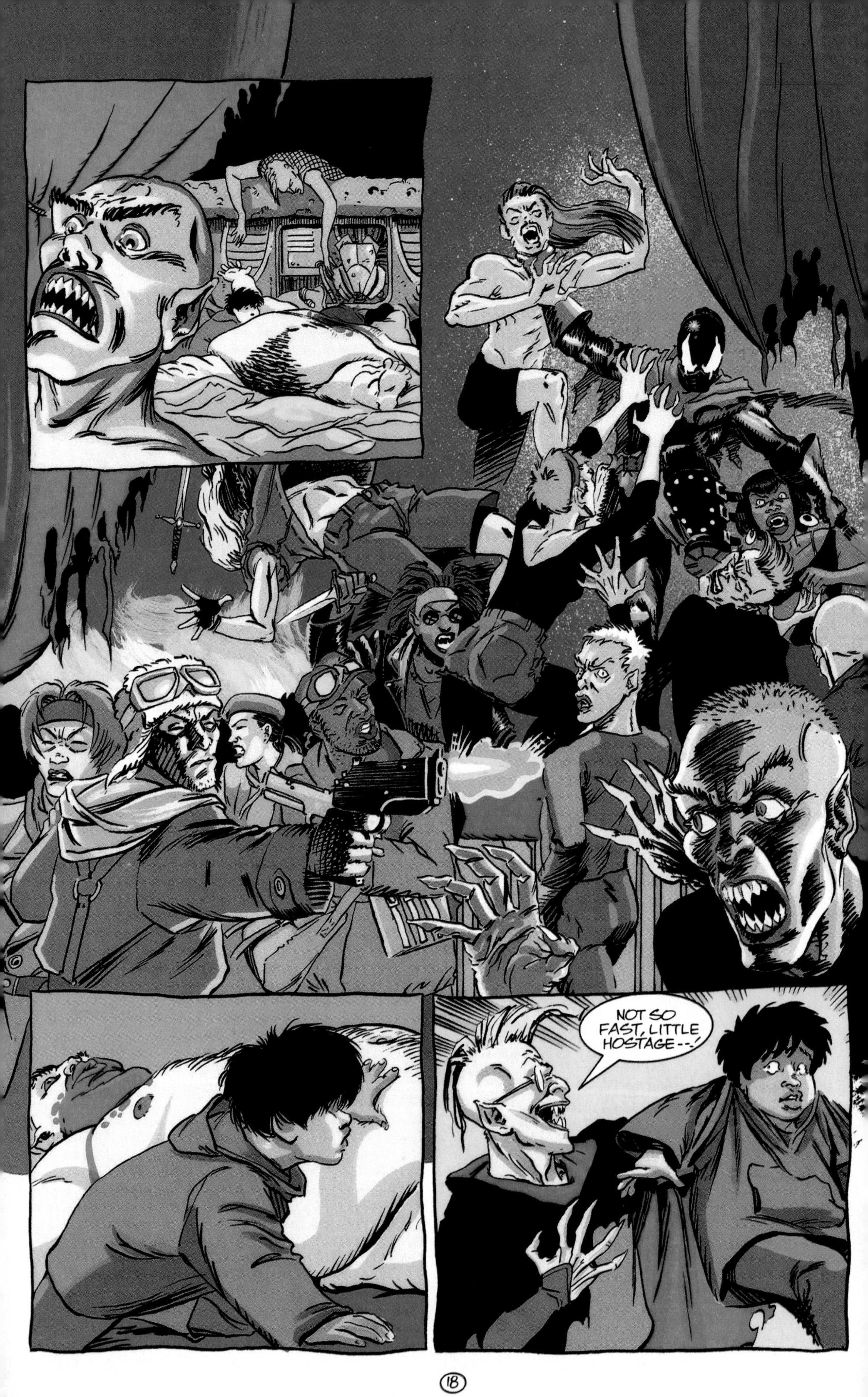
NOT SO FAST, LITTLE HOSTAGE--!

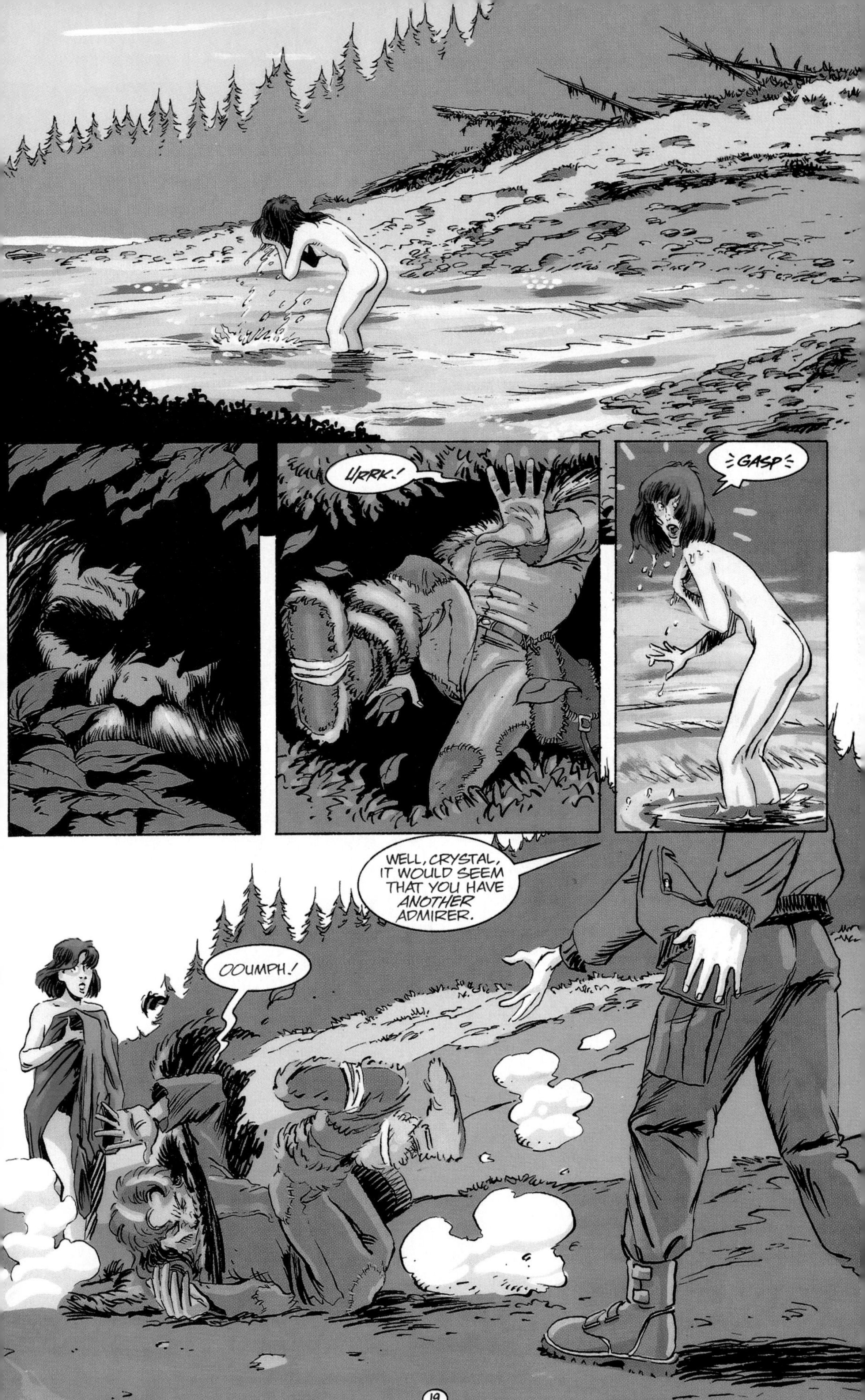
URRK!
GASP
WELL, CRYSTAL, IT WOULD SEEM THAT YOU HAVE ANOTHER ADMIRER.
OOUMPH!

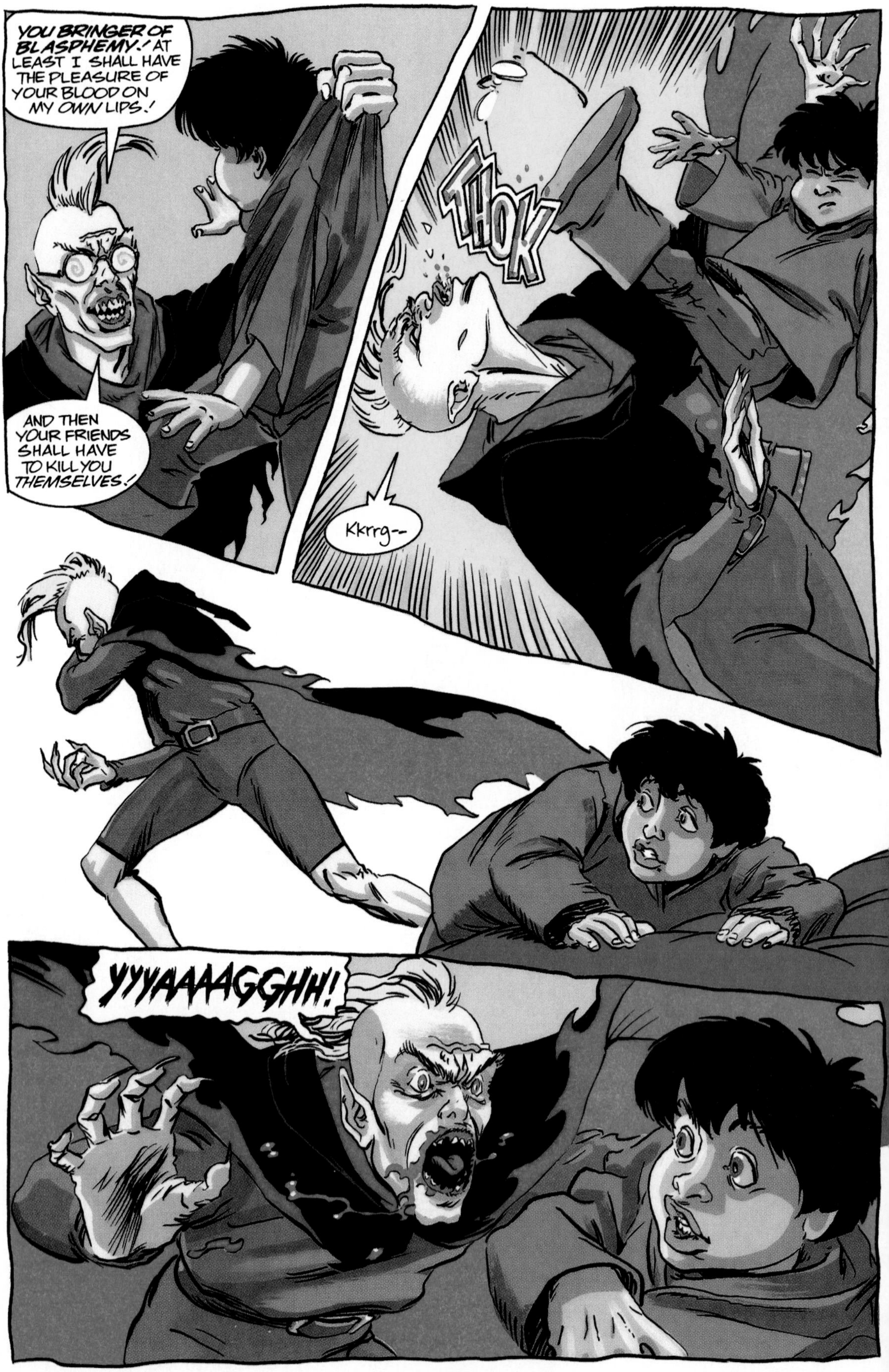
YOU BRINGER OF BLASPHEMY! AT LEAST I SHALL HAVE THE PLEASURE OF YOUR BLOOD ON MY OWN LIPS!
AND THEN YOUR FRIENDS SHALL HAVE TO KILL YOU THEMSELVES!
THOK
Kkrrg--
YYYAAAAGGHH!

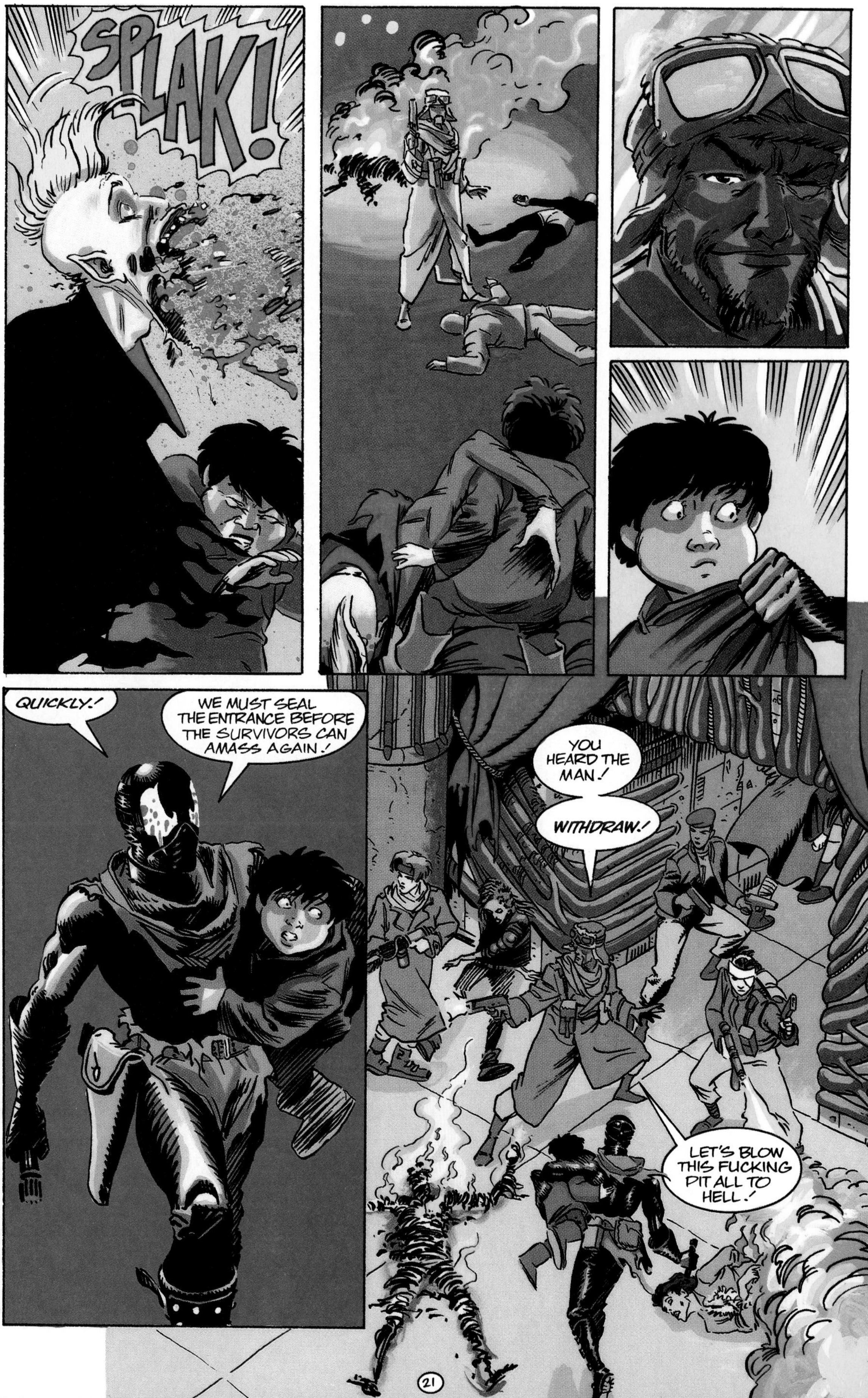

SPLAK!
QUICKLY!
WE MUST SEAL THE ENTRANCE BEFORE THE SURVIVORS CAN AMASS AGAIN!
YOU HEARD THE MAN!
WITHDRAW!
LET'S BLOW THIS FUCKING PIT ALL TO HELL!

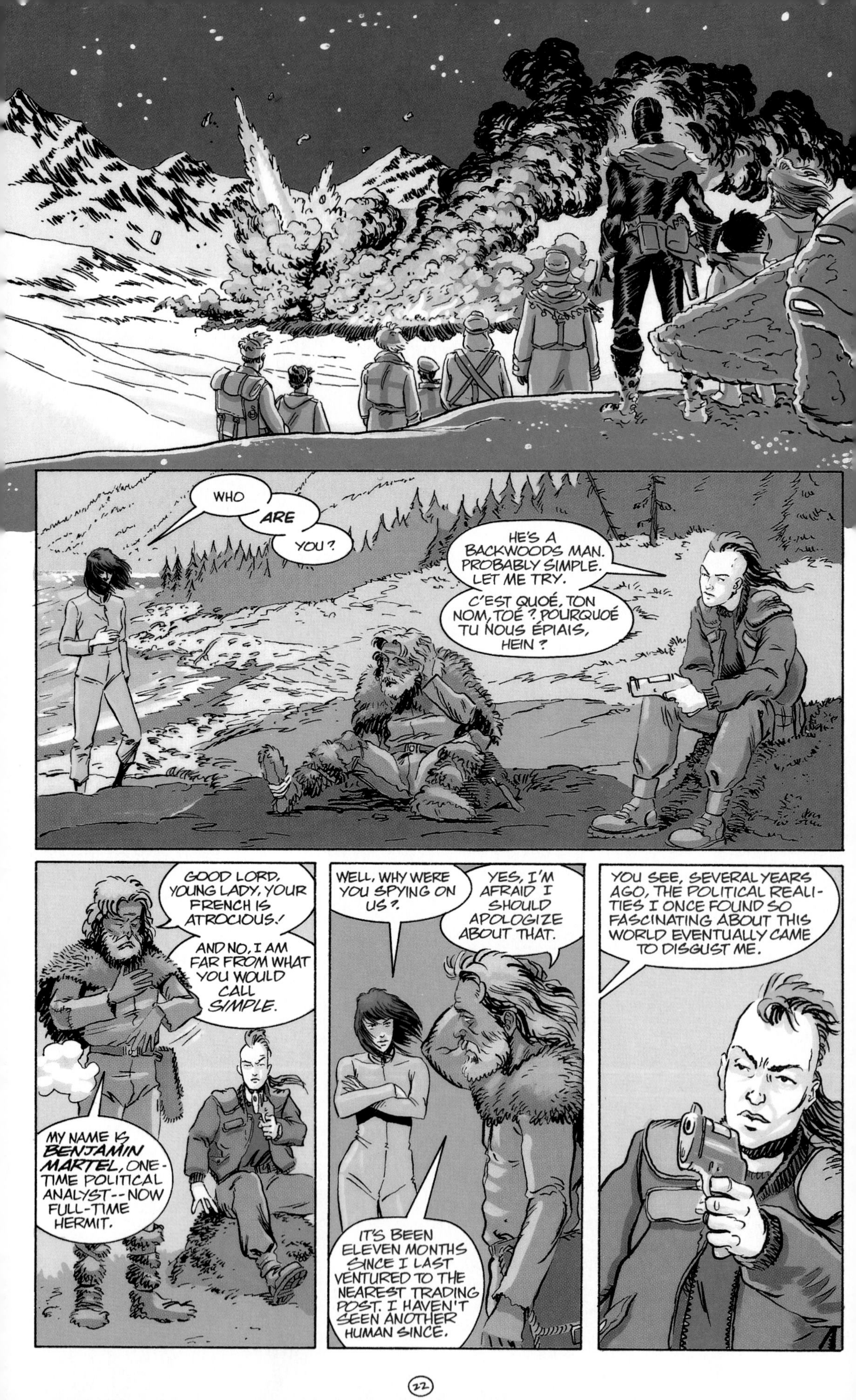
WHO ARE YOU?
HE'S A BACKWOODS MAN. PROBABLY SIMPLE. LET ME TRY.
C'EST QUOÉ, TON NOM, TOÉ? POURQUOÉ TU NOUS ÉPIAIS, HEIN?
GOOD LORD, YOUNG LADY, YOUR FRENCH IS ATROCIOUS!
AND NO, I AM FAR FROM WHAT YOU WOULD CALL SIMPLE.
MY NAME IS BENJAMIN MARTEL, ONE-TIME POLITICAL ANALYST--NOW FULL-TIME HERMIT.
WELL, WHY WERE YOU SPYING ON US?
YES, I'M AFRAID I SHOULD APOLOGIZE ABOUT THAT.
IT'S BEEN ELEVEN MONTHS SINCE I LAST VENTURED TO THE NEAREST TRADING POST. I HAVEN'T SEEN ANOTHER HUMAN SINCE.
YOU SEE, SEVERAL YEARS AGO, THE POLITICAL REALITIES I ONCE FOUND SO FASCINATING ABOUT THIS WORLD EVENTUALLY CAME TO DISGUST ME.

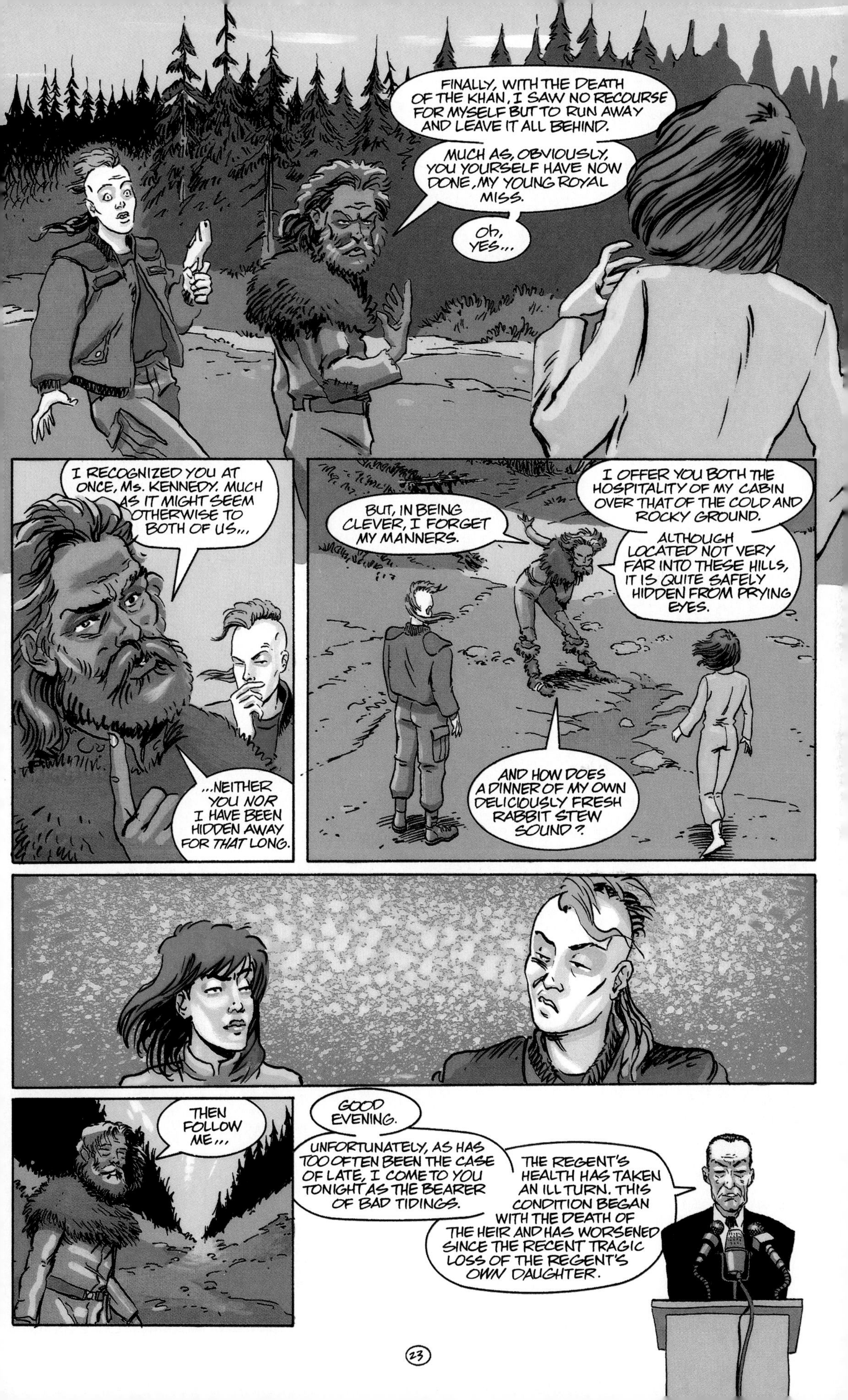
FINALLY, WITH THE DEATH OF THE KHAN, I SAW NO RECOURSE FOR MYSELF BUT TO RUN AWAY AND LEAVE IT ALL BEHIND.
MUCH AS, OBVIOUSLY, YOU YOURSELF HAVE NOW DONE, MY YOUNG ROYAL MISS.
Oh, YES...
I RECOGNIZED YOU AT ONCE, Ms. KENNEDY. MUCH AS IT MIGHT SEEM OTHERWISE TO BOTH OF US...
...NEITHER YOU NOR I HAVE BEEN HIDDEN AWAY FOR THAT LONG.
BUT, IN BEING CLEVER, I FORGET MY MANNERS.
I OFFER YOU BOTH THE HOSPITALITY OF MY CABIN OVER THAT OF THE COLD AND ROCKY GROUND.
ALTHOUGH LOCATED NOT VERY FAR INTO THESE HILLS, IT IS QUITE SAFELY HIDDEN FROM PRYING EYES.
AND HOW DOES A DINNER OF MY OWN DELICIOUSLY FRESH RABBIT STEW SOUND?
THEN FOLLOW ME...
GOOD EVENING.
UNFORTUNATELY, AS HAS TOO OFTEN BEEN THE CASE OF LATE, I COME TO YOU TONIGHT AS THE BEARER OF BAD TIDINGS.
THE REGENT'S HEALTH HAS TAKEN AN ILL TURN. THIS CONDITION BEGAN WITH THE DEATH OF THE HEIR AND HAS WORSENED SINCE THE RECENT TRAGIC LOSS OF THE REGENT'S OWN DAUGHTER.

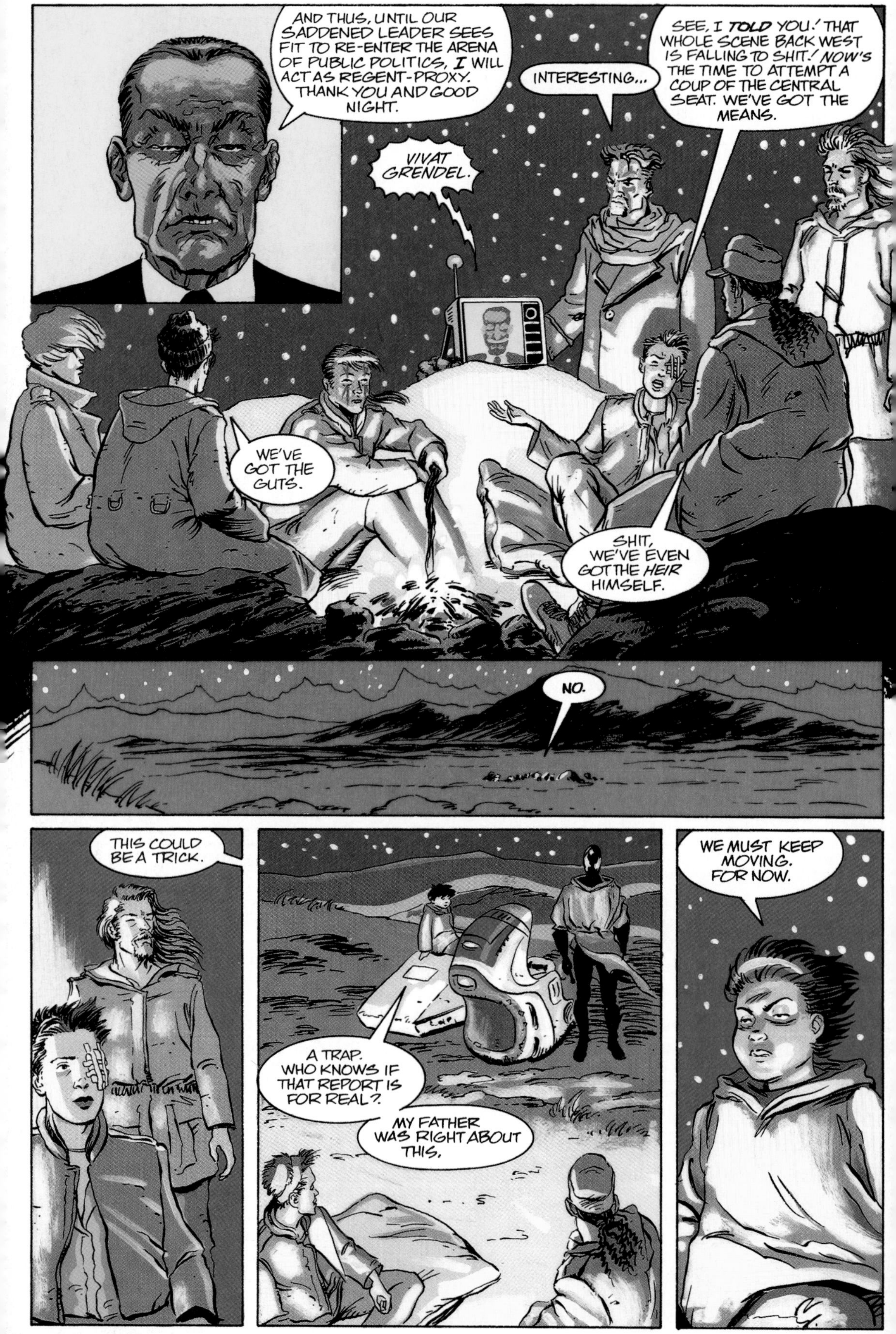
AND THUS, UNTIL OUR SADDENED LEADER SEES FIT TO RE-ENTER THE ARENA OF PUBLIC POLITICS, I WILL ACT AS REGENT-PROXY. THANK YOU AND GOOD NIGHT.
VIVAT GRENDEL.
INTERESTING...
SEE, I TOLD YOU! THAT WHOLE SCENE BACK WEST IS FALLING TO SHIT! NOW'S THE TIME TO ATTEMPT A COUP OF THE CENTRAL SEAT. WE'VE GOT THE MEANS.
WE'VE GOT THE GUTS.
SHIT, WE'VE EVEN GOT THE HEIR HIMSELF.
NO.
THIS COULD BE A TRICK.
A TRAP. WHO KNOWS IF THAT REPORT IS FOR REAL?
MY FATHER WAS RIGHT ABOUT THIS.
WE MUST KEEP MOVING. FOR NOW.

# CHAPTER 10
# DEVIL
## *in the house*

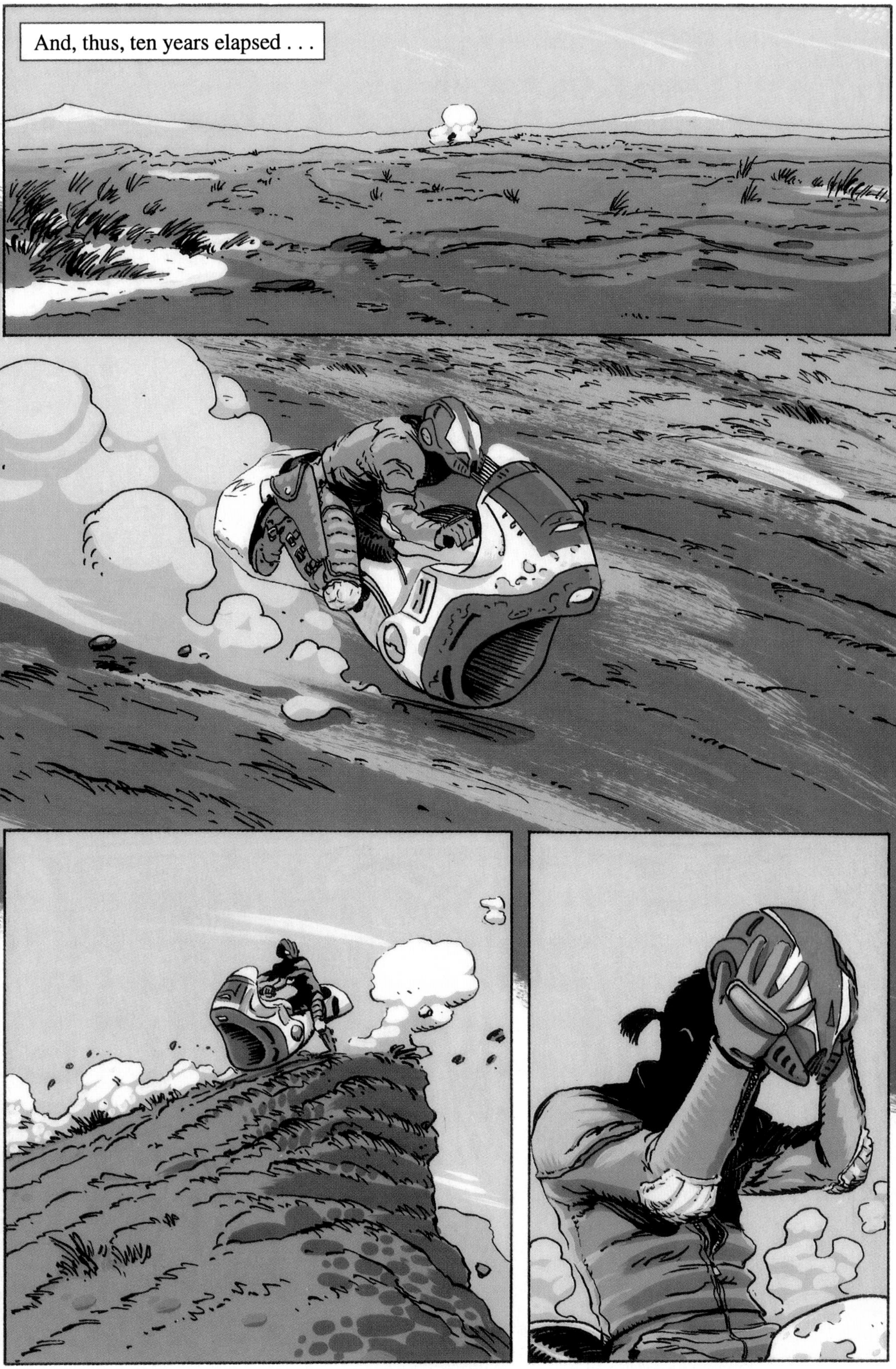
And, thus, ten years elapsed . . .

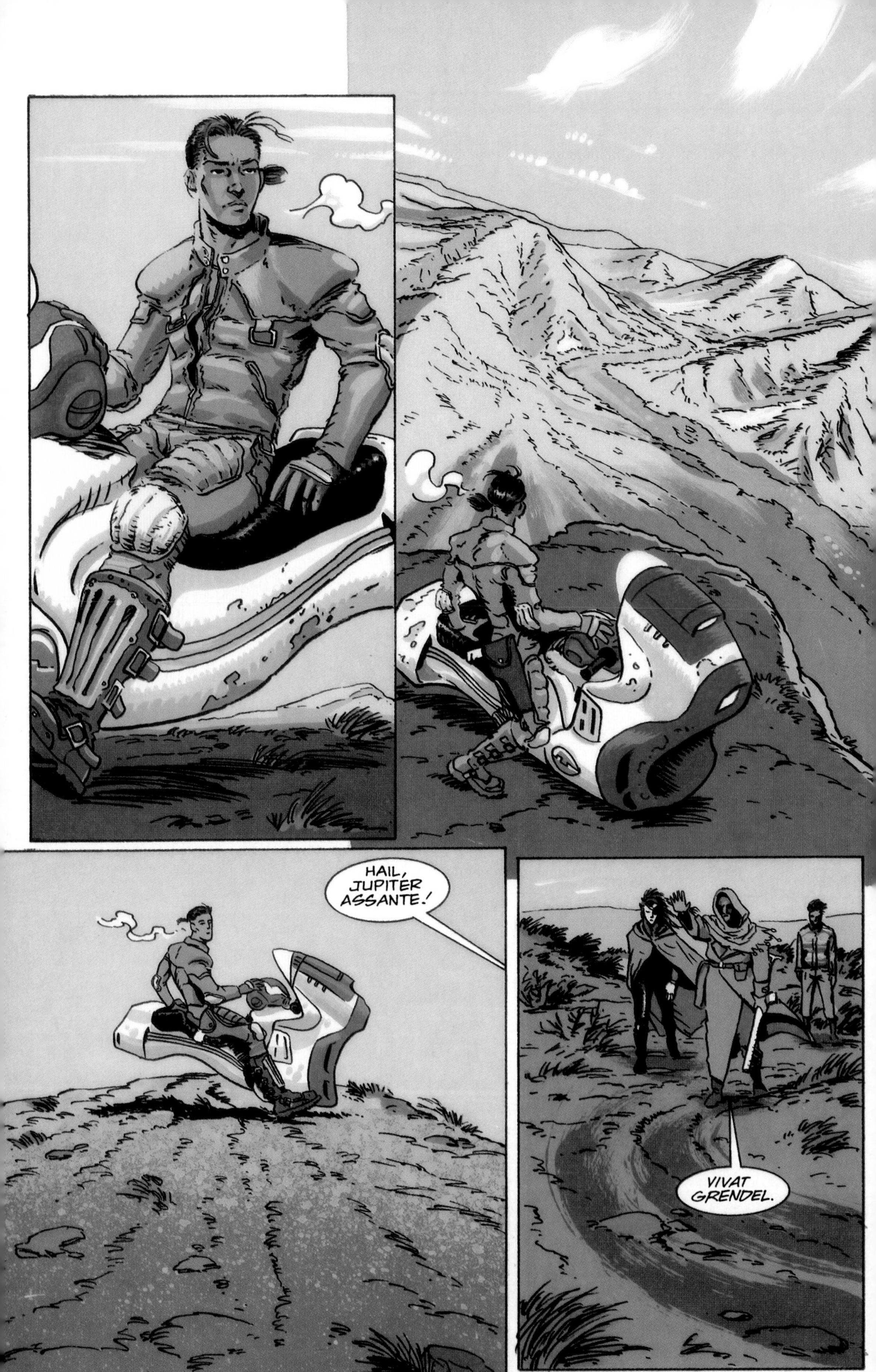
HAIL, JUPITER ASSANTE!
VIVAT GRENDEL.

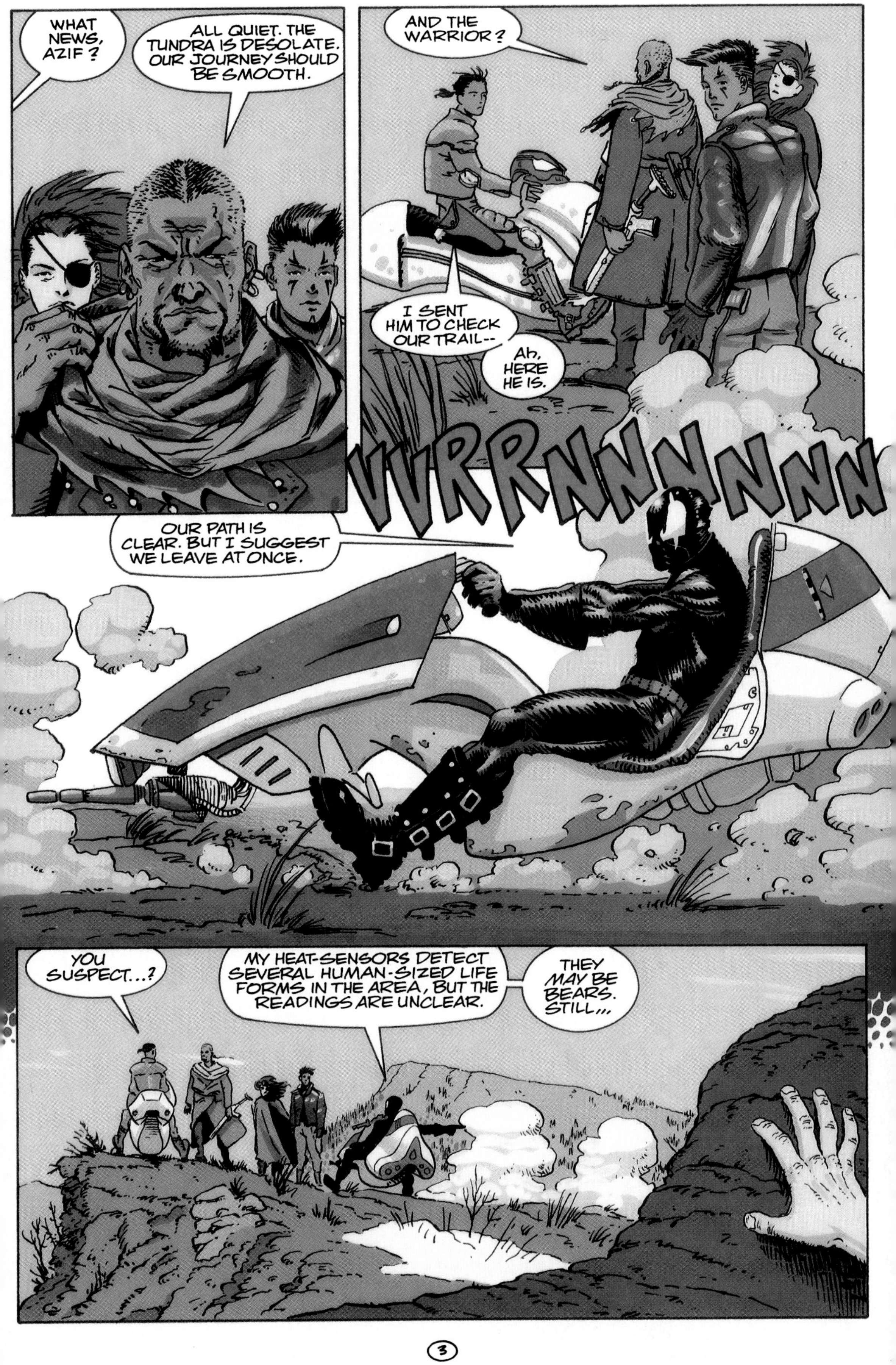
WHAT NEWS, AZIF?
ALL QUIET. THE TUNDRA IS DESOLATE. OUR JOURNEY SHOULD BE SMOOTH.
AND THE WARRIOR?
I SENT HIM TO CHECK OUR TRAIL--
Ah, HERE HE IS.
VVRRNNNNNNN
OUR PATH IS CLEAR. BUT I SUGGEST WE LEAVE AT ONCE.
YOU SUSPECT...?
MY HEAT-SENSORS DETECT SEVERAL HUMAN-SIZED LIFE FORMS IN THE AREA, BUT THE READINGS ARE UNCLEAR.
THEY MAY BE BEARS. STILL,,,

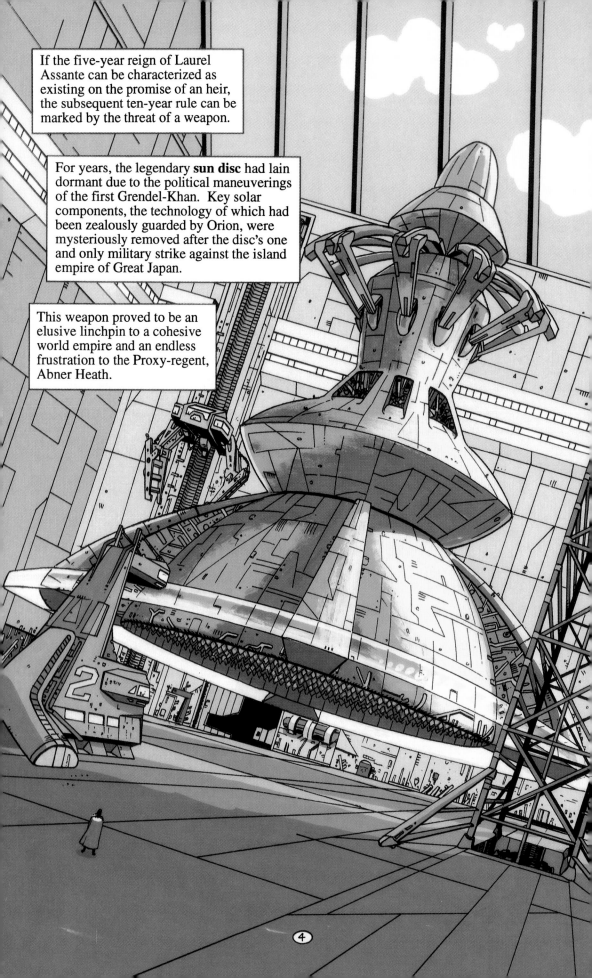

If the five-year reign of Laurel Assante can be characterized as existing on the promise of an heir, the subsequent ten-year rule can be marked by the threat of a weapon.

For years, the legendary **sun disc** had lain dormant due to the political maneuverings of the first Grendel-Khan. Key solar components, the technology of which had been zealously guarded by Orion, were mysteriously removed after the disc's one and only military strike against the island empire of Great Japan.

This weapon proved to be an elusive linchpin to a cohesive world empire and an endless frustration to the Proxy-regent, Abner Heath.

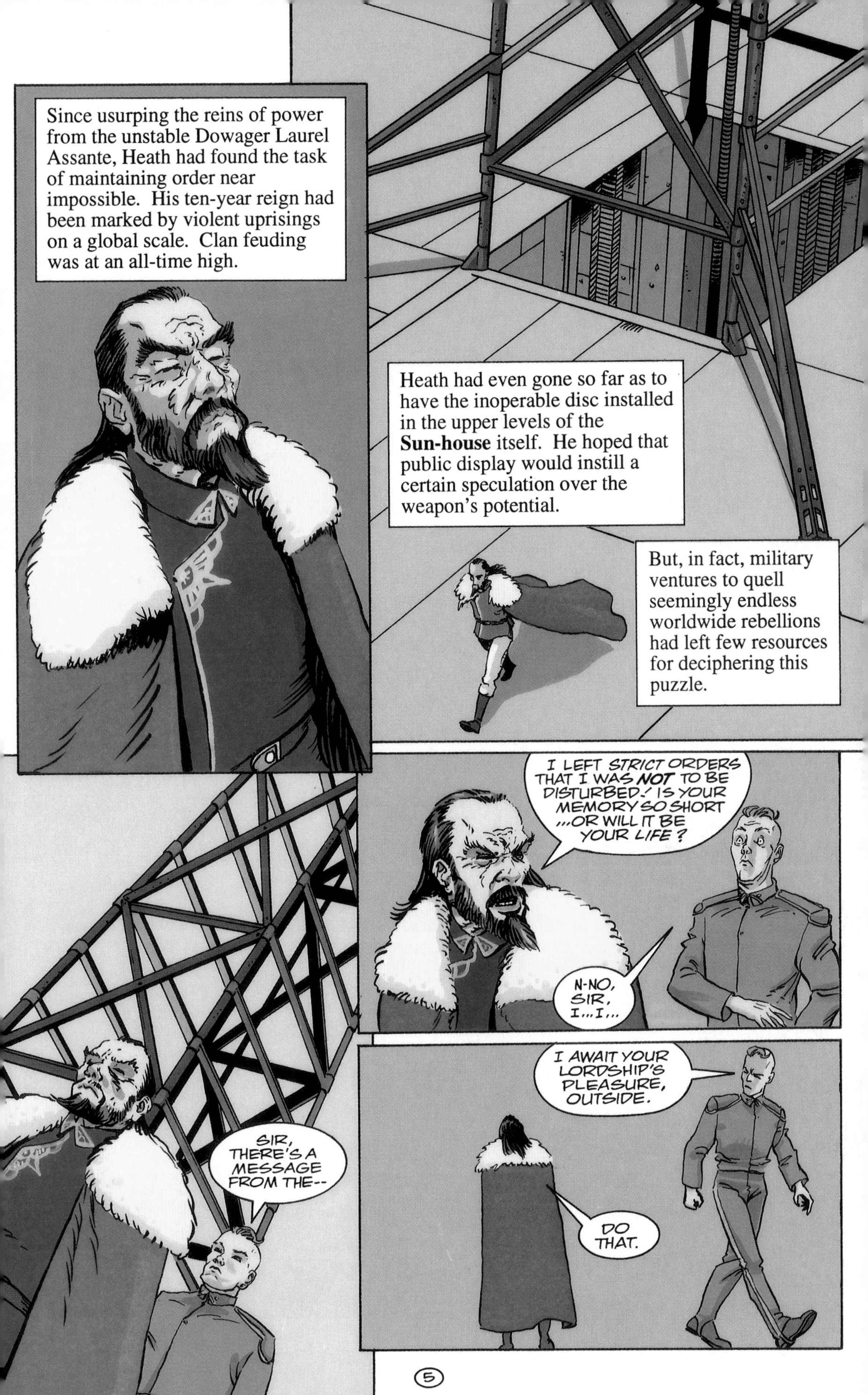

Since usurping the reins of power from the unstable Dowager Laurel Assante, Heath had found the task of maintaining order near impossible. His ten-year reign had been marked by violent uprisings on a global scale. Clan feuding was at an all-time high.
Heath had even gone so far as to have the inoperable disc installed in the upper levels of the Sun-house itself. He hoped that public display would instill a certain speculation over the weapon's potential.
But, in fact, military ventures to quell seemingly endless worldwide rebellions had left few resources for deciphering this puzzle.
SIR, THERE'S A MESSAGE FROM THE--
I LEFT STRICT ORDERS THAT I WAS NOT TO BE DISTURBED! IS YOUR MEMORY SO SHORT ...OR WILL IT BE YOUR LIFE?
N-NO, SIR, I...I...
I AWAIT YOUR LORDSHIP'S PLEASURE, OUTSIDE.
DO THAT.

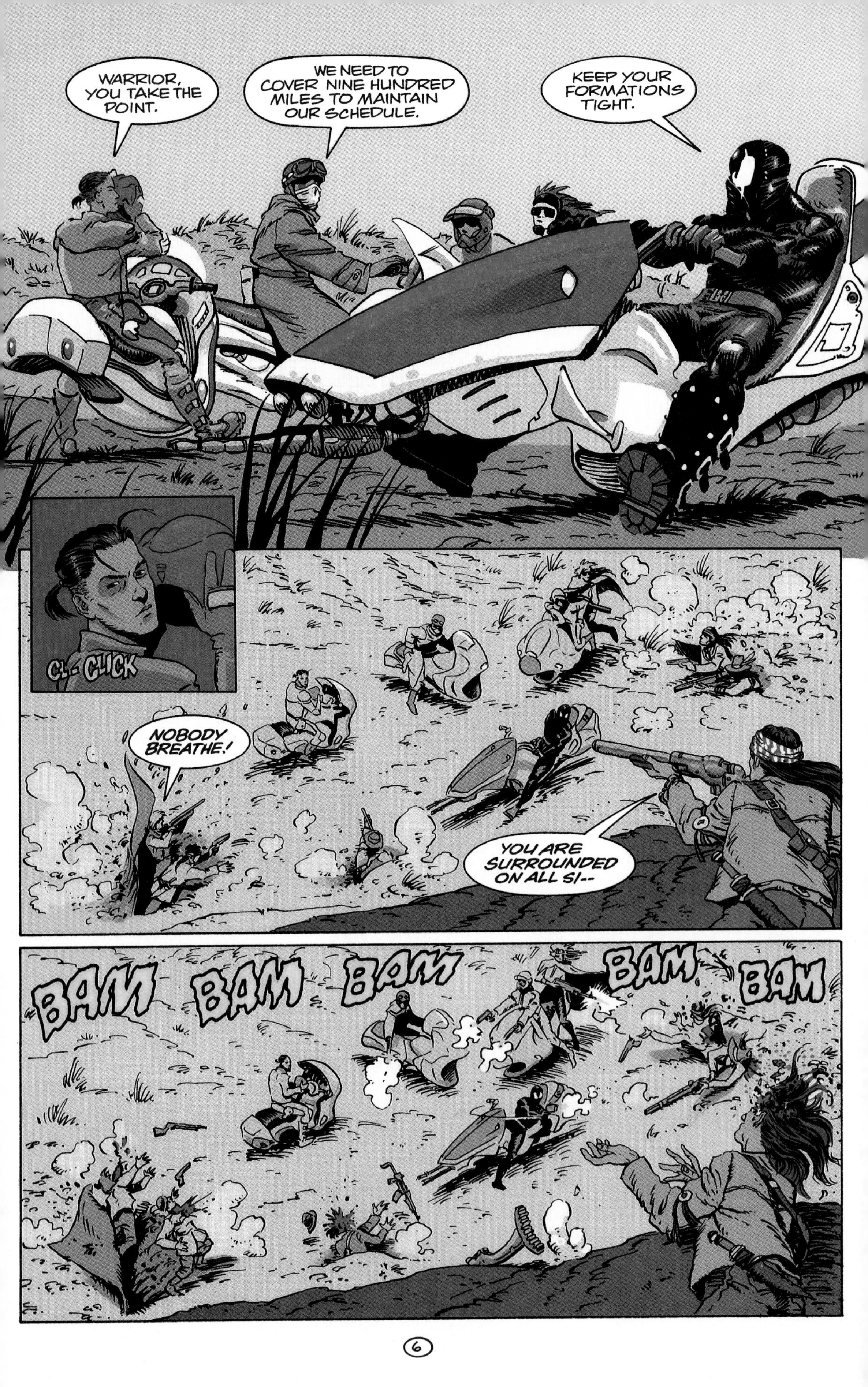
WARRIOR, YOU TAKE THE POINT.
WE NEED TO COVER NINE HUNDRED MILES TO MAINTAIN OUR SCHEDULE.
KEEP YOUR FORMATIONS TIGHT.
CL-CLICK
NOBODY BREATHE.!
YOU ARE SURROUNDED ON ALL SI--
BAM BAM BAM BAM BAM

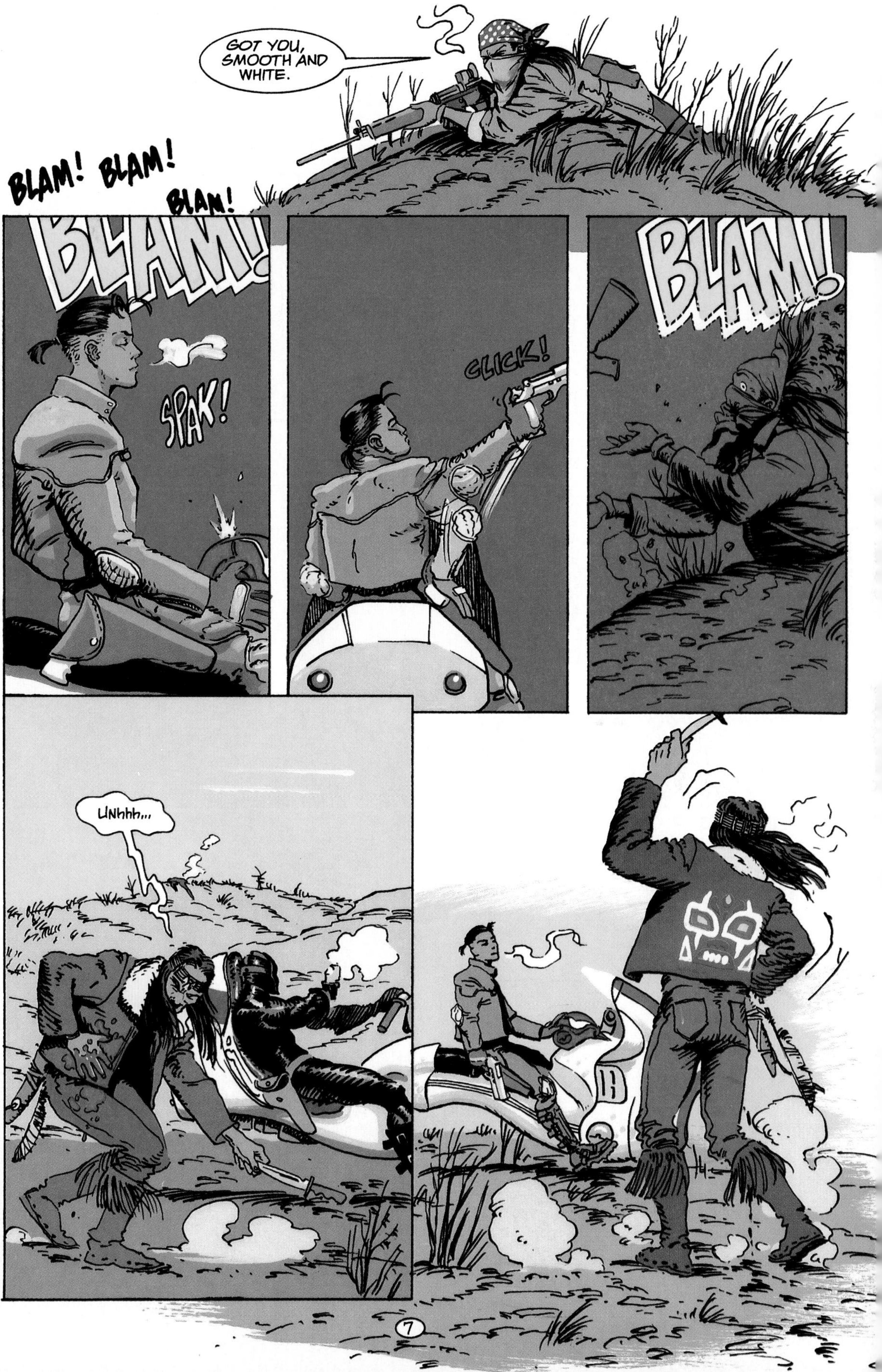
GOT YOU, SMOOTH AND WHITE.
BLAM! BLAM!
BLAM!
BLAM!
SPAK!
CLICK!
BLAM!
Unhhh...

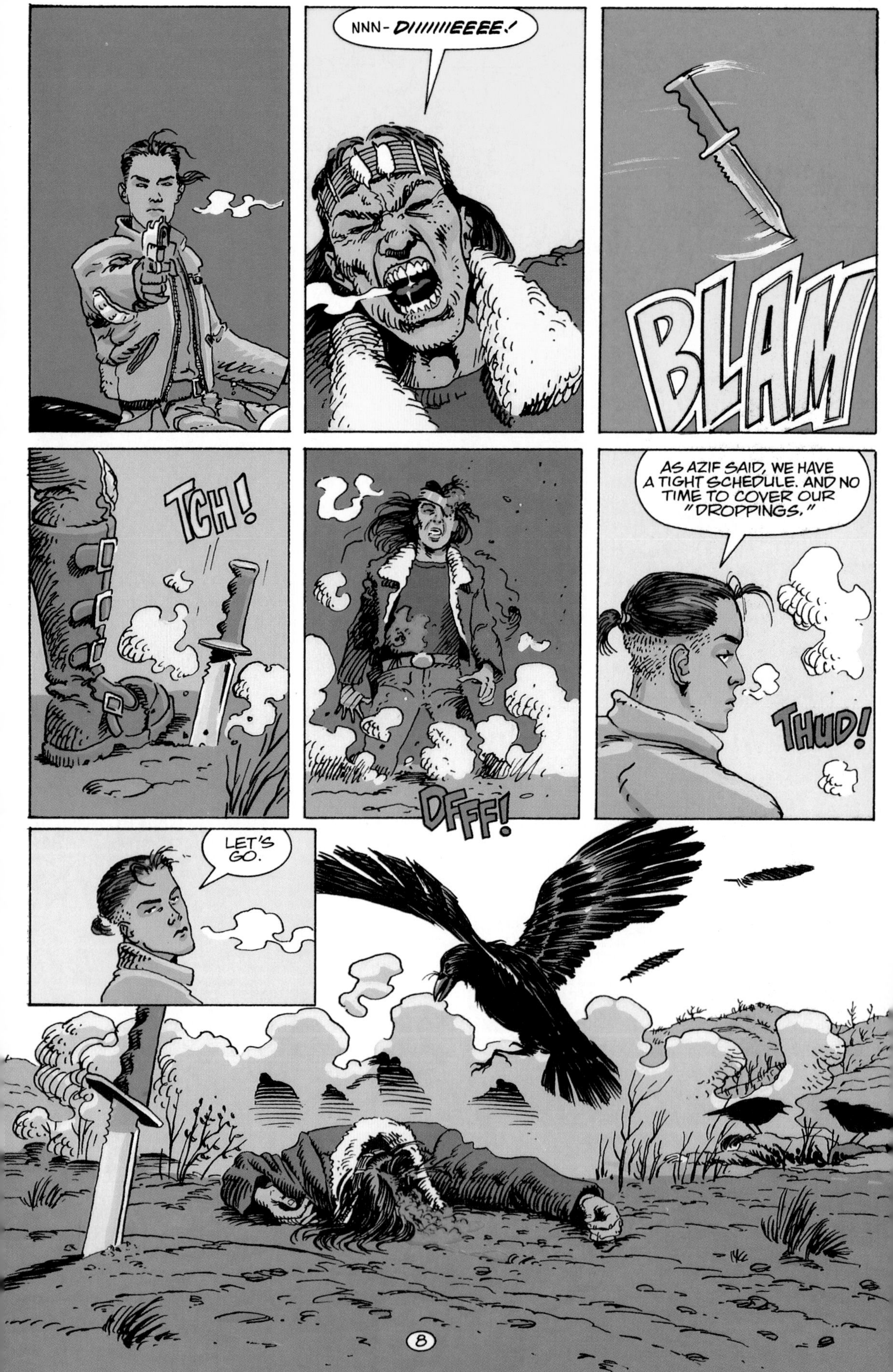
NNN-DIIIIIIEEEE!
BLAM
TCH!
DFFFF!
AS AZIF SAID, WE HAVE A TIGHT SCHEDULE. AND NO TIME TO COVER OUR "DROPPINGS."
THUD!
LET'S GO.

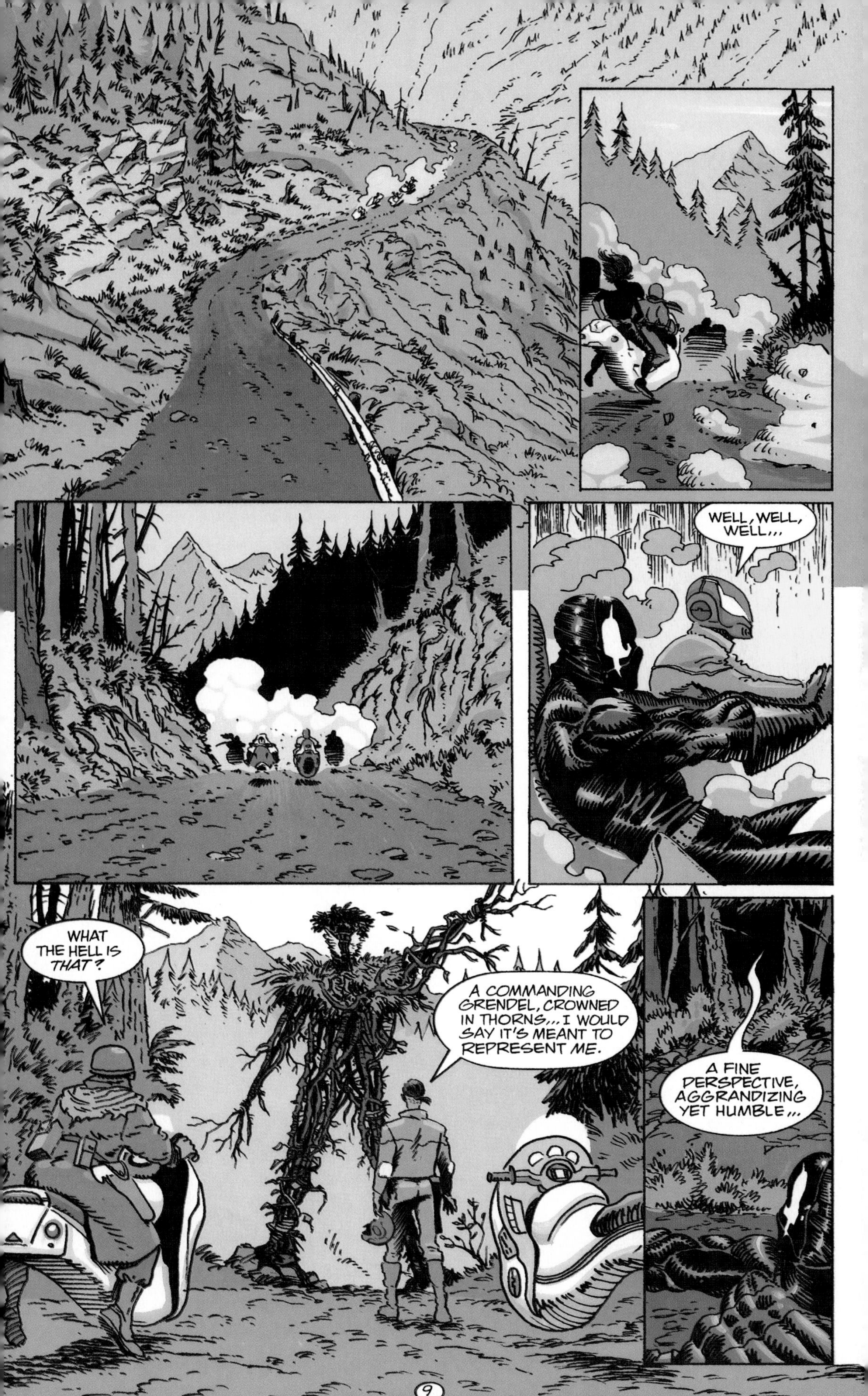
WELL, WELL, WELL...
WHAT THE HELL IS THAT?
A COMMANDING GRENDEL, CROWNED IN THORNS... I WOULD SAY IT'S MEANT TO REPRESENT ME.
A FINE PERSPECTIVE, AGGRANDIZING YET HUMBLE...

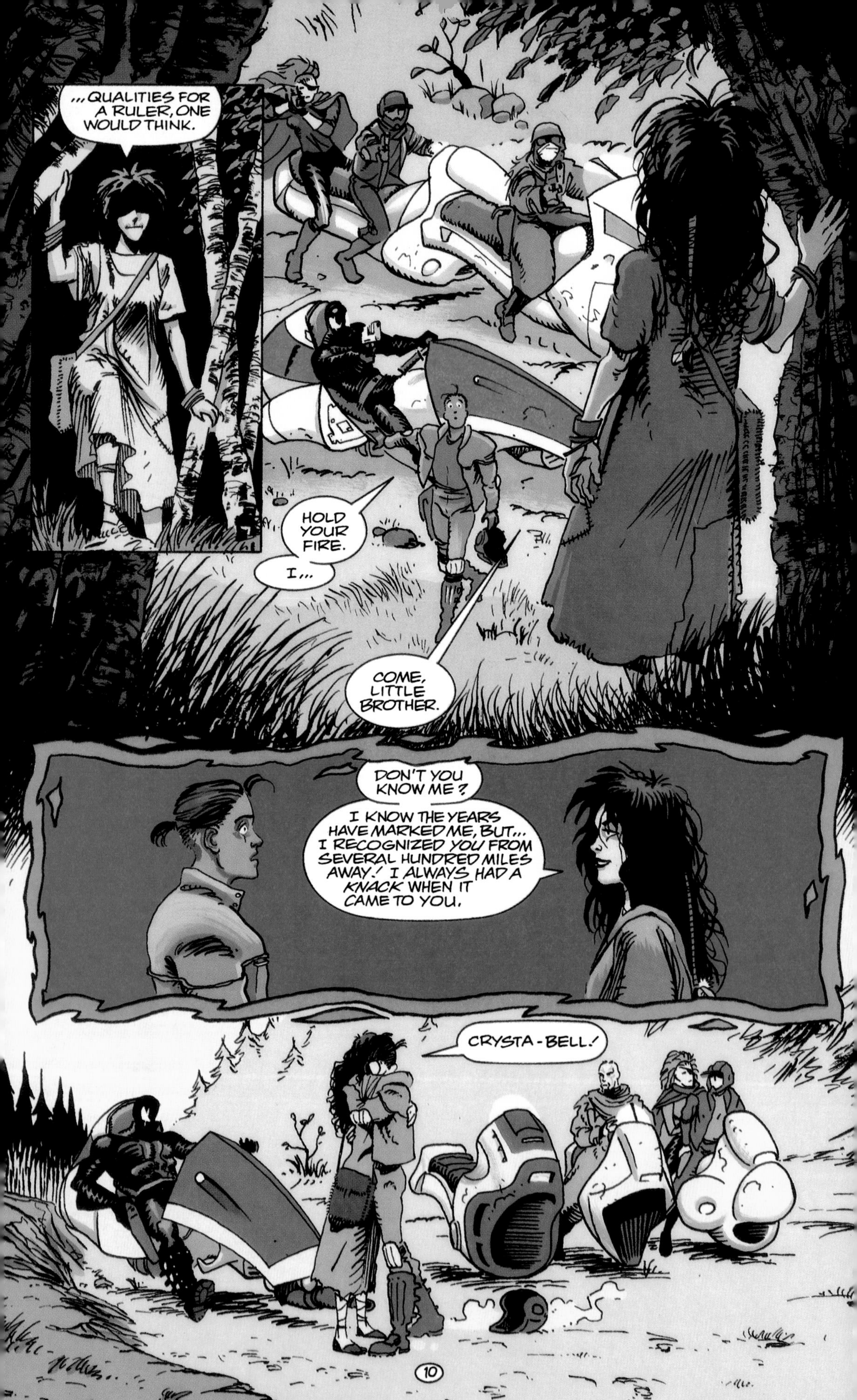
...QUALITIES FOR A RULER, ONE WOULD THINK.
HOLD YOUR FIRE.
I...
COME, LITTLE BROTHER.
DON'T YOU KNOW ME?
I KNOW THE YEARS HAVE MARKED ME, BUT... I RECOGNIZED *YOU* FROM SEVERAL HUNDRED MILES AWAY! I ALWAYS HAD A *KNACK* WHEN IT CAME TO YOU.
CRYSTA-BELL!

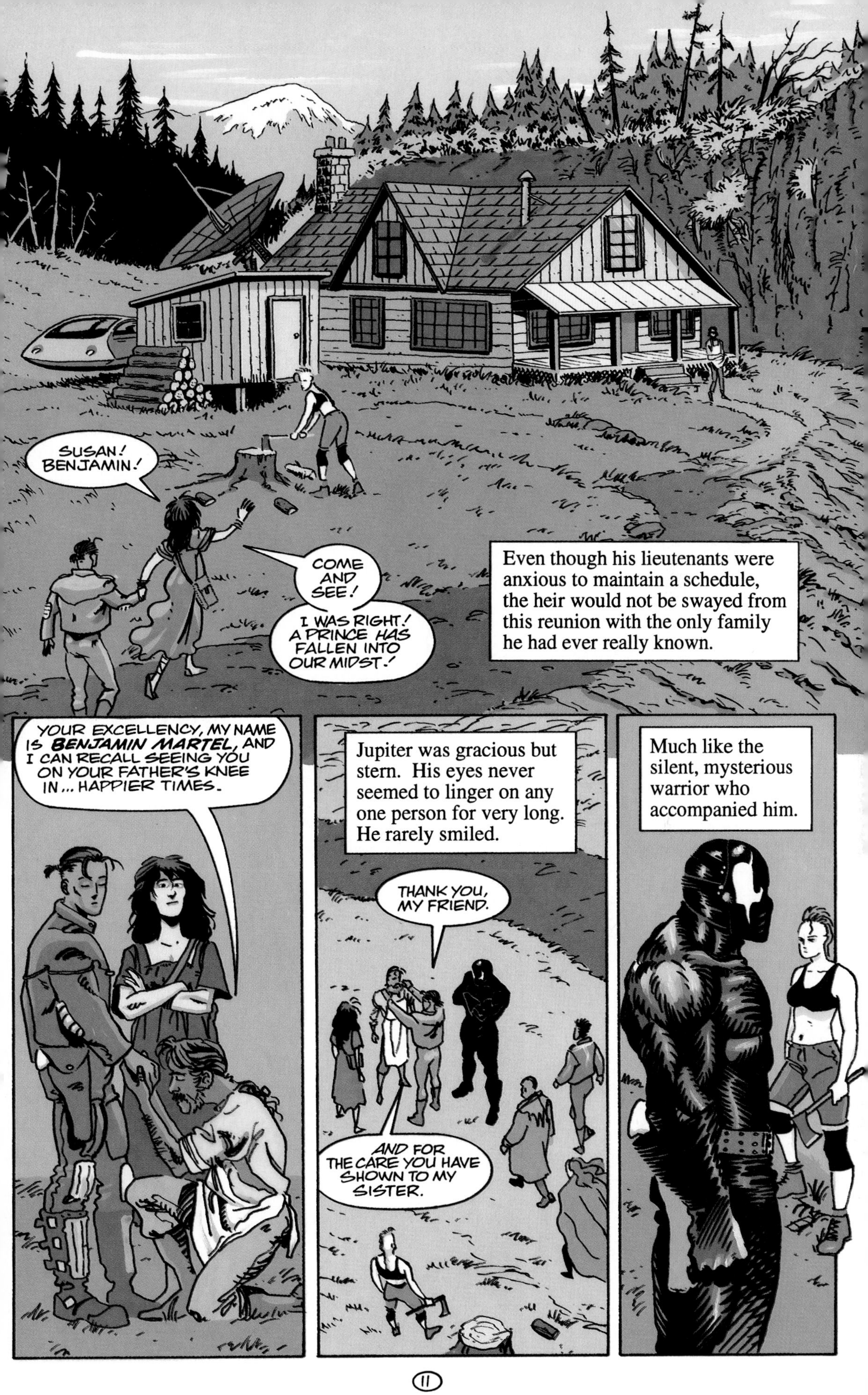
SUSAN! BENJAMIN!
COME AND SEE!
I WAS RIGHT! A PRINCE HAS FALLEN INTO OUR MIDST!
Even though his lieutenants were anxious to maintain a schedule, the heir would not be swayed from this reunion with the only family he had ever really known.
YOUR EXCELLENCY, MY NAME IS BENJAMIN MARTEL, AND I CAN RECALL SEEING YOU ON YOUR FATHER'S KNEE IN... HAPPIER TIMES.
Jupiter was gracious but stern. His eyes never seemed to linger on any one person for very long. He rarely smiled.
THANK YOU, MY FRIEND.
AND FOR THE CARE YOU HAVE SHOWN TO MY SISTER.
Much like the silent, mysterious warrior who accompanied him.

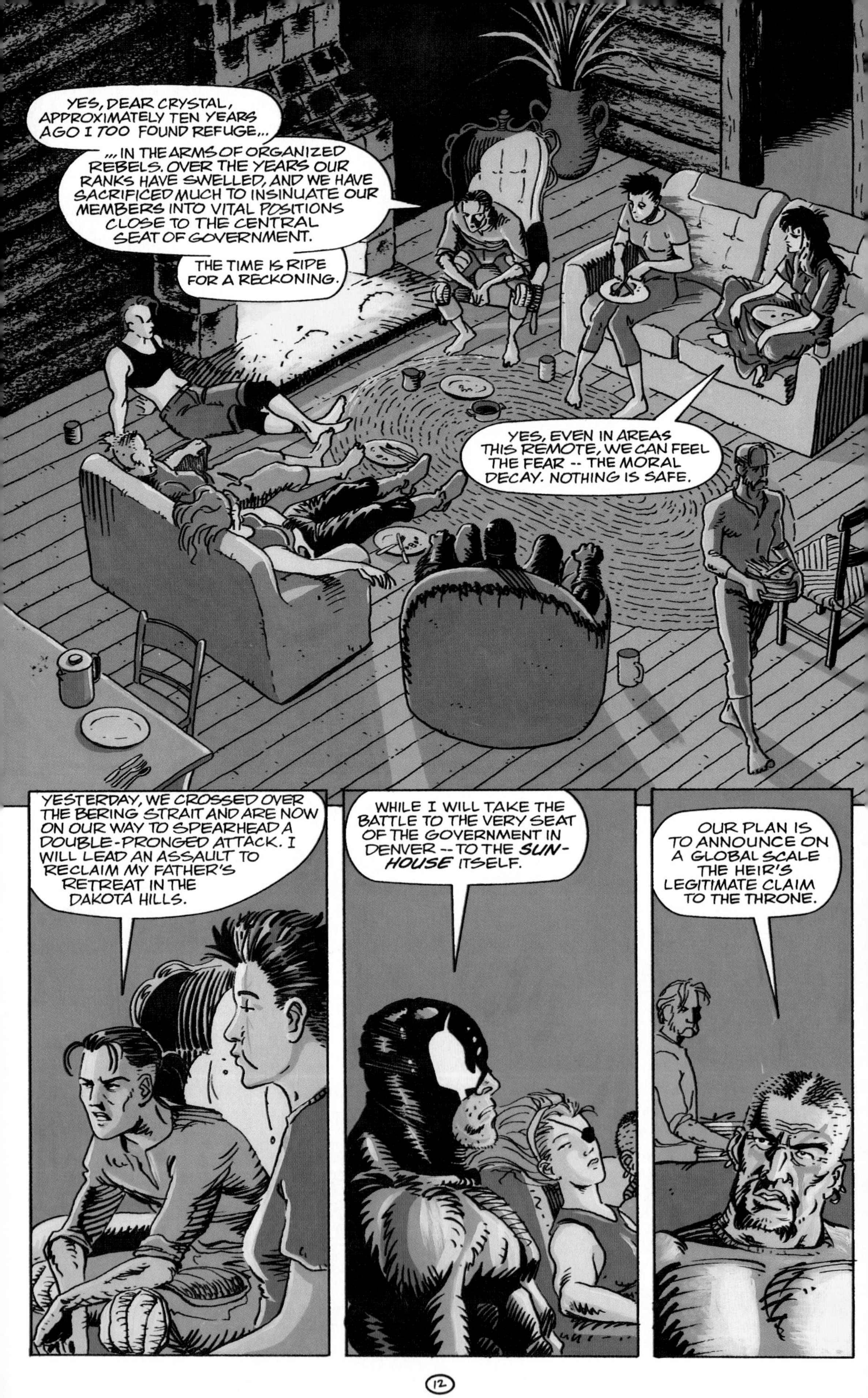

YES, DEAR CRYSTAL, APPROXIMATELY TEN YEARS AGO I *TOO* FOUND REFUGE...
...IN THE ARMS OF ORGANIZED REBELS. OVER THE YEARS OUR RANKS HAVE SWELLED, AND WE HAVE SACRIFICED MUCH TO INSINUATE OUR MEMBERS INTO VITAL POSITIONS CLOSE TO THE CENTRAL SEAT OF GOVERNMENT.
THE TIME IS RIPE FOR A RECKONING.
YES, EVEN IN AREAS THIS REMOTE, WE CAN FEEL THE FEAR -- THE MORAL DECAY. NOTHING IS SAFE.
YESTERDAY, WE CROSSED OVER THE BERING STRAIT AND ARE NOW ON OUR WAY TO SPEARHEAD A DOUBLE-PRONGED ATTACK. I WILL LEAD AN ASSAULT TO RECLAIM MY FATHER'S RETREAT IN THE DAKOTA HILLS.
WHILE I WILL TAKE THE BATTLE TO THE VERY SEAT OF THE GOVERNMENT IN DENVER -- TO THE *SUN-HOUSE* ITSELF.
OUR PLAN IS TO ANNOUNCE ON A GLOBAL SCALE THE HEIR'S LEGITIMATE CLAIM TO THE THRONE.

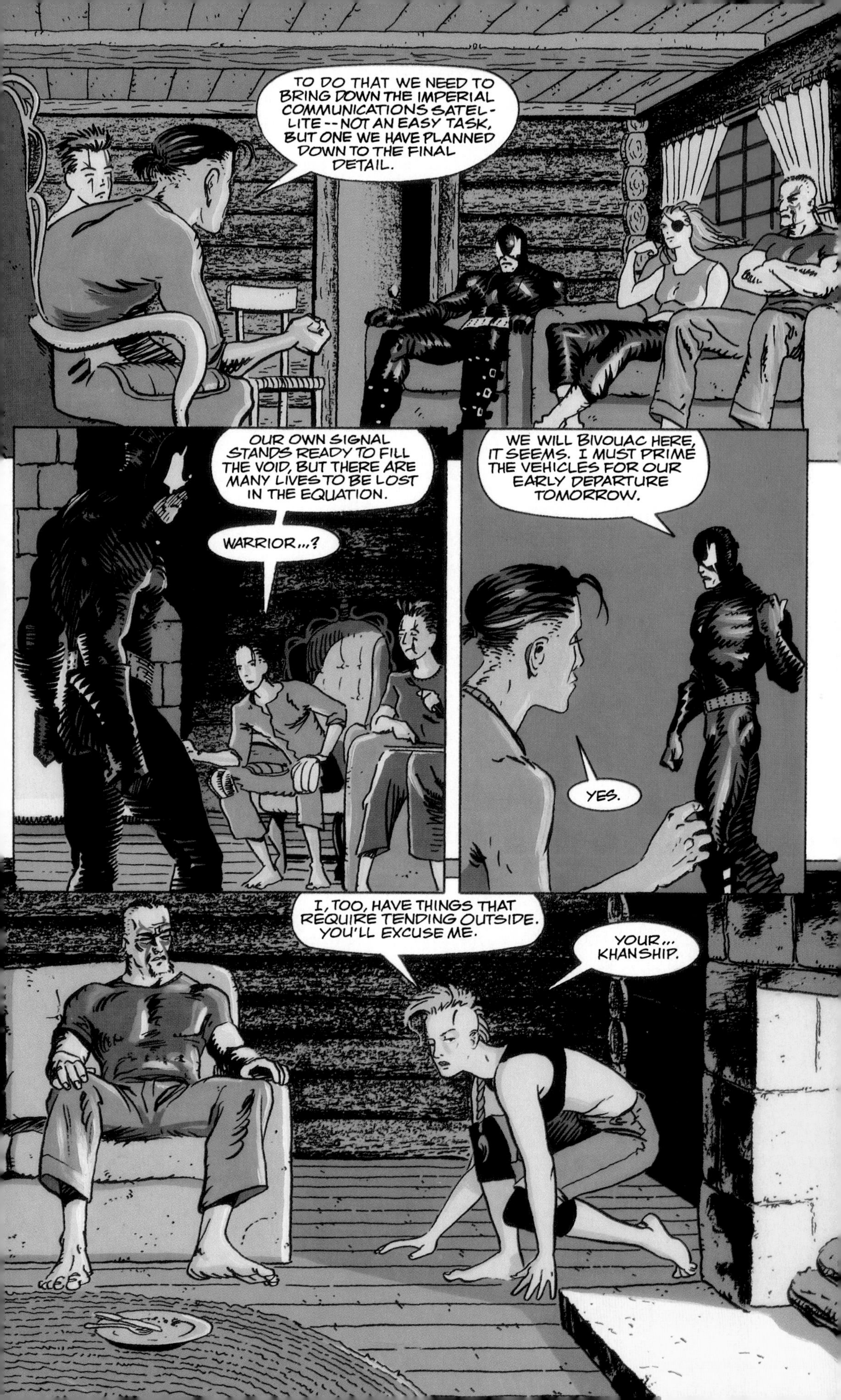
TO DO THAT WE NEED TO BRING DOWN THE IMPERIAL COMMUNICATIONS SATEL-LITE--NOT AN EASY TASK, BUT ONE WE HAVE PLANNED DOWN TO THE FINAL DETAIL.
OUR OWN SIGNAL STANDS READY TO FILL THE VOID, BUT THERE ARE MANY LIVES TO BE LOST IN THE EQUATION.
WARRIOR...?
WE WILL BIVOUAC HERE, IT SEEMS. I MUST PRIME THE VEHICLES FOR OUR EARLY DEPARTURE TOMORROW.
YES.
I, TOO, HAVE THINGS THAT REQUIRE TENDING OUTSIDE. YOU'LL EXCUSE ME.
YOUR... KHANSHIP.

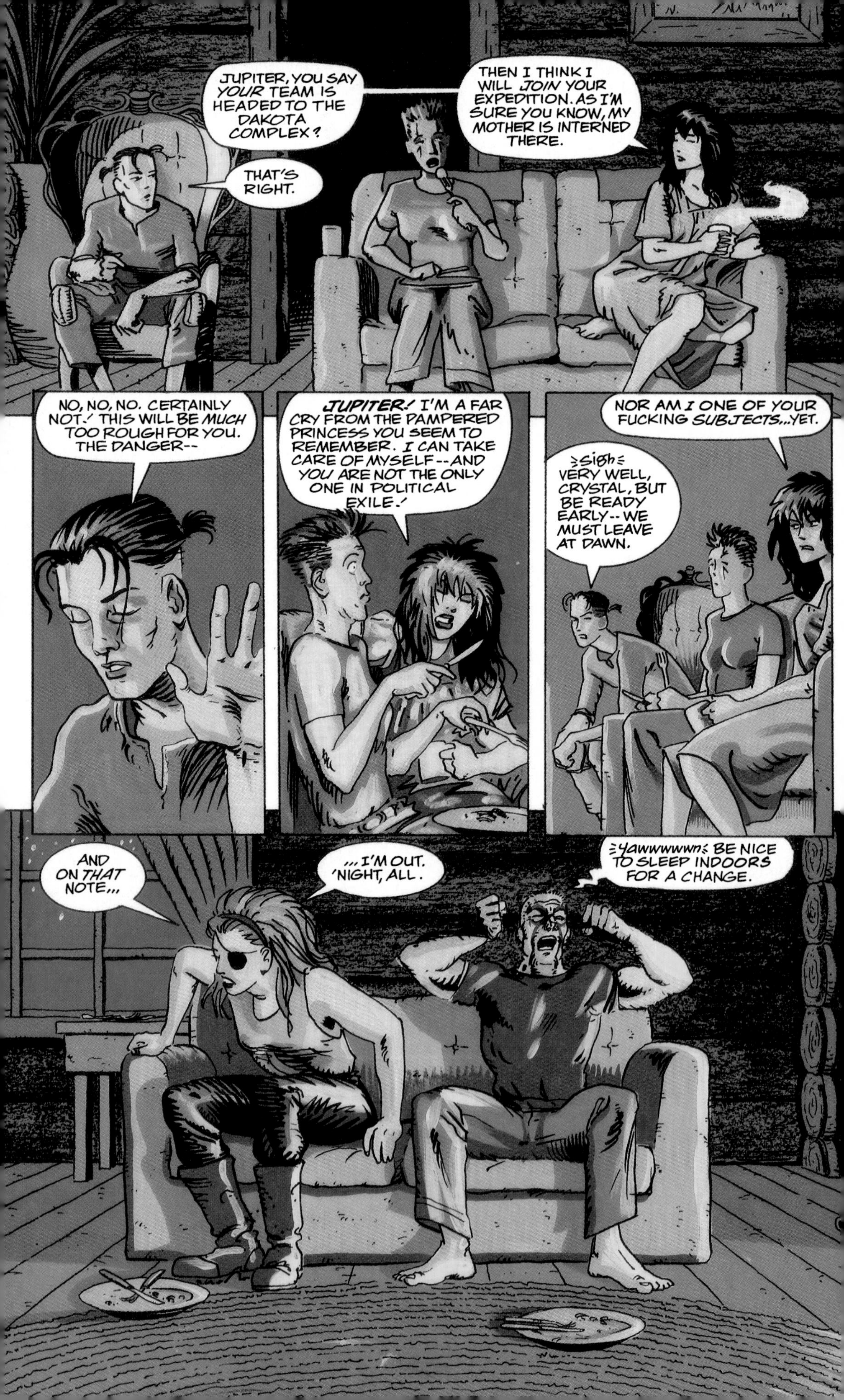
JUPITER, YOU SAY YOUR TEAM IS HEADED TO THE DAKOTA COMPLEX?
THAT'S RIGHT.
THEN I THINK I WILL JOIN YOUR EXPEDITION. AS I'M SURE YOU KNOW, MY MOTHER IS INTERNED THERE.
NO, NO, NO. CERTAINLY NOT! THIS WILL BE MUCH TOO ROUGH FOR YOU. THE DANGER--
JUPITER! I'M A FAR CRY FROM THE PAMPERED PRINCESS YOU SEEM TO REMEMBER. I CAN TAKE CARE OF MYSELF--AND YOU ARE NOT THE ONLY ONE IN POLITICAL EXILE!
NOR AM I ONE OF YOUR FUCKING SUBJECTS...YET.
sigh
VERY WELL, CRYSTAL, BUT BE READY EARLY--WE MUST LEAVE AT DAWN.
AND ON THAT NOTE...
...I'M OUT. 'NIGHT, ALL.
yawwwwwn
BE NICE TO SLEEP INDOORS FOR A CHANGE.

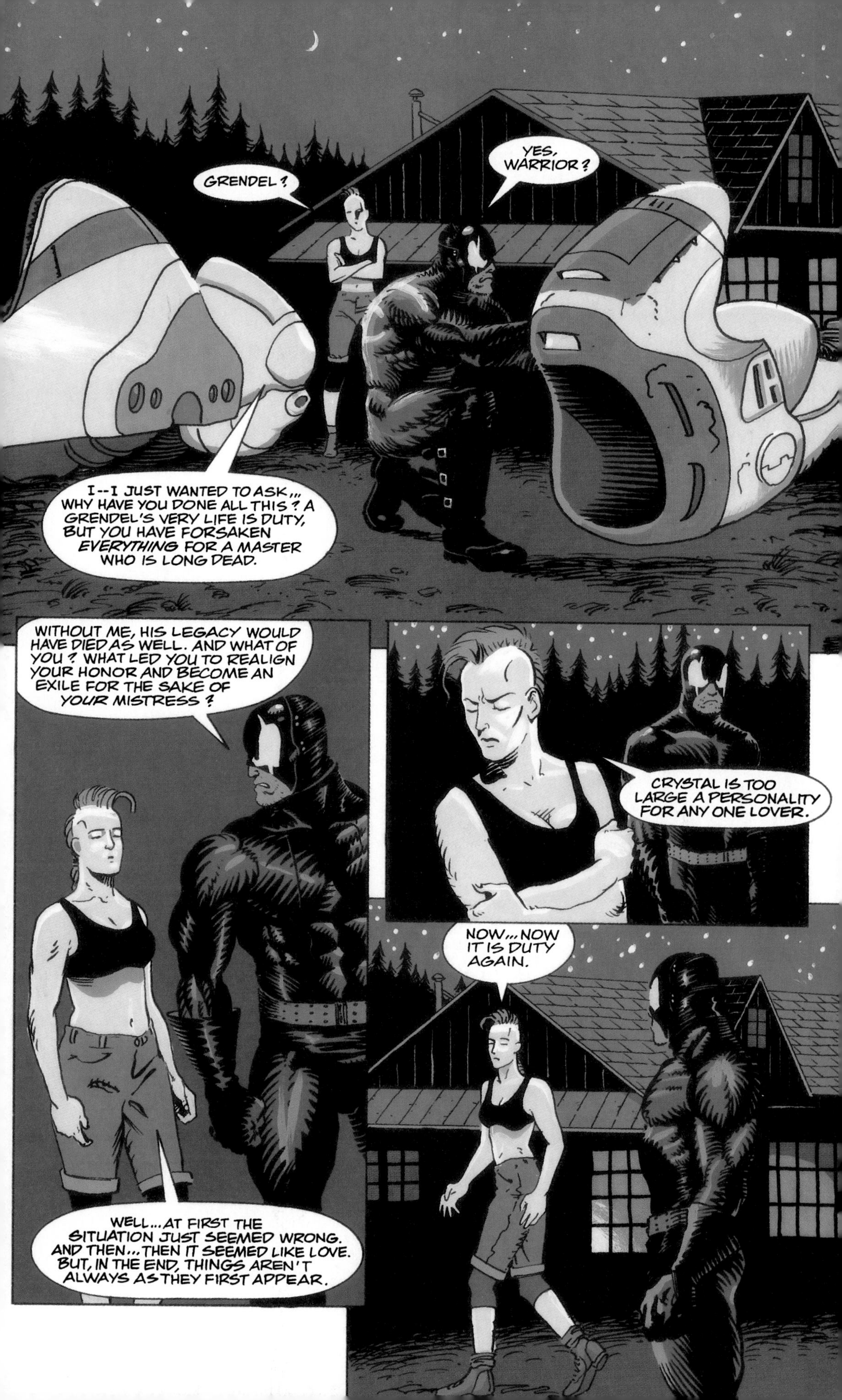
GRENDEL?
YES, WARRIOR?
I--I JUST WANTED TO ASK... WHY HAVE YOU DONE ALL THIS? A GRENDEL'S VERY LIFE IS DUTY, BUT YOU HAVE FORSAKEN *EVERYTHING* FOR A MASTER WHO IS LONG DEAD.
WITHOUT ME, HIS LEGACY WOULD HAVE DIED AS WELL. AND WHAT OF YOU? WHAT LED YOU TO REALIGN YOUR HONOR AND BECOME AN EXILE FOR THE SAKE OF *YOUR* MISTRESS?
WELL... AT FIRST THE SITUATION JUST SEEMED WRONG. AND THEN... THEN IT SEEMED LIKE LOVE. BUT, IN THE END, THINGS AREN'T ALWAYS AS THEY FIRST APPEAR.
CRYSTAL IS TOO LARGE A PERSONALITY FOR ANY ONE LOVER.
NOW... NOW IT IS DUTY AGAIN.

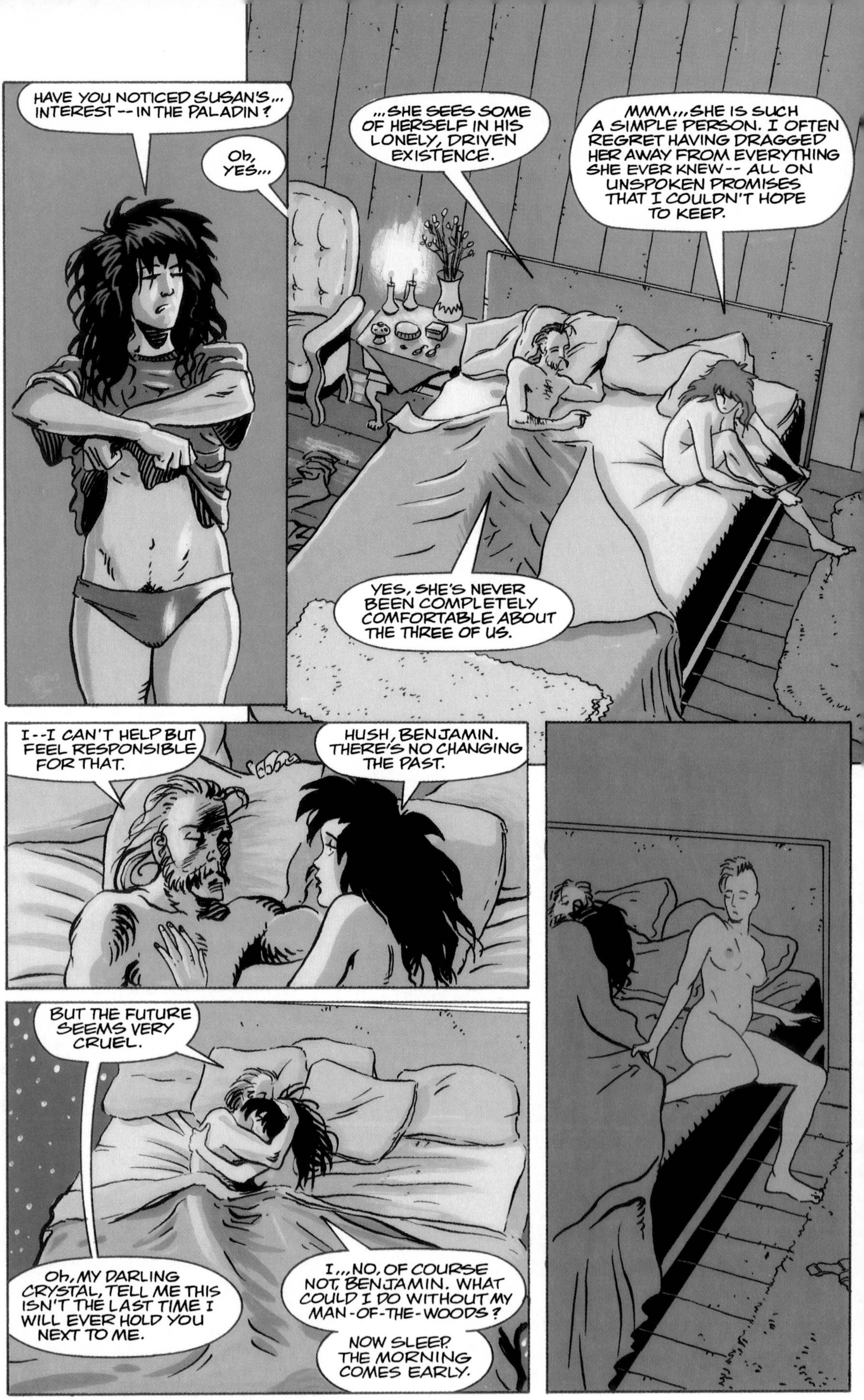
HAVE YOU NOTICED SUSAN'S... INTEREST -- IN THE PALADIN?
Oh, YES...
...SHE SEES SOME OF HERSELF IN HIS LONELY, DRIVEN EXISTENCE.
MMM...SHE IS SUCH A SIMPLE PERSON. I OFTEN REGRET HAVING DRAGGED HER AWAY FROM EVERYTHING SHE EVER KNEW -- ALL ON UNSPOKEN PROMISES THAT I COULDN'T HOPE TO KEEP.
YES, SHE'S NEVER BEEN COMPLETELY COMFORTABLE ABOUT THE THREE OF US.
I--I CAN'T HELP BUT FEEL RESPONSIBLE FOR THAT.
HUSH, BENJAMIN. THERE'S NO CHANGING THE PAST.
BUT THE FUTURE SEEMS VERY CRUEL.
Oh, MY DARLING CRYSTAL, TELL ME THIS ISN'T THE LAST TIME I WILL EVER HOLD YOU NEXT TO ME.
I...NO, OF COURSE NOT, BENJAMIN. WHAT COULD I DO WITHOUT MY MAN-OF-THE-WOODS?
NOW SLEEP. THE MORNING COMES EARLY.

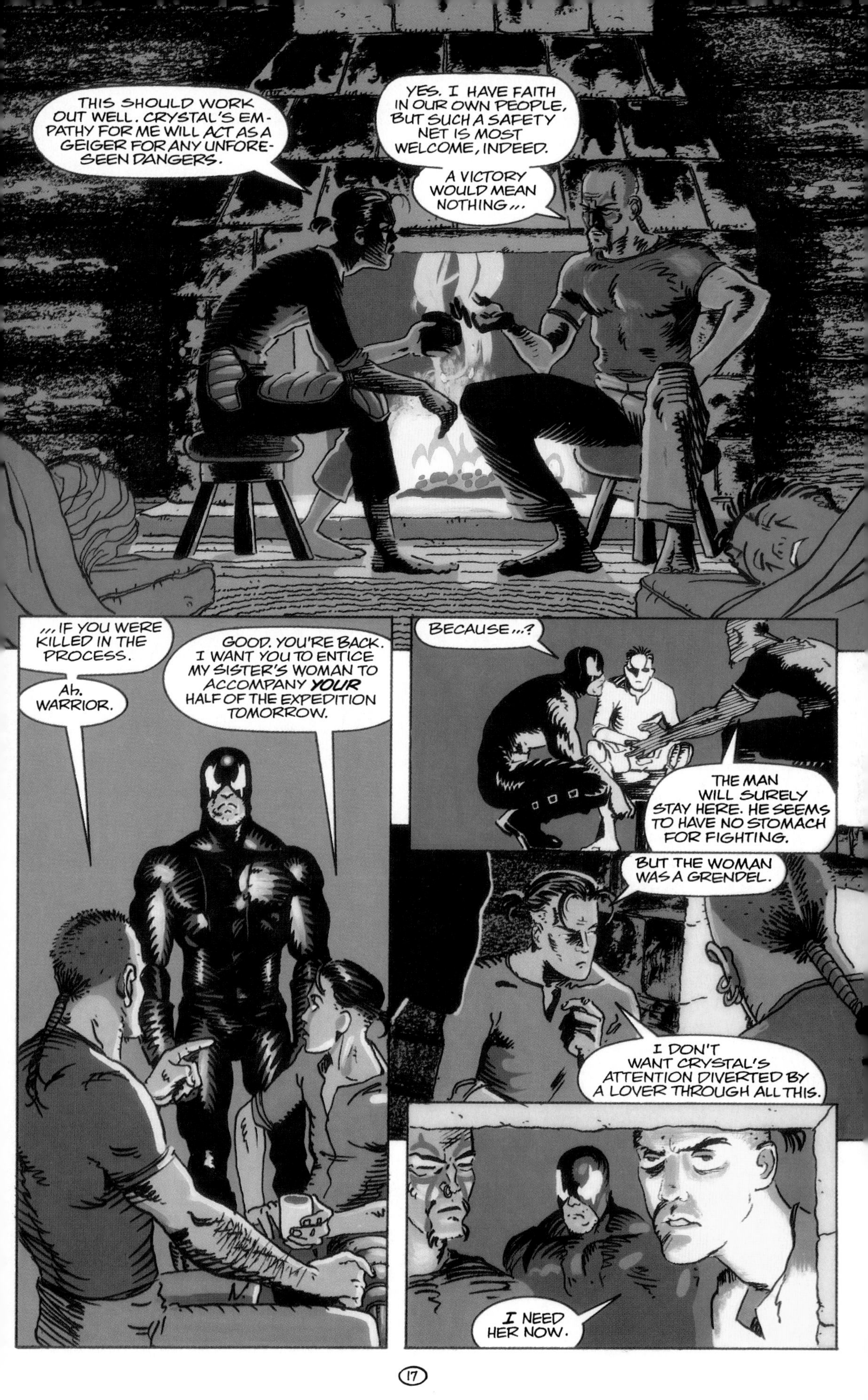
THIS SHOULD WORK OUT WELL. CRYSTAL'S EMPATHY FOR ME WILL ACT AS A GEIGER FOR ANY UNFORESEEN DANGERS.
YES. I HAVE FAITH IN OUR OWN PEOPLE, BUT SUCH A SAFETY NET IS MOST WELCOME, INDEED.
A VICTORY WOULD MEAN NOTHING...
...IF YOU WERE KILLED IN THE PROCESS.
Ah. WARRIOR.
GOOD. YOU'RE BACK. I WANT YOU TO ENTICE MY SISTER'S WOMAN TO ACCOMPANY YOUR HALF OF THE EXPEDITION TOMORROW.
BECAUSE...?
THE MAN WILL SURELY STAY HERE. HE SEEMS TO HAVE NO STOMACH FOR FIGHTING.
BUT THE WOMAN WAS A GRENDEL.
I DON'T WANT CRYSTAL'S ATTENTION DIVERTED BY A LOVER THROUGH ALL THIS.
I NEED HER NOW.

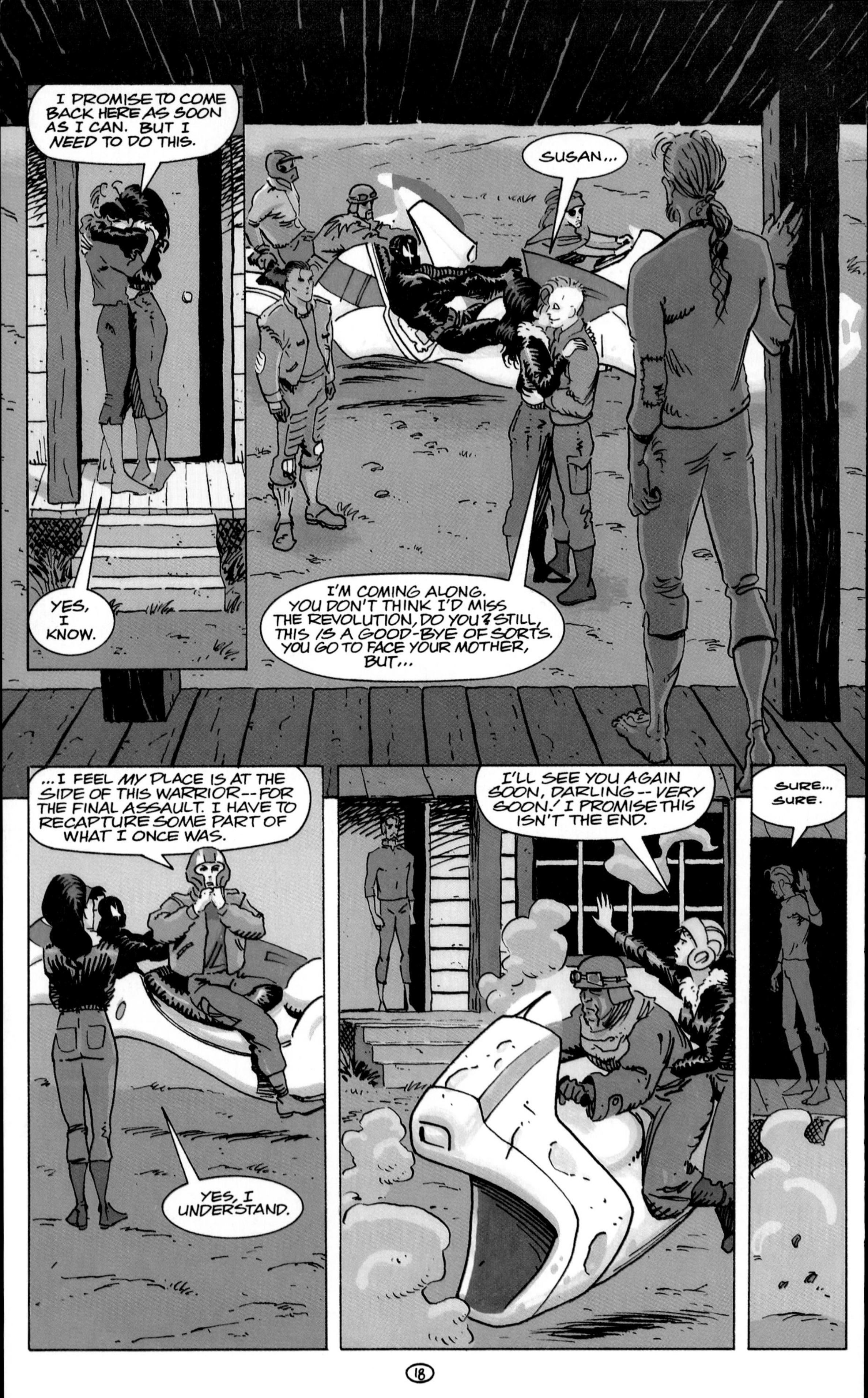
I PROMISE TO COME BACK HERE AS SOON AS I CAN. BUT I NEED TO DO THIS.
YES, I KNOW.
SUSAN...
I'M COMING ALONG. YOU DON'T THINK I'D MISS THE REVOLUTION, DO YOU? STILL, THIS IS A GOOD-BYE OF SORTS. YOU GO TO FACE YOUR MOTHER, BUT...
...I FEEL MY PLACE IS AT THE SIDE OF THIS WARRIOR--FOR THE FINAL ASSAULT. I HAVE TO RECAPTURE SOME PART OF WHAT I ONCE WAS.
YES, I UNDERSTAND.
I'LL SEE YOU AGAIN SOON, DARLING--VERY SOON! I PROMISE THIS ISN'T THE END.
SURE... SURE.

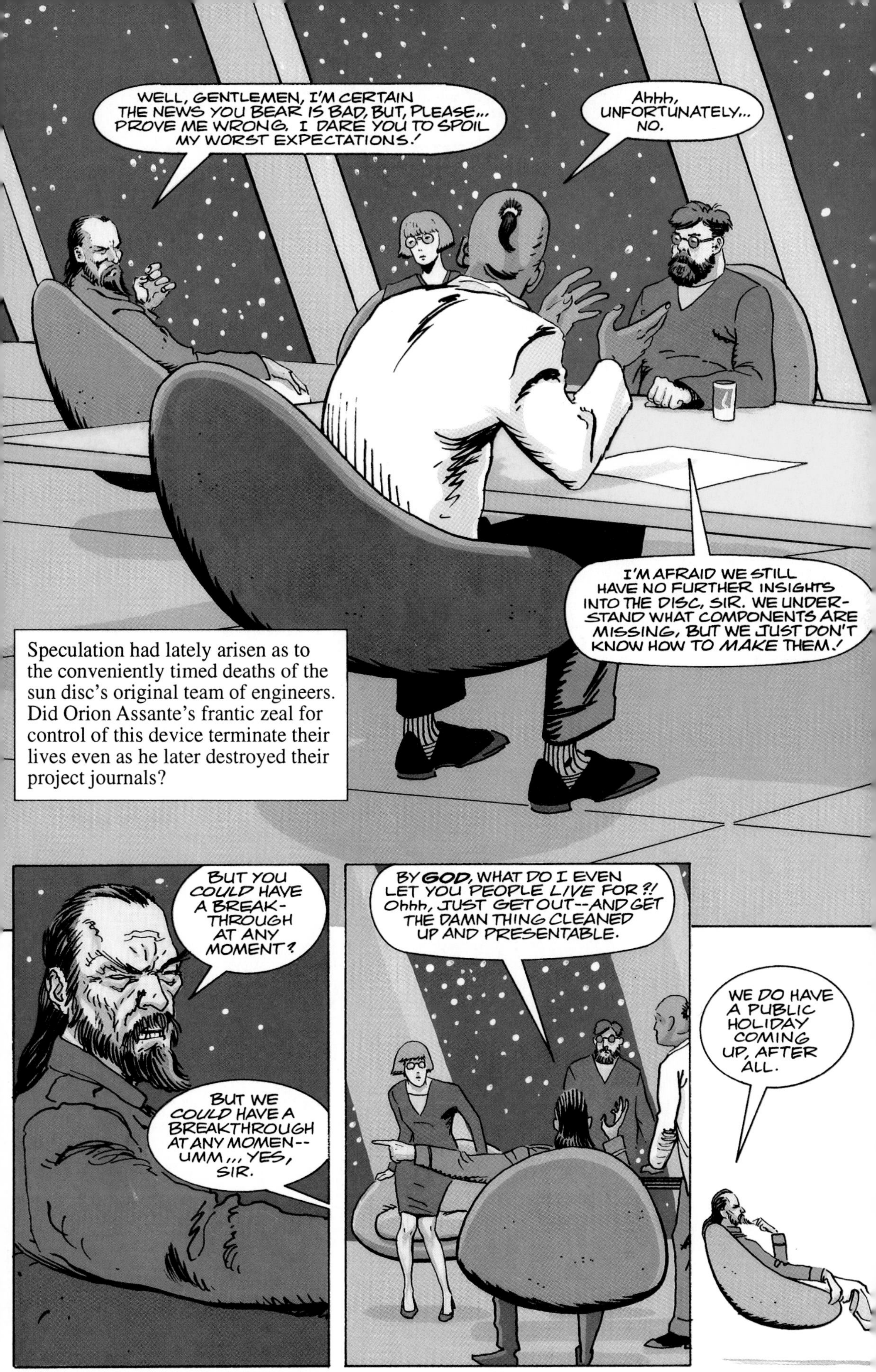
WELL, GENTLEMEN, I'M CERTAIN THE NEWS YOU BEAR IS BAD, BUT, PLEASE... PROVE ME WRONG. I DARE YOU TO SPOIL MY WORST EXPECTATIONS.!
Ahhh, UNFORTUNATELY... NO.
I'M AFRAID WE STILL HAVE NO FURTHER INSIGHTS INTO THE DISC, SIR. WE UNDERSTAND WHAT COMPONENTS ARE MISSING, BUT WE JUST DON'T KNOW HOW TO *MAKE* THEM.!
Speculation had lately arisen as to the conveniently timed deaths of the sun disc's original team of engineers. Did Orion Assante's frantic zeal for control of this device terminate their lives even as he later destroyed their project journals?
BUT YOU *COULD* HAVE A BREAKTHROUGH AT ANY MOMENT?
BUT WE *COULD* HAVE A BREAKTHROUGH AT ANY MOMEN-- UMM... YES, SIR.
BY **GOD**, WHAT DO I EVEN LET YOU PEOPLE *LIVE* FOR?! Ohhh, JUST GET OUT--AND GET THE DAMN THING CLEANED UP AND PRESENTABLE.
WE *DO* HAVE A PUBLIC HOLIDAY COMING UP, AFTER ALL.

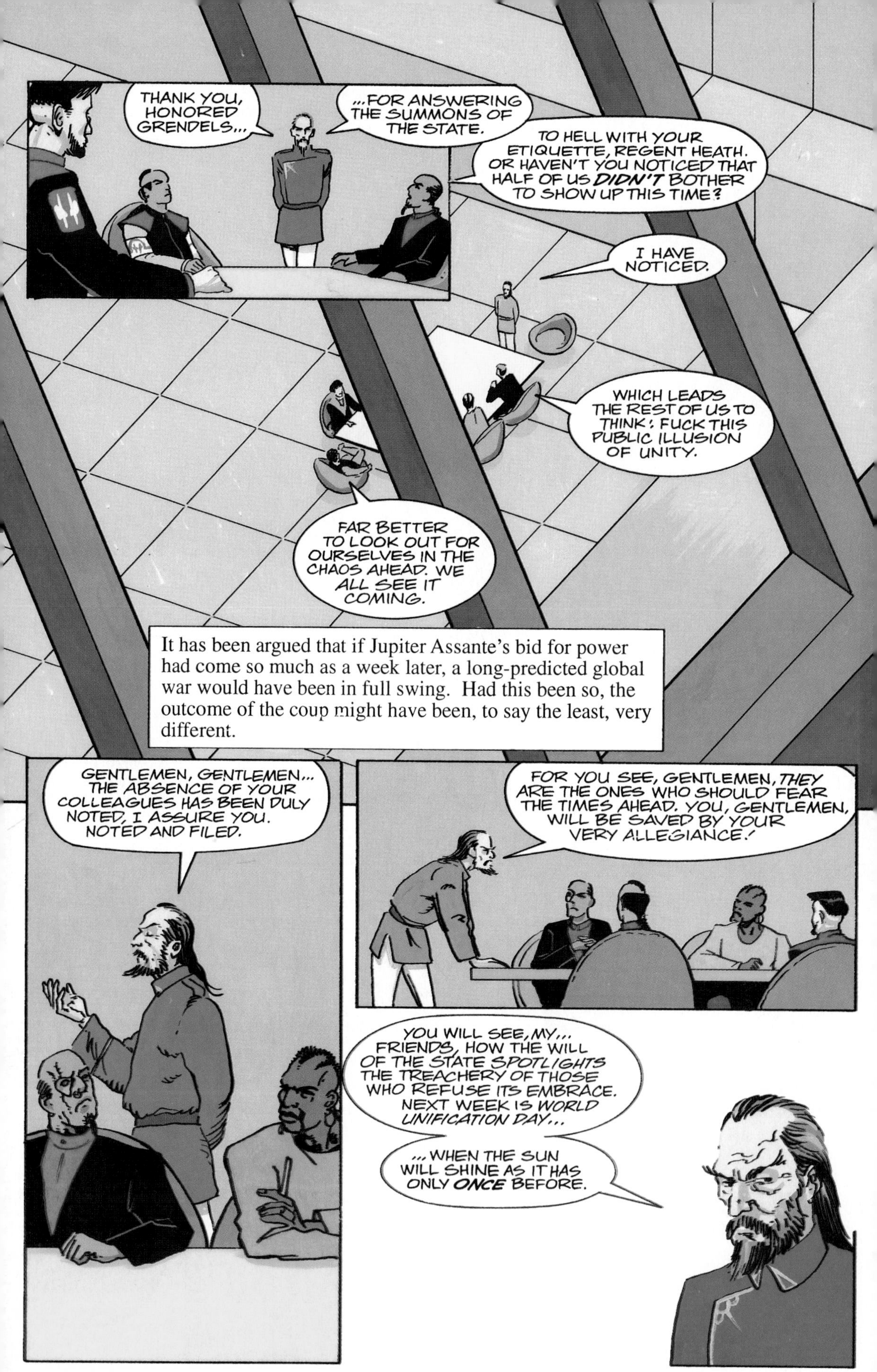
THANK YOU, HONORED GRENDELS...
...FOR ANSWERING THE SUMMONS OF THE STATE.
TO HELL WITH YOUR ETIQUETTE, REGENT HEATH. OR HAVEN'T YOU NOTICED THAT HALF OF US DIDN'T BOTHER TO SHOW UP THIS TIME?
I HAVE NOTICED.
WHICH LEADS THE REST OF US TO THINK: FUCK THIS PUBLIC ILLUSION OF UNITY.
FAR BETTER TO LOOK OUT FOR OURSELVES IN THE CHAOS AHEAD. WE ALL SEE IT COMING.
It has been argued that if Jupiter Assante's bid for power had come so much as a week later, a long-predicted global war would have been in full swing. Had this been so, the outcome of the coup might have been, to say the least, very different.
GENTLEMEN, GENTLEMEN... THE ABSENCE OF YOUR COLLEAGUES HAS BEEN DULY NOTED, I ASSURE YOU. NOTED AND FILED.
FOR YOU SEE, GENTLEMEN, THEY ARE THE ONES WHO SHOULD FEAR THE TIMES AHEAD. YOU, GENTLEMEN, WILL BE SAVED BY YOUR VERY ALLEGIANCE!
YOU WILL SEE, MY... FRIENDS, HOW THE WILL OF THE STATE SPOTLIGHTS THE TREACHERY OF THOSE WHO REFUSE ITS EMBRACE. NEXT WEEK IS WORLD UNIFICATION DAY...
...WHEN THE SUN WILL SHINE AS IT HAS ONLY ONCE BEFORE.

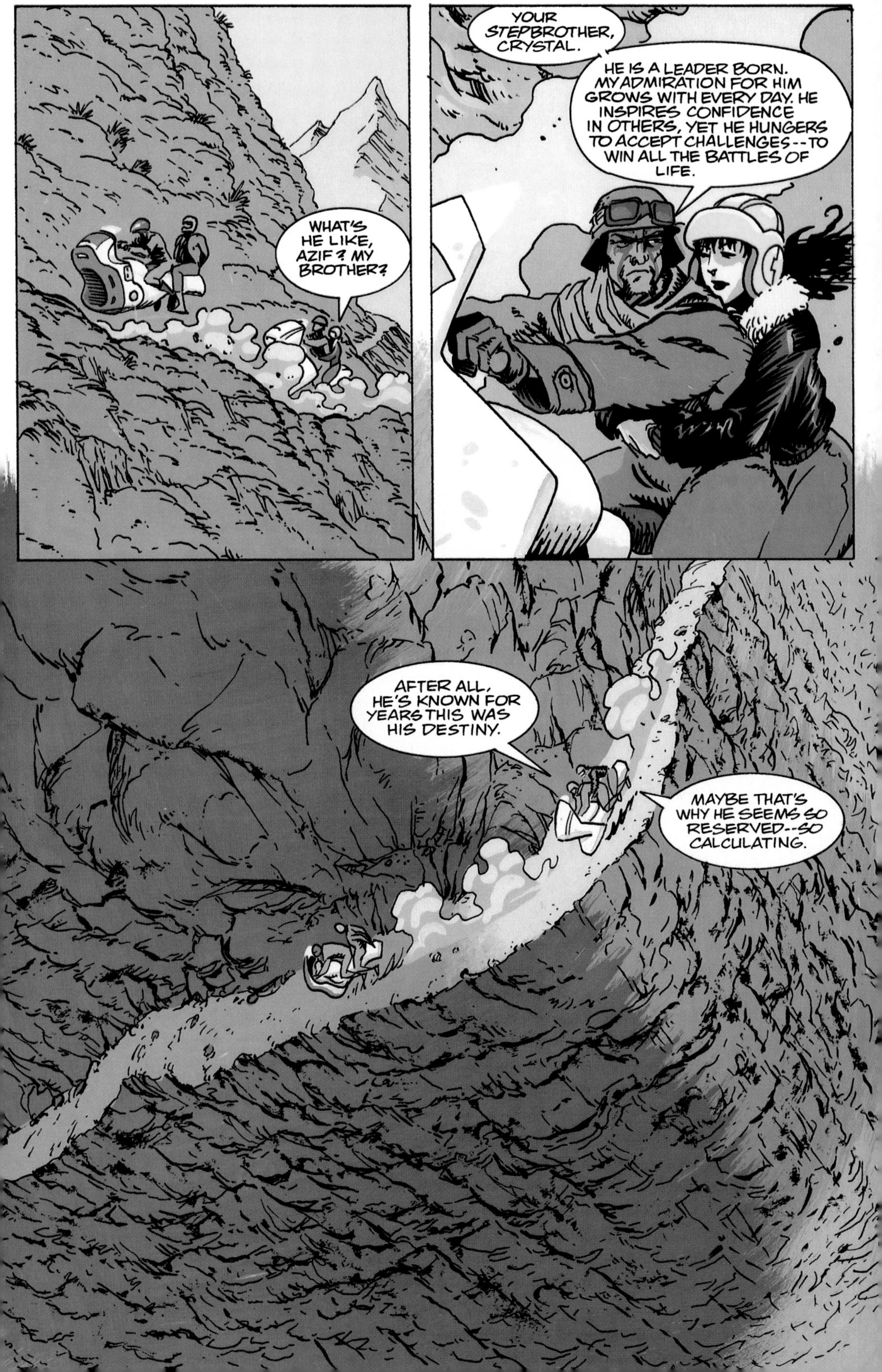
WHAT'S HE LIKE, AZIF? MY BROTHER?
YOUR STEPBROTHER, CRYSTAL.
HE IS A LEADER BORN. MY ADMIRATION FOR HIM GROWS WITH EVERY DAY. HE INSPIRES CONFIDENCE IN OTHERS, YET HE HUNGERS TO ACCEPT CHALLENGES--TO WIN ALL THE BATTLES OF LIFE.
AFTER ALL, HE'S KNOWN FOR YEARS THIS WAS HIS DESTINY.
MAYBE THAT'S WHY HE SEEMS SO RESERVED--SO CALCULATING.

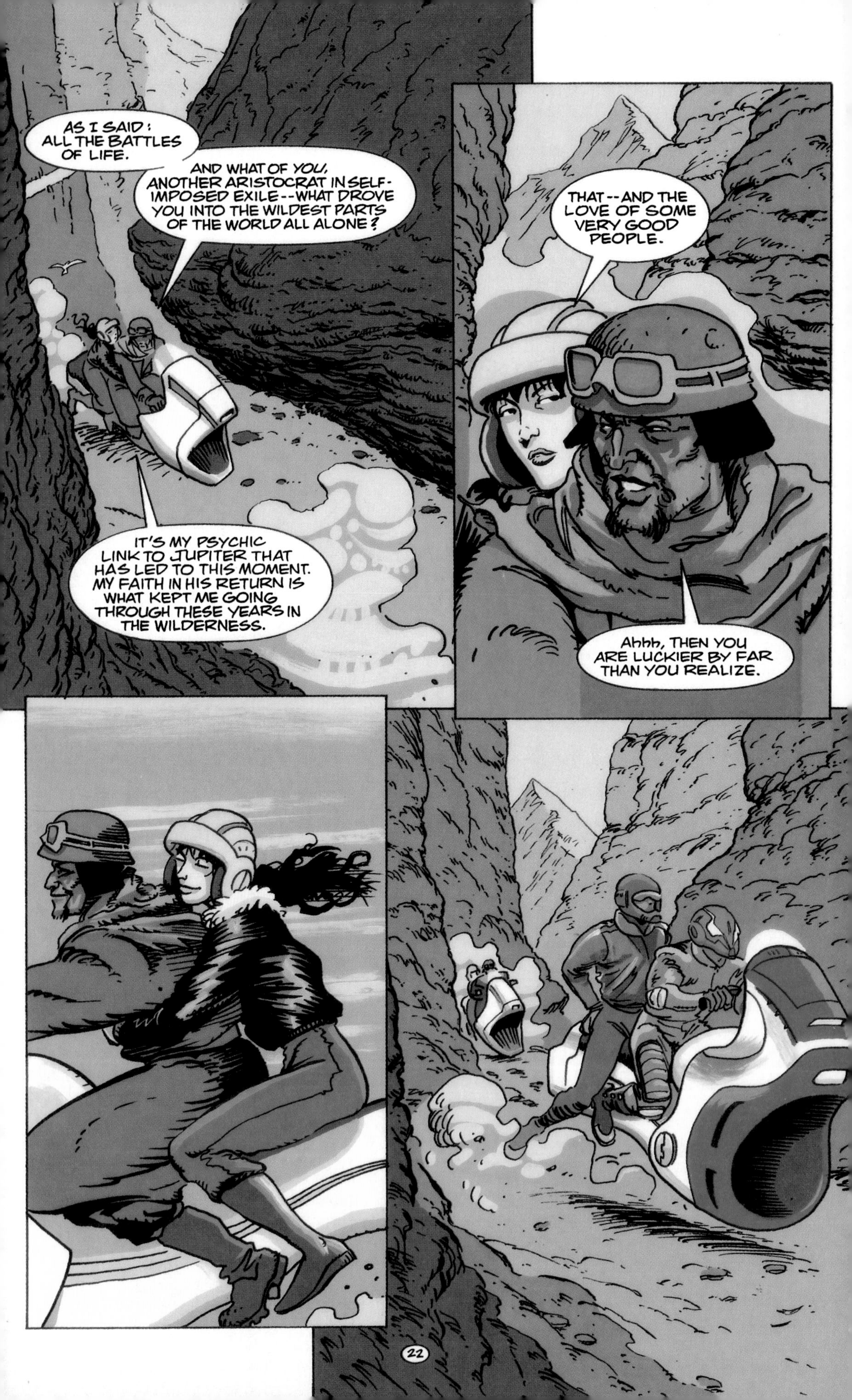
AS I SAID: ALL THE BATTLES OF LIFE.
AND WHAT OF YOU, ANOTHER ARISTOCRAT IN SELF-IMPOSED EXILE--WHAT DROVE YOU INTO THE WILDEST PARTS OF THE WORLD ALL ALONE?
IT'S MY PSYCHIC LINK TO JUPITER THAT HAS LED TO THIS MOMENT. MY FAITH IN HIS RETURN IS WHAT KEPT ME GOING THROUGH THESE YEARS IN THE WILDERNESS.
THAT--AND THE LOVE OF SOME VERY GOOD PEOPLE.
Ahhh, THEN YOU ARE LUCKIER BY FAR THAN YOU REALIZE.

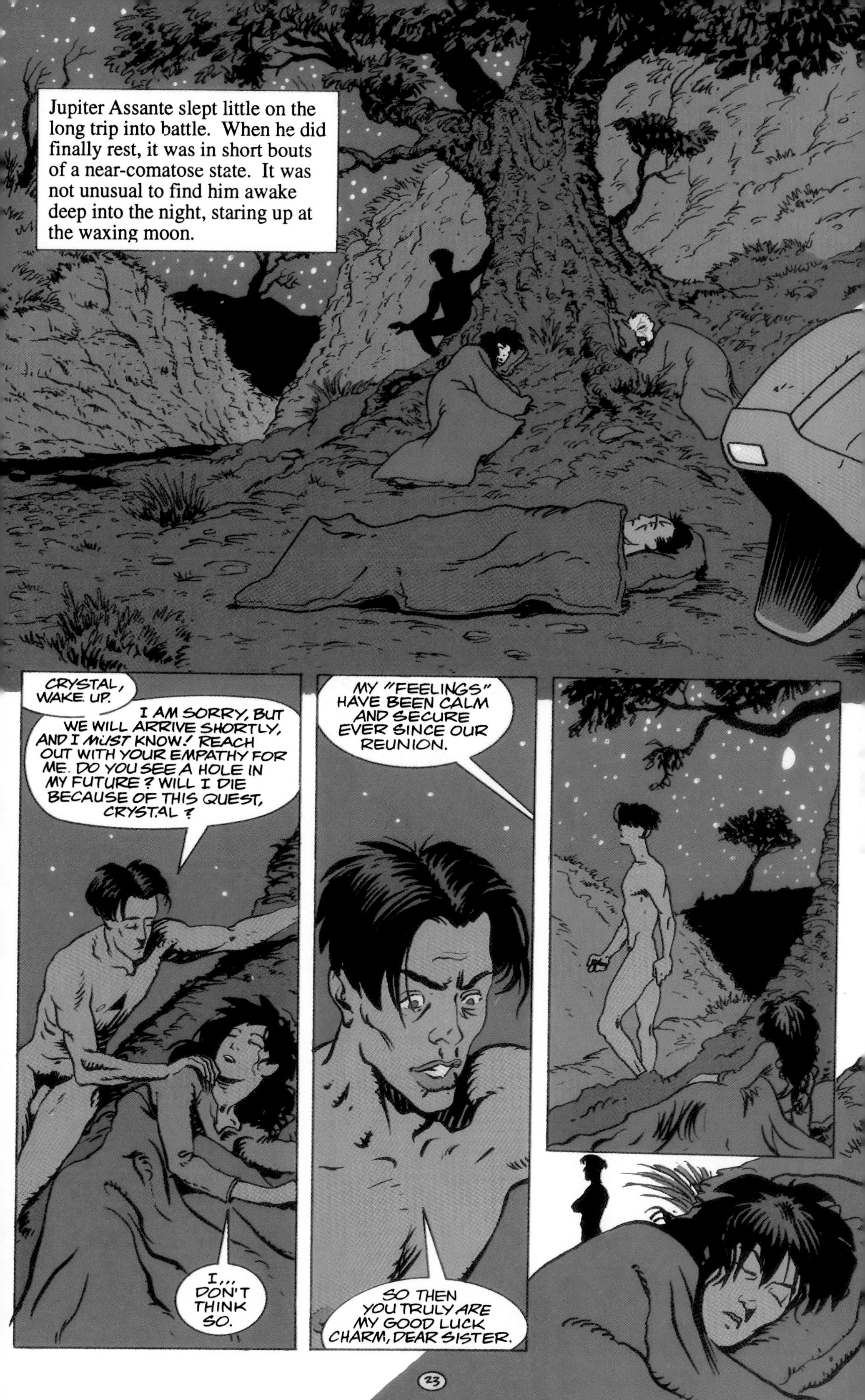
Jupiter Assante slept little on the long trip into battle. When he did finally rest, it was in short bouts of a near-comatose state. It was not unusual to find him awake deep into the night, staring up at the waxing moon.
CRYSTAL, WAKE UP.
I AM SORRY, BUT WE WILL ARRIVE SHORTLY, AND I MUST KNOW! REACH OUT WITH YOUR EMPATHY FOR ME. DO YOU SEE A HOLE IN MY FUTURE? WILL I DIE BECAUSE OF THIS QUEST, CRYSTAL?
I,,, DON'T THINK SO.
MY "FEELINGS" HAVE BEEN CALM AND SECURE EVER SINCE OUR REUNION.
SO THEN YOU TRULY ARE MY GOOD LUCK CHARM, DEAR SISTER.

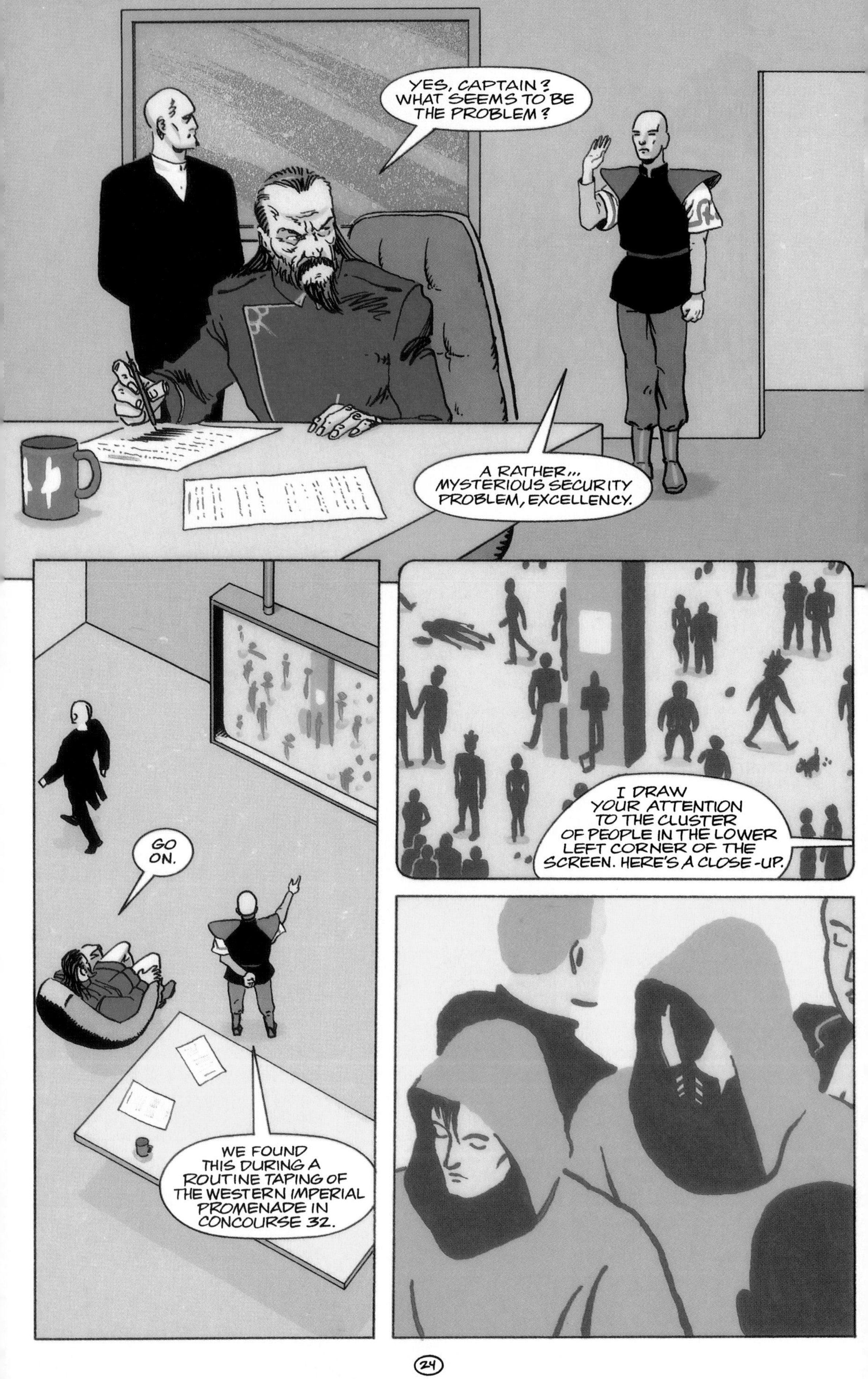
YES, CAPTAIN? WHAT SEEMS TO BE THE PROBLEM?
A RATHER... MYSTERIOUS SECURITY PROBLEM, EXCELLENCY.
GO ON.
WE FOUND THIS DURING A ROUTINE TAPING OF THE WESTERN IMPERIAL PROMENADE IN CONCOURSE 32.
I DRAW YOUR ATTENTION TO THE CLUSTER OF PEOPLE IN THE LOWER LEFT CORNER OF THE SCREEN. HERE'S A CLOSE-UP.

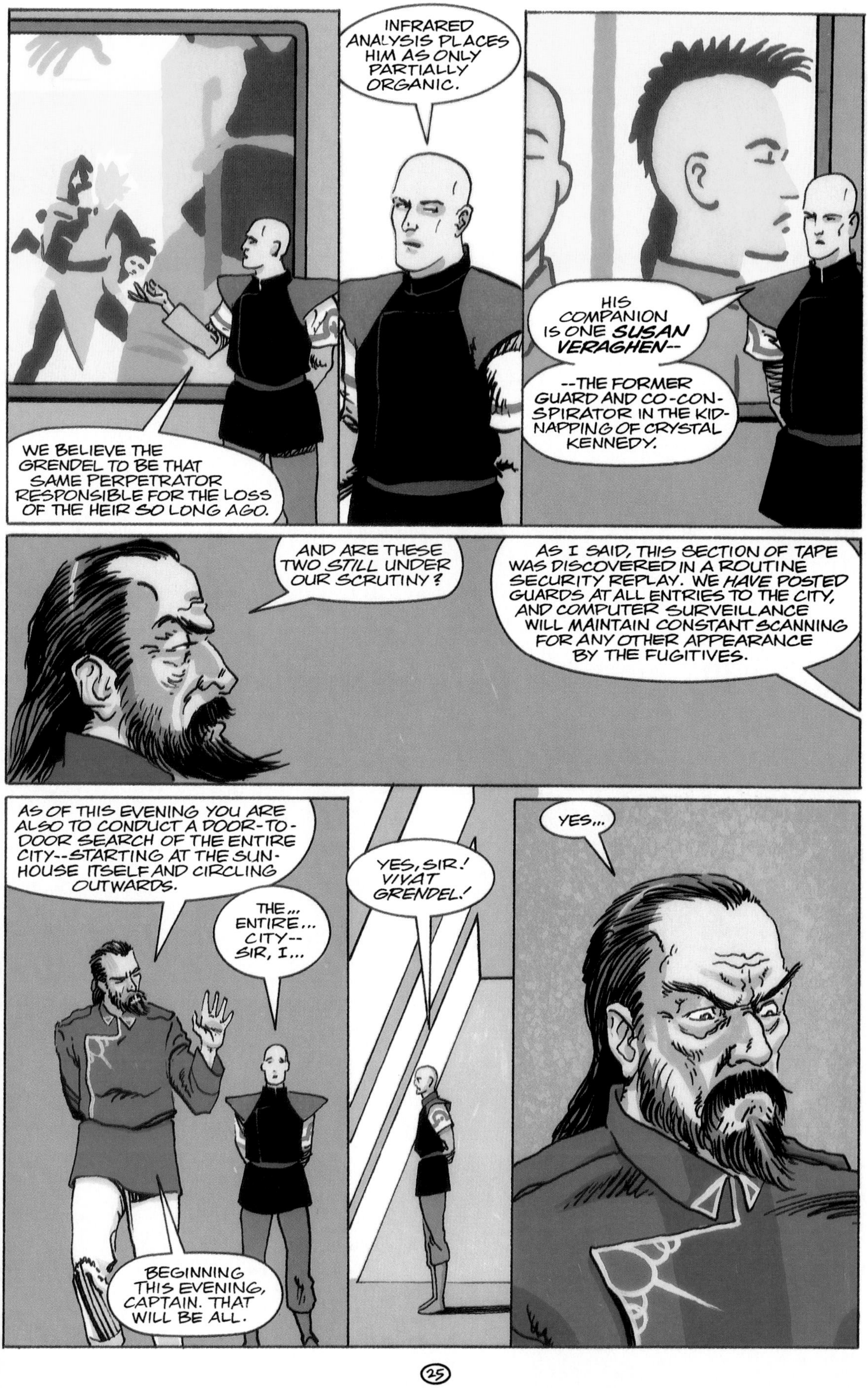
WE BELIEVE THE GRENDEL TO BE THAT SAME PERPETRATOR RESPONSIBLE FOR THE LOSS OF THE HEIR SO LONG AGO.
INFRARED ANALYSIS PLACES HIM AS ONLY PARTIALLY ORGANIC.
HIS COMPANION IS ONE SUSAN VERAGHEN--
--THE FORMER GUARD AND CO-CONSPIRATOR IN THE KIDNAPPING OF CRYSTAL KENNEDY.
AND ARE THESE TWO STILL UNDER OUR SCRUTINY?
AS I SAID, THIS SECTION OF TAPE WAS DISCOVERED IN A ROUTINE SECURITY REPLAY. WE HAVE POSTED GUARDS AT ALL ENTRIES TO THE CITY, AND COMPUTER SURVEILLANCE WILL MAINTAIN CONSTANT SCANNING FOR ANY OTHER APPEARANCE BY THE FUGITIVES.
AS OF THIS EVENING YOU ARE ALSO TO CONDUCT A DOOR-TO-DOOR SEARCH OF THE ENTIRE CITY--STARTING AT THE SUNHOUSE ITSELF AND CIRCLING OUTWARDS.
THE... ENTIRE... CITY-- SIR, I...
BEGINNING THIS EVENING, CAPTAIN. THAT WILL BE ALL.
YES, SIR! VIVAT GRENDEL!
YES...

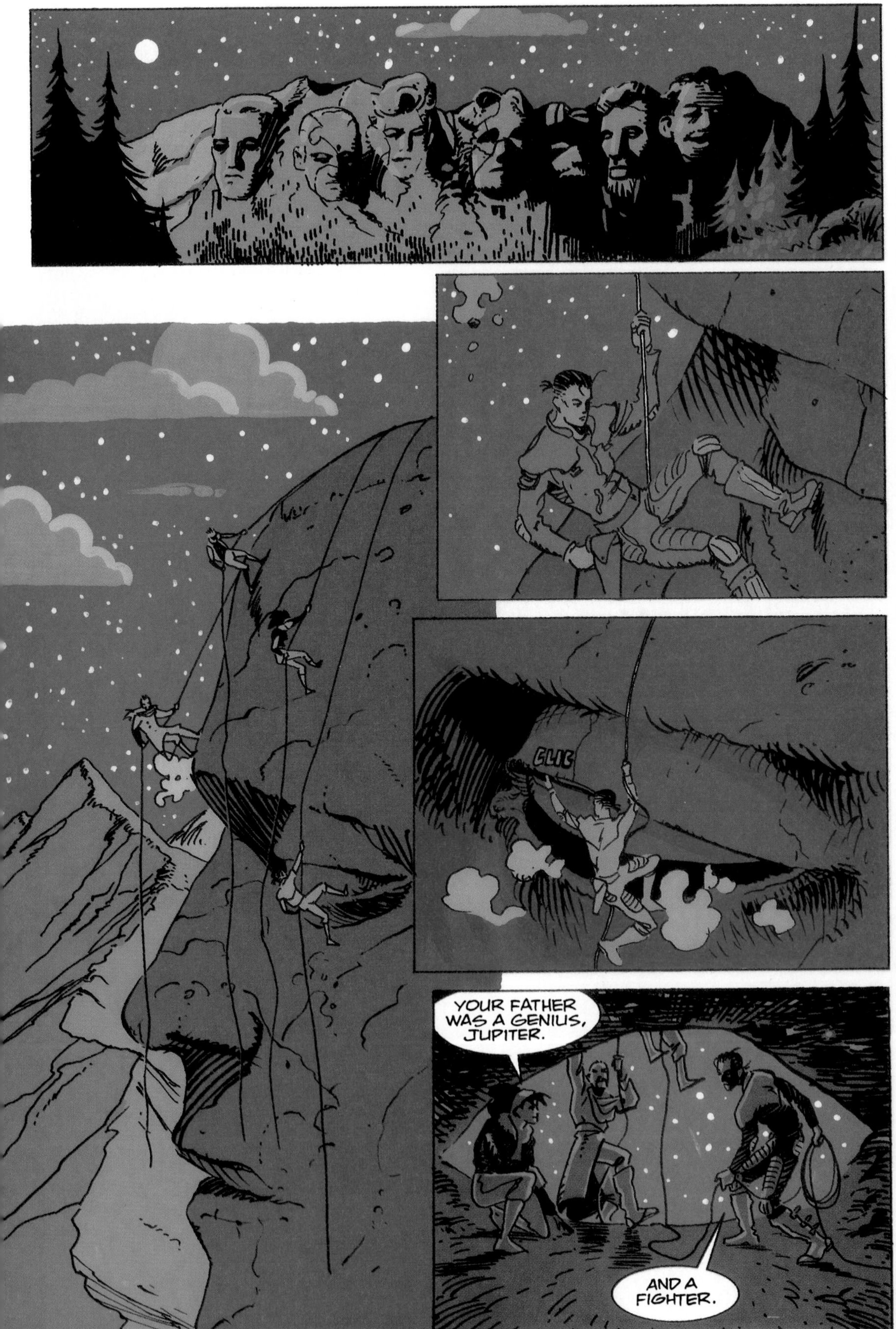
CLIC
YOUR FATHER WAS A GENIUS, JUPITER.
AND A FIGHTER.

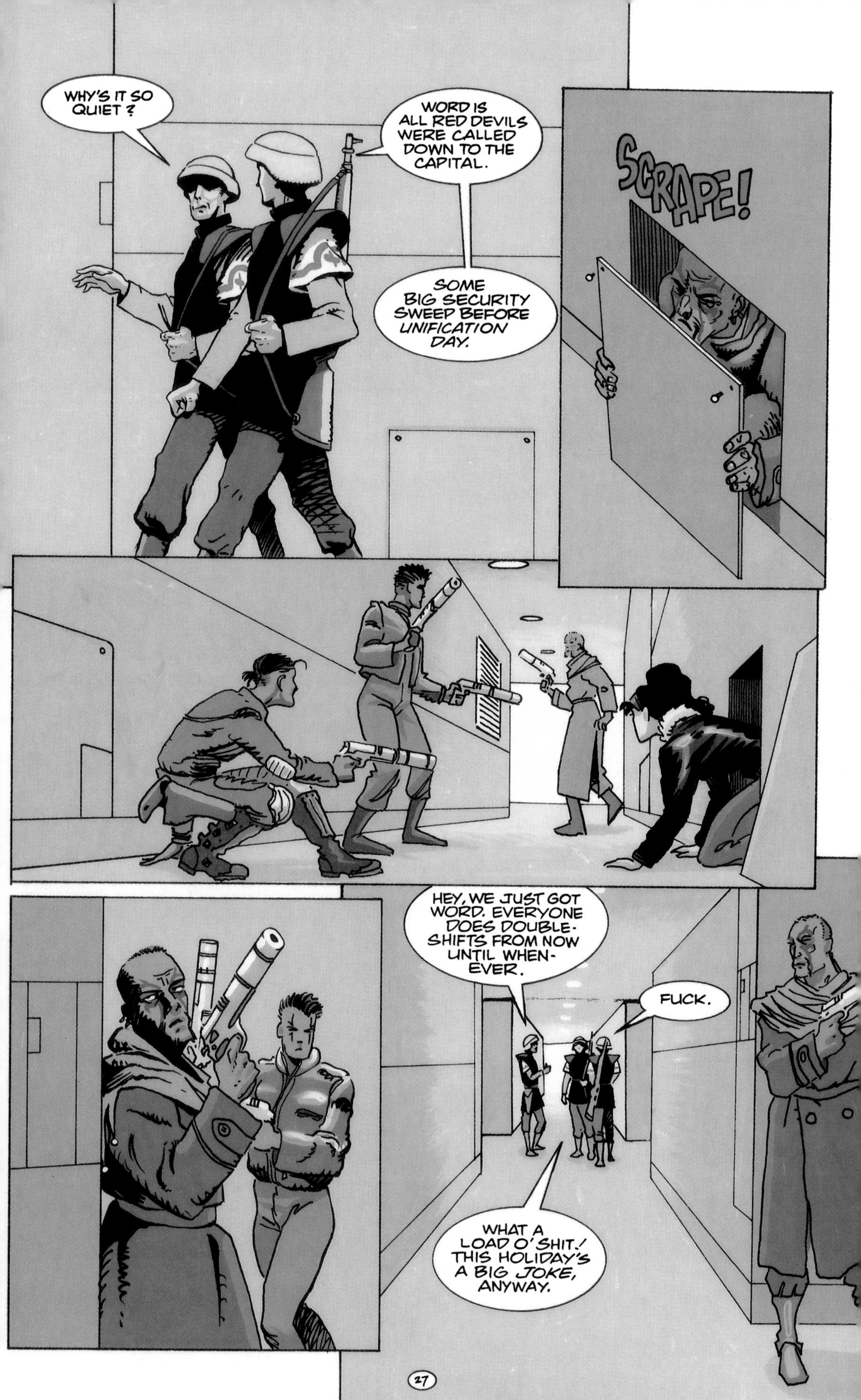
WHY'S IT SO QUIET ?
WORD IS ALL RED DEVILS WERE CALLED DOWN TO THE CAPITAL.
SOME BIG SECURITY SWEEP BEFORE UNIFICATION DAY.
SCRAPE!
HEY, WE JUST GOT WORD. EVERYONE DOES DOUBLE-SHIFTS FROM NOW UNTIL WHEN-EVER.
FUCK.
WHAT A LOAD O' SHIT! THIS HOLIDAY'S A BIG JOKE, ANYWAY.

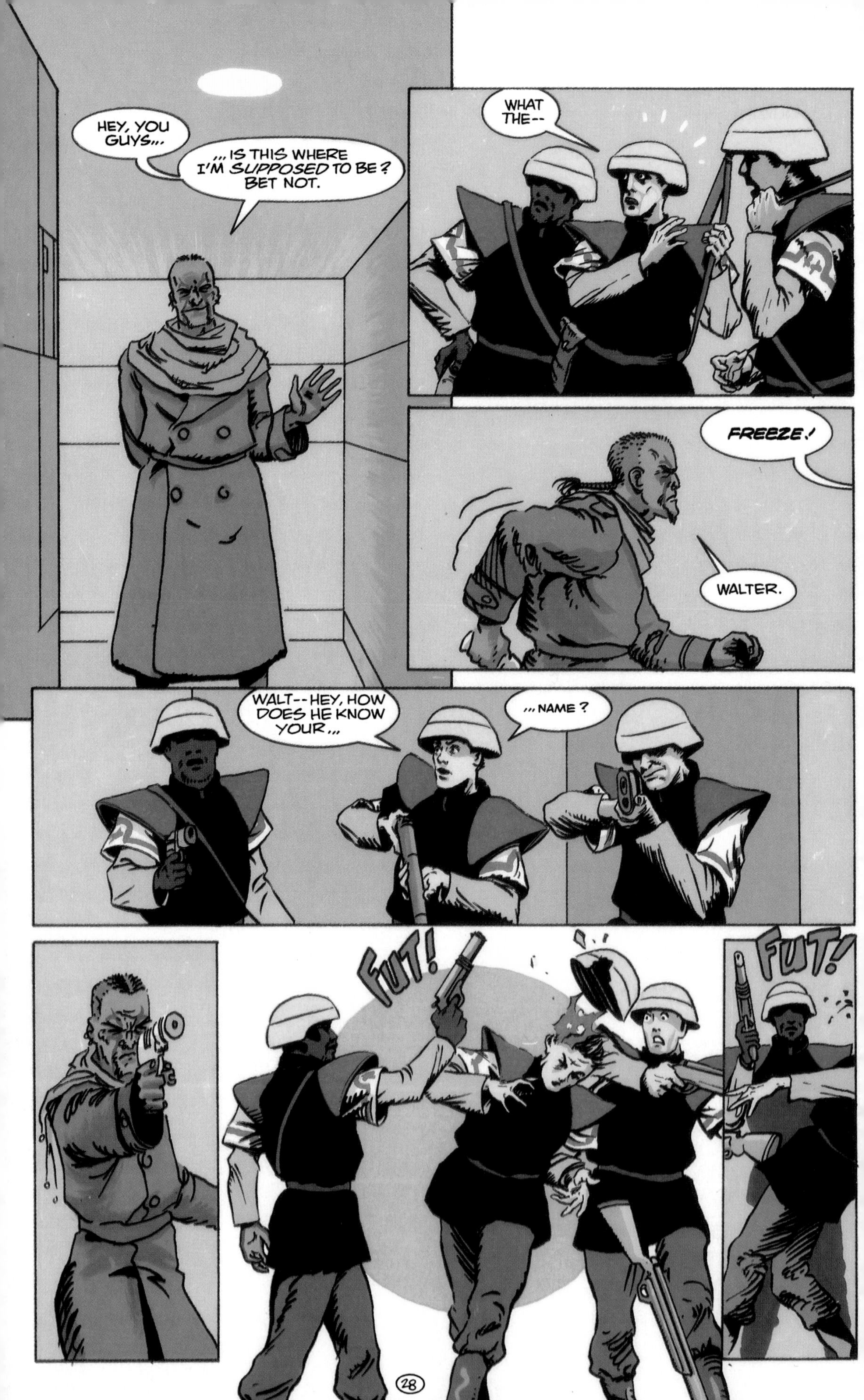
HEY, YOU GUYS,,,
,,, IS THIS WHERE I'M SUPPOSED TO BE? BET NOT.
WHAT THE--
FREEZE!
WALTER.
WALT--HEY, HOW DOES HE KNOW YOUR,,,
,,, NAME?
FUT!
FUT!

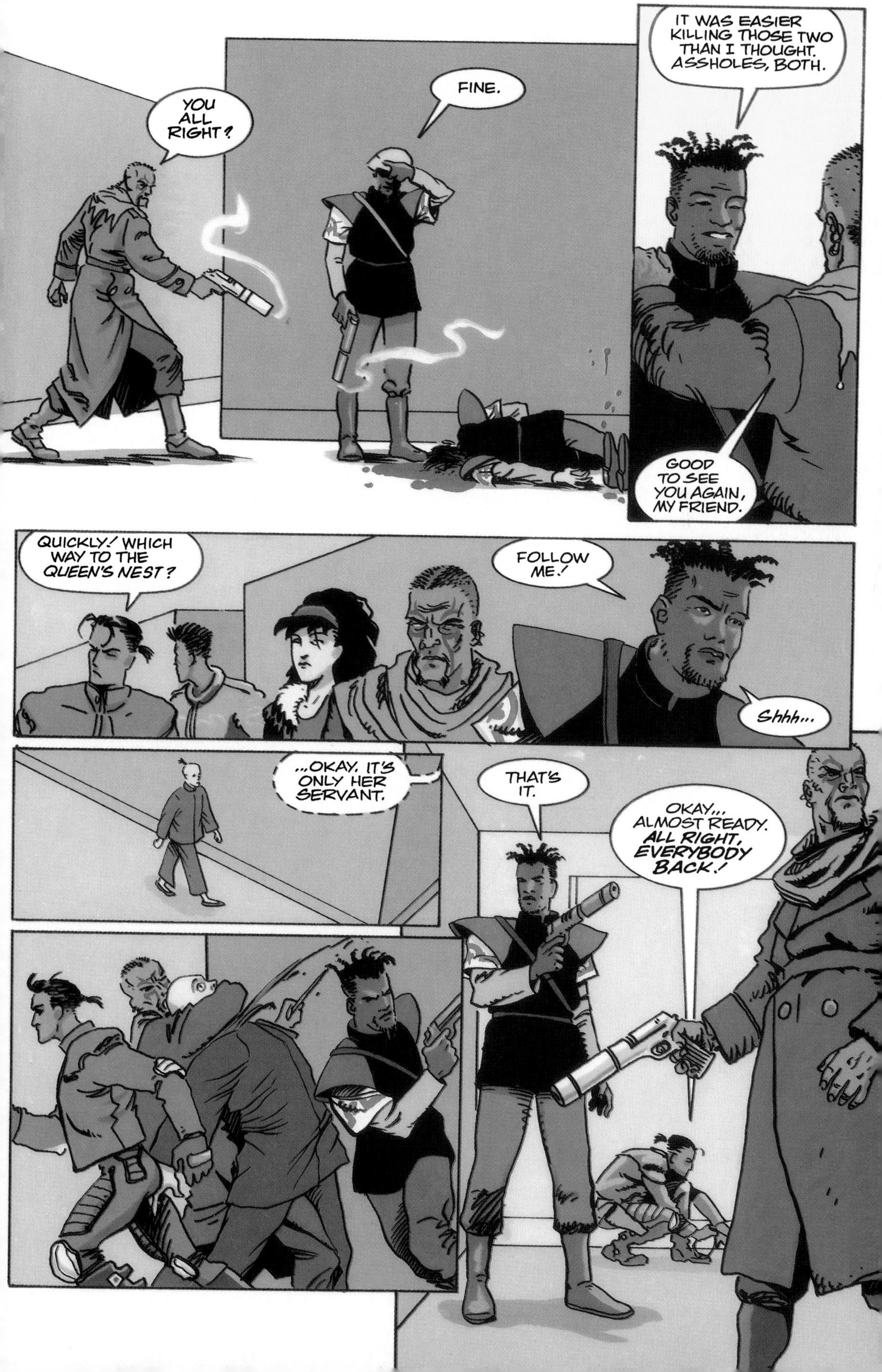
YOU ALL RIGHT?
FINE.
IT WAS EASIER KILLING THOSE TWO THAN I THOUGHT. ASSHOLES, BOTH.
GOOD TO SEE YOU AGAIN, MY FRIEND.
QUICKLY! WHICH WAY TO THE QUEEN'S NEST?
FOLLOW ME.!
Shhh...
...OKAY. IT'S ONLY HER SERVANT.
THAT'S IT.
OKAY... ALMOST READY. ALL RIGHT, EVERYBODY BACK.!

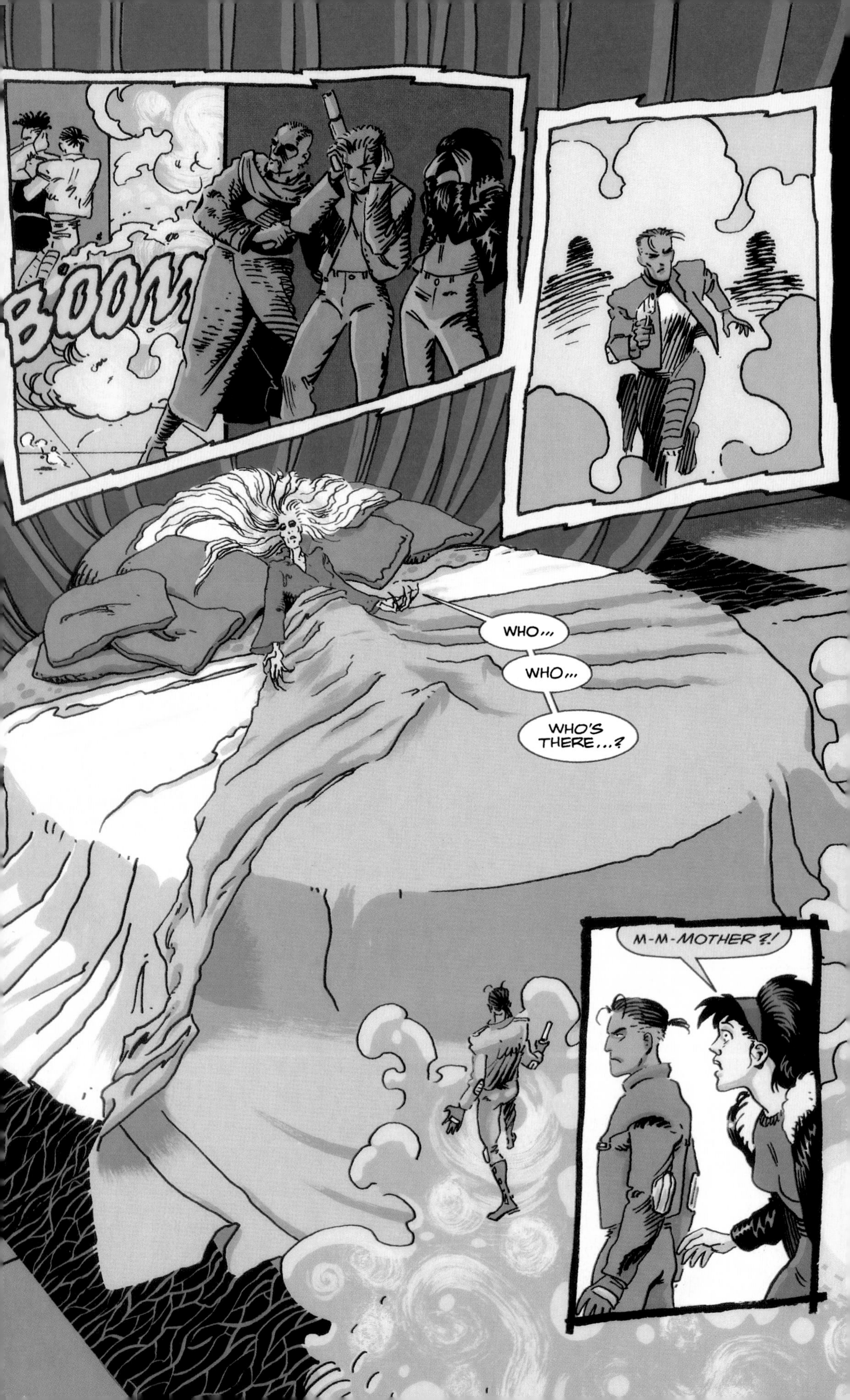
BOOM
WHO...
WHO...
WHO'S THERE...?
M-M-MOTHER?!

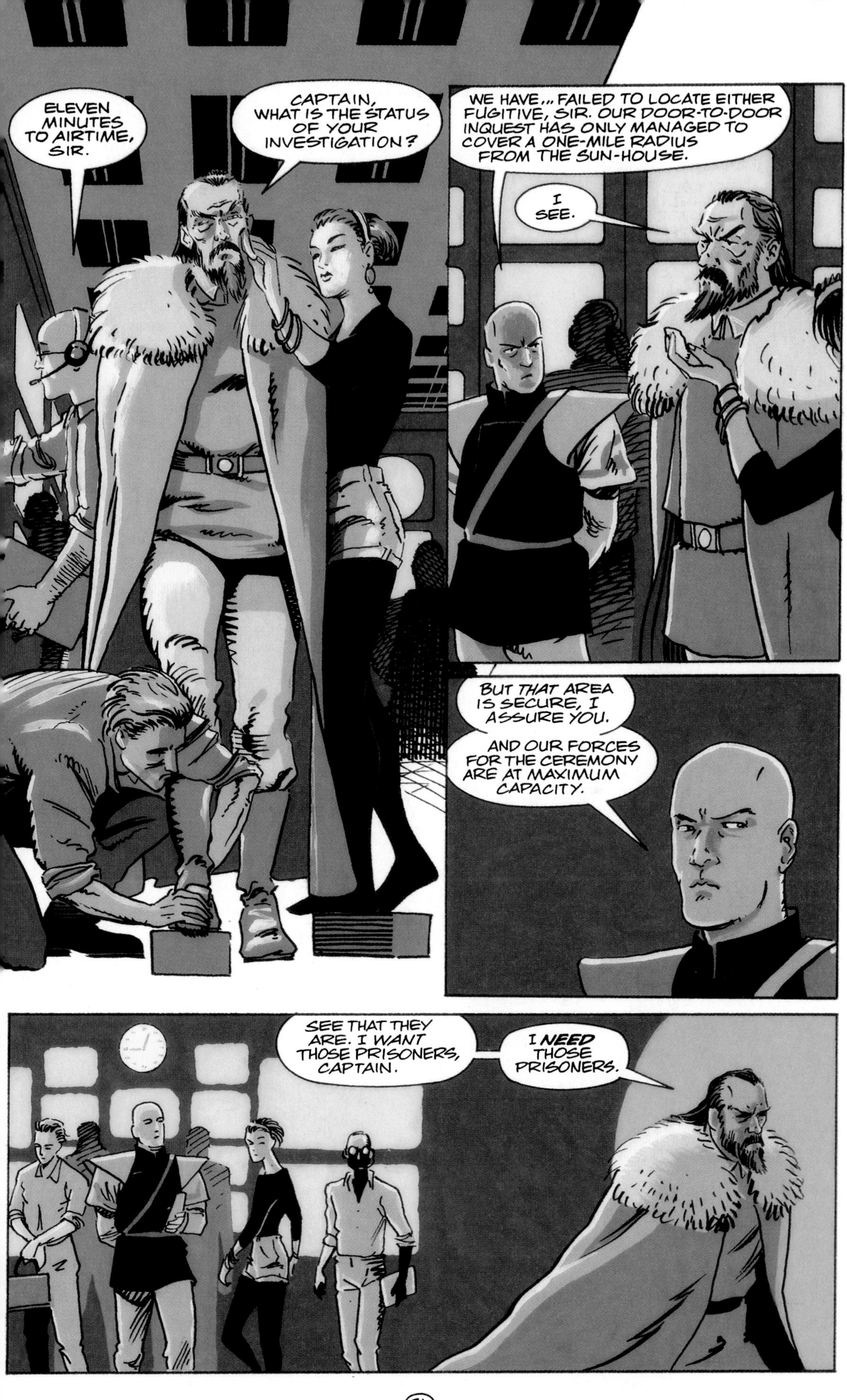
ELEVEN MINUTES TO AIRTIME, SIR.
CAPTAIN, WHAT IS THE STATUS OF YOUR INVESTIGATION?
WE HAVE... FAILED TO LOCATE EITHER FUGITIVE, SIR. OUR DOOR-TO-DOOR INQUEST HAS ONLY MANAGED TO COVER A ONE-MILE RADIUS FROM THE SUN-HOUSE.
I SEE.
BUT *THAT* AREA IS SECURE, I ASSURE YOU.
AND OUR FORCES FOR THE CEREMONY ARE AT MAXIMUM CAPACITY.
SEE THAT THEY ARE. I *WANT* THOSE PRISONERS, CAPTAIN.
I ***NEED*** THOSE PRISONERS.

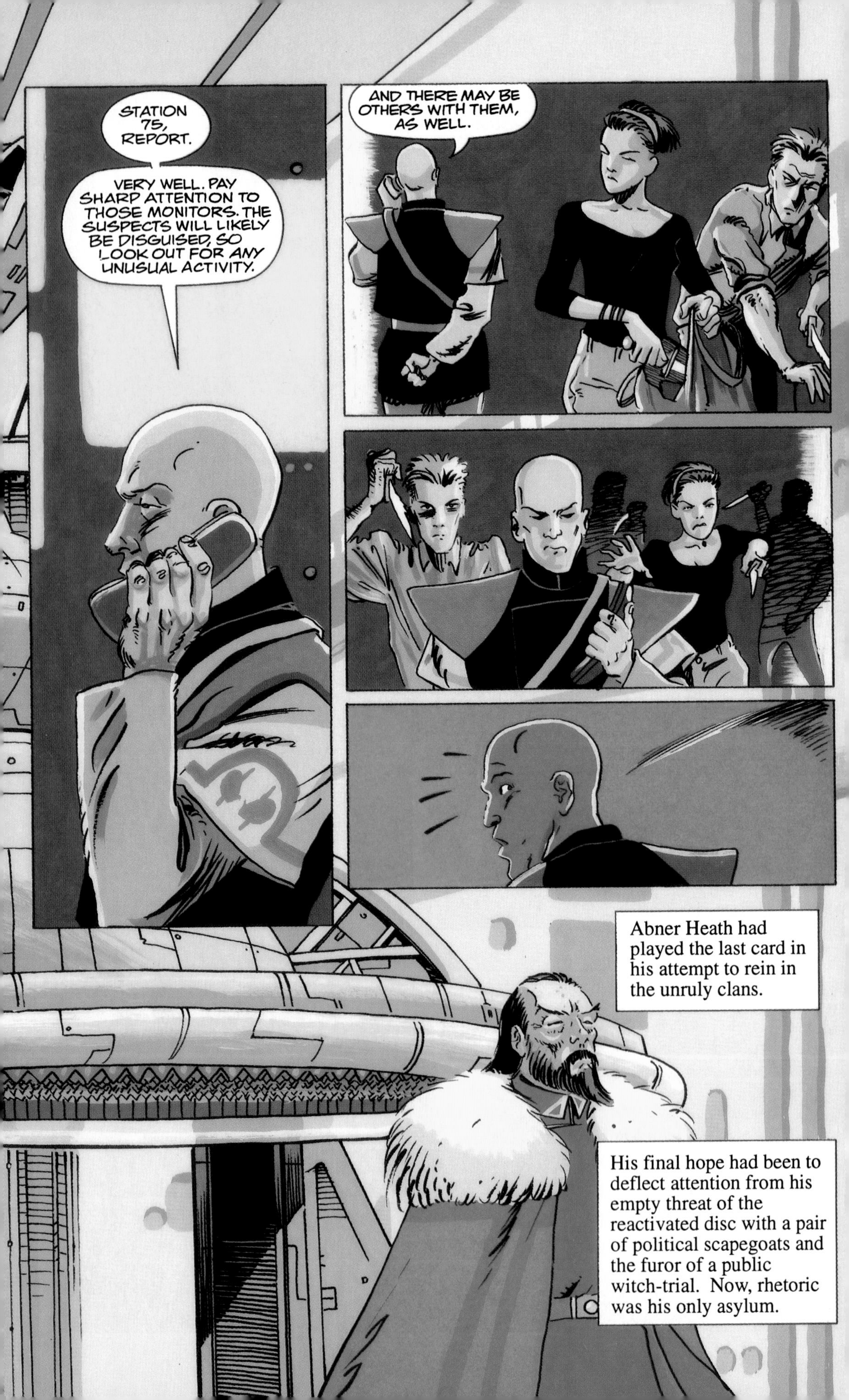
STATION 75, REPORT.
VERY WELL. PAY SHARP ATTENTION TO THOSE MONITORS. THE SUSPECTS WILL LIKELY BE DISGUISED, SO LOOK OUT FOR ANY UNUSUAL ACTIVITY.
AND THERE MAY BE OTHERS WITH THEM, AS WELL.
Abner Heath had played the last card in his attempt to rein in the unruly clans.
His final hope had been to deflect attention from his empty threat of the reactivated disc with a pair of political scapegoats and the furor of a public witch-trial. Now, rhetoric was his only asylum.

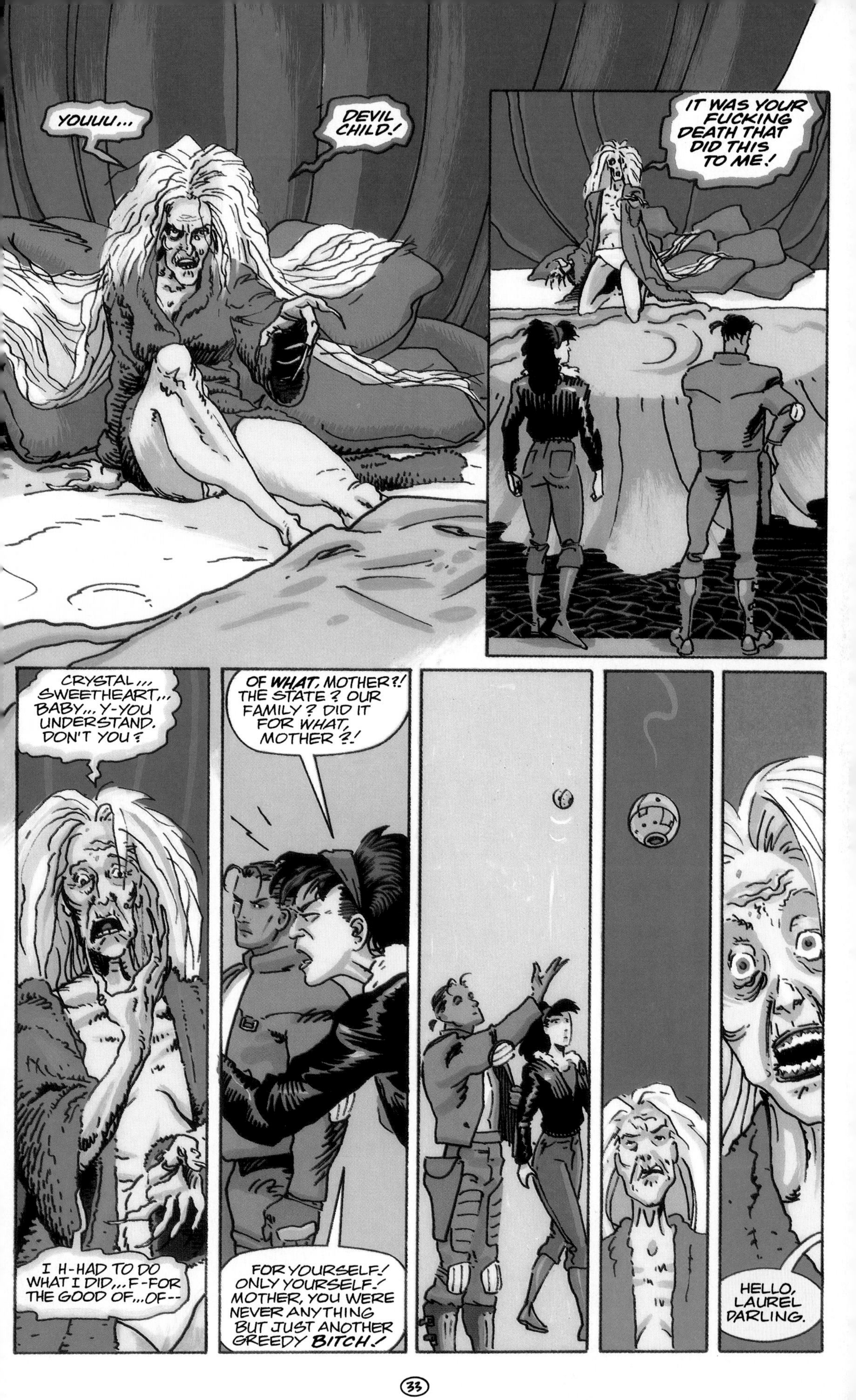
YOUUU...
DEVIL CHILD!
IT WAS YOUR FUCKING DEATH THAT DID THIS TO ME!
CRYSTAL... SWEETHEART... BABY... Y-YOU UNDERSTAND. DON'T YOU?
I H-HAD TO DO WHAT I DID... F-FOR THE GOOD OF...OF--
OF WHAT, MOTHER?! THE STATE? OUR FAMILY? DID IT FOR WHAT, MOTHER?!
FOR YOURSELF! ONLY YOURSELF! MOTHER, YOU WERE NEVER ANYTHING BUT JUST ANOTHER GREEDY BITCH!
HELLO, LAUREL DARLING.

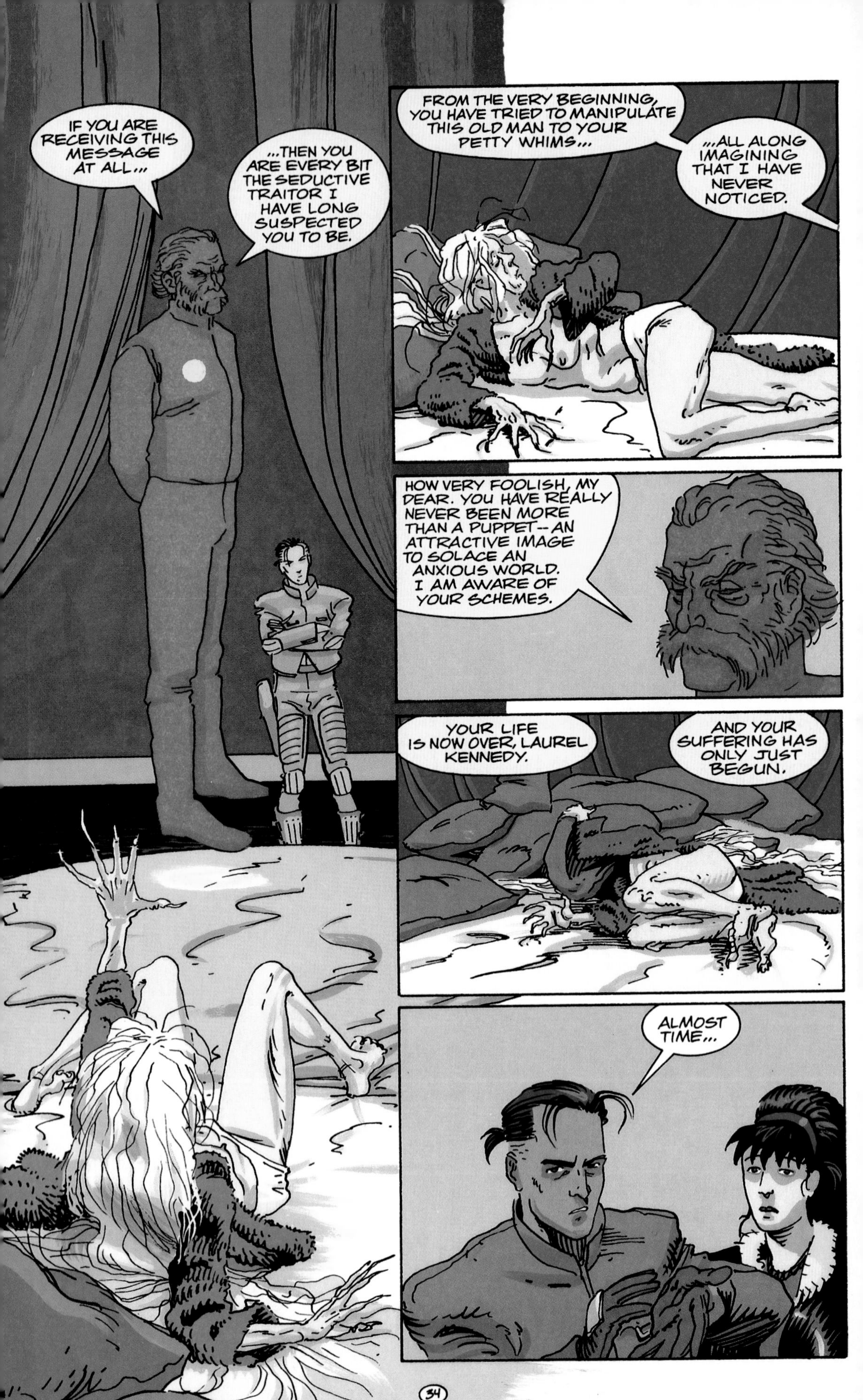
IF YOU ARE RECEIVING THIS MESSAGE AT ALL...
...THEN YOU ARE EVERY BIT THE SEDUCTIVE TRAITOR I HAVE LONG SUSPECTED YOU TO BE.
FROM THE VERY BEGINNING, YOU HAVE TRIED TO MANIPULATE THIS OLD MAN TO YOUR PETTY WHIMS...
...ALL ALONG IMAGINING THAT I HAVE NEVER NOTICED.
HOW VERY FOOLISH, MY DEAR. YOU HAVE REALLY NEVER BEEN MORE THAN A PUPPET-- AN ATTRACTIVE IMAGE TO SOLACE AN ANXIOUS WORLD. I AM AWARE OF YOUR SCHEMES.
YOUR LIFE IS NOW OVER, LAUREL KENNEDY.
AND YOUR SUFFERING HAS ONLY JUST BEGUN.
ALMOST TIME...

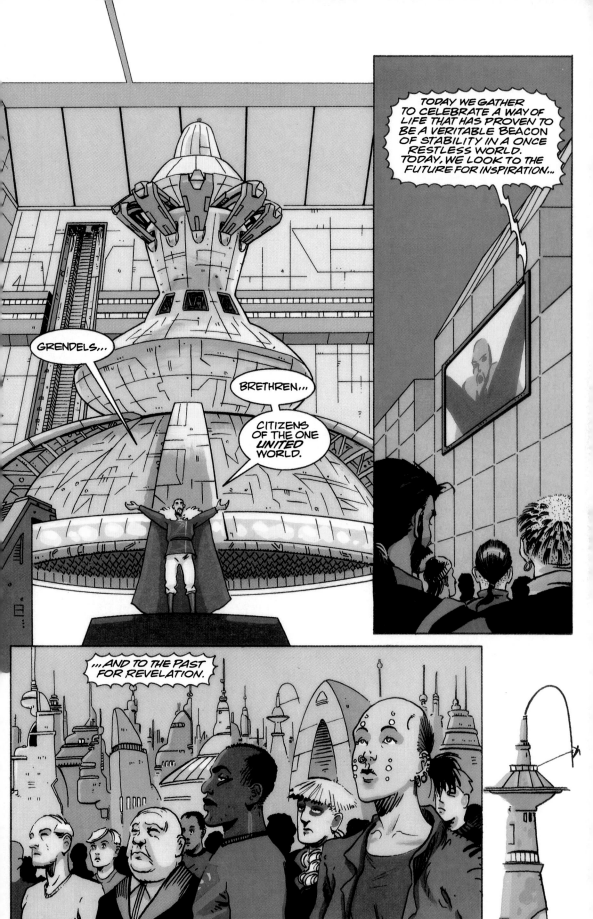

TODAY WE GATHER TO CELEBRATE A WAY OF LIFE THAT HAS PROVEN TO BE A VERITABLE BEACON OF STABILITY IN A ONCE RESTLESS WORLD. TODAY, WE LOOK TO THE FUTURE FOR INSPIRATION...

GRENDELS...

BRETHREN...

CITIZENS OF THE ONE UNITED WORLD.

...AND TO THE PAST FOR REVELATION.

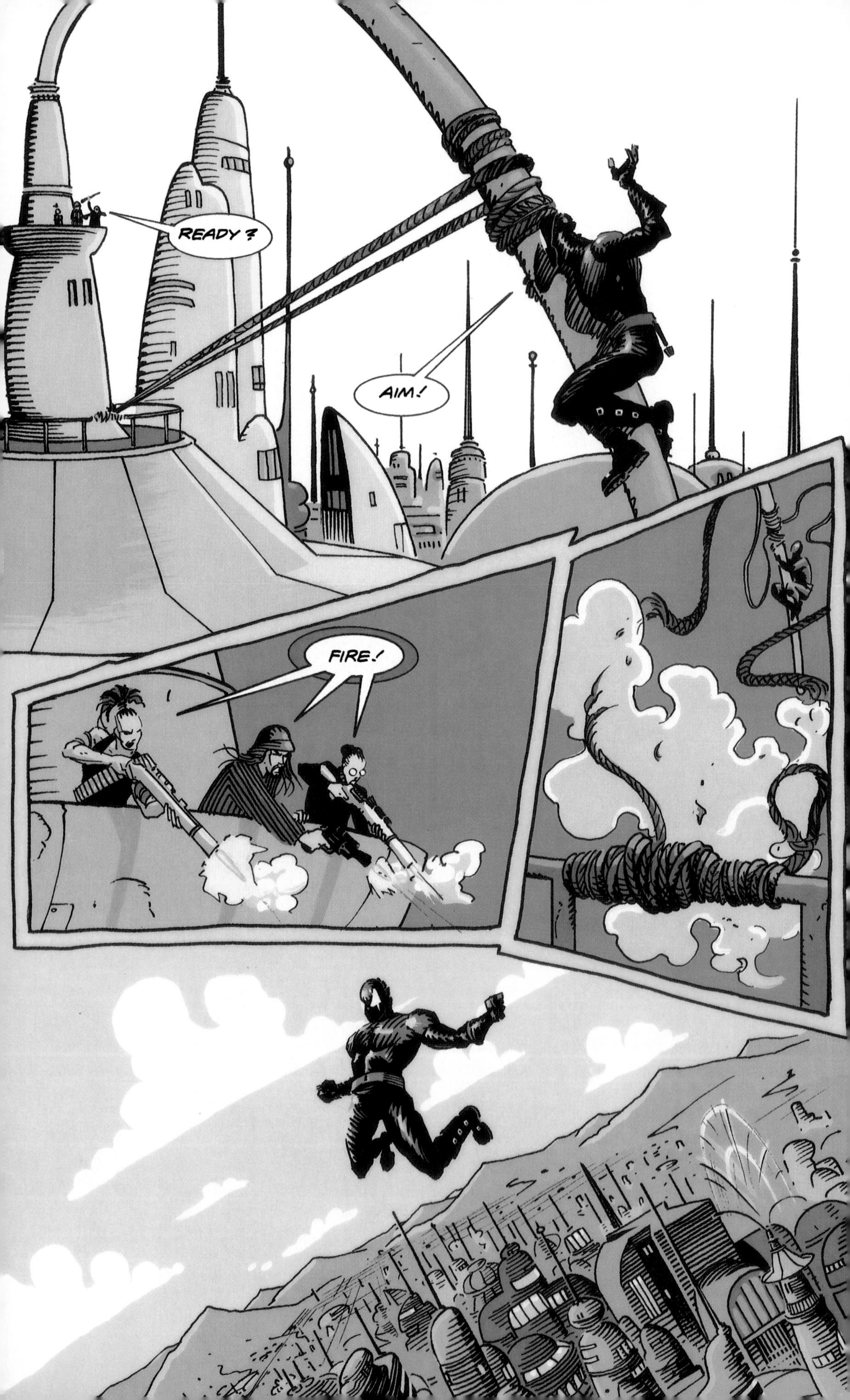
READY ?
AIM!
FIRE!

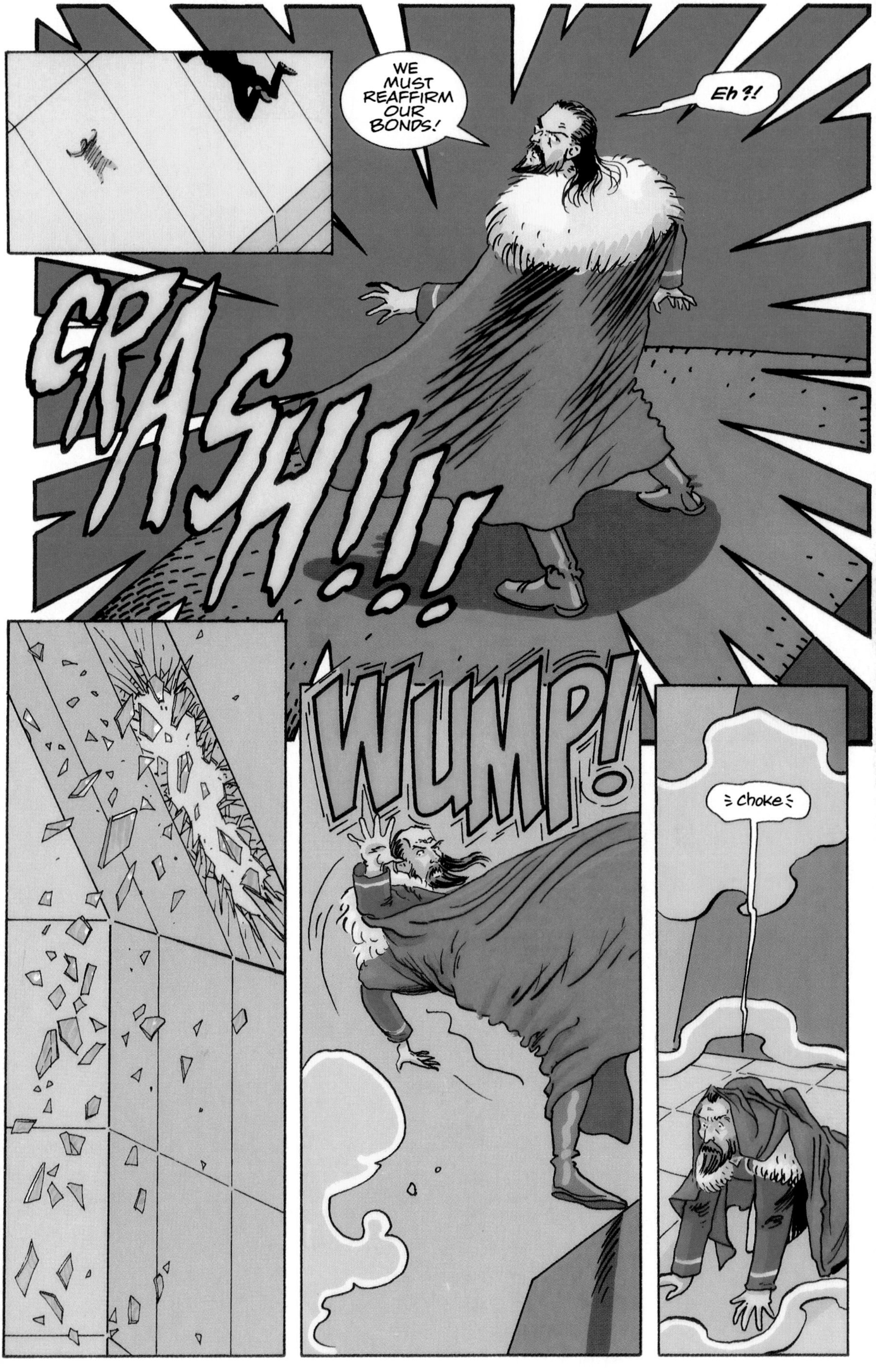
WE MUST REAFFIRM OUR BONDS!
Eh?!
CRASH!!!
WUMP!
Choke

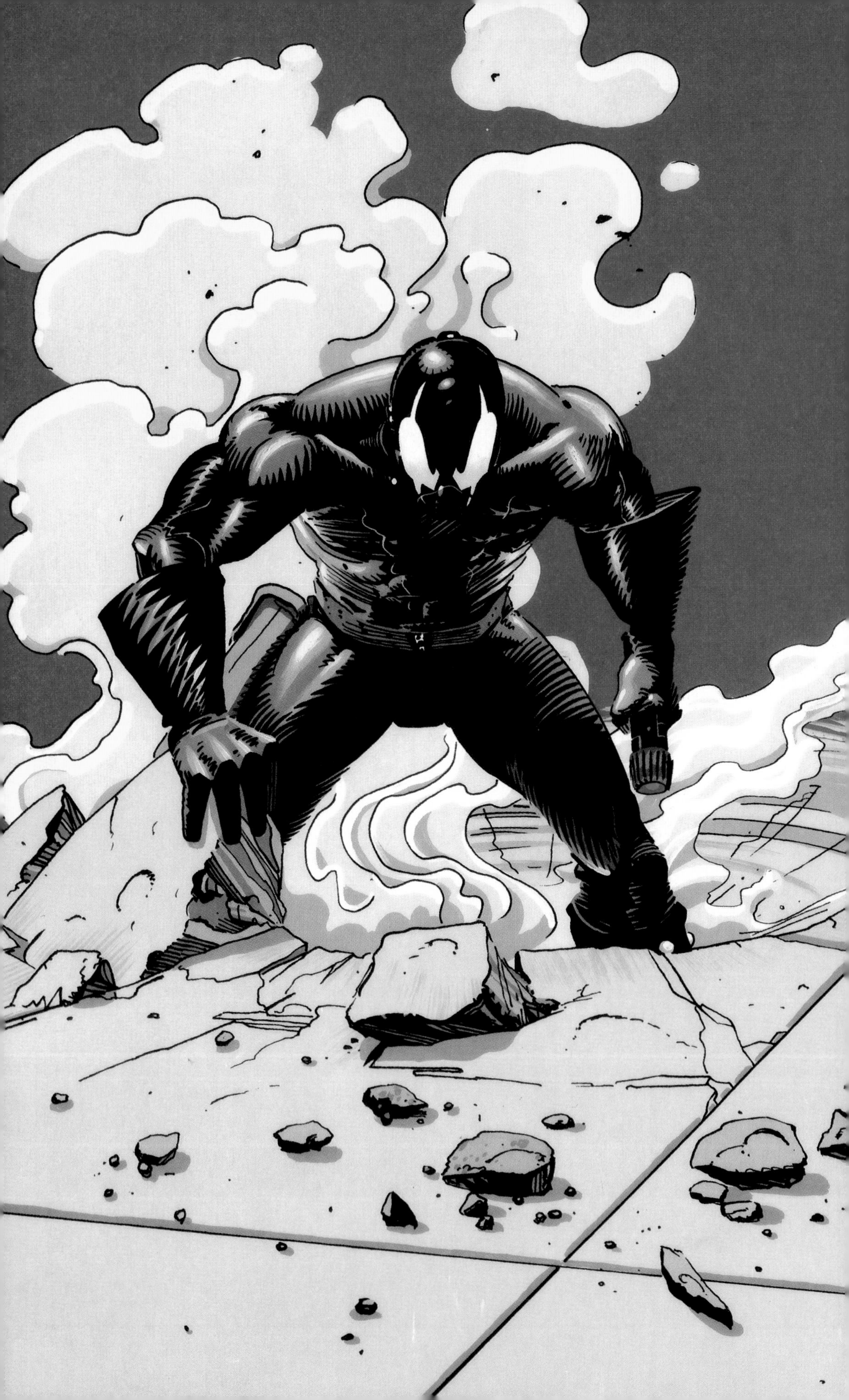

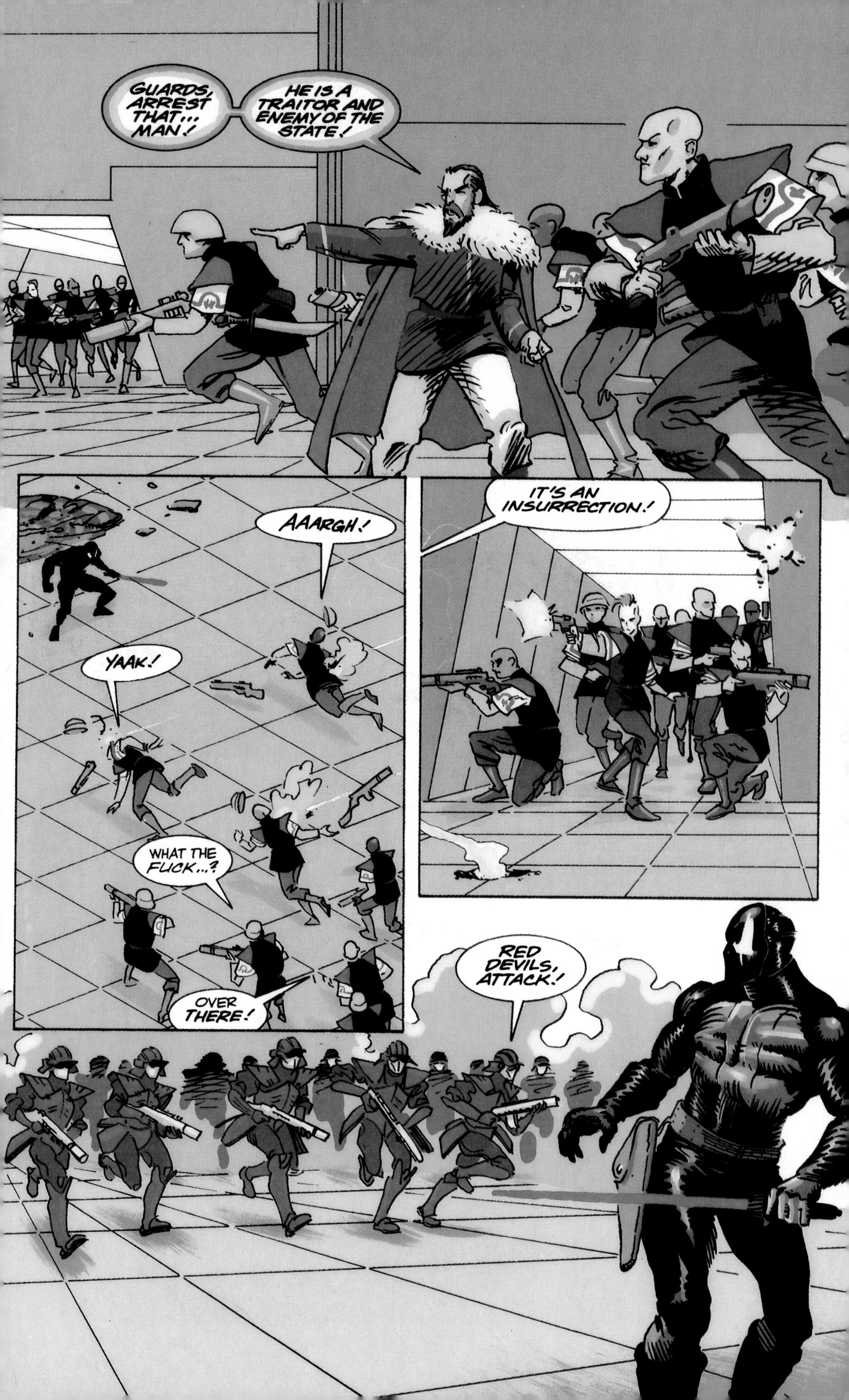
GUARDS, ARREST THAT... MAN!
HE IS A TRAITOR AND ENEMY OF THE STATE!
AAARGH!
YAAK!
WHAT THE FUCK...?
OVER THERE!
IT'S AN INSURRECTION!
RED DEVILS, ATTACK!

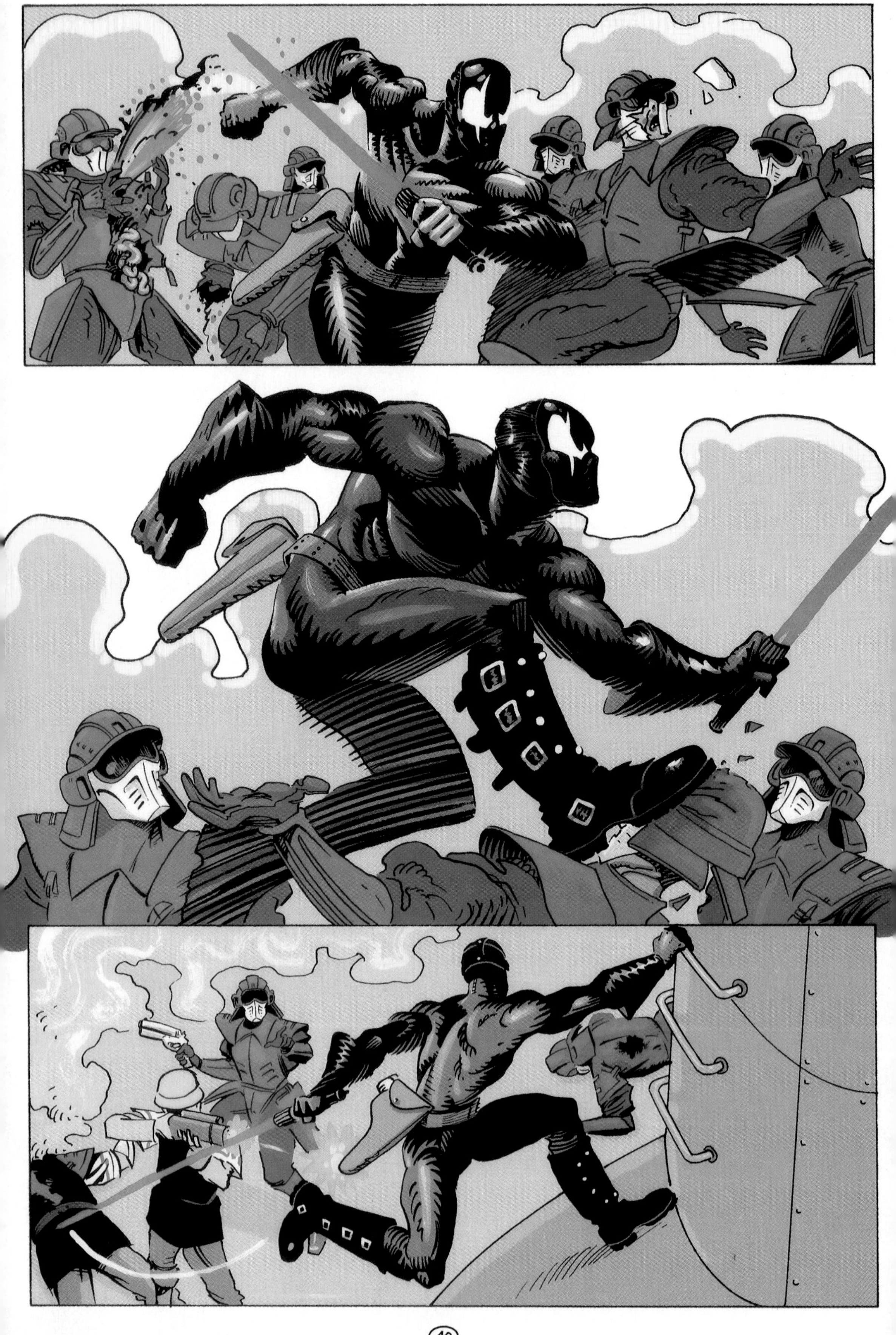

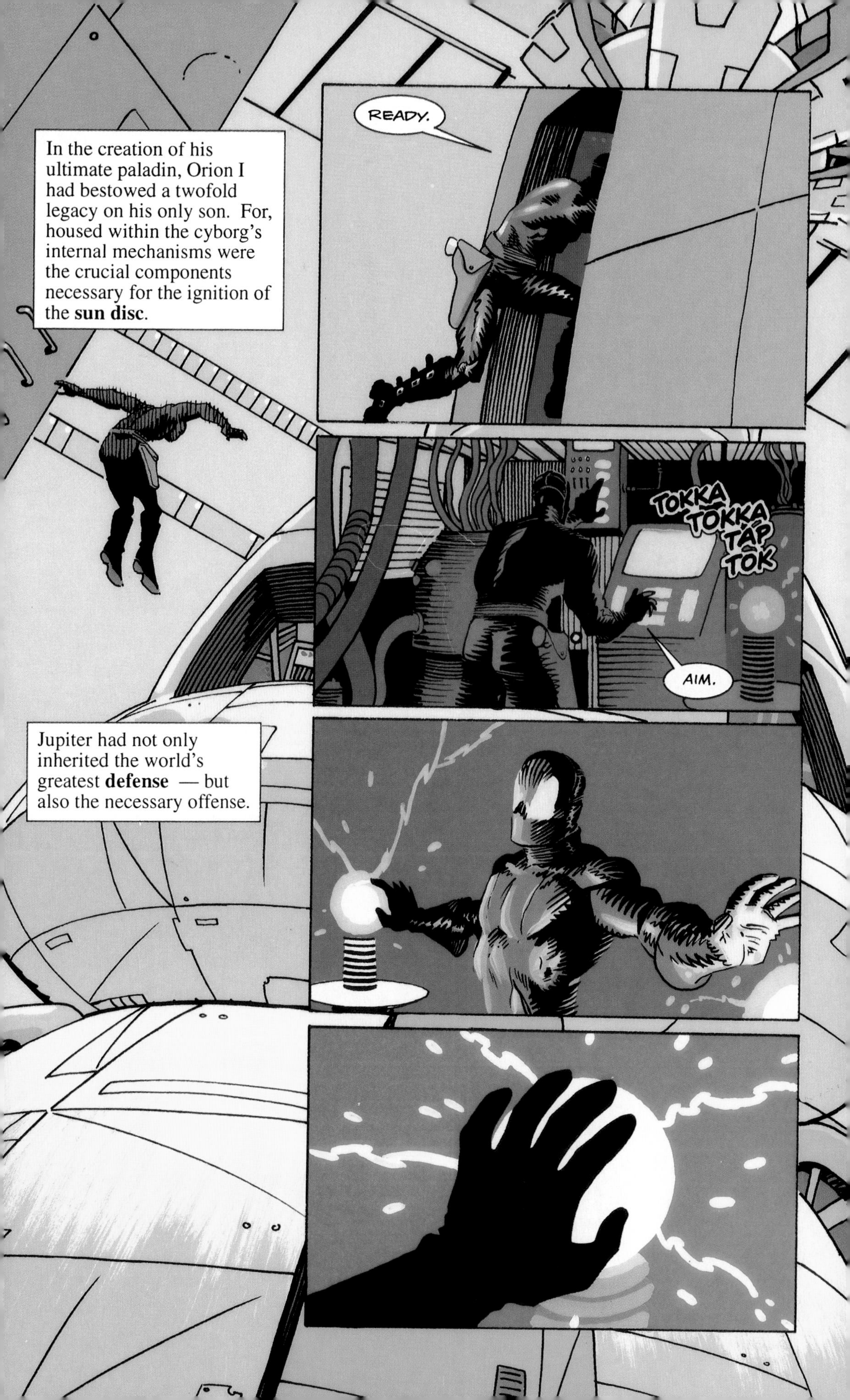
In the creation of his ultimate paladin, Orion I had bestowed a twofold legacy on his only son. For, housed within the cyborg's internal mechanisms were the crucial components necessary for the ignition of the **sun disc**.
READY.
TOKKA TOKKA TAP TOK
AIM.
Jupiter had not only inherited the world's greatest **defense** — but also the necessary offense.

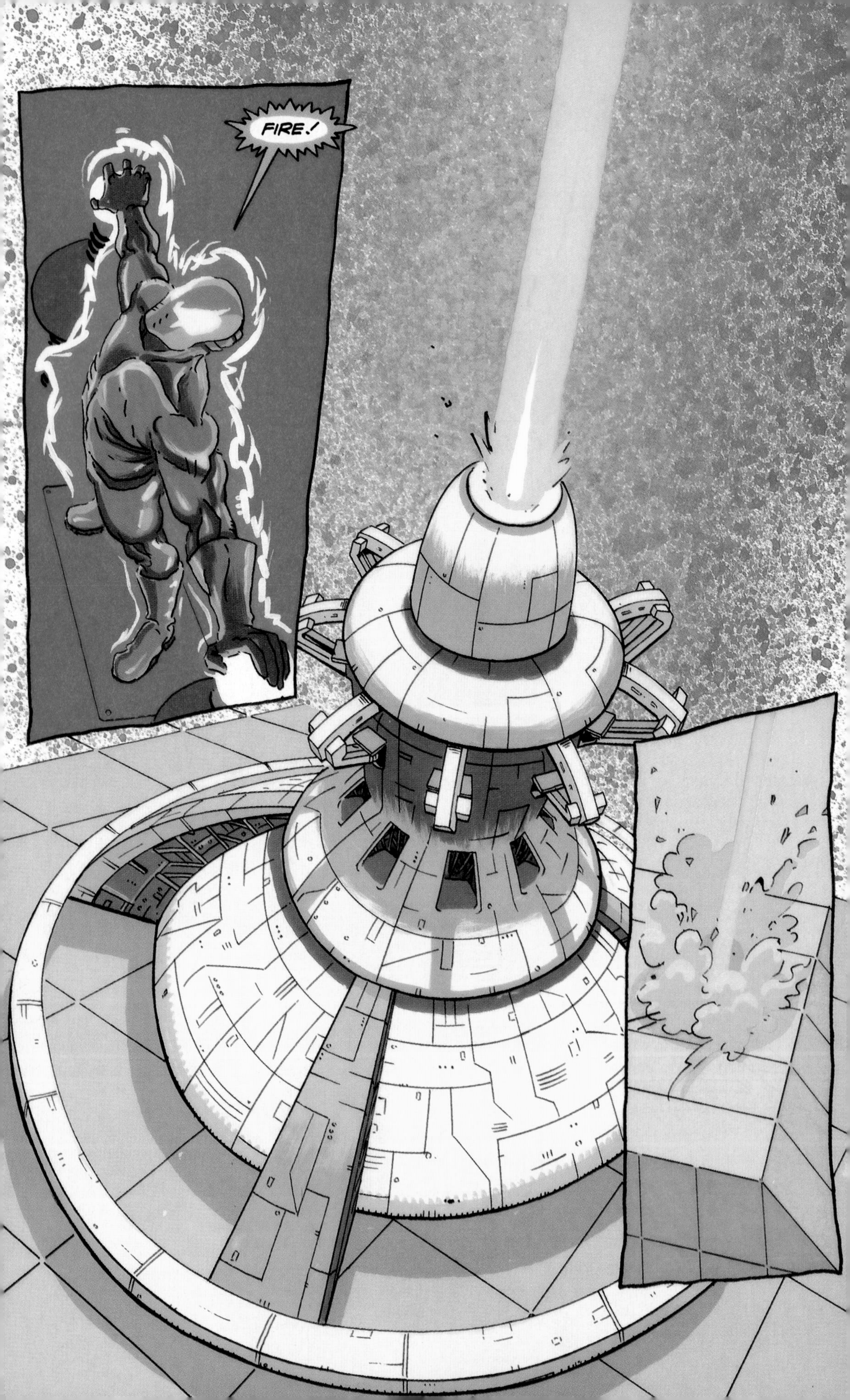
FIRE!

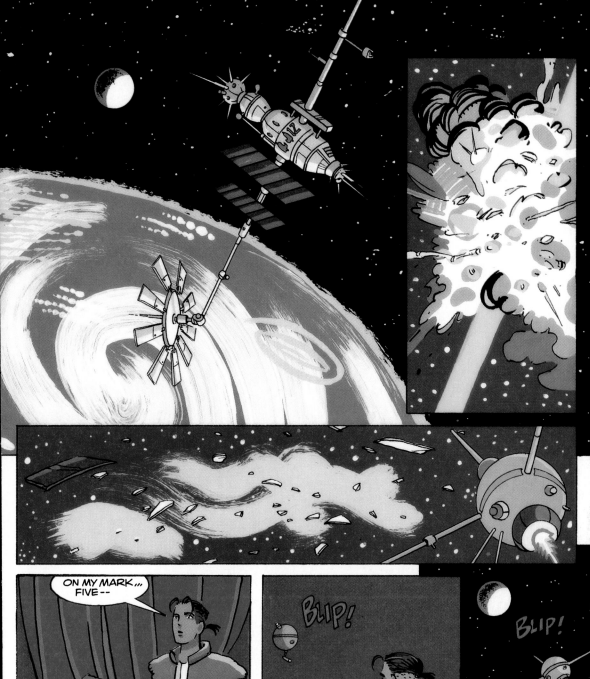

ON MY MARK... FIVE--

--FOUR--

--THREE--

--TWO--

--ONE:

BLIP!

BLIP!

"TRANSMIT."

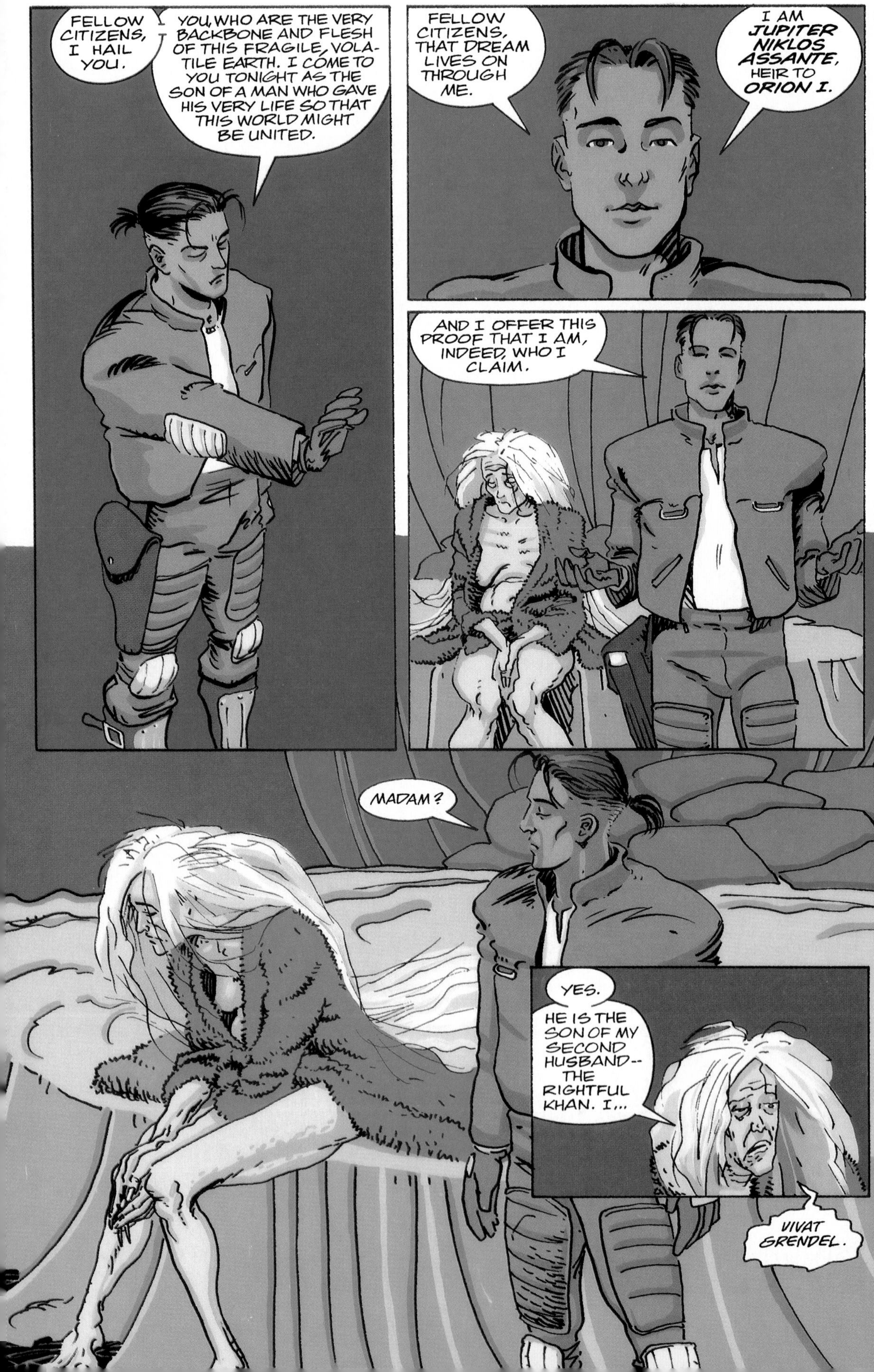
FELLOW CITIZENS, I HAIL YOU.
YOU, WHO ARE THE VERY BACKBONE AND FLESH OF THIS FRAGILE, VOLATILE EARTH. I COME TO YOU TONIGHT AS THE SON OF A MAN WHO GAVE HIS VERY LIFE SO THAT THIS WORLD MIGHT BE UNITED.
FELLOW CITIZENS, THAT DREAM LIVES ON THROUGH ME.
I AM JUPITER NIKLOS ASSANTE, HEIR TO ORION I.
AND I OFFER THIS PROOF THAT I AM, INDEED, WHO I CLAIM.
MADAM?
YES.
HE IS THE SON OF MY SECOND HUSBAND-- THE RIGHTFUL KHAN. I,..
VIVAT GRENDEL.

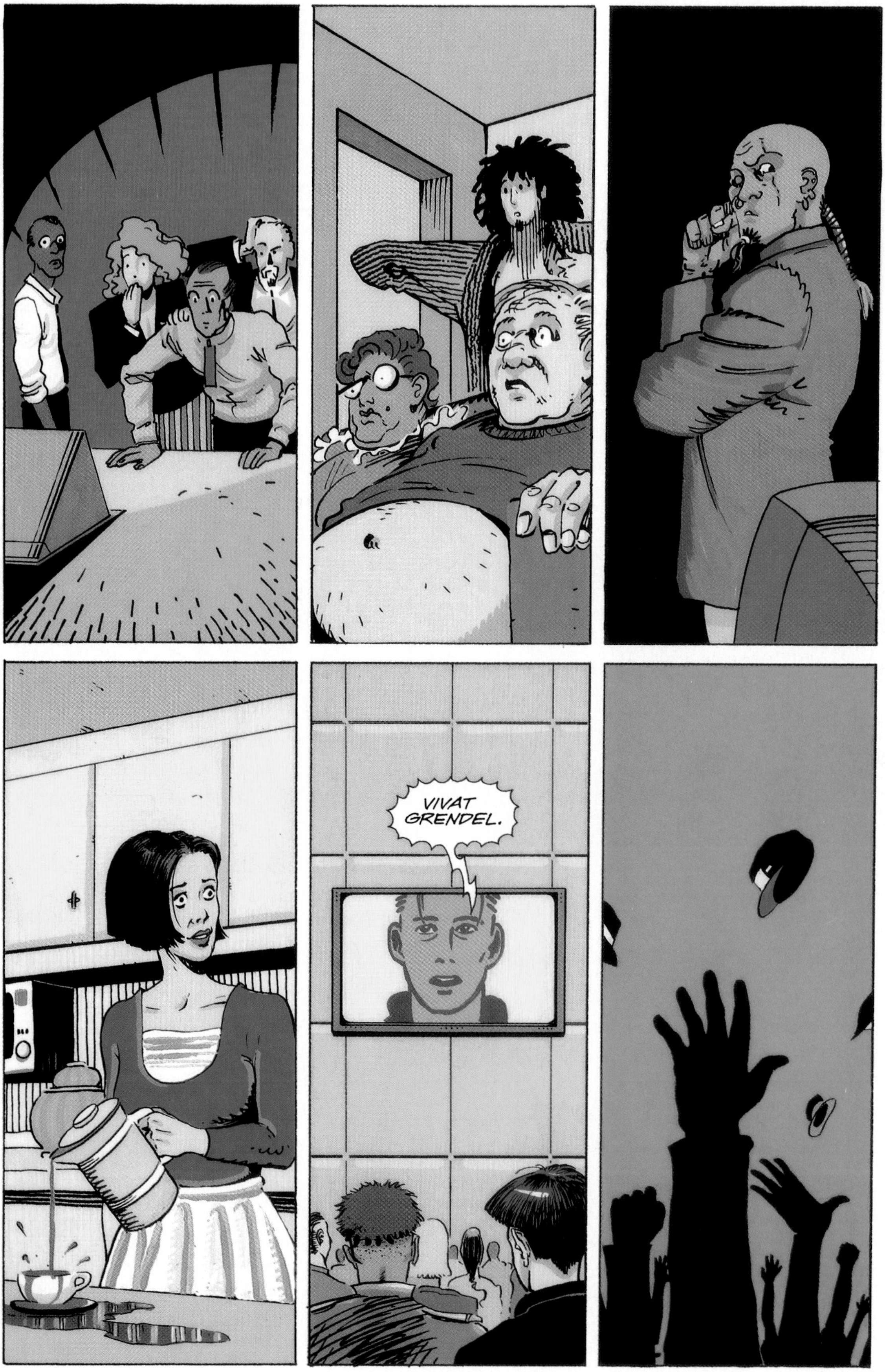
VIVAT GRENDEL.

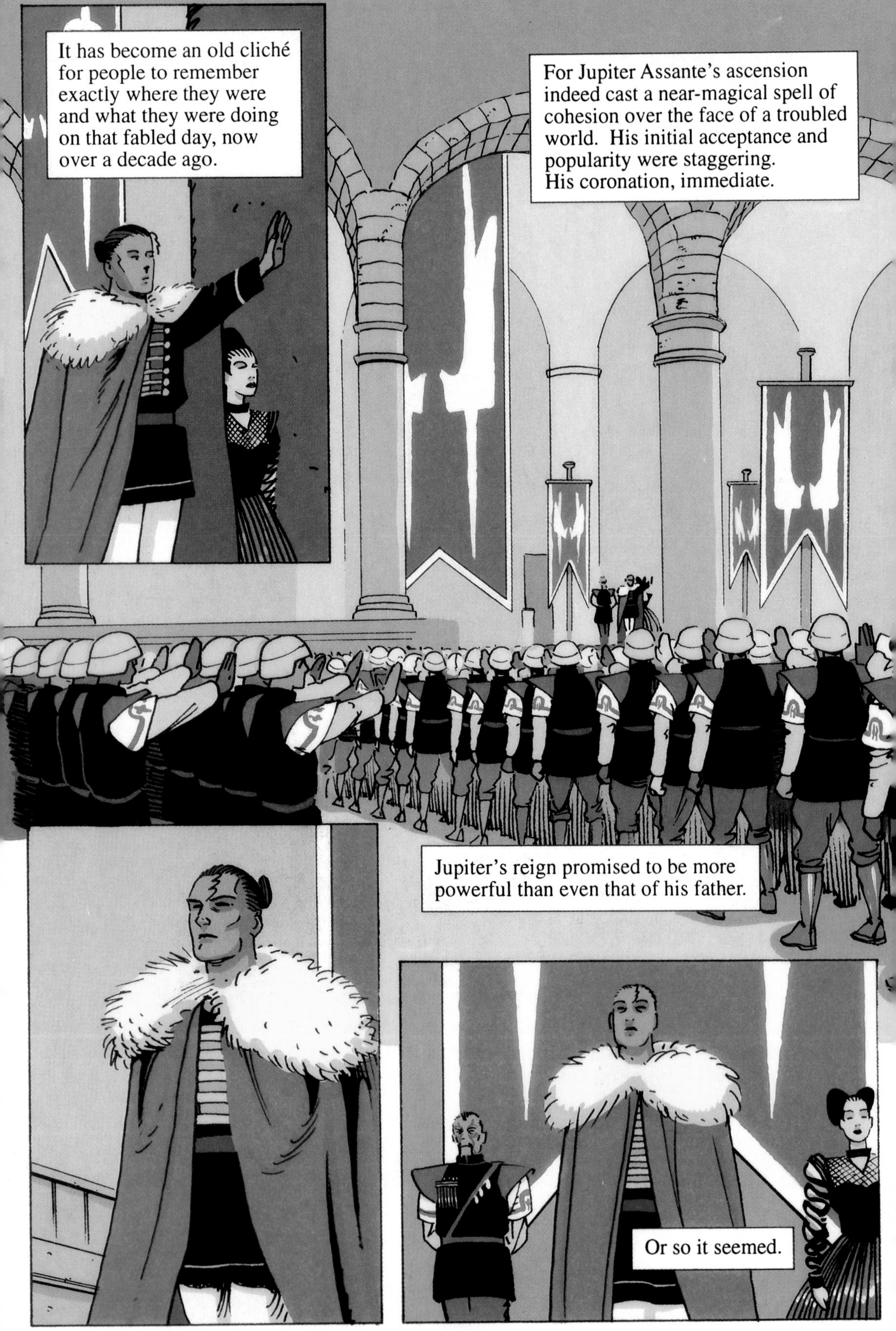
It has become an old cliché for people to remember exactly where they were and what they were doing on that fabled day, now over a decade ago.
For Jupiter Assante's ascension indeed cast a near-magical spell of cohesion over the face of a troubled world. His initial acceptance and popularity were staggering. His coronation, immediate.
Jupiter's reign promised to be more powerful than even that of his father.
Or so it seemed.

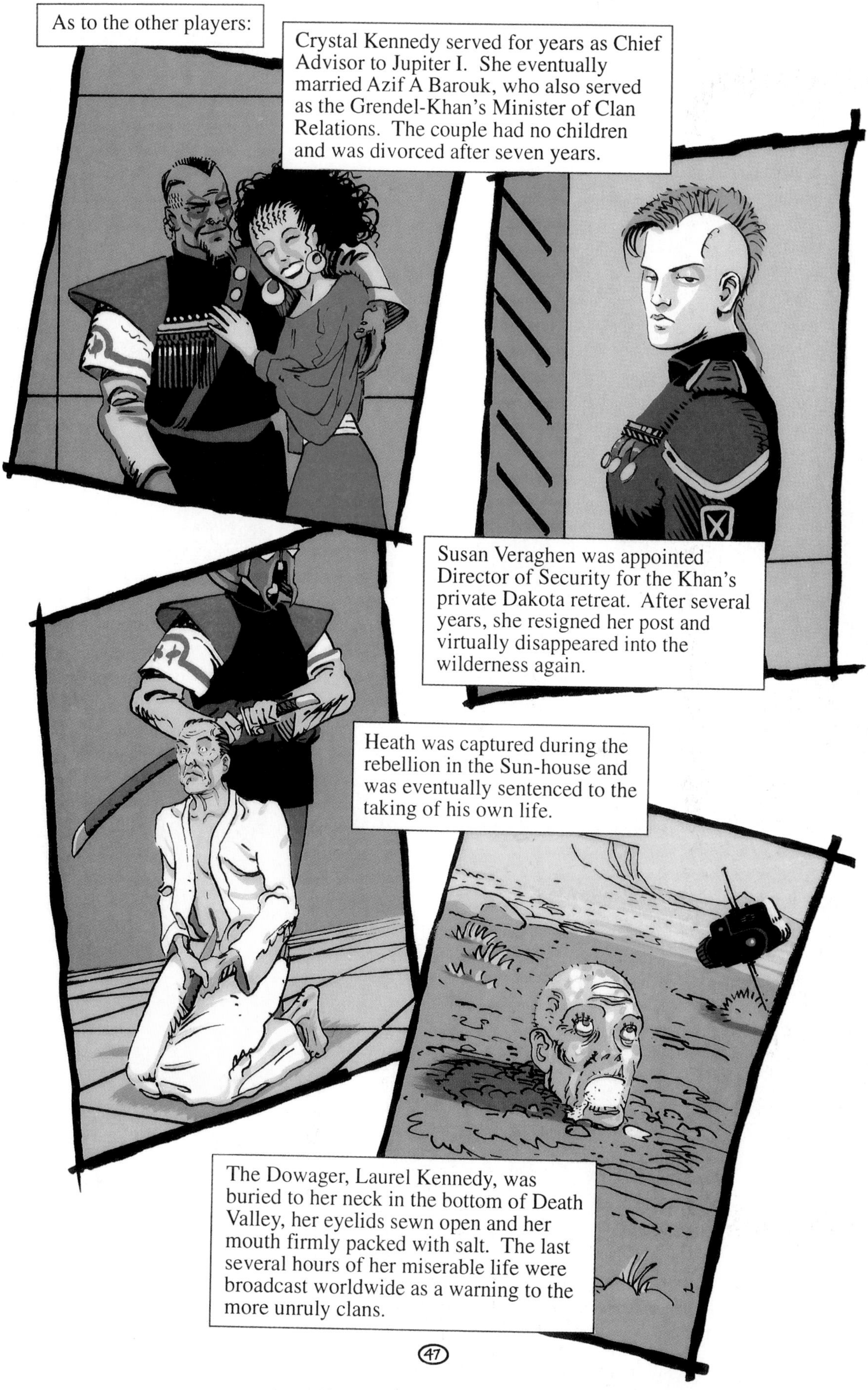
As to the other players:
Crystal Kennedy served for years as Chief Advisor to Jupiter I. She eventually married Azif A Barouk, who also served as the Grendel-Khan's Minister of Clan Relations. The couple had no children and was divorced after seven years.
Susan Veraghen was appointed Director of Security for the Khan's private Dakota retreat. After several years, she resigned her post and virtually disappeared into the wilderness again.
Heath was captured during the rebellion in the Sun-house and was eventually sentenced to the taking of his own life.
The Dowager, Laurel Kennedy, was buried to her neck in the bottom of Death Valley, her eyelids sewn open and her mouth firmly packed with salt. The last several hours of her miserable life were broadcast worldwide as a warning to the more unruly clans.

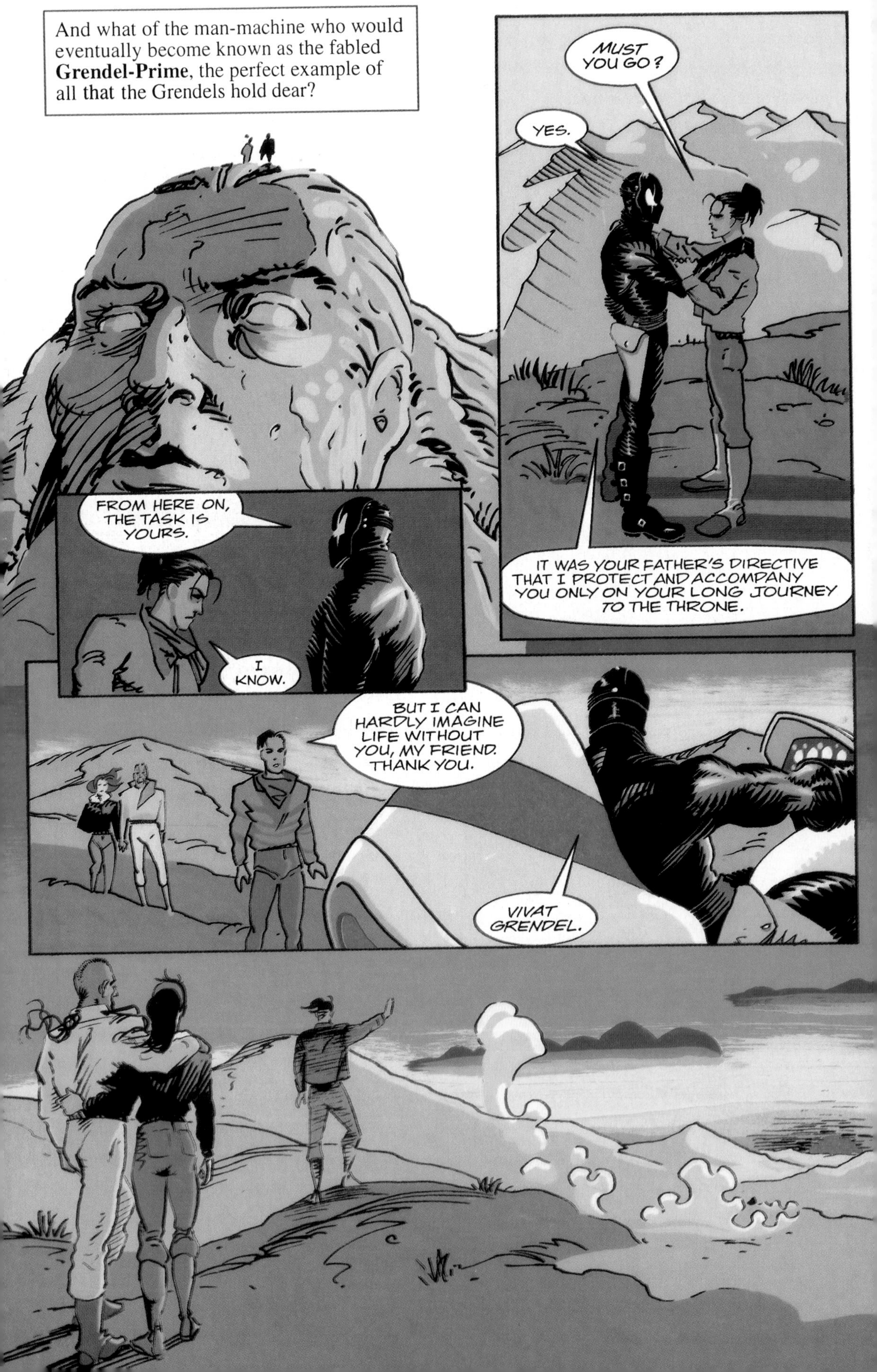
And what of the man-machine who would eventually become known as the fabled **Grendel-Prime**, the perfect example of all that the Grendels hold dear?
FROM HERE ON, THE TASK IS YOURS.
I KNOW.
MUST YOU GO?
YES.
IT WAS YOUR FATHER'S DIRECTIVE THAT I PROTECT AND ACCOMPANY YOU ONLY ON YOUR LONG JOURNEY TO THE THRONE.
BUT I CAN HARDLY IMAGINE LIFE WITHOUT YOU, MY FRIEND. THANK YOU.
VIVAT GRENDEL.

Although legends abound of encounters with Grendel-Prime, there has been no documented contact with him since that fateful day so long ago.Scientists can only speculate as to the possible life span of such a creature; conceivably, his existence could go on for centuries. In any event, his effect on the ultimate continuation of the Grendel identity cannot be overemphasized. In the face of an entire world of adversity, here is a being who not only miraculously endured but also saw to fruition the hopes and aspirations of the very race.

Who knows what effect he will next inspire when again he chooses to dabble in the fiery vortex of human affairs?

*excerpt from*
*The Life and Lineage of Jupiter Assante: Book I*
by Crystal Kennedy Martel

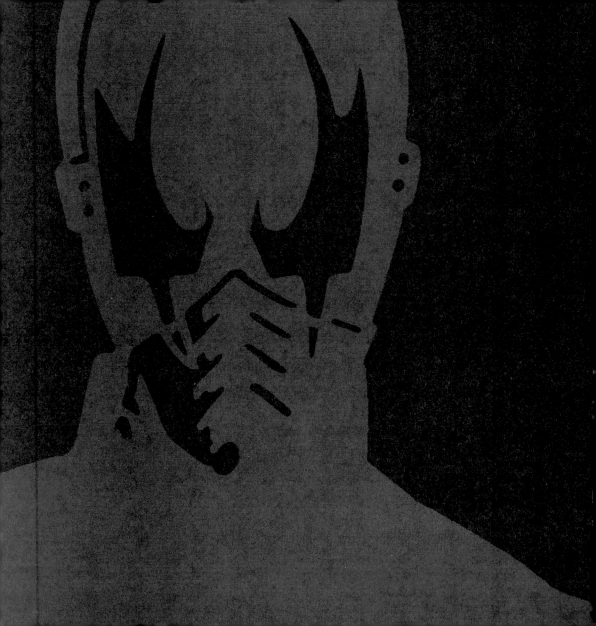

# GRENDEL

### warchild

## PORTRAITS OF GRENDEL-PRIME FROM:

*arthur* ADAMS

*tim* BRADSTREET

*cully* HAMNER

*kelley* JONES

*cam* KENNEDY

*doug* MAHNKE

*kevin* O'NEILL

*john* SNYDER III

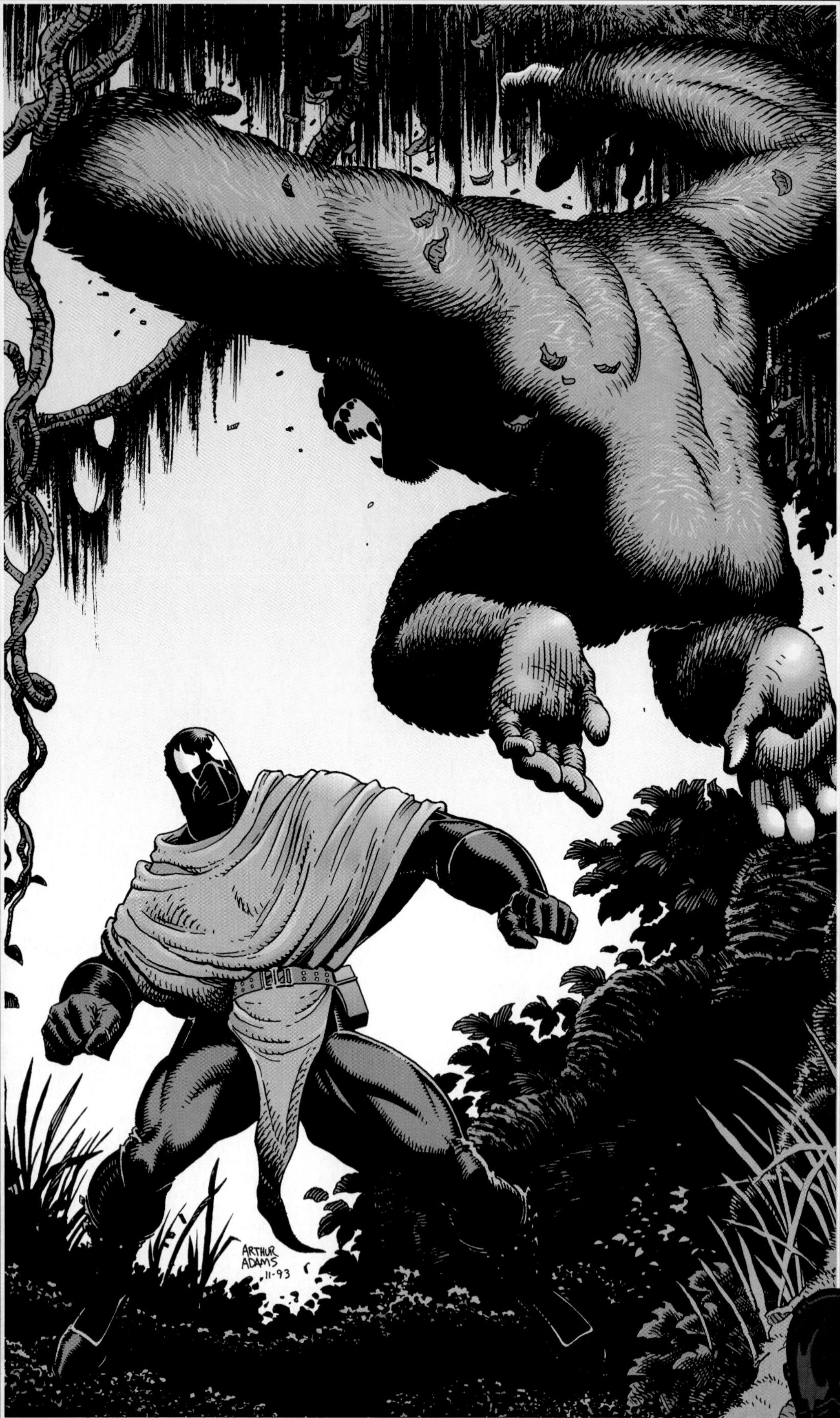
ARTHUR
ADAMS
11-93

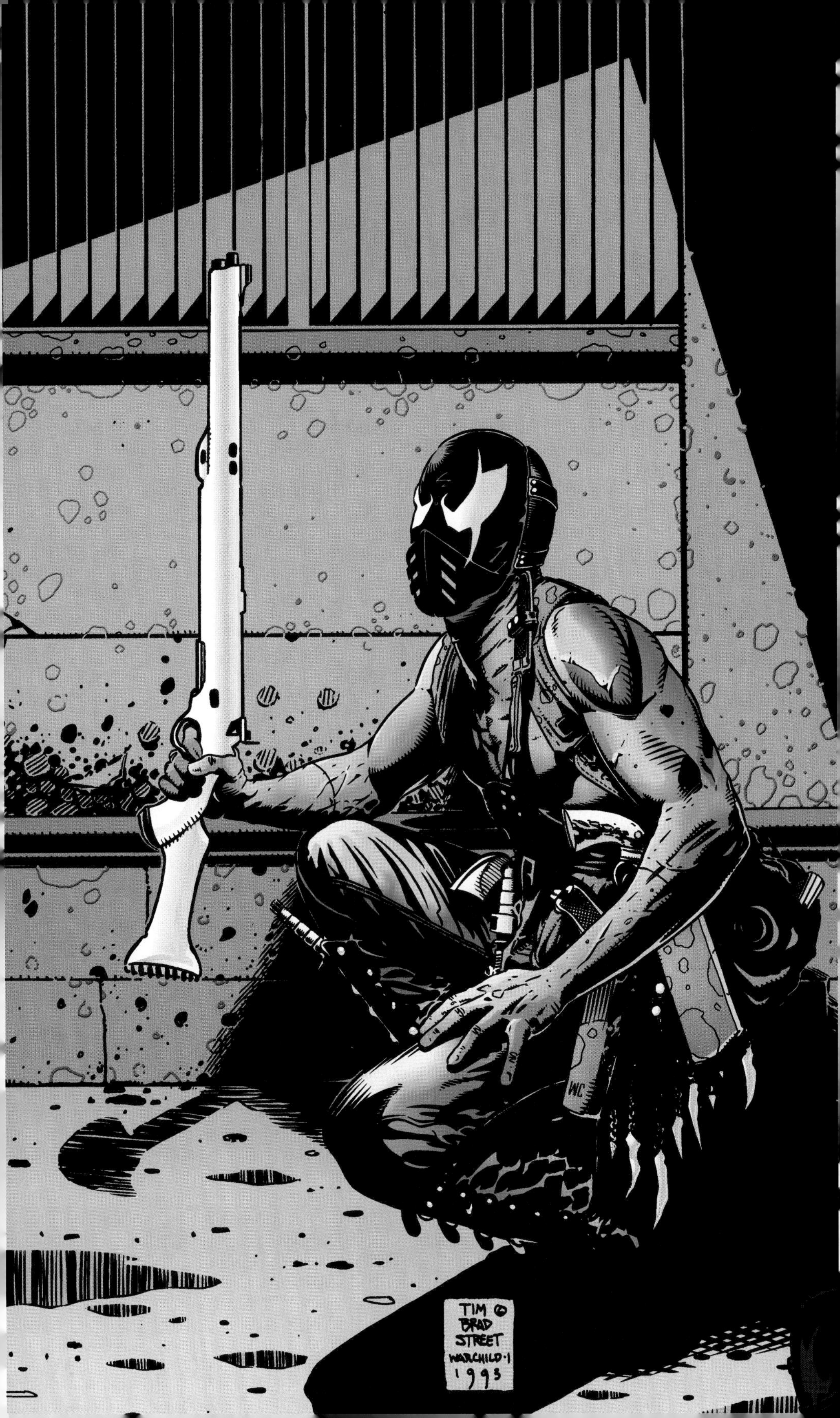
WC
TIM ©
BRAD
STREET
WARCHILD·1
1993

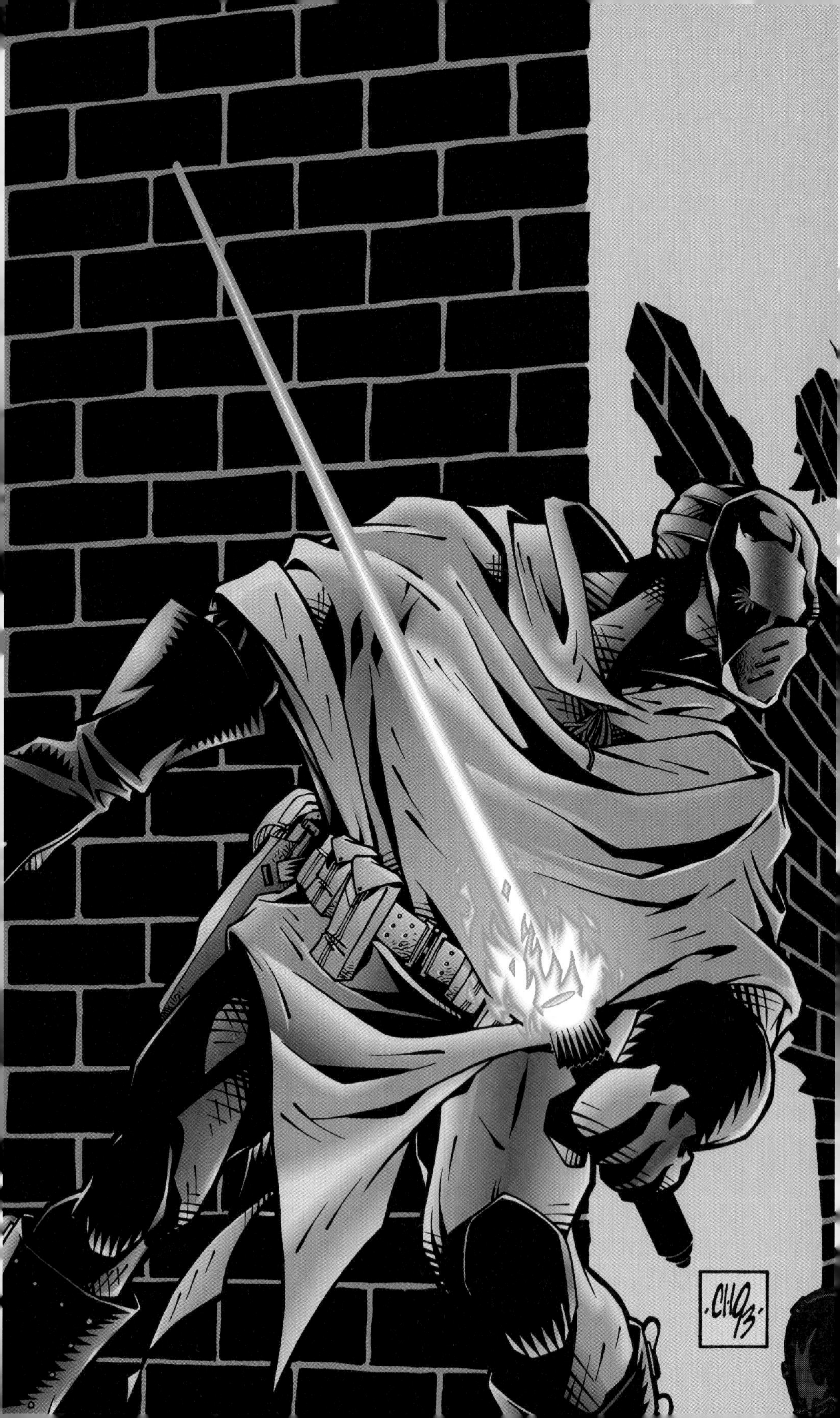

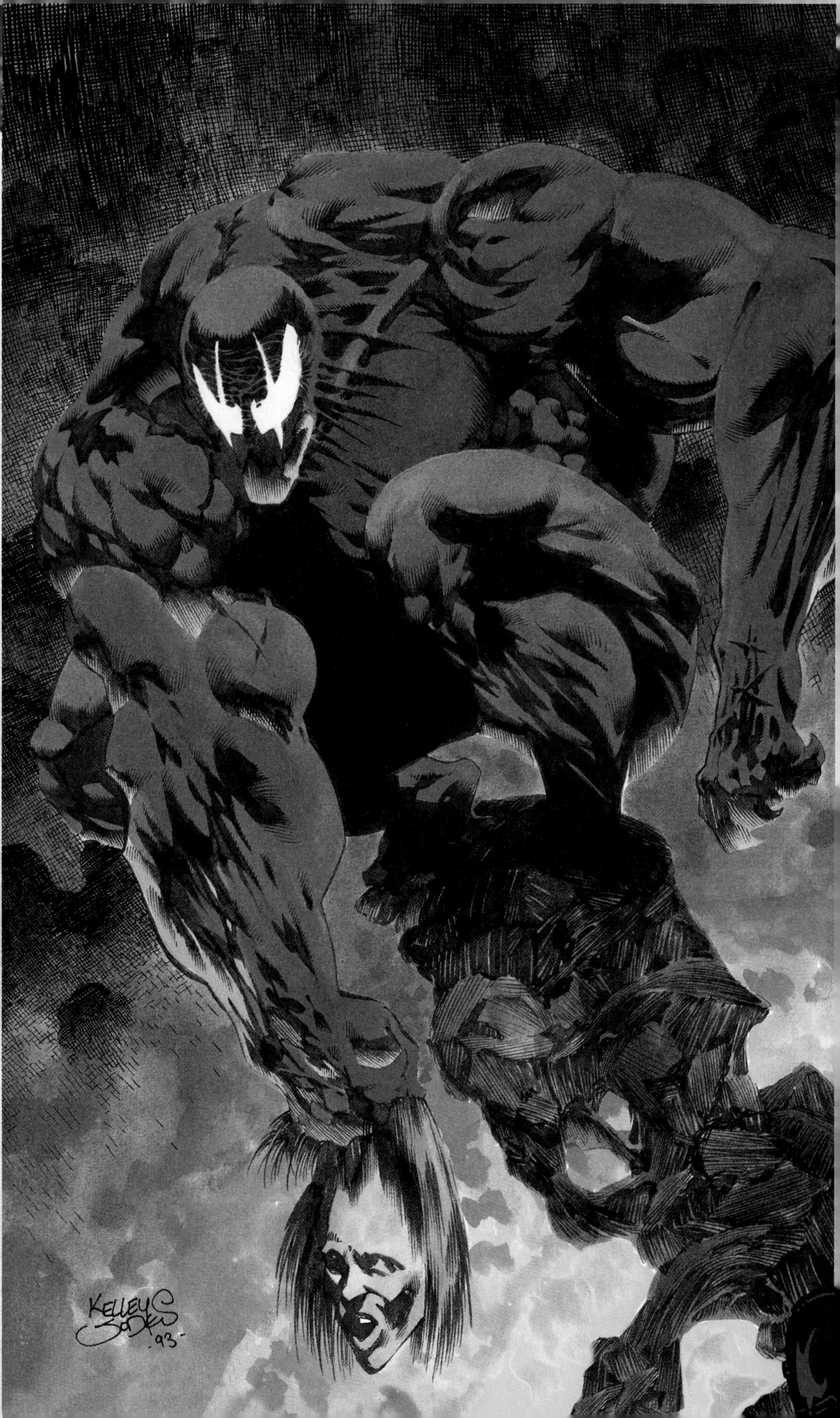

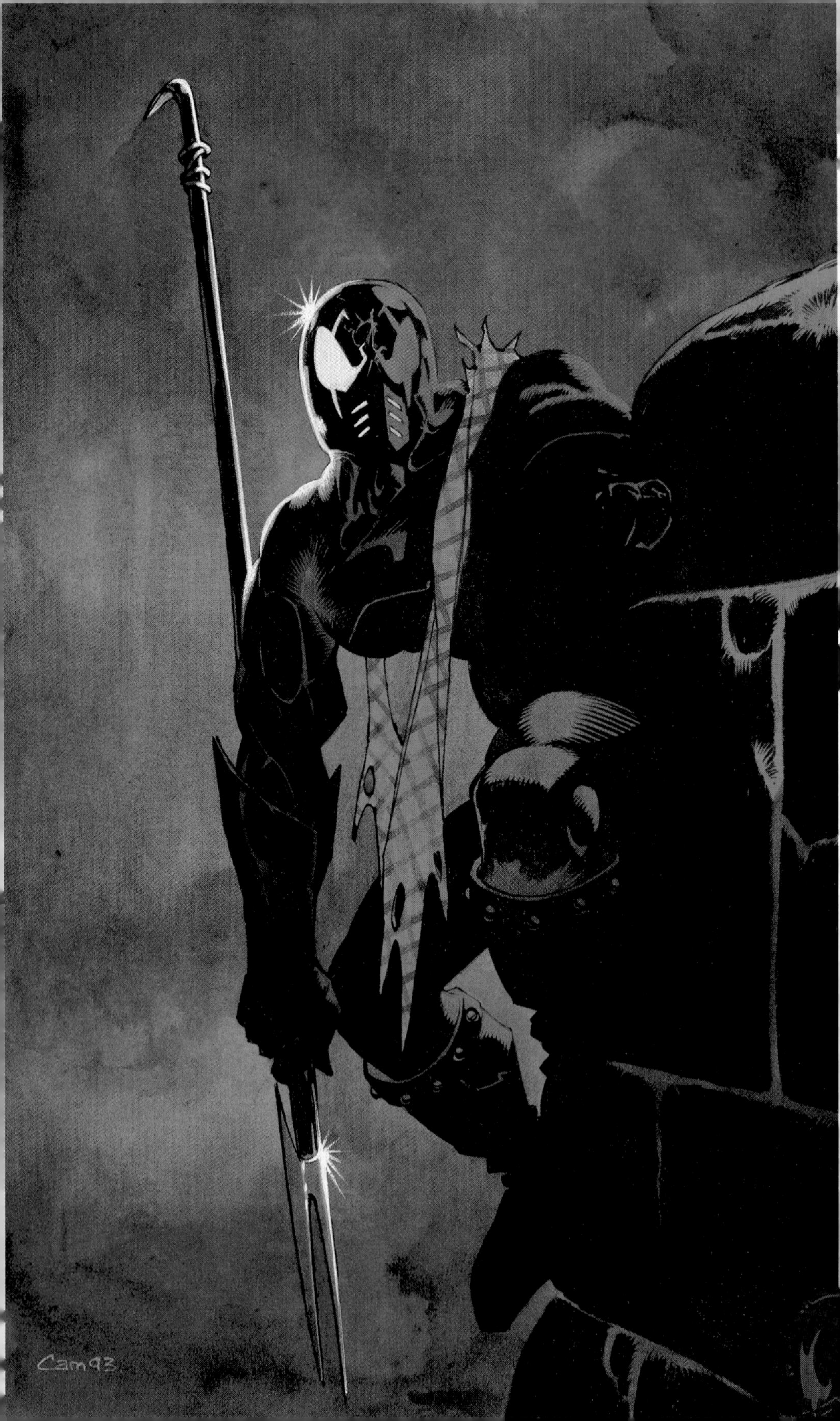
Cam93.

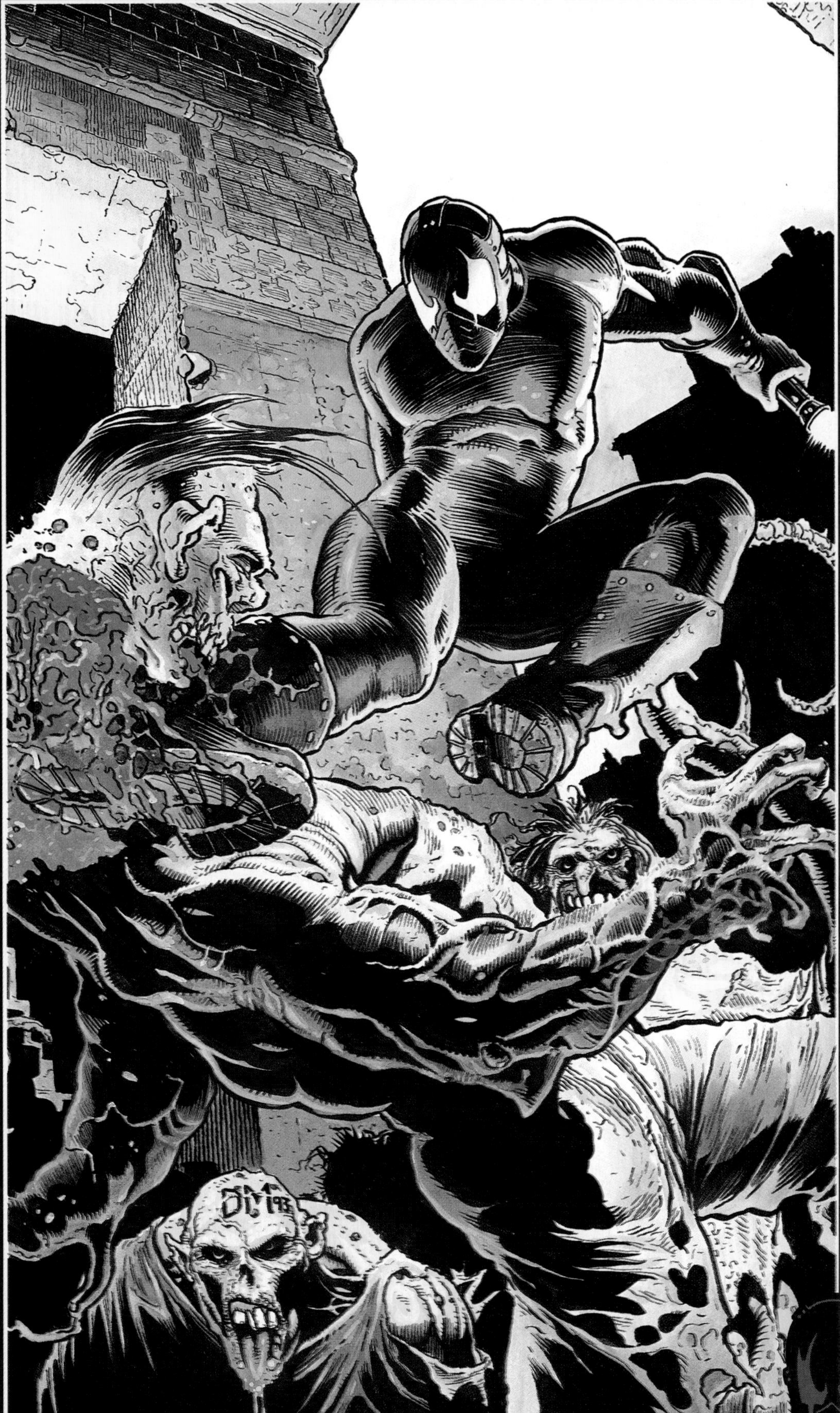

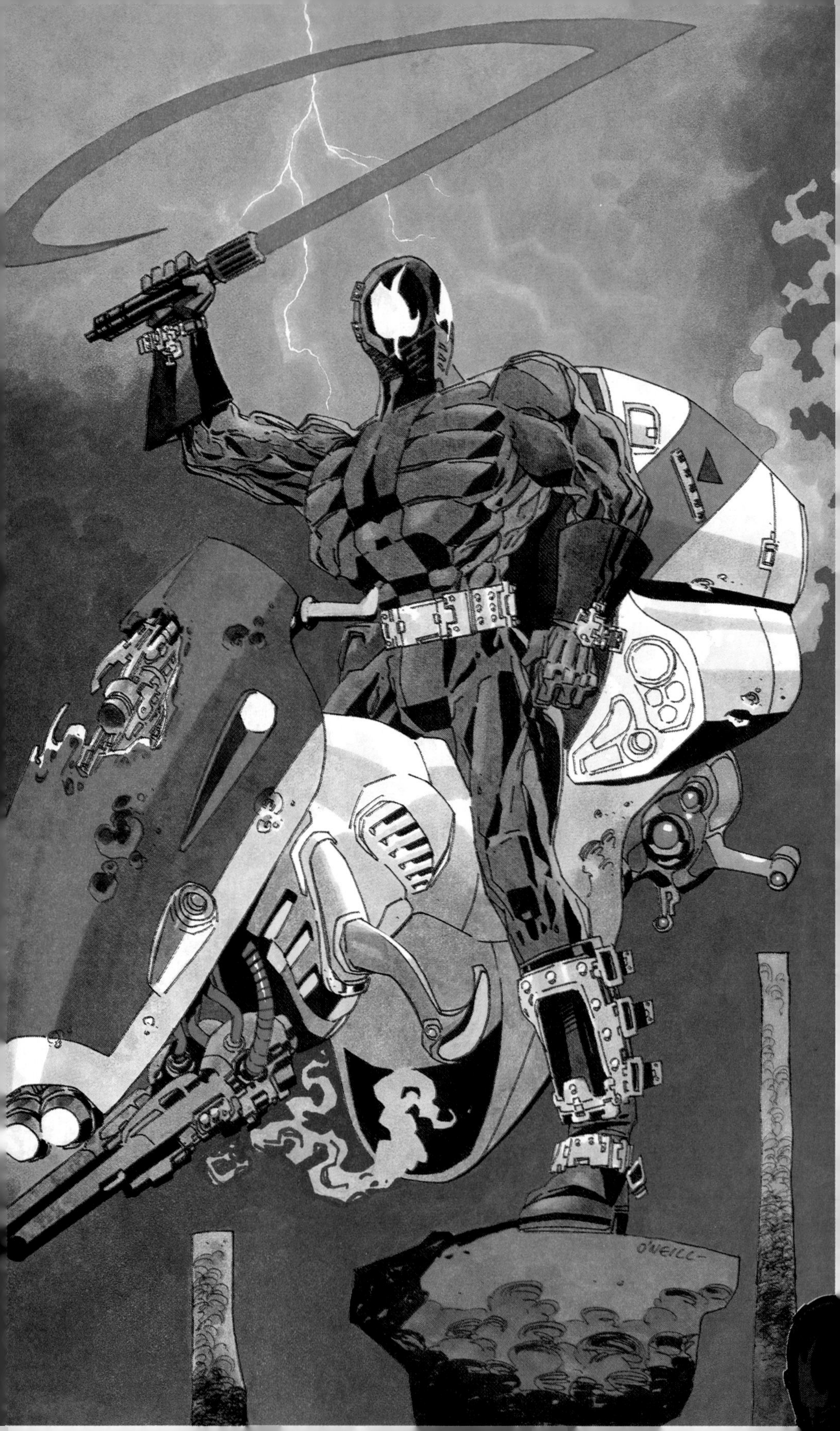
O'NEILL

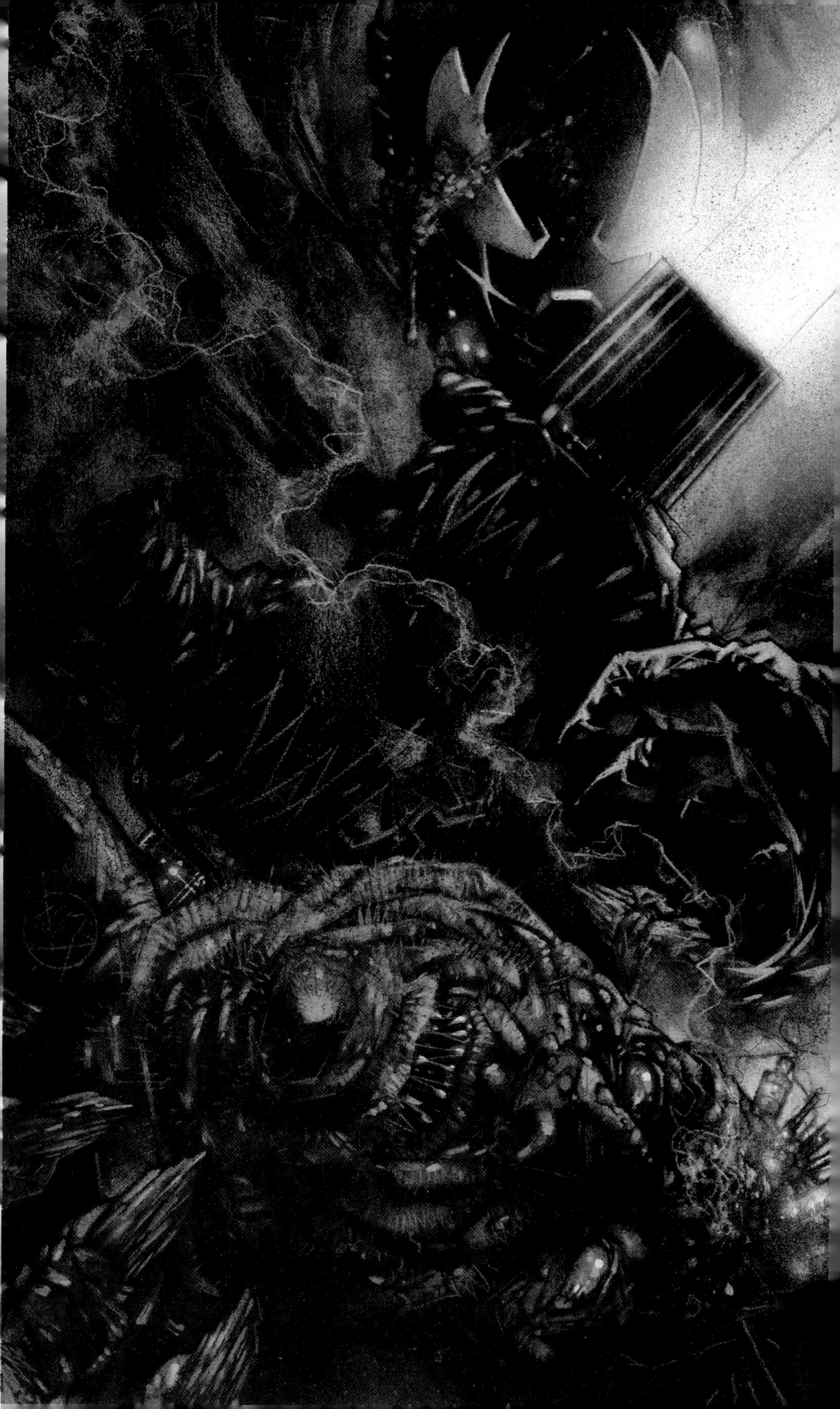

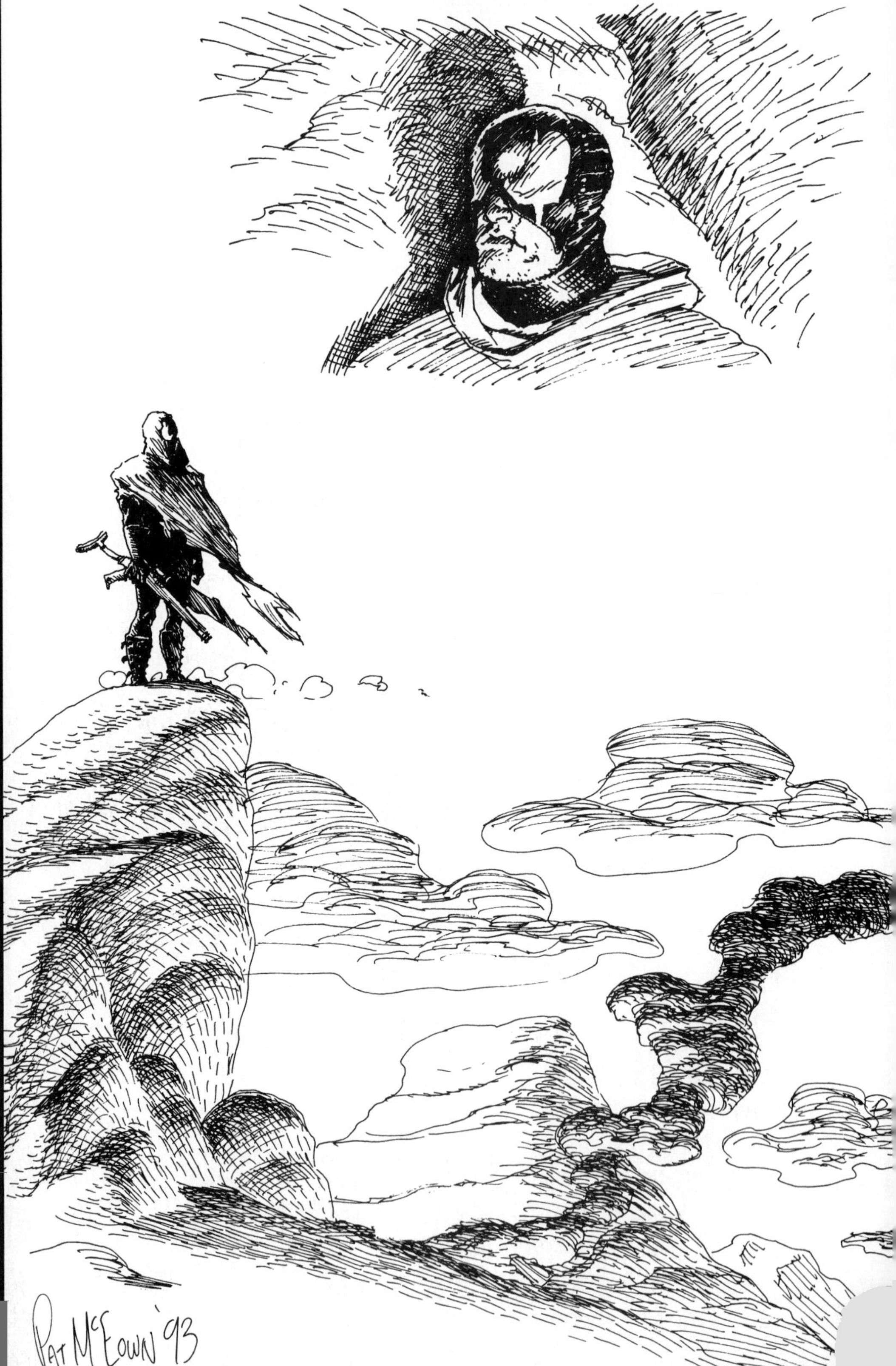
Pat McEown '93

## SKETCHES OF GRENDEL-PRIME FROM:

# *patrick* McEOWN

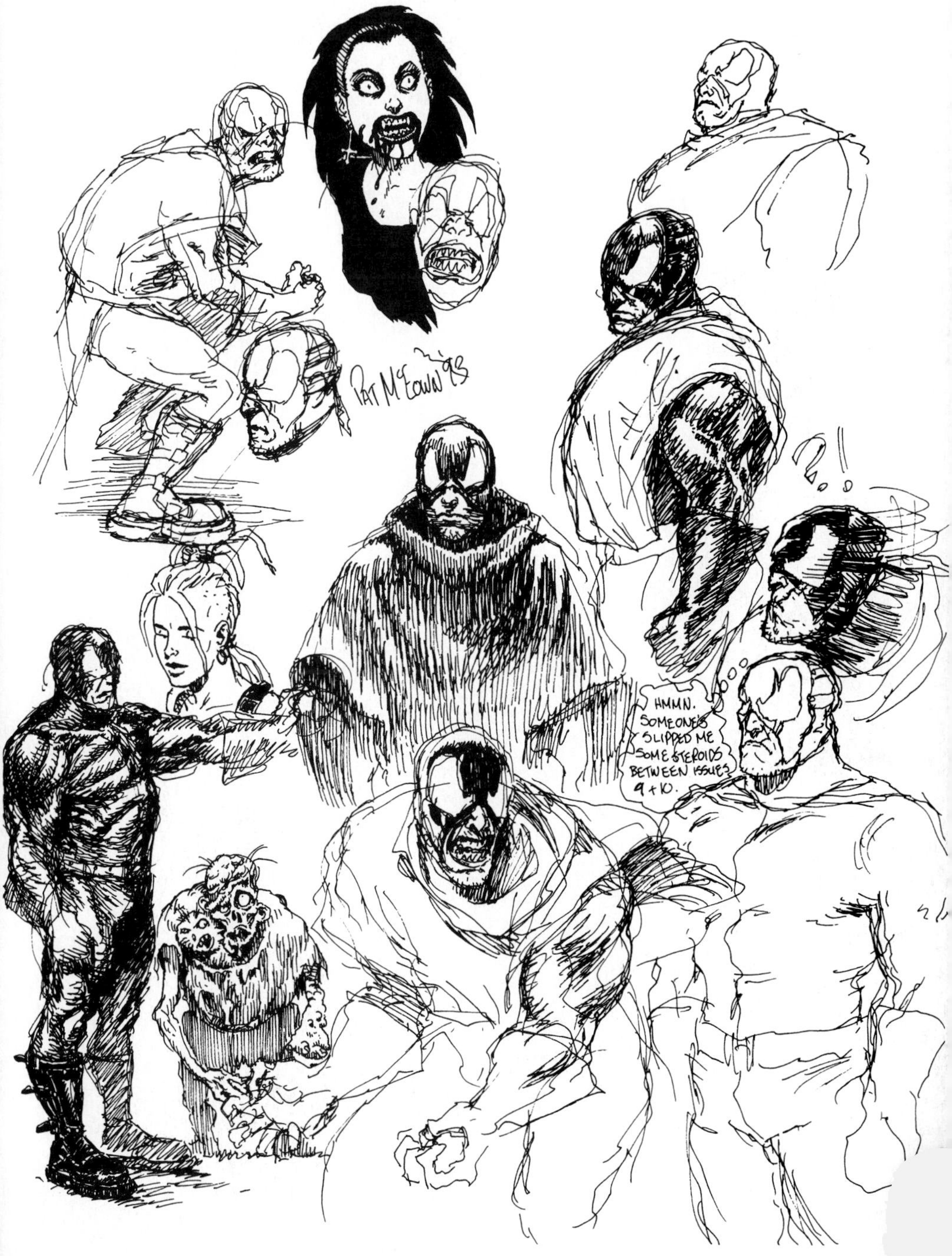
PAT McEOWN '93
?!!
HMMN. SOMEONE'S SLIPPED ME SOME STEROIDS BETWEEN ISSUES 9 + 10.

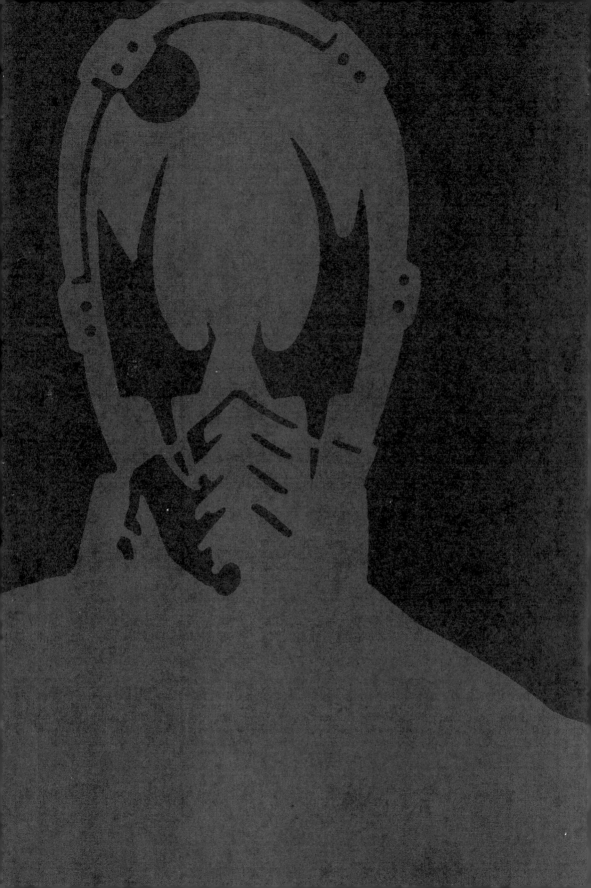